A MIDSUMMER NIGHT'S DREAM

THE GARLAND
SHAKESPEARE BIBLIOGRAPHIES
(General Editor: William Godshalk)
Number 12

GARLAND REFERENCE LIBRARY
OF THE HUMANITIES
Volume 440

The Garland
Shakespeare Bibliographies
William Godshalk, *General Editor*

Number 1:
King Lear
    compiled by Larry S. Champion

Number 2:
Four Plays Ascribed to Shakespeare
Edward III
Sir Thomas More
Cardenio
The Two Noble Kinsmen
    compiled by G. Harold Metz

Number 3:
Cymbeline
    compiled by Henry E. Jacobs

Number 4:
Henry V
    compiled by Joseph Candido
    and Charles R. Forker

Number 5:
King Henry VI
Parts 1, 2, and 3
    compiled by Judith Hinchcliffe

Number 6:
Love's Labor's Lost
    compiled by Nancy Lenz Harvey
    and Anna Kirwan Carey

Number 7:
Hamlet in the 1950s
    compiled by Randal F. Robinson

Number 8:
As You Like It
    compiled by Jay L. Halio
    and Barbara C. Millard

Number 9:
Merchant of Venice
    compiled by Thomas Wheeler

Number 10:
Timon of Athens
    compiled by John J. Ruszkiewicz

Number 11:
Richard III
    compiled by James A. Moore

Number 12:
A Midsummer Night's Dream
    compiled by D. Allen Carroll
    and Gary Jay Williams

A MIDSUMMER NIGHT'S DREAM
An Annotated Bibliography

D. Allen Carroll
Gary Jay Williams

GARLAND PUBLISHING, INC. • NEW YORK & LONDON
1986

Library of Congress Cataloging-in-Publication Data
Carroll, D. Allen (Daniel Allen), 1938–
A midsummer night's dream.

(The Garland Shakespeare bibliographies ; no. 12)
(Garland reference library of the humanities ; v. 440)
Includes index.
1. Shakespeare, William, 1564–1616.   Midsummer
night's dream—Bibliography.   I. Williams, Gary Jay.
II. Title.   III. Series.   IV. Series: Garland
reference library of the humanities ; v. 440.
Z8812.M5C37   1986   [PR2827]   822.3'3   86-4469
ISBN 0-8240-9073-X (alk. paper)

Printed on acid-free, 250-year-life paper
Manufactured in the United States of America

CONTENTS

PREFACE

In 1978 Lawrence Davidow, then Acquisitions Editor at Garland Publishing, invited me to edit a series of annotated bibliographies surveying Shakespeare scholarship published from 1940 until the present. Major contributions published before that period would also be included. We planned that each bibliography would be as comprehensive as possible, fully annotated, cross-referenced, and thoroughly indexed. Each would be divided into major sections that indicate the dominant critical and scholarly concerns of the play being discussed; these large divisions would be subdivided if such subdivision might be useful to the reader. The general format would thus have to remain flexible so that the form of each bibliography could reflect its contents. Although the authors would be presented with copies of our "Tentative Guidelines," we rejected a rigorous conformity to a style sheet in favor of humane, scholarly decisions based on individual perceptions and requirements. We desired a fairly uniform series of high quality, but we did not want to stifle creative initiative.

We emphasized that we wished complete surveys of current knowledge and critical opinion presented in such a way that the reader could retrieve that information rapidly and easily. To help the reader sift through large quantities of material, each bibliography would contain an Introduction that would trace briefly the history of recent criticism and research, as well as indicate new areas to be explored, if such areas had become apparent during the author's work on the project. Finally, the Introduction would make clear any special decisions made or procedures followed by the author in compiling and ordering his or her bibliography.

These were our plans, which now come to fruition in the individual bibliographies of the plays. We wish to thank all those who made this series possible, especially Ralph Carlson, Pam Chergotis, and Julia Johnson. Perhaps, however, our greatest thanks must go to the authors themselves, who, during the frequent meetings of the Garland Shakespeare Authors, came to act as a board of editors. Many of the most difficult questions confronting the series were raised and answered at those meetings. And, of course, we must acknowledge with thanks the hard work that went into the compiling, reading, and writing done by our authors.

October 9, 1980   W. L. GODSHALK
                                                         University of Cincinnati
                                                         General Editor

INTRODUCTION

I

What strikes us first about all this industry since 1940 is how seriously it takes the *Dream*. There is no longer enough of a compliment to be heard in Edward Dowden's "quaint and charming" (1904, item 741a) or in J. B. Priestley's "only so much gossamer and moonlight" (1925, item 13). Certainly no one today accepts the unkind version of this older view, as given, for example, by Hazelton Spencer in 1940, that the play is "not of high artistic purpose and belief," is "too glittering with poetic tinsel, and . . . essentially trivial" (item 23). Some few before our time did find moral and spiritual depths, Georg Brandes for one, who thought the *Dream* a great symbol with "the germs of a whole philosophy . . . latent in the wayward love-scenes" (1898, item 6). But at the onset of our period such was a minority view. For Peter Alexander in 1939 there was "no deep significance in the magic juice, no profound interpretation of life in the adventures of the lovers" (item 19); for Forrest Reid in 1941 there was none of the "supposed profound qualities" (item 28). Our own age, however, has decided that something very worthwhile is in the *Dream* and has made many and various efforts to find it out. There has been, on average, a published comment on the *Dream* (excluding reviews of productions) every ten days and a production of the play, by conservative estimate, every six weeks. The major difference between past and present, which has to do with interpretation and the expression of ourselves, reflects attitudes peculiar to our way of reading texts. Scholars have added little to our knowledge of the text or of social and literary backgrounds, although they have refined traditional opinions. Generalists have gone on introducing the play in responsible ways to those who have never before encountered it. Translators, adaptors, directors, actors, composers, illustrators, and critics have been very busy

and given us much to think about. For much of what is new
in all this work our debt is to the critics, with whom we
begin. They have found the play profound and complex.

    The key to interpretation has been our reaction to
Theseus' benign skepticism (at the beginning of Act Five)
over the young lovers' claim to a mysterious, illuminating
experience and to his lofty disdain for the imaginative
flights of lunatic, lover, and poet--"his smile at the
extravagances of undisciplined fancy" (G. Wilson Knight,
1932, item 15). The simple, early reading took Theseus to
be Shakespeare's spokesman, the sober voice of cool
reason, and the controlling idea therefore to be something
like "the lawlessness and laughableness of love" (E. K.
Chambers, 1905, item 12), its irrationality (Thomas Marc
Parrott, 1938, item 757), which is set off in the play by
the mature, rational love of Theseus and Hippolyta, the
fairies being a remarkable and pleasing device to help
dramatize this point. But the lovers did have the strange
adventure they describe, we insist. It leads to marriage, an
institution the play emphasizes at beginning and end and
one which most take to be idealized in the play.
Accordingly, we credit Hippolyta's view, which is the
opposite of Theseus', that the lovers' story contains
something more "than fancy's images," indeed "something of
great constancy." Moreover, for us the fairies, by
streaming on stage to bless the marriage beds after
Theseus' departure, appear to represent Shakespeare's last
word on what constitutes reality, at least *within* the play.
Theseus' bemused detachment cannot be taken as a guide to
the total experience of the play.

    It therefore no longer suffices, as it once did, to say
simply that the play treats love's follies, mocking or
cherishing them. Our response is to the total love
experience, one in which the mistakes of that night,
however ridiculous they are, produce a serious, permanent
love which has something glorious about it. We balance that
love which is "random, inexplicable, woodlike and Puckish"
(Alvin Kernan, 1974, item 452) with that which is inspired,
and see the whole experience at last as conditioned by
social reality and sanctioned by divine blessing. Thus we
have declared the *Dream* to be about the "miracle of love"
(Harold C. Goddard, 1951, item 79), about "the mystery
signified by and associated with marriage" (Paul A. Olson,
1957, item 145), about "the meaning of love between men
and women as the most basic of all human relationships"

(Irving Ribner, 1966, item 906), about "the reality of love" (L. A. Beaurline, 1978, item 522), about "love in relation to marriage" (Harold F. Brooks, 1979, item 960). The precise connection between the lovers' confusion and this ultimate value has not been easy to define. For Stanley Wells it is an impression, one "difficult to rationalize," that the lovers have had a learning experience (1967, item 913); for M. M. Reese it is the sense that they are "better people" for their dream of love (1970, item 931). Primarily it is a reaction to the strength of the resonances, sacral and joyous, of the unions in the end, which we perceive to balance and then absorb the disharmonies which go before. Certainly no one now would repeat, as Norman E. McClure did in 1937, E. K. Chambers' old view that the play shows love "not an integral part of life, but an amusing disturbance and kind of lunacy of the brain" (items 756 and 1905, item 12).

A number of critics, attaching to the unseen fairy world a high value as symbol, have sensed in this love a power beyond that of infatuation, beyond the mysteries of true or even married love, and well beyond ridicule. This power is that of the Christian Vision itself. So Harold C. Goddard implied, in 1951, with his conviction that the play shows the world of the sense to be "but the surface of a vaster unseen world" (item 79). Frank Kermode was more specific in an influential 1961 essay. For him Bottom's waking moment, so full as it is with garbled Pauline echoes, complicates the moral from the simple "love-is-a-kind-of-madness" to one mixed with the "love of God" and with "blindness as a means to grace" (item 182). Kermode found this theme treated "with an intense sophistication" and the whole play, in consequence, of a "marked intellectual content." Others since then have pursued this idea. The play's vision, for J. A. Bryant, Jr., is "a fleeting recollection of the heaven we lost when we surrendered our innocence" (1964, item 224). From its forest, for W. Moelwyn Merchant, comes "a ritual vision of a life sacramentally informed with love" (1972, item 406); from its Bottom, for Thomas B. Stroup, comes the discovery of "the bottom of God's secrets" (1978, item 544). Bottom, as "the carrier of divine mysteries" (Richard Cody, 1969, item 335), as "the receptacle and bearer of transcendental values" (William Willeford, 1969, item 351), has been the means "to some hidden truth" (Stephen Smith, 1977, item 516) for all sorts of mystical readings--and the main reason why the *Dream*, among the comedies, has been the principal

beneficiary of what Richard Levin has roundly condemned
as the trend in modern criticism toward "thematic elevation"
(1979, item 561a). Few adopt a Christian interpretation, but
many do try to sort out allusions to the Christian faith and
to solve the vexing problem of what they contribute to the
play's meaning. This higher love, as might be expected,
several critics define as the Neoplatonist's realization of
heavenly beauty: "a recognition between companion souls
. . . [of] the beauty of their divine self-nature," according
to John Vyvyan (1961, item 187), "the union of the soul
with divine beauty," according to Peter J. Zacharias (1971,
item 390). The mistakes of that night, for these critics,
represent the comic possibilities of the confused, searching
soul.

Equally evident recently has been a tendency to admit to
the presence of impulses from love's other side. Of a low,
dark, sexual element, Jan Kott's 1964 essay (item 239), the
most distinctive piece on the play in our era, is an
extreme, controversial statement. For Kott the play's "love
is mad," its Eros one of "Ugliness" in which all the
characters are promiscuous, and the whole a nightmarish
orgy of the grotesque and depraved, "a most truthful,
brutal, and violent play." Most critics have dismissed this
reading as wrong in its single-mindedness and urgency.
But Kott has made a difference. For a full decade some
reaction to him was obligatory, and the result has been, on
the whole, that we see more in the play than we saw
before. Kott has undoubtedly provided a check to excesses
in the other direction and has had an emphatic if uneven
and impermanent effect on productions. Few are willing to
believe, with S. M. Farrow in his summing-up for a 1972
school text, that the play's love is "a violent impersonal
force that irons the humanity out of people, reducing them
to animals, monsters, even things" (item 935), or with
David Ormerod, that the play depicts (within the limits of
stage convention) "an act of coitus between woman and ass"
(1978, item 538). Most, however, do believe, with David
Bevington, that in the play "the dark side of love is seldom
far away" (item 523)--an attitude rarely if ever taken
before Kott.

This suggestion of the salacious and threatening has
become part of a separate, related issue, one a little older
and germane to a number of interpretations, and that is
whether the fairies are sinister or not, and if so, the
extent to which. G. Wilson Knight, comparing the play to

Macbeth, wrote in 1932 of its "nightmare" atmosphere, of a fairyland "troubled" even while sweet (item 15). Later, in 1954, Tyrone Guthrie thought the fairies ought to be not merely pretty but dark and dangerous (item 828). The notion is at least as early as G. K. Chesterton, for whom a modern man, after seeing the play acted properly, "would feel shaken to his marrow if he had to walk home from the theatre through a country lane" (1904, item 7). Within the scale of opinions today, the inclination seems to be toward a position close to the traditional, categorical assumption of benevolence (given in Minor White Latham, 1930, item 14 and in K. M. Briggs, 1959, item 635) and away from that of Kott and, say, Stephen Fender, for whom the fairies have a "horrifying power" (1968, item 322). We seem not quite so anxious as W. Moelwyn Merchant was in 1961 to discover a method in productions for combining "the terror and the dignified grace of the fairy world" (item 183). Harold F. Brooks, in 1979, can find little evidence of any such darker features (item 960). Whatever is felt as "potentially dangerous" (David P. Young, 1966, item 303), most would agree, ought to be controlled by the operation of fairy benevolence and thus not seriously disturb our sense of well being. In any case, the fairies will never again be the tinsel-and-gauze variety of the sometimes past.

A second major contribution of recent critics, primarily those of the sixties and seventies, has been to focus attention onto a different theme, one taken to be more inclusive than love. Committed to the doctrine that good art shapes the experience it reflects into a single idea, and finding much in the play not strictly about love, many have taken imagination to be the central theme--the nature and transforming power of the imagination. With this larger theme critics have been able to account for the whole of Theseus' famous speech, which is about the imagination, not love, for the matter having to do with rehearsing and performing the playlet, for much about the nature and function of the fairies, as well as for the vagaries of love. And they have been able to reject early impressions of disunity, such as those of Robert Adger Law, in 1943, for whom there was no "organic unity" among the four groups in the play (item 37), and of Ernest Schanzer, in 1951, for whom there was no "close relation" between the main theme (love, for him) and the playlet (item 80). Some think it about the imagination in general: "the apprehension [of] imaginative truth," which to D. F. McKenzie is a "heavenly understanding through imagination," one not to be explained, only felt (1964, item 244). For most, though, it is about two specific functions of the imagination: "the heart of the comedy, its most pervasive unifying element," as R. W. Dent argued in a 1964 essay often cited and much praised, "is the partially contrasting role of imagination in love and art" (item 227).

In the years following Dent, and under his influence, discussion has tended to center on art, not love, that is, on the play's self-consciousness about creativity and on a presumed personal involvement by Shakespeare. David P. Young, for instance, has wondered if the play may not, "since it contains an inner play and discussions of drama, poetry, and the imagination, represent a very conscious effort on the part of the dramatist to advance the scope and level of his art and thus be a vital source of our understanding of Shakespeare's own ideas about the character and pursuit of his art" (1966, item 303). Both Dent and Young have called the *Dream* Shakespeare's "Defense of Dramatic Poesy." For James L. Calderwood and Norman Rabkin the *Dream* is about "the art and value of play-making and -viewing," about "the role of the imagination in play-making and play-watching" (1971, item 367; 1967, item 313). Thus when Bottom awakes, according to J. Denis Huston, it is Shakespeare who awakes to his own creative powers (1973, item 426). Needless to say, this approach has proved very congenial to critics. Many take little note of the caprice of love, its sweetness or sublimity; they watch, rather, a "fond pageant" performed under the direction of the playwright-surrogate Oberon and stage-managed by Puck. For them the magic of the play is actually the magic of theatre (Anthony Dawson, 1978, item 526). More and more, discussion has dealt with the multiple levels of theatrical being and the complexities of dramatic illusion, much to our benefit, for the most part, but in some cases producing readings too intricate for comprehension. For Albert Cook, to give one example, Bottom "articulates his inarticulateness by staging the incapacity to act." His playlet offers "the implied significative ridiculousness of ontological distortion" through a "splendid counterpointing of divergencies" (1976, item 487). This idea of the play commenting on itself, being about "the epistemology of the theater" (James L. Calderwood, 1971, item 367), L. A. Beaurline, for one, thinks "tiresomely overdeveloped in our time" (1978, item 522).

Readings such as these, which always find a "celebration of creativity" (Charles R. Lyons, 1971, item 377), like those which find the "miracle of Love," must accommodate an opposite attitude evident in much of the play. Theseus seems to deny to the imagination and art any high value, the mechanicals bungle their playlet, and Puck's epilogue permits us to think "this weak and idle theme, no more yielding but a dream." But critics now take such disclaimers to reflect Shakespeare's basic courtesy, his habitual modesty--a joke at his own expense--and to register, possibly, a deep-seated ambivalence in him and in his time toward the arts. The play's very triumph as a product of the imagination proclaims its real attitude. The burden of criticism, at all times, has been to marvel at and seek means to explain (1) how harmoniously the play's unlikely parts are brought together--Theseus and Hippolyta, young lovers, mechanicals, and fairies--(2) how exquisite the fairies are, and (3) how beautiful the verse. The entire play, therefore, as Rabkin reads it, constitutes "an ironic refutation of its thesis that the imagination is to be despised" (1967, item 313).

Since it is through Theseus that Shakespeare seems to belittle both love and art, what in older views is called a "recoil from romanticism" (H. B. Charlton, 1938, item 18), Theseus has been the subject of much debate. His skepticism does assume an awkward dimension, one which almost every critic of late has noticed. He is a shadow too, "a shadow questioning the validity of shadows" (Philip Edwards, 1968, item 321), himself a creation from "antique fable" and unconsciously involved in "fairy toys" yet believing in neither (R. W. Dent, 1964, item 227). Some simply pronounce him wrong: "the greatest ass of all" (Stephen Fender, 1968, item 322), with the joke at his, not Shakespeare's, expense (Anne Barton, 1974, item 941). Every real or apparent flaw in his character has been probed. But efforts to diminish his character have not been very successful. He may no longer be Edward Dowden's "grand ideal figure" (1875, item 4), but to many his voice remains one of "sanity, cool reason, common sense" (H. B. Charlton, 1938, item 18), "that of a ruler, magisterial, intelligent, and also compassionate" (R. A. Foakes, 1972, item 398). His description of how the poet's imagination works still carries conviction not only as superb in itself but also as a precise account of Shakespeare's own method in the play (Kenneth Muir, 1970, item 360), the conclusion of his speech, by implication, contradicting its beginning.

He may intend his remarks as censure, but his "eloquence, summoned like Balaam to curse, blesses altogether" (Harold F. Brooks, 1979, item 960). One may well wish, with D. J. Palmer, "that Shakespeare (or Theseus) had not left such an important point merely 'implicit'" (1973, item 724). His disdain, which is undeniable, is usually given the benefit of partial truth, his conscious verdict and the element it represents in the play allowed a place.

The result has been that interpretation has had to admit to a final complexity, a balance of attitudes which has been perceived to generate paradox. There is a "doubleness" about the *Dream*, according to C. L. Barber (1959, item 158), its romantic love, for Stephen Fender, either "a laughable delusion or an intimation of something truer than the literal world," or poised between both (1968, item 322), its perception of the power of art, for Philip Edwards, "a balance between belief and ridicule" (1968, item 321). We are made, says Ernest Gilman, "simultaneously conscious of the power and precariousness of the dramatic illusion" (1979, item 527). The *Dream* reveals, to Alvin B. Kernan, *both* Shakespeare's modesty about the higher claims for his theatrical art *and* his belief (which is Sidney's) that "in place of nature's brazen world the poet creates a golden one" (1979, item 577). The play's ending, to R. Chris Hassel, reflects a "splendid ambiguity" (1970, item 356). And the overall ambiguity, scholars have reminded us, toward love, art, and the imagination in general, is exactly that of Shakespeare's time. Given the "multivalency of the perspective," our task has become that of defining a felt synthesis between the Thesean and Hippolytan views, between the Athenian and forest worlds. We want, to give one example of the problem, "to explore the rich implications of the [Pauline] echoes without overdoing it" (Ronald F. Miller, 1975, item 477).

What would appear to be a weakness in the play, an inconsistency, we have therefore made into a virtue, and in doing so have made the play intellectual and difficult. "If you choose to look for them," Robert Speaight has observed, taking us back to Georg Brandes, "there are metaphysics in the *Dream*" (1977, item 517). They are not, we may add, easy of access or reducible to paraphrase. "The real meaning of *Dream*," according to Stephen Fender, "is that no one 'meaning' can be extracted from [its] puzzles" (1968, item 322). What is complicated we have taken to be mysterious, what inexplicable we have taken to

be ineffable. It is *because* "the play insists on its own
silliness: that we are forced, given our analytical reflexes,
"by a species of paradox to take it seriously" (Anthony
Dawson, 1978, item 526). What we praise in the *Dream* are
modern virtues--deep unity and complexity. Our method has
described a *Dream* which has the "astonishing effect of
unsounded depths" (J. Percy Smith, 1972, item 413).

In 1904 Chesterton was curious as to how the *Dream*
could be both "mysteriously charitable" and "cynical" (item
7). But in the main our interpretation is peculiarly our
own. For the eighteenth century the play was a fantastical,
even exquisite piece of nonsense, simple and beautiful. For
the nineteenth century, following Hazlett, Shakespeare was
here a poet, not a metaphysician or even much of a
dramatist (1817, item 1a). "In part a perfect piece of lyrical
poetry," Dowden described it, "in part a very imperfect
drama" (1895, item 5), or simply, "the poem" (1875, item
4). We ourselves take it to be a play, but we read it as if
it were a poem. As late as 1935 de la Mare could call it
"perhaps the least intellectual of the plays" (item 16).
Writing in 1954, Derek A. Traversi, a model of the close
reader, could find in the *Dream* "barely more than a
delicate, tenuous piece of decoration"; in 1967, however,
after we had changed our minds, he found in its conclusion
"something rather more than mere surface decoration," and
in the whole of "this great comedy" a complicated life
"disturbingly endowed with a reality of its own" (1969, item
346).

Precisely what this "something rather more" is we
obviously have trouble saying. Charles Knight thought the
play "must be left to its own influences" (1851, item 2),
and Swinburne thought it "outside as well as above all
possible or imaginable criticism" (1909, item 8). And like
earlier critics in the presence of this "great luminous flood
of poetry" (Logan Pearsall Smith, 1950, item 1001), we have
on occasion responded rather more poetically than
analytically. But our offerings in this vein (Louis
Zukovsky, 1963, item 217; Theodore Weiss, 1971, item 387a)
do not compare with those which we constantly quote:
Hazlitt, in reverie--"the reading of this play is like
wandering in a grove by moonlight; the descriptions
breathe a sweetness like odours thrown from beds of
flowers" (item 1a); and Coleridge, in ecstacy--"O what
wealth, what wild luxuriance, yet what compression and
condensation of English fancy" (item 1b). Undaunted by the

difficulty, we have tried all possible and imaginable criticism.

Certain features, formal and otherwise, have received constant and detailed attention. No discussion ignores the recurrent imagery of moon, flora and fauna, sight, transformation, and dream. Comment on any one of these would fill a volume. We are particularly and profitably occupied with ways the play uses and is itself like the dream experience. The pattern of the plot we have described, comparing it to a dance (Enid Welsford, 1927, item 575; G. K. Hunger, 1962, item 195), to a game (William Gibson, 1978, item 526a), and to structures spatial (Una Ellis-Fermor, 1960, item 166), geometric (David P. Young, 1966, item 303), and mathematic (Ralph G. Stanton, 1967, item 315). The five-act structure we have studied for its Renaissance (Marco Mincoff, 1965, item 279) and neo-Terentian (John T. Low, 1974, item 454) characteristics. We have made much of the overall "rhythmic movement," in Northrop Frye's words, "from normal world to green world and back again" (1957, item 142), of the superstitions surrounding the two holidays (Midsummer Eve, May Day) and, following the lead of C. L. Barber (1959, item 158), of the customs and pageantry associated with these holidays. (Most now think May Day is the holiday setting, but all assume the atmosphere combines elements of both.) Frye and Barber rank with Kermode, Kott, and Dent for the mark they have made in our time on studies of the *Dream*. We have, moreover, made a great effort to clarify what Robert Graves has called the play's "extraordinary mythographic jumble" (1948, item 55). Especially suggestive, for example, are two recent studies of the way the Theseus-Minotaur myth informs the whole play (David Ormerod, 1978, item 538; M. E. Lamb, 1979, item 561). All the discussion of the Circe-Diana-Lucina associations in Hippolyta (see, for example, Madeleine Doran, 1960, item 638) seem unlikely to produce any agreement as to her make-up and thus whether she represents "the forces of the lower passions in man" (Paul A. Olson, 1957, item 145) or else the urgings of some higher element to which she would have Bottom ascend (David Bevington, 1978, item 523). And we have continued the old disputes over two small issues: the number and distribution of nights and the condition and visibility of the moon--disputes which Ernest Schanzer has labeled "efflorescences of the absurd" (1955, item 124).

Among characters, Bottom, as would be expected, has inspired the fullest treatment. Everyone acknowledges that he is the play's finest creation and Shakespeare's first great comic character. The mixture in him of the "artist" as inspired romantic (J. B. Priestley, 1925, item 13) and the pragmatist, "prosaic to the backbone" (S. C. Sen Gupta, 1950, item 72), which forms the basis of discussions about him, has defied final analysis, as if he were, in Chesterton's early view, "greater and more mysterious than Hamlet" (1904, item 7). With him as with much in the play we must resort to paradox: he possesses, according to William J. Martz, "an equivalent of stature, the staturelessness" (1971, item 378), is "both absurd in essence," as noted above, and "the carrier of divine mysteries" (Richard Cody, 1969, item 335)--in all the means "to some hidden truth" which is alluded to in the play, "though he is not himself aware of it" (Stephen L. Smith, 1977, item 516). Most agree, apparently, after centuries of mistaking the acting tradition, that he is the clown-simpleton, not the droll-knowing wag (John Palmer, 1946, item 46; Nevill Coghill, 1954, item 108). Showing how his playlet relates to the rest of the play and itemizing its purposes in general (see, for example, Kenneth Muir, 1954, item 616), or its particular targets and the methods of its burlesque (see, for example, J. W. Robinson, 1964, item 651), have been constant and useful exercises.

The absence of personalities among the four young lovers is now no longer, as it was in the past, a cause for apology. What appeared to de la Mare and others to be "shallow, stumbling, bald, and vacant" about their verse (1940, item 148), we take instead to be happily appropriate in a play which resembles comic-opera (Kenneth Muir, 1979, item 562). Distanced by their verse, the lovers are for us generic mankind in love, more structural than individual, more formal than personal (J. L. Styan, 1960, item 174a). And their contribution to the comedy is considered to be just as significant as that of the fairies and mechanicals, which was not the case in the nineteenth and early twentieth centuries.

There are various specialized approaches to the play. We have a psychoanalytic reading, Weston A. Gui's, to mention the most comprehensive, which sees the play as Bottom's dream of his Oedipal difficulty and Puck "actually the penis of the father" (1952, item 84). Curiously for a play which would seem so susceptible to the method, neither this essay nor any other has proved very satisfactory (see Norman N. Holland, 1966, item 290). We have a Jungian view, which detects a mandala-like character about the process of identification which takes place (Franz Riklin, 1968, item 329; Alex Aronson, 1972, item 319); a Marxist, which sees a fantasy for "creating complete social poise" (Elliot Krieger, 1979, item 560); a structuralist, which considers the "primary disjunction" to be between frustration and desire, with Hippolyta's menstrual cycle having a disturbing effect (Jean Paris, 1973, item 404); a feminist, which finds "all women in the play . . . castrated" (Biodun Iginla, 1978, item 532); and several mythic readings, which see the play as a revelation of one or another myth of the mysteries of Nature (Elizabeth Sewell, 1960, item 172; Karl Kerényi, 1961, item 181). Alongside these we find countless introductions, not designed for specialists, many of which are excellent. Thomas McFarland's essay, to single out one, which makes no pretense to originality, provides a sensible overview. For him, *Dream* is "very possibly the happiest work of literature ever conceived" (1972, item 404). The introductions of David Bevington (1973, item 938) and Anne Barton (1974, item 941) could serve as models. Among the many plot summaries, to mention another minor form, that of Alfred Harbage (1963, item 1036) is simply delightful. At the other extreme, we continue the scholarly and critical pursuit of every nuance of every detail in the play. Typical is Hallett Smith's note (1976, item 678). Bottom's "sucking dove" (I.ii.77-78), he thinks, recalls a slip made by a professional actor who mixed "the sucking lamb or harmless dove" in *2 Henry VI* (III.i.71), a slip noticed in Chamberlain's *Booke of Mistakes* (1637).

Some speculation persists as to the possibility of a political allegory, although this approach is not now very fashionable. Here the crux is the speech known as "Oberon's Vision" (II.i.148-68), "the most famous of all tributes to Queen Elizabeth" (George Lyman Kittredge, 1936, item 954). With either of the two most familiar and responsible readings, little progress has been made. In Edith Rickert's view (1923, item 574), (1) Oberon's Vision recounts the festivities of Elvetham in 1591; (2) the play, like the festivities, was inspired by and reflects the Earl of Hertford's futile attempts to ingratiate himself with the Queen after his son ("the changeling boy") by Catherine Grey had been declared illegitimate; and (3) Bottom is King James of Scotland. This reading E. K. Chambers thought "quite incredible" (1930, item 576) and Hardin Craig thought "the most credible of all accounts so far advanced" (1948, item 54). In the older idea of N. J. Halpin (1843, item 568), Oberon's Vision refers to the festivities at Kenilworth in 1575 and Leicester's attempts to win Elizabeth's heart. Opinion seems about equally divided between the two interpretations, but few undertake the discussion with much enthusiasm. Many prefer to think that Oberon alludes to neither of the two specific events (Elvetham or Kenilworth) but rather to that *kind* of entertainment. Lately developed notions that the play is about the Elizabeth-Essex affair (Maureen Duffey, 1972, item 670) or the Alençon affair, with Bottom as Alençon (Marion A. Taylor, 1973, item 673), have not caught on. While there exists a certain amount of good will toward this approach, it gets relatively little attention, almost none anymore in general introductions.

As regards the date, nothing has altered our assumption that the play was written between 1594, not early, and 1596, not late, either narrowing this range or placing an emphasis within it, unless Harold F. Brooks' recent preference for the winter of 1595-96 should gather support (1979, item 960). Most seem to believe *Romeo*, the companion play, precedes *Dream* (but see Stanley Wells, 1967, item 913). Uncertainty has led some simply to identify both plays with a "lyrical group" written about this time, which includes *Richard II*. Few think there is enough evidence to indicate that the play contains layers of earlier work. John Dover Wilson, who developed the modern version of this theory (1924, item 748), thought the play written in 1592 or before, much revised (the Bottom and fairy scenes added) in 1594, and then probably revised again in 1598. Later, after de la Mare judged some of the poetry unworthy of the master, the dialogue of the young lovers in particular (1940, item 16), Wilson extended his theory to deny Shakespeare's presence in the early layer (1948, item 598). The clear evidence for revision in Theseus' speech (V.i.1-84), most agree, following W. W. Greg (1955, item 695), reflects an afterthought, not a new conception. The apparently duplicated ending has been taken to be a minor adaptation designed to fit the play, after its private performance, for the public stage, or else not there at all (Stanley Wells, 1967, item 913). Wells finds it "credible that *Dream* was always intended for the public theater."

Most continue to believe, despite the absence of any hard evidence, that Shakespeare wrote this play to be performed as part of the celebrations for the marriage of some noble couple. Of the ten or so marriages that have been offered in the past as the occasion, three remain serious candidates: Mary, Countess of Southampton and Sir Thomas Heneage on 2 May 1594; Elizabeth Carey and William, Earl of Derby on 26 January 1595; and Elizabeth Carey and Thomas, son of Henry, Lord Berkeley on 19 February 1596. Most avoid a solid commitment to any one of the three, though Harold F. Brooks' case for Carey-Berkeley (1979, item 960), which is strong, may have an effect.

There is widespread agreement about the text and therefore little comment. Thomas Fisher's quarto of 1600 (Q1), now the copy-text, was printed from a promptbook possibly in Shakespeare's hand (John Dover Wilson, 1924, item 748) or from foul papers (W. W. Greg, 1955, item 695), perhaps in a late stage (Robert K. Turner, Jr., 1962, item 699). James Roberts' quarto of 1619 (Q2) was a page-for-page reprint with a few corrections and added stage directions. The First Folio (1623) was based on a copy of Q2 which either had been compared with the promptbook or else had been annotated to serve as one.

Work of late has not uncovered the source of the play or lengthened appreciably the list which witnesses to a good deal of reading around on Shakespeare's part (available in Geoffrey Bullough, 1957, item 630; and see Kenneth Muir, 1957 and 1977, item 631). There has, however, been a large output on the uses made of these sources. Among many, four issues in particular have occupied scholars: (1) the connections, depending on which came first, between *Dream* and Anthony Munday's *John a Kent* (I. A. Shapiro, 1955, item 623; Nevill Coghill, 1964, item 648); (2) the question of whether Thomas Mouffet's *The Silkewormes, and Their Flies* (published in 1599, though apparently written much earlier) is or is not a source (Douglas Bush, 1932, item 578; A. S. T. Fisher, 1949, item 600; Kenneth Muir, 1954, item 615; Bullough, 1957, item 630; Katherine Duncan-Jones, 1981, item 685h); (3) the extent and kind of influence exerted by "The Knight's Tale" (T. W. Baldwin, 1959, item 634; Larry S. Champion, 1968, item 658; Ann Thompson, 1978, item 683); and (4) the precise nature of Shakespeare's reliance on Ovid (with over a dozen discussions). Otherwise, scholars have labored to detect hints from specific works taken up in *Dream*, to describe the general debt to predecessors such as Lyly and Greene, to compare *Dream* with other Shakespeare plays, especially *Romeo* and *The Tempest*, and to work over and over the several literary modes--farcical, comic, and romantic--which inform its being in a process which goes on diffuse and unabated.

Following the guidelines set down for these Garland bibliographies we have tried to be as comprehensive as possible for the period 1940-1979. We have, moreover, provided enough important items from before and after this period to insure that its place in the total history of response to the play can be appreciated. With a list of this size, needless to say, many changes had to be made after the whole had been organized and entries numbered. Items appeared late, came to our attention late, or else emerged as worthy of inclusion after the whole was before us. Low-case letters after numbers usually identify places where adjustments for these reasons were made. The section on editions and translations (V.), in keeping with the practice of the series, includes only complete or collected works published in English-speaking countries. An effort has been made, however, to list all individual editions and translations whatever the origins, even when copies could not be seen and full descriptions could not be got.

To the compilers of the special bibliographies, lists, and catalogues which appear in that section (IV.), my debt is great, as it is of course to the sponsors and makers of the annual lists on which all who study Shakespeare rely and without which this task would have been unimaginable--*Shakespeare Quarterly, International MLA Bibliography, Shakespeare Jahrbuch* (Heidelberg and Weimar), and *MHRA*. For assistance with foreign language material I am grateful to Professors Susanne Lenz of Wurzburg University, Tetsuo Anzai of Sophia University, and David E. Lee and John C. Osborne of the University of Tennessee. For their patience and efficiency I am indebted to the staff of Interlibrary Services of the University of Tennessee Library. For introducing me to the marvels of a main frame and laser printing, I must thank Ann Wilson. And for financial assistance all along the way I acknowledge the help of the Trustees of the John C. Hodges Better English Fund.

D. Allen Carroll
The University of Tennessee, Knoxville

II

The section of this bibliography entitled "Stage History and the Sister Arts" is designed chiefly to guide the user to materials about the play's stage history since the Restoration, with special concentration on productions from 1940 through 1983. The section will also guide the user to materials about film and television versions of the play, about performances of opera and ballet adaptations of the play, and about musical compositions and paintings, prints, and illustrations inspired by the play. A brief survey of the play's theatrical history is provided here, followed by an explanation of the format and guidelines for this section of the bibliography.

In its life in the theatre since the Globe, *A Midsummer Night's Dream* has undergone more metamorphoses than Ovid ever dreamed of and never more often than in this century. Today and within living memory, the play must be counted as one of the most frequently produced of Shakespeare's plays. But it was not always so. From 1662 until 1840, the play was seen on the English-speaking stage only in the form of operatic or quasi-operatic adaptations; nothing like the full text was played for nearly two hundred years. One suspects, in fact, that the appeal of this play, written about 1595, may have waned down the years from the beginning of James I's reign through Charles I's. In the interregnum, "Pyramus and Thisbe" emerged as a "droll" in clandestine performances (item 961). English companies touring in Germany carried the mechanicals' play in their repertoires, and there it eventually took the native form of Andreas Gryphius's *Herr Peter Squentz* (items 1040, T1102).

Early in the English Restoration, the play--in what version we do not know--seemed wholly "insipid" to Samuel Pepys when he saw it performed by the King's Company (items T1082, T1187). Thereafter, it makes no recorded stage appearance until Purcell's opera *The Fairy Queen* in 1692 (items 962, T1290, T1343a, and index). The most salient feature of this Baroque creation at Dorset Garden Theatre was not the play itself but the four elaborate and expensive entertainments of song, dance, and scenic spectacle that were placed at the ends of Acts II through V. It was for these that Henry Purcell wrote most of his score. These are intermezzi-like spectacles that are brought out by command of the fairy royalty at the end of each act, and the acts of the play seem rather like preambles to them.

In the eighteenth century, the play was variously dismantled for several operatic adaptations. "Pyramus and Thisbe" was borrowed out of the play, with the mechanicals being given songs, to create two popular one-act musical jests that poked fun at the new London rage for the Italian opera (items 963, 964, T1351). David Garrick's production of *The Fairies* at Drury Lane in 1755, with music by John Christopher Smith, used only the fairies and the young lovers, omitting Bottom and the mechanicals (item 965). It was relatively successful, certainly more so than the next adaptation, which offered the fullest version of the play given on the eighteenth century stage. That version was seen at Garrick's Drury Lane in 1763 under the title *Midsummer Night's Dream* (see item 967). It featured more of the text but was still furnished with thirty-three songs, five more than the previous version. For the critic for the *St. James Chronicle*, the result was "an odd romantic performance" that gave "a lively picture of the ungoverned imagination of the great poet." It lasted for one night. Like Theseus, audiences of the Enlightenment seemed to have found Shakespeare's fable "more strange than true." While a musical score was the standard means of dealing with the irrational and the supernatural, it could not create faith in Shakespeare's blend of Greeks and fairies, court lovers and crude artisans, Athenians and Elizabethans.

Romanticism brought a fuller literary appreciation of Shakespeare, but the stage was slow to follow. The play was discussed by the early German Romantic critics, and Goethe incorporated Oberon, Titania, Puck, and Ariel into the strange intermezzo of his "Walpurgis Night's Dream" in *Faust*, part one. But the full text of the play was not seen in the theatres of Germany or England until the 1840s. In the 1790s, Henry Fuseli created some rather sensual images of sexual dreaming in his painting and his engravings of Oberon, Titania, and Bottom in the 1790s (see item T1444), but of course no such images reached the stage until well into the twentieth century.

The first revival of the play in the nineteenth century was yet another operatic adaptation. It was created by Sir Frederick Reynolds, who reshaped it for musical pleasures and scenic grandeur on the huge Covent Garden stage (items 969, T1270, T1351). Sir Henry Rowley Bishop provided the music--an arrangement of songs from the previous adaptations, ten of his own, and some twelve more from other composers. The scenic elaborations included some manifestations of the romantic scenic pictorialism with which the play would long be associated. It was this production that brought on William Hazlitt's famous complaint that Shakespeare's poetry could never be realized upon the stage. The Reynolds-Bishop version was successful, however, and it was in Reynolds' version that the play was seen over the next two decades, including the first appearance of the play in the United States--at the Park Theatre in 1826 (item T1364).

It was finally in 1840 that Elizabeth Vestris brought the play to the stage relatively whole. "Madame" Vestris, light opera darling of London and a very resourceful theatre manager who was experienced in staging fairy pantomimes at the Olympic Theatre, brought out the new production in her second season as manager of Covent Garden (items 970, T1312, T1418, T1451). Notable on her staff were costumer James Robinson Planché and scene painter John Henderson Grieve. Her text, prepared by Planché, was more complete than any stage text had been since the interregnum, albeit embellished with fourteen songs. Vestris set many precedents, essentially creating the Victorian theatrical pattern for this play. It was staged with the splendors of Romantic pictorialism: Periclean palaces for Theseus, English forests, panoramas, and transformation scenes. Then, too, Vestris herself played the breeches role of Oberon, and this set the pattern. Hereafter, with one exception, women played the role of Oberon for the rest of the century. For Victorians, a female fairy king was just that much closer to being ethereal.

Felix Mendelssohn composed his famous overture for the play in 1827; Alfred Bunn and Vestris used the overture for their productions in 1833 and 1840, respectively (item T1351). Mendelssohn then created the incidental music for Ludwig Tieck's full-text production in 1843 in Potsdam (item T1102). Tieck's staging was notable for the main setting that included a fixed architectural unit of galleries and stairs: It was an attempt to get closer to Shakespeare's stage, an experiment Tieck had long dreamed of. Mendelssohn's music became almost inseparable from Shakespeare's play; it was still being used in major productions over a century later. It also was the inspiration for the Balanchine ballet, created in 1962 (item T1214a).

In 1853, Samuel Phelps created a dream-like staging at Sadler's Wells Theatre that seemed nearly ideal to his critics. A soft green scrim was placed across the proscenium for all the forest scenes, and, with carefully orchestrated gas lighting and a gliding panorama, the sylvan views melted one into another in a dream-like sequence. There were no extraneous songs here. Phelps's own effective portrait of Bottom blended well into his tastefully managed production (items T1270, T1286).

Charles Kean's 1856 production at the Princess's Theatre was a scenic elaboration upon Vestris's pattern, with much more of the text cut to make way for the pictures, which he had preserved for posterity in watercolors (items 973, T1270, T1418, T1491). They represent the splendor of mid-century English scene painting and the earnestness of Kean's antiquarian research.

In the United States between 1850 and 1888, there were four major, elaborate productions by William Burton, Thomas Barry (item 972), Laura Keene (item 974), and Augustin Daly (items 978, T1315, T1364). As with their British counterparts, some American producers tended to a tasteful blend of romantic forests and antiquarian splendor and some to the novelty effects of fairy pantomimes. The elaborations included crescent moons rising over a sleeping Titania and slow sunrises over the sleeping lovers; Puck rose from the earth on a mushroom, and fairies actually flew, sometimes in formations. There were chariots for the fairy royalty and panoramas of fairyland, real hounds to accompany Theseus and real ships for the argonaut, electric fairy wands that blinked and asses' ears that wiggled.

Sir Herbert Beerbohm Tree's production of 1900 at Her Majesty's Theatre was all that a Victorian might dream of, an illustrated family album of Shakespeare's fairy tale (item T1490a). It was an elaborate recapitulation and affirmation of the century's pictorial traditions for the play; it was intentionally so, aimed in some part at such new dissenters as William Poel and George Bernard Shaw. With it, the century clock struck midnight, said George Odell ruefully (item T1270).

The 1914 production of Harley Granville-Barker was an attempt to break from the pictorial tradition (see items T1149, T1392, T1401, T1497, and index). Granville-Barker wanted to place the emphasis upon Shakespeare's word

music. But he saw no virtue in the austerely bare platform
stage of Poel. The problem, said Barker, was "to invent a
new hieroglyphic language of scenery." His confidence in
the poetry led him to the use of the full text of the play,
and his designer, Norman Wilkinson, provided simplified,
suggestive settings that made possible the fluid,
uninterrupted flow of the play. For Titania's bower, there
was a small green knoll at center, over which hung a
circlet of diaphanous blue-green curtains, and behind it,
where there had once been mighty English beeches, were
folded draperies, laced lightly with floral lines in the *l'art
nouveau* style. The fairies were a radical departure from
the familiar Victorian iconography. "The fairies are the
director's test," Granville-Barker wrote in the preface to
his acting edition of the play. (Could they henceforth no
longer exist without inventive directors?) His were fantastic
creatures, gilded from head to foot and styled like
Cambodian idols out of Leon Bakst. They danced not to
Mendelssohn but to old English folk tunes, arranged by
Cecil Sharp. They were the production's most controversial
feature. Not until the Peter Brook staging of the play in
1970 would there be a production of it so hotly debated by
critics and audiences, one so clearly signalling cultural
changes, and one so influential. For traditionalists, like
Odell, the Granville-Barker production was a nightmare
bred of modernism, a desecration of sacred Shakespeare
(item T1270). There were those for whom it was a breath of
fresh air at a wake, but many critics welcomed the
experiment more than the results. One unmoved critic in
New York, where the production played in 1915, found in it
"a world arbitrarily made" (item T1401). In all, the
production was an amalgam of many influences, including
Poel, Max Reinhardt, and the new stagecraft; there were
even some traditional rose petals at the end from Benson.
While it was a sophisticated and intellectually resourceful
production, it seems not to have been a magical one. But
Granville-Barker's Savoy Theatre experiments with
Shakespeare were a necessary break from literalism in
search of a stage more hospitable to poetic metaphor and
were influential. Among other things Barker also brought to
English Shakespearean production the new art theatre
aesthetic, including its ideal of a director in whom
centralized artistic control resided.

The Granville-Barker production was not the end of
moonlight and Mendelssohn. Before Granville-Barker, the
play, staged in the traditional manner, though with some

simplifications, had become a fond and widely seen perennial in the repertoires of Sir Frank Benson (item T1198a) and Sir Philip Ben Greet (items 979, T1237). *A Midsummer Night's Dream* celebrated Shakespeare's birthday at Stratford-upon-Avon, was given in London at Christmas as a seasonal confection of fairies, and was played on the American Chautauqua circuit. As such, it was often an introduction to Shakespeare for the young, and that did not change after World War I. In Basil Dean's Christmas *Dream* at Drury Lane in 1924, dozens of fairy children were delivered by backstage hydraulic lifts to a point from which they could enter and descend the high staircases of a Grecian palace out of Sir Alma-Tadema for the final fairy revel (items T1249, T1310). Robert Atkins' productions at the Old Vic and in the outdoor theatre at Regent's Park in the nineteen-thirties relied heavily upon Mendelssohn and gauzy fairies and upon his own slow, resonant Bottom (item T1249, T1125).

But there were productions closer in spirit to the Granville-Barker ideals, in which the scenery was being simplified and the text being played more swiftly. W. Bridges-Adams out at Stratford-upon-Avon was attempting both in the 'twenties and early 'thirties (items T1129, T1436). A new generation of talent was bringing new life to the play in these years: Sybil Thorndike was Hermia under Ben Greet; Edith Evans was Helena and Gwen Frangcon Davies was Titania under Basil Dean; and Baliol Holloway was Bottom under Andrew Leigh at the Old Vic. Audiences at the Old Vic in 1929 and 1931 saw John Gielgud as Oberon, Leslie French as Puck, Margaret Webster as Hermia, and Ralph Richardson as Bottom, under the direction of Harcourt Williams (item T1111). Williams was reading Granville-Barker's *Prefaces* (items 9, 11). He also was influenced by the idea of this play being originally produced for a court wedding, as John Masefield had pictured it in his *William Shakespeare* (1911). Williams gave his staging the flavor of an Elizabethan or Jacobean court masque. Designer Paul Smyth borrowed from Inigo Jones and arrayed the fairies in seaweed. This Jacobethan motif would be a recurring one in productions over the next half century. It evoked the golden age of the playwright and his queen and placed the emphasis upon the beauty of the poetry and the glory of the poet.

In 1937, Tyrone Guthrie and designer Oliver Messel brought out the play at the Old Vic dressed in all the old

Victorian iconography. It was produced at Christmas time, and, inside the Old Vic's grand proscenium, fairies were flown and fairies danced to Mendelssohn. Dancer Robert Helpmann played Oberon, giving him a slightly sinister appearance. His Titania was Vivian Leigh, in wings and rosebuds. The production, whether created with nostalgia or with tongue-slightly-in-cheek, was fondly received.

German director Max Reinhardt staged the play, his favorite, in some eleven varying versions between 1905 and his Hollywood film of 1935. They ranged from his neo-romantic staging of 1905, which featured a three-dimensional forest that turned on a revolving stage, to his production at the Salzburg Festival in 1927, which put the play in a Baroque world of twisting columns, staircases, and candelabra. It featured Reinhardt's stellar company that included Alexander Moissi as Oberon and Lili Darvas as Titania (items T1390a, T1523). Following several outdoor, pageant-proportion productions in Europe and the United States, Reinhardt, with former pupil William Dieterle, created the 1935 film of the play (item T1406, T1323). It may be said to be as extravagant a spectacle in its way as any nineteenth century stage production of the play had been, but more than that, as Jack Jorgens has shown in his detailed appreciation (item T1406), it is rich with many remarkably interpretative strokes. Bottom in the ass's head becomes a Narcissus figure. There are dark strains of imaginative erotic symbolism, such as the dream sequence dance in which the allegorical female figure of night is sexually conquered by a dark male figure of Night. In this respect, as Jorgens has noted, portions of Reinhardt's film prefigure the darker directorial treatments of the play to come in the 1960s. But Reinhardt also deploys trains of follies' girls as fairies and finds a diminutive orchestra of elves in the forest: the kitsch and the sublime are strange bedfellows. The cast featured a number of American stars, some of whom were surprisingly effective in Shakespeare in the new medium. Victor Jory was Oberon, James Cagney was Bottom, Mickey Rooney was Puck, Joe E. Brown was Flute and Thisby, and Olivia de Havilland was Hermia. The film did not achieve commercial success in its time, but it remains a landmark in Shakespearean film history as an early, creative attempt to marry Shakespeare's theatre of words to the film's world of visual images. The Reinhardt film had been preceded by seven silent film experiments with *A Midsummer Night's Dream* between 1906 and 1925, the last a strangely dark variation directed by Hans Neumann, with titles by Klabund (items T1283a, T1240).

In productions in the years following World War II, there were some elaborate attempts at romantic reaffirmation, some of which tentatively suggested an erotic side to the dream world. At Stratford-upon-Avon in 1949, director Michael Benthall and designer James Bailey created a sumptuous Renaissance court peopled with heroic figures, while the wood was exotically sensuous (item T1110). In the Old Vic production of 1951, Guthrie left Victoriana behind. Tanya Moiseiwitsch's grove of silvered bamboo stood for the forest, and a wild-appearing Titania took a very human interest in Bottom (item T1120). At Stratford-upon-Avon in 1954, George Devine offered a directorial vision of Oberon and Titania as beautiful and fearsome birds, which distressed some critics (item T1140).

The most lavishly romantic post-war version came in the 1954 production in which the Old Vic and the Sadler's Wells Ballet combined forces under director Michael Benthall (item T1138). One hundred strings played Mendelssohn, and Helpmann and Moira Shearer virtually danced the roles of Oberon and Titania. Stanley Holloway was Bottom. The scenery included a Bibiena-sized palace for Theseus and, for part of the forest chase, a proscenium-wide cobweb that filled the stage of the Metropolitan Opera House where the production played in New York. It was a sell-out, though critics found it a cumbersome anachronism. At Stratford, Ontario, in these years, Guthrie and Moiseiwitsch were creating a new, proscenium-less theatre for Shakespeare, where poetry and suggestion were to displace pictorial illusion (item T1146); *A Midsummer Night's Dream* would make its first appearance there in 1960 (item T1194). In Stratford, Connecticut, in 1958, the American Shakespeare Festival offered the first significant American production of the play in half a century (item T1172). Director Jack Landau and designer David Hays borrowed and elaborated upon the Jacobethan wedding motif. The skeletal setting on the new modified thrust stage was elegant. The general spirit of the production was traditionally romantic. The special strength of it, the feature that those who saw it often recall, was the very individualized portraits of Shakespeare's common men by the American actors. Among the mechanicals were Hiram Sherman as Bottom, later replaced by Bert Lahr for the tour of the production; Will

Geer as Snout; Morris Carnovsky as Quince; and Ellis Rabb as Starveling.

In the early 1960s, there were two important, neo-romantic adaptations of the play, the Benjamin Britten opera of 1960 (items 1026a, T1188, and index), with its delicate, modernist scoring, and the George Balanchine ballet of 1962, based on the Mendelssohn score (items T1241a, T1409). The opera has become a standard in the international repertoire, and the ballet is a perennial in the repertoire of the New York City Ballet. The success of the Mendelssohn-inspired ballet in particular has meant that there has been a continuum for the romantic stage image of the play from the mid-nineteenth century to the closing decades of the twentieth.

In the theatre, the image of the play itself underwent a radical change in the 1960s. The 'sixties may be said to have begun with Peter Hall's production of 1959 at Stratford-upon-Avon (item T1183). It was a popular and an evolving production, created and then adjusted in revivals through 1963, during the formative years of the new Royal Shakespeare Company. A keystone principle of the RSC was that Shakespeare's plays should be imbued somehow with the spirit of the contemporary world. Hall's *A Midsummer Night's Dream* was a transition production, with elements of the past and the future in it. In the premiere in 1959, there was Charles Laughton as Bottom, heavily in the star tradition, but among the young lovers there were Albert Finney and Vanessa Redgrave, confused and ungainly, sounding notes of the uncertainties of a new age. The fairies were urchins in Jacobean court dress, but down below their starched ruffs they were barefoot. The forces of the irrational forest seemed just beneath the surface of the decorous court. The fairy world was a somewhat erotic, albeit benevolent one, a sensuous dream-world that stood in dramatic contrast to the daylight world of rational, orderly Athens. In the Royal Court Theatre production in London in 1962 (item T1215) and in Joseph Papp's 1964 production that toured to street and park audiences in New York City's five boroughs (item T1243), the elements of the play that became especially prominent were the young lovers, fleeing authority, and the mechanicals, who increasingly were becoming sources of democratic authenticity as much as sources of amusement.

In 1966, American director John Hancock and artist Jim Dine created an off-Broadway production that mocked all the popular romantic traditions around the play and created an erotic antimasque of its own (items T1269, T1312). At one end of a rainbow that provided the proscenium frame, and which was painted in house enamels, sat a neon-lighted Wurlitzer juke-box that played Mendelssohn's "Wedding March" at sexually suggestive moments. Titania was costumed as the comic book Wonder Woman, and the mechanicals were hippie-inspired. Helena was played by a female impersonator, and there was leathery sexual decadence in the love between Theseus and Hippolyta. In contrast, at Stratford, Connecticut, in the 1967 summer Shakespeare festival, Cyril Ritchard directed a conventionally romantic production in which he starred, doubling as both Bottom and Oberon (item T1277).

In 1970, the Royal Shakespeare Company production directed by Peter Brook turned the play that most still remembered as Shakespeare's moonlit, delicate fairy play into what was, for most, an exuberant, breathtaking celebration of young love and the theatre itself (item T1314). That Oberon and Puck should be swinging joyously on trapezes high above an all-white setting, bathed in dazzling white light, seemed, for many, surprisingly natural. The production spoke to the heart of a teeming cultural revolution and can be best understood in the context of a socially tumultuous era. It was received with an especially rapturous enthusiasm by those in sympathy with the youth culture of the era. They found in it a liberation of Shakespeare from the pretentious pomp and irrelevant reverence of the past. For them it was a joyous affirmation of faith in young love in the midst of what seemed an unending series of betrayals of ideals and duplicities by the adult establishment. These seemed to be compounded daily in issues touching the war in Viet Nam and civil rights. Urgent reasons to challenge all received values and to create a new, open world seemed to come from all sides. Explicit in the Brook production's all-white setting by Sally Jacobs, with its trapeze-born fairies, its ladders where the lovers scampered, and its catwalks where rock musicians accompanied the action, was an overt rejection of traditional illusion-making in favor of a theatricality that enjoined audience faith at every turn. Its young lovers were uninhibited, anxious, wired for spontaneous combustion. When Bottom went off to Titania's bower, borne on the shoulders of the fairies, one of them

simulated a huge erection for him with an upthrust arm
between his legs. It was a Dionysian gesture that might
have come out of Antonin Artaud or Jan Kott (items 239,
T1307) and was not far from the spirit of the ecstasies of
Hair, the "American Tribal Love-Rock Musical" of 1968. To
conservative critics, the Brook production seemed mere
gimmickry, an arrogant, adolescent vulgarization of a
delicate masterpiece, "Brook's *Dream*" indeed, not
Shakespeare's. But audiences world-wide came to see it
when it toured, and all objections may be said to have been
effectively overwhelmed by its impact. It was decisive proof
of the validity of the Royal Shakespeare Company's credo,
and it may be said to have profoundly altered the course of
Shakespearean production internationally over the decade
and a half since. It remains a key reference point in the
continuing debate over the so-called "director's theatre"
and the issue of directorial freedom in the interpretation of
Shakespeare's plays.

Between 1970 and 1982, four stage productions stand
out, each marked by a distinctive, innovative directorial
approach. At Stratford, Ontario, in 1976 and 1977, director
Robin Phillips took the Elizabethan world motif one
elaborate, romantic step further (item T1396). The staging
suggested, using framing tableaux that featured a
"Glorianna" out of Nicholas Hilliard, that the play was
Elizabeth I's dream, one in which the queen saw herself as
both Titania and Hippolyta. These roles were doubled, with
Maggie Smith memorable in them. The fairy world was made
a mirror of the court world. In 1977, the Royal Shakespeare
Company ventured its first revival since the pre-emptive
Brook production. Director John Barton's version made a
strong and distinctly different impression with its fantasy
forest world of exotic, unfolding plants and its bizarre
woodsprite fairies, young in body but with balding heads
and wizened faced (T1411). Presiding in the forest was
Patrick Stewart's masculine Oberon, a near-nude, bronzed
Aztec god. Contrasting with the sensuous forest was a
severe, high Renaissance court, costumed all in black and
white. In 1981, Ron Daniels' production with the RSC
offered vestiges of a Victorian theatrical world and puppet
fairies that looked like broken Victorian dolls. In the hands
of black-garbed operators against a black cyclorama, they
darted like spectres, ineffably sad relics of belief.
Theseus's palace reminded some of a Pollock toy theatre
setting, the forest was the backstage of a Victorian
theatre, and there were touches of English pantomime and

limelight. Some critics found it an occasion for nostalgia, some were perplexed or even angered by the bizarre puppets, and some found it poignant and disquieting, marked by an anxiousness for love and reconciliation. Late in 1982, on the stage of the National Theatre of Great Britain's Cottesloe Theatre, Paul Scofield was a grizzled, ancient Oberon amid Elizabethan fairies who were centuries old (item T1517). In director Bill Bryden's wistful vision, they dwelled in the wood around a manor house inhabited by an Edwardian summer community, and they haunted comfortingly and benevolently.

Sources of information on all the productions mentioned above and on many more will be found in the theatre section of the bibliography. It contains basically two types of annotated entries: (1) those for books and articles about productions of the play, historical and contemporary, and (2) production entries for selected important productions of the play on the English-speaking stage between 1940 and 1982. The production entries are incorporated in the chronological listing with the publications, arranged alphabetically in any given year under the play's title. (When there is more than one production in a given year, they are listed in the order of the dates of openings.) Each production entry provides the opening date and place of the production, a partial list of the cast and production staff, a brief characterization of the production and its historical significance, and a list of theatre reviews. The productions selected for such annotations are those that represent the work of nationally or internationally known directors, actors, and designers and that have been reviewed by several critics of major newspapers, magazines, or journals. (A checklist of the productions for which there are production entries will be found immediately preceding the stage history section of the bibliography. The bibliography also contains sources of information on hundreds of other productions, access to which may be had through the index. A "T" preceding the item number indicates a stage history section entry, as in T1314.) Films, television productions, operas, and ballets derived from the play are also given production entries, though without reviews. Production entries also contain cross references to other relevant entries, including published photographs, films, or sound recordings of the productions. We have preferred this format to the customary reliance on review entries, with excerpts, to represent productions. Comparisons among a number of sources, including a number of reviews, will,

we believe, lead the user to a better understanding of a
production and its place historically. The reader may also
wish to consult the index under the names of theatres,
companies, directors, actors, designers, composers, or
reviewers for further information on stage productions, or
under the headings of ballet, opera, music, film, or art.
The entries also include representative recordings of the
Mendelssohn score and of the Henry Purcell and Benjamin
Britten operas.

In the listings of articles and books, the reader will find
information on hundreds of other productions, including
productions in the three centuries from the Elizabethan
period to 1940. In the section of the bibliography entitled
"Adaptations, Acting Editions, Synopses, Influence," the
reader will find listed the published texts of adaptations
from the Restoration to the present and any published,
performance-derived acting texts of the play itself. For
promptbooks and related production materials, the reader
should consult Charles Shattuck's *The Shakespeare
Promptbooks* (see items T1264 and T1303). The priority
overall has been coverage of professional productions on the
English-speaking stage, but there are items representing
productions in many different nations. There are a number
of items on German productions, especially from Ludwig
Tieck through Max Reinhardt.

The reader will also find in the stage history section
some publications containing discussions or descriptions of
art works related to this play and, however indirectly, to
productions of it. These include exhibition catalogues.
However, this bibliography cannot remedy the absence of a
comprehensive catalogue of works of art illustrating
Shakespeare's plays or inspired by them; such a reference
companion is much needed.

The user new to research in theatre history may want to
consult a general bibliography such as that provided in
Oscar Brockett's *History of Theatre*, Fourth Edition (1982)
or, for tools, Marion K. Whalon's *Performing Arts Research*
(1976). Many standard works in the field published before
1940 are entered in our bibliography under their post-1940
reprint dates and are fully cross-referenced. Further
bibliographical help may be found in items T1098, T1249,
T1312, T1351, and T1398. Those interested in locating any
of the films listed here should consult the listings in the
Shakespeare on Film Newsletter.

I am indebted to the *World Shakespeare Bibliography*, published annually by the *Shakespeare Quarterly*, to its predecessors, to the annual *MLA Bibliography*, and to the *International Bibliography of Theatre*. I am grateful to the staff of the Folger Shakespeare Library, who daily helped speed my work, and I am indebted to Jeanne Newlin of the Harvard Theatre Collection and Dorothy Swerdlove of the Theatre Research Collection of the New York Public Library at Lincoln Center. I am also grateful for the solicitous attentions of the staff of the Shakespeare Centre Library in Stratford-upon-Avon. A grant from the National Endowment for the Humanities helped make my work there possible. Charles Shattuck urged that the work be done, and D. Allen Carroll has been a patient believer and partner.

Gary Jay Williams
The Catholic University of America

I. CRITICISM

Criticism

1 Hazlitt, William. *"The Midsummer Night's Dream." Examiner,*
   21 January 1816. Reprinted, among other places, in *The*
   Complete Works of William Hazlitt. Ed. P. P. Howe, after
   the edition of A. R. Waller and Arnold Glover.
   Centenary Edition. Volume 5. London and Toronto: J. M.
   Dent and Sons, 1934, pp. 274-77.

   Provoked by Frederic Reynolds' spectacular Covent
   Garden adaptation (see item 969), Hazlitt attacks the effort
   to represent on stage the illusions and poetry of the
   Dream. "Poetry and the stage do not agree together." In
   the case of this play, the imagination "cannot sufficiently
   qualify the impression made upon the senses by the visual
   spectacle [with the result that] the dream becomes an
   unmanageable reality." "Fairies are not incredible, but
   fairies six feet high are so." Hazlitt is remembered
   particularly for the following complaint: "All that is fine in
   the play, was lost in the representation. The spirit was
   evaporated, the genius was fled; but the spectacle was
   fine: it was that which saved the play. Oh, ye
   scene-shifters, ye scene-painters, ye machinists and
   dressmakers, ye manufacturers of moon and stars that give
   no light, ye musical composers, ye men in the orchestra,
   fiddlers and trumpeters and players on the double drum
   and loud bassoon, rejoice! This is your triumph; it is not
   ours." (Hazlitt included the piece in his *A View of the*
   English Stage, 1818.) See item 1a.

1a _____. *Characters of Shakespeare's Plays.* London:
   C. H. Reynell and C. and J. Ollier, 1817. xxiii, 352 pp.
   Reprint. London: Oxford University Press, 1927; New
   York: Dutton, 1957.

Bottom, the most romantic of mechanics, has not had justice done him. He is "conceited, serious, and fantastical." Puck, unlike the moralistic Ariel, is a "mad-cap sprite, full of wantonness and mischief." With Oberon and his fairies we enter into "the empire of butterflies." Here we see Shakespeare not as a gloomy and heavy writer but rather as full of delicacy and sportive gaiety, a poet, not a metaphysician. There is in *Dream* "more sweetness and beauty of description than in the whole range of French poetry put together." Reading it is "like wandering in a grove by moonlight: the descriptions breathe a sweetness like odours thrown from beds of flowers." Read it we must, for it is not actable. "When acted, [it] is converted from a delightful fiction into a dull pantomime. All that is finest in the play is lost in the representation." Hazlitt is recalling the Frederic Reynolds adaptation and his review of it; see items 1 and 969.)

1b Coleridge, Samuel Taylor. *The Literary Remains of Samuel Taylor Coleridge*. Ed. H. N. Coleridge. Volume 2. London: William Pickering, 1836. Pp. 110-14. Available in a number of sources, including *Coleridge's Shakespearean Criticism*. Ed. Thomas Middleton Raysor. Volume 1. Cambridge: Harvard University Press, 1930, pp. 100-102, from which the quotations below are taken.

Coleridge is disturbed by Helena's "ungrateful treachery" and delighted by the meter, especially of the fairies' verse, some of which he scans and describes. His notes are remembered primarily for two quotations: first, of the atmosphere--"I am convinced that Shakespeare availed himself of the title of the play in his own mind [as] a *dream* throughout"--second, of Puck's penultimate speech ("Now the hungry lion roars")--"O what wealth, what wild luxuriance, and yet what compression and condensation of English fancy." Elsewhere (p. 227, ed. Raysor) he remarks that "the whole of *Dream* is one continued specimen of the lyrical dramatized."

2 Knight, Charles. *Studies of Shakspere*. London: Charles Knight, 1851. vii, 560. First published in 1849. Reprint. New York: AMS, 1971.

The text is "as perfect as it is possible to be." The date 1594. "Of all the dramas of Shakspere there is none more

entirely harmonious." Malone was wrong (in item 735) to
find the play youthful in its beauties, evidence of the
playwright's minority. On the contrary, "if any single
composition were required to exhibit the power of the
English language for purposes of poetry, that composition
would be the 'Midsummer-Night's Dream.'" "The death / Of
learning, late deceased in beggary" (V.i.52-53) probably
refers to Greene, not Spenser. The poetry of the play Dr.
Johnson, who lived in a prosaic age, could not appreciate
(in item 732). And Hazlitt was right (items 1-1a): *Dream* is
"not for the stage--at least not the modern stage," though
it reflects the true dramatic spirit. It is not, moreover,
readily accessible to critical analysis. "No--the
'Midsummer-Night's Dream' must be left to its own
influences." (Pp. 207-13)

3   Hudson, Henry Norman. *Shakespeare: His Life, Art, and
    Characters.* 2 volumes. Boston: Ginn Brothers, 1872.
    Reprint. New York: Haskell House, 1970; AMS, 1973.

The central or governing idea of the play is the dream,
which explains and justifies its distinctive features. It
accounts for the preponderance of the lyrical over the
dramatic, and thus the fact that the play cannot be very
successfully performed, for the mixing of lofty and low, of
beautiful and grotesque, of fancy and fact. It accounts for
the preternatural setting and for the blending of droll with
romantic. Puck is "a little dream god." The fairies, whose
souls are more natural and sensitive than rational and
moral, are a "sort of personified dreams" with a keen sense
of the ludicrous and absurd. All the four parts (Theseus
and Hippolyta, Young Lovers, Fairies, and Mechanicals) are
made to "blend in lyrical respondence," and parody each
other. "The play forms properly a class by itself: literature
has nothing else like it. . . . All is the land of dreams--a
place for dreamers, not critics."

4   Dowden, Edward. *Shakspere: A Critical Study of His Mind
    and Art.* London: Henry S. King, 1875. xvii, 434 pp.
    Reprint. London: Routledge and Kegan Paul, 1948, 1957,
    1967; New York: Capricorn Books, 1962.

The setting is the beginning of May; the title points to
the first performance, the midsummer, perhaps, of 1594.
Theseus, who is magnificent, is "a grand ideal figure, . .

. the heroic man of action" seen here in his leisure. Shakespeare admires Theseus and at the same time feels over him a "secret superiority" (pp. 66-72). The mechanicals' interlude is an indirect apology for Shakespeare's own imperfect representation of the fairy world in *Dream*. For Dowden, *Dream* is "the poem" (p. 68). Bottom is "incomparably a finer efflorescence of the absurd than any preceding character of Shakespeare's invention" (p. 361).

5 _____. *Introduction of Shakespeare*. New York: Charles Scribner's Sons, 1895. 136 pp. First published in 1893. Several reprints, including New York: AMS, 1970.

The single paragraph (pp. 59-60) observes that *Dream* is "in part a perfect piece of lyrical poetry, in part a very imperfect drama."

6 Brandes, Georg. *William Shakespeare. A Critical Study*. 2 volumes. Translated from the Danish by William Archer, Mary Morison, and Diana White. London: Heinemann, 1898. Numerous reprints, including New York: Ungar, 1963.

Dream, "the first consummate and immortal masterpiece which Shakespeare produced," is notable especially for its incomparable lyric poetry; indeed, it is "rather to be described as a dramatic lyric than a drama in the strict sense of the word." The mix of courtly, artisan, and supernatural is also remarkable. The surface provides, among other delights, the "playful irony" of the poet about his own art. Oberon's speech to Puck undoubtedly refers to the Kenilworth festival of 1575 and to Leicester's relations with the Queen and Lettice, Countess of Essex, in the allegorical manner of Lyly's *Endymion* (see item 568). It deals with "love as a dream, a fever, an illusion, an infatuation, and making merry, in especial, with the irrational nature of the instinct." "The germs of a whole philosophy are latent in the wayward love-scenes." (Pp. 76-86)

7 Chesterton, G. K. "*A Midsummer Night's Dream.*" *Good
   Words*, 45 (1904), 621-26. Reprint. *The Common Man.*
   New York: Sheed and Ward, 1950, 1960.

   Dream is a psychological study of a spirit that unites
   mankind, and in this sense is "the greatest of
   [Shakespeare's] plays." Its sentiment (which Shaw could
   not see) is the "mysticism of Happiness"; "it has amazing
   symmetry, . . . amazing artistic and moral beauty." "If
   that ending were acted properly any modern man would feel
   shaken to his marrow if he had to walk home from the
   theatre through a country lane." "Shakespeare contrives to
   make the whole matter mysteriously hilarious while it is
   palpably tragic, and mysteriously charitable, while it is in
   itself cynical." Chesterton analyzes the way it is like a
   dream and Bottom's character--at length and
   rhapsodically--"He is greater and more mysterious than
   Hamlet." And comments on the Englishness of it all.

8 Swinburne, Algernon Charles. *Shakespeare.* London and
   New York: Henry Frowde, Oxford University Press,
   1909. 83 pp. Reprints. Folcroft, Pa.: Folcroft Library
   Editions, 1974; Norwood, Pa.: Norwood Editions, 1975;
   Philadelphia: R. West, 1978.

   Among the few comments (pp. 33-34): *Dream* "is outside
   as well as above all possible or imaginable criticism." "It is
   probably or rather surely the most beautiful work of man."

9 Granville-Barker, Harley. "Preface." *"A Midsummer Night's
   Dream": An Acting Edition.* London: Heinemann, 1914,
   pp. iii-x. Reprinted in *More Prefaces to Shakespeare.*
   Ed. Edward M. Moore. Princeton: Princeton University
   Press, 1974.

   According to the "pious commentators," this play is
   "impossible" in the theatre. And it *is* poetic, "in every
   sense nearer to 'Venus and Adonis' than *Macbeth.*" The
   fault is not Shakespeare's or the theatre's; it is ours,
   especially our failure to appreciate verse in drama.
   Shakespeare's heart was in these passages of verse, these
   "screeds of word-music," and he is a dramatist of genius.
   They are therefore filled with excitement and spontaneity;
   they are poetry made dramatic. "The fairies are the
   producer's test." Children, who are untrained to speak,

should not be used. The fairies may look "pretty"; they must not startle. (Throughout, Granville-Barker is commenting on his own production at the Savoy Theatre in January 1914.)

10   Croce, Benedetto. *Ariosto, Shakespeare and Corneille*. Translated by Douglas Ainslie. London: George Allen & Unwin; New York: Henry Holt, 1920. viii, 440 pp. Reprint. New York: Russell and Russell, 1966.

On the balance between dream and reality is this "quintessence" of all the comedies of love. "The little drama seems born of a smile." It shows "the quick ardours, the inconstancies, the caprices, the illusions, the delusions, every sort of love folly" in a world equally real, equally fantastic. (Pp. 171-74)

11   Granville-Barker, Harley. "Preface." *A Midsummer Night's Dream*. London: Ernest Benn, 1924, pp. ix-lii. (Vol. 4 of *The Players' Shakespeare*.) Reprinted in *More Prefaces to Shakespeare*. Ed. Edward M. Moore. Princeton: Princeton University Press, 1974.

Offers a compromise for this play between the mechanism of the modern theatre and Shakespeare's stage-craft. His resource was the spoken word, not visual illusion. As for intervals, which are not made explicit in the text, a modern director may rely on his own sense of the rhythm of construction; the fewer the better. Details of the staging, particularly the possibility of a machine for Titania's bower, more conveniently fit the Elizabethan great hall than its public stage. However the play was performed, its verse, which is what matters, must be done with clarity of utterance and delicate phrasing. Elizabethan music, because somewhat unfamiliar and thus suggestive, is to be preferred, or else folk-music, not Mendelssohn. The designer is not to stress the classical, Athenian setting. Casting should take into account the variety and blend of voice-tones, for sheer sound is crucial with this play--"the limpid music of his verse." "Poetry, poetry; everything to serve and nothing to compete with it!" Oberon and Titania are "daintily ridiculous." In all we do not need "ingenious machinery, gauzes, lighting." We do seem to need children--trained ones. The scene with the young lovers wrangling (discussed at length) is full of diversified effects. With Bottom Shakespeare seems to have allowed for both rustic clown and buffoon; we, perhaps for the best, banish the droll. Concludes with a list of preferred textual variants.

12 Chambers, E. K. "*A Midsummer Night's Dream.*" *Shakespeare: A Survey*. London: Sidgwick and Jackson, 1925. Reprint. New York: Hill and Wang, 1958 and following (A Dramabook), pp. 77-87. (First published in 1905 as an introduction to the Red Letter Shakespeare.) Reprinted in *Shakespeare: Modern Essays in Criticism*. Ed. Leonard F. Dean. New York: Oxford University Press, 1957; (in German) *Shakespeare. Englische Essays aus 3 Jahrhunderten zum Verständis seiner Werke*. Ed. Ernst Theodor Sehrt. Stuttgart: Kröner, 1958.

We are not to assume that Shakespeare believed in the supernatural. The fairies, drawn from sources classical as well as local, are symbolic, representing the "unexplained element in the course of human affairs upon earth," which here is love. The theme of the play, which all the threads are woven together to display, is comic love, "the lawlessness and laughableness of love." The lovers are the Hes and Shes of the conventional love-story, Bottom "the first of Shakespeare's supreme comic creations."

13 Priestley, J. B. "Bully Bottom." *The English Comic Characters*. London: Bodley Head, 1925, pp. 1-17. Reprint. 1963.

An influential defense of Bottom, "the most substantial figure in the piece," against the view that he is "gross, stupid, and ignorant." In a play "which is only so much gossamer and moonlight," he certainly appears to be "a piece of humorous, bewildered flesh, gross, earthy." And yet among his associates, he is "the romantic, the poetical, the imaginative man," the only one who shows any passion for drama, his imagination catching fire at the idea of it. Then, with Titania, he's the honest weaver, of solid male flesh, and something of a humourist. Afterwards, however, waking from his dream, his sense of wonder expands so that his style breaks down under the stress of it. We take him for the butt. He just may be "solemnly taking us in and secretly laughing at us." Such would be very English,

and "there is indeed no more insular figure in all
Shakespeare's wide gallery."

14 Latham, Minor White. *The Elizabethan Fairies: The Fairies
    of Folklore and the Fairies of Shakespeare.* Columbia
    University Studies in English and Comparative
    Literature. New York: Columbia University Press, 1930.
    Reprint. New York: Octagon, 1972. ix, 313 pp.

        Treats in depth (Chapters 5 and 6) the origins and
    nature, appearance and characteristics, and influence of
    Shakespeare's fairies and Robin Goodfellow. Latham
    concludes, finding no mention before, that Shakespeare
    invented diminutive fairies and all such subsequently derive
    from him, and that he was responsible for the benevolence
    of his fairies (Spenser excepted) and of those after. "Every
    aspect of their wickedness and every sign of their devilish
    connection is omitted from their portrait." "Diminutive,
    pleasing, and picturesque sprites, with small garden names
    and small garden affairs, associated with moon-beams and
    butterflies, they present themselves as a new race of
    fairies." Robin was (before) neither identified with fairies
    nor a *puck* (demon, devil). He was "the most famous and
    the most esteemed of all the spirits and supernatural beings
    who haunted England." Both a forest sprite and a domestic,
    and possessed of a broom and a boisterous "ho, ho, ho!",
    he was a native, shape-shifting, nonmalicious, practical
    joker who went by numerous titles. For other discussions of
    the nature of the fairies see items 24, 29, 56, 124, 183,
    239, 280a, 303, 334, 347, 453, 477, 504, 523, 569, 587a,
    597, 629-30, 635, 642, 644, 647, 661, 754, 756, 760, 825, 828,
    855, 913, 934 and 960.

15 Knight, G. Wilson. *The Shakespearian Tempest.* London: H.
    Milford, Oxford University Press, 1932. xxiv, 332 pp.
    Reprint. 3rd ed. London: Methuen, 1953, 1960, 1971.

        A sustained consideration (pp. 141-69) of the interplay
    of imagery and symbolism which finds the *Dream* "especially
    complex and beautiful." Primarily concerned with
    atmosphere, Knight constantly observes the peculiar mixture
    of the fearsome with the delightful. "Continually this play
    suggests *Macbeth*; elves and gnomes take the place of
    witches and ghosts, and here our dark strands are inwoven
    with brighter ones, and the total effect is, as I have

observed, that of a dream whose fairyland is sweet even though it be troubled." The atmosphere of gloom and dread is the "playground for the purest comedy." Knight's method is to proceed through categories of images (become symbols). Here is his own outline (p. 161): "Starting with tempests and dissension, I have traced the moon and darkness suggestion; the atmosphere of *Macbeth*-like nightmare, the mistakes and tragic passions, the fearsome beasts; again, the birds with which these are contrasted, a contrast perfectly and beautifully symbolized in the Bottom-Titania union; the sparkling jewel-imagery applied to grass and flowers; finally, the dawn-poetry, the waking back to human life. I have yet to observe the music which interthreads our pattern. . . ."

16   de la Mare, Walter. "The *Dream.*" *Pleasures & Speculations.* London: Faber and Faber, 1940, pp. 270-305. Reprint. Freeport, N.Y.: Books for Libraries, 1969. First published as the introduction to *A Midsummer Night's Dream.* Ed. C. Aldred. Scholar's Library Edition. London: Macmillan, 1935.

"The most lyrical, it is also perhaps the least intellectual of the plays." It is called a dream, resembles a dream, and we should submit ourselves to it as we would to a dream. Even though designed for the stage, it is more profitably experienced by reading. "How straightforward yet how fantastic and original a story the *Dream* has to tell." (We are led slowly through the story while mention is made, from the scholars, of the various sources for the separate elements, of possibilities for topical allusions, and of clues to the date of composition.) It is all little more than a parody of the theme of love. Unlike the other characters, the young lovers are not individualized, are "tongue-tied and tedious," only intermittently real. "Something must be amiss with their speeches." *Dream* reveals "discords in style and inequalities of mere intelligence so extreme" that it must have been composed at different times or else redrafted or revised. We may assume that the first of the three layers of composition in Dover Wilson's theory (the 1592 layer; see item 748) was not written by Shakespeare at all. See items 148 and 598.

17   Spurgeon, Caroline F. E. *Shakespeare's Imagery and What It Tells Us.* New York: Macmillan; London: Cambridge

University Press, 1935. Reprint. Boston: Beacon Press, 1958 and thereafter (Beacon Paperback); London: Cambridge University Press, 1971. xvi, 408, xvi pp.

The index lists twenty-six scattered references to passages from *Dream*. The main comment (pp. 259-63), which is about atmosphere, stresses the way the high frequency of moon images (the word occurs twenty-eight times) and the large number of nature images, including animals and birds, supply "the dreaming and enchanted quality in the play, which is reinforced by woodland beauty."

18 Charlton, H. B. "*A Midsummer Night's Dream*." *Shakespearian Comedy*. London: Methuen, 1938, pp. 100-123. Numerous reprints. First published in *Bulletin of the John Rylands Library*, 22 (1933), 44-46, and as *A Midsummer Night's Dream*. Manchester: Manchester University Press, 1933; reprint. Philadelphia: Richard West, 1977.

An important comment on the play in general with special attention to its theme of love, to the nature of love, its history, and the Elizabethan sense thereof. *Dream* is "the first play [it is compared with earlier plays] in which [Shakespeare] showed contemporary man buffeted by the power felt then to be the primary factor of his existence, his response to the quality and might of love." The rustics are "straight from the bosom of Mother Earth" and "nothing finally perturbs Bottom." "The main incidents of the play present the fashion of romantic love and the ways of romantic lovers." "Sanity, cool reason, common sense, is the pledge of Theseus against the undue ravages of fancy and of sentiment in human nature. But in Bottom the place of this intellectual temper is supplied by the crude native matter of human instinct." "*Dream* is Shakespeare's first comic masterpiece"; in it is his "first considerable apprehension of the enduring attitude of comedy."

19 Alexander, Peter. *Shakespeare's Life and Art*. London: J. Nisbet, 1939. vi, 247 pp. Reprint. 1944; New York: New York University Press, 1961, 1967; Westport, Conn.: Greenwood Press, 1979.

Placing *Dream* at the beginning of the "Second Period"
(1594-99), Alexander finds most likely the guess that the
piece was for the marriage of Elizabeth Carey and Thomas
Berkeley on 19 February 1956; and lists topical allusions
(the bad weather, James's fear of the lion) to 1594. "The
date 1596 cannot be far out." The First Folio is based on a
copy of the Second Quarto which had been compared with a
copy in the theatre. Bottom is a man of lucidity, sanity,
and common sense, belonging to "the purest comedy of
character"; Theseus "an admirable point of repose" amidst
it all. "There is no deep significance in the magic juice, no
profound interpretation of life in the adventures of the
lovers." (Pp. 104-109) See items 218-18a.

20 Brooke, C. F. Tucker. "Shakespeare Remembers His Youth
   in Stratford." *Essays and Studies in Honor of Carleton
   Brown*. New York: New York University Press, 1940,
   pp. 253-56. Reprinted in *Essays on Shakespeare and
   Other Elizabethans*. Ed. Leicester Bradner. New Haven:
   Yale University Press, 1948. Reprint. Hamden, Conn.:
   Archon Books, 1969.

   Suggests that Mercutio's Queen Mab speech preceded
   Dream. On the question of which play came first see also
   items 373, 622, 641, 744 and 913.

21 Miller, Donald C. "Titania and the Changeling." *English
   Studies*, 22 (1940), 66-70.

   Argues that Titania has made the boy her lover and that
   she is to be equated with Diana.

22 Smith, Thomas Warnock. *Shakespeare: "A Midsummer
   Night's Dream."* Notes on Chosen English Texts. London:
   James Brodie, 1940. 56 pp. Reprint. 1945.

   Designed for students. Includes sections on characters,
   plot, structure, style, along with general and context
   questions.

23 Spencer, Hazelton. *The Art and Life of William
   Shakespeare*. New York: Harcourt, Brace, 1940. xx, 495

14 _Criticism_

pp. Reprint. London: G. Bell and Sons, 1948; New
York: Barnes & Noble, 1970.

A general introduction (pp. 232-39) which seeks to
minimize the extent of the play's achievement. Typical of its
attitude are the following: "While the beauties of this play
are exquisite, they are works of craftsmanship, not of high
artistic purpose and belief." "The _Dream_ is a little too
romantic (in the worst sense), too glittering with poetic
tinsel, and . . . essentially trivial." "[It] is a romantic
comedy with farcical episodes. Unfortunately, each of these
elements obscures the other." "It defines, not poetry, but
charm." "[It is] the best of the lowest order of romantic
comedy."

24 Bickersteth, G. L. "The Philosophy of Shakespeare." _The
Aberdeen University Review_, 28 (1941), 84-92, 173-83.

Uses _Dream_ (pp. 174-75) to illustrate the phase of
Shakespeare's thought in which the operation of the fancy,
as opposed to stubborn matter-of-fact, is explored.

25 Falckenberg, Otto. "Zur Frage der Inszenierung [Staging]
des _Sommernachtstraum_." _Shakespeare Jahrbuch_, 77
(1941), 116-22. Also published as "Der neue
Sommernachtstraum. Gedanken zum Problem der
Inszenierung." _Münchener Neueste Nachrichten_, 16 March
1941, p. 4.

Falckenberg explains how he abandoned the illusionistic
effects of 19th century productions, emphasizing instead the
text. He wanted the stage empty to insure maximum freedom
of movement for the actors. Schlegel's translation he
considers a masterpiece, though it does not bring out
strongly enough the demonic, dangerous elements of the
play, thus the necessity for the Schröder translation.
Oberon alone, as a symbol of the genius of Shakespeare,
knows the magic formula for controlling the powers he
unleashes. On German translations see also items 26-27,
29-30, 128, 140, 207, 216, 446 and 528.

26 Gopfert, Herbert George. "Über Rudolf Alexander
Schröders Verdeutschung [Translation] von Shakespeares

Sommernachtstraum." Die Neue Literatur, 62 (1941),
258-61.

Compares Schröder's translation unfavorably with that of
Schlegel. See also item 25.

27 Lazenby, Marion Candler. *The Influence of Wieland and
Eschenburg on Schlegel's Shakespeare Translation.*
Baltimore: Johns Hopkins University, 1941. 37 pp.

Dream, Schlegel's first translation and one of six plays
here examined, was heavily dependent on Wieland and
Eschenburg, more so than Schlegel acknowledged. See item
25.

27a Ness, Frederic W. *The Use of Rhyme in Shakespeare's
Plays.* Yale Studies in English, 95. New Haven: Yale
University Press, 1941. Reprint. [Hamden, Conn.:]
Archon, 1969. x, 168 pp.

In *Dream* Shakespeare uses extended rhymed passages
with careful deliberation in support of the pervading
atmosphere of lyricism and romanticism and to differentiate
certain groups of characters. Throughout the play
distinctions in spoken medium are carefully kept. (Ness
gives in detail precisely when the lovers begin to rhyme
and stop and suggests why.) The trochaic tetrameter of the
fairies, he agrees with others, *is* the fairy dialect of
English literature. Mysterious are its charms. (Pp. 81-84)
For other discussions of rhyme see items 39, 488 and 508.

28 Reid, Forrest. "Some Reflections on *A Midsummer Night's
Dream." Retrospective Adventures.* London: Faber and
Faber, 1941, pp. 76-80.

One should mark the poetic and simple qualities of the
play, which are many, not its few dramatic and supposed
profound qualities. "I have had my private performance
[that is, reading], and it has left me with no desire for a
public one." The play's simply a fairy tale, not Brandes'
"great symbol" (item 6), and Theseus is merely a puppet
with a simple purpose, not Dowden's "heroic warrior and
man of action" (item 4).

29   Schröder, Rudolf Alexander. "Ein Wort zu Shakespeares
      Sommernachtstraum" [Remarks on Shakespeare's
      Midsummer Night's Dream]. *Hamburgischches Jahrbuch
      für Theater und Musik.* Hamburg: Broschek, 1941, pp.
      45-57. Reprinted in *Gesammelte Werke.* Volume 2. Berlin
      and Frankfurt: Suhrkamp, 1952, pp. 237-48.

      Discusses ways in which Shakespeare establishes a
      fairyland atmosphere in which no harm can come to the
      characters. He asks in an aside whether Wall and Moon are
      not a jibe at those who criticized the simplicity of the
      Elizabethan stage. Within this fairy-tale world Shakespeare
      introduces reality adroitly, as in the names he gives the
      elves and the gamut of emotions felt by the lovers. The
      presentation of Bottom and company and Theseus' words at
      the beginning of Act V are examples of masterful dramatic
      economy. In a comparison of *Dream* with *The Tempest* he
      finds that both lead through a whole world and that the mix
      of spirit and human world is present more naively in
      Dream. He uses daybreak in Act IV to illustrate how the
      fairy world and reality are interwoven, and ends with
      comments on his translation of *Dream.* See item 25.

30   Sehrt, Ernst Theodor. "Der entromantisierte
      'Sommernachtstraum': Zu Rudolf Alexander Schröders
      Neuubertragung" [The Deromanticized *Dream*: On R. A.
      S.'s New Translation]. *Germanisch-romanische* Monats-
      schrift, 29 (1941), 201-209.

      A careful comparison of the standard A. W. Schlegel
      translation with Schröder's reveals that the latter is more
      faithful to Shakespeare's rhyme and meter, achieves greater
      fidelity of vocabulary, and supplants some of Schlegel's
      lyricism with allegory in the manner of Shakespeare. But
      Schröder also exaggerates and at times draws lines more
      drastically than Shakespeare. The Baroque words Schröder
      employs often have associations for German readers which
      are not appropriate to Shakespeare's world. The translation
      deserves to be set alongside Schlegel's, but will not replace
      it. See also item 25.

31   Smythe, P. E. *"A Midsummer Night's Dream": Critical
      Notes, Appreciation and Exercises.* Sydney: College
      Press, 1941. 29 pp.

An introduction, with summaries and questions, designed as "private coaching" for students.

32 Sternberger, Dolf. "'Puck' Zum deutschen *Sommernachtstraum*" ["Puck": A Note on the German *Midsummer Night's Dream*]. *Frankfurter Zeitung*, 1941, nos. 8/9. (German--not seen)

33 Brown, Ivor. *A Word in Your Ear.* London: J. Cape, 1942. 136 pp. Reprint. 1944; New York: E. P. Dutton, 1945; Westport, Conn.: Greenwood Press, 1978.

Regrets (under *woodbine*) the loss of the word *woodbine* (II.i.251). It is not to be equated with *honeysuckle*. See item 45.

34 Entry Deleted.

35 Feely, Joseph Martin. *A Cypher Idyll anent The Little Western Flower.* Rochester, N. Y.: [privately printed], 1942. 82 pp.

An extended effort to "decypher" the section having to do with the changeling child (II.i.121-37) and with Oberon's Vision (II.i.148-68) in order to recover its hidden meaning. The allusion is taken generally to refer to Leicester's relationship with the Queen and his marriage to Lettice Knollys (see item 568). Titania is equated with the Queen. And Frances Bacon is discovered, although he is not identified with any character in the play. Most of the argument has to do not with what is discovered but with the method of decipherment. On Bacon see also items 591a and 609a.

36 Kökeritz , Helge. "Shakespeare's *night-rule.*" *Language*, 18 (1942), 40-44.

"Phonologically *rule* in the Shakespearean compound *night-rule* (III.ii.5) is merely a variant of *revel* ; *night-rule* accordingly means 'nightly merry-making or diversion.'" This information is also in his *Shakespeare's*

Pronunciation (New Haven: Yale U. P., 1953, etc.), pp. 189, 325.

37 Law, Robert Adger. "The 'pre-conceived pattern' of *A Midsummer Night's Dream.*" *Studies in English* (University of Texas), 23 (1943), 5-14.

Cannot praise the construction of *Dream* so highly as others do or find organic unity in the four themes of the plot. Shakespeare, rather, follows a pattern set by two or more of his predecessors (Lyly and Greene are discussed) in comedy. The four groups remain solidified and independent of each other at the last as at the first. See also items 184 and 282.

38 Lemmonnier, Léon. *Shakespeare.* Paris: Éditions Jules Tallandier, 1943. 473 pp.

Speculates (in Chapter 15) as to the Derby (William Stanley) influence on the play. *Dream* seems to reproduce the love relationships of different patrons of Shakespeare. "Bridget de Vere aime Lord Herbert, qui aime Mary Fitton, qui aime Derby, qui aime Elizabeth de Vere, qui aime Southampton, lequel en aime peut-être une autre." The mechanicals' part may have been suggested by the dramatic festival at Chester (associated with Derby) which included *Balaam and His Ass.* See items 611a and 626.

38a Lloyd, Francis V., Jr. "Shakespeare in Junior High." *English Journal,* 36 (June 1943), 337-38.

Experience producing "Pyramus and Thisbe" suggests that Shakespeare is not too difficult for junior high students to perform well and audiences to receive favorably.

39 Maas, P. "Note on 'M. L. R.' 1943, p. 128." *Modern Language Review,* 39 (1944), 179.

Quotes V.i.158-59 (*Thisbe-secretly*) to qualify Percy Simpson's statement that Shakespeare avoided rhyming a masculine ending with a feminine one.

40 Baldensperger, Fernand. *La Vie et l'oeuvre de William Shakespeare*. Montréal: Les Éditions de l'arbre, 1945. 262 pp. (French)

Dream demonstrates a strong moral: that marriage, not infatuation, is the authentic experience. In making this point Shakespeare doubtless was supporting a will growing more and more emphatic in the Queen that her court should not permit or condone the "*galanterie*" of the French and Italian courts. (Pp. 102-110)

41 Casamian, Louis. *L'Humour de Shakespeare*. Paris: Aubier, 1945. 233 pp. (French)

In Bottom Shakespeare recalls the clown to his simple (nonprofessional) foolishness, purifying and exalting him to a new level of art. The key to his humour is his self-possession. Puck's detached view of mortal activities makes him almost god-like and thus makes Shakespeare philosophical. (Pp. 37-39, 48-49)

42 Horne, Herman Harrell. *Shakespeare's Philosophy of Love*. Raleigh, N. C.: Edwards & Broughton, 1945. xviii, 205 pp.

Shakespeare is "having fun with love" by having it a species of fairy enchantment (one way, though not the best, of understanding love). (Pp. 42-47)

43 Entry Deleted.

44 Troubridge, St. Vincent, Bernard Redding, and A. S. E. Ackermann. "Nine Men's Morris." *Notes and Queries*, 188 (1945), 40-41.

In response to a query about the nature of the game (mentioned at II.i.98), these three notes give a list of helpful sources and quote a description from *Shakespeare's England*.

45 Harrison, Thomas P., Jr. "Flower Lore in Spenser and
    Shakespeare: Two Notes." *Modern Language Quarterly*, 7
    (1946), 175-78.

    Shakespeare may have had the rose in mind for "Cupid's
    Flower"--as in Henry Lyte's *Newe Herbal* (1578). "Dian's
    bud" may represent a combination of *Agnus castus*,
    associated with chastity, and *Artemisia*, associated with the
    deity. For other discussions of the plant imagery see items
    15, 17, 33, 89, 230, 276, 338, 445, 503, 541, 632, 670 and
    682.

46 Palmer, John. "Bottom." *Comic Characters of Shakespeare*.
    London: Macmillan, 1946, pp. 92-109. Reprint. 1947,
    1949, 1953, 1956, 1959, 1961. New York: St. Martin's,
    1956, 1962.

    Bottom alone sustains "the triple illusion" ("classical
    antiquity, rural Britain, and the kingdom of the fairies") of
    the play, supporting its gossamer structure. He is
    imperturbable, ingenuous, full of sheer enthusiasm and
    good-fellowship, and "has an unerring sense of the fitness
    of things." He is not a "self-centered, conceited person--as
    he is so unfairly charged with being." He, like all parts,
    should be presented with simplicity and innocence. For two
    hundred years, the failure to do his part right rendered
    the play incoherent. He has been victimized by "the
    clodpole tradition of the professionally funny man."

47 Schröder, Rudolf Alexander. "Das Menschenbild in
    Shakespeares *Sommernachtstraum*." *Zeitwende*, 18
    (1946/47), 86-97, 172-83. Reprinted in *Gesammelte
    Werke*. Volume 2. Berlin and Frankfurt: Suhrkamp,
    1952, pp. 248-80.

    Schröder asks what the higher idea is which has made
    this one of the most popular stage plays in Germany. In
    Shakespeare there is a Catholic element--the view that all
    worldly events emanate from Divine Providence--, a
    Protestant element--spiritual uproar, doubt and
    individualism--, and a pagan element, which shows both a
    classical and popular face in *Dream*. The combination makes
    Shakespeare the greatest writer of Humanism. Schröder
    examines these four elements within the scenic and spiritual
    structure of *Dream*. He points out confusion in the setting

(the reference to 1 May is, perhaps, a joke directed against the Puritans). Playing the devil's advocate, he determines that the personae are no more reputable than the calendar, that the classical mythology is a mishmash and the fairies and elves a questionable lot. The fifth act shows the human characters poised, elegant, and desirous of amusement, so the play-within-a-play reveals the audience to us. Several lines which put these dubious events in a kinder light are Bottom's stammering attempts to explain his dream and Theseus' words in V.i.214-15, both of which Schröder interprets as comments on all human activity. A sense of agape, of confidence and security pervades the play.

48 Watkins, Ronald. *Moonlight at the Globe: An Essay in Shakespeare Production.* London: Michael Joseph, 1946. 135 pp.

See item T1103.

49 Chambrun, Clara Longworth, Comtesse de. *Shakespeare Retrouvé: Sa vie; son oeuvre.* Paris: Libraire Larousse, 1947. Translated and revised by the author as *Shakespeare: A Portrait Restored.* London: Hollis and Carter, 1956; New York: P. J. Kennedy & Sons, 1957. x, 406 pp.

This brief introduction (pp. 82-83) takes the play to have been many times corrected and altered, the date of the Second Quarto to be 1609, and the marriages it helped celebrate to have been several, beginning with that of Essex and Sir Philip Sidney's widow in 1589.

50 Reyher, Paul. *Essai sur les Idées dans l'oeuvre de Shakespeare.* Bibliothèque des Langues Modernes, I. Paris: Marcel Didier, 1947. xxix, 662 pp. (French)

Quotes Sidney, Lyly, and Greene to show that *Dream* reflects a contemporary view as to the follies of love and contrasts the worlds of dream and reality in the play. (Pp. 57-63, 164-73)

51 Winsteadt, Richard. "The East in English Literature." *Indian Arts and Letters,* 21 (1947), 1-12.

Mentions Shakespeare's notion of India as a fairy-land in
Dream.

52 Wood, Stanley. *The New Teaching of Shakespeare in
    Schools*. London: Gill, 1947. 57 pp.

    Centers "new teaching" in the child and gives lessons on
    Julius Caesar and *Dream* (pp. 20-26) with tips on how not
    to teach (pp. 33-34).

53 Yoder, Audrey. *Animal Analogy in Shakespeare's Character
    Portrayal*. New York: King's Crown Press at Columbia
    University, 1947. x, 150 pp. Reprint. New York: AMS,
    1975.

    From the text and old theatrical accounts, we can
    surmise that Snug's lion costume must have had a mane and
    fastened down the front and that Bottom's piece resembled a
    sketch of an ass's head later drawn by Inigo Jones. (Pp.
    65-73, 84-89) For other discussions of animal imagery see
    items 15, 17, 107, 239, 391, 421, 433 and 619.

54 Craig, Hardin. *An Interpretation of Shakespeare*. New
    York: Dryden Press; Columbia, Mo.: Lucas Brothers
    Publishers, 1948. Reprint. New York: Citadel Press,
    1949. xii, 400 pp.

    Praises *Dream* for its masterful weaving together of
    various apparently unrelated plots into one story, quoting
    Dr. Johnson's enlightened common sense on the matter of
    unities. Edith Rickert's reading (that the play was inspired
    by and reflects the Earl of Hertford's effort to have the
    Queen declare his son legitimate--see item 574) is "the most
    credible of all accounts so far advanced," and thus the
    original play may be dated 1591. He also suggests that
    there are various levels of language (p. 35). It is "a
    culmination of Shakespeare's early achievements in comedy."
    (Pp. 35-38)

55 Graves, Robert. *The White Goddess: A Historical Grammar
    of Poetic Myth*. London: Faber and Faber; New York:
    Creative Age Press, 1948. 496 pp. Reprint. London:
    Faber and Faber, 1952.

For a sincere and accurate portrayal of the White Goddess one must not be misled by "the extraordinary mythographic jumble" of *Dream*. The whimsical fairies are the three fates; Robin is Hercules; Bottom is the Wild Ass of Dionysus; and Titania the Queen of Heaven. (P. 353) For other discussions of mythic elements and readings see items 47, 74, 142, 144, 181, 316, 329, 331, 335, 353, 391, 424, 432, 451, 457-8, 516, 538, 551, 555, 561, 618, 655, 672, 674 and 684.

56 Lindsay, Jack. "Shakespeare and Tom Thumb." *Life and Letters*, 58 (1948), 119-27.

The ancient folk tradition of Tom Thumb provides the clue to "the psychic meaning" (Tom as potent, irresponsible phallus) and is the source Shakespeare drew on for reducing the size of the fairies. See item 14.

57 Partridge, Eric. *Shakespeare's Bawdy: A Literary & Psychological Essay and a Comprehensive Glossary.* London: Routledge and Kegan Paul, 1947; New York: E. P. Dutton, 1948. ix, 226 pp. Rev. and Enlarged. 1955. Reprint. 1956, 1960, 1968.

Finds *Dream* "a pretty 'safe' play, hence a favourite in school examinations" (p. 53). Gives fewer than twenty references to the play in his glossary and these quite modest (*bed, burn, desire,* for examples). For other discussions of bawdy see items 154, 194, 204, 338b, 364a, 434, 444, 474, 511, 550 and 552.

58 Sitwell, Edith. "Some Notes on the Texture of *A Midsummer Night's Dream.*" *A Notebook on William Shakespeare.* London: Macmillan, 1948, pp. 186-93. Reprint. 1962.

Analyzes the poetic properties, especially sound properties, of various lines, including at length the Lysander-Hermia exchange (I.i.128-49) and "Over hill, over dale" (II.i.2-15).

59 West, E. J. "On a Purely Playful Hypothesis Concerning the Composition of 'Midsummer Night's Dream.'" *College English,* 9 (1948), 247-49.

Shakespeare reworked parts and devices he had found "theatrically valid" in *Love's Labour's Lost* and used the same cast. For other comparisons with this play see items 82, 101, 229, 282, 305, 311, 320, 333, 355, 372, 387a, 400, 414, 429, 436, 484-85, 643, 675, 756, 828, 913 and 960.

60   Fiedler, Leslie A. "The Defense of the Illusion and the Creation of Myth: Device and Symbol in the Plays of Shakespeare." In *English Institute Essays: 1948*. Ed. D. A. Robertson, Jr. New York: Columbia University Press, 1949, pp. 74-94. Reprinted as "Shakespeare and the Paradox of Illusion." *No! In Thunder: Essays on Myth and Literature*. Boston: Beacon Press, 1960.

The play-within-a-play is a "technical or structural myth" in which the artist justifies his art, defends the illusion of art. The failure of the illusion in the last plays becomes the revelation of a higher truth (all death is a hoax). In *Dream* the playlet is a "stunt to maintain a precarious illusion . . . of the larger production." ("The peripheral vulgar characters . . . seem to exist so often in Shakespeare, like Negroes in Hollywood films, largely to amuse the gentry.") For other discussions of the play-within see items 64, 80, 101, 122, 130, 157, 165, 172, 199, 307, 319, 400, 411, 415, 428, 449, 461, 482, 484, 496, 504, 535, 557, 572, 578, 613, 615-16, 618a, 641, 651, 657, 663, 676, 683, 685 and 802.

61   Frye, Northrop. "The Argument of Comedy." *English Institute Essays 1948*. New York: Columbia University Press, 1949, pp. 58-73. Reprint. *Shakespeare: Modern Essays in Criticism*. Ed. Leonard F. Dean. Rev. ed. New York: Oxford University Press, 1967. *Shakespeare's Comedies: An Anthology of Modern Criticism*. Ed. Laurence Lerner. Harmondsworth, Middlesex, and Baltimore: Penguin, 1967. *Essays in Shakespearean Criticism*. Ed. James L. Calderwood and Harold E. Toliver. Englewood Cliffs, N. J.: Prentice-Hall, 1970.

See item 142.

62   Halliday, F. E. *Shakespeare and His Critics*. London: Duckworth, 1949. 522 pp. Reprint. 1950. Rev. ed. New York: Schocken Books, 1958, 1965. 336 pp.

Provides (pp. 374-77 of the 1949 edition) passages from John Spencer, Samuel Pepys, Samuel Johnson (see item 732), Samuel Taylor Coleridge (see item 1b), William Hazlitt (see item 1), and Benedetto Croce (see item 10).

62a "*A Midsummer Night's Dream*" [filmstrip]. *The Shakespeare Series*. Del Mar, Calif.: Young America Films, 1949. Distributed by McGraw-Hill Films (New York, N. Y.). Code: 403403, 53 fr., b/w, 35 mm. (not seen)

An introduction to the play with photos from the Max Reinhardt 1935 movie. According to the catalogue description, "the play sequences enable students to analyze and study the main themes, to identify characters and plots, and to understand relationships." With teacher's guide.

63 Parrott, Thomas Marc. "*A Midsummer Night's Dream*." *Shakespearean Comedy*. London and New York: Oxford University Press, 1949, pp. 125-33. Reprint. New York: Russell & Russell, 1962.

This introduction touches on most of the critical and scholarly concerns of the play. *Dream* "surpasses the other comedies of the prentice period," an advance in part due to the period of the plague when Shakespeare was successful with his Ovidian poems. Parrott dates *Dream* late 1594; takes the marriage it celebrates to be that of William Stanley, Earl of Derby, on 26 January 1595; believes there is a double-ending; and quotes at length the relevant source portion of Montemayor's *Diana* as part of a running commentary on sources. Bottom is a pragmatist with "not a trace of romantic sentiment" in him. "Nowhere in all Shakespeare's works do we hear singing in so carefree a strain." The play "has never enjoyed great success upon the stage." (Parrott had used some of this material in his 1938 edition of Shakespeare; see item 757.)

64 Pettet, E. C. "Shakespeare's Detachment from Romance." *Shakespeare and the Romance Tradition*. London: Staples, 1949, pp. 101-135. Reprint. London: Methuen, 1970.

Dream (pp. 109-114) is one of the group of "Romantic Comedies" the general characteristics of which are given in Chapter 4. At the same time the play evinces a certain "detachment" toward romanticism, a smiling at what is cherished, through an awareness of its opposites, fickleness and inconstancy. *Dream* "contains a strong note of criticism and interrogation, which is announced insistently, even monotonously, in the very first scene." Bottom serves, as other characters before him had, "to embody a mundane, broadly comic antithesis to the romance world," and his playlet is "a murderous burlesque of romance." After giving the shaping attitude toward love behind the play, Pettet concludes that "the romantic claims for its moral and spiritual elevation . . . are grossly exaggerated."

65 Potts, L. J. *Comedy*. New York and London: Hutchinson University Library, 1949. 174 pp. Several reprints.

To illustrate a notion of comedy, Potts quotes and analyzes part of III.i (Titania waking with Bottom), stressing the incongruity, the simplicity of Bottom, "the fatuity of the exquisite Titania." "This scene, ranging from crude farce to high poetical comedy, tells us all we need to know about the comic mode." (Pp. 22-26)

66 Saitō, Takeshi. *Shakespeare Kenkyū* [A Study of Shakespeare]. Tokyo: Kenkyūsha, 1949. Ch. 9, Sect. 2. (Japanese)

"What makes this early work noteworthy is the beauty of the dreamlike atmosphere on the one hand, and on the other, the considerable compositional skill in manipulating complicated plot."

67 Stauffer, Donald A. *Shakespeare's World of Images: The Development of His Moral Ideas*. New York: W. W. Norton, 1949. 393 pp. Reprint. Bloomington and London: Indiana University Press, 1966 (A Midland Book).

One quotation will illustrate the kind of comments on *Dream* in a brief section (pp. 49-53) of a chapter on "The School of Love": "the theme of love is multiplied and divided and diversified into myriad gambolings and dartings and involutions and returns and jokes. . . . Love is physical, mental, blind, rash, fickle, loyal, doting, modest, miserable, natural, true, faithful, a dove and a serpent, a madness, a mystery, . . . an enchantment, a curse and a blessing." For Stauffer the play reconciles desire and order.

68   Carrère, Félix. "L'Imagination dans le Théâtre de Shakespeare." *Les Langues Modernes,* 44 (1950), 100-13. (French)

Imagination can be destructive (as in certain plays) and constructive (as in *Dream* and *The Tempest*). See item 149.

69   Pettet, E. C. "Shakespeare's Conception of Poetry." *Essays and Studies,* n.s. 3 (1950), 29-46.

A general analysis of Shakespeare's theory of poetry based on passages in his works indicates that the last part of Theseus' speech (V.i.2-22) qualifies the commonplace double notion of poetry as *feigning* and *furor* presented earlier in the speech. First, the poet's fantasy has an "altogether exceptional range" (it idealizes, for example), and second, it is "controlled" (thus truly creative). Theseus' words are, for the most part, but a poetic version of Sidney's. Remarkably, though, whenever Shakespeare speaks of poetry he ignores the overt moral and didactic emphasis of contemporary theory.

70   Pogson, Beryl. "*A Midsummer Night's Dream.*" *In the East My Pleasure Lies: An Esoteric Interpretation of Some Plays of Shakespeare.* London: Stuart & Richards, 1950, pp. 70-77. Rev. ed. London: Coole Book Service, 1963. Reprint. Folcroft, Pa.: Folcroft Library Editions, 1974; New York: Haskell House, 1974.

Theseus, having himself escaped from the labyrinth of passion, with its Bull Monster, representing the lower nature of man, can best rescue the young lovers who wander there. An "ideal set up for the audience," he is "the clue to the teaching" of the play. Under his guidance the lovers awake from passion to a new point of view which makes them ready for marriage. The whole is an indictment of Eros, the frenzy of love. The mechanicals' production, which provides "a moral example," lays bare the madness, absurdity, and potential for tragedy which love causes. See item 55.

71 Sanders, Gerald. *A Shakespeare Primer*. New York and Toronto: Rinehart, 1950. 224 pp. Reprint. 1959; New York: AMS, 1972.

A brief introduction. Some scenes, it is observed, are "too close to farce and the entire play too full of fantasy to warrant our classing it among Shakespeare's greatest comedies." It is nonetheless a delightful play to see and read. (Pp. 92-94)

72 Sen Gupta, S. C. *Shakespearian Comedy*. Calcutta, New York, and London: Oxford University Press, 1950. xi, 281 pp. Reprint. 1967.

Bottom, the one great character in the play, "marks the limitation of Theseus' philosophy, because, though cool reason will not approve of him, he is perfectly sane, and though he has something of the poet and the lunatic and is made love to by a fairy Queen, . . . his imagination will stoutly refuse to body forth the forms of things unknown." He is not Priestley's "artist" (see item 13); he is "prosaic to the backbone," unromantic and mechanical, "a realist . . . [who] does not understand reality," which makes him "a mixture of contradictory traits." (Pp. 59-62, 115-25).

73 Schomerus, Hans. "Der Kobold und die Güte Gottes" [The Sprite and God's Goodness]. *Zeitwende*, 22 (1950/51), 177-78. (German--not seen)

Apparently contains an interpretation of the moral of *Dream*.

73a Alexander, Peter. *A Shakespeare Primer*. London: James Nisbet, 1951. [x[, 182 pp.

"*Dream* is in some respects the most perfect of Shakespeare's comic devisings," Alexander says in this one-paragraph comment (p. 82). It is its own kind, with an enchantment which transforms human values and which criticism cannot reach.

74 Barber, C. L. "The Saturnalian Pattern in Shakespeare's Comedy." *Sewanee Review,* 59 (1951), 593-611.

The material here on *Dream* reappears in the author's *Shakespeare's Festive Comedy* (item 158).

75 Budde, Fritz. "Shakespeare und die Frage der Raumbühne" [Shakespeare and the Question of the Spatial-Stage]. *Shakespeare-Studien. Festschrift für Heinrich Mutschmann.* Ed. Walther Fischer and Karl Wentersdorf. Marburg: Elwert, 1951, pp. 21-47. (German)

Concentrates on the range of places and scenes in *Dream* and *Hamlet,* contrasting the "limitations" demanded by French dramaturgy with the "openness" of Shakespearean drama, and using *Dream* (pp. 24-36) as one example. The wedding feast, it is argued, is the "center of gravity" and focal point of all love motifs and plots.

76 Chute, Marchette. *An Introduction to Shakespeare.* New York: Dutton, 1951. 123 pp.

A brief (pp. 49-51) appreciation of the play, especially of its mix of the fairy world and the real. Shakespeare is praised for setting Bottom into this fairyland and for his "gentle courtesy" even toward fools.

77 Crane, Milton. *Shakespeare's Prose.* Chicago: University of Chicago Press, 1951. 219 pp.

"In no other play are prose and the several forms of verse so skillfully blended." The various styles (discussed on pp. 72-77) of expression help distinguish the different worlds (identified as four concentric circles). The royal and hapless lovers speak blank verse for the most part; the fairies speak blank verse occasionally but the rhymed octosyllabic line primarily; the mechanicals speak good, simple, direct prose, but for the bastard verses of their playlet. The mingling of prose and verse in the last scene is, "for delicacy and skill, unmatched in Shakespeare's work." For other discussions of prose see items 133, 139, 449 and 508.

78 Eardley-Wilmot, H. "'Write Me a Prologue.'" *English*, 8
    (1951), 272-74.

    Through Quince (and in other ways) Shakespeare shows
    prologues are absurd and clumsy devices.

79 Goddard, Harold C. "*A Midsummer Night's Dream*." *The
    Meaning of Shakespeare*. Chicago and London: University
    of Chicago Press, 1951, pp. 74-80. Reprint. 1969, 1973;
    2 volumes. Phoenix Edition, 1960.

    Dream announces "for the first time in overt and
    unmistakable fashion the conviction that underlies every one
    of his supreme Tragedies: that this world of sense . . . is
    but the surface of a vaster unseen world by which the
    actions of men are affected or overruled." Hippolyta "holds
    that the miracles of love are even greater than those of
    fancy, and because the same miracle takes place at the same
    time in more than one mind she believes that they testify to
    something solid and lasting that emerges from this 'airy
    nothing.'" The four "subjects" of the play--dream, play,
    love, art--are the four main aspects under which
    Imagination, the main theme, reveals itself. Imagination
    carries the sense, too, of Vision. Goddard compares *Dream*
    with *The Tempest*. The hound passage (IV.i.102-26) is as
    nearly perfect a metaphor for the play as can be conceived.

80 Schanzer, Ernest. "The Central Theme of *A Midsummer
    Night's Dream*." *University of Toronto Quarterly*, 20
    (1951), 233-38.

    The central theme is "the ridiculing of a certain kind of
    madness, a love-madness," one which ignores the evidence
    of the senses and the support of reason. With the
    Oberon-Titania quarrel we are dealing with lovers' quarrels
    in general (not the particular deviation which is the play's
    theme). "Nor is there any close relation between the main
    theme and the 'very tragical mirth' of Pyramus and
    Thisbe." It burlesques romantic love in general.

81 Desai, Chintamani N. *Shakespearean Comedy*. Indore City:
    Agra University Press, 1952. 204 pp. Reprint.
    Philadelphia: R. West, 1973; New York: AMS, 1975.

Dream is referred to briefly *passim*. A two-paragraph description of Bottom (on pp. 188-89) notes that while Shakespeare may have "meant him to be a fool," at least in the early scenes, Bottom quickly grows up, becoming bold and sensible, and thus truly comic, freed from the traditional motif of the clown.

82 Evans, B. Ifor. *The Language of Shakespeare's Plays.* Bloomington: Indiana University Press; London: Methuen, 1952. xi, 216 pp. Reprint. 1959, 1964.

In the *Dream* Shakespeare allows himself moments of simple, direct language in contrast with *Love's Labour's Lost* wherein his verse is almost totally the basis for the witty and decorative. Here the style is various (which is illustrated, pp. 45-52), and the transitions from one style to another produce some brilliant effects. "No passage of criticism can compete with [Theseus' speech] in showing the origins and effects of poetic imagery." The moonlight passages, an example of such effects, seems "to evoke the inner meaning of the *Dream.*" With this play, the rural theme, the basis of so much of the poetry of the early plays, passes.

83 Frye, Northrop. "Comic Myth in Shakespeare." *Proceedings and Transactions of the Royal Society of Canada,* 3rd series, 46, no. 2 (1952), 47-58. Reprinted in *Discussions of Shakespeare's Romantic Comedy.* Ed. Herbert Weil, Jr. Boston: D. C. Heath, 1966.

See item 142.

84 Gui, Weston A. "Bottom's Dream." *American Imago,* 9 (1952), 251-305.

A Freudian reading of Bottom's experience with Titania and other dream elements in the play in order to get at its meaning and the libidinous life of Shakespeare. Details of the play--taken to be Bottom's dream at large--reveal his jealousy of a sibling rival (the changeling boy), his Oedipal relationship with Oberon and Titania, and his failure to achieve sexual satisfaction. The moon is "the desirable but chaste and unattainable mother." The level of Bottom's erotic fantasy and of the regression is oral. The physical

confusion of the four lovers is a primal scene as it would
be observed by the child Bottom. Puck is "actually the
penis of the father." "Bottom's problems are basically those
of coping with oral trauma at the mother's breast and the
achievement of an identification with the father against
whom he has been thrust in phallic competition." See items
196 and 209.

84a Lease, Ruth, and Geraldine B. Siks. "Use of Shakespeare's
     Plays." *Creative Dramatics in Home, School, and
     Community.* New York: Harper & Bros., 1952, pp.
     96-97.

     Junior high students may enjoy creating the artisan and
     fairy scenes, but the scenes with the lovers should not be
     attempted.

85   Nicoll, Allardyce. *Shakespeare.* Home Study Books. London:
     Methuen, 1952. 181 pp. Reprint. 1961.

     Dream is "all a tissue of earlier material, and all
     magnificently new spun," and all bound together by "the
     theme of errors." In it Shakespeare first clearly introduces
     one of his most potent preoccupations--the theme of
     appearance and reality--which is the source of much of the
     inner quality of his later dramas, both comic and tragic.
     This "double vision" is evident in his treatment of the moon
     in *Dream.* We must certainly go beyond Theseus'
     levelheadedness to something more. (Pp. 104-107)

86   Schmidt, Karlernst. *Die Bühnenprobe* [Rehearsal] *als
     Lustspieltyp in der englischen Literatur.* Halle:
     Niemeyer, 1952. 32 pp. (German--not seen)

     A study of the "rehearsal" as a conventional element in
     English comedies. Contains a few comments on *Dream.*

87   Weilgart, Wolfgang J. *Shakespeare Psychognostic: Character
     Evolution and Transformation.* Tokyo: Hokuseido Press,
     1952. viii, 276 pp. Reprint. New York: AMS, 1972;
     Folcroft, Pa.: Folcroft Library Editions, 1974; Tokyo:
     Hokuseido Press, 1976.

A brief account (pp. 33-35) of the psychology of
change: "all lose one another's love and have to win it back
again through humiliation and eventual reform." Includes
page references to other places (such as "Enchantment,
Magic," "Infidelity") where the play is discussed as part of
the large discussion called "Types and Transformations."

88 Yoshida, Kenichi. *Sheikusupia* [Shakespeare]. Tokyo: Ikeda
Shoten, 1952. Ch. 3. Reprints. Tokyo: Tarumi Shobō,
1956, 1958, 1961; *Selected Writings of Yoshida Kenichi*.
Tokyo: Shinchōsha, 1961; *Collected Writings of Yoshida
Kenichi*. Tokyo: Shūeisha, 1978. (Japanese)

Points out the enthusiasm Shakespeare seems to feel
about his newly-discovered command of fine words, a
perfect vehicle to convey brilliant poetic images and verbal
music.

89 Hammerle, Karl. "Das Laubenmotiv bei Shakespeare und
Spenser und die Frage: Wer waren Bottom und die Little
Western Flower?" [The Arbor-Motif in Shakespeare and
Spenser and the Question: Who Were Bottom and the
Little Western Flower?]. *Anglia*, 71 (1952/53), 310-30.
(German)

Notes similarities between Spenser's description of
Acrasia's Bower of Bliss (*Faerie Queene*, II.v.29) and
Titania's arbor (II.ii.249ff.) and her woodbine-honeysuckle
sexual imagery (IV.i.41-43). Establishes a connection
between Spenser's "sad Amaranthus, made a flower of late"
(*Faerie Queene* III.vi.45) and *Dream*'s "little western
flower" (II.i.166) by identifying the flower from its
description as "Love-lies-bleeding," a member of the
amaranth family. On the basis of echoes from Spenser's
Prolog to Book III in Bottom's discourse on his "dream,"
Hammerle decides that Bottom and Quince, representing two
aspects of a single person, as do Gloriana and Belphoebe,
are in fact meant to be Edmund Spenser. Hammerle is thus
able to identify the "western flower" as Elizabeth Carey,
for whose wedding Hammerle thinks the *Dream* was written.
See also items 45, 110, 122 and 151a. For other comments on
the influence of Spenser see items 187, 500, 570, 574, 620,
670, 673, 732, 738, 744 and 960.

90-99   Entries Deleted.

100   Bluestone, Max. "An Anti-Jewish Pun in *A Midsummer
      Night's Dream*, III.i.97." *Notes and Queries*, 198 (1953),
      325-29.

      "Most brisky *juvenal*" puns "*Jew venal*."

101   Frye, Northrop. "Characterization in Shakespearian
      Comedy." *Shakespeare Quarterly*, 4 (1953), 271-77.

      Character depends on function in dramatic structure.
      With comedy there are basically four types of characters,
      the four lovers in our comedy being "eiron characters" (of
      the neutral sort), heroes and heroines. More interesting,
      however, is the "tricky slave" version of the type of which
      Puck is an example. See item 142.

102   Heninger, S. K., Jr. "'Wondrous Strange Snow'--*MND*,
      V.I.66." *MLN*, 68 (1953), 481-83.

      Theseus' phrase, long a crux, not only scans but also
      aptly describes a current notion of how the formation of
      snow depended on the presence of both heat and cold--a
      prodigy of nature.

103   Kökeritz, Helge. *Shakespeare's Pronunciation*. New Haven:
      Yale University Press; London: Geoffrey Cumberlege,
      Oxford University Press, 1953. Reprint. New Haven:
      Yale University Press, 1960, 1974. xv, 516 pp.

      Provides (pp. 349-53) a phonetic transcript of I.ii and
      II.i.249-67 ("I know a bank"). See item 36.

104   Litten, Heinz W. "Shakespeare als Beleuchtungsmeister"
      [Shakespeare as Master of Illumination]. *Heute und
      Morgen* (Schwerin), 1953, pp. 671-75. (German--not
      seen)

      Apparently in part on *Dream*.

104a Parrott, Thomas Marc. "Shakespeare Comedies"
       [audio-cassette]. *Shakespeare's Critics Speak*. New
       York: Jeffrey Norton Publishers, 1953. Cassette 23096,
       23 min.

    Dream and *Merchant* show Shakespeare a master of
romantic comedy, no longer an apprentice, the *Dream* (of
1594) being his first masterpiece, written while he had the
leisure during the plague. The central theme is love treated
not as a passion but rather as a fancy, and the four
strands are interwoven in order to show this pattern.
Theseus is a real character--something of an English
gentleman--one of the few real characters in the play.
Bottom is the other, one surely taken by Shakespeare from
real life. One thinks of the play as poetry, not as strict
drama. Some few comparisons and contrasts are drawn
between the two comedies.

105 Siegel, Paul N. "*A Midsummer Night's Dream* and the
       Wedding Guests." *Shakespeare Quarterly*, 4 (1953),
       139-44. Reprinted in the author's *Shakespeare in His
       Time and Ours*. Notre Dame: University of Notre Dame
       Press, 1968.

    Reading *Dream* with the original occasion in mind, that
is, becoming in effect one of those wedding guests, adds a
"teasing piquancy" to the experience. Theseus and
Hippolyta suggest the "august bridegroom and bride whose
wedding was being celebrated." Theseus "looks down with
humorous condescension and benevolent tolerance upon the
lovers and their moon-struck madness." Paradoxically he is
himself a "king of shadows," and there is much he cannot
comprehend. After the play-within-the-play both the actual
marriage and the play's marriages would be consummated.
In many ways the playlet comments on and is like *Dream*
itself--"a presentation in little of *Dream*." It asks that
Dream be regarded with imaginative understanding and
sympathy.

106 Spalding, K. J. *The Philosophy of Shakespeare*. New York:
       Philosophical Library; Oxford: George Ronald, 1953. viii,
       191 pp.

    Summarizes (pp. 63-67) the play with an emphasis on
Oberon as an incarnation of Power, a practical King of

Fairies who is endowed with the powers of heaven and concerned for the affairs of men, in an ongoing discussion of the development of the "Statesman" character in Shakespeare.

107   Strix [*pseud*.]. "Those Choughs." *Spectator*, no. 6545, 4 December 1953, pp. 655-56.

Gives responses to the query what is meant by "russet-pated choughs" (III.ii.21). While they may be "grey-headed jackdaws," they seem rather to be a mix of "simple-minded" shore-birds (ducks, gulls, and waders). See two responses: Henry Willink, ibid., no. 6546 (11 December 1953), p. 697, and A. P. Rossiter, ibid., no. 6547 (18 December 1953), pp. 726-27. See item 53.

108   Coghill, Nevill. "Wags, Clowns and Jesters." *More Talking of Shakespeare*. Ed. John Garrett. London: Hodder and Stoughton, 1954, pp. 1-16. Reprint. New York: Theater Arts Books, 1959; London: Longmans, 1959.

The foundation-stone for the character of Bottom, like that of all characters inspired by Shakespeare's desire to give scope to Will Kemp's talents, is "simpletonism." He is the simpleton, not the knowing wag. Built over this basic innocence is his genius as an artist (first noticed by Priestley; see item 13), which is his preoccupation with *style*.

108a   De Banke, Cecile. *Shakespearean Stage Production: Then and Now. A Manual for the Scholar-Player*. New York: McGraw-Hill, 1952. Reprint. London: Hutchinson, 1954. xviii, 342 pp.

There are suggestions about the use of the inner stage in Act IV (pp. 37-39), about the dancing (p. 253), and about when and what sort of music might be played, specific tunes being recommended for specific songs (pp. 290-94).

109   Halliday, F. E. *The Poetry of Shakespeare's Plays*. London: Gerald Duckworth, 1954. 196 pp.

The language of the lovers is "curiously archaic, literary and conventional"; but otherwise the style of *Dream* (that is, the diction, rhythm, and imagery) is much more natural, direct, and original than such had been in earlier plays and represents a beginning of the "more complex and dramatic" style which, further developed in *The Merchant of Venice*, will be characteristic of Shakespeare at his best. Hippolyta's foul-weather speech (II.i.81-117, analyzed in some detail) "is not dramatic poetry, but it is narrative poetry such as had never been heard in English." (Pp. 93-96)

110 Hammerle, Karl. "Das Titanialager des *Sommernachtstraumes* als Nachhall des Topos von *locus amoenus*" [Titania's Couch in *Dream* as an Echo of the Topos of the *locus amoenus*]. *Shakespeare Jahrbuch* (Weimar), 90 (1954), 279-84. (German)

In an earlier article (item 89) Hammerle tried to demonstrate that Titania's bower is taken from the "Arber greene" of the Bowre of Blisse and from the Bowre of Venus in the Garden of Adonis in Spenser's *Faerie Queene*. Further investigation has convinced him that these details were only segments of a broader circle of motifs and that Shakespeare was presenting a "total dramatization" of the *locus amoenus*, primarily in the form established in the *Faerie Queene*. This consisted of building up various elements of the *locus amoenus* around the Titania-Bottom idyll. See also items 101, 122 and 153.

111 Hudson, A. K. *Shakespeare and the Classroom*. London: Heinemann, 1954. xii, 116 pp. Rev. ed. 1960, 1963, 1966.

How *Dream* can and has been taught to students eleven years old--it ought to be stage centered. A lesson plan is given. (Chapter 2)

112 Hunter, Edwin R. *Shakspere and Common Sense*. Boston: Christopher Publishing House, 1954. 312 pp.

Comments briefly (pp. 103-5) on Theseus' speech ("Shakespeare is not speaking his own mind") and trips through (pp. 168-79) the playlet noticing humorous details

of "creative ignorance and honest bumbling" in this
burlesque of playing and play-making. See item 60.

113 Jaggard, G. Q. *An Informative Pamphlet on William
     Shakespeare's "A Midsummer Night's Dream,"* etc. Before
     the Curtain Rises, No. 6. Stratford: Jaggard, The
     Shakespeare Press, 1954. 4 pp.

     An introduction for those attending the Festival
     production.

113a Kahdy, Nell. "Eighth Grade Shakespeare." *High School
      Journal,* 38 (October 1954), 7-8.

      Describes a class project to produce a *Dream* revised for
      puppets. Gives an account of building a stage, designing
      scenery, and learning the voice parts. "A happy experience
      with Mr. Shakespeare!"

113b Krutch, Joseph Wood, educational director. *"A Midsummer
      Night's Dream": An Introduction to the Play* [film].
      Chicago: Coronet Instructional Films, 1954. 16 mm., 1 1/4
      reels, 15 min., col., b/w. (not seen)

      The film combines information about the play with
      dramatized excerpts from different places in it. It tries to
      explain for secondary students what the play is about, who
      the characters are, and what we need to know to enjoy
      seeing or reading it. With study guide.

114 Litten, Heinz W. "Noch einmal *Sommernachtstraum*" [*A
     Midsummer Night's Dream* Once More]. *Heute und Morgen*
     (Schwerin), 1954, pp. 33-38. (German--not seen)

115 Masefield, John. *William Shakespeare.* London: Heinemann;
     New York, Macmillan, 1954. vii. 184 pp. Reprint.
     Heinemann, 1961, 1969. Greenwich, Conn.: Fawcett,
     1964.

     A brief guide (pp. 57-59) to the play is followed by
     several remarks. *Dream* may well have been written for an
     occasion since its divisions could have been rehearsed

separately without great disturbance to the routine of a theatrical company. The playlet should not be willfully made a mockery; the manners of the courtiers in response seem to us outrageous. Surely the boy who played Hermia also played Moth, Falstaff's boy, and Maria. For other Masefield comments see items 769 and 905.

116 Meader, William G. *Courtship in Shakespeare: The Relation to the Tradition of Courtly Love.* New York: King's Crown Press of Columbia University, 1954. Reprint. New York: Octagon Books, 1971. 266 pp.

In brief comments scattered throughout suggests that *Dream* is typical of Shakespeare's treatment of the causes and effects of love: the power of the eyes (p. 67), the charm of the voice (p. 69), the fast pace of the heart (p. 95), the deification of the loved one (p. 101), the dream which develops the love (p. 114), the paleness of the lover (p. 116), and the willingness of the lover to die rather than suffer deprivation (p. 124). See items 662 and 667.

117 Paris, Jean. *Shakespeare par lui-même*. Écrivains de toujours. Paris: Éditions du Seuil, 1954. Translated by Richard Seaver as *Shakespeare*. Evergreen Profile Book, 10. New York: Grove; London: Evergreen, 1960. 191 pp.

The phases of the moon in the play reveal the "cosmic mechanism of initiation" of the Orphic mysteries. Before being initiated into the "light of salvation," the mortals must experience the bond between love, dream, and death. In the end all return to Theseus' palace "to celebrate the redeeming marriage and bury the old moon," and this whole metamorphosis of the moon is recalled for us "at random in the allegory of Pyramus and Thisbe." (Pp. 106-109) For other esoteric readings see items 70, 335, 551, 618 and 666.

118 Vierig, H. "Der Mensch ist ein Esel . . . . Betrachtungen über Shakespeare und seine Zeit an Hand einer Szene aus dem *Sommernachtstraum*" [Man is an Ass . . . . Observations on Shakespeare and His Time on the Basis of a Scene from *Dream*]. *Gestaltung und Gestalten* (Dresden), 9 (1954), 75-81. (German--not seen)

119   Boas, Guy. *Shakespeare and the Young Actor: A Guide to Production*. London: Rockliff, 1955. Reprint. London: Baurie and Rockliff, 1961. xi, 140 pp.

      Describes (pp. 45-49) a production at Sloane School, Chelsea. See item T1144a.

120   Fredén, Gustaf. "En strand där timjan blommar wild [A bank where the wild thyme blows]. En studie i Shakespeare--dramats bakgrund." *Orestes och försoningen* [Orestes and Reconciliation]. Lund, 1955, pp. 85-108. (Swedish--not seen)

121   Gerhardt, Mia I. "Het toneelstuk in het toneelstuk" [The Play-within-the-Play]. *Lavende Talen*, 1955, pp. 258-75. (Dutch--not seen)

122   Hammerle, Karl. "Shakespeares platonische Wende" [Shakespeare's Platonic Turn]. *Anglo-Americana: Festschrift zum 70. Geburtstag von Professor Dr. Leo Hibler-Lebmannsport*. Herausgegeben von Dr. Karl Brunner. Wiener Beiträge für englischen Philologie, 42. Vienna and Stuttgart: Wilhelm Braumüller, 1955, pp. 62-71.

      There are things in *Dream* which can only be understood if one assumes Shakespeare's deep interest in the new Platonism. London artisans could not have been the models for the play because mystery plays were suppressed in 1559 and the bourgeoise prevented the rise of a popular theatre tradition. In the artisans' play Shakespeare directs his satire against Spenser, whom he accuses of taking a workman's approach to poetry. In Shakespeare's view the true poet is inspired by the "fine frenzy" of Platonic madness. See also items 89, 101, 110 and 153. For other discussions of Platonic (and Neoplatonic) elements see items 187, 229, 325, 335, 390, 450, 469, 618 and 621.

122a Liu, James. "Elizabethan and Yuan: A Brief Comparison of Some Conventions in Poetic Drama." *China Society Occasional Papers*, 8 (1955), 5-6. (not seen)

      Apparently has some remarks on *Dream*.

123 Lynch, William F. "Theology and the Imagination III: The
    Problem of Comedy." *Thought*, 30 (1955), 18-36.

    Quotes (pp. 30-31) the scene of Bottom's transformation
    as an illustration of "the abandonment of the human as a
    way into being," part of a larger comment on the place of
    the comic in a Christian world.

124 Schanzer, Ernest. "The Moon and the Fairies in *A
    Midsummer Night's Dream*." *University of Toronto
    Quarterly*, 24 (1955), 234-46. A longer, French version
    appears in *OEvres Complètes de Shakespeare*. Ed Pierre
    Leyris and Henri Evans. Paris: Formes et Reflets, 1958;
    and a shorter version in *Shakespeare: The Comedies. A
    Collection of Critical Essays*. Ed. Kenneth Muir.
    Twentieth Century Views. Englewood Cliffs, N. J.:
    Prentice-Hall, 1965.

    On the significance of the title and May Day setting, the
    central theme ("love-madness"), the moon associations, and
    the nature of the three sorts of fairies. On both nights
    fairies were thought to be particularly powerful and
    witchcraft practiced. Midsummer Night had three special
    suggestions: flower magic, lovers' dreams, and madness.
    The moon is designed to create an atmosphere (magic,
    dreams, illusion) rather than to underline a theme. To some
    extent Titania merges with the moon and suggests chastity
    (Diana). Titania and Oberon are not diminutive. The fairies
    are not (as Chambers thought; see item 12) given to
    "childish irresponsibility and lawlessness" but rather are
    "accomplished and ceremonious courtiers." They were not
    played by children (unless by apprentice boys). Efforts to
    grasp the number of days or condition of the moon are
    "efflorescences of the absurd." See item 14.

125 Schmidtbonn, Wilhelm. "Die Fahrt in [Journey into] den
    Sommernachtstraum." In *Das festliche Haus: Das
    Düsseldorfer Schauspielhaus Dumont-Lindemann. Spiegel
    und Ausdruck der Zeit*. Ed. Kurt Loup. Cologne and
    Berlin: Klepenhauer & Witsch, 1955, pp. 122-24.
    (German)

    Gives several reasons why the Düsseldorf Schauspielhaus
    company chose *Dream* as the play it wished to present to
    500 guests from Bonn. A longer version originally appeared

in *Die Masken*, 1, no. 35 (1905/6), 1-4, a Programmzeit-
schrift for the playhouse.

126   Straumann, Heinrich. "Shakespeare und der verblendete
      Mensch" [Shakespeare and the Blinded Man]. *Neue
      Zürcher Zeitung*, no. 1638, 18 June 1955, p. 8.
      (German)

      On the common theme of men made blind in *Dream* and
      two other Shakespeare plays.

127   Bonnard, George A. "Shakespeare's Purpose in
      Midsummer-Night's Dream." *Shakespeare Jahrbuch*
      (Weimar), 92 (1956), 268-79.

      It would be difficult to imagine a more fantastic
      combination of heterogeneous elements drawn from all kinds
      of sources. Shakespeare must have had a definite purpose.
      Theseus and Hippolyta "stand for good honest human love
      shorn of any romantic nonsense, . . . for experience,
      intelligent use of it, good sense and reason." The fairies
      stand for the fancy and sense impressions unchecked by
      reason, common sense, or moral impulses. The lovers and
      artisans, at two extremes of the social scale, fall between
      these two types, influenced now by the one and now by the
      other. From the normal world, which is healthy and
      sensible, we move into the dream-world, where laws of
      space and time are suspended, behavior is unreasonable,
      and delusions prevail, and from it we move back into the
      normal world. In the end "the right sort of love" has
      triumphed over "the delusions of youthful fancy. . . . But
      [even] if sense thus celebrates its victory over nonsense,
      [still] illusions, dreams, [and] fancies of all kinds cannot
      be suppressed but will sprout again and proliferate at the
      slightest provocation." The poet wants also to show that
      they can be a blessing.

128   Candidus, Irmentraud, and Erika Roller. "*Der
      Sommernachtstraum* in deutscher Übersetzung von
      Wieland bis Flatter" [*Dream* in German Translation from
      Wieland to Flatter]. *Shakespeare Jahrbuch* (Weimar), 92
      (1956), 128-45. (German)

German translations from the first--Wieland's--to the most recent--Flatter's in 1952--are discussed. Both the internal qualities of the texts and the intellectual and artistic climate from which they sprang are considered. Although A. W. Schlegel, A. Böttger and F. Gundolf have succeeded best in capturing Shakespeare, Richard Flatter conveys the dramatic qualities most accurately, especially those communicated by the meter. Gundolf's rendering of the Pyramus-Thisbe play is influenced by his belief that it is not simply nonsense, but rather a production of simple souls reaching for the sublime. See item 140, especially, and item 25.

129 Dillingham, William B. "Bottom: The Third Ingredient." *Emory University Quarterly*, 12 (1956), 230-37.

The commonplace reality of Bottom and company connects the classical and romantic worlds of the play.

130 Grinstein, Alexander. "The Dramatic Device: A Play with a Play." *Journal of the American Psychoanalytic Association*, 4 (1956), 49-52.

The device (as represented primarily by *Hamlet*) is related to "a familiar psychological mechanism seen in dream work, a dream within a dream."

131 Myers, Henry Alonzo. "*Romeo and Juliet* and *A Midsummer Night's Dream*." *Tragedy: A View of Life*. Ithaca: Cornell University Press, 1956, pp. 110-128. Reprinted in *Aspects of Drama: A Handbook*. Ed. Sylvan Barnet, Morton Berman, and William Burto. Boston and Toronto: Little, Brown, 1962.

Compares *Dream* and *Romeo* in order to show that the genius of tragedy is the same as that of comedy--"that the function of tragedy is to reveal a just order in our joys and sorrows and the function of comedy to turn disorder into soothing laughter." *Dream*'s effect is the consequence of a special mix in views of love: common sense, non-sense, and fantasy. For other comparisons between the two plays see items 20, 170, 205-6, 246, 352, 372-3, 381, 387a, 412, 415, 420, 449, 482, 488, 572, 575a, 616, 630, 636, 675, 756, 759, 936 and 960.

132 Nemerov, Howard. "The Marriage of Theseus and
     Hippolyta." *Kenyon Review,* 18 (1956), 633-41.

     Theseus' speech is "neither distinguished nor
     illuminating," and Nemerov comments at length on Theseus'
     stance--his lofty disdain for art. He's saved from "being
     merely an outsized bore" by the fact that he is himself a
     lover and his speech is poetry. Nemerov defends
     Hippolyta's response and offers an extensive paraphrase of
     it. Together Theseus and Hippolyta bring two views of
     poetry into a marriage. "The poetry of Theseus is rational,
     civic-minded, discursive, and tends constantly to approach
     prose. The poetry of Hippolyta is magical, fabulous,
     dramatic, and constantly approaches music." For Theseus
     art is "entertainment," for Hippolyta it is "mystery."

133 Tschopp, Elisabeth. *Zur Verteilung von Vers und Prosa in
     Shakespeares Dramen* [On the Distribution of Verse and
     Prose in Shakespeare's Plays]. Schweizer anglistische
     Arbeiten, 41. Winterthur: Keller; Bern: Francke Verlag,
     1956. vii, 118 pp. (German)

     Proposes to determine the type of content associated with
     the distribution of prose and verse. *Dream* is discussed
     first (pp. 25-28) because it presents no problem. Tschopp
     concludes (p. 28) that there is a clear distinction in the
     play between prose and verse, the former being the medium
     of the doltish actors, the latter of the spirit world and the
     court. Members of the court do switch to prose to comment
     on the play while the actors fracture verse. In three
     passages there is conversation between representatives of
     these different spheres. The representative of the court
     adjusts to the prose of the artisans, but there is no such
     accommodation when Titania and Bottom converse, and they
     talk past one another. See also item 77.

134 Babler, O. F. "Shakespeare's *Midsummer Night's Dream* in
     Czech and Slovakian." *Notes and Queries,* 202 (1957),
     151-53.

     Lists dates, productions, and publication information for
     the following translators: Frantisek Doucha, Josef V.
     Sládek, Bohumil Stepánek, Erik A. Saudek, Jiří Valja, and
     (Slovakian) Pavel Országh Huiezdoslav. See also item 191.

135 Biancotti, Angiolo. *Guglielmo Shakespeare.* Torino, etc.:
Società Editrice Internazionale, 1957. vi, 303 pp.
(Italian)

A general introduction to the play (pp. 188-92).

136 Brodersen, Chr. N. "Omkring 'En Skaero sommernatsdröm'"
[About *Dream*]. *Vendsyssel Tidende* (Hiörring,
Denmark), 12 December 1957. (Danish--not seen)

137 Brown, John Russell. "Love's Truth and the Judgements of
A Midsummer Night's Dream and *Much Ado About
Nothing.*" *Shakespeare and His Comedies.* London:
Methuen, 1957. Rev. ed. 1962, 1964, 1968, pp. 82-123.

The play is a study of the way lovers' see, that is,
their special vision, which has its own truth. We are led
"to recognize the absurdity, privacy, and 'truth' of human
imagination." "The play's greatest triumph is the manner in
which our unerring acceptance of the illusion of drama is
used as a kind of flesh-and-blood image of the acceptance
which is appropriate to the strange and private 'truth' of
those who enact the play of love."

138 Cecil, Lord David. "Shakespearean Comedy." *The Fine Art
of Reading and Other Literary Studies.* London:
Constable; Indianapolis: Bobbs-Merrill, 1957, pp. 37-106.
Reprint. Indianapolis: Charter Books, 1964. Reprinted in
Discussions of Shakespeare's Romantic Comedy. Ed
Herbert Weil, Jr. Boston: D. C. Heath, 1966.

All the elements of romantic comedy are presented in
extreme form in *Dream* (discussed on pp. 52-61). It is "the
diagram and parable of its type." The deep sense of
integration and harmony, a blend "most startling," is
provided by the symmetry of its form and by the dream-like
atmosphere. "The whole play is, as it were, set to a music
which lulls the prosaic spirit of disbelief to sleep." By its
spirit of laughter and by its eye for character, the play
avoids the dullness of much fantasy. There are things
stranger than the common sense of Theseus can conceive.

139 Fisher, Peter F. "The Argument of *A Midsummer Night's Dream.*" *Shakespeare Quarterly*, 8 (1957), 307-310.

The four worlds of *Dream* focus attention on its argument: the polar opposition of passion (the lovers) and reason (the Athenian court), of instinct (the mechanicals) and fantasy (the fairies). The denouement leaves reason supreme, with passion in subordination, entertained by instinct, with fantasy as a commentator. The four worlds are represented by four "languages"--prose for instinct, blank verse for reason, couplets for passion, song for fantasy. See also item 77.

140 Flatter, Richard, and Irmentraud Candidus. "Eine Berichtigung und eine Antwort" [A Correction and a Response]. *Shakespeare Jahrbuch* (Weimar), 93 (1957), 214-15. (German)

Flatter takes exception to a statement by Candidus in her article on *Dream* translations (item 128), to wit that he has at points purposely combined the best of previous translations, specifically those of A. W. Schlegel, F. Gundolf, and A. Böttger. He describes the circumstances which led to his translation and acknowledges his debt to Schlegel but maintains that he translated freely and had no knowledge of the other two works. Candidus emphasizes that she never meant to imply that plagiarism was involved and is convinced that the similarities are accidental. See also item 25.

141 Foakes, R. A. "Atavism and Anticipation in Shakespeare's Style. III." *Essays in Criticism*, 7 (1957), 455-57.

Agrees with Schanzer (item 148) that because of their verse we laugh at the young lovers and adds that because of it we accept the ardor of their passion--a double effect.

142 Frye, Northrop. *Anatomy of Criticism: Four Essays.* Princeton: Princeton University Press, 1957. Several reprints, including New York: Atheneum, 1968. 383 pp.

The most influential remarks on *Dream* occur in the section "The Mythos of Spring: Comedy" in the Third Essay (pp. 163-86). Here is outlined the formulaic construction of

comedy: its movement from an old society to a new one, its
festive conclusion, the obstacle to be overcome, usually
parental, by young lovers, the inclusion of all characters in
the renewed society, which is one controlled by youth and
freedom--all of which are aspects of *Dream*. Puck is the
tricky slave (*eiron*) figure. *Dream* belongs in the fourth (of
six) phase of comedy in which we move from "the world of
experience into the ideal world of innocence and romance."
The action gives a "rhythmic movement from normal world to
green world and back again," the green world being
analogous to the dream world of desire at odds with
experience. The plot of this type of comedy has been
assimilated "to the ritual theme of the triumph of life and
love over the waste land."

Some of this material appears in "The Argument of
Comedy" (item 61), in "Characterization in Shakespearean
Comedy" (item 101), and in "Comic Myth in Shakespeare"
(item 83). See also items 55, 273-74 and 393.

142a Gerstner-Hirzel, Arthur. *The Economy of Action and Words
in Shakespeare's Plays*. The Cooper Monographs on
English and American Language and Literature, 2. Ed.
H. Lüdeke. Bern: Francke, 1957. 134 pp.

Reviews the gestures and actions implied by the texts of
the plays. *Dream*, which is mentioned only in passing, has
95 implicit or explicit gestures per 1000 lines (p. 87). To
show that it is "full of metrical and gestic dainties" (p. 65)
offers an analysis of the song "Over hill, over dale" (II.i)
in which the metre is taken to suggest the various gaits
and rests of the fairy singing.

143 Leech, Clifford. "Shakespeare's Use of a Five-Act
Structure." *Die Neueren Sprachen*, n.s. 6 (1957),
249-63.

A case can be made for seeing many of Shakespeare's
plays (more than T. W. Baldwin considered in
Shakespeare's Five-Act Structure, 1947), including *Dream*,
as having five-act patterns. "Act" in the stage-direction
"*They sleepe all the Act*" at the end of Act III may mean
"Act-interval," and thus the play originally had intervals.

144   Luserke, Martin. *Pan--Apollon--Prospero: "Ein
       Mittsommernachtstraum," "Die* Wintersage" [*The Winter's
       Tale*] *und "Der Sturm"*: [*The Tempest*]: *Zur Dramaturgie
       von Shakespeare-Spielen.* Hamburg: Hans Christian,
       1957. 224 pp. (German)

       Luserke applies his forty years of practical theatre
       experience to Shakespeare's plays. Shakespeare's style is
       intimately related to early cult plays and the popular use of
       masks. Theatre has to be a unity of language, music, and
       choreography, not illusionistic scenery. Luserke illustrates
       how Oberon's "Since once I sat . . . fancy-free"
       (II.i.148-74) is a whole melodrama rather than simple
       declamation (pp. 143-49). *Dream* has its full effect when the
       myth of the elves is de-Romanticized and when the elves
       seem to inhabit a reality coexistent with our own. The
       production must culminate in a high point where the hour of
       Pan is felt. Dialogue at the beginning and end was added
       for the benefit of Whitehall; it undermines the mythic effect
       and should be dropped. (Chapter 7) See items 55 and 117.

144a   Lüthi, Max. "*Ein Sommernachtstraum.*" *Shakespeares
       Dramen.* Berlin: Walter de Gruyter, 1957, pp. 156-70.
       (German)

       A general chapter sees *Dream* as "the first comedy in
       which Shakespeare's genius is fully developed." Particular
       emphasis is on the variations on the same themes (love,
       rejection, chaos, reestablishment of order, transformation of
       evil into good) in the various worlds presented (elf/nature,
       courtiers', noble lovers', rustics').

145   Olson, Paul A. "*A Midsummer Night's Dream* and the
       Meaning of Court Marriage." *ELH*, 24 (1957), 95-119.
       Reprinted in *Shakespeare's Comedies: An Anthology of
       Modern Criticism.* Ed. Laurence Lerner. Harmondsworth,
       Middlesex, and Baltimore: Penguin, 1967.

       The play is a serious dramatic allegory, masque-like,
       "best understood in terms of 16th century marriage
       doctrines" on the relationship between Reason and Love in
       marriage. In structure, character, and emblem the play
       shows the conflict between these traditional opposites
       (including male and female, earthy and spiritual love, order
       and chaos), with right rule reflected in Theseus and

Hippolyta, condemned in "Pyramus and Thisbe," achieved in the fairies and four lovers. Numerous details are taken to carry appropriate significances. When Oberon speaks of having sported with the morning's love, "he introduces an image which has behind it an accumulated tradition of references to the sun of God's charity." Titania stands for "the forces of the lower passions in man," Oberon for Reason. Bottom with ass's head is the carnal man. "Shakespeare's purpose was to bring to life certain truths about wedlock." See items 182 and 457.

146 Ōyama, Toshikazu. *Shakespeare Ningenkan Kenkyū* [A Study of Shakespeare's View of Man or Human Nature]. Tokyo: Shinozaki Shorin, 1957. Ch. 2, Sect. i. (Japanese)

Emphasizes the lyrical element as a factor unifying the romantic and realistic, and defines it as a step in Shakespeare's deepening understanding of human nature from the outward, mechanical approach in the earliest works to the inward, psychological grasp in the mature plays.

147 Popovic, D. "Vil'em Sekspir: *San letnje noci*" [*A Midsummer Night's Dream*]. *Letopis matice srpske* (Novi Sad), 379 (1957), 626-30. (Serbian--not seen)

148 Schanzer, Ernest. "Atavism and Anticipation in Shakespeare's Style." *Essays in Criticism*, 7 (1957), 242-56.

Argues that the verse of the young lovers is purposefully ridiculous, in response to de la Mare (item 16) who, finding it "shallow, stumbling, bald, and vacant," refused to accept it as Shakespeare's. See also item 141.

149 Sorell, Walter. "Shakespeare and the Dance." *Shakespeare Quarterly*, 8 (1957), 367-84, especially 381-84.

Dream, like *The Tempest*, is "dance wrapped in poetic words." Sorell describes a Bergomask dance and suggests the style of dancing and music which would be appropriate in modern productions of the play. For music, he recommends Carl Orff and Henry Purcell over Mendelssohn.

See also items 394 and 575. For other comparisons with *The
Tempest* see items 1a, 29, 68, 79, 149, 172, 208, 239, 296,
316, 328a, 334, 357, 362, 386, 388, 412, 414, 458, 461, 475,
497, 505, 526, 531, 566g, 575a, 618, 756, 913 and 1068a.

150   Brett-Evans, David. "Der 'Sommernachtstraum' in
      Deutschland 1600-1650" [*Dream* in Germany 1600-1650].
      Zeitschrift für deutsche Philologie, 77 (1958), 371-83.
      (German)

      A succinct review and evaluation of theories on how the
      Dream was transmitted in Germany and how Quince became
      one of the most popular figures on the 17th century German
      stage. He emphasizes the independent popularity since the
      Middle Ages of the Pyramus-Thisbe story in Germany. See
      items 25 and 60.

151   Gestetner, J. M. *Shakespeare's "A Midsummer Night's
      Dream."* New Issue. London: Pitman, 1958. Originally
      published in 1927.

      A commentary and questionnaire. Designed for students.

151a Hammerle, Karl. "Ein Muttermal des deutschen Pyramus und
      die Spenserechos in *A Midsummer Night's Dream*" [A
      Birthmark of the German Pyramus and the Spenser
      Echoes in *Dream*]. *Festschrift zum 70. Geburtstag von
      Friedrich Wild*. Ed. Karl Brunner et al. Wiener Beiträge
      zür englischen Philologie, 66. Vienna and Stuttgart:
      Wilhelm Braumüller, 1958, pp. 52-66. (German)

      Studies similarities of diction and syntax between *Dream*
      and *The Faerie Queene*, seeing the diction and rhetoric of
      the "Pyramus and Thisbe" playlet as a satire on Spenser's
      highly mannered style in Books I-III (inversion, postnominal
      adjectives, ellipses of pronouns and articles, archaisms,
      exaggerated alliteration, etc.). He notes difficulties
      encountered by Wieland, Schlegel, and later translators in
      rendering these linguistic anomalies. See also items 89, 101,
      110 and 122.

152 Hillegass, Clifton K. *Cliff's Notes on Shakespeare's "A Midsummer Night's Dream."* Lincoln, Neb.: Cliff's Notes, 1958. Rev. ed. 1961.

Scene-by-scene synopsis, summary of characters, comment on the structure of the play, and review questions and answers. Designed for students. Item 566a is either a revision or later version.

153 Hindenberg, Gisela. *"Der Traum in Drama Shakespeares"* [The Dream in Shakespeare's Plays]. Dissertation. Göttingen, 1958. 208 pp. (German--not seen)

154 Hulme, Hilda M. "Three Notes [including *Dream* II.i.54]." *Journal of English and Germanic Philology,* 57 (1958), 721-25.

"Tailour" by association with "yard" and "tail" came to carry certain obscene suggestions such as "penis" and "vagina" which may have some bearing on Puck's line. "Posteriors," one such bawdy sense, seems to be required by the line. See items 194 and 474.

155 Knight, G. Wilson. *The Sovereign Flower.* London: Methuen; New York: Barnes & Noble, 1958. Reprint. 1966. 324 pp.

Comments briefly (p. 184) on selected names. The sound of the name *Oberon* and the suggestiveness of *Titania,* the Greek names, and *Puck* help deepen our understanding of the play. For other discussions of names see items 444, 504, 528, 533a, 544, 550, 566-67, 571, 617, and 686-87.

156 Entry Deleted.

157 Nelson, Robert J. *Play Within a Play: The Dramatist's Conception of His Art: Shakespeare to Anouilh.* Yale Romanic Studies, 2nd series, 5. New Haven: Yale University Press; Paris: Presses Universitaires de France, 1958. xiii, 182 pp.

The play-within-the-play reflects Shakespeare's self-consciousness about theatrical conventions for dramatic illusion, but it does so playfully without that "sense of metaphysical anguish we usually associate with the play scene in *Hamlet*." (Pp. 11-17) See item 60.

158 Barber, C. L. "May Games and Metamorphoses on a Midsummer Night." *Shakespeare's Festive Comedy: A Study of Dramatic Form and Its Relation to Social Custom.* Princeton: Princeton University Press, 1959, pp. 119-62. Reprint. Cleveland: World Publishing, 1963 (Meridian Books); Princeton, 1972.

Discusses the numerous ties between the play and time-honored customs of Maying, contemporary pageantry, and the magic associated with Midsummer's Eve; in such elements Shakespeare is handling "with supreme skill just what was most commonplace." May game gave the out-and-back pattern for the whole; Oberon is May King, Titania a Summer Lady. The Fairies are "embodiments of the May-game experience or eros in men and women"; "any superstitious tendency to believe in their literal reality is mocked." The folly of fantasy is the general subject. The lovers in the whirl of release are "tossed about by a force [love's power] which puts them beside themselves to take them beyond themselves." The pervasive imagery of dissolution and "metamorphic metaphors" (melting, etc.) suggest how identity is lost and changed. The whole moves from release to clarification. The play has its skeptical side (which romantics miss), a "doubleness." We are not allowed to think that the fairies are real even though they walk about and have names. As to the powers of fancy, the double awareness occurs in Theseus' speech--it can create, but, after all, only from airy nothing. Wit offsets plot tensions and passions. In the playlet, Shakespeare "captures the naïveté of folk dramatics and makes it serve his controlling purpose as a final variant of imaginative aberration."

159 Entry Deleted.

160 Elling, Christian. *Shakespeare: Indsyn i hans Verden og dens Poesi* [Shakespeare: Insight Into His World and Poetry. Scenery]. Copenhagen: Gyldendal, 1959. 164 pp. (Danish)

Briefly, on Oberon's "I know a bank" speech (pp. 66 and 73).

161 Imam, Syed Mehdi. "Studies of Shakespeare's Plays: IV. *A Midsummer Night's Dream.*" *Mother India,* Sept. 1959, pp. 72-75; Oct. 1959, pp. 58-64. (not seen)

Apparently takes *Dream* to be "the gateway to the comedies"; the devices of comedy exemplified in it are situation, complication, reversals, crisis, harmonization, and discovery.

162 Pearce, T. M. "Shakespeare's *A Midsummer Night's Dream,* IV, i, 214-215." *Explicator,* 18 (1959), no. 8.

Bottom's lines recall 1 Corinthians 2:9. He is reflecting, wisely though in garbled fashion, that only a fool can think knowledge stems mainly from the senses rather than the spirit. See items 183, 406, 544 and 566.

163 Reynolds, Lou Agnes, and Paul Sawyer. "Folk Medicine and the Four Fairies of *A Midsummer Night's Dream.*" *Shakespeare Quarterly,* 10 (1959), 513-21.

Folk medicine clarifies the appropriateness of the names (each represents an item used in household remedies) and the humor of Bottom's conversations with the fairies in Act III. There is no greeting for Moth because moths had to be killed to become medicinal. See item 14.

164 Seiden, Melvin. "Shakespeare's Comic Dream World: *A Midsummer Night's Dream.*" *Kansas Magazine,* 1959, pp. 84-90.

Dream is like serious dream; its mode the inconsequential. "The unity is that of the off-center, logical illogical, soberly nonsensical *gestalt* of the dream-fiction." "Hippolyta's point of view [toward the playlet] will appear even more obtuse if it is pitted against Theseus' superb description of the power and function of the imagination."

165   Brown, Arthur. "The Play Within a Play: An Elizabethan
       Dramatic Device." *Essays and Studies,* n.s. 13 (1960),
       36-48.

       Gives briefly (pp. 47-48) the function of the
       playlet--one of "the most successful of its
       [play-within-a-play] appearances in the whole of Elizabethan
       comedy, if not the most successful of all." It is an integral
       part of the play's theme (gentle satire of the pangs of
       romantic love). See item 60.

166   Ellis-Fermor, Una. "The Nature of Plot in Drama." *Essays
       and Studies,* n.s. 13 (1960), 65-81.

       From one of the manuscript chapters of Miss
       Ellis-Fermor's uncompleted *Shakespeare the Dramatist.* She
       comments briefly on the impressions of a world and a life
       conveyed by the range and spatial groupings of characters.
       "Each figure in a play whose spatial structure is of this
       kind is like an illuminated point, independent and set at a
       distance from each of the others; yet seemingly endless
       patterns now suggest themselves by linking each to several
       others and the central figure to all."

166a   Emery, John P. "The Theme of *A Midsummer Night's
       Dream.*" *English Leaflet,* 59 (1960), 1-3. (not seen)

       Apparently the theme is identified as the importance of
       both realism and antithetical romance in the life of every
       individual.

167   Evans, Bertrand. "All Shall Be Well: The Way Found."
       Shakespeare's Comedies. Oxford: Clarendon Press, 1960,
       pp. 33-46. Numerous reprints.

       A study of the effects of one comic device--discrepant
       awareness--used repeatedly, of the various levels of
       knowing in audience and characters. The magic juice, to
       give one example of the kind of comment made, "is primarily
       responsible for the fact that at some time in the action each
       of [the principal persons] stands on a level of awareness
       below ours, and for the fact that we hold advantage over
       some person or persons during seven of the nine scenes."
       The climax occurs during III.ii through IV.i, that is, when

"the greatest number of participants are ignorant of the greatest number of facts in a situation that has attained its greatest complexity." Bottom is discussed at some length from this point of view.

168   Granlid, Hans O. *"En* Midsommarnattsdröm." *Tidning för Sveriges lävoverk* (Stockholm), 60, no. 17 (1960), 544. (Swedish--not seen)

169   Hewett, R. P. *Reading and Response: An Approach to the Criticism of Literature.* London: Harrap, 1960. 254 pp. Numerous reprints.

Quotes and examines in detail (pp. 102-6) Titania's foul weather speech (II.i.81-117) in order to demonstrate for students of the sixth form how to read a passage from the drama. The speech is described as a rhetorical set-piece of "lyric charm" and "rich elaboration," with "unquestionable beauty and delicacy," but with "relatively little dramatic purpose."

169a   Holland, Norman N. "Freud on Shakespeare." *PMLA,* 75 (1960), 163-73.

Freud made six separate comments on *Dream* (noticed here in a paragraph on p. 171). He thought the treatment of Titania quite suggestive, the play concerned with "the maliciousness of objects" (as in the thinking of children and primitives), and Theseus' speech (V.i.2-22) a true description of creativity. See also items 252, 290 and 556.

170   Holmes, Martin. *Shakespeare's Public: The Touchstone of His Genius.* London: John Murray, 1960. xiv, 237 pp.

Both style and resources required suggest an original country-house audience. Theseus resembles the lord of an English manor. The playlet represents a country effort at the latest London success *(Romeo).* Boy actors were probably brought around for the occasion. And London audiences would have accepted whatever difficulties arose as a result of the special circumstance of its origins. (Pp. 38-43) See item 131.

171   Maitra, Sitamsu. *Shakespeare's Comic Idea.* Calcutta: K. L.
        Mukhopadhyay, 1960. 100 pp.

        Makes one comment about *Dream* (on p. 70): it shows
        "the comic idea of Shakespeare as primarily being one of a
        relationship of accommodation between the New Individual
        [of the Renaissance] and the existing order with its
        necessary concomitant of temporary escape from this order
        [through the new value of constancy in love] wherever the
        situation so demands and until it is changed for the
        better."

172   Sewell, Elizabeth. *The Orphic Voice: Poetry and Natural
        History.* New Haven: Yale University Press, 1960. viii,
        463 pp. Reprint. London: Routledge and Kegan Paul,
        1961. New York: Harper & Row, 1971 (Harper
        Torchbook).

        Dream is a dramatized expression of the claim of the
        myth of Orpheus that poetry has power and place in the
        living universe. It is, like *The Tempest*, "an experimental
        essay on myth and mind and universe." The playlet is an
        example of "palpable-gross ciphering," turning myth into
        burlesque and laughter; at least it does not bore, as do the
        philosophical interpretations of Bacon and Chapman. In the
        last moment of the play, with the return of the fairies,
        Shakespeare shifts from parody back to sincere
        hieroglyphic, bringing myth to life. In all he manages to
        include precisely what Bacon wants to reject--"poetry,
        theater, dreams, and shadows"--enlarging the category of
        rationality. One can almost "hear the dry voice of Bacon" in
        the start and finish of Theseus' famous speech (V.i.1-22).

        The scope of natural subject matter in *Dream* easily
        matches that given by Bacon. And the love which is the
        theme of the play can be taken as the fertility of nature.
        In the simple naturalness of their names and callings and in
        their effort toward learning language and acting, the
        mechanicals dove-tail into the whole universe of the play.
        "They have struggled up out of the vegetable and animal
        into the human condition." Bottom, who may be the clue to
        the true interpretation of the play, is "the mind working
        with language," trying to make forms of its own with which
        to understand those of nature. The fairies are forms of
        nature and the mind turned into myth. See items 55, 117
        and 149.

173 *Shakespeare et le* Théâtre Élizabéthain *en France depuis Cinquante Ans. Études Anglaises*, 13, no. 2 (1960), *passim.* (French)

The entire volume is devoted to the topic of its title. Scattered throughout the various articles are comments on French productions and translations of *Dream* with the emphasis on the recent past. There is no index. See also items 176, T1209 and T1238.

174 Shalvi, Alice. [On Three Shakespearean Comedies]. *Bamah* (Jerusalem), 1, no. 4 (1960). (Hebrew--not seen)

On *Dream, As You Like It,* and *Twelfth Night.*

174a Styan, J. L. *The Elements of Drama.* Cambridge: University Press, 1960. viii, 306. Reprint. 1963, 1967, 1969. Also in Robert W. Corrigan and James L. Rosenberg, eds. *The Context and Craft of Drama.* San Francisco and Scranton, Pa.: Chandler, 1964.

The play, about the irrationality of love, in its gentle reprimand allows us no sympathy with any kind or degree of love--"all pleasing preconceptions and misconceptions are fretted and disparaged." We ourselves can identify only with the "rational onlookers" Theseus and Hippolyta, and observe in the others various assumptions about love repudiated. Character here, as in romantic comedies, is "more structural than individual, more general and formal than personal." (Pp. 178-80)

175 Volkenstein, V. [Playwriting]. 2nd ed. Moscow: Sovetsky pisatel, 1960. (Russian--not seen)

Pages 29-32 are on *Dream.*

176 White, Kenneth S. "Two French Versions of *A Midsummer Night's Dream.*" *French Review*, 33 (1960), 341-50.

A close comparison of the versions of Georges Neveux (1945, item 785) and Jean-Louis and Jules Supervielle (1959, item 858). The Neveux is rather personal, avoids direct translation (it is termed a "texte français"), is seriously condensed, and emphasizes action. The Supervielles' is more literal, attempts to find close French equivalents so as to preserve the original texture, and emphasizes the poetic qualities of the play. The Neveux translation seldom carries one's fancy; that of the Supervielles is "a rare and noteworthy accomplishment." See also item 173.

177   Zitner, Sheldon P. "The Worlds of *A Midsummer Night's Dream.*" *South Atlantic Quarterly,* 59 (1960), 396-403.

The strength of the play is in its "structure"--the firm management of its multiple worlds, these being "of power, of love, of work, of faery, of illusion." The links between these are loose; complications within them are not allowed to develop. Its holiday release is special, "the drama of avoidance"; it refuses the serious.

178   Bryant, J. A., Jr. "Hippolyta's View." *Hippolyta's View: Some Christian Aspects of Shakespeare's Plays.* Lexington: University of Kentucky Press, 1961, pp. 1-18.

Theseus and Hippolyta refer to two different kinds of poetry best understood in terms of medieval typology. Theseus describes allegory, wherein the "poet accommodates or translates into concrete terms something that is otherwise unperceived"; in Hippolyta's view the poet "begins, not with an abstract formulation, but with things as they seem to be in their concreteness," a method Dante called the "allegory of the theologians." Hippolyta accepts the lovers' story because it "has the individual vitality to assume a life of its own . . . and command belief." In her view poetry is "symbols through which we cannot see."

179   del Tufo, Joseph P., S. J. "The Structure of Shakespearean Comedy." Ph.D. dissertation, Fordham University, 1961. *DA,* 22 (1961), 4004.

Endeavors to show how the theme of each of five plays, including *Dream,* determines its nature. Plot, character, levels of reality, and sources are considered, and each play is compared with the other four.

180 Iser, Wolfgang. "Das Spiel im Spiel. Formen dramatischer
     Illusion bei Shakespeare" [The Play-within-the-Play.
     Forms of Dramatic Illusion in Shakespeare]. *Archiv für
     das Studium der neueren Sprachen und Literatur*, 198,
     no. 4 (1961), 209-226.

     Iser first defines the function of the play-within-the-
     play at this time: it is an attempt to grasp the dimensions
     of theatre following the demise of the cult play. He analyzes
     the use in both *Dream* and *Hamlet*. The internal play
     derives its meaning from its context. The artisans' play
     shows that anyone who cannot transform himself will never
     open up a world beyond his own limitations. Man determines
     himself through his protean character, the precarious
     nature of which is lightly touched upon. *Dream* is a comedy
     because fantastic transformations replace the activity that is
     the precondition to any real self-actuation. See item 60.

181 Kerényi, Karl. "Die Mythologie in Shakespeares
     Sommernachtstraum" [Mythology in Shakespeare's
     Midsummer Night's Dream]. *Neue Zeitschrift für Musik*,
     122 (1961), 349-51.

     Kerényi has nothing new to add to the sources, but
     wishes to discuss the entire drama from the standpoint of
     mythology. He considers this "mythic writing," that is,
     writing from the source that creates mythology rather than
     an imitation of mythology. Shakespeare's thrust is towards a
     myth of nature. On midsummer's night the world stands
     open and is ready for the entry of spirits and gods. On
     this evening the writer creates an Attic night in May--no
     other month is quite so pagan for him. The lower class
     characters are there to show that they, too, are caught up
     in the myth. The high point is in the conflict between
     Oberon and Titania, and a calculated low point is the story
     of Pyramus and Thisbe, which Keréyni feels is a conscious
     parody of contemporary imitations of mythic art. See item
     55.

182 Kermode, Frank. "The Mature Comedies." *Early
     Shakespeare*. Stratford-upon-Avon Studies, 3. Ed. John
     Russell Brown and Bernard Harris. London: Edward
     Arnold; New York: St. Martin's, 1961, pp. 211-27.
     Reprint. New York: Schocken Books, 1966. This article
     appears as Chapter 9 in Kermode's *Shakespeare,*

Spenser, Donne. Renaissance Essays. London: Routledge
and Kegan Paul; New York: Viking, 1971.

The play is of "marked intellectual content," its theme
("the disorders of fantasy [imagination]") treated with "an
intense sophistication," and the plot "a reflection of an
elaborate and ingenious thematic development." It is
Shakespeare's "best comedy." Bottom's moment of insight
(IV.i.202) complicates the moral from the simple
"love-is-a-kind-of-madness pattern" to one mixed with the
"love of God" and with blindness "as a means to grace."
Theseus cannot understand this matter and may be wrong.
There are comments on the importance of Apuleius' *Golden
Ass* as a source (see item 591) and some praise of Olson's
essay (item 145).

183   Merchant, W. Moelwyn. "*A Midsummer Night's Dream*: A
      Visual Re-creation." *Early Shakespeare*. Stratford-upon-
      Avon Studies, 3. Ed. John Russell Brown and Bernard
      Harris. London: Edward Arnold; New York: St.
      Martin's, 1961, pp. 165-85. Reprint. New York:
      Schocken Books, 1966.

Traces the treatment of the play in its theatrical history
and at the hands of engravers and painters (there are
figures and plates) in order to reveal the variety of
attempts made to catch its spirit and the consequent degree
of uncertainty about some of its themes. From this strange
"visual history," which includes, among many others,
considerations of works by Hogarth, Reynolds, and Fuseli,
we learn much about the "uneasy, disjointed course" of the
play in significant productions from Purcell's *The Fairy
Queen* (1692) to Benjamin Britten's operatic adaptation
(1960). In all there is no coherent tradition. There has
been no agreement as to the relation between fantasy and
Athenian fact, no total vision of the play, and no method
for combining "the terror and the dignified grace of the
fairy world." The play has eluded authoritative presentation
in each of the three quite different kinds of treatment:
"straight" performance (frequently tending to spectacle),
cut versions, and operatic versions (although Britten's
version is "the richest and most faithful interpretation . . .
in our generation"). Bottom, who, like the lovers, has a
new vision in the waking world, joins more than a hint of
St. John's first epistle with the more obvious 1 Corinthians

2:9 source. See also items 162, 406, 544, 566, T1182 and, a repeat entry, T1203.

184   Mincoff, Marco. "Shakespeare and Lyly." *Shakespeare Survey*, 14 (1961), 20-24.

Shakespeare is indebted in general to Lyly for the comic principle behind what one may call the main plot of the early comedies, for the structural pattern, that peculiar blend of a romantic comedy of courtship with a strain of low-comedy genre scenes, and for the strain of witty repartee. He transmutes Lyly's love into something more human and acceptable, his Cupid mythology into "friendly, benevolent" fairies, and his structure into a greater "complexity of interwoven strains." For other comparisons with Lyly see items 6, 37, 50, 184, 229, 236, 275, 282, 303, 355, 504, 568, 574, 581, 631, 643, 652, 670, 673-74, 680, 685n, 744, 746 and 960.

185   Sehrt, Ernst Theodor. *Wandlungen der Shakespeareschen Komödie* [Changes in Shakespeare's Comedy]. Kleine Vandenhoeck-Reihe 105. Göttingen: Vandenhoeck & Rupprecht, 1961. 66 pp. (German)

It is more difficult to find a core for Shakespeare's comedies than for the history plays or tragedies, but the concept of "play" (*Spiel*) is one which might serve as a focus. The idea of play was important for the life and philosophy of the time. Sehrt treats the comedies in chronological order and determines that there is a progression from the comic hero who is sovereign in his environment to the hero who is conscious of his vulnerability before God. Play is evident in many places in *Dream*. The sport of Oberon and Puck is not harmonious; it is inspired by jealousy and creates confusion. *Dream* differs from Shakespeare's earlier comedies in that man is dominated by the uncanny atmosphere and his vulnerability appears as the essence of his inner self. But this state of exposure is only temporary, and the order of the daytime world prevails. For other discussions of game-play elements see item 429.

186 Sen Gupta, A. C. *The Whirligig of Time: The Problem of
     Duration in Shakespeare's Plays*. Bombay: Orient
     Longmans; Mystic, Conn: Verry, 1961. ix, 201 pp.

     Finds (pp. 91-93) no "central thread in the tangled plot"
     and no central character but rather "the contrast of
     different attitudes" toward love and other topics. Thus any
     precise linear time is not to be expected.

187 Vyvyan, John. "Theseus and Hippolyta" and "*A Midsummer
     Night's Dream*." *Shakespeare and Platonic Beauty*. New
     York: Barnes & Noble; London: Chatto & Windus, 1961,
     pp. 7-14, 77-91.

     Hippolyta's "something of great constancy" is beauty;
     "behind it lies a great part of the Neo-Platonist philosophy
     of the Renaissance." The play stands as a parable of the
     Renaissance Neoplatonist thought; its leading idea is that
     "love on earth is a recognition between companion souls,
     who may at least perceive in one another, if they have true
     love-sight, the beauty of their divine self-nature." The
     confusion of the lovers is capable of deeply serious
     interpretation: the comic possibilities of the bewilderment of
     the searching soul. Comparisons are drawn with *Two
     Gentlemen*. The way to true self-knowledge is through
     perfect constancy in love achieved through a series of tests
     or trials. "The inner meaning" of all the early comedies is
     "the ascent or pilgrimage to heavenly beauty." The
     influence of Spenser's *Hymne in Honour of Beautie* is taken
     to be direct. For other comparisons with *Two Gentlemen* see
     items 235, 282, 305, 320, 355, 415, 489, 634 and 660. See
     also item 122.

187a Zimansky, C. A. "*A Midsummer Night's Dream*"
      [audio-cassette]. Ames, Iowa: State University of Iowa,
      1961. Distributed by National Center for Audio Tapes
      (Boulder, Colorado). Cassettes 0226-21, -22, -23. 50
      min. each. (not heard)

      Three lectures, designed for senior high students and
      adults.

188 Atherton, John. *William Shakespeare: "A Midsummer Night's Dream."* Guides to English Literature. London: Holton Educational Publications, 1962. iv, 60 pp.

For students. A scene-by-scene interpretation, with also sections on character, on "topics," and with specimen questions.

189 Berkeley, David S. *A Guide to Shakespeare's Comedies and Histories.* Stillwater, Oklahoma: Mrs. Ruth Bradley, 1962. 81 pp. (Companion volume) *Key to A Guide to Shakespeare's Comedies and Histories.* Stillwater, Oklahoma: Mrs. Ruth Bradley, 1962. 105 pp. (not seen)

Questions and answers on specific scenes and on the play in general.

190 Dabril, Lucien. *Sur les pas de Shakespeare "Tout est bien qui finit bien," "Un songe des nuits d'été," "La véridique histoire d'Henri VIII"* [On the Trail of Shakespeare: *All's Well That Ends Well, A Midsummer Night's Dream, Henry VIII*]. Paris: Nouv. Éd. latines, 1962. (French--not seen)

191 Dedinský, M. M. "Huiezdoslav ako prekladateľ drám." *Slovenské divadlo* (Bratislava), 10, no. 1 (1962), 1-16.

Analyzes dramatic translations of the Slovak poet Pavel Országh Huiezdoslav, including his *Dream* (1903). See also item 134.

192 Frye, Northrop. "Recognition in *The Winter's Tale.*" *Essays on Shakespeare and Elizabethan Drama in Honor of Hardin Craig.* Ed. Richard Hosley. Columbia: University of Missouri Press, 1962, pp. 235-46. Reprint. 1963, 1970.

Gives in passing a few remarks on *Dream.* Hippolyta has the "critical ability" in the family; Theseus is "a smiling public man past his first youth." The "middle world" of the play belongs to the fairies--the world of nature, of Eros and Adonis.

193   Herbert, T. Walter. "Dislocation and the Modest Demand in
      A Midsummer Night's Dream." *Renaissance Papers 1961.*
      Ed. George Walton Williams. [n.p.]: Southeastern
      Renaissance Conference, 1962, pp. 31-36.

      Invites notice of the astonishing steps whereby in the
      early scenes we are taken from the palace of Theseus in
      Athens to the home of an artisan which seems very English
      and thence into fairyland. George Peele, in *The Old Wives
      Tale*, had used the same devices before a similarly
      sophisticated audience. Chaucer had set the "loftily
      romantic Athens of Theseus" next to a world of English
      workingmen and had placed a story about fairyland in the
      mouth of an approving Wife of Bath. The audience would
      have been comfortable with such dislocations. Some of this
      material reappears in Chapter 1 of the author's *Oberon's
      Mazèd World* (item 504).

194   Hulme, Hilda M. *Explorations in Shakespeare's Language:
      Some Problems of Lexical Meaning in the Dramatic Text.*
      London: Longmans, Green, 1962; New York: Barnes &
      Noble, 1963. xii, 351 pp. Reprint (in which *Lexical*
      becomes *Word*). London: Longman, 1977.

      The index gives only four references to *Dream*. The only
      one which takes up more than a sentence is that which
      gives the obscene suggestion of *tailour* (II.i.54), which had
      been published before (item 154). See also items 57 and
      474.

195   Hunter, G. K. *Shakespeare: The Later Comedies.* Writers
      and Their Works, 143. London: Longmans, Green, 1962.
      Reprint. 1969. 60 pp. *Modern Essays in Criticism.* Ed.
      Leonard F. Dean. Rev. ed. London: Oxford University
      Press, 1967.

      Like the later romantic comedies, *Dream* is "centred on
      Love, but it moves by exposing the varieties of love,
      rather than [like the other comedies] by working them
      against one another in a process of argument." The pattern
      (which is like a dance) matters more than the psychological
      state of the dancers. It is a process of "pairing off." The
      lovers have no personalities; passion is reduced to a comic
      level; and the verse itself, which many have objected to,
      helps "distance" the scenes of the lovers' cross-purposes.

Seen against the royal pair and the fairies, their love is
irrational. But their innocence (sense of wonder) seems a
virtue when compared with the ignorance of the
mechanicals. What Shakespeare has done is present a
pattern of attitudes (for example, the lovers' levity set
against Bottom's aplomb), none of which is central and all
of which cast light on the others. The play works by
contrast rather than by interaction. The fairies are new not
only in their smallness and the absence of mischief as their
mode (but for Puck) but also in their concern with "*order*
in a quasi-human fashion." Theseus and Hippolyta represent
the "idea of achieved self-possession," the image of
"harmonious control over brute impulse." (Pp. 7-20)

196   Jacobson, Gerald F. "A Note on Shakespeare's *Midsummer
        Night's Dream.*" *American Imago*, 19 (1962), 21-26.

        Continues Gui's analysis (see item 84) by considering
Dream from the woman's point of view. Its "elucidation of
the psychosexual development of women" exposes especially
Hermia's Oedipal conflicts which are resolved in the end.
See Morton Kaplan's response (item 209). See also items 252
and 290.

197   Kersten, Dorelies. "Shakespeares Puck." *Shakespeare
        Jahrbuch* (Weimar), 98 (1962), 189-200 (German)

        Puck appears in six of the play's nine scenes, more
often than any other character besides the lovers. In his
essence and in the characteristics he possesses, he mirrors
the essential elements which constitute the atmosphere of
Dream and thus he reflects the drama itself. In addition, he
serves a dramatic function in the plot and is used by
Shakespeare in the artistic development of the drama,
uniting the diverse spheres and speeding the pace of
events. He plays the role of mediator between the viewer
and the work, and he reveals the sense of the work to the
audience.

198   Komiyama, Hiroshi. [*Midsummer Night's Dream*--The
        Characteristics of a Court Play.] *Kasei Gakuen Kenky u
        Kiyo*, 1 (1962), 30-38. (Japanese--not seen)

199   Righter [Barton], Anne. *Shakespeare and the Idea of the
      Play*. London: Chatto & Windus, 1962. 223 pp. Reprint.
      New York: Barnes & Noble, 1963. Reset.
      Harmondsworth, Middlesex, and Baltimore: Penguin
      Books, 1967. 199 pp. Several other reprints.

      Bottom and associates "have extraordinarily literal minds;
      . . . and they cannot tear their attention away from the
      audience. . . . In its obsession with the presence of the
      audience, the little tragicomedy seems to parody those older
      dramas written before the idea of the self-contained play
      had been commonly accepted. The medieval tradition of
      direct address, whether employed in the service of
      exposition or of simple contact with the spectators,
      obviously represented for Shakespeare an effective way of
      demolishing dramatic illusion." (Pp. 145-47) See item 60.

200   Söderwall, Margreta. "Notes on Some Shakespeare Editions:
      With Special Reference to *A Midsummer Night's Dream*."
      Moderna Språk, 56 (1962), 125-34.

      Brief descriptions of J. W. Lever's New Swan edition
      (item 870), The London Shakespeare (item 843), The Folger
      Library General Reader's Shakespeare (item 854), The New
      Stratford Shakespeare (item 828), and her own (item 858a).
      Söderwall concludes with a plea for the use of bilingual
      editions by non-English speaking students.

201   Torvalds, Ole. "Poeten, älskaren och galningen av idel
      fantasi besta . . ." ["The lunatic, the lover and the
      poet are of imagination all compact"]. *Åbo
      underrättelser*, 7 September 1962. (Swedish--not seen)

202   Wood, James O. "Shakespeare the Unobservant?"
      Shakespeare Newsletter, 12 (1962), 49.

      Certain details in *Dream*, the pervasive contradiction of
      the looked-for new and full moons, the visibility of Venus
      at midnight, are inconsistent with commonplace, readily
      observable facts of science. Shakespeare's "science" was of
      another order. On this same topic see items 302, 332, 385,
      389, 513 and 685d.

203   Brown, John Russell. "Mr. Pinter's Shakespeare." *The Critical Quarterly*, 5 (1963), 251-65.

In Bottom's climactic soliloquy (IV.i.199ff.) character-revelation is as important as thematic clarification (which many have noted). Like Bottom, the soliloquy is "practical, courageous, and egotistically romantic."

204   Cutts, John P. "'The Fierce Vexation of [*Midsummer Night's*] Dreame.'" *Shakespeare Quarterly*, 14 (1963), 183-85.

On the symbolical use of "love in idlenesse" and "Dians bud." The one (according to Gerarde) serves to cure "the French disease," the other brings on chastity. For other discussions of flowers see item 45.

205   Gamal, Saad M. "*A Midsummer Night's Dream* and *Romeo and Juliet*: Some Parallels." *Cairo Studies in English*, 1963/1966, pp. 109-17.

Classifies parallels under three headings: thematic, structural, and linguistic. For other comparisons between the two plays see item 131.

206   Guido, Augusto. *Struttura e personaggi nel "Sogno delle notte di mezza estate"* [Structure and Character in the *Dream*]. Lectura Shakespeareana Scaligera. Florence: F. Le Monnier, 1963. 18 pp. (Italian)

Discusses *Dream* as a manifest success, noting in particular its relationship with *Romeo*. See item 131.

207   Itkonen, Kyösti. "Englischer Einfluss auf die Sprache der Wielandschen Übersetzung des *Sommernachtstraum*" (1762) [English Influence on the Wieland Translation of *Dream* (1762)]. *Neuphilologische Mitteilungen*, 64 (1963), 1-15. (German)

Primarily an alphabetical list with commentary of words and phrases from C. M. Wieland's *Dream* translation which are literal translations from the English rather than true

German equivalents. Several borrowings from English syntax are also noted. See also item 25.

208 Kantak, V. Y. "The Poor Player . . ." *Literary Criterion* (Mysore), 6, no. 1 (1963), 153-63.

The diverse progeny of the imagination in *Dream* is kept in balance by the two "purveyors of realism." Bottom's feeling for Earth never deserts him, and Theseus' verdict is firmly against all forms of mid-summer madness. His speech (V.i.1-22), however, contains a "certain ambiguity," and in any case his is not the play's last word on the topic. In *The Tempest* the products of the imagination seem to gain in seriousness and reality. See item 149.

209 Kaplan, Morton. "*The American Imago* in Retrospect: An Article-Review." *Literature & Psychology*, 13 (1963), 112-16.

Summarizes and attacks Gerald F. Jacobson's interpretation (item 196). "[It] adds no insight into the play as aesthetic creation and ultimately produces one psychoanalyzed Shakespeare for every play." See also item 290.

210 LeWinter, Oswald, ed. *Shakespeare in Europe*. Cleveland and New York: Meridian Books, 1963. 382 pp.

Reprints (in translation, pp. 286-95) Bjørnstjerne Bjørnson's defense of his production (at Christiania Theatre in Spring, 1965) against hostile reviews. Bjørnson attacks those who require elaborate, artificial scenery and devalue the power of the poetry.

211 Purdom, C. B. *What Happens in Shakespeare: A New Interpretation*. New York: Roy Publishers; London: John Baker, 1963. 192 pp.

The play lacks "the essential element" of drama, a protagonist, and yet has fine poetry and theatricality (pp. 92-93).

212 Quennell, Peter. *Shakespeare: A Biography*. Cleveland and
New York: World; London: Weidenfeld, 1963. 384 pp.
Reprint. New York: Avon, 1964.

In a general comment (pp. 168-74) touches on the theme
("the illusory nature of love"), the mood ("dream-like"),
and the characters. Lists the sources, quoting portions of
Scot's *Discoverie*.

213 Shalvi, Alice. [Shadow and Reality in *A Midsummer Night's
Dream*]. *Bamah* (Jerusalem), 4, no. 22 (1963), 7-12.
(Hebrew--not seen)

Item 314 may be an English translation of this article.

214 Talbert, Ernest William. "*Love's Labour's Lost* and *A
Midsummer Night's Dream*." *Elizabethan Drama and
Shakespeare's Early Plays: An Essay in Historical
Criticism*. Chapel Hill: University of North Carolina
Press, 1963, pp. 235-61. Reprint. New York: Gordian
Press, 1973.

"Shakespeare's tendency to write patterned sequences
[here given in brief] seems to constitute his structural
principle in his drama, rather than any adherence to
academic precepts about protasis, epitasis, and catastrophe
or any modification of structural movements derived from
the tradition of the mystery or morality." Here he draws
upon folk merriment, the character-types and comic
gestures: for the Robin Goodfellow, the ass's head, for
Bottom (a "principal comedian and his crew"), and others.

215 Turck, Susanne. *Shakespeares "Midsummer Night's Dream"*:
Handreichungen für den Lehrer [Shakespeare's *Dream*:
Manual for the Teacher]. Der Neusprachliche Unterricht
in Wissenschaft und Praxis, 8. Dortmund: Lensing, 1963.
66 pp. (German--not seen)

For secondary school teachers.

216 Wendt, Ernst. "Sommernachtsspiele. Zadek inszenierte den
Shakespeare in der Übersetzung von Erich Fried"
[Summer-night-plays. Zadek Stages Shakespeare in the

Translation of Erich Fried]. *Theater heute*, 4, no. 6
(1963), 32-33. (German--not seen)

See item 25.

217   Zukofsky, Louis and Celia. *Bottom: On Shakespeare*. 2
         volumes. Volume 1 by Louis Zukofsky. Austin: Ark
         Press of Texas University Press, 1963.

All of Shakespeare gives expression to his idea of
"Love's mind"--a concept impossible to define precisely but
ever present and developing, influencing lines and words.
Part One relies heavily on Helena's speech (I.i.232-39) as
the basis for a general discussion of love in Shakespeare;
and throughout the book *Dream* is quoted over and over
again as typifying aspects of Shakespeare's idea of love and
in connection with a variety of related topics. Zukofsky
presents his material in a highly mannered style: a collage
of quotations and aphoristic comments arranged in an
alphabetical listing of topics from "A-bomb and H" to "Z
(signature)." Bottom he compares with Hamlet (pp. 22-24),
since love, being blind, is tragic, involving errors. ("The
theme of *Hamlet* [is that] Hamlet knows love and cannot
have it.") Characteristic of the style are the remarks on
Thisbe's "I kiss the wall's hole, not your lips at
all"--"These words edge pleasure, innocence and terror.
They canter towards a thoughtful, sensuous and
pre-archaic wall at once" (p. 34). Constant attention is
given to eyes (see, for example, pp. 283-84).

218   Alexander, Peter. *Alexander's Introductions to
         Shakespeare*. London and Glasgow: Collins; New York:
         W. W. Norton, 1964. 192 pp.

This (pp. 67-68) is the introduction to Alexander's
Tudor Edition (Collins, 1951; item 817). The sketch of
Theseus is "attractive and free of malice." Shakespeare
does not resent the attitude of the Duke toward the
mechanicals' playlet. His own art doubtless had met with
such condescension. *Dream* may indeed have been designed
for a specific marriage (but probably not three marriages),
with the Queen present and boys playing the parts of
fairies. See item 19.

218a _____. *Shakespeare.* The Home University Library
   of Modern Knowledge, 252. London and New York:
   Oxford University Press, 1964. [viii], 271 pp.

   We may surmise, according to Alexander (pp. 133-35),
   that *Dream* was performed for the wedding of Elizabeth
   Carey, grand-daughter of the Lord Chamberlain and a
   favorite of Queen Elizabeth, to Thomas Berkeley on 19
   February 1596; we may thus understand how children would
   be available to take the fairy roles and the Queen be
   present for the performance. But we have no record of the
   celebrations. This play combines Shakespeare's skill in
   construction with his growing sense of characterization and
   his poetic powers. (These remarks seem to be a reduced
   version of those in *Shakespeare's Life and Art*--item 19.)

219 Ben-Ya'acov, A. [Two Hebrew Translations of *Midsummer
   Night's Dream.*] *Yediot Ah'ronot* (Tel Aviv), 14 August
   1964. (Hebrew--not seen)

   Compares the Hebrew translations of Ephraim Broido
   (item 887) and Tcherni Carmi (item 888). See also items
   221, 248 and 254.

220 Brinkmann, Karl. *Erläuterungen zu Shakespeares "Ein
   Sommernachtstraum"* [Explications of Shakespeare's
   Dream]. Dr. W. Königs Erläuterungen zu den
   Klassikern, 80. Rev. ed. Hollfeld/Oberfranken: Bange,
   1964. 72 pp. (German)

   Annotations for teachers and students.

221 Broida, Ephraim. [A World of Dream and a World of
   Reality.] *la-Merhay* (Tel Aviv), 22 May 1964.
   (Hebrew--not seen)

   Apparently on the translator's interpretation of *Dream*
   (see item 887). See also items 219, 248 and 254.

222 Brown, Arthur. "Shakespeare's Treatment of Comedy."
   Shakespeare's World. Ed. James Sutherland and Joel
   Hurstfield. London: Arnold; New York: St. Martin's,
   1964, pp. 79-95.

Briefly (pp. 90-91) comments on the general intent of
Dream. "It is difficult to believe that Shakespeare was
doing anything but enjoy himself." "We are not encouraged
to accept Theseus' verdict on events, nor are we, on the
other hand, encouraged to reject it. The events are
presented to us through the eyes of all the interested
parties, and we may please ourselves what we do or think
about it all."

223   Brown, John Russell. [*A Midsummer Night's Dream.*]
       Te'atron (Haifa), 9 (June, 1964), 8-11. (Hebrew--not
       seen)

224   Bryant, J. A., Jr. "The Importance of *A Midsummer
       Night's Dream.*" *Ball State Teachers College Forum*, 5
       (1964), 3-9.

       Concentrates on the special vision of the play: "our
       vision of order emerging from disorder, our fleeting
       recollection of the heaven we lost when we surrendered our
       innocence, our assurance of the inevitability of our return
       there, and our recognition of the brotherhood of all who
       elect to make that passage." The time setting is not at all
       May Day. Theseus and Hippolyta are found "bickering" in
       the opening lines.

225   Burgess, Anthony. *Nothing Like the Sun: A Story of
       Shakespeare's Love-Life*. London: Heinemann; New York:
       W. W. Norton, 1964. Reprint. Harmondsworth,
       Middlesex: Penguin Books, 1966. 234 pp. There are
       several reprints.

       The imagined account of the inspiration for the play
       occurs on pages 144-48.

226   Conn, Naomi, "The Promise of Arcadia: Nature and the
       Natural Man in Shakespeare's Comedies." *Shakespeare
       Encomium: 1564-1964*. Ed. Anne Paolucci. The City
       College Papers, 1. New York: City College, 1964, pp.
       113-22.

       On nature's power in the comedies to control disorder as
       suggested by, and under the influence of, the pastoral

settings. In *Dream*, which is discussed in one paragraph, it is the power of moonlight in an enchanted forest to bring about a resolution to the excesses of love.

227 Dent, R. W. "Imagination in *A Midsummer Night's Dream.*" *Shakespeare Quarterly*, 15 (1964), 115-29, and *Shakespeare 400: Essays by American Scholars on the Anniversary of the Poet's Birth.* Ed. James G. McManaway. New York: Holt, Rinehart, and Winston, 1964, pp. 115-19.

The play is unified not by its comment on the irrationality of love but rather by "the partially contrasting role of imagination in love and in art." Poetic art, as the playlet ironically demonstrates and *Dream* itself confirms, "is in accord with discretion, and its creations are capable of universal appreciation, both as beautiful and as meaningful." Shakespeare discriminates between lover and poet even if Theseus does not. The entire play implies a view contrary to that of Theseus, despite the humility of the epilogue. The play is his "closest approximation to a 'Defense of Dramatic Poesy.'"

228 Eastman, A. M., and G. B. Harrison, eds. "*A Midsummer Night's Dream.*" *Shakespeare's Critics from Johnson to Auden: A Medley of Judgments.* Ann Arbor: University of Michigan Press, 1964, pp. 261-67.

Gives short selections from E. K. Chambers (1905, 1925; item 12), J. B. Priestley (1925; item 13), Enid Welsford (1927; item 595), S. C. Sen Gupta (1950; item 72), and C. L. Barber (1959; item 158).

229 Ferrara, Fernando. *Shakespeare e la commedia.* Bari: Adriatica Editrice, 1964. 428 pp. (Italian)

In Chapter 3 of the second part (pp. 187-209), Section 1 notices elements from other early plays (particularly *Love's Labour's Lost*) harmonized in *Dream*. Special emphasis is on masquing and Lyly's influence. Section 2 analyzes the levels of fantasy and reality suggested in the mechanicals' performance and the last act in general. Section 3 discusses the meaning of Theseus' speech on the imagination in

74 *Criticism*

Neoplatonic (citing Ficino) and rhetorical (*elocutio, inventio*) terms. See items 59, 122 and 184.

230 Gardner, Martin. *The Ambidextrous Universe*. New York: Basic Books, 1964. x, 294 pp. Numerous reprints.

In the "mixed-up violent left-right embrace of the bindweed [that is, the "woodbine" of IV.i.41-42, which is related to the morning-glory] and honeysuckle," the one coils in a right-handed helix, the other in a left-handed. The two flowers coil in opposite ways, Gardner notes in passing. (Pp. 53-54, and note, pp. 62-63)

231 Grace, William J. *Approaching Shakespeare*. New York: Basic Books, 1964. 248 pp.

Uses *Dream* in places to illustrate selected aspects of Shakespeare's art: his use of comic distortion (Bottom and Titania, pp. 47-49), of special verbal effects ("I know a bank," pp. 91-92), and of traditional materials which he varies (the fairies, pp. 146-49).

232 Grivelet, Michel. "Les Français, La Lune, et Shakespeare." *Europe*, 417 (1964), 94-102. (French)

On the difficulty the French have in grasping Shakespearean comedy and on the function of the moon in several comedies. In *Dream* the moon suggests the dark and foreboding, not Diana but Hecate.

233 Harwood, A. C. *Shakespeare's Prophetic Mind*. [London]: Rudolf Steiner Press, 1964. 63 pp.

As regards the concern of the book--"metaphysical powers"--*Dream* is "entirely innocent." Theseus' speech, however, is interesting as it contains perhaps "the earliest use of the word imagination as meaning a creative faculty and not merely a picture of the mind." (Pp. 30-33)

234 Herbert, T. Walter. "Invitations to Cosmic Laughter in *A Midsummer Night's Dream*." *Shakespearean Essays*. Ed. Norman Sanders and Alwin Thaler. Tennessee Studies in

Literature, Special No. 2. Knoxville: University of
Tennessee Press, 1964, pp. 29-39.

The material reappears in slightly altered form in
Chapters 2 and 4 of the author's *Oberon's Mazèd World*
(item 504).

235 Iyengar, K. R. Srinivasa. *Shakespeare: His World and His
Art*. Bombay and New York: Asia, 1964. xvi, 712 pp.

The play's treatment of love differs from that of the
other early plays, especially *Two Gentlemen*. Shakespeare
may have played Theseus. A general introduction (pp.
164-71). See item 187.

236 Jones, David Edwards. "Shakespeare's Apprenticeship in
Comedy." Ph.D. dissertation, University of Minnesota,
1963. *DA*, 25 (1964), 2491-92.

Assesses the relationship between *Dream* (the fifth play
considered) and its models, especially Lyly, with comments
on its independence and mastery as compared to the other
early plays. See item 184.

237 Kagan, L. V. [*A Midsummer Night's Dream* and the Theme
of the Beauty of Human Nature in the Early Comedies of
Shakespeare.] *Naučnye doklady Vyssej školy*, 7 (1964),
83-94. (Russian--not seen)

237a Kéry, László. *Shakespeare vígjátékai* [Shakespeare's
Comedies]. Budapest: Gondolat, 1964. 381 pp.
(Hungarian--not seen)

See item 238.

238 _____. "Shakespearian Comedy." *Acta Litteraria
Academiae Scientiarum Hungaricae*, 6 (1964), 245-66.

Introduces the comedies and critical ideas about them to
Hungarian readers. Of *Dream*, covered in one paragraph on
pages 252-53, the only generalization not usually found in
comments on the play is this: "The theme of love is

introduced in several ways; among others, in a variation
which flashes some light on the tragic situation of lovers
determined by a class society." The article is a summary of
the author's book on the comedies (item 237a).

239   Kott, Jan. "Titania and the Ass's Head." *Shakespeare Our*
        Contemporary. Translated by Boleslaw Taborski. Garden
        City, N. Y.: Anchor Books, 1966. London: Methuen;
        New York: Doubleday, 1964, pp. 213-36. New York: W.
        W. Norton, 1974. First published as *Szkice O*
        Scekspirze. Warsaw: Państwowe Wydawnictwo Naukowe,
        1964. (This essay appeared in numerous places in
        numerous languages in 1964.)

        The play is a nightmarish orgy of the grotesque and
depraved, including animal-human hybrids, revealing the
true nature of Eros when uncensored by the day. Puck is,
like Ariel, a menacing devil, "a fawn, a devil, and
Harlequin, all combined." "The most erotic of Shakespeare's
plays . . . [and] the eroticism [is] expressed . . .
brutally." "The reduction of characters to love partners
seems to me to be the most peculiar characteristic of this
cruel dream; and perhaps its most modern quality." "The
behaviour of all the characters . . . is promiscuous." "A
most truthful, brutal, and violent play." It is an "Eros of
ugliness, born through desire and culminating in folly."
The main theme is the "passing through animality." *Dream*
is a bestiary. "I imagine Titania's court as consisting of old
men and women, toothless and shaking, their mouths wet
with saliva, who sniggering procure a monster for their
mistress." Titania longs for animal love, and gets it. The
grotesqueries are compared to visions of Bosch and
characters of Goya. "The world is mad, and love is mad."
For responses, see items 287-88, 325, 340, 349, 391, 405,
444, 504, 520, 523, 566x, 566v and 960.

240   Leech, Clifford. "Shakespeare's Comic Dukes." *Review of*
        English Literature, 5, no. 2 (1964), 101-14.

        Duke Theseus resembles Solinus in *The Comedy of*
Errors in that both appear as part of the framework of
their respective comedies and both, arbitrarily, extenuate
the law. Theseus is rather more eloquent. The playwright
has handled him "with restraint, giving him an authority, a
kindliness, as well as a habit of condescension, a tinge of

self-importance, and a moment of arbitrary decision." For
other comparisons with *Errors* see items 247, 282, 305, 320,
355, 387a, 415, 429, 515 and 634.

241 Leech, Clifford. "Shakespeare's Greeks." *Stratford Papers
     on Shakespeare (1963)*. Ed. B. A. W. Jackson. Toronto:
     W. J. Gage, 1964, pp. 1-20.

In *Dream*, discussed briefly as one of the plays with
Hellenistic settings, "Shakespeare was encouraged both to
technical experiment and to certain, but varying, oddness
in his presentation of human beings."

242 Leoff, Eve. *Shakespeare's "A Midsummer Night's Dream."*
     Monarch Notes. New York: Monarch Press, 1964. 88 pp.
     Later title: *Review Notes and Study Guide to
     Shakespeare's "A Midsummer Night's* Dream."

Introduction, brief summary, detailed summary, critical
commentary, essay questions and answers. Designed for
students.

243 Lindsay, Noel. "Teorías sobre la obra de Shakespeare"
     [Theories on the Work of Shakespeare]. *México en la
     Cultura* (Supplemento de Novedades), 13 December 1964,
     p. 6. (Spanish--not seen)

244 McKenzie, D. F. "Shakespeare's Dream of Knowledge."
     Landfall, 18 (1964), 40-48.

Dream is much more sophisticated, more intellectually
stimulating, than the "tinsel and gossamer" nineteenth
century tradition understood. Its larger concern,
enveloping that of love itself as a theme, is the nature of
illusion. Like *Winter's Tale*, with which it compares, it
"strives to promote in us a direct apprehension of
imaginative truth," and thereby to justify Shakespeare's
art. In the midst of the play, in the woods, "by a
persistent complication of the many orders of imaginative
sight we are offered a most searching examination of the
connection between illusion and reality." We are led from a
lower, disordered imaginative world, based on sense, to one
ordered by a higher imagination, based on understanding,

which is also the third of Castiglione's three kinds of love. Theseus is "right in stressing the dangers and absurdities of the lower imagination, the mere acceptance of illusion, whether in love or art; and wrong in failing to allow of a higher imaginative truth." Through Bottom's awareness of the power of illusion, we awake to and are brought "into communion with the higher reality of which our present world is only the merest shadow." "The secret of the dream world, the nature of the illusion, cannot be explained but only felt."

245   Mendl, R. W. S. *Revelation in Shakespeare*. London: John Calder, 1964. 223 pp.

Notes (pp. 56-58) a few Christian elements amidst all the pagan ones. "[A] kinship with Nature in her sweetest aspect brings the play, albeit unconsciously, near to God."

246   Milward, Peter. "*A Midsummer Night's Dream.*" *An Introduction to Shakespeare's Plays*. Tokyo: Kenkyusha, 1964, pp. 59-65. Reprint. Folcroft, Pa.: Folcroft Press, 1970.

In *Romeo* Shakespeare's treatment of love had been emotional and perhaps too involved with the immediate situation; here in *Dream* his attitude has become more detached, objective, and even critical. "He has come to view human love as a game of hide-and-seek, in part tragic, in part comic, yet disclosing the serious ideal of the Golden World which is the supreme object of romantic comedy in Dante's definition." The theme of love is developed in stages through the separate groups of characters. Even in the young lovers we can detect several kinds of love. For other discussions of *Romeo* see item 131.

247   Nemoianu, Vergil. "Cazuri de paralelism in structură dramatică shakespeariana. Consideratii cu privire la sensul lor" [Parallelisms in Shakespeare's Dramatic Structure. Some Notes on Their Significance]. *Analele Universităţii Bucuresti*. Seria Stiinte sociale, filologie (1964), pp. 187-98. (Rumanian--not seen)

Apparently an investigation into the dramatic structure of *Errors*, *Dream*, and *Lear*.

248 [One Root, Two Translations]. *Davar* (Tel Aviv), 10 July 1964. (Hebrew--not seen)

Compares the translations of Tcherni Carmi (item 888) and Ephraim Broido (item 887) of *Dream*. See also items 219, 221 and 254.

249 Oshima, Yoshimure. [Love in *A Midsummer Night's Dream*]. *Eibungaku Shi*, 7 (1964), 12-19. (Japanese--not seen)

250 Palkó, István. [The Significance of *A Midsummer Night's Dream*.] *Életünk*, 1 (1964), 79-96. Reprint. *Magyar Pszichologiai Szemle*, 23 (1967), 77-85. (Hungarian--not seen)

Apparently an ethnographical, mythological, and psychological interpretation.

251 Entry Deleted.

252 Ravich, Robert A. "A Psychoanalytic Study of Shakespeare's Early Plays." *Psychoanalytic Quarterly*, 33 (1964), 388-410.

In brief comments (pp. 405-10) finds "a more frankly Oedipal situation . . . portrayed than in *Hamlet*" (Bottom with Titania with Oberon removed) and "Bottom's dream too shocking to bear interpretation." For other psychoanalytic readings see items 84, 169a, 196, 209, 290, 329, 391, 397, 424, 556 and 726d.

253 _____. "'Such seething brains, such shaping fantasies.'" *Abbottempo*, 2 (19 August 1964), 28-35.

Quotes Theseus' speech as a point of departure for a discussion of Shakespeare's general attitudes toward insanity.

254 Shalvi, Alice. [Shakespearean Translations into Hebrew.] *ha-Aretz* (Tel Aviv), 5 December 1964. (Hebrew--not seen)

Compares the translations of Techrni Carmi (item 888)
and Ephraim Broido (item 887). See also items 219, 221 and
248.

255   Tal, H. [Various Critics on *A Midsummer Night's Dream*.]
      Davar (Tel Aviv), 10 July 1964. (Hebrew--not seen)

      Quotations from Johnson, Coleridge, Hazlitt et al.

256   Trousdale, Marion. *"A Midsummer Night's Dream": A
      Scene-by-Scene Analysis, with Critical Commentary*.
      Study Master. New York: American R. D. M., 1964. 47
      pp.

      With notes and questions on each scene, critical
      appraisals, summary of characters, suggested study topics,
      and sample answers to questions raised. Designed for
      students.

257   Colwell, C. Carter. *"Midsummer Night's Dream"*
      [audio-cassette]. [n.d.] Distributed by
      Everett/Edwards, Inc. (DeLand, Florida), Cassette 705,
      and Listening Library (Old Greenwich, Conn.). Cassette
      WS79cx, no. 5. 35 min. (not heard)

      A lecture.

258   *"A Midsummer Night's Dream"* [audio-cassette]. Distributed
      by Center for Cassette Studies, Inc. (New York, N.
      Y.), [n.d.]. Cassette No. 775, 58 min. (not heard)

      According to the catalogue description, Dick Powell and
      Jean Muir discuss the following questions: What is the
      reason for Oberon's dispute with Titania? How does Puck
      create the error that provides the comedy? Why is Bottom
      given the head of an ass? And how does Shakespeare
      resolve all problems of the lovers?

259-66   Entries Deleted.

267 Anson, John Seller. "Dramatic Conventions in Shakespeare's Middle Comedies." Ph.D. dissertation, University of California, Berkeley, 1964. *DA*, 25 (1965), 4122.

Dream (discussed briefly) achieved for Shakespeare a move away from the sense of sophisticated superiority toward conventions found in his romantic sources and toward the special form of his subsequent comedies (here called "utopian").

268 Araya, Guillermo. "Shakespeare y Góngora parodian la fábula de Píramo y Tisbe" [Shakespeare and Gongora Parody the Plot of Pyramus and Thisbe]. *En homenaje a Eleázar Huerta*. Estudias Fililógicos, 1. Valdivia: Univ. Austral de Chile, 1965, pp. 19-40. (Spanish--not seen)

269 Baxter, John S. "Present Mirth: Shakespeare's Romantic Comedies." *Queen's Quarterly*, 72 (1965), 52-77.

The comedies have been treated in the last one hundred and fifty years "as the handsome, intelligent, but relatively docile young ladies in the Shakespearean household." To show that the comedies are largely an inducement to good fun, quotes the "court scene" with Bottom and the fairies. Here Bottom "assumes an air of aristocratic *ennui* in relation to Titania's courtiers and contrives to be at one and the same time the essence of princely gentility and graciousness and the embodiment of the democratic spirit." Baxter also describes the last moment of the play for its atmosphere and the importance it gives to the promise of children. Shakespearean comedy "begins in escapism [and] ends in vision and profound hope."

270 Black, Matthew Wilson. *William Shakespeare, "A Midsummer Night's Dream": An Outline Guide to the Play*. New York: Barnes & Noble, 1965. 121 pp. Rev. ed., 1967.

Adapted by the staff of Barnes & Noble from an original work by Black. Contains summaries and discussions, analyses of theme, "Kinds of Unreality," setting, time sequence, "Dramatic Purpose of Each Scene," and character sketches. Designed for students. Item 566a seems to be a revision.

271   Calderwood, James L. "*A Midsummer Night's Dream*: The
       Illusion of Drama." *Modern Language Quarterly*, 26
       (1965), 506-22.

       This article reappears, "newly corrected and
       augmented," in the author's *Shakespearean Metadrama* (item
       367), which see.

272   Choe, Jaisou. *Shakespeare's Art as Order of Life*. New
       York: Vantage, 1965. 199 pp.

       Concludes (pp. 60-61) that the function of comedy for
       Shakespeare as manifested by *Dream* "was not so much to
       provide fun and laughter as to give a full and harmonious
       sense of happiness."

273   Frye, Northrop. *A Natural Perspective: The Development of
       Shakespearean Comedy and Romance*. New York and
       London: Columbia University Press, 1965. xiv, 159 pp.
       Reprint. New York: Harcourt, Brace, & World. [n.d.].

       Continues and develops ideas set out in *Anatomy of
       Criticism* (item 142). There are in Chapter 4 scattered,
       brief comments on *Dream*. The comic drive leads to a new
       social identity, replacing the original irrational and
       tyrannical society with a new one crystallized around the
       marriage of the central characters. The conventions in the
       structure of romantic comedy are closely related to its
       primitive basis in the movement toward rebirth and renewal
       of the powers of nature, from winter to spring, darkness to
       dawn. The imagery of comedy is cyclical. "The action moves
       from a world of parental tyranny and irrational law into a
       forest." The forest is a dream, golden, green, magical
       world, with the fairies representing the cyclical processes
       of nature, the world having a "miraculous and irresistible
       reviving power." See also item 274.

274   _____. "Nature and Nothing." *Essays on
       Shakespeare*. Ed. Gerald W. Chapman. Princeton:
       Princeton University Press, 1965, pp. 35-58.

       Briefly comments (pp. 50-55) on the collision between a
       natural (forest) society and an obstructive or anti-comic
       society and on the general structure of the romantic

comedies. The natural society takes over its rival and informs it with its own comic spirit. See also items 142 and 273.

275 Gabler, Hans Walter. *Zur Funktion dramatischer und literarischer Parodie im elisabethanischen Drama: Beiträge zur Interpretation ausgewählter Dramen aus dem Werk Lylys, Marlowes und Greenes und Frühwerk Shakespeares* [On the Dramatic and Literary Function of Parody in Elizabethan Drama: Contributions to the Interpretation of Selected Plays of Lyly, Marlowe and Greene and the Early Work of Shakespeare]. Dissertation, Munich, 1965. Reinheim/Odenwald: the author, 1966. (German--not seen)

Contains a chapter on *Dream* (pp. 154-61) with special emphasis on the function of parody.

276 Hilliard, Addie Suggs. "Shakespeare's Botanical Imagery: Its Meaning to the Elizabethan Audience and Its Dramatic Function in the Plays." Ph.D. dissertation, University of Tennessee, 1964. *DA*, 25 (1965), 5906.

Analyzes and appraises Shakespeare's knowledge of botany and attempts to infer what average Elizabethans knew about plants in order to understand the function of plants in the plays. *Dream* is treated in Chapter 3, on botanical imagery used as background. See item 45.

277 Lyons, Charles Ray. "Shakespeare and the Ambiguity of Love's Triumph." Ph.D. dissertation, Stanford University, 1964. *DA*, 25 (1965), 5909.

Studies the basic ambiguity of love in the comedies, of marriage in particular, which "seems to pose a paradox: love is the source of integration and disintegration, the promise of immortality and the loss of the self." The social integration brought about by love in the romantic comedies exists "only within the greater perspective of an awareness of human mortality and the deliquescence of love." *Dream* is one of the early comedies discussed. Presumably the material on *Dream* is the same as that printed in the 1971 book of this title and a 1971 article (see item 377).

278   Matthäi, Hans Rudolf. *Das Liebesmotiv in den Komödien*
      Shakespeares [The Love Motif in the Comedies of
      Shakespeare]. Dissertation, Frankfurt, 1965. 317 pp.
      (German--not seen)

      The material on *Dream* is on pages 99-129.

279   Mincoff, Marco. "Shakespeare's Comedies and the Five-Act
      Structure." *Bulletin de la Faculté des Lettres de*
      Strasbourg, 63 (1965), 919-34.

      Dream reflects an obvious balance in its structure, with
      Act I the prologue, Act V the epilogue, Act III a climax of
      misunderstandings and squabbles, flanked by two acts
      which give the preparation and allayment of such tension.
      This five-act structure reflects Renaissance models (with
      the point of greatest tension in the middle), not classical.

280   Murerji, Ena. "A Shakespearian Theory of Poetry."
      Shakespeare: A Book of Homage. Calcutta: Jadavpur
      University, 1965, pp. 150-53.

      Takes Shakespeare's theory of the imagination to be
      defined by Theseus: "the concept of ecstatic imagination
      that transforms and transcends the limitations of facts,"
      and finds Theseus not sarcastic but cool and sensible.

280a Schanzer, Ernest. "*A Midsummer Night's Dream*"
      [audio-cassette]. *Shakespeare's Critics Speak*. New
      York: Jeffrey Norton Publishers, 1965. Retaped, 1977.
      Cassette 23097, 19 min.

      A general introduction, using Theseus' speech as a
      springboard. The tiny fairies were Shakespeare's invention,
      and he tempered their traditional fearfulness. The
      wonderful design--surpassing anything in classical
      comedy--is likewise his invention. No source will ever be
      found. Not love but rather "love-madness" is the central
      theme, that is, love cut off from judgment and the senses.
      Puck is like Cupid, the juice standing for the arrow.
      Bottom and Titania are an emblem of this madness.

281 Vardi, Dov. *Shakespeare u-Mahzotav* [Shakespeare and His
     Plays]. Nerhavia, Israel: Sifriyat Po'alim, 1965. 368 pp.
     (Hebrew--not seen)

     Includes an essay on *Dream*.

282 Bonazza, Blaze Odell. *"A Midsummer Night's Dream."*
     Shakespeare's Early Comedies: A Structural Analysis.
     Studies in English Literature, 9. The Hague: Mouton,
     1966, pp. 105-24.

     The Comedy of Errors, Love's Labour's Lost, and *Two
     Gentlemen,* three early comedies, experiment with four
     types of plots in preparation for *Dream* which fully
     orchestrates all four in a movement toward greater
     complexity. The plots are (A) the enveloping action, (B)
     the romantic love story, (C) the parodying subplot, and
     (D) the atmosphere-providing plot (Oberon versus Titania
     in *Dream*). In *Dream* Shakespeare used "the changes of
     identity of Plautine comedy, the elegance and beauty of
     language of court comedy, the parodying subplot of Lyly,
     and the complicated romantic plot of the Sidney-Greene
     school of romance rendered acceptable on the stage by an
     agreeable dramatic climate of his own devising." See items
     59, 187, 240 and 184. For discussions of the influence of
     Robert Greene see items 37, 50, 275, 282, 303, 355, 407,
     583, 654, 697, 742, 760 and 897.

283 Brown, John Russell. *Shakespeare's Plays in Performance.*
     London: Edward Arnold, [1966]; New York: St. Martin's
     Press, 1967. x, 244 pp. Illustrated. Reprint.
     Harmondsworth, Middlesex: Penguin Books, 1966, 1969.

     Analyzes the texts of selected plays and productions to
     show inherent production values, alternating between close
     reading and stage history. He argues that in Oberon's "We
     are spirits of another sort," meter, rhythm, diction,
     syntax, and phrasing will provide "the long controlled
     sound" that gives the fairy king authority. In an analysis
     of Bottom's character, his inner nature is said to be
     revealed to us in a sequence that is progressively intimate,
     leading ultimately to our full, amused understanding of his
     performance as Pyramus. There are a few brief references
     to stage business in the 1959 production of *Midsummer*

Night's Dream at Stratford-upon-Avon, directed by Peter
Hall. There is another entry on this item at T1267.

284   Campbell, Oscar James, and Edward G. Quinn, eds. "*A
        Midsummer Night's Dream.*" *The Reader's Encyclopedia of
        Shakespeare*. New York: Thomas Y. Crowell, 1966, pp.
        540-50.

        Helen Delpar gives summary comments on text (Q1 is
        probably from the annotated foul papers), date (1594-1595),
        sources, topical allusions, and a plot synopsis. There are
        critical comments from Charles Knight, Thomas Kenny,
        Georg Brandes, E. K. Chambers, John Russell Brown,
        C. L. Barber, and Wolfgang Clemen. A stage history of the
        play in England and America is by Maureen Grice (see item
        T1267a). In his comment Campbell accepts the possibility of
        two textual layers, the early one consisting of the dialogue
        of the lovers and other passages of wooden rhymed verse,
        the later consisting of the lines written in celebration of
        "the allegorically described wedding" and the "bursts of
        verbal music." This second, "upper level" may contain
        "half-buried topical allusions and personal satire." The
        theme is that "Love is a wholly irrational passion." Theseus
        is no Greek tyrant, but a thoroughly English gentleman.
        Puck's part exhibits such a variety of styles, now
        mechanical, now magical, that it must have been revised.
        Campbell also accepts as probable Edith Rickert's thesis
        (see item 574) that *Dream* alludes to the Elvetham festival in
        Oberon's Vision (II.i.148-68) and is, to some extent, a
        political allegory of Hertford's efforts to have his son by
        Lady Catherine Grey ("the changeling boy") declared
        legitimate by the Queen. Moreover, as Rickert had argued,
        Bottom's remark about the fear of a lion alludes to King
        James' fear, and Bottom is, from time to time, James.
        Puck's epilogue, he adds, constitutes a plea for pardon for
        such topical liberties as these. (Much of this material is
        presented in items 807 and 900.)

285   D'Amico, Jack Paul. "Symbolic Patterns of Action in Certain
        Shakespearean Comedies." Ph.D. dissertation, State
        University of New York, Buffalo, 1966. *DA* 27 (1966),
        744A.

        Investigates the analogy between the play metaphor and
        the whole play in order to consider the value and function

of poetic drama. "A willingness to identify poetic drama within the play with a trick, equivocation, or special form of madness is combined with the metaphoric assertion that poetry can grow in its own way to something of great constancy."

286 Evans, Bertrand. *Teaching Shakespeare in the High Schools*. New York: Macmillan, 1966. vi, 306 pp.

Discusses placement, approach, emphases of presentation and discussion, and accompanying and following activities in the teaching of *Dream* in the high school, insisting that the "highbrow" quality of the play, "all that is finest," would be difficult for ninth and tenth graders--even perhaps for high schoolers--and suggesting therefore that it would be better taught to seventh or eighth graders or else to seniors. Certainly versions of teaching which emphasize Bottom only should be avoided. (Pp. 191-208)

287 Fricker, Robert. "Shakespeare und das Drama des Absurden" [Shakespeare and the Drama of the Absurd]. *Shakespeare Jahrbuch* (Heidelberg), 1966, 7-29. (German)

The article is in reaction to Jan Kott's interpretation (see item 239). Fricker does not view *Dream* as a precursor of absurdist drama since it does not present a world devoid of all sense and alienated from God. Some elements in *Dream* might seem to bear out insights of depth psychology, but the love chase is so stylized that it resembles an elegant dance more than a Walpurgis Night. The world of day is as valid as the wild woods; it is a question of how man reacts. In any case, the surrender to the brutal, elementary side of amorous life is not irreversible, as is often the case in modern literature.

288 Haas, Rudolf. "Über das Thema des *Midsummer Night's Dream*." *Literatur, Kultur, Gesellschaft in England und Amerika. Friedrich Schubel zum 60 Geburtstag*. Ed. Gerhard Müller-Schwefe and Konrad Tuzinski. Frankfurt: Diesterweg, 1966, pp. 309-19. (German)

Studies the philosophical and religious and moral aspects of the theme of love in *Dream* with special emphasis on the

significance of marriage. Haas summarizes the views of Carl
Orff (see item 149), Jan Kott (see item 239), and Karl
Kerényi (see item 181), who see in *Dream* "a pan-daemonic
nature myth" revolving around the Eros theme, before
presenting his own view of it as primarily an encomium to
marriage (the confusion of the night resulting in a new
constantia as the constancy of love ripens to marriage).

288a "The Great Plays: *A Midsummer Night's Dream*"
      [audio-cassette]. *Meet Mr. Shakespeare*. New York: New
      York Board of Education, 1966. Distributed by National
      Center for Audio Tapes (Boulder, Colo.). Cassette No.
      0135-16, 15 min. (not heard)

289   Hart, John A. "Foolery Shines Everywhere: The Fool's
      Function in the Romantic Comedies." *"Starre of Poets":
      Discussions of Shakespeare*. Carnegie Series in English,
      10. Pittsburgh: Carnegie Institute of Technology, 1966,
      pp. 31-34.

      Discusses the function of the artisans. They are
"common sense, the reasonableness of Theseus carried to
absurd literal-mindedness," agents who work, ironically, to
help qualify Theseus' original intolerance.

290   Holland, Norman N. *Psychoanalysis and Shakespeare*. New
      York: McGraw-Hill, 1966. viii, 412 pp.

      Summarizes (pp. 243-46) the positions of Gui, Jacobson,
and (in reaction to both) Kaplan (see items 84, 196, 209),
and observes that there are no adequate psychoanalytic
readings as yet. Scattered throughout the book are
numerous observations based on psychoanalytic findings.
See item 252.

291   Jackson, Margaret Y. "'High Comedy' in Shakespeare." *CLA
      Journal*, 10 (1966), 11-22.

      Many elements of Shakespeare's comedy, including much,
though not all, from *Dream*, would fit George Meredith's
notion of "high comedy": "that it is aimed at the intellect,
evoking thoughtful laughter; it flourishes in cultivated
society; and it represents women on an equal footing with

men." The dialogue between Helena and Demetrius
(II.i.188-244), for example, is "indeed the quintessence of
high comedy."

292   Jayne, Sears. "The Dreaming of *The Shrew*." *Shakespeare
      Quarterly*, 17 (1966), 41-56.

      Draws several parallels between *Dream* and *The Shrew* as
      regards how dreams work in order to suggest the way *The
      Shrew*'s Induction functions and should be completed.
      Hermia's dream (II.ii.144-49) is in microcosm what we see
      enlarged in Sly's situation, namely, a character who dreams
      a dream motivated by his inner state of fear, desire, hate,
      etc., and who acts out his dream before us. Bottom's dream
      of his ass's head may be taken to parallel closely Sly's (we
      see Bottom before, during, and after), and we might learn
      from Bottom's proposal what would have been expected of
      Sly. For other comparisons with *The Shrew* see items 292,
      320, 355, 378, 387a and 566u.

292a Kadushin, Charles. "Shakespeare & Sociology." *Columbia
      University Forum*, 9 (Spring 1966), 25-31.

      A sociologist reports on reactions throughout the five
      boroughs to the New York Shakespeare Festival's Mobile
      Theatre interracial production of *Dream* in 1964.
      Approximately 70,000 saw the play in 57 free performances.
      Between 80 and 90 per cent liked something about it. It is
      concluded that the masses will come to hear and see high
      culture, that there is no clear relationship between
      appreciation and understanding of what was going on, and
      that a "debased version" of the play did not result. The
      article summarizes a larger report underwritten by the
      Twentieth Century Fund on this experiment of presenting
      art to the masses. It also discusses the difficulties of doing
      social research into the arts. For another comment see item
      T1255.

293   Miller, Raeburn. "The Persons of Moonshine: *A Midsummer
      Night's Dream* and the 'Disfigurement' of Realities."
      Explorations of Literature. Ed. Rima D. Reck. Baton
      Rouge: Louisiana State University Press, 1966, pp.
      25-31.

Through the interrelations brought on by their forest
experience each of the three groups, illustrating a special
form of unreality (personal, public, and wholly
imaginative), learns its own nature and thus clarifies its
own confusions in a "return to the surer patterns of the
city, the rational world."

294 Nemerov, Howard. "Bottom's Dream." *Virginia Quarterly
     Review*, 42 (1966), 555-75.

Observes in passing, as part of a general discussion of
play and fact in poetry, that there is no better definition
of poetry than Bottom's "It shall be called Bottom's dream,
because it hath no bottom."

295 *Notes on William Shakespeare's "A Midsummer Night's
     Dream."* Study-Aid Series. London: Methuen
     Educational, 1966. 41 pp.

There are sections on plot, reading Shakespeare, and
character, with self-testing questions and answers.
Designed for students.

296 Nugent, Mary Ellen. "Puck and Ariel." *Listener*, no. 7
     (1966), 74-79. (not seen)

Apparently finds Puck childlike, mischievous, and
critical; Ariel adult, mysterious, and sympathetic. See item
149.

297 Phialas, Peter G. "*A Midsummer Night's Dream.*"
     *Shakespeare's Romantic Comedies: The Development of
     Their Form and Meaning*. Chapel Hill: University of
     North Carolina Press, 1966, pp. 102-33.

The overriding idea is "inconstancy in love"; as such
the *Dream* has a place within the larger, all-encompassing
idea of the comedies: "the proper attitude, shorn of
extremes, to love." Various extreme attitudes toward love
occur in the play. Theseus and Hippolyta represent the
golden mean. *Dream* is compared with other early plays.

298 Presson, Robert K. "Some Traditional Instances of Setting
   in Shakespeare's Plays." *Modern Language Review*, 61
   (1966), 12-22.

   Brief comments (*passim*) on the "organically
contributory" forest setting of *Dream*.

299 Sinclair, Alexander R. "Shakespeare's Word-play in Arany's
   Translations." *Acta Litteraria Academiae Scientiarum
   Hungaricae*, 8 (1966), 454-63. (not seen)

   Apparently on Arany János' translation, dating from the
second part of the 19th century, still thought by many to
be the best in Hungarian.

300 Thakur, Damodar. "A New Look at *A Midsummer Night's
   Dream*." *Indian Journal of English Studies*, 7 (1966),
   24-32.

   Summary observations which find touches of homeliness,
of reality, of the common and uncourtly in the play and a
"core of seriousness" in the possibility of contemporary
allusions. Titania may be Elizabeth and the "rose distil'd"
(I.i.76) an allusion to her.

301 Wells, Stanley. "Happy Endings in Shakespeare."
   Shakespeare Jahrbuch (Heidelberg), 1966, 103-23.

   A general discussion with little space given to *Dream*.
Wells thinks the theory of alternative endings to be "quite
mistaken," there being no redundancy. For other comments
on this theory see items 63, 330, 645, 748, 776 and 843.

302 Wood, James O. "'Finde out moone-shine, finde out
   moone-shine.'" *Notes and Queries*, 211 (1966), 128-30.

   The moon was full and Quince might have found out
moonshine from an almanac of 1594 or 1595 for Midsummer
Night, June 23. See items 332, 385, 389, 513 and 685d.

303 Young, David P. *Something of Great Constancy: The Art of
   "A Midsummer Night's* Dream." New Haven: Yale

University Press, 1966. The section on structure (pp.
86-106) is reprinted in *Modern Shakespearean Criticism*.
Ed. Alvin B. Kernan. New York: Harcourt, Brace, &
World, 1970, and in *Essays in Shakespearean Criticism*.
Ed. James L. Calderwood and Harold E. Toliver.
Englewood Cliffs, N. J.: Prentice-Hall, 1970. (The book
is based on a 1965 Yale dissertation.)

Prologue. Young intends--through "a more thorough
examination than [the *Dream*] has had to date"--"to
establish the importance of *Dream* in the development of
Shakespeare's art, to redefine its place in the canon, and
to emphasize its significance as a source of knowledge of
Shakespeare's attitude toward drama, poetry, and the
imagination."

1. Backgrounds. Here Young examines the dramatic and
nondramatic resources with emphasis on the manipulation of
audience response to accomplish particular dramatic ends.
The episode of Titania's waking illustrates treatment of the
familiar in a novel and surprising way.

The Nondramatic Background. The three kinds of
celebrations--royal marriage and the May and Midsummer
holidays--create the festive ambience and the basis for
audience expectation. (Shakespeare "has deliberately
created a blurring of time in the play in order to dismiss
calendar time and establish a more elusive festival time.")
Folklore is given force and respectability through a blend
with myth (lore with learning, local with classical),
especially through the moon, fairies, and Puck. Of the
fairies: "their benevolent presence . . . serves to
emphasize the comic context only if they are recognized as
potentially dangerous."

The Dramatic Background. Poetic moments and aspects of
dramaturgy from earlier plays illustrate the kinds of
conventions satirized in the playlet. Elements from the two
traditions represented by Greene and Lyly: the Popular
theatre (clowning, magic, variety movement, inclusiveness)
and the Coterie theatre (elegance and wit, metamorphosis,
symmetry, consistency) merged easily into a happy
synthesis, one attempted before, but one in which by its
success *Dream* constitutes a self-conscious breakthrough.

2. The Concord of This Discord. "Takes up stylistic and structural achievements that made possible the wedding of such diverse comic materials."

Style. The variety of styles helps set off individuals and groupings, makes for subtle or sharp transitions, and this variety is evidence neither of extensive revision nor of other hands. The variety is harmonized by iterative imagery (moon, etc.), frequent "panoramas" (glimpses of activities or landscapes), and by the style of "profusion," especially in lists--all of which bring concord in the sense of wonder.

Structure. Young finds a "minimization of time" and emphasizes, rather, spatial aspects: positioning of character groups, levels of awareness, spheres of action--the metaphors of geometry being especially useful (circles, etc.) for purposes of analysis. Of particular value is the way characters or groups "mirror" others and contribute through mimicry, parody, and exaggeration. The reflective function of the mechanicals is considered in detail. Shakespeare developed a comedy "of multiple interest in which he achieved organic unity not by subordination of one element to another . . . but by a careful thematic control through which diverse elements were shown to be facets of the same idea."

3. Bottom's Dream. Shakespeare compares his art with the dream, as was commonly done, to suggest its trivial nature; but the experience of the dream in the play does not permit the conventional association. Bottom is right to sense a mystery in his experience and his own limitations in expressing it. The orthodox view of the superiority of reason over the imagination is similarly reexamined and called into question. Theseus is wrong; Hippolyta has the last word. She defends art itself as well as the consistency of the lovers' story. Art works alongside Nature as a concern of the play. Other familiar oppositions occur and "begin to break down and mingle under the playwright's influence."

Epilogue. Young finally views the play from a distance to suggest its place in intellectual history and Shakespeare's art. Its use of "polarities held in balance, unresolved opposites," anticipates the literary concerns of the seventeenth century. If the *Dream* is Shakespeare's *ars poetica*, as it seems to be, then it is one of his most important plays.

304   Allen, John A. "Bottom and Titania." *Shakespeare
        Quarterly*, 18 (1967), 107-17.

        Analyzes Bottom's role in an effort to account for the
potency of the tableau of Bottom in the arms of the Fairy
Queen. We find Bottom funny "because he combines
humanity and asshood and thus comments obliquely upon the
peculiar qualities of each species in comparison with the
other." With Bottom in her arms, Titania resembles more the
doting mother than the goddess of procreation which is her
rightful function. Inspired by his recent experience,
changed by it, Bottom is capable of comprehending the
point of his playlet, the triumph of love over death. Bottom
is both emblem of mortal grossness and representative of
the ideal of sacrifice for love.

305   Hamilton, A. C. "The Resolution of the Early Period." *The
        Early Shakespeare*. San Marino, Calif.: Huntington
        Library, 1967, pp. 216-33.

        Studies *Dream*'s relationship with the earlier comedies to
show why and how it "accommodates all responses, from the
romantic to the realistic and from the most imaginative to
the most literal." It derives its central plot device from *The
Comedy of Errors*, its love and friendship theme from *Two
Gentlemen*, its emphasis on spectacle from *Love's Labour's
Lost*. Three of the four distinct worlds of *Dream* are related
to the earlier three comedies: Theseus can be identified
with the Duke of *Errors*, the young lovers with those of
Two Gentlemen, and Bottom, who stands for common sense,
with Costard of *Love's Labour's Lost*. The fourth world,
that of the fairies, unique to *Dream*, resolves the other
three into a larger unity. *Dream* is "the most satisfying and
complete of the early works." For other comparisons with
these plays see items 59, 187 and 240.

306   Hawkins, Sherman. "The Two Worlds of Shakespearean
        Comedy." *Shakespeare Studies*, 3 (1967), 62-80.

        Qualifies Northrop Frye's Green World-Normal World
pattern (see item 142) to make it fit comedies in addition to
the four it obviously fits. These other comedies, which
offer an "alternate pattern," have intrusions from outside,
rather than escapes, and willfulness from within the lovers
themselves as sources of repression. They have "closed"

rather than "green" worlds. Sometimes these kinds of plays overlap in their patterns. While the *Dream* fits Frye's pattern, it has some characteristics of the "closed" sort--the lovers, for example, in their "alternating attraction and repulsion." "The closed world of *The Alchemist* is a green world seen from inside, a satiric inversion of *Dream*, in which Subtle and Face, like Oberon and Puck, stage-manage a green (or golden) world of illusions."

307   Holleran, James V. "The Pyramus-Thisbe Theme in *A Midsummer Night's Dream.*" *California English Journal*, no. 1 (1967), 20-26.

The playlet "serves to enlarge and conclude" the general commentary on love and marriage--indeed, "emerges as the most profound observation on love," the various types of which are discussed. Ironically, "profound love exists between Pyramus and Thisbe which is far deeper than they [the courtly audience] are capable of understanding." See item 60.

308   Jameson, Thomas. "Some Undercover Literary Skirmishing." *The Hidden Shakespeare: A Study of the Poet's Undercover Activity in the Theatre.* New York: Funk & Wagnalls, 1967, pp. 132-61. Reprint. New York: Minerva Press, 1968, 1969.

On the assumed superiority of the upper class and of Theseus in particular in reacting to the mechanicals' playlet. Shakespeare gives "a fairly good-humored reflection on the behavior of the influential Tudor patron of art." Later, in other plays, Shakespeare will not be quite so tolerant. When speaking of art, Theseus "did not entirely know what he was talking about." See item 60.

309   Lerner, Laurence, ed. *Shakespeare's Comedies: An Anthology of Modern Criticism.* Harmondsworth, Middlesex, and Baltimore: Penguin, 1967. 346 pp.

Prints selections from Sir Arthur Quiller-Couch (item 748), Enid Welsford (item 575), and Paul A. Olson (item 145).

310 Lhôte, Jean Marie. *Shakespeare dans les tarots et autres
     lieux, ou tentative de divagation cohérente à la fois
     théoretique et practique au travers du "Songe d'une nuit
     d'été"* [Shakespeare in the Tarot Cards and Other
     Places, or An Attempt at a Coherent Bypath Both
     Theoretical and Practical through *Dream*]. Paris: J.-J.
     Pauvert, 1967. Also in *Bizarre*, 43-44 (June 1967),
     1-100. (French)

     An investigation into the appropriateness of using the
     images of the Tarot cards as the basis for designing the
     sets and costumes of the play, on the possible influence of
     the cards as suggested by some remarkable similarities
     between the cards and the play. Based on a production in
     August 1964, directed by Jacques Falguières, by the
     Théâtre Universitaire de Marseille. A "Supplement
     Complementaire" makes suggestions about translating certain
     passages. See item 893.

311 Okado, Mineo. [From *Love's Labour's Lost* to *A Midsummer
     Night's Dream*--An Essay on Shakespeare's Romantic
     Comedy (2).] *Kyoyobu Bulletin* (Nagoya University), 11
     (1967), 224-36. (Japanese--not seen)

312 Oyama, Toshiko. "Love and Its Rhetoric in *A Midsummer
     Night's Dream.*" *Anglica* (Osaka), 6, no. 4 (1967), 1-19.
     Reprinted in the author's *Shakespeare's World of Words*.
     Tokyo: Shinozaki-Shorin, 1975.

     Argues that love is not merely the theme but an
     organizing and developing factor as well. "Everything is
     drawn to the center of Shakespeare's world of comedy. Love
     with its various phases is the means by which Shakespeare
     intends to express his idea of comedy." Abstracted in
     Shakespeare Newsletter, 19 (1969), 42.

313 Rabkin, Norman. *Shakespeare and the Common
     Understanding*. New York: The Free Press; London:
     Collier-Macmillan, 1967. xii, 267 pp.

     Dream reflects (pp. 200-205) Shakespeare's ambivalence
     toward art. In it he "triumphantly yet ironically"
     acknowledges the common role of "imagination, the intuitive,
     suprarational element of the mind, in love and art." Like

love, art must be viewed "complementarily"; the entire play
constitutes an ironic refutation of its thesis that the
imagination is to be despised. The moon (the basis for this
discussion) is not a consistent symbol. It suggests meanings
which work against each other and this tends to support
Dent's view (item 227) that *Dream* is "a play about the role
of imagination in play-making and play-watching."

314 Shalvi, Alice. "Shadow and Substance in *A Midsummer
     Night's Dream*." *The World & Art of Shakespeare*. Ed.
     A. A. Mendilow and Alice Shalvi. Jerusalem: Israel
     Universities Press; New York: D. Davey, 1967, pp.
     83-88. Published also in Hebrew, Tel Aviv: Hakibbutz
     Hameuchad, 1966.

     A general introduction to the play which deals with the
     separate planes of reality (Athens and woods) and the
     several groups of characters. The farcical events of the
     night are taken to mock and satirize the excesses of
     romantic love. The play is also concerned with the
     relationship between art and reality, with the function and
     purpose of drama and the interaction of the playwright and
     his public. The artisans are incapable of distinguishing
     between art and reality. For Hippolyta (V.i.23-27) it is the
     shaping of what the imagination has conceived which makes
     credible what is otherwise strange and marvelous. Both
     Athens and fairy world fuse in the end with the reality of
     the Elizabethan audience. (This may be a translation of item
     213.)

315 Stanton, Ralph G. "*A Midsummer Night's Dream*--A
     Structural Study." *Psychological Reports*, 20 (1967),
     657-58.

     Employs a graphical schema to depict the play's group
     structures and interpersonal relationships.

316 Weimann, Robert. "Niederer Mythos und poetische
     Phantasie: Puck und Ariel." *Shakespeare und die
     Tradition des Volkstheaters: Soziologie, Dramaturgie,
     Gestaltung* [Shakespeare and the Tradition of the
     Popular Theatre: Sociology, Dramatic Technique, Artistic
     Realization]. Berlin: Henscherlverlag, 1967, pp. 313-31.
     Revised as "Puck und Ariel: Mythos und poetische

Phantasie." *Shakespeare Jahrbuch* (Weimar), 104 (1968),
17-33, which is reprinted as "Shakespeares
'Sommernachtstraum' and 'Sturm'" in *Phantasie und
Nachahmung: Drei Studien zum Verhältnis von Dichtung,
Utopie und Mythos* [Phantasy and Imitation: Three
Studies on the Relationship of Fiction, Utopia and Myth].
Halle (Saale): Mitteldeutscher Verlag, 1976, pp. 63-84.
The original essay, revised and translated, appears as
"Popular Myth and Dramatic Poetry: Robin and Puck," in
Weimann's *Shakespeare and the Popular Tradition in the
Theater: Studies in the Social Dimension of Dramatic
Form and Function.* Ed. [and trans.] Robert Schwartz.
Baltimore and London: Johns Hopkins University Press,
1978, pp. 192-96.

Weimann's comments on the relationship between popular
myth and *Dream* are put forth in three different forms (the
article of 1976 is a verbatim reprint of the *Jahrbuch* essay
of 1968). The book of 1967 treats the same material as the
Jahrbuch essay but with a more detailed description of
analogous developments in other areas of the theatre and
with more examples to illustrate the status of the Robin
Goodfellow figure in the popular and literary traditions of
the time. The English translation adds nothing new to this
particular section and is shortened considerably, first by
omitting an analysis of passages from *The Tempest* and
second by deleting some important comments on the method
Shakespeare employs in transforming popular myth (1967,
pp. 322-25).

In his *Jahrbuch* essay Weimann warns against an
allegorical or one-dimensional interpretation of Puck and
suggests the figure is something Hegel called "sinnliches
Bewusstsein [sensual consciousness]." The book (1967)
sketches similarities between what Dick Tarlton did with
popular tradition of the clown and what Shakespeare did
with popular mythology. The inspiration for Shakespeare's
treatment cannot be found in earlier Tudor drama, which
was allegorical or biblical rather than mythological. The
creature of lower mythology had lived on in the popular
imagination, and the new element was now their use in
literature. This was not possible until the second half of
the sixteenth century. Robin Goodfellow was not an exotic
fairy from a courtly romance, but one close to home and to
nature. In spite of the association of his name with the
devil, Robin was basically a good spirit and became a
folk-hero of popular Renaissance literature, combining

mythic and satiric elements in the manner of the *mimus* tradition or the wordplays of popular theatre. When Shakespeare found him, Puck had long been transformed from a figure of pure popular myth. Ovid's *Metamorphosis* is also a source for Shakespeare's treatment of Puck. Shakespeare smiles at myth but not at the power of mythic imagination. Only later, in *The Tempest*, does he exploit the full potential of myth by creating his own mythic being, Caliban. See item 55 for other readings which stress myth.

317 Westlund, Joseph Emanuel. "Thematic Structure in Shakespeare's Middle Comedies." Ph.D. dissertation, University of California, Berkeley, 1966. *DA*, 28 (1967), 206A.

Attempts to see the play whole, to find its "thematic structure," not to view characters or plot as separate from other elements. *Dream* is about "the uses and abuses of the imagination." It is one of six comedies studied.

318 Entry Deleted.

319 Berlin, Normand. *The Base String: The Underworld in Elizabethan Drama.* Rutherford, N. J.: Fairleigh Dickinson University Press, 1968. 244 pp.

In *Dream* Shakespeare's ability to fragment society and allow one part to reflect another meaningfully is seen for the first time. The artisans' playlet mocks Shakespeare's own play, literally and laughingly bringing the moon "down to earth." (Pp. 172-74)

320 Cutts, John P. "*A Midsummer Night's Dream.*" *The Shattered Glass: A Dramatic Pattern in Shakespeare's Early Plays.* Detroit: Wayne State University Press, 1968, pp. 49-55.

The characters of *Dream* suffer from delusions of various sorts. Examples are: Theseus only imagines he is in love with Hippolyta (she's a conquest), and he is otherwise not very rational. There is something more than baby-love in the attraction to the changeling boy: he resembles too closely Ganymede. And Titania is in a "love-lorn state" over

Theseus which is "betrayed by her every move." Similar
delusions occur in the other early plays: *The Shrew, Love's
Labour's Lost, Two Gentlemen, Errors.* See items 59, 187,
240 and 292 for other comparisons with these plays.

321   Edwards, Philip. *Shakespeare and the Confines of Art.*
      London: Methuen; New York: Barnes & Noble, 1968. vi,
      170 pp.

      Wonders what to make of the ironic level suggested by
      Theseus' speech, the playlet, and Puck's epilogue. Theseus'
      skepticism assumes "an awkward dimension," since *he* is a
      shadow too. "A shadow questioning the validity of
      shadows," Theseus expects very little of art, does not
      "believe in it," and is "not much distressed by the patent
      foolishness of what Bottom and his friends present." "The
      whole play affirms the power of art, and certain characters
      and incidents in the play question the power of art. The
      balance between belief and ridicule is finely maintained."
      With its concentric circles, the play must force its audience
      to wonder who sits above and watches it. (Pp. 51-56)

322   Fender, Stephen. *Shakespeare: "A Midsummer Night's
      Dream."* Studies in English Literature, 35. London:
      Edward Arnold, 1968. 64 pp.

      1. Introduction: Play or Opera? "Operatic" versions of
      the play (here noticed) and productions which can be
      described with words like "delightful" and "enchanting"
      inevitably attempt to "smooth out complexities of tone in the
      original" (p. 9). They remove the "fairies' horrifying
      power," and otherwise miss verbal effects which are as
      important as the sequence of events. It would seem that
      Theseus the man of reason controls natural forces in the
      end of this play (Act IV). But his simple, limited grasp of
      what has gone on in the woods, though he *ought* to know
      given his past history, will not do as a standard for
      interpretation. In Act IV he only ratifies in human terms a
      solution already established by the supernatural powers. We
      must question the face value of the play.

      2. Character and Emblem. The complexity rises not from
      the development of characters--here, as in Chaucer's "
      Knight's Tale," characters are emblems to be defined, not
      persons to be presented realistically. It rises from the

"morally ambivalent" (p. 20) nature of these emblems, each with the potential for both good and evil. The romantic love of the play is either "a laughable delusion or an intimation of something truer than the literal world" (p. 24), or both. Theseus' rationality, similarly ambivalent, enables him to rule a city but restricts him from understanding the power of the imagination. And the fairies, themselves ambivalent, especially Titania, are capable of both beneficence and malevolence.

3. Wood and Wit. "Inexorably the characters in the wood are forced to come to terms with forces within themselves which they never knew existed and in the process to disregard old social, verbal and fictional formulae which are no longer adequate to deal with their new insights" (p. 33). Both lovers and mechanicals are badly suited to their environments (the woods, acting). "They enter the wood speaking in a highly organized, witty, complicated manner, and leave it speaking much more simply" (p. 36). All along, "the courtly style degenerates" as the lovers learn about themselves and, through their barbaric behavior, about the ambivalence of romantic love.

4. Strategic Puzzles. In Act 5 the lovers return to the reasonableness of Athens, putting behind, even forgetting their imaginative experience, so that they can satirize a pageant which should remind them of their own adventures. The play offers three responses to the wood experience, each with a certain validity, each, to an extent, cancelling the others out. Theseus dismisses as a kind of madness the lovers' story. We know he is wrong, although out of context (the play) he is right. Bottom has a vision of the supernatural but one which he cannot express. (Puck's epilogue reminds us of the validity of this golden world.) Hippolyta admits the story is improbable but sees a certain consistency in it. "Shakespeare uses complexity--or the illusion of complexity--as a dramatic device. . . . The real meaning of *Dream* is that no one 'meaning' can be extracted from the puzzles with which a fiction presents its audience" (p. 61). See item 347.

323   Entry Deleted.

324   Lee, Marion Hartshorn. "Playing *A Midsummer Night's Dream*: An Introduction to Period Acting for American

College Students." Ph.D. dissertation, Columbia
University, 1967. *DA*, 28 (1968), 4304A.

   Dream is used to introduce undergraduate actors to the
"major problems and approaches to the acting of one
Shakespearean play." "Such sources as publications,
recordings, films, filmstrips, photographs, unpublished
lectures, production notes and interviews were utilized to
select significant material."

325   MacOwan, Michael. "The Sad Case of Professor Kott."
      Drama, 88 (Spring 1968), 30-37.

   Attacks Jan Kott's view (item 239) of Shakespeare in
general and his reading of *Dream*, the chapter "perhaps the
most Kottian of the whole book," in particular. "Kott relies
on bald, repetitive assertion rather than logical reasoning;
he ignores or distorts opinions opposite to his own; he
constantly manipulates facts to suit theories and colors his
whole book with a pervasive, gloating salacity sometimes on
the edge of hysteria." He does not seem to *hear*
Shakespeare's English, misses altogether the humor of the
playlet, ignores Oberon's presence and beneficent purpose,
and denies the truth of Shakespeare's love, that it is not
brutal eroticism but rather idealized in the Platonic mode of
Elizabeth's day.

325a   *A Midsummer Night's Dream* [filmstrip]. Goleta, Calif.:
       Tenth Muse, Inc., 1968. LC no. 78-734545, 50 fr., col.,
       35 mm. (not seen)

   Explores the play as seen through the eyes of a
contemporary director. Includes plot summary, exploration
of stagecraft, lighting and other aspects of production.
With teachers' guide and script.

326   Ogawa, Kazuo. [Shakespeare on Imagination.] *The Rising
      Generation*, 114, no. 3 (1968), 12-14; no. 4, 12-15; no.
      5, 18-21. (Japanese--not seen)

   Apparently discusses Theseus' speech on the
imagination.

327 Olson, Elder. *The Theory of Comedy.* Bloomington: Indiana
    University Press, 1968. Reprint. 1975, 1980. 145 pp.

    Describes (pp. 96-98) the "magnificent architecture" of
    the three plots with each having an undertaking,
    interference, and happy conclusion, and all with no
    extraneous elements. Everything is fitted to function.

328 Pasquale, Pasquale di, Jr. "Coleridge's Framework of
    Objectivity and Eliot's Objective Correlative." *Journal of
    Aesthetic and Art Criticism,* 26 (1968), 489-500.

    Uses Theseus' speech to start his discussion. Coleridge's
    "framework of objectivity" is the equivalent of
    Shakespeare's "local habitation and a name."

329 Riklin, Franz. "Shakespeare's *A Midsummer Night's Dream:*
    ein Beitrag zum Individuationsprozess" [A Contribution
    to the Process of Individuation]. With an English
    translation by Andrea Dykes. *The Reality of the Psyche:
    The Proceedings of Third International Congress for
    Analytical Psychology.* Ed. Joseph B. Wheelwright. New
    York: G. P. Putnam's Sons, 1968, pp. 262-92.

    A Jungian analysis which reads the play as a dream
    exhibiting a mandala-like character about the process of
    individuation. Mythological connections are made with each
    of the leading characters in order to show connections with
    shadow, anima, self, and collective consciousness. The play
    "depicts the critical situation [leading to ego unification]
    caused by the integration of the anima into the masculine
    world of collective consciousness or into the animus world of
    the woman." See also items 55 and 391 for similar readings.

330 Ringler, William A., Jr. "The Number of Actors in
    Shakespeare's Early Plays." *The Seventeenth-Century
    Stage: A Collection of Critical Essays.* Ed. Gerald Eades
    Bentley. Chicago and London: University of Chicago
    Press, 1968, pp. 110-34.

    Finds a total of 23 parts, 22 speaking, and presents a
    "Doubling Chart." A cast of 11 adults and 4 boys would
    mean that the mechanicals doubled for the fairies; thus the
    effect was "not one of literal diminutive beauty" but rather

of something like "bulky grotesquerie." Ringler sees no
need for the dual ending Fleay found. On doubling see item
549a.

331   Robinson, James E. "The Ritual and Rhetoric of *A
      Midsummer Night's Dream.*" *PMLA,* 83 (1968), 380-91.

      Dream is based both on ritualistic (festive, processional,
      mythic) and on rhetorical (argumentative, connective,
      imitative) theories of comedy as is evident in the context,
      dramatic action, and language of the play. Robinson draws
      a detailed distinction between the two modes and then shows
      their unity which rests in the relations of nature to
      experience. The comedy combines faith (from the one) and
      understanding (from the other). He ends with an analysis
      of the "play of Pyramus and Thisby" (p. 391).

332   Stevenson, W. H. "'Finde out moone-shine, Find out
      moone-shine.'" *Notes and Queries,* 213 (1968), 131-32.

      In response to James O. Wood's "the moon is evidently at
      least very near full, for it is overhead at midnight" (item
      302): the moon in Britain is never overhead and a full moon
      never high at midsummer. See items 385, 389, 513 and
      685d.

333   Vickers, Brian. *The Artistry of Shakespeare's Prose.*
      London: Methuen; New York: Barnes & Noble, 1968. ix,
      452 pp.

      Shakespeare (pp. 65-71) through speech characterizes
      only one of the rustics, Bottom. He is given to malaprops
      (*hypallage* in particular) and *synoeciosis* (a form of
      oxymoron), and his speech as an ass fits his character
      (*decorum*). The simplicity and artlessness of his speech
      suggest a gentle kindliness. Bottom differs from Armado,
      with whom for characterizing speech he might be compared,
      because with Bottom Shakespeare moves to internal
      characterization. The stylistic symmetries of his waking
      speech (IV.ii.204 ff.), for example, "do not mock him--they
      anatomize the process of his thought" (here analyzed). See
      item 77.

334   Blount, Dale Melotte. "Shakespeare's Use of the Folklore of
       Fairies and Magic in *A Midsummer Night's Dream* and *The
       Tempest.*" Ph.D. dissertation, Indiana University, 1969.
       DAI, 30 (1969), 679A-680A.

       Depicts ways Shakespeare drew on traditional fairy and
       magic lore (Ch. 2) and demonstrates the different dramatic
       functions of folklore (Ch. 4). "The idea of magic in both
       plays implies superhuman or supernatural effects, connotes
       the mysteriously enchanting, inexplicable experience and
       thereby makes possible manifold themes which the poet
       never consciously envisioned." See items 14 and 149.

335   Cody, Richard. "*A Midsummer Night's Dream*: Bottom
       Translated." *The Landscape of the Mind: Pastoralism and
       Platonic Theory in Tasso's "Aminta" and Shakespeare's
       Early Comedies.* Oxford: Clarendon Press, 1969, pp.
       127-50.

       Dream is a serio-comic blend of the pastoral and Platonic
       in the Orphic tradition. Through the "language of night
       and dreams" (p. 15) it rehearses the mysteries supposed to
       be inherent in mythological fables. In it, "by virtue of the
       pseudo-Orphic unction of Shakespeare's style, a pastoral
       theocracy of Diana, Venus, and Cupid, Apollo and Bacchus,
       Hercules and Orpheus visibly impends." The structure
       follows the pastoral rhythm of dramatic action: *emanatio,
       raptio,* and *remeatio.* It moves from Diana through Apollo
       and Bacchus to Venus. The Bottom-Titania episode suggests
       the Midas fable and encomia of the ass as "both absurd in
       essence and the carrier of divine mysteries." The whole is
       a drama of "pastoral esotericism" which celebrates, finally,
       the poet's art. See items 55, 117 and 122 for similar
       studies.

336   Homan, Sidney R. "The Single World of *A Midsummer
       Night's Dream.*" *Bucknell Review,* 17 (1969), 72-84.

       Critics are wrong to view the play as, in effect, a
       debate between the two worlds of Theseus (Athens, reason,
       repression) and Oberon (woods and expanding universe,
       passion, freedom) which forces us to choose one. The
       worlds are not so much "antithetical as synthetic," integral
       parts of a single world (though Oberon's is larger). The
       forest is at times a projection of the collective

unconsciousness of the mortals and an extension of the real. The lovers, ironically, perceive this truer, larger reality, though later they forget it, and Bottom is allowed a vision of it. Lover and poet share a priceless gift in experiencing and creating this larger reality. Whereas lunatic and lover abandon their reason unawares, the artist consciously uses reason in conjunction with the imagination. Art initiates us into a fuller awareness of what constitutes total reality.

337   Katayama, Haruko. [A Tradition of Season Plays in Shakespeare.] *Mulberry* (Aichi Kenritsu University), 19 (1969), 33-34. (Japanese--not seen)

338   Kerr, Jessica. *Shakespeare's Flowers*. Illustrated by Anne Ophelia Dowden. New York: Thomas Y. Crowell; London: Longmans, 1969. Hammondsworth: Kestrel, 1974. 85 pp.

Large, colored illustrations with accompanying commentary. Index gives fifteen references to *Dream*. For a list of other discussions of plants see item 45.

338a Leech, Clifford. "The Function of Locality in the Plays of Shakespeare and His Contemporaries." *The Elizabethan Theatre: Papers Given at the International Conference on Elizabethan Theatre Held at the University of Waterloo, Ontario, in July 1968*. Ed David Galloway. Toronto: Macmillan, 1969; Hamden, Conn.: Archon, 1970, 103-116.

Very briefly, locality serves, among other functions, to "frame" the play, "with Athens at either end of the Wood, yet with the Wood coming to the palace to offer a final blessing."

338b Leech, Clifford. "Chinks." *The Times Literary Supplement*. 25 December 1969.

"Chinks" in *Romeo* (I.v.19) has a double meaning, one bawdy, as it seems to have in *Dream* (in the playlet). For other bawdy see items 57, 443 especially, and 444.

339 Leimberg, Inge. "Shakespeares Komödien und Sidneys
'Goldene Welt.'" *Shakespeare Jahrbuch* (Heidelberg),
1969, 174-97. (German)

Analyzes the importance of Sidney's definition of poetry
for Shakespeare's comedies. *Dream* is mentioned only twice,
and then to suggest the author's thesis that Shakespeare
created a "golden world" in his comedies which is similar to
that found in contemporary pastoral poetry.

340 Lewis, Allan. "*A Midsummer Night's Dream*--Fairy Fantasy
or Erotic Nightmare?" *Educational Theatre Journal*, 21
(1969), 251-58.

Reviews recent trends in *Dream* stage interpretation
(with the examples of Cyril Ritchard, John Hancock) in
order to show that a variety of interpretations is possible.
Lewis finds especially defensible the view that the play
admits a dark side of human sexual nature, though he
objects to the interpretation of Jan Kott's which finds so
much black humor (item 239). *Dream* should be neither
cruel and animal nor sentimental. It may be that Theseus is
"the bawdy libertine in a dark comedy of sexual
anonymity"; at least this part of Kott's view we should not
reject outright. (This seems to be the paper presented as
"Shakespearian Comedy and Social Comment: *A Midsummer
Night's Dream*" at the 13th International Shakespeare
Conference in September 1968 and abstracted in
Shakespeare Newsletter, 19 [1969], 48.) (See repeat
annotation at T1298.)

341 Mirek, Roman. "Erotyka w komediach Szekspira. *Sen nocy
letniej. Wieczor Trzech Kroli. Jak qam sie podoba*"
[Eroticism in Shakespeare's Comedies: *A Midsummer
Night's Dream, Twelfth Night, As You Like It*]. *Przeglad
Lekarski*, 25 (1969), 391-95. (Polish--not seen)

342 Miyauchi, Bunshichi. [Young Shakespeare.] *Cultural
Science Review of Kagoshima University*, 5 (1969),
117-96. (Japanese--not seen)

Apparently surveys the early plays.

342a Pyle, Fitzroy. *"The Winter's Tale"*: *A Commentary on*
      Structure. London: Routledge & Kegan Paul, 1969; New
      York: Barnes & Noble, 1969. xv, 195 pp.

      Shakespeare may have thought of the two plays as
      resembling each other in title and in the combination of
      courtly and romantic settings. Both have Ovid as a source.
      Paulina is like Hippolyta in her ability to believe in what
      may transcend reason (pp. 2-3). Oberon and Prospero are
      both princes who command beings similar to each other and
      who control events (p. 142). *The Tempest* "can be seen as
      the tragi-comic correlative of" the *Dream* (pp. 142-43).

343   Elledge, Scott. *"A Midsummer Night's Dream."* *Teaching*
      Shakespeare. Ed. Arthur Mizener. New York and
      Toronto: New American Library, 1969 (A Mentor Book),
      pp. 159-81.

      Elledge's introduction urges that students be introduced
      first to the holidays involved and the idea of the occasion
      celebrated (marriage). Then they ought to try to answer
      two questions: *What is the play about?* It is about
      characters, plot, and setting, and in special ways, but it is
      also about love and hate, illusion and reality, waking and
      dreaming, and so on--Elledge's list of such antitheses is
      long. *How does it work?* Here a detailed study is required.
      Elledge to some extent shows how it works in the full
      summary of the action which follows his introduction. He
      demonstrates what students ought to be able to see. For
      Elledge "this lighthearted play should be taken seriously."
      It is "an almost miraculous revelation of the ways in which
      man's imagination may be more useful and humane than his
      reason." There are short-answer questions, questions for
      discussion, and a sample test.

344   Takei, Naoe. [On *A Midsummer Night's Dream*.] *A*
      Shakespeare Handbook. Ed. Jirō Ozu. Tokyo: Nanundō,
      1969, pp. 181-92. (Japanese)

      General introduction dealing with the date, history of
      productions, plot, and characteristic qualities.

345 Taylor, Michael. "The Darker Purpose of *A Midsummer Night's Dream.*" *Studies in English Literature*, 9 (1969), 259-73.

Along with our recognition of the obvious innocent delights of *Dream*'s dream world, Taylor says, we should also recognize an unfestive reality whose constituents are human pettiness and its concomitant, a stubborn intractability. In ironic fashion both the "good" and the impish fairies reflect not only the play's "gossamer web" charm, but are anthropomorphized in such a manner as to be equally human in their concern for petty triumph--hence the acerbity of the quarrel between Oberon and Titania. Their "jangling" is similar to that of the human lovers Hermia, Lysander, Helena, and Demetrius. Even the more noble and, in a sense, ideally representative human lovers, Theseus and Hippolyta, are touched by complacency and irrationalism, modifying somewhat our delight in the perfect harmony of their union. Out of this discord, however, like Helena's "comforts from the East," comes concord, a harmony which in retrospect the play makes seem inevitable. An awareness of the presence both of disharmony and of concord is essential to a full understanding of Shakespeare's purpose, particularly to make relevant its darker aspect (the disharmony of human triviality).

346 Traversi, Derek A. *An Approach to Shakespeare*. 3rd ed. rev. and expanded. Garden City, N. Y.: Doubleday, 1969. xxii, 674 pp. Also issued in two volumes, with *Dream* in Volume 1, pp. 139-59.

Contains (pp. 130-48) a reading of the play from beginning to end which gives special emphasis to the contrast between reason (as represented by Theseus and Athens) and the follies and incongruities of love (as represented by the characters in the woods). The play turns out to require a harmonizing of the various visions of love. Theseus balances the demands of reason and the spiritual. The "web of confusion" which takes place in the middle of the play exhibits the nature of passion. "There is indeed a sinister element in this fairy realm, one associated with the action of 'blood' and the darker side of the passions, not in any way less real than that of lyrical fancy and poetic decoration to which we can all respond." We are treated to love's excesses and the web of unreason and

return, with the lovers, suitably chastened and
enlightened. The love carries with it, however, "a glimpse
of the divine element in human life; and at this point
[Bottom waking] the ridiculous and the sublime meet in
what is perhaps the play's deepest, most profound moment.
. . ." The superstitions of the conclusion offer something
"more than mere surface decoration." They suggest a world
and love "disturbingly endowed with a reality of its own."

347 Warren, Roger. "Three Notes on *A Midsummer Night's
     Dream.*" *Notes and Queries*, 214 (1969), 130-34.

     1) Accuses Stephen Fender (item 322) of making comedy
     too "solemn" and of instances of "grotesque
     over-interpretation." Warren objects to the notion that
     fairies are malevolent, the place sinister, and to the
     assumption that the play's about "the nature of art," hiding
     its meaning in puzzles. 2) The conceits of Titania's
     "season" speech (II.i.81-117) are not pageantic but rather
     are vivid and immediate. 3) "transfigur'd" (V.i.24)
     suggests something more than simply *altered* or *changed* ;
     it implies a new mental state where affections *are revealed*
     without any deception in their true nature.

348 Weidinger, Anton. "Traum und Wirklichkeit einer tollen
     Nacht. Zu Shakespeares Komödie *Ein Sommernachtstraum*"
     [Dream and Reality of a Mad Night. On Shakespeare's
     Comedy *A Midsummer Night's Dream*]. *Neue Wege*, 234,
     no. 24 (1969), 20. (German--not seen)

349 Weil, Herbert S., Jr. "Comic Structure and Tonal
     Manipulation in Shakespeare and Some Modern Plays."
     Shakespeare Survey, 22 (1969), 27-33.

     The *Dream*, among other plays by Shakespeare,
     resembles certain disturbing modern plays (by Albee,
     Genet, and others) especially in its ending wherein the
     affirmation is not necessarily unmixed with qualification. Jan
     Kott may not be right (see item 239), but alternative
     perspectives do need our attention. Perhaps "multiplicity"
     of attitudes we should accept as a "formal principle for
     Shakespearian comedy."

350 Wickham, Glynne. "*A Midsummer Night's Dream*: The Setting
     and the Text." *Shakespeare's Dramatic Heritage:*
     Collected Studies in Mediaeval, Tudor and Shakespearean
     Drama. London: Routledge & Kegan Paul; New York:
     Barnes & Noble, 1969, pp. 180-90.

     Dream is a "complex parable" in a significant setting.
     Reason dominates Athens, emotion the wood, and the whole
     is a "discussion of adolescent attitudes to sex" (which can
     be compared with Milton's *Comus* and Fletcher's *The Faithful*
     Shepherdess). The story of the mechanicals allows for the
     farcical (Bottom and Titania) and tragic ("Pyramus and
     Thisbe") potentialities of infatuation in a comic frame.
     Three or four simple, commonly used emblems were
     required: a throne, three or four trees, a mossy bank, and
     possibly an arbor. A stage using these emblems is
     described.

351 Willeford, William. *The Fool and His Sceptre: A Study in*
     Clowns, Jesters and Their Audience. London: Edward
     Arnold; Evanston: Northwestern University Press, 1969.
     xxii, 265 pp.

     Several remarks (especially pp. 137-42) on Bottom as
     fool and his dream as a kind of folly. He is "the receptacle
     and bearer of a transcendent value that, instead of being
     made accessible to social life, is 'deranged, distorted, and
     ostensibly lost in the fool's own being."

352 Wilson, F. P. "Shakespeare's Comedies." *Shakespearian and*
     Other Studies. Ed. Helen Gardner. Oxford: Clarendon
     Press, 1969, pp. 54-99, especially 77-80.

     In lyricism and dramatic ideas, *Dream* resembles *Romeo*.
     Dream is a "miracle of construction." It contains almost all
     the variations which occur in his comedies on the theme of
     love. While not Shakespeare's, Theseus' voice of cool reason
     is necessary for balance before and after a midsummer
     night.

353 Asimov, Isaac. *Asimov's Guide To Shakespeare.* 2 Volumes.
     Volume 1: *The Greek, Roman, and Italian Plays.* Garden
     City, N. Y.: Doubleday, 1970.

Explains (pp. 17-51) the allusions in the play (which are
listed as part of a running plot summary), especially those
mythological, and gives other kinds of information. In
circling the earth at a rate of 37,500 miles per hour, Puck
would exceed the escape velocity.

354   Fergusson, Francis. *Shakespeare: The Pattern in His
      Carpet*. New York: Delacorte Press, 1970. Pp. 120-27.
      Reprint. New York: Delta/Dell, 1971.

      An introduction to the play, the same used for the
      Laurel Shakespeare (item 860).

355   Habicht, Werner. "*A Midsummer Night's Dream*." *Das
      englische Drama: vom Mittelalter bis zur Gegenwart*. Ed.
      Dieter Mehl. Volume 1. Dusseldorf: August Bagel, 1970,
      pp. 79-95, 375-78. (German)

      Sketches the changing fashions in performance and
      cultural approaches. *Dream* is a mixture of the styles of
      Comedy of Errors (Plautine farce), *Love's Labour's Lost*
      (courtly comedy, à la John Lyly), *Two Gentlemen of Verona*
      (romanesque fantasy), and *Taming of the Shrew* (British
      farce tradition). Then, after a brief account of the
      probable sources and of the disparate verse forms and
      language choices, Habicht places *Dream* in the British
      tradition of the hybrid comedy (as with Lyly, Greene). He
      regards the marriage of Theseus and Hippolyta to be the
      key to the drama but dismisses as unfounded the notion
      that it was written for a specific wedding. He analyzes
      various persistent themes which derive from the Theseus
      point of departure and fuse the separate plot elements into
      a harmonious whole: the conflict of the old and the new
      (waning moon/new moon, Egeus/Hermia), the paradox of
      subjective and objective reality (fancy, imagination/reason),
      the paradox of the forest (freedom from social
      constraints/chaos, beauty/terror), animal imagery and
      metamorphosis, and the paradoxical mirroring of character
      and speeches (Bottom/Puck). The dominant theme, he
      thinks, is "what for Theseus is a past he has vanquished
      and what rebellious youth must again and again experience
      anew--the unalterable, irrational process of the development
      of love from the conflict of the sexes and generations." See
      items 59, 187, 240 and 292 for other comparisons with these
      plays.

356   Hassel, R. Chris. "Shakespeare's Comic Epilogues:
         Invitations to Festive Communion." *Shakespeare Jahrbuch*
         (Heidelberg), (1970), 160-69.

         The four comedies with festive epilogues (*Dream, Love's
         Labour's Lost, As You Like It, Twelfth Night*) all admit the
         imperfectibility of man and at the same time glory in it as
         the secret of man's greatness. These epilogues reflect the
         invitation to the Christian communion, which is based upon
         the same essential paradox about man. *Dream* ends with
         both these real and imagined qualities of man at one in
         Puck's appeal for acceptance in his epilogue and in the
         combination of the real (Athens) and the imagined (the
         fairies). It is a "splendid ambiguity" with which to end the
         play. (This material reappears with modifications in the
         author's *Faith and Folly in Shakespeare's Romantic
         Comedies,* item 566h.)

357   Hawkins, Harriett. "Fabulous Counterfeits: Dramatic
         Construction and Dramatic Perspectives in *The Spanish
         Tragedy, A Midsummer Night's Dream,* and *The
         Tempest.*" *Shakespeare Studies,* 6 (1970), 51-65.

         In both these comedies Shakespeare seems to examine his
         own "so potent art." He brings together the topics of
         magic, imagination, dreams, and especially the nature of
         dramatic illusion. Kyd's *Spanish Tragedy* offers an
         interesting precedent (not necessarily a source) for the
         dramatic organization and emphasis of the two comedies. It
         may have bequeathed to Shakespeare "the multiple levels of
         dramatic action, and the multiple perspectives on dramatic
         action." In all three plays superhuman characters show a
         dual perspective, at once questioning and predicting the
         ultimate outcome. In all we are reminded of "the essentially
         arbitrary, amoral and unjust nature of both tragic and
         comic forms." *Dream* attacks the validity of every level of
         reality it brilliantly creates. It takes all the assumptions of
         its audience and violates them in surprising ways: clashing
         perspectives combine to give us comic harmony. (This
         material reappears with modifications as Chapter 2 of the
         author's *Likenesses of Truth in Elizabethan and Restoration
         Drama* [1972]--item 402.)

358   Jochums, Milford C. "Artificial Motivation in *A Midsummer
      Night's Dream.*" *Illinois State University Journal*, 32
      (1970), 16-21.

      The fairy world not only controls the world of men but
      also provides external motivation for the progress of the
      action of the play. Oberon resolves his quarrel with
      Titania, corrects Puck's negligence, cures Demetrius'
      "sickness," and in general brings about a new order.

359   "*A Midsummer Night's Dream*" [filmstrip]. *Simply
      Shakespeare*. Holyoke, Mass.: Scott Education Division,
      1970. Distributed by Prentice-Hall Media, Inc.
      (Tarrytown, N. Y.). 90 fr., col., 35 mm. (not seen)

      Apparently presents a children's comedian who narrates
      the story with the accent on the comedy. Designed for the
      primary grades.

359a "*A Midsummer Night's Dream*--An Introduction" [film].
      Shakespeare. England: Seabourne Enterprises, Ltd.,
      1970. Distributed by Broadcasting Foundation of America
      Educational Media (New York, N. Y.). Cat. no. 10734,
      25.5 min., col., 16 mm. (not seen)

      Apparently several scenes are performed by an English
      company to introduce first-time readers to the comedy.
      Brief narrative bridges connect the scenes. With study
      guide.

360   Muir, Kenneth. "Shakespeare's Poets." *Shakespeare Survey*,
      23 (1970), 92-94. Reprinted with slight revisions in
      Shakespeare the Professional and Related Studies.
      London: Heinemann; Totowa, N. J.: Rowman and
      Littlefield, 1973, pp. 22-40.

      Theseus should not be taken as Shakespeare's
      spokesman; he is "wrong, even about the lovers." What
      Theseus intends as a gibe against poetry is a precise
      account of Shakespeare's method in the play.

361 Neely, Carol Thomas. "Speaking True: Shakespeare's Use of the Elements of Pastoral Romance." Ph.D. dissertation, Yale University, 1969. *DA*, 30 (1970), 3433A.

Chapter 2 comments on how *Dream* (among other pastoral plays) includes and reconciles conflicting elements through its pastoral style.

362 Neubauer, Patricia. "An Exploration in Esthetics: Five Aspects of Two Shakespearean Plays." *The Barnes Foundation Journal of the Art Department*, 1 (1970), 43-62.

The five aspects are expression (meaning overall theme), decoration (poetic devices such as alliteration and assonance), illustration (the way character and event are revealed in time), unity, and variety. *Dream* and *Tempest*, because both are fantastic, are used to illustrate the aspects.

363 Rohmer, Rolf. "Beiträge zum Kolloquium über das Thema 'Erbe-Gegenwart-Prognose.'" *Shakespeare Jahrbuch* (Weimar), 106 (1970), 63-68.

Praises the effort made in the Weimar production of the play to show processes at work in the development of society in the future, particularly in the rustics' scenes. Cited as examples in this staging are the use of a cart on the stage for the Pyramus and Thisbe drama, the "mercantile" attitude of the rustics when Bottom fails to appear on time, and the rustics' attitude toward their courtly audience.

364 Shaaber, M. A. "The Comic View of Life in Shakespeare's Comedies." *The Drama of the Renaissance: Essays for Leicester Bradner*. Ed. Elmer M. Blistein. Providence: Brown University Press, 1970, pp. 165-78.

The comic in *Dream* (and four other romantic comedies) is "as palpable, as pervasive as the romantic" and deserves at least as much the stress. Love is not taken seriously as much as it is disparaged; it is the prime joke. Love is, after all, inflicted on Titania as a punishment. Shakespeare's most basic view of love is a detached acceptance of both comic and romantic, of the folly and the glory.

364a Shand, G. B. "Chinks." *The Times Literary Supplement.*
      29 January 1970.

      Bottom and Flute should converse through the "chink" of
      two fingers. (See items 338b and 443.) E. A. M. Coleman
      (in item 444) rejects this notion.

365   Torbarina, Josip. "Ivanjska noć u djelu Držića i
      Shakespeare" [St. John's Eve in the Works of Drzic and
      Shakespeare]. *Forum* (Zagreb), 20 (1970), 5-20.
      (Croatian--not seen)

366   Uchiyama, Tomobumi. [On the Diction of *A Midsummer
      Night's Dream.*] *Jimbun Kagaku Ronshū* (Shinshū
      Daigaku), 5 (1970), 33-45. (Japanese)

      Analyzes the three-fold verbal pattern of the play--of
      decorative blank verse of the noblemen, prose of the
      artisans (including malapropisms and comic imitation of
      hyperboles), and rhymed tetrameters of the fairies.

367   Calderwood, James L. "*A Midsummer Night's Dream*: Art's
      Illusory Sacrifice." *Shakespearean Metadrama: The
      Argument of the Play in "Titus Andronicus," "Love's
      Labour's Lost," "Romeo and Juliet," "A Midsummer
      Night's Dream," and "Richard II."* Minneapolis:
      University of Minnesota Press, 1971, pp. 120-48.

      Dream "explores the nature of dramatic illusion as the
      point of convergence for play and audience and does so
      with an almost Pirandello-like engrossment in the
      epistemology of the theatre" (p. 10). It is about the art
      and value of play-making and play-viewing. Theseus and
      Oberon are sorts of playwright-producers. Finally
      Shakespeare was less concerned to claim priority for either
      reason or imagination than to suggest "how man arrives at a
      rational life without forfeiting the liberating virtues of the
      imaginative vision." "The modesty of Shakespeare's epilogue
      is transformed by humorous irony into something of this
      order: 'If it makes you feel more "reasonable," adopt

Theseus' view and regard the play as an idle dream--at
best a way of passing time; but like the lovers who also
converted drama into dream, whether you realize it or not,
you have experienced something here of enduring value and
with a reality of its own.'" See item 271.

368 Comtois, Mary Elizabeth. "*A Midsummer Night's Dream*: A
        Study in Criticism." Ph.D. dissertation, University of
        Colorado, 1970. *DAI*, 31 (1971), 4940A.

        Studies the numerous and complex relationships of the
parts of the play to the whole, how multiplicity and
diversity are integrated to form an organic unit ("organistic
criticism"), *Dream* being used to demonstrate the critical
theory.

369 Dent, Alan. *World of Shakespeare: Plants*. Reading,
        England: Osprey, 1971; New York: Taplinger, 1971.
        Reprint. Taplinger, 1973. 124 pp.

        The index has twenty-seven references to *Dream*. See
item 45 for other discussions of plants.

370 Donker, Marjorie Jean. "The Visual Imagery of Courtly
        Festival in Shakespeare's Drama." Ph.D. dissertation,
        University of Washington, 1970. *DAI*, 32 (1971), 386A.

        "In the *Dream*, Shakespeare manipulates the visual
imagery of the celebration of the wedding of Theseus and
Hippolyta to reinforce the contrast between the world of
nature and the world of art, the civilized world of ordered
ceremony that contains and sanctions Eros."

371 Entry Deleted.

372 Farnham, Willard. *The Shakespearean Grotesque: Its
        Genesis and Transformations*. Oxford: Clarendon Press,
        1971. [10 & plate], 176 pp.

        The treatment of the mechanicals (pp. 75-79) is superior
to that of the low performers in *Love's Labour's Lost*
because *Dream* "contrives to give the grotesque low a due

place among the orders of life and a quality that draws
fellow feeling from life other than its own, however much it
also draws laughter." Bottom (compared to Falstaff) is "a
hero among his fellows simply because he sees and does
things with a superior naïvety of naturalness that comes
from animality." Shakespeare just may have turned from the
"grotesque 'Pyramus'" playlet to the love tragedy *Romeo*.
The two plays show an "extraordinary extension of the
joining of grotesque and non-grotesque beyond the bounds
of a single play."

373   Harrison, Thomas P. "*Romeo and Juliet, A Midsummer
        Night's Dream*: Companion Plays." *Texas Studies in
        Literature and Language*, 13 (1971), 209-13.

        In language, imagery, and situation, the two plays are
        similar--"complete counterparts." (*Dream* is assumed to be
        first.) See item 131 for other comparisons.

374   _____. "Shakespeare's Glowworms." *Shakespeare
        Quarterly*, 22 (1971), 395-96.

        The glowworms at III.i.163, with light in their eyes, are
        a West Indian, not European, species.

375   Hermann, István. [The Nuptials of Theseus. Shakespeare
        and the Myth.] *Világosság* (Budapest), 3 (1970),
        161-66. (Hungarian--not seen)

376   Homan, Sidney. "When the Theater Turns to Itself." *New
        Literary History*, 2 (1971), 407-17.

        Dream is one of several examples of moments when
        Shakespeare turns to metaphors taken from the theatre,
        especially in the playlet and epilogue, with resulting
        ambiguities as to what is real. "Our own reality is suspect
        as a fraud, a dream." He thus "mocks human pretences to
        know the boundaries of reality."

377   Lyons, Charles R. "*A Midsummer Night's Dream*: The
        Paradox of Love's Triumph." *East West Review* (Kyoto),
        4 (1971), 102-25. Also published as Chapter 1 of

Shakespeare and the Ambiguity of Love's Triumph. The
Hague: Mouton, 1971. Lyons has a 1964 Stanford
dissertation with this title (item 277).

The essay attempts to examine and clarify aspects of the
ambiguity of the end of *Dream*. The conventional comic
triumph of love is complicated both by imagery and by the
structural contrast between the illusory and the real. The
concept of love in the play is equivocal, is both of high
value and of high folly. Theseus' skepticism (V.i.4-22) as
to the value of the imagination is in tension with what
appears (in his own speech) to be a "latent celebration of
creativity" (and thus of love). He cannot provide a final,
rational perspective. Bottom accepts the mystery of his
dream and thereby in effect the paradox of the play: the
illusion and reality of love. For a moment at the end of the
play we have the illusion of infinite happiness (love's
triumph), but Puck, speaking in a double voice (as Puck
and as an actor), returns us to the actual world of the
spectators' experience in which folly and death are present.

378   Martz, William J. "Bottom and Paradox Compounded."
      Shakespeare's Universe of Comedy. New York: David
      Lewis, 1971, pp. 61-79. Reprint. New York: Revisionist
      Press, 1979.

Analyzes our delight with the mechanicals, especially
with Bottom (going over each of his five appearances), the
question being to what extent we identify with them and
him. Paradoxically, we both identify with and maintain a
comic distance. The mechanicals, who would seem the least
likely to show imagination, show it in abundance and are a
triumph of human fellowship and communication over
ineptness. What Bottom possesses is "an equivalent of
stature, the stature of staturelessness. This stature of
staturelessness is, more specifically, an embodiment of
qualities, innocence, lyricism, poetic beauty, universal
love, personal freedom as the choice of simpleness and
duty." Bottom has not possessed Titania sexually; his
vision speech refers "to the immortal aspects of the mortal
act"--"Shakespeare's joke." Through the three groups of
characters we meet in the first three scenes, we enter into
a world which is not farce (*Dream* is constantly contrasted
with *The Shrew*); we are closer to the action, in a world
which has "a quality of warmth." While much is absurd, in

Theseus, the young lovers, fairies, and mechanicals, we
feel a "bemused and tolerant interest."

379 Milward, Peter. "Teaching Shakespeare in Japan."
    Shakespeare Quarterly, 25 (1971), 228-33.

    Dream is the favorite comedy of Japanese students.

380 Entry Deleted.

381 Richmond, Hugh M. "Bottom as Romeo." *Shakespeare's
    Sexual Comedy: A Mirror for Lovers*. Indianapolis:
    Bobbs-Merrill, 1971, pp. 102-122.

    Dream is Shakespeare's "verdict on the sexual conduct of
    Romeo." Bottom, in his flexibility, responsiveness, and
    rueful acceptance of all is much more worthy as a model for
    the young than Romeo, who is "a catalyst of disaster, and
    something close to a mass murderer." The passion of the
    young lovers is sentimental and destructive; they
    "positively solicit difficulty, tension, and separation." "No
    significant character in the play is wholly exempt from this
    sadomasochistic type of sexuality--unless indeed it be
    Bottom." For a similar approach see item 131.

382 Scholes, Robert, and Carl H. Klaus. *Elements of Drama*.
    New York and London: Oxford University Press, 1971.
    78 pp.

    Uses *Dream* (*passim*) as one of four plays to illustrate
    elements such as the use of narrative and meditation
    techniques, multiple modes (romance, comedy, farce), and
    the nature of dialogue and character.

383 Schulz, Volker. *Studien zum Komischen in Shakespeares
    Komödien* [Studies in the Comic in Shakespeare's
    Comedies]. Impulse der Forschung, 3. Darmstadt:
    Wissenschaftliche Buchgesellschaft, 1971. 243 pp.
    (German)

    "A systematic survey of the whole range of devices used
    . . . to achieve comic effect," based on the idea that there

are "eight main types" of comedy. *Dream* is not one of the comedies studies closely. (An English summary is in Habicht: item 720)

384 Sinko, Grzegorz. "Noc świętojańska czy noc Walpurgi?" [A Midsummer's Eve or a Walpurgisnacht?]. *Miesięcznik literacki*, 6, no. 4 (1971), 72-77. (Polish--not seen)

385 Taylor, Neil. "'Finde out moone-shine, Finde out moone-shine.'" *Notes and Queries*, 216 (1971), 134-36.

Argues for "the plausibility of the action lasting at least four nights," although there is a confusing timelessness in the woods, and believes there is a new moon on the wedding night. See items 302, 332, 389, 513 and 685d which address the same issue.

386 Toliver, Harold E. "Shakespeare's Inner Plays and the Social Contract." *Pastoral Forms and Attitudes*. Berkeley: University of California Press, 1971, pp. 82-115.

Dream (covered on pp. 82-93), *The Tempest*, and *As You Like It* are discussed in a chapter together because they are "especially typical of Renaissance pastoral themes in their exposure of nobles to rustics and in their concern with contrasts between art and nature." The moon, which presides over all, illuminates the basic dualities of the play (court and forest, art and nature, imagination and reason, love and authority); it may work, for example, in either of two ways--to strengthen the bonds of love or to disrupt rational vision and provoke fickleness. Under the influence of the moon, social order and language disintegrate only to reassert themselves in authority and good sense with the return to court. But the benefits of the forest, which are tolerance and amusement in the face of contrarieties as encouraged by the free play of the imagination, make themselves felt in the court in the conclusion.

387 Weiner, Andrew D. "'Multiforme Uniforme': *A Midsummer Night's Dream*." *ELH*, 38 (1971), 329-49.

The poet's imagination reduces "multiformity to uniformity" by enfolding them in form--the spectators' imagination does so through an apprehension of the formal structure. The play thus can be primarily about "the mysteries signified by and associated with marriage" (Olson, item 145) and yet also be about much more. It can even be "Shakespeare's *Defense of Poesie.*" Hippolyta's response to Theseus' derision, if we consider Sidney's *Defense,* acknowledges the poet's power to present not merely "fairy toys" but "the eternal and unchanging truths governing the universe, whether we call them Platonic Ideas or embodiments of Christian Sapience."

387a Weiss, Theodore. "So Musical a Discord: *A Midsummer Night's Dream.*" *The Breath of Clowns and Kings: Shakespeare's Early Comedies and Histories.* London: Chatto & Windus; New York: Atheneum, 1971, pp. 75-110. Reprint. New York: Atheneum, 1974.

A long, lyrical comment, not easily summarized, on the play's action and mood and in praise of Shakespeare's success. Typical is the following: "To wed Bottom--rock bottom reality or earthiness--to Titania--ethereality itself--by love, by moonlight and the essence of a magical flower, this is what great poetry is made of in its ability to discover the compatibility, the unity, the community of all things. For all its absurdity this match is endearing and idyllic, the momentary conjunction of earth and moon in a twilit music, that of poetry." The mechanicals are the "genius of loutishness distilled"--"delectable toads and newts in an imaginary garden." Special attention is given to the presence of magic and the moon, to the general immersion of human in nature, and to the way *Dream* develops out of early comedies (*Comedy of Errors, Love's Labour's Lost, The Taming of the Shrew*) and relates to *Romeo and Juliet.*

388 Wild, Henry Douglas. *Shakespeare: Prophet for Our Time.* Wheaton, Ill., etc.: Theosophical Publishing House, 1971. xii, 129 pp.

Joins *Dream* with *The Tempest* (pp. 75-87) to perceive "an extended meditation on man's unfolding knowledge of himself." In the one (to paraphrase Hugo) man is slave to forces not understood; in the other he has mastered these forces. The poet's intention was to make us "aware of our whole psychic process"--from animal-like (Bottom) to supermanhood (Prospero). "Shakespeare invites us to approach our mystery and the living of it as a form of yoga." Bottom's dream intimates the "animalistic in one direction and godlike in the other."

389 Wood, James O. "'Finde out moone-shine, finde out moone-shine.'" *Notes and Queries*, 216 (1971), 464.

Defends his case of "a fulling moon" planned "from the start" against the reservations of W. H. Stevenson and Neil Taylor (items 332, 385). Taylor replies (to Stevenson) that a new moon would *not* be visible for the first few days and (to Wood) that Puck's remark that the "wolfe beholds the moone" is not meant to be taken literally. See items 202, 302, 332, 385, 513 and 685d which address the same issue.

390 Zacharias, Peter J. "An Analysis of the Motif of Death and Revival in the Tragicomedies of Shakespeare, Daniel, and Fletcher." Ph.D. dissertation, Michigan State University, 1970. *DAI*, 31 (1971), 6028A-6029A.

Takes the motif in *Dream* "to point to the Neoplatonic mystery of the union of the soul with divine beauty." See item 122 for a similar reading.

391 Aronson, Alex. "Eros: Sons and Mothers." *Psyche & Symbol in Shakespeare*. Bloomington and London: Indiana University Press, 1972, pp. 193-228, esp. pp. 204-12. Reprint. 1980.

A Jungian reading which sees the wood experience as reflecting the disordered libido form which "they wake up to a new, transformed present in which they are, once more, themselves--though they do not know what made this self-discovery possible." Puck, a Mercurius or Trickster-figure, represents the unconscious, presided over by Oberon. Theseus represents consciousness. Tree and Ass are traditional fertility symbols, as Jung observed. Accepts Kott's notion (item 239) of animality. See also items 55, 80a and 329.

392   Berry, Ralph. "The Dream and the Play." *Shakespeare's*
      Comedies: Explorations in Form. Princeton: Princeton
      University Press, 1972, pp. 89-110.

      The play dramatizes two symbols--the dream and the
      play--which makes "illusion" the term best adapted to
      describe the theme. Theseus' support of Egeus in the
      beginning would not have seemed monstrous to an
      Elizabethan audience. He provides the frame of values:
      "strong for laws in public, ready to try techniques of
      conciliation in private." The play stresses moon, dream,
      and eye imagery (Berry discusses eye imagery at length),
      all of which as used suggest illusion, notably the illusion of
      love. The play is Shakespeare's Allegory of Love; the best
      epigraph for it is H. L. Mencken's "Love. The illusion that
      one woman is any different from another." Bottom's playlet
      provides an intellectual "critique of the mechanics of
      illusion," and thus complements the main enquiry of the
      play: "how reality is to be assessed, how the evidence of
      one's eyes is to be judged." "The lovers declare illusion to
      be reality; the actors declare reality to be illusion." The
      two symbols (play and dream) display a natural antipathy
      (the playlet satirizes the love of the main action); but they
      also converge, "embrace at the last," in reconciliation. The
      play thus does not finally satirize love.

393   _____. "Shakespearean Comedy and Northrop Frye."
      Essays in Criticism, 22 (1972), 33-40.

      Objects to Frye's view (item 142) that Shakespearean
      comedy, *Dream* in particular, begins in a "harsh or
      irrational law." The law is "perfectly defensible, and is in
      fact defended by the courteous and rational Theseus. . . .
      Egeus has a case."

394   Brissenden, Alan. "Shakespeare and Dance." *Stratford*
      Papers 1968-69. Ed. B. A. W. Jackson. Hamilton, Ont.:
      McMaster University Library Press; Shannon: Irish
      University Press, 1972, pp. 85-96.

      Considers actual dancing and references to dancing in
      Dream and other plays with special attention to the dance of
      Oberon and Titania, the bergomask of the mechanicals, and
      the carole of the fairies at the end. Much of the motion of
      the play, especially of the fairies, is dance-like. "Given the

circumstances of having available boys who could dance and sing, Shakespeare made dancing an essential part of the plot, a summarizing action and a universal symbol instead of leaving it the merely delectable embellishment it might have been." On the dance see also items 149, 195, 442a and 575.

395   Brown, John Russell. "The Presentation of Comedy: The First Ten Plays." *Shakespearian Comedy*. Ed. Malcolm Bradbury and David Palmer. Stratford-upon-Avon Studies 14. London: Edward Arnold; New York: Crane, Russell, 1972. Pp. 9-30.

Comments briefly (pp. 12-13) on the wide focus of the opening of the play, on the "dispersal of dramatic interest."

396   Clemen, Wolfgang. *Shakespeare's Dramatic Art: Collected Essays*. London: Methuen; New York: Barnes & Noble, 1972. ix, 236 pp.

Uses *Dream* to illustrate Coleridge's observation that in his first scenes Shakespeare "takes the opportunity of sowing germs, the full development of which appears at a future time." We are given exposition, preparation for the mood and theme through imagery and key-words, and we get three of the four plots. No supernatural element is introduced, but we are prepared for such by Theseus' harsh sentence, unreal in the world of comedy. (Pp. 11-18)

397   Faber, M. D. "Hermia's Dream: Royal Road to *A Midsummer Night's Dream*." *Literature and Psychology*, 22 (1972), 179-90.

Gets at the total meaning of the play through Hermia's dream, with its "rich and multiple meanings." The dream expresses an erotic wish, involving Lysander, and operates through disguise, distortion, etc. The play works the same way, having something *outside* (the love-juice, for example) stand for something *inside*. The whole has finally to do with "the problem of setting boundaries between male and female." See items 252 and 556.

398   Foakes, R. A. "The Owl and the Cuckoo: Voices of
      Maturity in Shakespeare's Comedies." *Shakespearian
      Comedy*. Ed. Malcolm Bradbury and David Palmer.
      Stratford-upon-Avon Studies 14. London: Edward
      Arnold; New York: Crane, Russell, 1972, pp. 121-41.

      Considers Theseus, paradoxically, the "spokesman for
'cool reason' who nevertheless speaks the most magical
verse in the play." Theseus bridges life and art,
"reminding us of the need for reason." "The paradox
embodied in the *Dream* is that the voice of reason is
necessary." His voice is "that of a ruler, magisterial,
intelligent, and also compassionate."

399   Goldman, Arnold Lawrence. "The Structure of Time in
      Shakespearean Comedy." Ph.D. dissertation, University
      of Minnesota, 1972. *DAI*, 33 (1972), 2934A.

      Dream is one of four comedies used to demonstrate that
"cyclical time" opposes and finally assimilates "linear time."
Dream, the paradigm of Shakespearean comic structure,
begins at the end of a solar and lunar period, when a law
grown old, represented by the *senex* Egeus, prevents
marriages and threatens youth with death. An intercalary
dreamlike carnival obliterates established forms and permits
the creation of a new community based on love. For other
discussions of time see items 302-3, 332, 385, 389, 476,
510, 513 and 634.

400   Grivelet, Michel. "Shakespeare et 'The Play within the
      Play.'" *Revue des Sciences Humaines*, 145 (1972), 35-52.
      (French)

      Though he seems to be making fun of the comedians,
Shakespeare is in fact showing his disapproval of the
aristocrats who watch the playlet in their mistreatment of
the players. The plays within are flawed, it is true, but
they reflect the new capacities of drama of the time.
Bottom's part, for example, has a special poignancy to it,
and the pageant of the nine worthies (in *Love's Labour's
Lost*) functions as a miniature emblem of that whole play.
(*Dream* is considered on pp. 40-45.) See items 59 and 60.

401 Hart, John A. "Father-Daughter as Device in Shakespeare's Romantic Comedies." *In Honor of Austin Wright.* Carnegie Series in English, 12. Pittsburgh: Carnegie-Mellon University, 1972, pp. 51-61.

Once the conflict between father and daughter (Egeus and Hermia) gets the play going, it is shunted aside, with little made of it; we do catch a hint of reminder in Thisbe's predicament.

402 Hawkins, Harriett. "'See here my show': Theatrical Illusions and Realities in *The Spanish Tragedy, A Midsummer Night's Dream* and *The Tempest.*" *Likenesses of Truth in Elizabethan and Restoration Drama.* Oxford: Clarendon Press, 1972, pp. 27-50.

See item 357.

403 Ishikawa, Minoru. [The Love Theme in *A Midsummer Night's Dream*--An Essay on Shakespeare's Dramaturgy.] *Hiyoshi Kiyō* (Keiōgijuku Daigaku), 13 (February 1972), 6-17. (Japanese)

Discusses the theme of love as the unifying factor and the structural basis of the play.

404 McFarland, Thomas. "And All Things Shall Be Peace: The Happiness of *A Midsummer-Night's Dream.*" *Shakespeare's Pastoral Comedy.* Chapel Hill: University of North Carolina Press, 1972, pp. 78-97.

Largely a discussion of the mood of the play--the goodness, happiness, and benignity, not to mention beauty--which renders no comic motivation a serious source of anxiety. We are interested, however, in the play-within-a-play preparation, and our laughter at the playlet "confirms [our] existence in paradise." Constantly McFarland denies any validity to Jan Kott's interpretation (see item 239). *Dream* is "very possibly the happiest work of literature ever conceived." Its darkness is "but a symbol of soft and benign exhilaration."

405   Maclean, Hugh. "Shakespeare in the Classroom: Titles and
      the Text." *English Record*, 23, no. 1 (1972), 27-33.

      Briefly (pp. 31-32) on using the title of *Dream* as a
      point of departure for teaching and on the moon image.

405a May, Robin. *Who's Who in Shakespeare*. London: Elm Tree
      Books, 1972; New York: Taplinger, 1973. x, 109 pp.

      A dictionary of the characters in Shakespeare's plays
      which lists and describes in some detail every major
      character in *Dream*. In most cases the description includes
      both a quick evaluation of the character and a summary of
      the plot line in which the character is involved.

406   Merchant, W. Moelwyn. *Comedy*. The Critical Idiom Series,
      21. London: Methuen, 1972. x, 92 pp.

      Considers *Dream* in the context of Northrop Frye's
      "green world" theory (item 142) and, assuming Bottom to be
      alluding to St. John's first epistle, has him leave the green
      world with something similar to that which the lovers take
      away--"a ritual vision of a life sacramentally informed with
      love." (Pp. 55-57) See items 162, 186, 544, 566 and 610 for
      other discussions of Bottom's allusions.

407   Mortenson, Peter. "*Friar Bacon and Friar Bungay*: Festive
      Comedy and 'Three-Form'd Luna.'" *English Literary
      Renaissance*, 2 (1972), 194-207.

      Notes in passing (p. 196) that *Friar Bacon* "is a festive
      comedy, provides multiple plots, utilizes the image of
      three-formed Luna, and ends in a celebratory pageant and
      masque"--and thus is to be compared with *Dream*. See item
      282.

408   Muir, Kenneth. "Didacticism in Shakespearean Comedy:
      Renaissance Theory and Practice." *Review of National
      Literatures*, 3, no. 2 (1972), 39-53.

      In one paragraph (pp. 48-49) Muir summarizes the
      didactic element in the play ("something besides delight").
      We are led to sympathetic laughter at the absurdities of

people in love and at the badness of amateur acting and of poetasters. "The magic juice is a symbol of the volatile enchantment brought about by sexual desire, particularly in adolescence."

409   Rose, Mark. "Contexts and Designs." *Shakespearean Design*. Cambridge: The Belknap Press of Harvard University Press, 1972, pp. 1-26.

Dream suggests that Shakespeare had "a strong sense of spatial form and quite remarkable powers of organization, . . . did not normally count lines but that he did have a feeling for the general 'mass' of a scene." *Dream* is triadic in shape (Athens-Forest-Athens) or, more accurately, of five-parts (Athens-Workmen-Forest-Workmen-Athens), with the union of Bottom and Titania at the very center of the Forest sequence.

410   Schabert, Ina. *Shakespeare-Handbuch: Die Zeit, Der Mensch, Das Werk, Die Nachwelt*. Stuttgart: Kröner, 1972. xvi, 904 pp. (German)

An introduction to the comedies by Manfred Pfister (pp. 388-446) contains an interpretation and bibliography and a special chapter on *Dream* (pp. 459-65) which surveys the different editions and Shakespeare's sources. Pfister treats *Dream* sketchily (pp. 411-17) in terms of 1) text and dating, 2) sources, 3) analysis and interpretation, and 4) influence on later works. The emphasis is on Shakespeare's blending of four separate plot-lines (Theseus-Hippolyta, young lovers, mechanicals, and Oberon-Titania), variations on the central theme (love), and use of contrasts (dreaming-waking, night-day, reason-folly, order-chaos). A highly selective bibliography is appended.

411   Schmitt-von Mühlenfels, Franz. *Pyramus and Thisbe. Rezeptionstypen eines Ovidischen Stoffes in Literatur, Kunst und Musik* [Pyramus and Thisbe. Examples of the Reception of an Ovidian Motif in Literature, Art and Music]. Studien zum Fortwirken der Antike, 6. Heidelberg: Carl Winter, 1972. 164 pp., 34 pl. (German)

A typological--not chronological--study of the story as it appears in all the arts. Chapters are on Ovid's account, the moralization of the story, its treatment as a celebration of love, as a tragedy, and as a comedy (the parodies). Shakespeare's playlet ought not to be seen solely as an isolated production but should be brought into relation with the history of an Ovidian theme which "exemplifies various features of the cultural history of 2000 years." See item 60.

412 Smith, Hallett. "*A Midsummer Night's Dream* and *The Tempest*." *Shakespeare's Romances: A Study in Some Ways of the Imagination*. San Marino, Calif.: Huntington Library, 1972, pp. 121-44.

After briefly linking *Dream* with *Romeo* (the latter probably came first), compares *Dream* with *The Tempest*. Both plays have elaborate, strange landscapes, the greatest possible contrasts of characters, a presiding mage (Oberon is taken by many to be very like Prospero), and much ado about dreams and illusions in contrast with waking and reality mixed with a strong interest in the stage. *Dream* is discussed first, then *The Tempest*. See items 131 and 149 for other comparisons with these plays.

413 Smith, J. Percy. "Imaginary Forces and the Ways of Comedy." *Stratford Papers 1968-69*. Ed. B. A. W. Jackson. Hamilton, Ont.: McMaster University Library Press; Shannon: Irish University Press, 1972, pp. 1-20.

Examines several of the reflections on poetry and the theatre in *Dream*. Theseus' inclusion of the poet on his list is not Shakespeare's joke at the expense of his own craft; the speech (V.i.2-22) gives the imagination a "new function, making it positively creative." Shakespeare had come to realize the value of the imagination to poets and actors. The movement away from court and back and the varying and intermingling levels of experience (dream-within-dream, play-within-play) produce the "astonishing effect of unsounded depths." We have been invited to participate in a dream, an act of the imagination.

414 Wells, Stanley. "Shakespeare Without Sources." *Shakespearian Comedy*. Ed. Malcolm Bradbury and David Palmer. Stratford-upon-Avon Studies 14. London: Edward Arnold; New York: Crane, Russell, 1972, pp. 58-74.

Love's Labour's Lost, *Dream*, and *The Tempest* which have no narrative source have certain techniques and ideas in common: grouped characters, structural parallels (plays-within-plays), minimal psychological development in the characters, moral concerns, a set "place apart," and a preoccupation with art. All, too, seem inspired by special occasions. "The resemblances among these three plays may suggest that, left to his own inventive powers, Shakespeare was apt to confine himself to a comparatively narrow range of techniques and themes." See items 59 and 149 for similar comparisons.

415 Willson, Robert F., Jr. "Burlesque Tone in *A Midsummer Night's Dream* or the Play from Bottom Up." *Lock Haven Review*, 13 (1972), 115-27.

Sets out in great detail the parallels between the plot of the young lovers and that of the playlet in order to show that the latter is intended to parody the former. In fact, it is argued, a strong case can be made for seeing burlesque and parody as the point of view intended in presenting the lovers' plot and that of Oberon and Titania as well. Many of the events involving the lovers are staples of such burlesque plays as *Ralph Roister Doister* and *The Knight of the Burning Pestle*. Suggested as being among specific works parodied are Golding's Ovid, Shakespeare's *Comedy of Errors*, *Two Gentlemen*, and *Romeo*. The spirit of parody pervades almost every level of the play. See items 131, 187, 240 and 484 for similar comparisons.

416 Yamagushi, Yoshirō. [On the Folklore in *A Midsummer Night's Dream*.] *Kiyō* (Awoyama Gakuin Joshi Tanki Daigaku), 26 (November 1972), 15-24. (Japanese)

Describes the folklore background, with special reference to May festivities and magic of herbs.

417 Zimbardo, R. A. "Regeneration and Reconciliation in *A Midsummer Night's Dream*." *Shakespeare Studies*, 6 (1972), 35-50.

The central idea of reconciliation is "shaped by the interaction of two themes: that of permanence in mutability . . . and that of discordia concors." In general, summer

and winter, male and female, reason and imagination--all
meet and are reconciled. The moon, symbol of continuity in
change, presides, and each of the plots brings concordance
out of seeming opposites. Male and female qualities mixed
paradoxically in Theseus and Hippolyta come together, on a
higher plane, in Oberon and Titania. The lovers resolve the
conflict between law and love. And the playlet draws
together objective reality with subjective fantasy.

418   Adland, David. *The Group Approach to Shakespeare: "A
       Midsummer Night's Dream."* London: Longmans, 1973. 142
       pp.

       The book aims to "bring the acting experience into the
       class-room or the drama hall." It provides "practical
       material for every scene in the play," that is, background
       matter, glosses, suggestions about blocking, voice, and
       gesture, and teaching devices.

419   Cope, Jackson I. "Theater of the Dream: Dante's *Commedia*,
       Jonson's Satirist, and Shakespeare's Sage." *The Theater
       and the Drama: From Metaphor to Form in Renaissance
       Drama*. Baltimore and London: Johns Hopkins University
       Press, 1973, pp. 211-44.

       Dream is "a mythic play which both suggests and blurs
       its relation to folk ritual by presenting a play-within-a-play
       which interacts with dreams-within-a-dream." The relation
       of play and dream is discussed in the play in terms of the
       aesthetics of the imagination, terms which reflect precisely
       the debate on the subject going on among Italian critics
       (Mazzoni, Bulgarini) as to whether dream and art are vain
       or significant. Shakespeare demonstrates that poetry's truth
       transcends reason.

420   Danek, Robert Matthew. "The Symbolism of Perverse
       Marriage in Shakespearean Drama." Ph.D. dissertation,
       Indiana University, 1973. *DAI*, 34 (1973), 1854A.

       Contrasts (Ch. 2) the marriage norm of *Dream* with that
       of *Romeo*. In the latter there are similar conflicts but in a
       tragic context, one in which the sacramental power of
       marriage to unite the lovers with society is not permitted to
       operate.

421 Dent, Alan. *World of Shakespeare: Animals & Monsters.*
Reading, England: Osprey, 1972; New York: Taplinger,
1973. 160 pp.

The index gives twenty-three references to *Dream.* See
item 53.

421a _____. *World of Shakespeare: Sports and Pastimes.*
Reading, England: Osprey, 1973; Taplinger, 1974. 111
pp.

Cites five allusions to sports and pastimes in *Dream.*

422 Fawcett, Sharon. *The Imagination of Awakening: Endings of
Some of Shakespeare's Comic Plays. Archai*, no. 2.
Coquitlam, British Columbia: Archai Publications, 1973.
ii, 49 pp.

On how the numerous contraries in the play
(dream-reality, etc.) relate to and partake of each other,
especially the ambiguity of the end, which is a synthesis,
"a metaphorical remarriage of two artificially separated
worlds." (Pp. 22-30)

423 Finkelstein, Sidney. *Who Needs Shakespeare?* New York:
International Publishers, 1973. 261 pp.

Summarizes the play. (Pp. 56-57)

424 Goldstein, Melvin. "Identity Crises in a Midsummer
Nightmare: Comedy as Terror in Disguise."
Psychoanalytic Review, 60 (1973), 169-204.

The lovers must work through madness (here defined in
psychoanalytic terms), which is represented by a variety of
forms of disguises, to their authentic selves, at which point
they are ready to join the community in marriage.
Language, with its multiple meanings, many unconscious,
reflects the stages in the movement to the true self
(especially the word *figured*). Much of the discussion is
based on psychoanalytic tenets and motifs from mythology.
See items 55 and 252.

425   Hiraiwa, Norio. [Oberon and Shakespeare.] *Gaikokugo
      Kenkyū* 10 (March 1973), 13-25. (Japanese)

      Emphasizes Oberon's unifying function as an agent of
      God's harmonizing power, with imagination as its metaphor.

426   Huston, J. Denis. "Bottom Waking: Shakespeare's 'Most
      Rare Vision.'" *Studies in English Literature*, 13 (1973),
      208-22.

      "When Bottom awakens alone in Act 4 of *Dream*," Huston
      says, "Shakespeare focuses many of the themes and actions
      of the play into a moment of dramatic and thematic
      intensity. First, by raising Bottom up from a formless mass
      on an apparently empty stage, Shakespeare makes his
      audience aware of the basic challenge facing any dramatist,
      who must find some way to fill a stage with life. Then, as
      he moves Bottom frantically about in search of lost
      companions, Shakespeare bodies forth the raw energies of
      imaginative excitement which the artist must harness within
      the limits of his form and medium. Finally, when
      Shakespeare brings Bottom at last to a stop, alone in the
      center of the stage that he has been trying to seize for
      himself since his initial entrance, the language of his
      subsequent soliloquy suggests visionary experience.
      Fleetingly the themes of love, dream, revelation, and
      art--themes which treat of nothing less than Shakespeare's
      play as a whole--are gathered together in a dramatic
      moment of vision which passes all understanding, which has
      'no bottom.'"

427   Mandel, Jerome. "Dream and Imagination in Shakespeare."
      Shakespeare Quarterly, 24 (1973), 61-68.

      Shakespeare's plays (such as *Dream*) are like dreams to
      the audiences, and thereby have some of the higher
      revelations the Renaissance found in dreams. Further, the
      audience participates in making real-like the plays and at
      the same time learns something about the real world.

428   Miller, Sara Ann Mason. "Shakespeare as a Critic: His
      Satire of Literary Language, Themes, Characters, and
      Conventions." Ph.D. dissertation, University of
      Mississippi, 1973. *DAI*, 34 (1973), 1864A-1865A.

Chapter 1 explores the satire of literary language and aspects of popular drama in the "Pyramus" portion of *Dream*. Shakespeare summarizes most of the features of popular drama--its use of bombastic language, incongruous titles, over-long explanations of the action at hand, characters which are abstractions, and tedious death scenes. See item 60.

429   Miola, Robert. "Early Shakespearean Comedy: *sub specie ludi*." *Thoth*, 14, no. 1 (1973-1974), 23-36.

Three comedies--*Dream*, *Love's Labour's Lost*, and *Comedy of Errors*--are basically ludic (like a game) rather than mimetic (like life). To show how these plays proceed, one may profit by ideas from Plato, Vladimir Nabokov, and Johan Huizinga about play and its tripartite structure (*Initiation Ludi, In Media Ludi, Terminus Ludi*). Like play, *Dream* begins with a central agon (Egeus against the young lovers); its middle occupies a playground (the woods) removed from everyday life; its ending establishes (through marriage) a new social community. This kind of play both instructs and delights. For other discussions of game-play elements see items 79, 158, 467, 516, 526a, 534 and 547.

430   Muir, Kenneth. "Shakespeare's Poets." *Shakespeare the Professional and Related Studies*. London: Heinemann; Totowa, N. J.: Rowman and Littlefield, 1973, pp. 22-40.

Reprints item 360.

431   Ozaki, Yoshiharu. [The Structure of *A Midsummer Night's Dream* and the Audience.] *Kenkyū Nempō* (Nara Joshi Daigaku), 16 (1973), 28-52. (Japanese)

Analyzes the metadramatic aspect of the play, emphasizing that the play is an exploration of the nature and meaning of dramatic imagination.

432   Paris, Jean. "Clefs d'un songe." *La Critique genérative, change*, 16-17 (September 1973). An English translation "The Key to a Dream" appears in *Sub-stance*, 4 (1973), 3-25. A condensed version is part of the introduction to *Le Songe d'une nuit d'été*, etc. Ed. Jean Paris. Livre de

Poche classique. Paris: Gallimard, 1971. The full version
occurs in the author's *Univers Parallèles: I-Théâtre*.
Paris: Éditions du Seuil, 1975. (French)

A complicated structuralist reading which sees the
"primary disjunction," out of which it all emerges and
repeated at all levels, to be between desire and frustration,
especially sexual. Hippolyta's menstrual cycle prohibits
consummation at the outset. "If menstrual equals
monstrous," etc. "The most critical sexual prohibition
appears therefore linked to the lady's [Thisbe's] veil
maculated with blood. . . . Symbolically, this is where
Dream begins." Discusses transformations, inversions,
conjunctions, and repetitions throughout, calling on the
mythic in general as well as C. L. Barber's discussion (item
158) and Jean-Marie Lhôte's analysis (see item 310) of the
components of the play as analogous to that of the Tarot
cards, and stressing the playlet. Consummation takes place
after the play.

433   Rowland, Beryl. *Animals with Human Faces: A Guide to
      Animal Symbolism*. Knoxville: University of Tennessee
      Press, 1973. xix, 192 pp.

      Briefly (p. 24) on how "Bottom bears traces of the ass's
      peculiar ancestry," with special attention to his singing.
      See also items 566kk and 603.

434   Sider, John Wm. "The Serious Elements of Shakespeare's
      Comedies." *Shakespeare Quarterly*, 24 (1973), 1-11.

      With *Dream* (p. 2) we are moved by curiosity as to what
      will happen and by romantic sentiment rather than by
      profound sympathy.

435   Sorum, Judith Ann. "Shakespeare and Molière: A
      Comparison of Their Comic Worlds." Ph.D. dissertation,
      Michigan State University, 1973. *DAI*, 34 (1973),
      3357A-3358A.

      Dream and three other comedies serve as the basis for
      the Shakespearean side (Chapter 2). Shakespeare's comic
      world goes well beyond that of Molière, including all he has
      for setting, theme, and character and much, much more.

436 Swinden, Patrick. *"A Midsummer Night's Dream." An
     Introduction to Shakespeare's Comedies*. London:
     Macmillan; New York: Barnes & Noble, 1973, pp. 51-64.

   In *Dream* the "flat narrative-conversational plane" of
Love's Labour's Lost (the two plays are compared and
contrasted) is replaced by a "series of mobile perspectives"
here suggested by a diagram. The various "planes" of the
play "cut across and get entangled" with each other. Our
senses must strain to see what is dark, to grasp the
conflicting evidence of the size of the fairies, to
comprehend the vast space and time suggested, even to
grasp Puck's contradictory nature and powers. "The life of
the imagination is . . . at once capricious and healing,
deranging and, finally, conducive to harmony." We are like
the "shadows."

437 Tyler, Parker. "The Education of a Prince: The Elements in
     Drama." *Prose* (New York), 6 (1973), 185-215.

   Dream (pp. 196-98) in its apparent natural
"anarchy"--mixing of classes--actually gives a "more
comprehensive order of nature" than might appear.
Shakespeare believed in an emergent aristocracy of nature
which "transcends any static concept" of social or natural
order, one symbolized in Theseus' acceptance of the rustics
and in Bottom's relations with Titania.

438 Weathers, Martha Bell. *"A Midsummer Night's Dream* and the
     Dream Perspective: An Historical Analysis." Ph.D.
     dissertation, Rice University, 1973. *DAI*, 34 (1973),
     1260A.

   "Examines the dramatic, comic function of the dream
perspective . . . utilizing an historical critical approach."
Chapter 1 considers the ways drama can be said to be like
a dream. Chapter 2 demonstrates that the Renaissance
viewed the dream as many faceted. Chapter 3 shows how
the metaphor of dream works for laughter and delight in
the play. And Chapter 4 explores the meaning of the play
as a dream experience. "The play's subject is primarily the
transforming power of the imagination and its ability to
generate a 'golden' world out of a 'brazen' one."

439   Wilson, Elkin Calhoun. *Shakespeare, Santayana, and the
      Comic.* University: University of Alabama Press; London:
      George Allen & Unwin, 1973. viii, 191 pp.

      Summarizes the play (pp. 67-74) in order to show that it
      integrates the various modes of the comic (two of the modes
      being the farcical and the romantic).

440   Yamamoto, Iwata. [Reading *A Midsummer Night's Dream.*]
      Jimbungaku Ronso (Yokohama Ichiritsu Daigaku), 24, no.
      1 (April 1973), 27-76. (Japanese)

      Running commentary on various topics in the play, such
      as a midsummer season, the opening speeches,
      love-in-idleness, Helena and Demetrius, Bottom, "fine
      frenzy," the epilogue, and the like.

441   Bandera, Casáreo. "Literature and Desire: Poetic Frenzy
      and the Love Potion." *Mosaic*, 8, no. 2 (1974-75), 33-52.

      As the exchange between Lysander and Hermia
      (I.i.132-51) suggests, it is in the nature of love that
      obstacles (frequently illusory) are felt to be present
      perpetually (pp. 43-44).

442   Bilton, Peter. *Commentary and Control in Shakespeare's
      Plays.* Norwegian Studies in English, 19. Oslo:
      Universitetsforlaget; New York: Humanities Press, 1974.
      247 pp.

      In the play certain devices protect us from threatening
      emotions. Theseus' and Oberon's power and control prevent
      us from fearing that anyone will come to grief. Moreover,
      Bottom, like Shakespeare, is concerned that we "not be *too*
      carried away by illusion." (Pp. 81-84)

442a Brown, John Russell, and J. R. Mulryne. "Patterns and
      Character in *A Midsummer Night's Dream*" (Tract A) and
      "Fantasy and Imagination in *A Midsummer Night's Dream*"
      (Tract B) [Audio-cassette]. Mount Vernon, N. Y.:
      Audio Learning, 1974. Audio-Cassette ELA001, 55 min.

Intending their remarks for a general, perhaps student audience, the two speakers discuss such topics as the rhythm of the play from court to forest and back, its dance-pattern of motion and bonding (with no misfits or excluded figures), the levels of being in the play (from real to fantastic), and the natures of selected characters, especially Puck and Bottom. They take the play to be about the power, variety, and precariousness of love. A Supplementary Booklet of eight pages, by John Sutherland and Keith Walker, gives a Summary of the Discussion, Commentary, Questions, and Further Reading.

443 Clayton, Thomas. "'Fie What a Question's That If Thou Wert Near A Lewd Interpreter': The Wall Scene in *A Midsummer Night's Dream*." *Shakespeare Studies*, 7 (1974), 101-13.

While Wall may indeed spread his fingers, as is usually done in performances, he should also spread his legs in order properly to discharge his part. Much in the text suggests that this stance makes dramatic and poetic sense. See item 364a. E. A. M. Coleman (in item 444) rejects this motion.

444 Coleman, E. A. M. *The Dramatic Use of Bawdy in Shakespeare*. London: Longman, 1974. x, 230 pp.

"There are in the play, at a cautious estimate, about nine demonstrable instances of bawdy"--each of which is identified. All but two are from the artisans, who are rarely allowed to show any awareness of their own comic lines. The choice of the word *hole* (in the playlet) seems deliberate. *Bottom* does not suggest *buttocks*. Sexuality and bawdy do have a role in the play (unrecognized in Mendelssohnian interpretations), for "midsummer madness is amoral" and "there is a distasteful side to Titania's doting *mésalliance* with the ass-headed Bottom." But we are not to view the play through the "baleful spectacles" of Jan Kott (item 239). Kott has, however, "proved sufficiently influential to place the image of the *Dream* in need of repair." (Pp. 27-31, 171) See also items 57 and 155.

445 Doran, Madeleine. "Titania's Wood." *Rice University Studies*. 60, no. 2 (1974), 55-70.

On the woodland setting--how it is created and what
purposes it serves, how "the formal, the traditional, the
immediately observed are fused," especially flowers and the
moon, and how homely and literary, realistic and fantastic
are allied. There is an extensive comment on the details of
several passages describing the woods, the discussion of
the flowers of Titania's bower being particularly long and
involved. With the moon (which has several pages devoted
to its classical origins and function in the play) one should
not, like Bottom, look too closely at the calendar, or, for
that matter, at the mythographers. Though sources can be
found for much in the woods of the play, the result is
thoroughly the product of Shakespeare's invention. One of
Sidney's poets, he has created "another nature," making
the brazen one golden.

446 Engler, Balz. *Rudolf Alexander Schröders Übersetzungen
     von Shakespeares Dramen* [R. A. S.' Translations of
     Shakespeare's Plays]. The Cooper Monographs, 18.
     Bern: Francke, 1974. 231 pp. (German)

     A study of Schröder's method of translating and the
     problems of translating into German. Schröder took *Dream*
     to be about the "dangers of unchecked imagination, of the
     temptation by evil forces." There is an English summary in
     Habicht, 1975 (published in 1976): see item 720. See also
     item 25.

447 Garber, Marjorie B. "Spirits of Another Sort: *A Midsummer
     Night's Dream.*" *Dream in Shakespeare: From Metaphor to
     Metamorphosis*. New Haven and London: Yale University
     Press, 1974, pp. 59-87.

     Dream is "a play consciously concerned with dreaming; it
     reverses the categories of reality and illusion, sleeping and
     waking, art and nature, to touch upon the central theme of
     the dream which is truer than reality." All the
     transformations in the play bring about self-knowledge, of
     which the dream is chief (perhaps *vision* is a better word).
     The world of the wood over which Oberon presides is
     nothing more than a dramatic metaphor for the dream world
     of the subconscious and irrational. The whole recalls the
     medieval Dream Vision, with its god of love, journeying
     lovers, enchanted garden, and May morning. (Based on a
     1969 Yale dissertation abstracted in *DAI*, 31 [1970], 1227A.)

448   Hamel, Guy A. "Structure in Elizabethan Drama." Ph.D.
      dissertation, University of Toronto, 1972. *DAI*, 34
      (1974), 5101A-5102A.

      Devotes a chapter to the two kinds of structure in the
      play; *process*--the sense of quantitative structure gained
      by an audience as it experiences the play; and
      product--the eventual recognition of its shape as a
      construct. "The structure of *Dream* viewed as a product
      forms a series of concentric circles representing the levels
      of influence of the four groups of characters. The
      development of the play sets comic against tragic impulses
      in a way that celebrates the primacy of the comic force in
      each sphere. The dialectical mode of the process by
      duplicating the same conflict . . . at each level is the
      means of revealing the structure of the product."

449   Hasler, Jörg. "Parody and Self-Parody in the 'Pyramus and
      Thisbe' Interlude." *Shakespeare's Theatrical Notation:
      The Comedies*. The Cooper Monographs, Theatrical
      Physiognomy Series, 21. Bern: Francke, 1974, pp.
      78-95.

      Examines the dramaturgy of Peter Quince and shows that
      the joke is not entirely at the expense of the mechanicals or
      their stage audience. Shakespeare in fact caricatures his
      own techniques. The methods "he normally applies so
      discreetly become glaringly, ridiculously obvious" (pp.
      14-15). The rustics by their pointing in the rehearsal scene
      ("this green plot," "that brake") parody Shakespeare's own
      traffic with word-scenery. In all their three scenes we are
      constantly invited to compare similar iterations in his other
      plays (especially *Romeo*, which the playlet parodies). There
      are striking verbal parallels which coincide with a stark
      contrast in tone and atmosphere. A special chapter (6) on
      endings connects the opening of *Dream* with the closing
      speeches, and with the latter notices the clues to stage
      business. See items 60 and 131.

450   Henze, Richard. "*A Midsummer Night's Dream*: Analogous
      Image." *Shakespeare Studies*, 7 (1974), 115-23.

      Distinguishes between Theseus' conception of the poetic
      imagination and that which emerges from the play as a
      whole. Shakespeare accepted neither Platonic frenzy nor

Aristotelian ideal imitation of the truth as the basis for art.
His play emphasizes the poet's *art* rather than his
inspiration and *common images* rather than ideal ones.
Shakespeare's poet is less a divine creator than Sidney's,
less frenzied than Theseus', but he is just as surely a
poet. Imagination is the major theme of the play.

451   Isaacs, Neil D., and Jack E. Reese. "Dithyramb and Paean
      in *A Midsummer Night's Dream.*" *English Studies*, 55
      (1974), 351-57.

      Dream seems patterned on a Dionysian celebration, a
      Dithyramb, in which Apollonian order is suspended to be
      replaced by inverted procedures, the king's place is
      assumed by a master of revels or lord of misrule, and
      broad license of behavior allows or actually demands
      intoxication, promiscuity, and abandoned music and
      dancing. The young lovers break the rules of order by
      entering the woods. The fairies personify elements of
      misrule. And Bottom is the Lord of Misrule or Disorder--a
      comic version of satyr or centaur. Reminders of the
      Dionysian "rites" are found to be abundant in the play.
      Dream is "the most thoroughly and explicitly ritualistic of
      Shakespeare's plays." See items 55 and 117.

452   Kernan, Alvin. "From the city to the woods: *A Midsummer
      Night's Dream.*" *The "Revels" History of Drama in
      English, 1576-1613.* Ed. J. Leeds Barroll, Alexander
      Leggatt, Richard Hosley. Volume 3. London: Methuen,
      1975, pp. 311-19.

      Here we "see clearly for the first time the complete
      rhythm of human experience which is the essence of
      Shakespearian comedy." To go deeper into the woods for
      the lovers is to go "deeper into total commitment to
      passion." Titania and Oberon reflect past and since
      suppressed qualities of Hippolyta (man-killer) and Theseus
      (seducer). "There is about love . . . something random,
      inexplicable, woodlike and Puckish, and something like
      Oberon and Titania in the strength of will with which lovers
      insist on having their way." The withdrawal in the end
      involves a return to the world of the city wherein
      "orderliness can be adjusted to natural impulses to provide
      for a satisfactory *human* life." The woods have the same
      effect on Bottom and company.

453 Leggatt, Alexander. *"A Midsummer Night's Dream."*
     Shakespeare's Comedy of Love. London: Methuen, 1974,
     pp. 89-115.

     Bottom and Titania present the play's most striking
image, he with his cheerful equanimity, she in the grip of
passion, the keynote being their innocence. Each is totally
absorbed in his or her own world, and such is also true of
each of the four groups of the play. Each is preoccupied
with its own limited problems, largely unaware of the
others. Relative to the whole play, each is innocent. And
each provides a context for the others. Each has its own
special view of things, which we experience. The play
suggests the workings of perception. We observe and enjoy
the special, limited perceptions of the separate groups. The
lovers are so deeply in love that they are unaware of the
very conventions they express, the mechanicals so
embroiled in convention (tragedy) that they damage the
experience the convention should embody. Theseus can
provide no objective authority: He scoffs at art yet
(quoting G. K. Hunter) "himself is just another such
antique fable." The fairies are limited to activities of the
night and even then are not involved with its darkest and
most shameful secrets, and are otherwise not infallible.
These worlds border on each other, ultimately appearing to
us as one world. A darker world of passion, terror and
chaos never breaks the thin line which separates it from
this comic world. It is the harmony of these various
perspectives, including that of art, which in the play is
itself limited, that gives the play its special delight.

454 Low, John T. *Shakespeare's Folio Comedies*. Norwood, Pa.:
     Norwood Editions, 1974. 188 pp. Reprint. Folcroft, Pa.:
     Folcroft Library Editions, 1978.

     Divides each comedy into three movements ("the
neo-Terentian pattern") and gives a scene-by-scene
analysis. For *Dream* the first movement ends with II.ii, the
second with III.ii. (Pp. 87-94)

455 McElveen, Idris Baker. "Shakespeare and Renaissance
     Concepts of the Imagination." Ph.D. dissertation,
     University of South Carolina, 1973. *DAI*, 35 (1974),
     409A-410A.

The belief that dreams were the product of an imaginative faculty that remains active even when one is asleep is helpful in understanding *Dream*. By shifting the perspective from one group of characters to another, Shakespeare confuses the senses of the playgoer and enchants him into a dream-like state. Both the characters and the audience are thus dreamers, and their actual and illusory worlds become one through the powers of the imagination. *Dream* is one of four plays discussed.

456   Oku, Yasuko. "*A Midsummer Night's Dream*: A Happy
        Comedy." *Studies in English Literature* (English Literary
        Society of Japan). English Number, 1974, pp. 3-26.

        Points out the contrast between Art (civilization) and Nature (man's natural desires) and argues that the play represents its resolution in the final scenes, concluding that the "play is a 'happy' comedy, not in the sense it presents life as happy, but in the sense it embodies the eagerness to realize and enjoy humanly possible forms of happiness on earth."

457   Pearson, D'Orsay W. "'Unkinde' Theseus: A Study in
        Renaissance Mythography." *English Literary Renaissance*,
        4 (1974), 276-98.

        "One of the most significant 'myths' confronting the serious student of the *Dream* is that of the metamorphosed Theseus, whose medieval and Renaissance image as an unnatural, perfidious, and unfaithful lover and father overshadowed his military or political reputation. The classical, medieval, and Renaissance sources available to Shakespeare stress Theseus' extreme sensuality as well as his lack of paternal devotion. Shakespeare seems to have anticipated audience awareness of Theseus' reputation as a part of the response he expected for the *Dream*, beginning with Theseus' opening speech, which uses images of ingratitude to portray his eagerness for marriage, moves to his lack of compassion for the plight of Hermia and Lysander, and on to his neglect of state affairs. Even his abrupt and unmotivated shift to compassion at the end of the play takes on a strong ironic dimension because of his previous actions and his legendary reputation as perfidious lover and cruel father." See items 55, 538 and 561 for other views of Theseus.

458 Richer, Jean. "Le rituel et les noms dans *Le songe d'une nuit de la mi-été.*" *Annales de la Faculeté des Lettres et Science Humaines de Nice*, 22 (1974), 7-18. (French)

Like *The Tempest, Dream* can be read as a "rituel de renouvellement de l'année." Various mythological associations of ass, other motifs, and names reveal the ritual shape of the play. *Titania* carries the sense "titled she-ass." The true date--based on the animal-zodiacal signs--should be 22-24 June. See items 53, 55 and 149 for other such readings.

459 Turner, Robert Y. *Shakespeare's Apprenticeship*. Chicago: University of Chicago Press, 1974. vii, 193 pp.

Dream, dated 1594-95, ends the period of apprenticeship and is his first masterpiece. Turner discusses (pp. 189-92, 217-19) the development of the art through the early plays up to this success, concentrating in particular on the nature of the laughter at the end of *Dream* (in the playlet and the epilogue), wherein the laughter of scorn is itself ridiculed, on how and the extent to which we ourselves are involved, and on the nature of the verbal wit of the playlet.

460 Entry Deleted.

461 Willson, Robert F., Jr. "The Plays Within *A Midsummer Night's Dream* and *The Tempest.*" *Shakespeare Jahrbuch* (Weimar), 110 (1974), 101-11.

In *Dream*, among other functions of burlesque and parody, the playlet reveals the sexual side of love, a realistic corrective to the romantic. The qualities of burlesque and parody disappear with *The Tempest*, however, where the play-within through a highly symbolic style stresses the harmony of a philosophic vision, and represents Prospero's wishes for Ferdinand and Miranda. See items 60 and 149.

462 Entry Deleted.

463   Cairncross, Andrew S. "'Spinner' (*M.N.D.* II.ii.21; *Romeo*
      I.iv.60)." *Notes and Queries,* 220 (1975), 166-67.

      The "spinner" is the "daddy-long-legs" or crane-fly, not
      the spider.

464   Crossley, Robert. "Education and Fantasy." *College
      English,* 37 (1975), 281-93.

      A brief discussion (on pp. 284-85) of Bottom's response
      to his vision. "His inarticulateness becomes a paradox: he
      makes an unwittingly articulate defence of silence as a
      strategy of response and he rationalizes a nonrational
      method for keeping faith with fantasy." In his silence,
      Bottom is the archetype of the adult reader of fantasy.
      Theseus, who has something to say about fantasy, is "the
      ass, the patched-fool, the man of truncated wisdom and
      practical discretions."

465   Date, Hisahiro. [A Note on *A Midsummer Night's Dream.*]
      Eibungaku-kai-shi (Ohtani Woman's University), 2
      (1975), 1-20. (Japanese--not seen)

      Apparently on two kinds of reason in the play.

466   Eddy, Darlene Mathis. "The Poet's Eye: Some
      Shakespearean Reflections." *Ball State University Forum,*
      16, no. 3 (1975), 3-11.

      Considers several "poised polarities" between *Dream* and
      Hamlet. The one reflects Platonic inspiration--in Theseus'
      speech; the other Aristotelian mimesis--in Hamlet's advice to
      the players. *Dream* shows life, *Hamlet* death. *Dream*
      "affirms joy, and the affirmation is tempered by a wise
      knowledge of sorrow; *Hamlet* perceives joy which is lost in
      a lament which pierces the spirit in its keen recognition."

467   Farrell, Kirby. "A Rite to Bay the Bear: Creation and
      Community in *A Midsummer Night's Dream.*"
      Shakespeare's Creation: The Language of Magic & Play.
      Amherst: University of Massachusetts Press, 1975, pp.
      97-116.

To reach a moment when they can be freely creative and join in authentic community with their lovers, themselves, and us, the lovers must abandon their harsh, limiting conventionality and self-ignorance and pass through a magical, wonderful experience of dissociation in the nighttime woods. Of the playlet: "we exorcise false postures and beliefs by virtually mocking the life out of the playlet's characters. . . . By clarifying the experience of the play proper (as the play in turn illuminates our lives), the demise of 'Pyramus' releases its audiences from sterile conventions. It signals a fresh beginning for the onlookers, a new ability to play."

468 Foster, Leslie D. "The Relation of Act Five to the Structure of *A Midsummer Night's Dream.*" *Michigan Academician*, 8 (1975-76), 191-206.

Studies the *process, agent, agency,* and *architectus* (these terms are defined) whereby the major characters change from tyrants to lovers (which change is taken to be the fundamental problem of the play) and the various problems of individual, sexual, and social identities which accompany this change. The final act brings about the social acceptance of the lovers (beyond their recently discovered sexual identities). Theseus changes from tyrant to lover (he's been insensitive and unimaginative before), Hippolyta noting and delighting in this change. And Bottom becomes more concerned with his audience (taking only one role) than with himself and as a result is accepted generously and imaginatively. These changes are wrought by the performance of the playlet.

469 Guilhamet, Leon. "*A Midsummer-Night's Dream* as the Imitation of an Action." *Studies in English Literature*, 15 (1975), 257-71.

Taking the Aristotelian *praxis* ("action") to mean "purpose" or "aim" (after Francis Fergusson), that is, essentially a psychic movement, sees the unity of *Dream* suggested by Theseus' exasperated question: "How shall we find the concord of this discord?" (V.i.60). "To find the concord of discord"--is the theme, the Neoplatonic and classical concept of *discordia concors*. Harmony works itself out on various levels--heroic, romantic, cosmic, and rude--each level (considered in turn) having its own particular purpose or movement which is obstructed. From the discord of death, for example, in the play's inept production in Act Five comes "a kind of ultimate concord: the harmony of laughter"; and this laughter removes the chief discordant note in human life, death.

470   Hamada, Shioko. "Nature in *A Midsummer Night's Dream.*" *Annual Report of Studies* (Shizuoka Eiwa Jogakuin Junior College), 7 (1975), 109-25.

Concludes that *Dream* "represents nature's real feature and quality, and nature's essential harmony is used as its unifying power as a comedy."

471   Hertel, Charles. "*A Midsummer Night's Dream* I.ii.113." *Explicator*, 33 (1975), Item 39.

The phrase "Hold or cut bowstrings" means "come what may." The longbowman either held the enemy (longbowmen never attack) or else, in defeat or rout, cut his bowstring to render the weapon useless to the enemy. Compare item 471qq.

472   Kernan, Alvin B. "Place and Plot in Shakespeare." *Shakespeare Newsletter*, 25 (1975), 37. (Abstract of paper given at the Third Annual Meeting of the Shakespeare Association of America in March 1975.)

Dream offers a paradigm of the two settings of Shakespeare plays. The plot shifts from city to country and back to city. Usually the characters find the city too constricting for their desires, move to the place of freedom which then becomes too confusing and fearsome, and then return to the first place.

473   Komiyama, Hiroshi. [Shadow and Substance in *A Midsummer Night's Dream.*] *Shuryu* (Doshisha University), 1975, pp. 168-81. (Japanese--not seen)

474   Lee, Virgil. "Puck's 'Tailor': A Mimic Pun?" *Shakespeare Quarterly*, 26 (1975), 55-57.

Among other connotations, the old aunt's "tailor" (II.i.51-57) carries sexual suggestions. (Anticipated by Hilda M. Hulme in item 154.) See also item 57.

475 Lengeler, Rainer. *Das Theater der leidenschaftlichen Phantasie. Shakespeares "Sommernachtstraum" als Spiegel seiner Dichtungstheorie* [Fancy's Theatre. Shakespeare's *Midsummer Night's Dream* as Mirror of His Poetics]. Habilitationsschrift, Kiel. Kieler Beiträge zur Anglistik und Amerikanistic, 11. Neümünster: Karl Wachholtz Verlag, 1975. 234 pp. (German)

This study attempts to get at Shakespeare's poetics through an analysis of the meaning of three "enacted metaphors": dream, drama, and magical transformations. Chapter 1 traces the meaning of these metaphors in the contexts of Elizabethan cosmology, psychology, and art theory. Chapter 2 shows how the three metaphors are used in scenes from *Richard II* and *The Tempest* to reveal the inner soul (hidden guilt, love). Chapter 3, which deals with scenes of nature animism in *Dream*, shows that the imagination in states of passion is instrumental in the manifestation of the supernatural. Chapter 4 offers "a continuous interpretation of *Dream* with emphasis on the interdependence of events and plots and the metadramatic implications of this interaction." The summaries of these last two chapters as they are given in Habicht, *English and American Studies in German* (see item 720), for 1975 (published in 1976), pp. 81-84, are themselves very difficult to understand and summarize. They have to do with the relationship between action and deep metaphor within the triangle of artist, play, and audience.

476 Link, Franz H. "Die Zeit [Time] in Shakespeares *A Midsummer Night's Dream* and *The Merchant of Venice*." *Shakespeare Jahrbuch* (Heidelberg), 1975, pp. 121-36. (German)

Examines the fictionalization of time in drama. Distinguishes different levels on which time is fictionalized and categorizes the various possibilities and effects of its use. The theory developed is applied to *Dream*. This appears as an appendix in the author's *Dramaturgie der Zeit* (item 510). See also item 399.

476a   May, Susan Hartman. "A Survey of the Criticism of *A
       Midsummer Night's Dream*." Ph.D. dissertation,
       University of Pennsylvania, 1974. *DAI*, 36 (1975), 278A.

       A massive presentation (1115 pp.) of attitudes and
       quotations from the enormous body of criticism in English,
       German, and French from 1662 to 1974 arranged
       discursively under 21 major headings (such as Setting,
       Atmosphere, Style, Duration of the Action, Fairies, etc.)
       and 81 minor headings. The intention is to neglect nothing
       of significance. Includes a detailed index and an extensive
       bibliography of early comments on the play.

477   Miller, Ronald F. "*A Midsummer Night's Dream*: The Fairies,
       Bottom, and the Mystery of Things." *Shakespeare
       Quarterly*, 26 (1975), 254-68.

       The fairies are not to be seen as blatant allegories of an
       unseen world which controls us, but rather as suggestive
       of the mysteriousness of our own existence in matters of
       love, luck, imagination, and even faith. "The problem is
       how to explore the rich implications of the [Pauline] echo
       [in Bottom's waking speech] without overdoing it." To find
       a specific insight of a large nature is to "run roughshod
       over the delicate distinctions which have characterized the
       mode of existence of these elusive beings." The effects of
       the fairies we may interpret in two ways: as a natural
       disorder mythologized and as the workings of some
       imminence behind events. "The important thing is the
       multivalency of the perspective." See item 14 for other
       discussions of fairies.

478   Opalski, Jósef. "Psychodeliczny *Sen nocy letniej*" [A
       Psychodelic *Midsummer Night's Dream*]. *Życie literackie*,
       25, no. 43 (1975), 7. (Polish--not seen)

479   Oyama, Toshiko. "Form and Rhetoric in Shakespearean
       Comedy." *Shakespeare Studies* (Tokyo), 11 (1975), 1-27.
       Reprinted in the author's *Shakespeare's World of Words*.
       Tokyo: Shinozaki-Shorin, 1975.

       Attributes the success of *Dream* not to its use of comic
       conventions but rather to the "power of words and
       rhetoric." The "concord of discord" is the essence of the

play. Provides a brief (pp. 8-14) statement of the main
themes and events.

480   Rodway, Allan. *English Comedy: Its Role and Nature from
      Chaucer to the Present Day*. Berkeley: University of
      California Press; London: Chatto & Windus, 1975. 288
      pp.

      While the element of farce is large, so that the play
      might not be supposed in the strict sense a comedy, it has,
      nonetheless, a serious theme: "namely that an imbalance of
      body, mind and emotions (or anything analogous to these)
      is undesirable." The play should be taken symbolically, but
      there is "no *fixed* symbolic significance, nor is any one
      character a model of the balance and harmony exemplified
      by the play itself; yet as a whole it has the effect of most
      dreams in being often experientially meaningful, though
      sometimes merely pleasurable." (Pp. 100-103)

480a Smith, Warren D. *Shakespeare's Playhouse Practice: A
      Handbook*. Hanover, N. H.: The University Press of
      New England for the University Press of Rhode Island,
      1975. xii, 119 pp.

      Gives ten or so references (there is an index) to places
      in *Dream* where we can assume Shakespeare is calling
      attention to the playhouse itself, to the movement of actors,
      especially onto and off of the stage, to the audience, and
      to special conventions of the theatre (when, for example,
      the daylight of a performance must be taken for night).

481   Snodgrass, W. D. "Moonshine and Sunny Beams:
      Ruminations on *A Midsummer Night's Dream*." *In Radical
      Pursuit: Critical Essays and Lectures*. New York: Harper
      & Row, 1975, pp. 203-240. Reprint. 1977, and in *The
      Writers Craft: Hopwood Lectures, 1965-81*. Ed. Robert
      A. Martin. Ann Arbor: Univ. of Michigan Press, 1982,
      pp. 144-80.

      A long, talky overview of most of the motifs of the play.
      There are large generalizations about culture and human
      nature, allusions to other literature, and constant attention
      to the texture, especially verbal, of the play. The play is
      seen to reflect tension between abstinence and indulgence,

between the sexes over who shall dominate, between fathers and children as to who rules and the extent to which. It is a play in which lovers hurt the ones they love and lovers love what is denied. "The play's purpose is, in part, to make us more eager for marriage and for bed; it does this partly by its mockery of Romantic Love. At the same time it helps reveal and expiate our fear of marriage, even of sex itself." There is much speculation about the culture and psychology of romantic love, acting, weaving, and the moon. Not uncharacteristic of the kind of comment made is the following: "Peter Quince--whose name echoes Penis Cunt--has trouble keeping Bottom in his place."

482   Traci, Philip. "Religious Controversy in *Romeo and Juliet*:
        The Play and Its Historical Context." *Michigan
        Academician*, 8 (1975-76), 319-25.

The playlet's parody of *Romeo* shows that the conflict of the earlier play was one of "a religiously mixed marriage" (Juliet is Jewish). Here Pyra*mass* is Popish, Thisbe Jewish (note "Elijah the *Tishbite*"). (This reading is tongue-in-cheek.) See also item 131.

483   Weld, John. "*A Midsummer Night's Dream.*" *Meaning in
        Comedy. Studies in Elizabethan Romantic Comedy.*
        Albany: State University of New York Press, 1975, pp.
        91-206.

Dream is a series of metaphors made dramatic through actions and characters that serve "to explain, to make funny, and to evaluate" what "gets into" people when they fall in love. The four lovers are "generic mankind": "they exemplify the passionate silliness and the happy ending of man as man." Their flight and pursuit to the wood is a figure of lovers' flight to and pursuit of the torment of passionate turmoil. The separate groups and actions in the woods--treated with a smile and sympathy--present "the disorder of passionate unreason by way of fantastic allegory." (In many ways *Dream* resembles the moralities.) Puck and Oberon represent, superficially, Fortune, whose caprices dominate passionate men, and profoundly, Providential design. All are wakened in the end by the harmonies of the passions subdued by reason. This harmony has not been produced by human reason (mankind in general remains passionate and absurd) but rather by that of a superior power. The knowledge of the illusory quality of the whole experience of love, which the playlet shows, enables us to avoid the tragedy potential in our passionate natures.

484 Willson, Robert F., Jr. "Shakespeare's Method in *A Midsummer Night's Dream* and *Love's Labour's Lost.*" *"Their Form Confounded": Studies in the Burlesque Play from Udall to Sheridan.* The Hague: Mouton, 1975, pp. 27-56.

The central plot of *Dream* is a burlesque treatment of the typical romance triangle with the ludicrous effect achieved by adding another woman and thus exaggerating the confusion. Theseus is the only sane one, his marriage ideal. He will not allow tragedy (brought on by the harsh Athenian law) to dampen the joy of his wedding ceremony. The love plot pokes fun at such romances as Chaucer's "Knight's Tale." Titania is made a lunatic in her licentiousness to illustrate Theseus' second class of those of imagination all compact. The mechanicals represent the third class, the poets. While the lovers' actions reflect a broad farcical treatment of romance, the mechanicals' playlet ridicules both the young lovers and certain popular tastes in literature. It spoofs the mixing of mirth and tragedy in Thomas Preston's *Cambises* and certain stylistic features of Golding's translation of Ovid (such as repetition, alliteration, inappropriate rhythm, and more), as well as Ovidian narratives in general. Three characteristics of the rustics associate them with their medieval predecessors, the dramatists of the morality school: their literal-mindedness, total sincerity, and concern with the reactions of the audience. They remind us of Nicholas Udall's *Ralph Roister Doister* (Bottom is like Rafe), George Peele's *The Old Wives' Tale,* and *Fulgens and Lucrece.* The second half of the essay, following a paragraph on ways the two plays are similar, discusses burlesque elements in *Love's Labour's Lost.* See also item 415 and 496.

485 Zimmerman, Heinz. *Die Personifikation in Drama Shakespeares.* Schriftenreihe der Deutschen Shakespeare-Gesellschaft West. N.s., 12. Heidelberg: Quelle & Meyer, 1975. 260 pp. (German)

Interprets Helena (I.i.222-45) as expressing the play's
theme in an emblematic way with her reference to "blind
Cupid," suggests that detailed characterization of the four
lovers was thereby rendered unnecessary, and views Puck's
actions as a concretization of the thematic emblem.
Zimmerman finds "love" less obviously and rhetorically
personified here than in *Love's Labour's Lost*. (Pp.
210-15) (There is a synopsis of the dissertation in Habicht, 1974,
item 720.)

486   Anzai, Tetsuo. [Dream, Theatre, and the World--Materials
      and Construction of *A Midsummer Night's Dream*.] *Sophia*
      (Sophia University), 25, no. 2 (1976), 58-79. (Japanese)

      Traces the emergence, through the fusion of various
heterogeneous traditions, of a typically Shakespearean comic
form as a parable of a spiritual metamorphosis.

486a Condee, Ralph Waterbury. "Goneril Without a White
      Beard." *Shakespeare on Film Newsletter*, 1, no. 1
      (1976), 1, 5, 7.

      Describes a Shakespeare course for non-majors at The
Pennsylvania State University in which the Peter Hall film
of *Dream* is one of seven films used. Once the films were
added the approval rate for the course jumped from 74% to
100%.

487   Cook, Albert. *Shakespeare's Enactment: The Dynamics of
      Renaissance Theatre*. Chicago: Swallow Press, 1976. xi,
      257 pp.

      In difficult, abstract generalizations, Cook discusses
(pp. 18-25) the "splendid counterpointing of divergencies"
in the play, the levels of theatrical being and exclusion,
and the complexities of illusion, giving special attention to
the lovers and the rustics. The latter, for example, are
"caught in an unperceived impossibility of incommunicable
make-believe." Bottom's failure to become Pyramus
"articulates his inarticulateness by staging the incapacity to
act." His playlet offers "the implied significative
ridiculousness of ontological distortion"; it is a
"metatheatrical relegation of tragedy to inarticulateness" (p.

122). Love is taken to be the single subject of the play and to function divergently for each of the four orders.

488 Doran, Madeleine. *Shakespeare's Dramatic Language*. Madison: University of Wisconsin Press, 1976. x, 254 pp.

Dream, Romeo, and *Richard II,* all perhaps of 1595, illustrate (pp. 11-16) Shakespeare's increasing mastery of dramatic style. *Dream,* largely of Shakespeare's own fabrication, is *Romeo* in a comic mood. Its setting is primarily experienced verbally. The fairies can be fully comprehended only in language, for they cannot be truly represented. Words make the wood, but they suggest both a heroic background and the world of farms and cottages. The uses of prose or meter (rimed or not), each with its special effect, are described. The scene with Bottom and Titania (III.i, IV.i) is "a triumph of orchestration" in diction, image, verse, and prose. See items 27a and 131.

488a Enstrom, Frederic A. "Humanism as the Key to Shakespeare's Relevance." *Focus: Teaching English in Southeastern Ohio*, 2 (May 1976), 46-52. (not seen)

Apparently uses *Hamlet* and *Dream* to illustrate the thesis that Shakespearean drama requires us to pierce the surface to search for the essence of the human experience.

489 Ford, Jane M. "The Father/Daughter/Suitor Triangle in Shakespeare, Dickens, Conrad, and Joyce." Ph.D. dissertation, State University of New York, Buffalo, 1975. *DAI*, 36 (1976), 4507A.

Dream, like *Two Gentlemen,* illustrates denunciation of the suitor by the father. See item 187.

490 Halio, Jay L. "Nightingales that Roar, Morrises Filled with Mud: The Dramatic Language of *A Midsummer Night's Dream*." *Shakespeare Newsletter*, 26 (1976), 35. (An abstract of a paper given at the Modern Language Association meeting on 28 December 1975)

The language of *Dream* is repeatedly undercut by its odd opposite: tenor by vehicle, tone by the actual sense of the

words. Hermia's series of oaths (I.i.169-78), Titania's foul
weather speech (II.i.81-117), Oberon's "I know a bank"
speech (II.ii.249-58), and the malapropisms of the
rustics--all exhibit this form of linguistic complexity.

491   Entry Deleted.

492   McCanles, Michael. "The Literal and the Metaphorical:
      Dialectic or Interchange." *PMLA*, 91 (1976), 279-90.

      In an effort to restate the relationship between literal
      and metaphoric, to find, among other aspects, two kinds of
      relations--dialectic and interchange--*Dream* is used as the
      example of the dialectic. Considers how the distinction
      between literal and metaphoric works with the two worlds
      (the play *and* the fiction it represents), the latter of which
      itself has two worlds (Athens, forest). What is metaphor in
      one (Athens) becomes literal in the other (forest)--"Bottom
      is an ass." The play (the first world) calls attention to
      itself as an artifice, existing *in* London. In these
      relationships a dialectic takes place. Real and fiction fuse in
      a "dizzying manner."

493   Naef, Irene. *Die Lieder in Shakespeares Komödien: Gehalt
      und Funktion* [The Songs in Shakespeare's Comedies:
      Substance and Function]. Dissertation, University of
      Zurich. Schweizer Anglistische Arbeiten, 86. Bern:
      Francke, 1976. 371 pp. (German)

      An examination of the individual songs in context
      followed by a summarizing section in which the diversity of
      the songs is ordered into categories, and general critical
      conclusions are advanced--in particular that the
      development of Shakespeare's use of songs shows their
      increasing integration into the structure of the plays.
      There is a summary in English (pp. 7-8).

494   Pagnini, Marcello. *Shakespeare e il Paradigma della
      Specularità: Lettura di due Campioni, "King Lear" e "A
      Midsummer Night's Dream."* Saggi critici, 3. Pisa: Pacini,
      1976. (Italian--not seen)

      On aspects of technique in the two plays.

495   Plummer, Denis Lee. "Generative Poesis: The Book and
      Child Metaphor in Renaissance Poetry." Ph.D.
      dissertation, University of Washington, 1975. *DAI*, 37
      (1976), 990A-91A.

      Applies theory of generative poesis to *Dream* (one of
      four "poems"). The theory pertains "to the sexual and
      aesthetic making of children and poems for the purpose of
      redeeming the earthly garden ravaged by Time."

496   Seufert, Robert George. "The Mirrored Art: Dramatic
      Parody on the Popular Tudor Stage." Ph.D. dissertation,
      Ohio University, 1975. *DAI*, 36 (1976), 7444A.

      Discusses parody in *Dream* (and four other plays) in
      order to deduce Elizabethan attitudes toward the nature and
      purpose of drama. The parodies in general imply a reaction
      against (1) amateurism and (2) artlessness (lack of decorum
      and failure to achieve a complex and intelligible pattern).
      See item 60 and 484.

497   Uchida, Yumi. [Fairy World in Shakespeare's Plays.] *Sella*
      (Shirayuri Joshi Daigaku), 5 (1976), 39-49.
      (Japanese--not seen)

      Apparently discusses the dramatic function of fairies in
      Dream and *The Tempest*.

498   Zesmer, David M. "*A Midsummer Night's Dream.*" *Guide to
      Shakespeare*. The Barnes & Noble Outline Series. New
      York: Barnes & Noble, 1976, pp. 107-112, 124-25.

      A brief introduction summarizing the play and giving
      comments from critics.

499   Arthos, John. "The Dream and the Vision." *Shakespeare's
      Use of Dream and Vision*. London: Bowes; Totowa, N.
      J.: Rowman and Littlefield, 1977, pp. 15-84.

      From many points of view--"from the events, from
      Bottom's words, from what Theseus says about fancy and
      lunacy and love and poetry, the play has been entertaining
      us with innumerable ways of looking at life as if it were a

dream, making us wonder if reality and dream are not
forever masking as the other." The events in the play work
out what must have been the troubles experienced
beforehand by Theseus and Hippolyta. Moods, details,
sequence of events all suggest the special illogic
experienced in dreams, attesting to Coleridge's view that
"Shakespeare availed himself of the title of this play in his
own mind, and worked upon it as a dream throughout."

500   Barthel, Carol. "Prince Arthur and Bottom the Weaver: The
      Renaissance Dream of the Fairy Queen." *Spenser:
      Classical, Medieval, Renaissance, and Modern*. Ed. David
      A. Richardson. Proceedings from a Special Session at the
      Twelfth Conference on Medieval Studies in Kalamazoo,
      Michigan, 5-8 May 1977. Cleveland: Cleveland State
      University, 1977, pp. 72-91. With commentary by Walter
      R. Davis. (microfiche)

      Finds a general reference to *Sir Thopas* in the
      appearance of a Fairy Queen to her mortal lover. Bottom is
      a parody of the hero of a fairy romance, possibly of Prince
      Arthur in Book I of *The Faerie Queene*. Comparisons are
      made with Spenser and Chaucer.

501   Bourg-Oulé, Anne Marie le. "*Le Songe d'une nuit d'été*:
      Perspectives de la fête" [Perspectives of the Festival].
      In Françoise Charpentier. "Poétique et langage
      dramatique." *Revue de littérature comparée* (Paris), 202
      (1977), 300-301. (French)

      The festival and dream elements are merely theatricalized
      covers for social conditions (Theseus' rule, the separation
      of classes) which are not ultimately disturbed. (Report of
      seminar presentation)

502   Colley, John Scott. "*Bartholomew Fair*: Ben Jonson's 'A
      Midsummer Night's Dream.'" *Comparative Drama*, 11
      (1977), 63-72.

      The plays resemble each other. "The daylight comic
      magic" of Jonson's play "works wonders" of transformation
      and regeneration "almost equal to the eye-drops and
      confusions mischievously administered by the invisible
      Puck." In both the acceptance of one's folly becomes the

prelude to self-knowledge. For other comparisons with this play see items 566mm-nn.

503 Fox, Levi. *An Illustrated Introduction to Shakespeare's Flowers*. Stratford-upon-Avon: Shakespeare Birthplace Trust, 1977. [32 pp.]

With colored plates accompanying relevant passages (several from *Dream*). See item 45 for a list of other items on plants.

504 Herbert, T. Walter. *Oberon's Mazéd World: A Judicious Young Elizabethan Contemplates "A Midsummer Night's Dream," With a Mind Shaped by the Learning of Christendom Modified by the New Naturalist Philosophy and Excited by the Vision of a Rich, Powerful England*. Baton Rouge: Louisiana State University Press, 1977. [xxvi], 200 pp.

Attempts to follow the reactions of an imaginary young, educated Londoner through a performance of *Dream* in 1595. The observations are primarily in his voice (first person plural). Above all, this mind is "full of notions about ancient and modern cosmologies" (p. 65).

Chapter 1 describes the way we are willingly teased into the fairy world from court and city--prepared by other plays, especially those of Peele and Lyly, and by Chaucer--and return in the end to a new Athens (before cruel, now full of mirth).

Chapter 2 perceives a pattern ("strange, admirable, and funny") in the selection of the names, a pattern suggestive of dreams, based on "error" or mistakes, strangely derived from familiar components. "*Demetrius* and *Lysander* sound crazily like a pair of names from "The Knight's Tale."

Chapter 3 considers the harmonious mix of the three components of Fairyland: folk tale, romance, and classical story and objects to Jan Kott's interpretation (item 239). The Olympian character of the unruly fairy rulers gives them a "celestial order" of amoral transcendence just as it does the unruly gods of Homer. The fairies are not witches, are not malevolent.

Chapter 4 contrasts the Babylonian world of the playlet with that in Ovid's and Chaucer's treatment of the story and with Athens. The world of the playlet is philosophically, terrifyingly naturalistic (Newtonian), more desolate than Ovid's world of "crass causality"; that of Chaucer and Athens is animistic, genial.

Chapter 5 discusses the animist and naturalist world models as they coexisted in the Renaissance common and scientific minds. Pyramus talking to the wall is the extreme animist, as the thrust of the whole play is generally. Oberon's Rule encourages "Questions of a Healthy Natural Order, Justice and Loving Tolerance."

Chapter 6 describes the fervor of scientific conversation and analyzes the mix of the two modes of thought, in mathematicians especially (John Dee in particular), who "like Quince and Bottom . . . unwittingly constructed a naturalist world and still talked of things other than business in an unconstructed animist language."

Chapter 7 applies the complications of thought among contemporaries to the various aspects of the play. It presents a "double antithesis": four world models, "the two contrasted worlds through which the Athenians and the Babylonians move and the false models they implicitly believe in." Bottom, animist in a naturalist world, contrasts with Lysander, naturalist in an animist world.

Chapter 8 suggests ways Bottom and Company reflect Londoners' "practical self-confidence and philosophical obtuseness." Bottom has traits of "great merchants, financiers," etc. "Doctor Faustus . . . paid with his soul for powers fully offered to [an uninterested] Bottom out of love."

Chapter 9 looks at "inductive structures," after describing some of the ways Elizabethans were acquiring the habit of mind. The double plot gave a chance for induction.

Chapter 10, in turning up the theoretical basis of the play, draws parallels between Oberon's powers and those of God. In Athens disproportion drives out disproportion and harmony is restored. Hippolyta "exemplifies the precious second article of the naturalist creed, respect for unexpected data." See items 193, 234 and 155.

505   Herz, Judith Scherer. "Play World and Real World: Dramatic
        Illusion and the Dream Metaphor." *English Studies in
        Canada* (Toronto), 3 (1977), 386-400.

        The play-as-dream topos clearly had a special fascination
for Shakespeare. It offered him a congenial viewpoint for
the exploration of the nature of dramatic illusion as well as
means for creating that illusion. In *Dream* the metaphor is
"the very central concern of the play" and the basis for its
form (as it is with *The Tempest*). The characters think
they dream what we see in the play. Each has a dream life
of his or her own and at the same time is a character in
the dream of another. There are three dream realms: the
whole play, the lovers' forest experience, and Bottom's.
Bottom stands at the intersection of dream and real world,
preventing the spectator from entering completely the
illusion, which ironically strengthens the illusion. *Dream* "is
a play about playing." But in the end it maintains the
distinction between reality and play-dream; in *The Tempest*,
however, "the equation of dream-play-reality is total." See
item 149.

506   Huntley, John F. "An Objective Test for Literary
        Comprehension." *College English*, 39 (1977), 361-67.

        Gives a 15 minute test on *Dream* which asks students to
place passages in chronological order.

507   Janakiram, Alur. *Reason and Love in Shakespeare: A
        Selective Study of Three Poems and Five Plays*. Andhra
        Pradesh, India: Triveni, 1977. Ch. 5.

        Looks at contemporary views as to the role of
"phantasy." At times it aided Will (and thus misled), at
times, Reason. Pierre Charron's remarks on the heat of the
imagination are compared with Theseus'. In general the play
asks us to contemplate the relationship between reason and
fantasy. The play makes them two allies rather than
adversaries.

508   Kupper, Hans Jörg. "A Local Habitation and a Name:
        Bemerkungen zum [Remarks on] *Sommernachtstraum*."
        Shakespeare Jahrbuch (Heidelberg), 1977, 51-69.
        (German)

After a brief survey of the treatments of Shakespeare's verse (Elisabeth Tschopp, item 133, and Brian Vickers, item 333), his verse and prose (Jörg Hasler, item 449), and rhymes (F. W. Ness, item 27a), Kupper examines the speeches of the lovers and reveals how the presence or absence of verse, *enjambement*, etc. led him to block their scenes. Kupper concedes that "verse characteristics" can only be determined generally. See item 77.

509   Lamoine, Georges. "Le thème du jeu dans *The Rape of the Lock*." *Bulletin de la Société d'Études Anglo-Americaines des XVIIe et XVIIIe Siècles*, 4 (June 1977), 21-45. (French--not seen)

Apparently comparisons are made with *Dream*.

510   Link, Franz H. "Die Zeit [Time] in Shakespeares *Sommernachtstraum* und *Kaufmann von Venedig*." *Dramaturgie der Zeit*. Rombach Hochschul Paperback, 87. Freiberg im Breisgau: Rombach, 1977, pp. 206-221. (German)

The essay is an appendix. There is an English summary of the book in it and one in Habicht, *English and American Studies in German* (1977), pp. 52-53 (see item 720). The essay is published separately in *Shakespeare Jahrbuch* (Heidelberg), 1975 (item 476).

511   McCall, John. *William Shakespeare: Spacious in the Possession of Dirt*. Washington: University Press of America, 1977. xxv, 348 pp.

Considers (pp. 196-200) *Dream* "quite mild, with just a few passages of inoffensive bawdy." Gives thirty-two citations with brief comments. "Pap" (V.i.287) is on the list. See item 57.

512   Nakamura, Yasue. [Song of Bottom.] *Helicon* (Ehime University), 29 (1977), 63-85. (Japanese--not seen)

Apparently discusses comical catharsis in *Dream*.

513 Paolucci, Anne. "The Lost Days in *A Midsummer Night's Dream*." *Shakespeare Quarterly*, 28 (1977), 317-26.

One may explain the apparent difficulty with the time scheme (27 April to 1 May) by a careful consideration of "a set of highly original clues" in the long, disorienting, "floating" night scene, especially of its "intervals of rest" and "reminders of sleep." Though all is subjected to the control of the moon, which is the fairies' element, when things familiar are temporarily destroyed, time does not stand still. We are provided the two end-points, before and after, at the beginning, and thus are alerted "to *awareness* of time and to the psychological effects we can expect in characters subject to such awareness." The events of Act II take place on the night of 28-29 April; Demetrius' interval of sleep (III.ii) the night of 29-30; the interval which marks the end of the wild chase and the proper regrouping the night of 30 April-1 May; the new moon and playlet the night of 1-2 May. Theseus marks the return of the normal diurnal cycle. For other discussions of the duration of the action and time see items 124, 302-3, 332, 385, 389, 399, 476-76a, 548, 567, 744, 752 and 874.

514 Ramsey, Clifford Earl. "*A Midsummer Night's Dream*." *Homer to Brecht: The European Epic and Dramatic Traditions*. Ed. Michael Seidel and Edward Mendelson. New Haven: Yale University Press, 1977, pp. 214-37.

Designed as an introduction to the play, this essay proceeds through the "scenic structure" (using Madeleine Doran's division into seven scenes; see item 855) in order to show that the organization is "everywhere expressive of diversity and variety and opposition, and yet at the same time paradoxically everywhere expressive also of harmony and concord and integration." It is the "dynamism" and "perspectivism" of the play and its affirmations which account for the play's deep hold on the contemporary imagination.

515 Scott, William O. *The God of Arts: Ruling Ideas in Shakespeare's Comedies*. Humanistic Studies, 48. Lawrence: University of Kansas Publications, 1977. 140 pp.

Of the seven steps which shape "characters' concepts of themselves" in the comedies (which are combined in most plays), *Dream* provides an example of the way forces outside--either supernatural or artistic or both--influence the characters toward self-awareness and their own good. Chance is willed by the characters, in contrast to *Errors*. (Pp. 48-50)

516   Smith, Stephen L. "*A Midsummer Night's Dream*: Shakespeare, Play and Metaplay." *Centennial Review*, 21 (1977), 194-209.

Dream can be read as a playful study of Shakespeare's ideas about play, of which a play is one form. It exhibits that conflict, contradiction, and uncertainty (these are illustrated from the play) which Johan Huizinga finds at the basis of play. It stands for the play before the love (foreplay) which consummates all these marriages. It reflects, too, the striving for order of the game. The fairies represent the mythopoeic mind seeing life as synthetic. To this world we may respond with Bottom the scientist or Theseus the psychologist or we may simply accept it, on faith, religiously. At selected moments we are teased by the play into the mystifying region between illusion and reality, drawn into the game, that is. "Shakespeare hints at and points the way to something deeper [than the ordinary world], some ultimately benevolent, game-playing spirit or mystery behind it all." Bottom, though he is not aware of it, is the means to "some hidden truth which is alluded to throughout the whole play." See item 429 for other discussions of game-play.

517   Speaight, Robert. *Shakespeare: The Man and His Achievement*. London: J. M. Dent; New York: Stein and Day, 1977. xi, 384 pp.

After considering (pp. 108-116) the miracle of the fusion of materials from such varied sources, Speaight trips through the play making light, suggestive comments all the way. E.g., of Bottom being transformed into an ass: he has also been "transformed into a gentleman." The Southampton-Heneage marriage of 2 May 1595 seems the likely one as an occasion for the play. We should look for a ceremony at which the Queen was *not* present. The analogy between Bottom's waking speech and that of a mystic communicating his Beatific Vision may or may not be accidental. "There are metaphysics in the *Dream* if you choose to look for them."

518 Stückle-Gerbes, Peter. "Mystification und Doublebind-Phänomene der Kommunikationstheorie bei Shakespeare: Kommunikationstheoretische Untersuchungen der dramatischen Dichtungen *Ein Sommernachtstraum* und *König Lear*" [Mystification and Double-bind-Phenomena in the Communication Theory of Shakespeare: Communication Theory Investigations of the Dramatic Works of *Dream* and *King Lear*]. Ph.D. dissertation, Medical Faculty, Heidelberg University, 1977. (German--not seen)

519 Willson, Robert F., Jr. *Shakespeare's Opening Scenes*. Salzburg Studies in English Literature. Elizabethan & Renaissance Studies, 66. Salzburg: Universität Salzburg, 1977. 217 pp.

Each character is defined in the opening scene in terms of his or her attitude (implied or expressed) toward the old and new moons which have certain symbolic values. "Lysander is running away not from the old moon but into its arms." (Pp. 49-59)

520 Yamada, Reiko. [*A Midsummer Night's Dream*--Harmony and Reality.] *Eigo Kenkyū* (Tokyo University), 12 (1977), 111-42. (Japanese)

Criticizes Jan Kott's interpretation (item 239), emphasizing the poetic catharsis wrought by imaginative transformation of reality into harmony. There is a summary in English.

521 Ansari, A. A. "Shakespeare's Allegory of Love." *Aligarh Journal of English Studies* (India), 3 (1978), 44-62.

The play explores "the various manifestations of the irrationality of love, governed by chaotic, subconscious impulses and drives." The wood is "the home of potent and dark energies," Titania's bower suggestive of "complete instinctual unity in the human," the dissension over the changeling the overt symbol of "irrational, antagonistic, submerged forces" in Oberon and Titania. Eye, moon, dream, and play support these notions.

522 Beaurline, L. A. *Jonson and Elizabethan Comedy: Essays in Dramatic Rhetoric*. San Marino: The Huntington Library, 1978. xi, 351 pp.

The play generates laughter and wonder (two kinds of awareness), sometimes separately, sometimes (with Bottom and Titania) together. Bottom's experience (the Corinthian texts are considered) is *like* a vision of paradise: but he does not have such "because he does not understand it." With the lovers, the audience sees "the natural perspective of human foolishness first and gets the wonderful supernatural insight later." Our reactions to the playlet combine laughter with a sense of courtesy (the actors are "deadly serious"). The play penetrates through Theseus' apparent jesting (the "self-deprecating joke" of Shakespeare's) to "the reality of love." "It begins with natural affection and ends in a contemplation of a wonderful, including spirit." (Pp. 86-102)

523 Bevington, David. "'But we are spirits of another sort' The Dark Side of Love and Magic in *A Midsummer Night's Dream*." *Medieval and Renaissance Studies*. Ed. Siegfried Wenzel. Medieval & Renaissance Series, 7. Chapel Hill: University of North Carolina Press, 1978, 80-92.

"The dark side of love is seldom very far away in this play." The "truly frightening illusions" of Puck and the regality of Oberon represent contrasting forces within the fairy kingdom. "Their chief power to do good lies in withholding the mischief of which they are capable." The forest is itself ambivalent, as is the moon, and the whole experience reflects inner, erotic desires, though Jan Kott (item 239) goes too far. An essential tension is between sexual desire and external restraint. Titania, "rather than descending into the realm of human passion and perversity, . . . has attempted to raise Bottom into her own." Dark and affirmative love are reconciled in the image of Titania and the Ass's head.

524 Clayton, Thomas. "Shakespeare's Cynophobia: A 'Collied'
    Addition to the Canine Catalogue." *Studies in English
    and American Literature*. Ed. John L. Cutler and
    Lawrence S. Thompson. *American Notes and Queries,*
    Supplement, Volume 1. Troy, N. Y.: Whitson, 1978, pp.
    60-64.

    Shakespeare's *collied* (I.i.145) is a "plurisignative"
    coinage that means both "blackened" and "dogged," and
    possibly as well the sense "to move the neck; to turn the
    head from side to side."

525 Cox, John D. "Homely Matter and Multiple Plots in Peele's
    Old Wives Tale." *Texas Studies in Literature and
    Language*, 20 (1978), 330-46.

    Cites in passing (p. 331) a number of parallels between
    Wives Tale and *Dream* to suggest that the former be given
    the "due" the latter has recently got. Both deal with
    popular folk material; both apologize disingenuously for
    themselves in their titles; both have been slow to win
    serious critical consideration. The one is not taken to be a
    source of the other.

526 Dawson, Anthony. *Indirections: Shakespeare and the Art of
    Illusion*. Toronto: University of Toronto Press, 1978.
    xv, 194 pp.

    Though there is no disguised manipulator in *Dream*, it is
    nonetheless through the manipulation of dramatic illusion
    that the play produces that clarification about experience
    which is its purpose, that reconciliation of opposites: love
    out of hate, sight out of blindness, and natural harmony
    out of chaos and disorder. The best way to focus on the
    use of illusion in the play is through (1) IV.i, when the
    lovers are wakened and the heroes arrive ("we get a
    metaphorical enactment of the central action of the play");
    (2) comparisons with *The Tempest*, Prospero's "revels"
    speech being like Puck's epilogue; and (3) the way the
    playlet comments on the whole play: "The play insists on its
    own silliness and hence, by a species of paradox, forces us
    to take it seriously, just as the [playlet] insists on its own
    seriousness and ends up being ridiculous." The magic of
    the play is actually the magic of theatre. (Pp. 62-70) See
    items 60 and 149.

526a   Gibson, William. *Shakespeare's Games*. New York:
       Atheneum, 1978. vii. 226 pp.

       Dream is a series of "moves" and "objects" on four levels
       with the "master promise" being that which animates every
       romantic comedy written--"boy meets girl, boy loses girl,
       boy gets girl"--"it is the spring at the center" of *Dream*.
       Oberon, for example, is a "move," Titania, an "object."
       The truth in this "forest" (the *Dream*) is savage: "man's
       reason is a dream, and sexual pairing is maniacal." (Pp.
       46-49) See item 429 for other discussions of game-play.

527   Gilman, Ernest B. "The Natural Perspective in
       Shakespearean Comedy: *Twelfth Night* and *A Midsummer
       Night's Dream*." *The Curious Perspective: Literary and
       Pictorial Wit in the Seventeenth Century*. New Haven and
       London: Yale University Press, 1978, pp. 129-66.

       In general this book finds a connection between the
       verbal wit of seventeenth century literature and the visual
       wit of the "curious perspective"--those pictures or devices
       which manipulated linear perspectives for special optical
       effects. *Dream*, it is argued, asks us to unite two
       conflicting perspectives, which reflect neatly from Bottom's
       double nature (he is human and beast). Bottom's dream
       suggests that there is both a bestial and a sacral dimension
       to the experience of love. These separate aspects belong to
       two separate clusters of opposed values that critics have
       noticed in the play: everyday and holiday, reason and love,
       reason and intuition, Athens and woods, and so on. Critics
       have generally assumed that the play favored one cluster or
       the other, that is, have been either Thesean or Hippolytan.
       The best criticism recognizes that the play balances these
       two points of view in a "comic equilibrium" which we can
       call "the double perspective" of comedy. The young lovers
       have such a double vision when they awake (IV.i.188-93).
       The audience of *Dream* does too, nudged back and forth
       across the border of the illusory and the real throughout
       the play, conscious of both, now enchanted, now detached.
       Shakespeare makes the audience "simultaneously conscious
       of the power and precariousness of the dramatic illusion."
       (This book is based on a 1976 Columbia University
       dissertation.)

528 Habicht, Werner. "Bottom Translated: Eine Anmerkung zur Geschichte deutscher Shakespeare-Übersetzungen" [A Note to the History of German Shakespeare Translation]. *Archiv*, 215 (1978), 86-89. (German)

On the problem of translating into German Bottom's name so that, on the one hand, its reference to his trade, weaving, is clear and, on the other, the pun on his bottomless dream and the sense of the expression "Bully Bottom" are suggested. Surveys all German versions of *Dream* from Andreas Gryphius (1657) to M. Hamburger (1971). See also item 25.

529 Handelsaltz, Michael. [An Ass's Head]. *Da'var ha-Shavu'ah* (Davar Daily, Tel Aviv), 23 June 1978. (Hebrew--not seen)

530 Handelsaltz, Michael. [A Midsummer Night's Dream of Erotic Madness]. *Da'var ha-Shavu'ah* (Davar Daily, Tel Aviv), 28 June 1978. (Hebrew--not seen)

531 Hibbard, G. R. "Adumbrations of *The Tempest* in *A Midsummer Night's Dream*." *Shakespeare Survey*, 31 (1978), 77-83.

The similarity between these plays has long been a commonplace of criticism. Indeed we might even think of them as "a distinct sub-species of Shakespearean comedy, magical comedy." In nature and function Puck and Ariel are similar--they are speedy spirits who can be invisible, seem able to control nature, serve masters whom they assist in plans for the good. The dominant feature of both plays, and that which sets them off from the rest of the *oeuvre*, is their use of magic for ends that are good, though the magic they draw on (one of the folk, one learned) is not the same. In *Dream* the magic makes little real difference with the lovers and Titania. Bottom is affected; he has a wonderful, inexplicable vision. His experience anticipates that of Alonso and Caliban, both of whom are moved by their experience when others are not. Both plays question the relationship between dream and waking consciousness, between dramatic illusion and reality. The dark suggestiveness of both plays, that of Puck's speech (V.i.368-76), for example, allows us, with Nicholas Rowe,

to join these two plays with *Hamlet* and *Macbeth*. See item
149 for other comparisons with *The Tempest*.

532   Iginla, Biodun. "Woman and Metaphor." *enclitic* (Department
      of French and Italian, University of Minnesota), 2, no. 1
      (1978), 27-37.

      The metaphors for women idealize, tame, mark, repress,
      and otherwise reduce or distance the threatening bodies of
      the women in a world dominated by men. "All the women in
      the play are castrated." For other studies of the place of
      women in the play see item 566s.

533   Iwasaki, Soji. [Iconography in *A Midsummer Night's
      Dream*]. *Eigo Seinen* (Tokyo), 124 (1978), 384-87.
      (Japanese--not seen)

      Elizabethan drama is "an iconographical fiction." *Dream*
      is a drama of Venus and Diana, and Puck is Cupid in
      disguise. See item 55 for a list of other discussions of
      mythological elements.

533a Levith, Murray J. *What's in Shakespeare's Names*. Hamden,
      Conn.: Archon Books, 1978. 147 pp.

      The names of the play are to be found in the myth of
      Theseus, in Plutarch, and in Ovid. A number of names are
      suggestive. *Hermia*, for example, suggests *Hermes*-Mercury,
      which perhaps accounts for her fiery personality. *Bottom* is
      taken to be a play on the anatomical *ass*. (Pp. 75-78) See
      item 155 for other discussions of names.

534   Moses, Joseph. "The Comic Compulsion." *Sewanee Review*,
      86 (1978), 84-100.

      Uses *Dream* to illustrate (pp. 96-100) a particular
      morphology of comedy, in which Moses sees "the comic as
      an abstract play of form perceived intellectually, a game
      whose rules are contradiction and antithesis" (p. 91). The
      play shows just what aspect of our erotic identities is
      appropriate to comedy: not the passion and boundless
      desire (which belongs to tragedy) but rather its bounded
      and limited counterpart--courtship and marriage. Comedy

reduces Eros to the proportions of conventional human behavior and then examines the limitations of the conventions. From the beginning of the play we have a comic duality--"a social *control* [the Athenian law] that becomes the condition for *discrepancy* [elopement]." This pattern of duality persists throughout the play. Even in the forest the lovers are subjected to the control of conventions and authority; faithlessness in these forest affairs is the chief example of contradiction. The contradiction inherent in the pattern of social authority is constantly illuminated by ironic examination, a perception which encourages us to accept these same kinds of difficulties in life.

535 Narita, Tatsuo. [Drama within Drama within Drama].
    Eibungaku-shi (Otani Women's University), 5 (1978),
    14-23. (Japanese--not seen)

    Discusses *Dream* and *As You Like It* ; if the world is a
    stage, "drama within drama" could be drama within drama
    within drama.

536 Nathan, Moshe. [*A Midsummer Night's Dream*]. *Ma'ariv* (Tel
    Aviv), 16 June 1978, pp. 32-33. (Hebrew--not seen)

537 Entry Deleted.

538 Ormerod, David. "*A Midsummer Night's Dream*: The Monster
    in the Labyrinth." *Shakespeare Studies*, 11 (1978),
    39-52.

    The myth of Theseus, "whose dynamic presence seems to
    have been hitherto unsuspected," with its constituent
    ingredients (Theseus, labyrinth, Minotaur) has been
    reworked and reassembled "so that the conflation of [its]
    overtones constitutes a new design." "To view the play this
    way is to observe it spring into a new and more acute focus
    and to bring together, holistically, the Athenian locale, the
    Duke and his Amazon bride-to-be, the Cretan maze
    transported across the seas for a renewed moral purpose,
    an updated Athenian tribute of youths and maidens, and,
    above all, a metamorphosed Minotaur in the half-beast,
    half-human figure of the transformed Bottom." The play
    depicts (within the limits of stage convention) "an act of

coitus between woman and ass." Fairies and young people were associated in the turf and hedge mazes of early England. The labyrinth is an icon of blinded wrong choice, the ass head, of passion. See also items 55 and 561.

539   Petronella, Vincent F. "Shakespeare's *A Midsummer Night's Dream*." *Explicator*, 37 (Fall 1978), 5-6.

The actors originally assigned the parts of parents in the playlet take other, symbolically appropriate parts in the final version, in keeping with the diminution of parental power in the play in general.

540   Riffaterre, Michael. *Semiotics of Poetry*. Bloomington and London: Indiana University Press, 1978. x, 213 pp.

Discusses (pp. 101-105) the significance for the French of the title "Bottom" of Rimbaud's prose poem. In the poem a lover becomes first a bird, then a bear, and finally a jackass. Shakespeare's text is what, for French readers' imagination, confers their significance upon all those animals (which taken together equal "the folly of love"). In French Bottom is "a notorious word." Its meaning (*derrière*) having long been suppressed in translations (the word *Bottom* has been used instead), it has acquired an especially heightened sense of that meaning; the jackass stands for "sex rampant" in a lover. See item 53.

541   Rydén, Mats. *Shakespearean Plant Names: Identifications and Interpretations*. Stockholm Studies in English, 43. Stockholm: Almquist & Wiksell International, 1978. 117 pp.

Lists the plants, concentrating on certain ones which are of special interest, their English and Latin names, and the difficulties of finding the right Swedish translation. There are sections on "Cowslip, Oxlip, and Primrose" (p. 72), "Eglantine and Muskrose" (p. 77), "Dian's bud and Cupid's flower" (p. 76). "Dian's bud" is identified with *Vitex agnus castus*, not with the *Artemisia vulgaris* (mugwort). "Cupid's flower" is the wild pansy (*Viola tricolor*). The difficulties with the "honeysuckle and woodbine" crux (II.i.251) are outlined in great detail (pp. 81-83). See items 45 and 685o.

542 Serio, John N. "Stevens, Shakespeare, and Peter Quince."
     Modern Language Studies, 9 (Winter 1978-79), 20-24.

     Examines the function of Quince in order to account for
     Stevens' use of him in a poem essentially meditative in
     spirit. The playlet shows, ironically, a love unwavering,
     eternal, with a serious function and thus expressing "the
     deepest truth in the play." In both poem and play Quince
     presents a brief drama illustrating the ideal nature of love,
     beauty, and art. See item 60.

543 Sillars, Stuart. "Phoebe and Phoebus: Bottom's Verbal
     Slip." *Notes and Queries*, 223 (1978), 125-26.

     "Phibbus' car" (I.ii.31), usually glossed as
     mispronounced *Phoebus'*, should be glossed *Phoebe's*, in
     reference to the moon.

544 Stroup, Thomas B. "Bottom's Name and His Epiphany."
     Shakespeare Quarterly, 29 (1978), 79-82.

     The phrase "the bottom of Goddes secretes" in 1
     Corinthians 2:11 (Geneva, 1557) is a source if not *the*
     source of the name. "Bottom has discovered the bottom of
     God's secrets--has realized that they are indeed
     bottomless." He has "recognized the reality of mysteries."
     See items 155, 162, 183, 406 and especially 566 on the same
     topic.

545 Sugimoto, Eiji. [Oberon's Power in *A Midsummer Night's
     Dream*]. *Eibun-gakkai-shi* (Sei Gakuin Women's Junior
     College), 10 (1978), 1-21. (Japanese--not seen)

     Oberon's all-unifying power governs the fairies,
     mechanics, and other elements.

546 Takayama, Hiroki. [Fairies and Mortals in *A Midsummer
     Night's Dream*]. *Kiyo* (Musashino Women's College), 13
     (1978), 115-25. (Japanese--not seen)

     Discusses the conflicts between fairies and mortals,
     reason and passion, men and women.

547   Van Laan, Thomas F. *Role-playing in Shakespeare.*
      Toronto: University of Toronto Press, 1978. x, 267 pp.

      Athens prevents the lovers from playing their desired
      roles, so they seek a more fitting setting. Fairyland, with
      the capacity of Oberon and Puck to change shapes, is
      characterized by fluidity. A number of "playlets" take place
      there before the lovers assume new, fixed roles in the end.
      In fairyland, even Bottom gets his heart's desire--several
      roles. (Pp. 53-59)

548   Yamada, Reiko. [Art and Artifice--A Note on Numbers Used
      in Three Shakespearean Dramas]. *Eigo Kenkyū* (Tokyo
      University), 13 (1978), 1-20. (Japanese--not seen)

      Apparently a study of the double-time scheme of *Dream,
      Hamlet,* and *Othello.* See item 399.

549   Alexander, Marguerite. "*A Midsummer Night's Dream.*" *A
      Reader's Guide to Shakespeare and His Contemporaries.*
      Pan Literature Guides. London and Sydney: Pan Books;
      New York: Barnes & Noble, 1979, pp. 50-57. (Also
      published with the title *An Introduction to Shakespeare
      and His Contemporaries*)

      Plot summary (4 pp.) and a brief critical commentary (4
      pp.) which stresses the appropriateness of the play for a
      wedding celebration, its remarkable structural symmetry, its
      masque-like qualities, and the symbolic values of Athens
      (reason) and the wood outside (imagination). Oberon is "an
      image of the poet, the spinner of dreams."

549a Booth, Stephen. "Speculations on Doubling in
      Shakespeare's Plays." *Shakespeare: The Theatrical
      Dimension.* Ed. Philip C. McGuire and David A.
      Samuelson. New York: AMS, 1979, pp. 103-131.

      The exchange between Oberon and Titania (II.i.60-81,
      106-114) in the dispute over the changeling boy seems
      "especially designed to hold a maximum number and variety
      of examples of changes and confusions of persona" (which
      are listed), and, therefore, an "explosion of categories"
      results when the actors playing Titania and Oberon double
      as Hippolyta and Theseus. Despite William Ringler's

arbitrary denial of this possibility (in item 330), it worked
well for Peter Brook's production (see item T1314)--he also
doubled Puck and Philostrate--and many have since done it.
In fact, the lines seem written to capitalize on it.

549b   Carroll, D. Allen. *"A Midsummer Night's Dream"* [Film].
       English Classics Series. Knoxville: University of
       Tennessee, 1979, 25 min.

       Lecture on principal themes and features of the play.
       Brief dramatizations illustrate the points being made.

550   Clayton, F. W. *The Hole in the Wall: A New Look at
       Shakespeare's Latin Base for "A Midsummer Night's
       Dream."* The Tenth Jackson Knight Memorial Lecture.
       Delivered at the University of Exeter, 13 June 1977.
       Exeter: The University, 1979. 32 pp.

       Presents a number of possibilities for wordplay, usually
       bawdy or scatological, in the playlet, primarily by
       associations made from a wide range of Latin texts,
       especially those of Ovid and Juvenal, but also by reference
       to parallel English texts, beginning with an effort to
       understand "wall's hole" (*tenui rima*). Clayton traces his
       own experience with Latin, with words and the unconscious,
       and with literature, his experience with *Dream* having
       started in an open-air, Armed Forces production of 1945.
       He makes linguistic associations with "*stones,* with *lime and
       hair knit up,*" *Limander, Snout,* "Most *brisky Juvenal,*"
       Demetrius (noting the classical instances of the name),
       bellows, Quince, lion, Bottom, and much more--which, he
       claims, his unconscious mind has been working on for
       thirty-two years.

551   Dufour, Gérard. *"Le Songe d'une nuit d'été* et le sacré."
       Aspects du sacré dans la littérature anglo-américaine.
       Reims: Centre de Recherche sur l'Imaginaire dans les
       Littératures de Langue Anglaise, Univ. de Reims, 1979,
       pp. 21-31. (French)

       Explores primitive, religious associations of motifs in
       Dream with special emphasis on the Ass in the history of
       ritual and myth. "L'union de Titania et de Bottom est une

véritable cérémonie initiatique dans la tradition des mystères éleusiens." See items 53 and 55.

552   Franke, Wolfgang. "The Logic of *Double Entendre* in *A Midsummer Night's Dream*." *Philological Quarterly*, 58 (1979), 282-97.

On the basis of a wide variety of evidence (satirical literature, folk songs, other plays) finds the possibility of sexual suggestions in the names of the mechanicals (*Snug, Flute, Quince*) and in their words (*lion, roaring, sword, die, weaver*). Their little playlet is a sexual comedy. They themselves are actually quite prim; they give only one deliberate pun of an indelicate nature ("crowns"). They are, however, made to appear utterly devoid of shame and prone to a kind of verbal exhibitionism. Their dialogue goes consistently on two levels of meaning. The discussion starts out in an effort to solve the problems of this crux: "Then know that I, as Snug the joiner am / A lion fell, nor else no lion's dam" (V.i.221-22). See item 57.

553   Friedrenreich, Kenneth. "Shakespeare, Marlowe, and Mummers." *American Notes and Queries*, 18, no. 4 (1979), 50-51.

Theseus' call for a surgeon (V.i.298) links Bottom, even unconsciously, to the clowns and boasters of the folkplays given at Midsummer who were slain to be revived by surgeons.

554   Entry Deleted.

555   Girard, René. "Myth and Ritual in Shakespeare: *A Midsummer Night's Dream*." *Textual Strategies: Perspectives in Post-Structuralist Criticism*. Ed. Josué V. Harari. Ithaca: Cornell University Press, 1979, pp. 189-212.

Takes the real theme to be certain destructive aspects of love, especially the violence in the loss of identity through "mimetic desire" (the desire to appropriate the absolute that the lover perceives). But this theme has been obscured by the power of worn-out myths of true love which audiences fall for. The lovers are saved by "the sheer luck of being in a comedy." Girard discusses such aspects as rhetoric, animal imagery, and the theme of reversal. Hippolyta is right; Theseus hears nothing.

556   Holland, Norman N. "Hermia's Dream." *Representing Shakespeare: New Psychoanalytic Essays*. Ed. Murray M. Schwartz and Coppélia Kahn. Baltimore: Johns Hopkins University Press, 1980, pp. 1-20. Reprint. 1982. Originally appeared in *The Annual of Psychoanalysis*, 7 (1979).

Gives three overlapping interpretations of the dream which together recapitulate the history of psychoanalytic criticism. The first, taking the dream as an actual dream, discovers its infantile bases in genital, anal, and oral phases, and notes Hermia's chief defence mechanism, the search for alternatives. The second, which considers the dream in the context of the play as a whole, notes how it is part of the larger theme of separation and fusion. The third, which, reflecting recent trends in criticism, sees the dream as a function of the audience's special need for self-structuring ("transactive criticism"), shows how the play's (and the dream's) themes (trust and betrayal, fusion and separation) make a particular impression upon Holland. See items 252 and 397.

557   Kernan, Alvin B. *The Playwright as Magician: Shakespeare's Image of the Poet in the English Public Theater*. New Haven: Yale University Press, 1979. vii, 164 pp.

More than any other play, *Dream* reveals *both* Shakespeare's modesty about higher claims for his theatrical art (through the bungling of the mechanicals' play and the limitations of the Athenian courtly audience) *and* his belief (which is Sidney's) that "in place of nature's brazen world the poet creates a golden one." Since the "real" and inadequate audience in the play (Athenian) is itself fictive, "we too may be only another player audience on another larger stage." "If *all* the world is a play, then one play may be as true as another; and if the conditions are right, as in Oberon's play [on the stage of his magical forest] but not in Bottom's, then the theatre may reveal the true

nature of the world and effect its transformation" (which is
the Renaissance ideal for art). (Pp. 74-79)

558   Komiya, Teruo. [The Minor Fairies in *A Midsummer Night's
       Dream*]. *Chiba Univ. Kyoyo-bu Kenkyū Hokoku*, B-12
       (1979), 85-103. (Japanese--not seen)

559   Kondo, Hikaru. "An Observation on the Language of *A
       Midsummer Night's Dream.*" *Eigo Kenkyū* (Tokyo
       University), 15 (1979), 23-52. (not seen)

560   Krieger, Elliot. "*A Midsummer Night's Dream.*" *A Marxist
       Study of Shakespeare's Comedies*. New York: Barnes &
       Noble; London: Macmillan, 1979, pp. 37-69.

       The forest is no escape but rather well within the
ambience of Athenian laws of decorum and propriety. The
juice symbolizes objective, social contents which cannot be
negated. In particular, the language of the lovers recreates
the Athenian prohibitions. The imagination helps separate
the self from the other, establishes an "hierarchical
separation between itself and the other social classes." The
flight to the forest, really one of "style and gesture,"
helps solidify Theseus' position as a figure of social
authority. "Authority itself releases and then reabsorbs the
aristocratic protagonists . . . into its administration of the
state." This process the fairies also certify. *Dream*
dramatizes a fantasy for "creating complete social poise."

561   Lamb, M. E. "*A Midsummer Night's Dream*: The Myth of
       Theseus and the Minotaur." *Texas Studies in Literature
       and Language*, 21 (1979), 478-91.

       This myth has a serious, complicated influence and
significance. The lovers wander in a forest-labyrinth.
Bottom is a comic minotaur *and* the thread leading out.
Though now no more, Theseus has been an irrational lover
(deserting Ariadne). This view encourages us to see that
the attitude toward love is mixed, ambivalent. Theseus'
speech does not address the nature of art (Hippolyta's
does); it addresses instead the experience of the artist.
The views are to be taken together. See also items 55 and,
especially, 538.

561a   Levin, Richard. *New Readings vs. Old Plays: Recent*
       Trends in the Reinterpretation of English Renaissance
       Drama. Chicago and London: University of Chicago
       Press, 1979. xiv, 277 pp.

       In the course of his account of the biases in criticism of
       the last thirty years, Levin makes twenty-six references to
       comments on or attitudes toward the *Dream* (see index). He
       uses Bottom's soliloquy to illustrate what the trend of
       discovering profundity has done to a single episode (on p.
       60). *Dream* has been "one of the principal beneficiaries of
       thematic elevation."

562   Muir, Kenneth. "Experiment: *A Midsummer Night's Dream.*"
       Shakespeare's Comic Sequence. Liverpool: Liverpool
       University Press; New York: Barnes & Noble, 1979, pp.
       42-50.

       Shakespeare may or may not have written the highly
       artificial verse in *Dream* ; but he was, in any case,
       responsible for its presence, and saw that, in a play whose
       effect is almost like that of comic opera, the crudity of
       such verse could be turned to good account. "The play is
       primarily a critique of love: the irrationality of adolescent
       passion, the function of imagination as an ingredient of
       love, and the necessity of consecration."

563   Schwartz, Robert Barnett. "Shakespeare's Parted Eye:
       Approaches to Meaning in the Sonnets and Plays." Ph.D.
       dissertation, University of Virginia, 1978. *DAI,* 40
       (1979), 3324A.

       Dream, As You Like It, Twelfth Night, and the sonnets
       are used to "explore what Shakespeare thought about
       thought." Meaning is the product of a complex constellation
       of elements like structure, theme, language, and the like,
       though it is not embodied in any one of these. What one
       experiences in these plays and poems are two states of
       awareness (to "know" and to "know well") which correlate
       with each other as kinds of movements to lead to a new
       level of experience in which paradoxes having to do with
       the flux of human emotions are transcended and ignored.

564   Smith, Jonathan C. "*A Midsummer Night's Dream* and the
      Allegory of Theologians." *Christianity and Literature*,
      28, no. 2 (1979), 15-23.

      The action of the *Dream* is "realistic in a topological
      sense," not symbolic in its imaginative treatment of love. It
      is representative, as Dante regarded his *Commedia*. Finds
      Theseus not an emblem of sanity and order but rather
      "prone to the same weaknesses" as the others in the play.
      Like the other lovers he undergoes a miraculous change
      from false to true love (and this love is a type of divine
      love). A miracle occurs. Titania's love for Bottom points to
      "a profound reflection of divine love in a woman."

565   Stempler, Cher, ed. *The Practical Bard: Classroom
      Curriculum for the Study of Shakespeare.* [Orlando,
      Fla.] The Shakespeare Institute, University of Central
      Florida, 1979. vi, 187 pp.

      Based on the workshop contributions of "sixty
      professionals." Cynthia Huggins offers a study guide, essay
      questions, written projects, activities, objective test
      questions, and an overview. Designed to provide an
      interdisciplinary approach (six other plays are covered).
      Supplement contains a note on "Composing Thematic Music
      for our Production of *A Midsummer Night's Dream*," by
      Craig Jon Alexander, with a sample ("You spotted
      snakes"). *Dream* was the focus of a summer's study by the
      group. (Pp. 1-28)

566   Willson, Robert F., Jr. "God's Secrets and Bottom's Name:
      A Reply." *Shakespeare Quarterly*, 30 (1979), 407-408.

      Questions Stroup's conclusion (item 544) that Bottom's
      dream has anything to do with "the bottom of Goddes
      secretes" (1 Cor. 2:11). Such is "to transform a witty
      romantic comedy into a morality play." The commonly
      accepted association of the name with the trade (noted first
      by Halliwell-Phillipps), along with certain connotative
      functions, will do. See also item 155.

566a Black, Matthew. "*A Midsummer Night's Dream*": *Notes.*
      Gary Carey, ed. James L. Roberts, consulting ed. Cliffs

Notes. Revised edition. Lincoln, Neb.: Cliffs Notes,
1980. 59 pp.

Introduction and guide for college students. The early
edition is item 152.

566b   Comtois, M. E. "The Hardiness of *A Midsummer Night's
       Dream.*" *Theatre Journal* (Columbia, Mo.), 32 (1980),
       305-311.

Comtois analyzes the play according to "its order of
actions and dynamics." The hardiness of the play--its
ability to survive an arduous and long production
history--derives from "a deeply integrated and
multidimensional design." The play's main idea is that of a
dream--dream gives shape to it. Its plot involves four
groups of characters, each with a public function to
perform and a private matter to resolve--so we have eight
patterns of action: all of which point to the marriage
celebration. Most of the scenes have their own inherent
forms (can stand alone) which contribute to the
entertainment value of the play. There are fourteen
movements or units (listed here) which taken together form
a pyramid for the structure.

566c   Draper, Ronald P. *William Shakespeare: "A Midsummer
       Night's Dream."* York Notes. London: Longman, 1980.
       87 pp.

Study guide designed for college students.

566d   Evans, T. M. "The Vernacular Labyrinth: Mazes and
       Amazement in Shakespeare and Peele." *Shakespeare
       Jahrbuch* (Heidelberg) (1980), 165-73.

Allusions to the maze in the *Dream*, drawing on
deep-seated associations in myth, ritual, and game
described in studies by C. L. Barber (item 158) and
Northrop Frye (see item 142), imply the loss of a traditional
path of wisdom and truth in the world and represent "a
disfunction in the psychological and spiritual sphere."
"Maze" is to be aligned with "amazement" in the play. And
the image of the maze is a structural analogue of the play

itself. In these respects the play resembles Peele's *Old Wives' Tale*.

566e   Falk, Florence. "Dream and Ritual in *A Midsummer Night's Dream.*" *Comparative Drama*, 14 (1980), 263-79.

Since the characters "see *narrowly*" at the outset, Oberon, the *shaman* figure, sets about, through the agency of the dream, to expand their mode of perception. The "Rites of passage" undertaken in the play conform in shape to those of village and bush described in Victor Turner's anthropological study of Ndembu culture in *The Ritual Process* (1969).

566f   Felheim, Marvin, and Philip Traci. *"A Midsummer Night's Dream." Realism in Shakespeare's Romantic Comedies: "O Heavenly Mingle."* Lanham, Md.: University Press of America, 1980, pp. 79-102.

The play is full of satiric and realistic aspects, as can be seen in each of the plots. Titania and Oberon, for example, are bickering "parents," and all the bickering is for a little boy. The plot of the mechanicals "incorporates those realistic elements which are the very essence and center of the whole play." These men are obsessed with reality. Their play is "satire upon the very nature of romantic love." The central idea of the play is change. We participate throughout with wonder in two worlds--the romantic and the realistic.

566g   Grene, Nicholas. *Shakespeare, Jonson, Moliére: The Comic Contract.* London: Macmillan; Totowa, N. J.: Barnes & Noble, 1980. xvii, 246 pp.

In Chapter 3 Grene looks at two plays, the *Dream* and *The Tempest*, to see what use Shakespeare makes of the authoritarian figures Theseus and Prospero (such figures are normally ridiculed in comedies, their authority subverted). Theseus is wise and humane, unlike the peremptory and tyrannic Egeus. While he shares control with Oberon (and the parts sometimes doubled), he is not to be identified with Oberon completely. The distinction must be maintained. Oberon's authority is arbitrary, divorced from human commitments. We must consider that the middle of the play takes place somewhere else than in Athens. Theseus shifts from compassionate but just magistrate to benign and merciful duke, as ultimately society vindicates what nature demands. Whatever he lacks in perspective, however limited his imagination, that limitation is necessary if he is to fulfill his proper function. The confidence we have in Theseus is required for the pattern of the comedy. Prospero is to be identified with Oberon, ruling over the powers of the night and doing so in an arbitrary and capricious way. Grene draws several comparisons and contrasts between the two. For other comparisons with *The Tempest* see item 149.

566h   Hassel, R. Chris, Jr. "'Most Rare Vision': Faith in *A Midsummer Night's Dream.*" *Faith and Folly in Shakespeare's Romantic Comedies.* Athens: University of Georgia Press, 1980, pp. 52-76.

Here Hassel provides a thorough analysis of this comedy as it gives expression to a Christian dimension in the comic vision. Through metaphor and allusion, especially to the words of St. Paul and of Erasmus in *The Praise of Folly*, Shakespeare underscores "this analogy between romantic and religious faith." The folly and faith of the one is similar to the folly and faith of the other. In this chapter he discusses first Bottom's waking experience, calling attention at length to its relationship with the Pauline text (and noticing other relevant texts). The biblical context helps us understand both the "absurdity and profundity" of Bottom's "brush with the transcendental." Then he discusses the young lovers as examples of Erasmian folly, and Theseus and others as presenters of the Pauline point of view. (Some of this material, and that from other places in the book, appeared earlier; see items 356 and 666.)

566i   Hawkes, Terence. "Comedy, Orality, and Duplicity: *A Midsummer Night's Dream* and *Twelfth Night.*" In *Shakespearean Comedy.* Ed. Maurice Charney. New York: New York Literary Forum, 1980, pp. 155-63.

Joins the ideas on comedy of Northrop Frye (see item 142), C. L. Barber (see item 158), and Mikhail Bakhtin into the "notion of a confusing 'green' 'topsy-turvy' Festive or Carnival world whose operation upon the normal world of everyday that it opposes involves a kind of redemptive duplicity . . . [in order] to change that world to a better place." Adds to this the idea that comedy is basically "oral" as an art, a mode "fundamentally interactive and interlocutory," requiring audience participation, and thereby provides, not merely entertainment or distraction, but positive involvement and engagement with the fabric of social life. *Dream* illustrates this idea of oral values in the drama of nonliterate society. Its playlet "offers a model of a comedy's best relationship to the community that generates it."

566j   Longo, Joseph A. "Myth in *A Midsummer Night's Dream*." *Élisabéthain*, 18 (1980), 17-27.

Traces the motifs of Apollonian sobriety and Dionysian madness through the play to their resolution in the concluding act by the power of the imagination in the idea of Theatre. With Puck as Orpheus Shakespeare brings the two motifs together. The nuances associated with the fables of Apollo, Dionysos, and Orpheus can be viewed as essential to the play. Cf. items 55, 117, 149 and 172.

566k   Nevo, Ruth. "Fancy's Images." *Comic Transformations in Shakespeare*. London and New York: Methuen, 1980, pp. 96-114.

At its start the play shows the mind, in its aspect as the image-making and image-perceiving faculty, to be "an errant faculty indeed, unstable, uncertain, wavering, and seeking anchorage among a welter of rival images and self-images." That one rival wants what the other has is "the comic disposition which the comic device exposes and exacerbates." It is about various sorts of rivalry, often shown in the form of mimicry.

566l   Riemer, A. P. *Antic Fables: Patterns of Evasion in Shakespeare's Comedies*. New York: St. Martin's Press; Sydney: Sydney University Press, 1980. ix, 229 pp.

"The play is notable for its discovery of individual accents for each group of characters--accents, moreover, which are immediately recognizable. Through their individual modes of speech, the characters carry about with them tokens of their basic isolation from the other orders of existence depicted in the play." There is indeed a wide range of effects. Riemer cautions as to what may seem to many as an "infinite suggestibility" in the play; such may be no more than the evocation of "cloud-cuckoo-land on the stage." He remarks on how the Theseus-Hippolyta exchange helps set up the conclusion of the play and explain the many transformations which take place in the play. The concern of the play with the nature of art is not put explicitly, but it is there nonetheless, insinuating itself onto our attention. Episodes in the play "explore the possibilities of illusion, trickery and the use of agencies . . . capable of transforming our normal perceptions."

566m   Roberts, Jeanne Addison. "Animals as Agents of Revelation: The Horizontalizing of the Chain of Being in Shakespeare's Comedies." *Shakespearean Comedy.* Ed. Maurice Charney. New York: New York Literary Forum, 1980, pp. 79-96.

Roberts, viewing in sequence the animal images of Shakespeare's plays, finds "a progression of thought that moves from the secure hierarchy of the Great Chain of Being, characteristic of the earlier plays, to the fleeting recognition at the end of *The Tempest* that the chain may be horizontal rather than vertical, and to the acceptance of the narrowing gap between man and animal." Bottom fits in the first stage of this progression, alongside the transformation of Falstaff in *Merry Wives*. With the change in these two we laugh "because man is superior to animal and joining the two forms seems absurd. . . . In both [these] cases there is an initial shock which relaxes into comedy and then moves beyond." (Some of this material appears in the author's *Shakespeare's English Comedy*, item 562a.)

566n   Vaughn, Jack A. "*A Midsummer Night's Dream.*" *Shakespeare's Comedies.* New York: Frederick Ungar, 1980 (paper, 1982), pp. 61-76.

A general introduction to the play which proceeds through the play, taking up each of the plots, and has a few general comments to make about other aspects of the play and stage history.

566o   Broock, Ursula. "Traum und Tag [Dream and Day] in
       Shakespeare's *A Midsummer Night's Dream.*" *Shakespeare
       Jahrbuch* (Weimar), 117 (1981), 68-84.

       Taking "fancy" to be the aesthetic unifying factor of the
       Dream, Broock focuses attention on the five characters who
       possess fancy and are thus susceptible to the magical world
       of elves: the four lovers and Bottom. Broock rejects Karl
       Elze's view (in 1868) that the five are passive objects of
       the magic of Oberon/Puck and attempts to demonstrate,
       through an analysis of the mental and emotional state of the
       lovers before they fall asleep and when they awaken, that
       they actively respond to the situations into which Oberon
       has placed them; Bottom, of course, does not sleep at any
       point in the *Dream* [?], but in his preoccupation with his
       role in the playlet he falls into a state of "creative
       intoxication" which renders him susceptible. Oberon and
       Puck are thus seen as "catalysts" which make possible the
       experiences of the five in the forest-night, which Broock
       sees not as a metaphorical expression for subjective
       perception of reality but as a construct which has an
       affinity to the dream.

566p   Comtois, M. E. "The Making of Farce Out of Fancy at the
       Center of *A Midsummer Night's Dream.*" *On Stage
       Studies: The Annual Publication of the Colorado
       Shakespeare Festival*, 5 (1981), 44-54.

       The story of Bottom and Titania, as seen through their
       scenes together (III.i, IV.i), is an example of pure farce,
       of Eric Bentley's "extreme case of the extremes." Comtois
       treats character, action, vision, and language, finding in
       them opposites and extreme versions thereof.

566q   Cox, Richard H. "Shakespeare: Poetic Understanding and
       Comic Action (A Weaver's Dream)." *The Artist and
       Political Vision.* Ed. Benjamin R. Barber and Michael J.
       Gargas McGrath. New Brunswick and London:
       Transaction Books, 1981, pp. 165-92.

       A "playfully serious set of conjectures" or "musings" on
       the *Dream*, taken to be a compelling and perplexing play,
       which is especially exercised by the philosophic nature of
       the content of the play and its implications for politics. How
       do we distinguish dream from reality in the play? Is there

concord in all this discord? Looks at Theseus as treated by Shakespeare, Plutarch, and Socrates. Gives particular attention to the artisans, who they are and what they mean, and to Bottom, especially in his waking moment. Draws constant comparisons with Greek literature and history, especially that which has to do with the high and low classes in society.

566r   Finch, G. J. "Shakespeare and the Nature of Metaphor."
        Ariel, 12 (1981), 3-19.

"The deep structure of Theseus's language works against his argument." Despite his own skeptical irony, the poet's, Shakespeare suggests here and demonstrates everywhere, is a miracle. The *Dream* is a "defence of dreaming." "The artistic imagination is . . . fundamentally maligned by Theseus." Theseus's speech serves as a start for a discussion of Shakespeare's use of metaphor.

566s   Garner, Shirley Nelson. "*A Midsummer Night's Dream*:
        'Jack shall have Jill;/Nought shall go ill.'" *Women's
        Studies*, 9 (1981), 47-63.

"The social and sexual implications of the return of the green world have gone unnoticed. What has not been so clearly seen is that the renewal at the end of the play affirms patriarchal order and hierarchy, insisting that the power of women must be circumscribed, and that it recognizes the tenuousness of heterosexuality as well." The men want "to attain the exclusive love of woman and, also, to accommodate their homoerotic desires." Egeus is particularly attracted to Demetrius. Central to the plot is breaking of the bonds of the women. The comic pattern suggests that men need to maintain their ties with other men and to sever women's bonds with each other. Cf., on the place of women in the play, items 532, 566t, 566x, 566gg and 566pp.

566t   Greer, Germaine. "Love and the Law." *Politics, Power, and
        Shakespeare*. Ed. Frances McNeely Leonard. Arlington,
        Texas: Texas Humanities Resource Center, University of
        Texas at Arlington, 1981, pp. 29-45.

The problem the play faces is how to "prop up human preferences one for another so that it *becomes* the lifeline of the family, the basis for fruitfulness." Diana, the goddess of chastity and fruitfulness, who presides over the play, must "win by harnessing enchantment." The play is about the conflict between anarchic sexual passion and family demands. On an insubstantial basis one must build a solid form and make it last. "Once the children come along, it really doesn't matter if you are a lunatic, a lover, or a poet: there is too much work to do." Throughout, Greer makes observations about sixteenth century sexual and marital practices. See item 566s.

566u   Huston, J. Dennis. "Parody and Play in *A Midsummer Night's Dream.*" *Shakespeare's Comedies of Play*. New York: Columbia University Press, 1981, pp. 94-121.

Part of this essay (pp. 98-107) was published earlier as an article (see item 426). In the *Dream*, unlike *The Shrew*, which Huston has been discussing, we are conscious not of a principal character (like Petruchio), but rather of the playwright's part in shaping his creation. Bottom is like Petruchio in many ways; through Bottom the comic hero is deflated, parodied, to show that the actor is subservient to the playwright. Shakespeare plays with the limitations of dramatic form in a series of parodies, Bottom being the main one. Shakespeare parodies the conventions which as dramatist he must use. He is "here mentally and dramatically playing with his art form, creating a play which conspicuously calls attention to itself, not only in the details of its comic underplot but also in the action of its love plot as well." It is his "most exuberantly self-reflexive comedy of play." See item 292 for other comparisons with *The Shrew*.

566v   Kott, Jan. "The Bottom Translation." *Assays: Critical Approaches to Medieval and Renaissance Texts*. Ed. Peggy A. Knapp and Michael A. Stugrin. Vol. 1. Pittsburgh: University of Pittsburgh Press, 1981, pp. 117-49. (Translated by Daniela Miedzyrzecka)

Kott is taken with the doubleness of the play, its simultaneous highness and lowness, reflections of each other. Beginning with the dual nature of Cupid and with a constant basis in two texts--Corinthians and *The Golden*

Ass--he ranges widely and at great heights over myth and literature, of Cupids, asses, Venuses, and other symbols, to show the presence in the play of the Neoplatonic and of Mikhail Bakhtin's *serio ludere* or carnivalesque. "Apuleius, Paul, and Erasmus [*The Praise of Folly*] meet in Bottom's monologue." To Kott "there will always remain two interpretations . . . : the light one and the dark." Its ecstasy works both ways. For Kott's other comment on the play see item 239.

566w   Lindblad, Ishrat. "The Autotelic Function of *A Midsummer Night's Dream.*" *Papers from the First Nordic Conference for English Studies: Oslo, 17-19 September 1980.* Ed. Stig Johansson Bjørn Tysdahl. Oslo: Institute of English Studies, University of Oslo, 1981, pp. 134-47.

An examination of the "self-reflexive activity" in the play--the play calling attention to itself as dream or as art--reveals how the justification of its own form emerges during the course of the play. In it we get, for example, several different views of an author's role in relation to his plots and characters, and we get spectators. Primarily, though, we get the artist's problem of imposing order on the disordered experience of human life. Concentrates finally on problems the mechanicals cannot solve in theirs but that Shakespeare solves nicely in his play. For similar studies see Index under Metadrama.

566x   Marcus, Mordecai. "*A Midsummer Night's Dream*: The Dialectic of Eros-Thanatos." *American Imago*, 38 (1981), 269-78.

The over-riding concern of the play is the theme of love-and-death--which "becomes a paradigm of fulfillment--a paradigm which overlaps the themes of order, reconciliation, and maturation in the play's plot." Neither Hugh M. Richmond (item 381) nor Jan Kott (item 239), both of whom have used this approach, have sufficiently explored it. Richmond found nothing positive, and Kott found too much violence. Love-and-death is a "paradigm of some ultimate condition of fulfillment in which love projects its chosen ones." It is a kind of "divine madness," and is part of the play's "aura or lyric undernote." There are references to Denis de Rougement and Norman O. Brown.

566y   Perkins, D. C., and J. Huke. *A Midsummer Night's
       Dream*. Notes and Comments. Walton-on-Thames: Celtic
       Revision Aids, 1981. iv, 119 pp. (not seen)

566z   Pitt, Angela. *Shakespeare's Women*. Newton Abbot and
       London: David & Charles; Totowa, N. J.: Barnes &
       Noble, 1981. 224 pp.

       Looks briefly (pp. 85-92) at the place of women in the
       play. Hermia and Helena are very similar in education and
       taste, but there are also differences between them: "Hermia
       is short, aggressive and unrelenting; Helena tall, anguished
       and a coward physically." Most interesting is the tacit
       assumption that Oberon's behavior toward Titania is
       justified. "Shakespeare has made it clear that nothing
       Titania can claim or do will justify the fundamental wrong
       she has committed: she has failed to submit to her
       husband's desires." Finally, in the play the "women become
       the conservative, sixteenth-century ideal: submissive and
       silent." (There are several black-and-white photographs of
       productions.) For other studies of the place of women in
       the play see 566s.

566aa Stewart, Garrett. "Shakespearean Dreamplay." *English
       Literary Renaissance*, 11 (1981), 44-69.

       "The focus of this essay is on the kind of language that
       tends to be spoken by Shakespearean characters when that
       language is most cognizant of itself as aesthetic discourse.
       . . . The hypothesis I wish to test, first with *A Midsummer
       Night's Dream* and then with *The Winter's Tale*, is that
       certain characters gravitate at moments of greatest
       intensity, moments closest to the ineffable, toward what
       might be called the metastyle of dream speech." The
       account Bottom gives of his adventure and the reaction of
       Leontes to the astonishing spectacle before him are each "a
       welling up into utterance of dream's metaphoric
       displacements and cryptic disorientation."

566bb Vickers, Brian, ed. *Shakespeare: The Critical Heritage*.
       The Critical Heritage Series. 6 vols. London: Routledge
       & Kegan Paul, 1974-1981. [Most recent volume in 1981;
       more volumes to follow.]

The series reprints excerpts from early criticism of Shakespeare. Here is a list of the critics whose comments on the *Dream* are included thus far and the places where their comments occur. Volume 1, covering 1623-1692, gives extracts from Samuel Pepys (p. 30) and Gerard Langbaine (pp. 421-22). Volume 2, covering 1693-1733, quotes from Charles Gildon (pp. 83, 242), Nicholas Rowe (pp. 197-98), Alexander Pope (pp. 410, 412), Lewis Theobald (pp. 428, 492f.), and William Warburton (p. 530). Volume 3, covering 1733-1752, quotes Warburton (pp. 90, 227, 230f.), William Collins (p. 113), Anonymous of 1747 (pp. 260f.), Peter Whalley (p. 280), John Upton (pp. 309, 311, 319), Thomas Seward (p. 386), Thomas Edwards (p. 400), and Thomas Gray (p. 448). Volume 4, covering 1753-1765, quotes Zachary Gray (p. 150f.), Christopher Smart (p. 204), Joseph Warton (p. 264), George Colman (p. 443), Benjamin Heath (pp. 553ff.), and George Steevens (p. 565). Volume 5, covering 1765-1774, gives extracts from Samuel Johnson (pp. 66, 101-102, 167), George Colman (p. 179), James Barclay (p. 234), Thomas Tyrwhitt (p. 240), Richard Farmer (p. 270), Edward Capell (pp. 305f.), William Duff (pp. 368, 372), and George Steevens (pp. 519, 548). Volume 6, covering 1774-1801, gives extracts from Francis Gentleman (pp. 105ff.), William Kenrick (p. 114), George Steevens (pp. 191ff.), Edward Capell (pp. 252, 265, 268), Edmund Malone (pp. 303, 523), Samuel Felton (p. 467), and Anonymous of 1789 (pp. 508, 510).

566cc Willson, Robert F., Jr. "The Chink in the Wall: Anticlimax and Dramatic Illusion in *A Midsummer Night's Dream.*" *Shakespeare Jahrbuch* (Weimar), 117 (1981), 85-90.

The *Dream* exploits the comic device of anti-climax or undercutting time and again. No one escapes some form of embarrassment or ridicule. The pattern of anticlimax starts when Theseus, after taking Egeus' part, turns aside with Egeus and Demetrius in "a hint of conciliation, of collective bargaining in private." Any serious issue thereafter in the play is not permitted to threaten. It is short-circuited--in the warm light of romantic love. In a related manner, Hippolyta's observation on the imagination undercuts Theseus's "somewhat self-satisfied judgment of this matter."

566dd   Black, James. "The Monster in Shakespeare's Landscape."
        The Elizabethan Theatre VIII. Ed. G. R. Hibbard. Port
        Credit, Ontario: P. D. Meany, 1982, pp. 51-68.

        Discusses monstrosity in the *Dream* and then in *Lear*,
        but draws few comparisons between the two plays. After
        beginning with the "swift rush for the open air and to a
        world which is upside-down," concentrates primarily on
        Bottom's transformation, the kind of impression it makes in
        the theatre, the general relevance of "hateful fantasies" and
        prodigies. The *Dream*, for Black, is a teratology--a
        narrative concerning prodigies, or a marvelous tale.

566ee   Collins, David G. "Beyond Reason in *A Midsummer Night's
        Dream*: Stratford, 1981." *Iowa State Journal of Research*,
        57, no. 2 (1982), 131-42.

        That the *Dream* is no "shimmering gossamer" but rather
        a play with substantial intellectual content is an assertion
        few serious students of Shakespeare would contest. "But
        there remains," Collins says, "considerable disagreement
        about what statement emerges from the action. Many critics
        view the play as a validation of the Christian humanist
        tradition wherein reason and order triumph over passion
        and disorder. Cultural changes in the past twenty years
        have, however, made possible another perception of the
        play. Much recent criticism has concentrated on Hippolyta's
        assertion that in the madness of the central action there is
        'something of great constancy.' What Shakespeare presents
        is in fact an alternative approach to the wisdom Theseus
        consciously seeks through reason. Bottom, the play's
        greatest fool, shows us that it is possible to *apprehend*
        what we cannot *comprehend*--that there are truths beyond
        the reach of reason, accessible only to 'initiates.' Peter
        Brook's 1971 production of the play demonstrated
        convincingly that such a reading works well on the stage,
        and Ron Nichol's RSC production in 1981 carried the work a
        set further."

566ff   Erlich, Bruce. "Queenly Shadows: On Mediation in Two
        Comedies." *Shakespeare Survey*, 35 (1982), 65-77.

        A complicated, detailed study of the way the structure
        of the play (the four lovers' situation, the forest-city
        dichotomy) creates a particular kind of myth which

responds to and in effect resolves real social problems
peculiar to the late Tudor period. It applies insights from
Marx and Levi-Strauss and attitudes toward the specific
social realignment of the (possible) marriage of the Earl of
Derby (the old aristocracy) with Elizabeth de Vere (the
new, being Burghley's granddaughter) in order to draw its
observation of the special balance achieved in the play's
conclusion.

566gg   Marshall, David. "Exchanging Visions: Reading *A
        Midsummer Night's Dream.*" *ELH*, 49 (1982), 543-75.

A long, involved essay which compares and contrasts the
kinds of perspectives or visions which audiences have had
of the play in performance with the idea of point of view or
perspective in the play itself. The play teaches us "how to
look"--we must exchange our own vision for that of others.
And this "exchange might be seen as an alternative to the
theft of visions," which occurs in the form of male tyranny
in the play.

566hh Mebane, John S. "Structure, Source, and Meaning in *A
        Midsummer Night's Dream.*" *Texas Studies in Literature
        and Language*, 24 (1982), 255-70.

This article combines several complementary types of
evidence: (1) A comparison between the *Dream* and
Chaucer's "Knight's Tale" reveals that Shakespeare deals in
an indirect, allusive fashion with philosophical questions
which Chaucer dealt with explicitly. (2) Symphonic
variations upon the theme of *discordia concors* in the
language of the play reinforce the philosophical implications

566ii   Parker, Douglas H. "'Limander' and 'Helen' in *A
        Midsummer Night's Dream.*" *Shakespeare Quarterly*, 33
        (1982), 99-101.

In the "Limander-Helen" blunder (V.i.194-95)
Shakespeare may have meant more than a simple, ignorant
effort at "Leander and Hero." "Thisby mistakes a figure of
faith, Hero, for Helen, a figure of infidelity in the name of
the prototype of infidelity." It may also be an unconscious
reference to the inconstant "Lysander" and the faithful
"Helena."

of its structure. (3) Shakespeare's use of dreams within the play and his typical use of reliably prophetic dreams in other works both suggest that the *Dream* is a revelatory dream-vision. (4) Shakespeare's playful use of the fairies as poetic shadows of genuine spiritual realities is a remarkably effective and enjoyable instance of the traditional practice of utilizing extravagant jests in order to deal with important truths, especially those which defy a purely rational comprehension.

566jj   Stansbury, Joan. "Characterization of the Four Young Lovers in *A Midsummer Night's Dream.*" *Shakespeare Survey*, 35 (1982), 57-63.

The four young lovers are individuals and not, in the usual view of them, "practically interchangeable." The women are contrasted physically, of course. "But the real distinction between the various lovers surely lies in their attitude to love, and their individual manner of speech." The quality of love, for example, between Demetrius and Helena at the beginning is inferior (forms of "dote" and "fond" describe it usually); and the lovers' forms of address (especially in their choice of "thou" or "you" forms) reveal the nature and depth of their love.

566kk   Wyrick, Deborah Baker. "The Ass Motif in *The Comedy of Errors* and *A Midsummer Night's Dream.*" *Shakespeare Quarterly*, 33 (1982), 432-48.

In the early comedies Shakespeare exploited the linguistic, thematic, and structural possibilities inherent in the word "ass." He transformed this "seemingly unassuming word into a complex verbal cipher." In the one section here devoted to *Dream*, Bottom is described as "the apotheosis of asininity"; he synthesizes the "admirable ass," the "foolish ass" and the "licentious ass" traditions--which traditions are traced in a section on background material relating to the symbolic associations of the ass. Bottom's transformation symbolizes "the primal pattern of the play--the dramatic recreation of the Apollonian-Dionysian dialectic." See items 433, 603, and 685j.

566ll   Bellringer, Alan W. "The Act of Change in *A Midsummer Night's Dream.*" *English Studies*, 64 (1983), 201-17.

A theme running throughout the play is the need to accept change and to respond positively to different situations. Through dreaming and acting people explore various alternative selves. "The point which the play as a whole makes is the superiority of adaptability over mere mutability in sexual relationships, in matters of love." The positive alternative to mutability is metamorphosis, exemplified in marriage, in magic, and in the art of acting.

566mm   Cohen, Ralph Alan. "The Strategy of Misdirection in *A Midsummer Night's Dream* and *Bartholomew Fair*." *Renaissance Papers 1982*. Ed. A. Leigh Deneef and M. Thomas Hester. Durham, N. C.: The Southeastern Renaissance Conference, 1983, pp. 65-75.

For all their obvious differences, these two plays, surprisingly, employ the same strategy of dramatic illusion. By constantly interrupting the dramatic moment and by framing the next and higher level of illusion in a strategy of misdirection, the plays lower the audience's guard against belief. "A dramatic moment is established, it is replaced by other material more challenging to belief, that new material is in turn replaced, and so on until the audience, constantly adjusting its view, soon loses sight of the original illusion as such and becomes ever less able to keep a distance from the play." In one play the loss of self occurs in dreaming, in the other at the Fair. See also, for comparisons with this play, items 502 and 566nn.

566nn   Craig, D. H. "The Idea of the Play in *A Midsummer Night's Dream* and *Bartholomew Fair*." *Jonson and Shakespeare*. Ed. Ian Donaldson. Canberra: Australian National University; Atlantic Highlands, N. J.: Humanities Press; London: Macmillan, 1983, pp. 89-101.

Shakespeare and Jonson use the same device (the play-within) to reflect sharply different views about plays and audiences. Craig discusses first one and then the other. In general he shows that Jonson forces us to be aware of the distinction between the world of the self-contained play and of the contrivances and mechanisms of the stage, whereas Shakespeare forces us to join with this awareness sympathy for both worlds, imaginative participation in each, and thus to bridge the gap. See previous item.

566oo Hartman, Vicki Shahly. "*A Midsummer Night's Dream*: A
       Gentle Concord to the Oedipal Problem." *American Imago*,
       40 (1983), 355-69.

       A Freudian reading which sees that most characters
       initially pursue impossible relationships which can be
       described as various Oedipal configurations. Characters are
       driven by the systematic self-defeating oedipal-type
       fascination with unobtainable partnerships. Throughout,
       however, Shakespeare proclaims the "futility" of Oedipal
       pursuit, and he offers finally a more appropriate love,
       marriage. Art, as Freud said, is a "path from phantasy
       back to reality."

566pp Montrose, Louis Adrian. "'Shaping Fantasies': Figurations
       of Gender and Power in Elizabethan Culture."
       Representations, 1, no. 2 (1983), 61-94.

       "Explores how the text of the *Dream* restructures its
       idealogical subtext." Considers the dialectic between the
       fantasies by which the play has been shaped and which it
       shapes--"within a specifically Elizabethan context of cultural
       production: the interplay between representations of gender
       and power in a stratified society in which authority is
       everywhere invested in men--everywhere, that is, except at
       the top." Relationships in the play having to do with
       gender/power are studied in detail as reflections of cultural
       bias: the *Dream* "dramatizes a set of claims which are
       repeated throughout Shakespeare's canon: claims for a
       spiritual kinship among men that is unmediated by women;
       for the procreative powers of men; and for the autogeny of
       men." At the same time that the play reproduces
       legitimating structures, it also reproduces challenges to
       these structures. The ending, for example, is undermined
       by dramatic ironies and a kind of inter-textual irony.
       Through such ironies the *Dream* discloses that "patriarchal
       norms are compensatory for the vulnerability of men to the
       powers of women." The discussion relies particularly on
       contemporary views of Elizabeth and of the Amazons. For
       similar readings see the list at 566s.

566qq Petersen, Carol J. "Bowstrings, Anyone?" *American Notes
       & Queries*, 21 (1983), 130-32.

After reviewing various interpretations of "hold, or cut bowstrings" (I.ii.104), suggests it is analogous to "fish or cut bait." Compare item 471.

566rr   Tassiter, Alyn. [On "and eke most lovely Jew" from *A Midsummer Night's Dream*]. *Bulletin of the New York Shakespeare Society*, 1, no. 7 (Jan. 1983), 15-16. (not seen)

Apparently explicates the line by reference to "Juvenall."

566ss   Walch, Günter. "*Ein Sommernachtstraum*: Komödienform und Rezeptionslenkung." *Shakespeare Jahrbuch* (Weimar), 119 (1983), 31-48.

After giving a summary of the reception of the *Dream*, Walch asserts that Shakespeare intentionally chose heterogeneous material in order to make the contradictions inherent in the material serve the purposes he wished to achieve and in so doing created a "comedy *sui generis* which has been misunderstood for the simple reason that it sets its own standards." Walch then examines the role of Theseus as an example of Shakespeare's "strategy." The allusions to Queen Elizabeth in Theseus' speech at V.i.91-105 and the difficulty of the case which Theseus must judge (Demetrius and Lysander are equal in every respect) are noted, and the presentation of Theseus as "judgment," the polar opposite of "fancy," is seen as an attempt by Shakespeare to render both judgment and fancy problematic. Walch also notes that Shakespeare took care to have the audience perceive Theseus from the outset as a wise and temperate ruler, not as the rash and treacherous man he was also represented to be in myths known to the audience. Walch believes, however, that at the end of the play, particularly in IV.i and V.i, Shakespeare reveals how limited Theseus is by his rationality and inability to conceive of a non-rational realm. The artisans, particularly Bottom, are thus superior to Theseus because the fairy world is not closed to them.

The final section of Walch's essay, in which he treats the form of the *Dream*, also reflects the Marxist bias, which demands unwarranted emphasis on the rustics, the only characters which could be construed as members of the

proletariat. Walch sees the heterogeneous groups not as
social ranks but as concentric spheres. In the innermost
(first) he places Bottom and the rustics, in the second the
pairs of lovers, in the third Theseus and Hippolyta, and in
the outermost (fourth) the elves, with Puck occupying the
innermost position, Oberon the outermost, and Titania
somewhere in between.

II. SOURCES, BACKGROUND, DATE

567 Halliwell[-Phillipps], James Orchard. *An Introduction to Shakespeare's "Midsummer Night's Dream."* London: William Pickering, 1841. Reprint. Folcroft, Pa.: Folcroft Library Editions, 1974. 104 pp.

Halliwell generalizes as to possible sources and influences, suggests specific meanings for details, and gives extracts from numerous contemporary literary sources and analogues. Chapter 1 considers the inconsistencies in the stages of the moon and time duration and title (the time setting is in fact May Day), which "do not in the least detract from the most beautiful poetical drama in this or any other language." Chapter 2 quotes accounts of the weather, from Simon Forman, John Stowe, and Thomas Churchyard, along with other evidence to support an autumn 1594 date. Chapter 3 makes "a few general observations" on the sources of the play at the same time insisting that it is finally Shakespeare's own invention. "The Knight's Tale," *The Legend of Good Women,* and Golding's translation of Ovid's *Metamorphoses* were obviously used. The tale of Midas as contained in a broadside based on Ovid Halliwell also thinks was influential. He reprints *The Merry Puck, or Robin Goodfellow* (the ballad), which he takes to pre-date the play (this ballad, which E. K. Chambers calls *The Mad Merry Prankes of Robin Goodfellow,* registered on 23 March 1631--see items 576); and he assumes the *Merry Prankes* (the prose history) which Chambers calls *Robin Goodfellow, his Mad Prankes and Merry Jests,* was registered on 25 April 1627) to pre-date and, in places, to have influenced the play. Chapter 4 connects Bottom's name with his trade: a *bottom* was a ball of thread wound upon a cylindrical body. Chapter 5 presents a brief stage history, disagreeing with the view that the play is unfit for the stage although admitting that it has rarely been performed successfully. Chapter 6 provides materials on the legend of the Man in the Moon. Chapter 7 conjectures on the "death of learning" allusion (V.i.52-53): Robert Greene seems likely. Chapter 8 makes observations on a dozen or so passages especially where questionable emendations have been offered, and reprints the first part of Fisher's 1600 quarto (Q1). Chapter 9 discusses the orthography of the name in order to show a preference for *Shakespeare*. An appendix reprints the prose political tract *The Midnight's Watch, or Robin Goodfellow* (1643).

568   Halpin, N. J. *Oberon's Vision in the "Midsummer-Night's Dream," Illustrated by a Comparison with Lyly's "Endymion."* London: The Shakespeare Society, 1843. Reprint. Nendeln: Kraus, 1966. vii, 108 pp.

A comparison of the two plays and a study of historical accounts of the Kenilworth festivities (by Robert Laneham, George Gascoigne, and William Dugdale), along with what we know about Leiscester's complex personal relations at the time, leads to the following conclusions: Oberon's Vision (II.i.148-68) refers to the Queen's visit to Kenilworth Castle in July 1575; to the "Princely Pleasures" on that occasion (a suggestion first made in print by James Boaden, in 1832 and again in 1837); to the attempts of Leicester ("Cupid," Lyly's "Endymion") to win Elizabeth ("the cold moon," Lyly's "Cynthia"); to his wavering passion for the Countess of Sheffield ("the earth," Lyly's "Tellus"); and finally to his intrigue with Lettice, Countess of Essex ("a little western flower," Lyly's "Floscula"), not with Mary, Queen of Scots, as Warburton had suggested, or with Amy Robsart, as Boaden had suggested. Shakespeare, at age eleven, is thought to have been present for the festivities. Part 1 gives the events and characters surrounding Kenilworth as they inform the allegory. Part 2 gives the allegory of *Endymion*. Part 3 makes the comparison between the allegories of the two plays. For attitudes toward this view see items 6, 35, 573-74, 586, 644, 668, 674, 740, 746, 750 and 960. For other comparisons with Lyly see item 184.

569   Halliwell[-Phillipps], James Orchard. *Illustrations of the Fairy Mythology of "A Midsummer Night's Dream."* London: The Shakespeare Society, 1845. Reprint. Nendeln: Kraus-Thomson, 1966; New York: AMS, 1970. xxii, 319 pp. Issued "with certain additions and corrections" with Joseph Ritson's *Fairy Tales, Legends, and Romances, Illustrating Shakespeare and Other*

English Writers. London: Frank & William Kerslake, 1875. Reprint. New York: AMS, 1972. xix, 320 pp.

"The principal early documents concerning the fairy mythology of England, as far as they can be considered in any way illustrative of Shakespeare" (p. ix). The introduction (pp. vii-xix) offers a few observations on "the probable extent of Shakespeare's obligations to the fairy creed of his own day" (p. xiv). It traces the history of the superstition as it existed in the age of Elizabeth. Shakespeare founded his elfin world on the prettiest of the people's traditions, not on literary notions, and clothed it in "the everlasting flowers of his own exuberant fancy." How innovative he was we shall probably never know. *The Mad Pranks and Merry Jests* though dated 1628 surely is earlier [but see E. K. Chambers, item 576]. Descriptions of fairies from Reginald Scot's *Discovery* (1584) and Thomas Nashe's *Terrors of the Night* (1594) and other places are quoted. See item 14.

570 Halliwell-Phillipps, J. O. *Memoranda on the "Midsummer Night's Dream," A.D. 1879 and A.D. 1855*. Brighton: Fleet and Bishop, 1879. 47 pp.

This small book reprints the introduction to Halliwell's *Dream* (item 738) and adds several observations which were the results of his reconsiderations. What he takes to be a quotation in the play from Spenser's *Faerie Queene*, Book VI ("Through hils and dales . . .") leads him to date *Dream* after 1596. A final note connects "the wier brake" below the church in Stratford with the woods of the play.

571 Sidgwick, Frank. *The Sources and Analogues of "A Midsummer-Night's Dream."* The Shakespeare Library. New York: Duffield; London: Chatto & Windus, 1908. 196 pp. Reprints. Folcroft Library Editions. Folcroft, Pa.: Folcroft Press, 1971, 1973; New York: AMS, 1973.

Chapter 1 gives what justification there is for taking "The Knight's Tale" as the source for the "sentimental" plot (that is, the Athenian plot); except for a few details, Shakespeare was not indebted to Chaucer. Chapter 2 mentions Reginald Scot's *Discovery of Witchcraft* (1584) and Lucius Apuleius' *The Golden Ass* (W. Adlington's translation, 1566, often printed) as they may have

suggested Bottom's translation (the "grotesque" plot),
though non-literary sources, it is urged, ought to be taken
seriously; and lists four previous versions, including that
of Ovid, for Pyramus and Thisbe. Chapter 3 traces the
origins of the names of the "fairy" plot, of the word *fairy*,
while finding that, but for his special treatment, most of
what Shakespeare knew about fairies came from the oral
tradition. (Sidgwick gives a long discussion of the fairies of
metrical romances, including summaries of the relevant
material.) For illustrative texts (pp. 69-193), mostly
excerpts, Sidgwick includes Arthur Golding's translation of
Ovid's Pyramus and Thisbe section, *Robin Good-Fellow, His
Mad Pranks and Merry Jests* (the prose tale, registered
1627), *Thomas of Erceldoune* ("fytte" 1), Reginald Scot's
Discovery (1584), Thomas Churchyard's "Strange Farlies"
(the ballad, published 1592), *The Mad Merry Pranks of
Robin Good-Fellow* (the broadside ballad registered 1631),
"Queen Mab" (from Ben Jonson's *A Satyr*, 1603), "The
Fairies' Farewell" (a ballad printed in 1648), "The Fairy
Queen" (poem from *The Mysteries of Love and Eloquence*,
1658), and Michael Drayton's *Nymphidia* (poem, published in
1627). For other general discussions of the sources see
items 561, 567, 576, 615, 630-31, 744, 747 and 960.

572   Hemingway, Samuel B. "The Relation of *A Midsummer
       Night's Dream* to *Romeo and Juliet*." *MLN*, 26 (1911),
       78-80.

       The interlude is "unquestionably a burlesque not only of
       the romantic tragedy of love in general but of *Romeo and
       Juliet* in particular." See items 60 and 131.

573   Chambers, E. K. "The Occasion of *A Midsummer Night's
       Dream*." *A Book of Homage to Shakespeare*. Ed. Israel
       Gollancz. Oxford: University Press, 1916, pp. 154-60.
       Reprinted in the author's *Shakespeare Gleanings*.
       Oxford: University Press, 1944. Reprint. Folcroft, Pa.:
       Folcroft Press, 1969.

       Considers carefully some of the events, attitudes, and
       personalities involved in the William Stanley, Earl of Derby,
       and Elizabeth Vere marriage of 26 January 1594 since it may
       have been the occasion and the basis for topical allusions in
       the play, though he remains "by no means convinced."
       Chambers suggests briefly that the Thomas

Berkeley-Elizabeth Carey wedding of 19 February 1596 be
given consideration, and rejects the old notion that
Oberon's Vision (II.i.148-68) alludes (Warburton) to Mary
Queen of Scots and the northern rebellion or (Halpin, item
568) to the intrigue of Leicester with the Countess of
Essex. If Shakespeare had any pageant in mind (of water-
and fireworks), it would have been that at Elvetham in
September 1591.

574 Rickert, Edith. "Political Propaganda and Satire in *A
     Midsummer Night's Dream.*" *Modern Philology*, 21 (1923),
     53-87, 133-54.

Act II.i.1-187 consists largely of political propaganda for
the Earl of Hertford's (Edward Seymour's) heir. The
pageantry in Oberon's Vision (II.i.148-68) fits much better
the fête at Elvetham in 1591, which was part of Hertford's
futile attempt to ingratiate himself with the Queen, than it
does that of Kenilworth in 1575, when we consider a
contemporary account and drawing. Hertford's son by Lady
Katherine Grey would have been next in line to succeed
Elizabeth, but the marriage of his parents had been
declared null and void by the Queen and he thus
illegitimate. He wanted his son declared legitimate, and thus
have some hope that the boy would succeed to the throne.
His mother ("the votaress") died in 1568. Oberon is Henry
VIII, Titania is Elizabeth, and Bottom is James of Scotland
(whom the play satirizes, he being a likely successor to
Elizabeth). Miss Rickert concludes with a list of the
principal facts on the basis of which this theory rests. 1)
About 100 lines in II.i.1-87 are topical. 2) The lines that
seem to refer to the Elvetham fête are preceded by lines
that parallel the story of Lady Katherine Grey, by others
that suggest the refusal of Elizabeth to submit to the will of
Henry VIII about the Suffolk heir, and by others that hint
at supernatural wrath due to this situation as causing the
abnormal weather of 1594-1595. 3) The generally accepted
reference to the lion-episode at Stirling is borne out by
other echoes from that occasion. (Malone had noticed a
possible allusion to the christening of Prince Henry on 30
August 1594 in the joke about the "lion among ladies"
[III.i.29]. Because James was afraid, the lion which was to
draw the chariot was replaced with a blackamore.) 4) Many
jokes either inappropriate to Bottom or obscure in
themselves are explained by striking peculiarities about the
person or history of King James. 5) If James's Pyramus

poem (quoted in the main argument) is, as there are strong
reasons for believing, the supposedly lost poem that he
sent to Elizabeth, it motivates the satire on his pretensions
to the English throne in the story of Pyramus and Thisbe,
and it also helps to explain why the figures of alliteration
and repetition, which he expounded with approval in his
critical treatise, should be so abundantly parodied in the
Interlude itself. 6) Study of the run-on lines makes it clear
that the Theseus and Fairy plots were written several years
after the Lovers plot, and that the whole play underwent
some later revision before 1600; internal evidence shows
that it could not have been finished before the early
summer of 1595; and although it bears all the marks of a
court play, there is no evidence that it was ever played
before the Queen. 7) In 1595 the affairs of Hertford were
at a crisis that warranted an attempt on his behalf; and the
situation of Elizabeth and James was such that satire
against him before her might have been planned. 8) The
Cecils had frequently used both drama and masque as
political tools, and the Cecils were adherents to the Suffolk
claim. 9) James was commonly satirized on the English stage
at this time. 10) *Dream* shows the influence of Spenser and
Lyly, both of whom wrote political allegory, and in turn it
influences a political allegory by Dekker (*The Whore of
Babylon*). 11) Shakespeare in *Hamlet* shows that he is
familiar with the political use of the drama; in *Henry V* he
shows his dislike of the Scots and admiration for Essex and
his ideas. 12) Shakespeare's part in the political game can
be explained through his relationship with Southampton,
friend of Essex, or with the Careys. For attitudes toward
this view see items 54, 284, 576, 673, 685g, 750, 807 and
900.

575   Welsford, Enid. *The Court Masque: A Study in the
      Relationship between Poetry & the Revels*. Cambridge:
      University Press, 1927. Pp. 331-32. Reprint. New York:
      Russell & Russell, 1962. The section on *Dream* is
      reprinted with lacunae in *Shakespeare's Comedies: An
      Anthology of Modern Criticism*. Ed. Laurence Lerner.
      London: Penguin, 1967.

      The music of the poetry, the scenic element, the
dance-like structure, the use of character-types, the
presence of "antimasque" elements in the rusticals are all
poetic transmutations from "floating recollections of Court

festivities." *Dream* "was the product of many earlier
masques and entertainments." See also items 149 and 394.

575a   Spurgeon, Caroline F. E. *Keats's Shakespeare: A
       Descriptive Study Based on New Material.* London:
       Humphrey Milford, Oxford University Press, 1928. viii,
       178 pp. There are numerous reprints.

       Dream and *The Tempest,* judging the marks and their
       wear in Keats's copy of Shakespeare, were by far the most
       read of the plays and along with *Romeo* his favorites (pp.
       5-6). *Dream* provided him with pictures or ideas and
       sometimes with "sweet sounds" for *Endymion* (pp. 15-16).
       (The lines influenced by *Dream* are listed on pages 62-65.)
       He especially loved the fairy poetry and songs, but shows
       no sign of appreciation of the comic part (p. 19). On
       Titania's foul weather speech (II.i.81-117) he has a long
       note, which concludes that "the thing is a piece of
       profound verdure" (p. 52). Keats's markings in *Dream* are
       printed on pages 86-105. For instances of specific influence
       see items 1005 and 1083.

576   Chambers, E. K. *William Shakespeare: A Study of Facts and
       Problems.* Volume 1. Oxford: Clarendon Press, 1930. Pp.
       356-63.

       Provides the basic bibliographic facts and speculates
       briefly as to the relationship among the three early texts.
       Q1, the Fisher quarto of 1600, is a fairly well-printed text
       and may be from the author's manuscript. Q2, the Roberts
       quarto of 1619, is from Q1, and F1 is from Q2, with the
       analysis of Dover Wilson suggesting that certain notes for a
       revival had been incorporated (item 748). Six weddings
       have been offered for the occasion: 1) Robert Devereux,
       Earl of Essex and Frances Lady Sidney in April or May
       1590, 2) Sir Thomas Heneage and Mary Countess of
       Southampton on 2 May 1594, 3) William Stanley, Earl of
       Derby and Elizabeth Vere at Greenwich on 26 January 1595,
       4) Thomas Berkeley and Elizabeth Carey at Blackfriars on
       19 February 1596, 5) Henry Wriothesley, Earl of
       Southampton and Elizabeth Vernon about February or
       August 1598, 6) Henry Lord Herbert and Anne Russell at
       Blackfriars on 16 June 1600. Chambers assesses without a
       certain conclusion the likelihood of each, finding that the
       Berkeley-Carey and Stanley-Vere weddings seem to fit a

date of 1594-1596. He does not find an allusion to Robert
Greene at V.i.52-53, suggesting instead Tasso, if any
particular death is intended. The bad weather of March
1594 is probably the basis for the allusion (II.i.81-117).
Chambers accepts the idea of revision in Act 5, though
rejects Dover Wilson's theory (see item 748) of extended
revision, and assumes the play to have been adapted for
the public stage. Edith Rickert's view is "quite incredible"
(see item 574). He lists quickly (in one paragraph) sources
and evidence of the early stage history and finds no
ground other than forgeries for assuming sixteenth-century
versions of the prose *Robin Goodfellow, his Mad Prankes
and Merry Jests,* registered on 25 April 1627, or of the
ballad *The Mad Merry Prankes of Robin Goodfellow,*
registered on 23 March 1631. Chambers describes the
misdating of the Roberts quarto ("1600" and not "1619") by
William Jaggard on pages 133-38.

577   McCloskey, F. H. "The Date of *A Midsummer Night's
      Dream.*" *MLN,* 46 (1931), 389-91.

      Takes Bottom's song (III.i) "The Woosel cocke" to be a
      parody of a poem called "a Mayde forsaken" published in
      The Arbour of Amorous Devices in 1594 and thus dates the
      play c. 1595.

578   Bush, Douglas. *Mythology and the Renaissance Tradition in
      English Poetry.* Rev. ed. New York: W. W. Norton,
      1963. xiv, 372 pp. First published, Minneapolis:
      University of Minnesota Press, 1932. Reprint. Pageant
      Book Company, 1957.

      Gives numerous details (scattered throughout) of the
      variety of Pyramus and Thisbe versions but does not
      discuss Shakespeare's version in particular. Absent from
      the 1963 revision is the following comment from 1932: "I
      have not found evidence" for Thomas Mouffet's *The
      Silkewormes, and Their Flies* as a source. For other views
      on this topic see items 600, 615, 630, 663 and 685h.

579   Simpson, Percy. "The 'Headless Bear' in Shakespeare and
      Burton." *Studies in Elizabethan Drama.* Oxford:
      Clarendon Press, 1955, pp. 89-94. Originally published
      in *Queens Quarterly* (Canada), 1932.

Finds a "headless bear" in a realistic 1613 pamphlet (later owned by Burton) which may reflect a superstition prompting Puck's usage (III.i.98-101). See item 650a.

580 Draper, John W. "The Date of *Midsommer Nights Dreame*." *MLN*, 53 (1938), 266-68. Reprinted in the author's *Stratford to Dogberry: Studies in Shakespeare's Earlier Plays*. Pittsburgh: University of Pittsburgh Press, 1961.

The numerous astronomical references fit consistently together to suggest that the comedy was written to be performed about 1 May 1595.

581 Baldwin, Charles Sears. "Pastoral and Rustic Comedy." *Renaissance Literary Theory and Practice: Classicism in the Rhetoric and Poetic of Italy, France, and England 1400-1600*. Ed. Donald Lemen Clark. New York: Columbia University Press, 1939, pp. 146-54.

Dream is "the dramatic solution of myth and pastoral, folklore and rustics, for court show" whereby Lyly's "pedantic encomium and clumsy dumb show, Peele's jolly rustics and half-fairies, become as antiquated as the many Elizabethan gropings through the moralities and pastoral." Shakespeare combined classical and romantic into one. See item 184, for Lyly connections with the play, and items 193, 484, 504 and 525 for Peele connections.

582 Kroepelin, H. "Das Niedersächsische [Lower Saxon Elements] in *Sommernachtstraum*." *Deutsche Allgemeine Zeitung* (Berlin), 25 September 1940. (German--not seen)

583 McNeal, Thomas H. "Studies in the Greene Shakspere Relationship." *Shakespeare Association Bulletin*, 15 (1940), 210-18.

In general (by burlesquing the dream vision and the Petrarchan *blazon*) and in various particulars (Bottom's "I have had a most rare vision"), *Dream* seems to satirize the poem *A Most Rare and Excellent Dreame* published in 1593 and usually attributed to Robert Greene. See item 282.

584   Wright, Celeste Turner. "The Amazons in Elizabethan
         Literature." *Studies in Philology*, 37 (1940), 433-56.

         Surveys attitudes about and allusions to Amazons, with a
      few notices of Hippolyta (pp. 436-37). Nothing is observed
      to be distinctive about Shakespeare's treatment.

585   Calthorpe, Fitzroy A. G. "'A fair vestal throned by the
         west.'" *Baconiana*, 26 (1942), 171-72.

         Such a reminiscence of the Elvethan fête as occurs in
      Dream can only mean that the poet "was privileged by right
      of birth and social rank." See items 35 and 574.

585a Ellison, Florence R. "Fairy Folk in *A Midsummer Night's
         Dream*." *Journal of the South-West Essex Technical
         College*, 1 (1942), 99-101.

         For his fairy material Shakespeare drew on many
      different sources. The several treated briefly and generally
      here are typically acknowledged and discussed in more
      detail elsewhere. For other studies of the fairy material see
      item 14.

586   Brooks, Alden. *Will Shakespeare and the Dyer's Hand*. New
         York: Charles Scribner's Sons, 1943. xx, 703 pp.

         Argues that the first version of *Dream* was a
      transformation of a fairy spectacle by Thomas Churchyard
      for the Queen's entertainment involving an allegory of
      Leicester and the quarrel over Alençon. The "western
      flower" was Lettice Knollys, the Kenilworth entertainment of
      July 1575, the ultimate inspiration. In the second version,
      Bottom and company are Shakespeare the actor and
      Pembroke's Men. Sir Edward Dyer wrote the play. (Pp.
      92-103) See item 568.

587   Law, Robert Adger. "The Text of 'Shakespeare's
         Plutarch.'" *Huntington Library Quarterly*, 6 (1943),
         197-203.

         Shakespeare probably used the 1579 edition for *Dream*;
      the 1595 was "almost certainly too late." (There are very

few differences between the two.) The spelling of Titania's list of ladies seems closer to 1579.

587a   Tucker, William John. "Irish Aspects of Shakespeare." *Catholic World*, 156 (1943), 698-704.

Nowhere is the "Celtic note" of natural magic (which Matthew Arnold found to be one of the characteristics of English poetry) seen more clearly than in Shakespeare's spirit-world, especially in *Dream*. There are several similarities (discussed briefly on p. 699) between the Celtic fairy-land of Ireland and its Shakespearean counterpart.

588   Baldwin, T. W. *William Shakspere's Small Latine & Lesse Greeke*. Volume 2. Urbana: University of Illinois Press, 1944.

The way Shakespeare uses "triple Hecate" suggests that he consulted both Golding's translation and Ovid. (Pp. 436-40) See items 608 and 599.

589   Le Comte, Edward S. *Endymion in England: The Literary History of a Greek Myth*. New York: Columbia University Press, King's Crown Press, 1944. xii, 189 pp.

Remarks in passing (p. 93) on similarities between Phoebe's promises to Endymion in Drayton's poem *Endymion and Phoebe* and Titania's promises to Bottom. William Brough's *Endymion*, a burlesque of 1860, recalls Titania and Bottom (p. 121).

590   Bethurum, Dorothy. "Shakespeare's Comment on Mediaeval Romance in *Midsummer-Night's Dream*." *MLN*, 60 (1945), 85-94.

"The Knight's Tale" supplied the only suggestion for the four lovers that Shakespeare needed, and he heightened the irony implicit in Chaucer's story to produce the lightest and gayest satire on medieval romance there is. The significant dependence, which is a matter largely of tone, does not admit of cataloguing as do the more obvious borrowings (which Frank Sidgwick, in item 571, and others have noted). Shakespeare needed only to follow out hints in

Chaucer of satire to produce his own burlesque. The four lovers are simply Chaucer's characters treated more realistically than the romantic conventions would permit. (The hint of Pyramus and Thisbe is there in "The Merchant's Tale.") Shakespeare may well have been parodying Chaucer's tale as it was present in the play Henslowe lists as *Palamon and Arcite*, performed in late 1594. For other discussions of "The Knight's Tale" as source see items 322, 454, 567, 571, 611, 630, 634, 648, 658, 683, 685r, 744, 747 and 754.

591   Generosa, Sister M. "Apuleius and *A Midsummer Night's
      Dream*: Analogue or Source, Which?" *Studies in
      Philology*, 42 (1945), 198-204.

      Maintains that a parallel of situation, not words, exists, and that Shakespeare knew *The Golden Ass*, either in Latin or in Adlington's 1566 translation. Both Bottom and Lucius are transformed into asses. The legend of Cupid and Psyche, used by Apuleius, may have provided hints for Puck. Titania resembles the woman loved by Lucius, though here Shakespeare refines the coarseness of Apuleius. For other discussions of Apuleius as source see items 182, 571, 592, 598, 630-31, 672, 685i, 685m, 754 and 960.

591a Melsome, W. S. *The Bacon-Shakespeare Anatomy*. London:
      Lapworth; New York: Russell F. Moore, 1945. xv, 250
      pp.

      Cites nine parallels in thought and phrasing between *Dream* and Francis Bacon's work to help prove that Shakespeare's plays were written by Bacon. See also items 35 and 609a.

592   Starnes, Dewitt T. "Shakespeare and Apuleius." *PMLA*, 60
      (1945), 1021-50.

      Argues (pp. 1030-32) that Shakespeare knew Apuleius, probably in the Adlington translation of 1566, that Bottom's transformation and Titania's falling in love with him could have been suggested by *The Golden Ass*. There are likenesses also in details and phrasing. Only the transformation is there in Reginald Scot's *Discovery of*

Witchcraft (1584). Both transformation and subsequent love are in *The Golden Ass*. See item 591.

593 Farzaad, M[asūd]. *Woodbine and Honeysuckle*. Hertford: Stephen Austin & Sons, 1946. 113 pp.

Part I is an effort to examine and clarify the "remarkably large--and confused--mass of critical material (both facts and conjecture) [which] has accumulated in the course of the centuries around this passage" (p. 2): "So doth the woodbine the sweet honeysuckle/ Gently entwist" (IV.i.41-42). Concludes that *woodpine* is the proper reading, with *wood* meaning "rough" or "forest." Gives the lines (41-43) from Titania to the fairies.

Part II (a series of specific observations) finds in II.ii.9-32 two different parts involving two different methods of delivery--the two quatrains forming a "roundel" and the remaining two stanzas (a lullaby) forming "a fairy song." The *ivy-elm topos* (IV.i.42-43) implies a marital and therefore chaste relationship between Bottom and Titania. Analyzes the crucial passage (II.ii.9-32) for its sound properties. The "I know a bank" passage (II.i.249-56) is recalled in the crucial passage (II.ii.9-32). Underscores the importance of scents in the "bank" passage. Both Jonson and Milton had *Dream* in mind for their flower passages: *The Vision of Delight, Comus*, 543-45, *Lycidas*, 142-47, *Paradise Lost*, IV, 689-705. See item 45.

594 Poirier, Michael. "Sidney's Influence upon *A Midsummer Night's Dream.*" *Studies in Philology*, 44 (1947), 483-89.

Detects echoes of *Arcadia* (1590) in Theseus' hound speech (IV.i.102-126) and of *Defence* in his description of the poet (V.i.2-27). For other connections between Sidney and *Dream* see items 50, 69, 282, 339, 387, 445, 450, 475, 557 and 595-6.

595 Thaler, Alwin. *Shakespeare and Sir Philip Sidney*. Cambridge: Harvard University Press, 1947. 100 pp.

There is a striking resemblance (pp. 8-9, 42-48) between two passages in *Dream*--Theseus' speech on the imagination (V.i.7-18) and on actors as shadows

(V.i.208-209)--and Sidney's disquisition on the subject in the *Defense*. See item 594.

596   Ribner, Irving. "A Note on Sidney's *Arcadia* and *A Midsummer Night's Dream.*" *Shakespeare Association Bulletin*, 23 (1948), 207-208.

The Philoclea-Zelmane-Basilius-Gynecia tangle constitutes a possible source for Shakespeare's lovers. See item 594.

597   Spence, Lewis. *The Fairy Tradition in Britain*. London and New York: Rider, 1948. 374 pp.

Chapter 1 describes the several species of English fairies, with sections devoted to Puck, Brownie, Robin Goodfellow, and Hobthrust, among others. Cites their various names, locations, activities, and the literature (including *Dream*) about them. See item 14.

598   Wilson, J. Dover. "Variations on the Theme of *Midsummer Night's Dream.*" *Tribute to Walter de la Mare on His Seventy-fifth Birthday*. London: Faber & Faber, 1948, pp. 25-43. Reprinted with additions in *Shakespeare's Happy Comedies*. London: Faber & Faber, 1962, pp. 184-220 (item 644).

Extends his theory of revision (see item 748) by declaring his belief that Shakespeare did not write the original play at all, and expresses his delight that de la Mare, "the poet above all others of this age," has agreed (in item 16) as to the weakness of some of the poetry of the play and thus of revision, denying Shakespeare's presence in the weak lines. The fairy plot, afterwards revised, was part of the original. Finds significant the influence of Cupid and Psyche from Apuleius' *Golden Ass*, translated by Adlington in 1566, for Bottom's transformation and the magic flower. In the early version Cupid had Puck's function. Even Oberon's retrospective speech (II.i.148-68) may have come from Apuleius' description of Venus. See item 591.

599   D[avenport]., A[rnold]. "Weever, Ovid and Shakespeare." *Notes and Queries*, 194 (1949), 524-25.

Considers the Picus and Circe episode in the *Metamorphoses* as a source of passages in *Venus and Adonis* and *Dream*. Such may account for the "wanton" (Circe rather than Diana) qualities in Titania. For other discussions of Ovid as source see items 316, 411, 415, 504, 550, 567, 588, 608-9, 611, 615, 624, 630, 635a, 638, 641, 647, 657-57a, 660a, 676, 680, 685, 685v, 747, 754 and 960.

600 Fisher, A. S. T. "The Source of Shakespeare's Interlude of Pyramus and Thisbe: A Neglected Poem." *Notes and Queries*, 194 (1949), 400-402.

Shakespeare read Thomas Mouffet's didactic poem *The Silkewormes, and Their Flies* (1599) in manuscript and was influenced by it, as is evident from the number of verbal parallels. There are other kinds of evidence as well: *bottom*, to give one example, is "the technical name for a silkworm's cocoon and occurs five times in Mouffet's poem." Margaret Farrand anticipated Fisher in *Studies in Philology*, 22 (1930), 333-43. See items 578, 615, 630, 663 and 685h.

601 Hotson, Leslie. "Manningham's 'Mid . . . .'" *Times Literary Supplement*, 9 September 1949, p. 585.

Calls attention to a deleted syllable which may suggest that Manningham began to write *Midsummer Night's Dream* in his *Diary* instead of *Twelfth Night*. The plays being similar, he may have mixed them in his mind.

602 Thomas, Sidney. "The Bad Weather in *Midsummer Night's Dream*." *MLN*, 64 (1949), 319-22.

Argues for a 1596 date as the basis for the bad-weather allusion (II.i.81-117), the rains being especially heavy that summer, according to contemporary accounts, and thus for fall or winter of 1596 as the date of the play. The occasion may have been the double wedding of the daughters of the Earl of Worcester on 8 November 1596.

603 Adolf, Helen. "The Ass and the Harp." *Speculum*, 25 (1950), 49-57.

Connects in passing (p. 54) singing Bottom to the proverb "the Ass and the Harp" (the ass cannot hear the beauty of the music), the origins of which are dealt with in depth. See items 433 and 566kk.

604   Blythe, Ronald. "Four Villages." *Essex Review*, 59 (1950), 212-15.

Describes Arthur Golding's home village, digressing into his life, talents, and influence on Shakespeare.

605   McManaway, James G. "Recent Studies in Shakespeare's Chronology." *Shakespeare Survey*, 3 (1950), 23-33.

E. K. Chambers (in item 576) suggested 1595-1596 as the date for *Dream*. Various scholars have dated it as early as 1591 and as late as 1600 based on theories which are the consequence of the play's appropriateness for a wedding celebration. Sidney Thomas (in item 602) has offered 1596 on the basis of what he takes to be the allusion in the foul weather passage (II.i.81-117).

606   Atherton, J. S. "Shakespeare's Latin, Two Notes." *Notes and Queries*, 196 (1951), 337.

Finds a Latin parallel in the Vulgate (Wisdom 2:1) for "a tedious brief scene" (V.i.53).

607   Bradbrook, M. C. *Shakespeare and Elizabethan Poetry*. London: Chatto & Windus, 1951. Reprint. 1961, 1965; Cambridge: University Press, 1979. Pp. 154-61.

Surveys quickly suggestions *Dream* took from a wide variety of impulses literary and otherwise, including what would later be called the *nocturnal* (the enchantments and mistakes of the night), and how in a host of ways it touched literature before and after. "The fun [of the playlet] puts both players and audiences together inside the jest of professional actors pretending to be mechanicals trying to be amateur actors before an unreal audience."

608 Sledd, James. "A Note on the Use of Renaissance
Dictionaries." *Modern Philology*, 49 (1951), 10-15.

In cautioning scholars as to the proper use of parallels,
considers that "triple Hecate," which Baldwin had found "so
striking" in Golding, is suggested in several dictionaries.
See item 588.

609 Venezky, Alice S. *Pageantry on the Shakespearean Stage.*
New York: Twayne, 1951. Reprint. *AMS,* 1972. 242 pp.

Describes (pp. 140-42) elements in the Elvetham
entertainment which seem to be reflected in *Dream,* all, it is
noted, occurring in the first scene of the second act, and
which are also influenced by Ovid. *Dream* has an affinity
with such pageants. Briefly compares (pp. 157-58) *John a
Kent and John a Cumber* ("produced about 1594") with
Dream. They share these ingredients: four crossed lovers,
the love-chase, magic, and one subplot entirely devoted to
the preparation and presentation of a show to celebrate a
wedding. See items 574, 599 and 623.

609a Burridge, W. "An Idol of the Theatre." *Baconiana,* 36
(1952), 33-36.

The results attained by Puck's trickery in *Dream* are
excellent stage representations of the results attained
through belief in a false notion or Baconian "idol of the
theatre." See also items 35 and 591a.

609b Mutschmann, Heinrich, and Karl Wentersdorf. *Shakespeare
and Catholicism.* New York: Sheed and Ward, 1952. xvii,
446 pp. (First published in German in 1950.)

Four places in *Dream* are taken to be evidence of
Shakespeare's Catholicism: the allusion to Holy Water (p.
227), to what happens to the souls of suicides after death
(p. 238), to the practice of blessing houses and marriage
beds (p. 257), and to the superiority of "God-devoted
chastity" to matrimony (p. 293). See items 649 and 672a.

610 Rashbrook, R. F. "Shakespeare and the Bible." *Notes and
Queries,* 197 (1952), 49-50.

Finds a sustained parallel in Bottom's speech "I have had a most rare vision" to 2 Corinthians 12:1-6 and possibly 1 Corinthians 1:27 as well as the oft-noted 1 Corinthians 2:9. See item 406 for other comments on this issue.

611 Thomson, J. A. K. *Shakespeare and the Classics*. London: George Allen & Unwin; New York: Barnes & Noble, 1952. Reprint. Westport, Conn.: Greenwood Press, 1978. 254 pp.

"There is no evidence that [Shakespeare] used "The Knight's Tale" in Chaucer or the last book of Statius' *Thebais*." Having listed the instances of classical allusions relevant to the subject of Shakespeare's classical scholarship, Thomson finds them "not numerous" and "in no sense recondite." "I ask this question," he concludes, "how could a man, who read Ovid's Latin with ease and pleasure, bear to read Golding instead?" (Pp. 77-81, 154) See items 590 and 599.

611a Titherley, A. W. *Shakespeare's Identity*. Winchester, England: Warren and Son, 1952. xi, 338 pp.

Argues (pp. 71-75) that William Stanley, 6th Earl of Derby, wrote *Dream*. It was performed at Greenwich on 26 January 1595 for Derby's marriage with Elizabeth de Vere. There are, moreover, Derby connections with the Elvetham festival, with the Chester mystery plays (*Balaam and His Ass* influenced the Bottom transformation), and with the character Theseus (Derby=Theseus). Oberon alludes (II.i.148-68) to Elvetham and a period when Derby who was secretly betrothed to Queen Elizabeth fell in love with Elizabeth de Vere. *Dream* is his "charming wedding gift" to the bride. See items 38 and 626.

612 Briggs, K. M. *The Personnel of Fairyland*. Oxford: Alden Press, 1953. Reprint. Cambridge: R. Bentley, 1954, 1971; Detroit: Singing Tree Press, 1971. 228 pp.

Gives a brief account of Robin Goodfellow (p. 219) and Puck (p. 215). "The names Robin Goodfellow, Robin Hood and Hobgoblin seem to be indiscriminately applied to the same character." Intended for children.

613   Hankins, John Erskine. *Shakespeare's Derived Imagery*. Lawrence, Kansas: University of Kansas Press, 1953. 289 pp. Reprint. New York: Octagon, 1967.

Traces a number of images (the index gives nine references to *Dream*), including those having to do with sleep, blot, "winding," and garment, to possible origins in Palingenius' *Zodiacus* as translated by Barnabe Googe in 1565.

613a Hammerle, Karl. "The Poet's Eye (*MND* V.i.12): Zur Auffassung Shakespeares vom Wesen des Dicters" [On Shakespeare's Concept of the Poet]. *Innsbrucker Beiträge zur Kulturwissenschaft* (Ammann-Festgabe I. Teil), 1 (1953), 101-7. (German)

Cites North's Plutarch, specifically Cassius' speech to Brutus, as a probable source of passages in *Love's Labour's Lost* and *Dream* in which Berowne and Theseus, respectively, compare the poet and the lover, emphasizing that both look "not with the eyes, but with the mind." See item 59.

614   Boughner, Daniel C. *The Braggart in Renaissance Comedy: A Study in Comparative Drama from Aristophanes to Shakespeare*. Minneapolis: University of Minnesota Press, 1954. ix, 328 pp.

Bottom's remarks (I.ii.30-42) point to *Hercules Furens* and other plays of Seneca in the Newton volume. Bottom would be a ranter, not a braggart. (Pp. 141-42)

615   Muir, Kenneth. "Pyramus and Thisbe: A Study in Shakespeare's Method." *Shakespeare Quarterly*, 5 (1954), 141-53.

There is evidence that Shakespeare was influenced by six or seven versions of the story: Golding's translation of Ovid; Ovid; J. Thomson's version in *A Handful of Pleasant Delites*; the anonymous version in *A Georgeous Gallery of Gallant Inventions*; the one in Chaucer's *The Legend of Good Women*; Dunstan Gale's *Pyramus and Thisbe* (1596 or 1597). He also may have known about or been influenced by Lydgate's and Gower's versions and by *Cambises*. Muir

devotes half of his space to arguing that Shakespeare
borrowed most from Thomas Mouffet's poem *The
Silkewormes, and Their Flies* (published in 1599). This
poem was written to advocate the cultivation of the silkworm
in England; silkworms feed on mulberry leaves, stained
forever, according to Ovid, by the blood of Pyramus and
Thisbe. Most of the Mouffet parallels Margaret Farrand had
given in *Studies in Philology*, 27 (1930), 233-43, and
Douglas Bush rejected in *MLN*, 46 (1931), 144-47. Muir's
essay appears with slight changes in his *Shakespeare's
Sources* (item 631). See also items 60, 578, 600, 616, 630,
663, 683 and 685h.

616 _____. "Shakespeare as Parodist." *Notes and
        Queries*, 199 (1954), 467-68.

        There are six purposes for which Shakespeare used the
sources of the Pyramus and Thisbe playlet: 1) to show that
lovers cannot rely on supernatural intervention (Oberon and
Puck had intervened with the young lovers) to save them
from their folly; 2) to arouse laughter by showing the
actors' inadequacy; 3) to show that *Romeo*, by depending
so heavily on accident, was unsatisfactory tragedy; 4) to
burlesque the original; 5) to reflect on the relation of life
to art; and 6) to compile "a kind of anthology of bad
poetry"--the choice examples being from the best-known
versions of the story. Shakespeare either consulted his
sources during composition or else, which is unlikely, "all
the versions he had read since childhood coalesced in his
mind." Repeated in the author's *Shakespeare's Sources*
(item 631). See also item 615 especially, and 131.

617 Spencer, Terence. "Three Shakespearean Notes." *Modern
        Language Review*, 49 (1954), 46-41.

        "I. The Vile Name of Demetrius." Shakespeare recalled
the Demetrius Poliorcetes whose amorous and sadistic
escapades are described in North's *Plutarch*. See item 679.

618 Arnold, Paul. "Fées, Elfes et Puissances: le 'Songe d'une
        Nuit d'Été.'" *Esotérisme de Shakespeare*. Paris: Mercure
        de France, 1955, pp. 100-17. Translated into German by
        Marie Mankiewicz as *Esoterik im Werke Shakespeares*.
        Berlin: K. H. Henssel, 1957. 268 pp. Much of the same

material reappears in abridged form in "L'Engagement."
*Clef pour Shakespeare: Esotérisme de l'oeuvre
shakespearienne*. Essais d'art et de philosophie. Paris:
Librairie Philosophique J. Vrin, 1977, pp. 90-102.
(French)

Assumes that for Shakespeare the fairies and Puck
reflect a reality serious and mysterious, that he believes in
their power (as against the position of skeptics such as
Reginald Scot), and that through them and the play he
takes a moderate stance against the anti-erotic views of
contemporary thinkers. Behind the elements of *Dream*
Arnold finds a good deal of esoteric lore which he takes to
be a direct comment on contemporary controversies.
Comparisons are drawn with *The Tempest*. See items 55 and
117.

618a   Bradbrook, M. C. *The Growth and Structure of
        Elizabethan Comedy*. London: Chatto & Windus, 1955.
        Reprint. 1961, 1962, 1973; Berkeley and Los Angeles:
        University of California Press, 1956; Baltimore: Penguin
        Books, 1963; New York: Humanities Press, 1973;
        Cambridge and New York: Cambridge University Press,
        1979. ix, 246 pp.

There are scattered comments on *Dream*. The discussion
of the popular romantic drama suggests the kind of play the
mechanicals think of: *Common Conditions, The Cobler's
Prophecy, Sir Clyomon and Sir Clamydes*, for examples (pp.
17, 24). In *Dream* Shakespeare is creating his own form (p.
75). The thrice-three Muses mourning for the death of
learning (V.i.52-53) actually appear in Richard Edwards'
Damon and Pithias (p. 222n.).

619   Cheney, David Raymond. "Animals in *A Midsummer Night's
       Dream*." Ph.D. dissertation, Iowa State University, 1955.
       DA, 15 (1955), 2188.

Undertakes to illustrate sixteenth century animal
connotations through the uses which occur in *Dream*. Part
One treats the sources of animal lore, Part Two the uses of
animals in the play, Part Three the possibility that certain
scenes and animal names would have been taken
allegorically. The suggested allegory supports Elizabeth's
policy of non-marriage and her refusal to name a successor.

An appendix considers that the topical allusion is to the weather of 1594 and is critical of the government's corn policies. See item 53.

620   Groom, Bernard. *The Diction of Poetry from Spenser to Bridges.* Toronto: Toronto University Press, 1955. viii, 284 pp.

There are a few comments scattered about on *Dream*. Shakespeare is "most Spenserian" in *Dream* (p. 17), a play which belongs to "the Spenserian period of Shakespeare's diction" (p. 18). In Demetrius' exclamation "O Helen! Goddess . . ." (III.ii.137-44) the epithets would have struck contemporaries as hakneyed (p. 31). See item 89.

621   Nitze, William A. "*A Midsummer Night's Dream,* V.I.4-17." *Modern Language Review,* 50 (1955), 495-97.

Shakespeare derived the madnesses of the lunatic, lover, and poet from the second discourse of Socrates in Plato's *Phaedrus,* perhaps in Ficino's Latin translation. See item 122.

622   Schanzer, Ernest. "*A Midsummer Night's Dream* and *Romeo and Juliet.*" *Notes and Queries,* 200 (1955), 13-14.

Since the idea that "the wall is down" (V.i.337) that parted their fathers appears in none of the sources of the Pyramus and Thisbe playlet--and *is* there in *Romeo*--Shakespeare had probably already written *Romeo*. See items 20 and 131.

623   Shapiro, I. A. "The Significance of a Date." *Shakespeare Survey,* 8 (1955), 100-105.

The date for Anthony Munday's *John a Kent and John a Cumber* should be 1590, not 1595 (Collier) or 1596 (Greg). Many have seen parallels between it and *Dream*. See also items 648, 906 and 960.

624   Wilkinson, L. P. *Ovid Recalled.* Cambridge: University Press, 1955. 483 pp.

Lists and explains details ("triple Hecate," images in the hound scene at IV.i.102-26, the schedule of "sports" supplied to Theseus) which seem to have been suggested by Ovid and makes some general comments about the influence of Ovid on the fairy world, including this: "the whole atmosphere is extraordinarily reminiscent of the *Metamorphoses.*" (Pp. 419-21) See item 599.

625 Braddy, Haldeen. "Shakespeare's Puck and Froissart's Orthon." *Shakespeare Quarterly,* 7 (1956), 276-80.

Since the two have so many characteristics in common, Froissart's influence is probable.

626 Evans, A. J. *Shakespeare's Magic Circle.* Westport, Conn.: Associated Book Sellers, 1956. 160 pp.

Argues that William Stanley, sixth Earl of Derby, wrote the play as a wedding present to his bride, Elizabeth de Vere, whom he married on 26 January 1595. The Queen may have considered and rejected Derby as her Consort; the "little western flower" (II.i.166) in Oberon's Vision thus would be de Vere. (Pp. 55-63) See items 38 and 611a.

627 Gesner, Carol. "The Greek Romance Materials in the Plays of Shakespeare." Ph.D. dissertation, Louisiana State University, 1956. *DA,* 16 (1956), 2162.

Dream has "verbal and incidental elements" which apparently have Greek romance affinities. See item 664a for an account of the published version.

628 Harrison, Thomas P. "Shakespeare and Marlowe's *Dido, Queen of Carthage.*" *Texas Studies in English,* 35 (1956), 57-63.

The predominating sensuous and lyric qualities of *Dido* made a first and extensive impression upon Shakespeare and unmistakably link the two plays (as was first noticed by Edgar I. Fripp in the *TLS* on 16 August 1928). Parallels can be found between passages wholly descriptive and ornamental and passages describing the supernatural. (Most of the article is concerned with the influence of *Dido* on *Antony and Cleopatra*.)

629   Briggs, K. M. "The English Fairies." *Folklore*, 68 (1957), 270-87.

Within an account of fairies (types, powers, temperaments) relevant in general to *Dream*, touches briefly (p. 283) on how the play reflects the "mild and cheerful temper" of the English nature fairies. See items 14, 612 and 642.

630   Bullough, Geoffrey, ed. "*A Midsummer Night's Dream*." *Narrative and Dramatic Sources of Shakespeare*. Volume 1. London: Routledge & Kegan Paul; New York: Columbia University Press, 1957, pp. 365-422.

The introduction quickly places the play in relation to others, dating it 1594 or 1595, assuming certain additions (Titania's weather speech, for example, may have been written later), and taking the time setting to be the night before May Day, the wedding for which it was written a summer wedding. Then discusses in detail the known sources for each of the five main ingredients: 1) Theseus and Hippolyta. Plutarch's version of Theseus gave "stability and poise" to the traditional, legendary figure drawn largely from Chaucer. 2) The four young lovers. 3) The fairy world. Bullough assumes "The Merchant's Tale" provided suggestions for the fairy monarchs. 4) The misadventures of Bottom. 5) *Pyramus and Thisbe*. Of the influence of Thomas Mouffet's poem *The Silkewormes, and Their Flies* Bullough is not convinced by Kenneth Muir (item 615), and is unwilling to venture as to whether *Romeo* or "Pyramus" came first. Sections from the following are reprinted: I. Chaucer's "The Knight's Tale" (Probable Source). II. Thomas North's translation of Plutarch's "Life of Theseus" (Probable Source) and the comparison of Theseus with Romulus. III. *Huon of Bourdeaux* (Lord Berners' translation, in the 1601 edition, Probable Source). IV, VII. Reginald Scot's *Discoverie of Witchcraft* (1584, Probable Source). V, VIII. The account of Midas and of Pyramus and Thisbe from Thomas Cooper's *Thesaurus* (Analogues). VI. William Adlington's translation of Apuleius' *Golden Ass* (Possible Source). IX. Pyramus and Thisbe in Arthur Golding's translation of Ovid's *Metamorphosis*

(Source). X. I. Thomson's poem "A New Sonet of Pyramus and Thisbe" (1584, Possible Source). XI. *The Tragedy of Pyramus and Thisbe* (seventeenth-century ms. play, Analogue). See item 571.

631   Muir, Kenneth. *Shakespeare's Sources: Comedies and Tragedies*. London: Methuen; New York: Hillary House, 1957. Pp. 31-47. Reprint. 1961, 1965, and, with revisions, as *The Sources of Shakespeare's Plays*. London: Methuen, 1977; New Haven: Yale University Press, 1977. Pp. 66-77.

Gives a brief, comprehensive discussion of the sources (there is no single source) and what they were used for. Shakespeare appears to have taken hints from Plutarch, Chaucer, Montemayor, Apuleius, Scot, and possibly Marlowe and Lyly. The material here having to do with the sources of "Pyramus and Thisbe" is drawn from earlier essays (items 615 and 616). The material on the rest of the play is dense with instances of possible debt. See item 571.

632   Demetz, Peter. "The Elm and the Vine: Notes Toward the History of a Marriage Topos." *PMLA*, 73 (1958), 521-32.

Traces the presence of this distinctive, traditional topos (suggesting the true union of husband and wife) in Western literature from the first century B.C. to the present. Shakespeare has ivy-and-elm at IV.i.42-43. Though he does not mention *Dream*, Demetz does notice (p. 530) "the popular Renaissance antithesis of ivy and vine" and the substitution in Goethe. See item 45.

633   Rossky, William. "Imagination in the English Renaissance: Psychology and Poetic." *Studies in the Renaissance*, 5 (1958), 49-73.

Examines contemporary psychological accounts of the imagination to show its disrepute and why and how this disrepute influenced poets in their expression of and justification of the imagination. Theseus' speech serves as a point of departure.

634   Baldwin, T. W. *On the Literary Genetics of Shakespere's
      Plays 1592-1594*. Urbana, Ill.: University of Illinois
      Press, 1959. Ch. 28.

      Investigates *Dream*'s affinities with other early
      plays--"as the last probable representative of early work."
      Comparisons of plot are made with *Errors* and *Two
      Gentlemen*, of setting and props with *Wives*. Neither *Dream*
      nor *Wives* was written for an occasion first. Argues for the
      importance of "The Knight's Tale" as a source. Theseus'
      reference to the poet was suggested by Plutarch. Equates
      Titania with Diana: "Oberon must bear all the blame!"
      Considers that "the new moon and the four days at the
      beginning are only a false start, a discarded plan."
      Speculates as to the contribution of some other play using
      the Chaucerian material. And assumes the weather passage
      and courtly compliment to the Queen to be "Christmas
      inserts" for a performance at court and thus dates the
      play, but for these inserts, by the early summer of 1594.
      About most of these points there has been a good deal of
      controversy. See items 187, 240 and 590.

635   Briggs, K. M. *The Anatomy of Puck: An Examination of
      Fairy Beliefs among Shakespeare's Contemporaries and
      Successors*. London: Routledge & Kegan Paul, 1959.
      Reprint. New York: Arno Press, 1977. xi, 284 pp.

      Mentions the numerous strands out of which the fairies
      are woven and then concentrates on the two innovative
      characteristics drawn not from romance but from folklore:
      the smallness of the fairies and their relative benevolence.
      "It is not only that they 'do not all the harm that seemingly
      they have power to do,' but they show an active kindness."
      They are given to some mischief (Puck), but are "sharply
      dissociated from the witches." Shakespeare has picked out
      "one strand in a varied web" (their benevolence) and
      asserts it against "the more formal doctrine." In general the
      fairies are "creatures of another order," "definite,
      clear-cut, and natural." (Pp. 44-55) See item 14.

635a Bush, Douglas. "Classical Myth in Shakespeare's Plays."
      *Elizabethan and Jacobean Studies Presented to Frank
      Percy Wilson in Honor of His Seventieth Birthday*. Ed.
      Herbert Davis and Helen Gardner. Oxford: Clarendon

Press, 1959, pp. 65-85. Reprint. Folcroft, Pa.: Folcroft Press, 1969.

A consideration of "the distribution, the function, and the changing quality" of allusions to classical myth. With *Dream* the allusions become in places more than rhetoric alone; they become poetry--Oberon's speech at III.ii.391 ff. ("Even till the eastern gate . . ."), Oberon's Vision (II.i.148-68), and Theseus' hounds' speech (IV.i.102-126). Shakespeare obviously was inspired away from simple allusion by his setting, derived from Chaucer, North's Plutarch, and his own Athenian world, and by his highly original "antimasque" of Pyramus and Thisbe.

636   Coghill, Nevill. "Shakespeare's Reading in Chaucer." *Elizabethan and Jacobean Studies Presented to Frank Percy Wilson in Honour of His Seventieth Birthday.* Ed. Herbert Davis and Helen Gardner. Oxford: Clarendon Press, 1959, pp. 86-99. Reprint. Folcroft, Pa.: Folcroft Press, 1969.

Traces the history of scholarly comment on Chaucer's influence on *Dream*, especially of "The Knight's Tale," noting when it has been found and when questioned, and that Richard Edwards' play *Palemon and Arcyte* has been taken to be the possible source for the Chaucerian matter in *Dream*. It is hard to prove that Shakespeare read, let alone loved, Chaucer, but the evidence ("finger-prints") is there. There is a "sudden concentration of Chaucerisms" in *Dream, Romeo,* and other works of the same time. "Towards his thirtieth year" Shakespeare must have come upon a copy of Chaucer "and devoured it." Image after image from the older poet imprinted itself on his thought. See items 571 and 590.

637   Reed, Robert R., Jr. "Nick Bottom, Dr. Faustus, and the Ass's Head." *Notes and Queries,* 204 (1959), 252-54.

The prose history of Dr. Faustus (1592) rather than Scot's *Discoverie* (1584) may have suggested Puck's use of an ass's head.

637a   Brownlee, A. *William Shakespeare and Robert Burton.* Reading, England: Bradley and Son, 1960. xi, 337 pp.

Argues that *Dream* was written by Robert Burton and
cites (pp. 146-51) 26 parallels between it and Burton's
writing to help prove the case. Brownlee's central
contention has not been generally accepted.

638   Doran, Madeleine. "*A Midsummer Night's Dream*: A
      Metamorphosis." *Rice Institute Pamphlet*, 46 (1960),
      113-35.

The "richness of the allusive texture" and the free use
of diverse materials, especially the classical ornamentation,
suggest that Shakespeare "meant to give his play a classical
flavor in keeping with its setting at the court of Theseus,
and so to fulfill the [Renaissance] artistic requirements of
verisimilitude and decorum." Theseus combines elements
from Chaucer, Ovid, Plutarch, and Elizabeth's courtiers to
become a Renaissance Prince. Titania has
Circe-Diana-Lucina associations.

639   Parry-Jones, D. "Ritual at a Welsh Healing Well." *Gwerin*, 3
      (1960), 56-57.

Describes a ritual observed about 1785 that mentions
near the river Clydach a dingle "called *Cwm-Puca*, or the
Hobgoblin's Dingle" which may have suggested *Puck*.
Legend connects Shakespeare with the area.

640   Savage, James E. "Notes on *A Midsummer Night's Dream*."
      University of Mississippi Studies in English, 2 (1961),
      65-78.

The likely occasion for the first performance was the
Thomas Berkeley-Elizabeth Carey wedding of 19 February
1596. The description of the hounds (IV.i.102-26) would
have been made as a compliment to Berkeley's father, Sir
Henry, who was devoted to hunting. Possible sources for
the passage are given. See items 657a and 671.

641   Doran, Madeleine. "Pyramus and Thisbe Once More." *Essays
      on Shakespeare and Elizabethan Drama in Honor of
      Hardin Craig*. Ed. Richard Hosley. Columbia: University
      of Missouri Press, 1962; London: Routledge & Kegan
      Paul, 1963, pp. 149-61.

Looks at two versions of the story, a widely known and
influential twelfth-century Norman *lai* and Giovanni Andrea
dell'Anguillara's popular mid-sixteenth-century Italian one in
order to note what survived and what varied between the
two points with a view to throwing some light on
Shakespeare's handling of the story. Shakespeare catches
the basic features of the story unchanged since Ovid's
time, but also certain features that were most amplified or
altogether new in post-Ovidian traditions. While these two
versions are good, those Shakespeare is certain to have
known are all bad. The subject of Pyramus and Thisbe had
become through countless retellings "especially ripe for
parody." (Speculations as to which came first, *Romeo* or
Dream, are futile.) See items 60 and 599.

642 Green, Roger Lancelyn. "Shakespeare and the Fairies."
     Folk-lore, 73 (1962), 89-103.

Supplements Kathleen Briggs (item 629) on fairies in
literature and folklore before and after Shakespeare,
considering origins and characteristics as they are
suggested by the play. Shakespeare did in a sense *invent*
the fairies, as Charles Lamb is reported to have written,
despite the evidence scholars have tried to bring forth to
the contrary. There was no great fairy literature before
him. The medieval literary conception of Fairyland remains
in *Dream* only as a vague kind of background. The
mythology behind Oberon and Titania is mixed, and his
fairy world in general made up out of floating traditions
popular and literary. He gave us a fairy-world "of kindly
powers, with a King and Queen who wish well to mortals,
who have the Puck as their faithful follower, and who are
beautiful and gracious beings--no longer evil, malicious, or
in league with Hell." Though there may have been a
popular tradition that has the fairies diminutive (there
certainly was one that had them dwarf-size), Shakespeare
seems to have been responsible for their extreme smallness
and for that subsequent fashion. See item 14.

643 Hunter, G. K. *John Lyly: The Humanist as Courtier*.
     London: Routledge & Kegan Paul, Cambridge: Harvard
     University Press, 1962. 376 pp.

Theseus' appreciation of his hounds may have been
prompted by the real hounds which were actually used at

230   Sources, Background, Date

Christ Church, Oxford, in 1566, for *Palamon and Arcite* (p. 113). Lyly's influence includes: the balancing of a number of self-contained groups who relate to a single theme ("love versus authority"), the use of the Lylian debate subject of imagination versus reason, and having plot rather than character bear much of the meaning. But with each of these elements Shakespeare's treatment diverges from Lyly's. *Dream* and *Love's Labour's Lost* are "completely Lylian in their construction" unlike other earlier plays, perhaps as a consequence of their aristocratic occasions. Discusses the theme of appearance and reality and Theseus' speech. (Pp. 316-30) See items 59 and 184.

644 Wilson, J. Dover. "A Postscript (1961). Variations on the Theme of *A Midsummer Night's Dream.*" *Shakespeare's Happy Comedies*. London: Faber & Faber; Evanston: Northwestern University Press, 1962, pp. 184-220. Reprint. 1969.

Dream, "if not the loveliest, is certainly the happiest, of all the Happy Comedies."

Section I praises the construction of the plot and treats each component, quoting at length Peter Alexander's humorous portrait of Bottom (from item 19). Of the fairies, Wilson doubts Minor White Latham's view (item 14) that Shakespeare was responsible for their tiny size and general benevolence.

Section II takes Oberon's Vision (II.i.148-68) to be a poetic version of the Kenilworth pageantry of 9-27 July 1575 when the Queen visited the Earl of Leicester, as Halpin had thought (item 568), giving excerpts from George Gascoigne and Robert Laneham describing that festival alongside lines from Oberon, and assumes Shakespeare, at eleven, would have been there. (E. K. Chambers, in item 573, thought Elvetham in 1591 the reference, if there is one.) The passage was not written for the Queen to hear, since it might have offended her, and was never spoken when she was present. May Day is the setting, and Wilson recommends the wedding as that between Sir Thomas Heneage and the Countess of Southampton, mother of Shakespeare's patron, on 2 May 1594. Other allusions suggest that of William Stanley, Earl of Derby, to Elizabeth Vere on 26 January 1595. Too, it may well have been

performed at that of Sir Thomas Berkeley and Elizabeth
Carey on 9 February 1596.

Section III reprints the essay of 1948 in tribute to Walter
de la Mare (item 598).

645   Rowse, A. L. *William Shakespeare: A Biography*. New York:
      Harper & Row; London: Macmillan, 1963. Reprint. New
      York: Pocket Books, 1965. xiv, 511 pp.

Considers the occasion to have been the wedding of
Mary, Countess of Southampton, and Sir Thomas Heneage
on 2 May 1594, and takes the lines which end "and dies in
single blessedness" (I.i.74-78) to be a reference not to
Elizabeth, who would not have been present, but to the
young Earl of Southampton. Titania at II.i.81-117 describes
the disastrously wet summer of 1594. Sees a
"double-ending," calls attention to the Warwickshire country
beliefs which are seen as influential, and assumes that
Shakespeare shows in Sonnets 18 and 106 that he is
thinking of "a summer story." (Pp. 202-11) See item 646.

645a Smith, Charles G. *Shakespeare's Proverb Lore*. Cambridge,
      Mass.: Harvard University Press, 1963. ix, 181 pp.

Cites five instances of proverbs or sententiae in *Dream*
from Leonard Culman's *Sententiae Puerlis*.

646   Spencer, T. J. B. *The Observer*. 6 October 1963. (not
      seen)

Apparently questions the validity of A. L. Rowse's
reasoning (item 645) that the Queen could not have been
present (whatever the occasion itself) because of
I.i.72ff.--and that the lines refer to Southampton and not
to the Queen.

647   Staton, Walter F., Jr. "Ovidian Elements in *A Midsummer
      Night's Dream*." *Huntington Library Quarterly*, 6 (1963),
      165-78.

Shakespeare drew upon Ovid not only for the skit but
also for elements in the fairy plot, a possibility which has

been ignored heretofore because scholars have been
preoccupied with the native fairy tradition as a source.
Elizabethans in fact saw the classical and native traditions
as a single one. Oberon is like Jupiter, Titania is "an
amalgam of several classical goddesses," especially Juno,
and Robin is like Mercury. Also in common with Ovidian
material are the quarrel over the child, the foul weather,
Oberon's revenge, and much more. Shakespeare used Ovid
for "romantic enrichment," but he also, in Titania's wooing
of Bottom, parodied imitators of Ovid, even himself in
Venus and Adonis. See item 599.

648   Coghill, Nevill. *Shakespeare's Professional Skills.*
        Cambridge: Cambridge University Press, 1964. xvi, 224
        pp.

        Chapter 2 (pp. 32-60) is a source-study of *Pericles* and
Dream (separately) in order to show that "Shakespeare was
at pains to give unified shape of a meaningful kind to the
plays he composed, and some of the means he used to do
so." The unity of *Dream* is "the most consummate in the
whole canon of Shakespeare's works." Coghill takes Anthony
Monday's *John a Kent and John a Cumber* as a serious
source, accepting as its date 1589 (see item 623; Greg had
suggested 1596, Collier 1595), and considers at length its
influence alongside that of various places in Chaucer,
especially the "Knight's" and "Merchant's" tales. Coghill
lists the notions Shakespeare found in Monday (p. 52).
Shakespeare found useful the rustic reception committee
(Turnop and his troupe) and their Masque of Welcome. In
Monday they are detachable; not so in Shakespeare. The
fairy-imp idea in Shrimp is perfected in Puck. But Monday
worked too quickly, did not know what he was about,
though he had some bright ideas. What Monday lacked was
Theseus and love (both provided by "The Knight's Tale")
and the notion of Pyramus and Thisbe (provided in *The
Legend of Good Women* and "The Merchant's Tale").
"Theseus, in Chaucer as in Shakespeare, is a piece of warm
greatness and stability, the unmoved mover of the human
side of both stories," "the only character Shakespeare took
over whole from Chaucer." See items 599 and 683.

649   Crehan, J. H., S.J. "Shakespeare and the *Sarum Ritual.*"
        Month, n.s. 32 (1964), 47-50.

Oberon's blessing (along with that of the fairies who join him) echoes the *Sarum Manual* marriage ceremony (the last phase, in the bedroom) and "would have reminded anyone . . . that he was witnessing something which had been done in England by a priest a generation back in the past." Did the marriage involve Recusants? See items 609b and 672a.

649a Ford, Gertrude C. *A Rose by Any Name*. New York: A. S. Barnes, 1964. xiv, 302 pp.

A sustained, versified claim that Edward de Vere, 17th Earl of Oxford, wrote Shakespeare's plays. The evidence is presented in the margin for assertions made in the poem. There are scattered references to *Dream*. Bottom is, for example (pp. 242-43), sometimes Alençon and sometimes Vere himself. Helena *and* Titania = Elizabeth; Hermia = Anne, Burghley's daughter. See items 586 and 673.

650 Kim, Sun-Sook. "The Sources of *A Midsummer Night's Dream*." *English Language and Literature*, 15 (1964), 63-73.

Surveys generally the sources, relying on early scholarship.

650a Rahter, Charles A. "Puck's Headless Bear--Revisited." *Susquehanna University Studies* (Selinsgrove, Pa.), 7 (1964), 127-32.

Reinforces Percy Simpson's suggestion (see item 579) that "headless bears" were well known in the mid-nineties. The Trundle pamphlet of 1613 on which Adams based his suggestion was in fact a reprint of a 1584 pamphlet.

651 Robinson, J. W. "Palpable Hot Ice: Dramatic Burlesque in *A Midsummer Night's Dream*." *Studies in Philology*, 61 (1964), 192-204.

Examines the targets and methods of the burlesque in the playlet: it is "both more precise than 'amateur acting' and less definite than Sussex' Men or *Damon and Pithias*." The clues followed are title, company, *dramatis personae*, and dramaturgy. Shakespeare burlesques the previous irregularity of his own profession and the hybrid play still evident in his day. See item 60.

652 Bradbrook, M. C. *English Dramatic Form: A History of Its Development*. London: Chatto & Windus; New York: Barnes & Noble, 1965. xii, 205 pp.

The effect on Shakespeare of a withdrawal into a courtly world during 1592-1594 was not unlike the withdrawal into the enchanted wood in many of his plays. A perspective such as this from his own life illuminates certain "courtly" aspects of *Dream*, Dream Vision elements of the enchanted wood, and other Lylian and Chaucerian influences. Bottom is the one character in the play who is "unmistakably gifted with the full range of human voice and human personality." A stage-struck artisan who finds himself playing before a "King and Queen," he is very like (Bradbrook hints) Shakespeare himself. (Pp. 72-77) See items 184 and 683.

653 Nosworthy, J. M. *Shakespeare's Occasional Plays: Their Origin and Transmission*. London: Edward Arnold; New York: Barnes & Noble, 1965. 238 pp.

Dream is not treated here since there is "no good reason for supposing" that it was composed to celebrate a nuptial (p. 3). It frequently resembles Henry Porter's *Two Angry Women of Abingdon* (c.1589), in situation, setting, character, and dialogue (p. 94n.).

654 Reed, Robert Rentoul, Jr. "Oberon, Puck, and Later Demons." *The Occult on the Tudor and Stuart Stage*. Boston: Christopher Publishing, 1965, pp. 194-233.

Shakespeare combines qualities of the puck (the mischievous) and Robin Goodfellow (the industrious) into one, and he relies on the conception of Oberon as one devoted to virtue. For these characters he was influenced by the prose folk tale *The Mad Pranks and Merry Jests of Robin Goodfellow*, printed prior to 1588, Reed says, apparently accepting J. Payne Collier's statement to that effect; E. K. Chambers rejected it in item 576. Shakespeare was also influenced by Robert Greene's *The Scottish History of James the Fourth* (c.1591). This chapter outlines the history of Oberon and the fairies on the stage during this

period: "a highly popular but short-lived theatrical vogue."
See item 14.

655 Thorne, William Barry. "The Influence of Folk-Drama upon
Shakespearian Comedy." Ph.D. dissertation, University
of Wisconsin, 1965. *DA*, 25 (1965), 6603.

Finds in *Dream*, one of eight plays discussed, the use of
a "normal world-green world" opposition drawn from such
early motifs as the mummers' play, Maying theme, "flight to
the Woods," misrule, and the primitive resurrection motif of
the rebirth of the year. See items 55 and 74.

656 Lee, G. M. "Plotinus and Shakespeare." *Notes and Queries*,
212 (1967), 134.

Plotinus' concept of "internal form" may have influenced
Theseus' speech on the imagination (V.i.14-18). See item
122.

657 Waldrop, Ian Douglas. "'Shakespeare's Metamorphoses': The
Influence of Ovid's Epic on *A Midsummer Night's Dream.*"
Ph.D. dissertation, University of Western Ontario
(London, Ontario), 1967.

"Chapter one investigates the general theme of
metamorphosis in the play and attempts to establish a firm
relationship between metamorphosis and the power of the
imagination. . . . The second chapter presents a condensed
survey of traditional fairy lore and submits the possibility
that Shakespeare's fairies possess a number of Ovidian
traits which critics have hitherto failed to discern. . . . A
third chapter . . . speculates that Ovid's portrait of
Theseus in the *Metamorphoses* may have been . . .
influential. Chapter four deals with the Ovidian
contributions to the main plot of *Dream*. It argues that the
love plot has been compounded from the chase motif in
several tales of the *Metamorphoses*. . . . The fifth chapter
surveys the history and popularity of the Pyramus and
Thisbe myth in Renaissance England with a view to
establishing the target of Shakespeare's burlesque in the
clowns' interlude." (Abstract) See item 599.

657a   Baldwin, T. W. "The Pedigree of Theseus' Pups:
       Midsummer Night's Dream, IV, i, 123-30." Shakespeare
       Jahrbuch (Heidelberg), 1968, 109-20.

       Theseus' hounds derive from actual and literary sources,
       from Shakespeare's own observation and from Arthur
       Golding's Metamorphoses. Their Latin antecedents can be
       traced in a number of "most erudite reference works." See
       item 640 and 671.

658   Champion, Larry S. "A Midsummer Night's Dream: The
       Problem of Source." Papers on Language and Literature,
       4 (1968), 13-19.

       Shakespeare used Chaucer's "Knight's Tale"as the
       prototype for a complete narrative in a much more
       substantial way than hitherto noticed to achieve "his
       greatest success in situation comedy." Rather than simply
       fusing three or four disparate strands of action to make his
       play, he has adapted the single plot of this chivalric
       romance. "The basic structure and sequence of events in
       the two stories run parallel from end to end, and these
       parallels have not been examined in the detail they
       deserve." Seven parallels are listed and then treated
       specifically for each work. (This material reappears with
       some modifications in Champion's Evolution of Shakespeare's
       Comedy; item 664.) See item 590.

659   Greenfield, Thelma N. "A Midsummer Night's Dream and The
       Praise of Folly." Comparative Literature, 20 (1968),
       236-44.

       Similarities between the two works in subject,
       perspective, motif, and proverbial lore seem notable, and
       certain parallels in concept and allusion allow for the
       suggestion that Shakespeare used Folly. Most interesting
       among the parallels are the image of the actors on stage
       who stand exposed as to their real identity and the state of
       the fool who has glimpsed paradise. "Both works within a
       comic context offer ironic but sublime hints of fleeting,
       non-rational modes of perception which give the fool, after
       all, his valid moment of triumph." Read together, the two
       prevent us from seeing the play as either a "pretty trifle"
       or else "a simplistic moral attack on human irrationality."

660 Kennedy, Judith M. *A Critical Edition of Yong's Translation of Montemayor's "Diana" and Gil Polo's "Enamoured Diana."* Oxford: Clarendon Press, 1968. Pp. xlvi-1.

The main plot of *Dream* is drawn from Jorge de Montemayor's Book I (a position taken by R. Tobler in *Shakespeare Jahrbuch*, 34 [1898], 358-66 and T. P. Harrison in *Texas Studies in English*, 6 [1926], 72-120), as that of *Two Gentlemen* is drawn from Book II. *Diana* provides a link therefore between the two plays. The love tangles of the plot Shakespeare borrowed, the humorous attitude to love, the friendship of Helena and Hermia, the herbs, the juice through which he unties the lovers' knots. Both are concerned with the problems of inconstancy and constancy of love, with the connection between love and reason, and have pastoral settings which are similarly infected with jealousy, the disease of love. See item 187.

660a Klose, Dietrich. "Shakespeare und Ovid." *Shakespeare Jahrbuch* (Heidelberg), 1968, 72-93. (German)

Studies Ovid's influence on Shakespeare in general with special emphasis (pp. 81ff.) on the use of the *Metamorphoses* in *Dream* in various aspects: name and character of Titania; character of Helena; dominant themes (magic sleep, dreams, forest, weddings); Pyramus and Thisbe, both as presented by Bottom and company and as inspiration/source of the Lysander-Hermia relationship; and metamorphosis *per se*, most strikingly in the case of Bottom but also as is evident more subtly in other characters. See item 590.

661 Henning, Standish. "The Fairies of *A Midsummer Night's Dream*." *Shakespeare Quarterly*, 20 (1969), 484-86.

Reginald Scot's *Discovery of Witchcraft* (1584) describes certain witches who share several characteristics with *Dream*'s fairies; they are, for example, extremely small, which may account for Shakespeare's "tiny" fairies. See item 14.

662 Russell, William M. "Courtly Love in Shakespeare's Romantic Comedies." Ph.D. dissertation, Catholic University of America, 1968. *DA*, 29 (1969), 4502A.

Studies the treatment of medieval traditions of courtly
love in, among other plays, *Dream.* Courtliness is
paradoxically both comic and serious. See item 116.

663   Willson, Robert F., Jr. "Golding's *Metamorphoses* and
      Shakespeare's Burlesque Method in *A Midsummer Night's
      Dream.*" *ELN,* 7 (1969), 18-25.

Challenges Kenneth Muir's belief that the playlet is a
conscious parody of Thomas Mouffet's *The Silkewormes, and
Their Flies* (1599--see item 615) by turning to clues and
hints for treating the tragic story in a comic way present
in Arthur Golding's translation of Ovid (1565). Shakespeare
parodies the regular vere form, pokes fun at the excessive
alliteration and assonance, and mocks the frequent
apostrophes. The mechanicals' omissions (the mulberry and
moral) reflect their lack of imagination and failure to
understand their material. See item 60, 578, 599, 600, 630
and 685h.

664   Champion, Larry S. *The Evolution of Shakespeare's
      Comedy: A Study in Dramatic Perspective.* Cambridge:
      Harvard University Press, 1970. 241 pp.

Repeats with modifications the 1968 article (item 658).
(Pp. 47-59)

664a Gesner, Carol. *Shakespeare & the Greek Romances: A
      Study of Origins.* Lexington, Ky.: University of
      Kentucky Press, 1970. 216 pp.

Finds (on p. 153) a connection between the *Ephesiaca*
fragment (containing the Ninus narrative) and the parody
of Pyramus and Thisbe. (This is, presumably, a
development of the dissertation at item 627.) See item 685a.

665   Biswas, Dinesh Chandra. *Shakespeare's Treatment of His
      Sources in the Comedies.* Calcutta: Jadaupur University
      Press, 1971. xi, 287 pp.

Discusses Theseus--in particular--as having been altered
from Chaucer and Plutarch in order that he may embody
"tolerance, common sense and sobriety." The source

materials are "so isolated and fragmentary that they do not convey any subtle or large significance and not one of the stories seems to have had any comic potentiality." In his sources Shakespeare did not find "love's ardour as well as its changefulness and irrationality"--which is his theme. (Pp. 46-52)

666 Hassel, R. Chris, Jr. "Saint Paul and Shakespeare's Romantic Comedies." *Thought*, 46 (1971), 371-88.

There is "a close and consistent affinity" between the thought of St. Paul and that of the romantic comedies. "Shakespeare uses commonplaces on religious faith to articulate the ideals of faith in love; he uses commonplaces about the Christian community to formulate the ideal comic community." In these comedies sapientia, that is, transcendental wisdom, is decisively chosen over scientia, that is, knowledge through reason and the senses. Bottom's waking exposition paradoxically expresses "the inexpressible wonder of love, by joining it directly and unmistakably to the inexpressible wonder of God and his love for us." (Much of this article reappears in the discussion of the Renaissance conflict of Reason and Faith in the early pages of the author's *Faith and Folly* [item 566h], which also has a chapter devoted to *Dream*.) See items 356 and 666.

667 Thompson, Karl F. *Modesty and Cunning: Shakespeare's Use of Literary Tradition*. Ann Arbor: University of Michigan Press, 1971. 176 pp.

Dream conforms to the *debat d'amour* (court-of-love) and "religion of love" conventions. Theseus governs a court of love and judges in a case of inconstancy (Demetrius'). He wisely restores the morally and conventionally correct situation that existed before the play began. Oberon's discordant court contrasts with Theseus'. (Pp. 57-59) See item 116.

668 Warren, Roger. "Shakespeare and the Princely Pleasures at Kenilworth." *Notes and Queries*, 216 (1971), 137-39.

Offers the impression, gathered from Robert Laneham's and George Gascoigne's accounts, that the entertainment at Kenilworth provided "the *kind* of interest which *may* have

helped Shakespeare to create the distinctive atmosphere of
Dream." See item 568.

669   Draper, John W. "The Queen Makes a Match and
      Shakespeare a Comedy." *Yearbook of English Studies,* 2
      (1972), 61-67.

      The presence of the new moon and Venus in conjunction
      and the reference to the "rite of May" suggest an actual
      date of 1 May 1595, and thus the wedding of Lady Dorothy
      Devereux, younger sister of the second Earl of Essex, to
      Henry Percy, ninth Earl of Northumberland, a match
      probably engineered by the Queen herself. (This marriage
      seems not to have been suggested before.)

670   Duffy, Maureen. *The Erotic World of Faery.* London:
      Hodder and Stoughton, 1972. 352 pp. Rev. ed. New
      York: Avon Books 1980 (A Discus Book).

      Notices the special influence of Lyly, his *Endymion* in
      particular, and Spenser's *Faerie Queene* at one layer of the
      play and, as a consequence, argues for an extensive
      political allegory. Titania is Elizabeth; Oberon is Essex;
      1956 the appropriate year; the "little changeling boy" is
      someone like Sir John Harington. Hippolyta is also
      Elizabeth, and Theseus an idealized Essex. The lovers are
      various young courtiers. Bottom is Raleigh. Much is made
      of the parallels with the Actaeon myth. Shakespeare's
      knowledge of flowers is belittled. These speculations are
      followed by an analysis of the play which contains much
      about the erotic psychology of its characters, especially the
      young lovers. The "thrice three muses" (V.i.52) alludes to
      Spenser's *Tears of the Muses.* (Pp. 139-59) See items 89
      and 184.

671   Henn, T. R. "The Ritual of the Hunt." *The Living Image:
      Shakespearean Essays.* London: Methuen, 1972, pp.
      41-44.

      On the music of the hounds, and on the stages and
      topography of the hunt, an understanding of which is
      necessary if we are to grasp certain moments in
      Shakespeare. The remarks of Theseus and Hippolyta at

IV.i.103-126 are glossed as a starting point for this brief
discussion. See items 640 and 657a.

672 McPeek, James A. S. "The Psyche Myth and *A Midsummer
    Night's Dream.*" *Shakespeare Quarterly*, 23 (1972),
    69-79.

Shakespeare must have relied on the pattern of the myth
as it appears in Lucius Apuleius's *Golden Ass,* perhaps in
the Latin original, certainly in William Adlington's 1566
translation. The similarities between *Dream* and Apuleius
(which are given in detail here) run deeper than that of a
series of casual resemblances, such as might be based on
vague recollecting. They reside not in the texture of the
language or in the structures of the works: they are in the
events and characters common to each. Shakespeare has
given the Psyche tale "a truly mythic translation," while
purging the original of its coarseness. See items 55 and
591.

672a Milward, Peter. *Shakespeare's Religious Background*.
     Bloomington and London: Indiana University Press, 1973.
     312 pp.

In a number of places mentioned in passing, *Dream*
reflects Shakespeare's sensitivity to his Catholic
background. See items 609b and 649.

673 Taylor, Marion A. *Bottom, Thou Art Translated: Political
    Allegory in "A Midsummer Night's Dream" and Related
    Literature*. Amsterdam: Rodopi, 1973. 253 pp.

On the basis of Elizabethan sensitivity to political
allegory, especially as it was present in Spenser, in the
Kenilworth and Elvetham festivities, and in Lyly, accepts
Edith Rickert's view (see item 574) of the Hertford basis
for the allusions of the play and adds one significant
variation (anticipated by Percy Allen in 1934 in *Anne Cecil,
Elizabeth and Oxford*, pp. 102-103): Bottom is (not King
James of Scotland, but rather) Alençon. Here is some of the
evidence. 1) Bottom's excessive use of the word *Mounsieur*.
2) A triple pun on *"French crowns"* (I.ii.90). 3) Bottom's
reference to Hercules (I.ii.25), it being one of Alençon's
names. 4) Bottom's willingness to play the lover. 5)

Bottom's willingness to play Thisbe, Alençon having been
slight and boyish. 6) Bottom's willingness to play the lion,
Alençon having been a "lion among ladies." Etc. Taylor also
identifies the actors who would have played the roles:
Kemp=Bottom, etc. (p. 214). See items 568, 574, 586 and
649a.

674 Purdon, Noel. "Myth in Action: The Substructure to *A
     Midsummer Night's Dream.*" *The Words of Mercury:
     Shakespeare and English Mythology of the Renaissance.*
     Salzburg Studies in English Literature. Elizabethan and
     Renaissance Studies, 39. Salzburg: Institut für Englische
     Sprache und Literatur, Universität Salzburg, 1974, pp.
     167-204.

     In a long study which ranges widely over Elizabethan
literature and is filled with mythological analogues (and is
itself a plea for this approach to literature), makes four
broad contentions about the play: 1) Shakespeare presents
as a point of reference for the events in the play the icon
of the moon; 2) that the central argument in the play is
about the desirability of marriage over the state of
virginity; Diana is patroness of marriage; 3) that 1) and 2)
are linked by means of a psychomachia between Cupid and
Diana which forms a mythological substructure to the play;
4) that the play is an attempt to take the Lylian drama of
mythology and give it new resonance and meaning by
testing the assumptions of illusion and reality within it.
Titania is an avatar of Diana. There is a long discussion of
the iconographic structures of the Kenilworth and Elvetham
festivities and Oberon's Vision (II.i.148-68). There are a
number of plates. On Elvetham see items 55, 568 and 574.

675 Salingar, Leo. *Shakespeare and the Traditions of Comedy.*
     London and New York: Cambridge University Press,
     1974, 1976. x, 356 pp.

     Deals with medieval, classical, and renaissance
backgrounds, making frequent mention of *Dream* (see
Index) but rarely dwelling on it. Pages 226-28, for
example, treat the background of Theseus' famous speech
("his skepticism is misplaced") and gives numerous parallels
with *Love's Labour's Lost,* primarily from the point of view
of Shakespeare's growing sense of what the imagination is.
Pages 277-78 show how the Pyramus and Thisbe playlet

reflects back on the stage spectators themselves in their earlier experience as "shadows" in the woods. Pages 313-14 suggest that the Athenian statute with which Theseus threatens Hermia comes from Arthur Brooke's *Romeus and Juliet* (1562, 1587) and reflects Elizabethan attitudes of *patria potestas*.

676 Van Emden, W. G. "Shakespeare and the French Pyramus and Thisbe Tradition, or Whatever Happened to Robin Starveling's Part?" *Forum for Modern Language Studies* (University of St. Andrews), 11 (1975), 193-204.

Links the playlet *via* the poem in *A Gorgeous Gallery of Gallant Inventions* with the French tradition, the features of which are summarized in detail, a tradition which derives largely from the Old French redaction of Ovid, *Piramus et Tisbe*. A number of signs of influence are investigated. Shakespeare drew on the poem for the idea of assigning the roles in the playlet of the parents. The notes here offer several references to other studies of the legend, including some by Van Emden. See item 60.

677 Briggs, K. M. *A Dictionary of Fairies: Hobgoblins, Brownies, Bogies and Other Supernatural Creatures.* London: Allen Lane; New York: Pantheon Books, 1976. xix, 481 pp.

Includes brief accounts of Robin Goodfellow ("in a sense he seemed to swallow all others and their names were made nicknames of his"), Puck Hobgoblin, Oberon, and Titania. See item 14.

678 Smith, Hallett. "Bottom's Sucking Dove, *Midsummer Night's Dream*, I.ii.82-3." *Notes and Queries*, 221 (1976), 152-53.

Bottom's "sucking dove" recalls a slip made by a professional actor who mixed "the sucking lamb or harmless dove" of *2 Henry VI*, III.i.71. The actor's slip is mentioned in Robert Chamberlain's *A New Booke of Mistakes* (1637).

679 Wells, Stanley. "A Note on Demetrius's *Vile Name*." *Cahiers Élizabéthains*, 10 (1976), 67-68.

In response to Terence Spencer (item 617), finds the Demetrius of *Titus* the more likely source for the name.

680   Scragg, Leah. "Shakespeare, Lyly and Ovid: The Influence of *Gallathea* on *A Midsummer Night's Dream."* *Shakespeare Survey*, 30 (1977), 125-34.

That Shakespeare was influenced by the generalized form of the Lyly plays has been amply illustrated (by R. Warwick Bond, for example, in *The Complete Works of John Lyly* [1902], ii, 297-98, and G. K. Hunter [see item 643]); the claim for the specific influence of one of his plays, *Gallathea,* on *Dream* ought to be advanced. The two plays exhibit numerous correspondences: of location, plot, character, and theme. The action opens in warm sunshine on the banks of the Humber where a harsh choice between virgin death and instant flight precipitates an exodus to a forest frequented by factious deities and by a group of apprentice artisans; there are forests in which the emotional confusions of vulnerable youth are compounded by the intervention of a mischief-loving spirit, triangular relationships are established; and a resolution, with its accompanying return to the external world, can be accomplished only by the metamorphosis of one of the lovers by the 'newly reconciled gods who marshal the characters toward a wedding feast in which all the social levels are to participate. *Gallathea* has four groups of characters, presiding deities whose quarrels have repercussions among humans, unusual fairies (Diana's nymphs), and apprentice/artisans who will provide entertainment for a wedding feast. But the relationship which may be most forcibly argued is the importance of the transformation theme in both plays--it informs action and language. The nature and extent of Ovid's influence on *Dream* has remained elusive because much of that influence was filtered through Lyly's sensibility. See items 184 and 599. A later version appears in item 685n.

681   Steele, Eugene. "Shakespeare, Goldoni, and the Clowns." *Comparative Drama*, 11 (1977), 209-26, esp. 215-17.

The two rehearsal scenes (I.ii.III.i) suggest methods of Shakespeare's own troupe and of *Commedia dell'Arte* (in the substitution, extemporizing).

682   Bradbrook, M. C. *Shakespeare: The Poet in His World*.
       London: Weidenfeld and Nicolson; New York: Columbia
       University Press, 1978. ix, 272 pp.

       The Queen was present and the marriage was that of
       Burghley's granddaughter Elizabeth Vere and William
       Stanley, Earl of Derby on 26 January 1595, or that of Lord
       Hunsdon's granddaughter Elizabeth Carey and Thomas
       Berkeley at Blackfriars on 19 February 1596. Describes
       from Stubbes and Malory the rites of May for lovers, and
       elements in the play (the world "dream," for example) as
       they have literary and folk traditions before Shakespeare.
       Titania's *bank* was "the grubbiest of frequently-used stage
       properties." (Pp. 112-19)

682a   Hankins, John Erskine. *Backgrounds of Shakespeare's
       Thought*. Hamden, Conn.: Archon Books, 1978. 296 pp.

       Hankins pauses over two places in particular in *Dream*,
       though there are a dozen or so references to the play
       scattered throughout. He suggests (pp. 40-48) some of the
       ways the spirits in *Dream* combine contemporary theories
       about elemental spirits, which he gives, with the traditions
       of popular fairy lore. They are governed by the moon.
       Puck, however, is a terrestrial spirit subordinate to spirits
       of the air. Hankins gives the literary sources for accounts
       of these various kinds of spirits. He also finds (pp. 91-95)
       in Theseus' speech (V.i.2-22) the distinction present in
       Aquinas and others between *apprehend* (what fantasy does)
       and *comprehend* (what reason does). See item 14.

683   Thompson, Ann. *Shakespeare's Chaucer: A Study in
       Literary Origins*. Liverpool: Liverpool University Press;
       New York: Barnes & Noble, 1978. x, 239 pp.

       Notes the borrowings of plot, names, and words from
       "The Knight's Tale," and the parallel treatment of Theseus
       ("in his role as the slightly aloof spectator, judge, and
       figure of authority *vis-à-vis* the lovers"), and comments on
       the relationship between the structures of the two works:
       "It is more a matter of variations on a number of themes [in
       Dream] than a close echoing of the poem's structure" (thus
       qualifying Larry S. Champion's view in item 658). A strong
       case can be made for the influence of "The Knight's Tale."
       Shakespeare, however, may have used the lost play *Palamon*

and Arcite, put on in 1594, more than we can now know.
The parallel between the Oberon and Titania quarrel and
that of Pluto and Proserpine in "The Merchant's Tale" is
weak. But there does seem to be support in *The Legend of
Good Women* in Chaucer's light tone for an influence on
Pyramus and Thisbe (in contrast to Kenneth Muir in item
615). Finally, there seems to be a fleeting reference at
IV.i.136-37 to *The Parlement of Foules.* (Pp. 88-94) For
other discussions of the influence of Chaucer see items 193,
322, 484, 500, 504, 567, 590, 615, 630-31, 634, 635a, 636,
638, 652, 658, 665, 747, 754, 897, 925 and 960.

684   Vlasopolos, Anca. "The Ritual of Midsummer: A Pattern for
      A Midsummer Night's Dream." *Renaissance Quarterly,* 31
      (1978), 21-29.

      Interpretations of *Dream* have suffered from a hesitation
or a downright refusal on the part of critics to consider the
full significance of the ritual of Midsummer, or Saint John's
Day, in Shakespeare's comedy. The play, like the ritual
which informs its structure, maintains a dual frame of
reference, Christian and pagan. Within this frame such
seemingly unrelated subjects as the moon and dew imagery,
the frequent references to eyes, and the business of magic
plants, particularly the peacemaking "Dians bud," become
thematic components of the comic movement toward
reconciliation of natural and lawful love. The lovers'
progression from the night of misrule to the light of the
holy day parallels the pagan nature of the Midsummer
festival and its Christian conclusion. The fertility rite of
Midsummer Eve draws the lovers at last into harmony with
each other and with the natural world. The dawn of Saint
John's Day brings about the lovers' integration into society
and into the community of religion which sanctifies their
union, assuring them and their issue a permanence beyond
that of generation. "Dians bud," the ritual associations
suggest, is not Agnus Castus (which has punitive
functions) but rather is the mugwort (motherwart, Saint
John's Plant, etc., which has medicinal functions and is
identified with Midsummer). See items 45 and 55.

685   Rudd, Niall. "Pyramus and Thisbe in Shakespeare and
      Ovid: *A Midsummer Night's Dream* and *Metamorphoses,*
      4.1-166.*" *Creative Imitation and Latin Literature.* Ed.

David West and Tony Woodman. Cambridge and New
York: Cambridge University Press, 1979, pp. 173-93.

Discusses at length the Ovidian influence in the play in
general (there is a general Ovidian ambience), in the
playlet in particular, which is gone over very carefully,
and the "ramifications" of the Ovidian tale in "their wider
and more subtle implications," finding a number of hints
from Ovid for lines in *Dream* not before noted. A number of
passages suggest that Shakespeare had read the original
Latin. The playlet parodies the Lysander-Hermia
relationship and at the same time "gently reminds us of the
tragic possibilities of romantic love." Here is how Rudd
condenses his thesis: the dramatist set out to show how
love can transpose, how Bottom was translated, transformed
and transported, and how the minds of all the characters
were transfigured. "The result was Shakespeare's
Metamorphoses--the most magical tribute that Ovid was ever
paid." See item 599.

685a   Sandy, Gerald N. "Ancient Prose Fiction and Minor Early
        English Novels." *Antike und Abendland*, 25 (1979),
        41-55.

        In an appendix (on p. 55), rejects Carol Gesner's
        identification (in item 664a) of the *Ephesiaca* fragment as a
        possible source for the Pyramus and Thisbe playlet.
        Suggests Ovid instead.

685aa   Tobin, J. J. M. "The Irony of 'Hermia' and 'Helena.'"
        American Notes and Queries, 17, no. 10 (1979), 154.

        Have with You to Saffron-Waldon (1596) is a possible
        source of some diction in *Dream.* Nashe uses "Hermia" and
        "Helena" for his heroines, two notoriously promiscuous
        women. In adopting the same names, Shakespeare uses
        nomenclature ironically, because his heroines are the victims
        of male promiscuity.

685b   Andreas, James R. "From Festivity to Spectacle: *The
        Canterbury Tales, Fragment I* and *A Midsummer Night's
        Dream.*" *The Upstart Crow*, 3 (1980), 19-26.

The fascinating interplay of serious and comic materials in the *Dream* is parallel to and yet different from that of *Fragment I*, wherein the "Miller's" and "Reeve's" tales follow the "Knight's." Both Chaucer and Shakespeare through their separate rude mechanicals offer a grotesque parody of what has gone before. With both we have a "dramatic interchange between elite and low." But what are polarities in Chaucer (high and low, romantic and grotesque, structure and anti-structure), which are maintained, in Shakespeare are resolved or absorbed "in solution within an elitist framework"; the festive, "gay" pastimes of the conclusion have become "entertainments to watch and to be judged by the 'gentils.'" The difference is a matter of comic tonality.

685c   Barkan, Leonard. "Diana and Actaeon: The Myth as
       Synthesis." *English Literary Renaissance*, 10 (1980),
       317-59.

A full study of the iconography and interpretation of the myth which concludes with a discussion of its relevance to this play. Shakespeare "juxtaposes all the profound associations of the Actaeon myth with the comic tradition concerning men who become, first spiritually and then physically, jackasses. The meeting of Bottom and Titania . . . is the fullest example in Renaissance literature of the [myth]: here we find the sublime aspect of the story re-created through comic bathos." In the Renaissance understanding of the story, prefigured in *The Golden Ass*, divine powers can find their basis in nature's dress. Bottom's transformation, his self-fulfillment, "recalls the Renaissance Actaeon who becomes animal and divine, fool and initiate in the same metamorphosis." The fullest range of associations, followed by the barking of Theseus's dogs, occurs at Bottom's waking.

685d   Brown, James Neil. "'A Calendar, A Calendar! Look in the
       Almanac.'" *Notes and Queries*, 225, n.s. 27 (1980),
       162-65.

Astrological references in the *Dream* suggest that the four-day period could be both 8-11 June 1594 and 29 April-1 May 1595. The play therefore was written in the spring of 1595 to celebrate a marriage of 1 May. Shakespeare may have been influenced by the astrology of

Spenser's *Epithalamion*. For other arguments based on this line see item 302 and the items listed there.

685e Burnett, Archie. "Miltonic Parallels." *Notes and Queries*, 225 (n.s. 27) (1980), 332-34.

Notes a parallel between "L'Allegro" (1.127)--"And pomp, and feast, and revelry"--and I.i.19--"With pomp, with triumph, and with revelling."

685f Wickham, Glynne. "*The Two Noble Kinsmen* or *A Midsummer Night's Dream, Part II?*" *The Elizabethan Theatre VII*. Ed. G. R. Hibbard. Hamden, Conn.: Archon Books, 1980, pp. 167-96.

The Two Noble Kinsmen is "organically connected to the emotional relationships" of the principal characters of the real-life funeral of Prince Henry in late 1612 and the marriage ceremony of Princess Elizabeth to the Elector of Palatine of the Rhine which followed soon thereafter in early 1613. Thus it is very similar to the *Dream*, itself generally acknowledged to have been written to celebrate a wedding. In *Kinsmen* Shakespeare chose another aspect of the story of Theseus and Hippolyta and begins with echoes of the song which closes the *Dream*. Comparison of the two plays, which Wickham proceeds to give, "becomes a perfectly legitimate exercise."

685g Bevington, David. "The Uses of Contemporary History in the Greek and Elizabethan Theatres." *Shakespeare's Art from a Comparative Perspective*. Ed. Wendell Aycock. Proceedings: Comparative Literature Symposium, Texas Tech Univ., Vol. 12. Lubbock: Texas Tech Press, 1981, esp. pp. 38-39.

Edith Rickert's thesis (see item 574), considered here in one long paragraph, "illustrates the common danger of seeing too much hidden meaning in Elizabethan drama."

685h Duncan-Jones, Katherine. "Pyramus and Thisbe: Shakespeare's Debt to Moffett Cancelled." *Review of English Studies*, 32 (1981), 296-301.

The theory that Thomas Mouffett's (sometimes Mouffet) poem *The Silkewormes, and Their Flies* (1599) is a source rests on very shaky foundations. The poem almost certainly was written near its date of publication and thus too late. Moreover, the poem is not "inherently ridiculous," as Muir thought (item 615), and thus a likely model for the Mechanicals' fooling; it seems to be quite good. Finally, we can easily dismiss the supposed "echoes." For other contributions to this discussion see items 578, 600, 615, 630, 663 and 960.

685i Mielle de Prinsac, Annie-Paule. "Le métamorphose de Bottom et *L'Ane d'Or*." *Études Anglais*, 34 (1981), 61-71.

Bottom's adventure echoes three or four passages in Adlington's translation of Apuleius' *Golden Ass*, which suggests that it is a primary source. For similar suggestions see item 591.

685j Rosenblum, Joseph. "Why an Ass?: Cesare Ripa's *Iconologia* As a Source for Bottom's Translation." *Shakespeare Quarterly*, 32 (1981), 357-59.

Adds to the list of the multitude of sources for Bottom's transformation the possible influence of a representation from Ripa, first published in Rome in 1593, showing Obstinance as a woman all in black, her head surrounded with a cloud, holding an Ass's head with both hands. There seem to Rosenblum to be other minor connections as well between Ripa and the play. Cf. item 566kk.

685k Shulman, Jeff I. "*Tell-Trothes New-years Gift* (1593): Another Source of *A Midsummer Night's Dream*." *Theatre Journal*, 33 (1981), 391-92.

This pamphlet constitutes a possible source since "it is the only reference to Robin predating the *Dream* that relates him directly to the themes of the play." In it Robin Goodfellow, a sort of fairy *praeceptor amoris*, attacks the causes and effects of jealousy, especially authoritarian parents and "mad-fondness and dotage."

685l   Entry deleted.

685m   Nosworthy, J. M. "Shakespeare's Pastoral Metamorphoses." *The Elizabethan Theatre VIII*. Ed. G. R. Hibbard. Port Credit, Ontario: P. D. Meany, 1982, pp. 90-113.

     Pursues Coleridge's observation that "Shakespeare availed himself of the title of this play in his own mind, and worked upon it as dream throughout" by noting the diversification of time, shape and dimension in the play, and its several nightmare elements. As for sources, Shakespeare's Puck may derive from Hodge in *The Two Angry Women of Abingdon*. Apuleius' *The Golden Ass* "affords a sufficient source for the whole Bottom-Titania relationship." The fact that Bottom, unlike Lucius, is only partly metamorphosed admits the possibility that the Centaurs and Minotaur of Plutarch's *Life of Theseus* influence Shakespeare. There are other minor obligations to this *Life* and the *Life of Demetrius*. See item 581.

685n   Scragg, Leah. *The Metamorphosis of "Gallathea": A Study in Creative Adaptation*. Washington, D. C.: Univ. Press of America, 1982. 141 pp.

     Chapter 4 expands the comparison between the *Dream* and Lyly's play which occurs in the 1977 article (item 680). For other comparisons with Lyly see item 184.

685o   Cohen, Marion. "'Dian's Bud' in *A Midsummer Night's Dream*, IV.i.72." *Notes and Queries*, 228, n.s. 30 (1983), 118-20.

     Since neither of the two flowers (Artemisia or mugwort and Agnus Castus) usually put forth as "Dian's Bud" (the antidote of "Love-in-Idleness") satisfies precisely the demands of the text, Cohen agrees with Mats Rydén (item 541) that the flower is probably a blend of several flowers--among which ought to be included Euphrasia or Eye-bright and Spurge or Virgin's nipple, a species of Euphoria. For other discussions of plants see item 45.

685p   Comtois, M. E. "Oberon's Plot of Intrigue." *Shakespeare
       and Renaissance Association of West Virginia: Selected
       Papers*, 8 (1983), 68. (not seen)

       An abstract, apparently on the influence of the Italian
       plot of intrigue on the fairy subplot.

685q   Hunter, William B. [Appendix to] *Milton's "Comus": Family
       Piece* . Troy, N. Y.: Whitston, 1983, pp. 95-101.

       In the first few lines of the *Dream* we learn that there
       will be a new moon in four days and Hippolyta and Theseus
       will marry on the fifth. There are no reasons in the play
       that follows for such specific information; in fact, the
       moonlight which is everywhere contradicts it. But if these
       characters represent in some sense a couple in the audience
       to be married, it is surely significant that on 18 February
       1596 there was a new moon; the next day saw the nuptials
       of Elizabeth Carey and Thomas Berkeley. Her grandfather,
       Lord Hunsdon, was the patron of Shakespeare's company.
       The play seems therefore to have been performed on
       Valentine's Day, 1596. Something of the epilogue probably
       was performed later, after the actual ceremony. The play
       may have been adapted for this occasion. (Other reasons
       are given to support the possibility of the Carey-Berkeley
       wedding.) For other suggestions that this marriage was the
       occasion see items in Index under Carey, Elizabeth.

685r   Roberts, Valerie S. "Ironic Reversal of Expectations in
       Chaucerian and Shakespearean Gardens." *Chaucerian
       Shakespeare: Adaptation and Transformation*. Ed. E.
       Talbot Donaldson and Judith J. Kollmann. Medieval and
       Renaissance Monograph Series, 2. [Detroit]: Pub. for
       the Michigan Consortium for Medieval and Early Modern
       Studies, 1983, pp. 97-117.

       Using as the basis for her discussion the garden *topos*,
       the *locus amoenus*, Roberts finds parallels between the
       "Knight's" and "Merchant's" tales and the *Dream*. The world
       and attitudes are closely related. They are pagan and, as
       regards love, are cynical. Love is foolish and cruel. The
       lovers are not finally influenced at all (taught, improved)
       by the forest retreat. For similar discussions see Index
       under Chaucer.

685s Schleiner, Winfried. "Imaginative Sources for Shakespeare's Puck." *Shakespeare Quarterly*, 36 (1983), 65-68.

Shakespeare may have been aware of an intermediate stage connecting the common noun and class *pookas/a puck* with the proper noun *Puck* and thus with the conception of his character. In an account published in 1593, a girl accused of witchcraft, just before her execution, acknowledged that she "willed" a spirit named "Pluck" to "goe torment [three sisters], but not hurt them"--a curious distinction present in Shakespeare.

685t Spisak, James W. "Pyramus and Thisbe in Chaucer and Shakespeare." *Chaucerian Shakespeare: Adaptation and Transformation*. Ed. E. Talbot Donaldson and Judith J. Kollmann. Medieval and Renaissance Monograph Series, 2. [Detroit]: Pub. for the Michigan Consortium for Medieval and Early Modern Studies, 1983, pp. 81-95.

Compares the two works. Of all the various writers Shakespeare drew upon, only Chaucer presented the material ironically, and this basic tone seems to be a more significant borrowing than the scattered verbal and rhetorical echoes that can be found elsewhere. In several ways Shakespeare differs from Chaucer. His method is outright burlesque, Chaucer's fragile irony. He's outrageous, Chaucer funny. His excesses are theatrical, Chaucer's narrative. Some of Shakespeare's wit may be at Chaucer's expense.

685u Langford, Larry. "*The Story Shall be Changed*: The Senecan Sources of *A Midsummer Night's Dream*." *Cahiers Élisabéthains*, 25 (1984), 37-52.

Shakespeare used Senecan sources for his comedies as well as for his tragedies. With the *Dream*, where the allusions are primarily thematic, though some are verbal, they help give shape and form to the theme of sexual possession and dominance. Suggestions from the love and fury of Hercules and Medea and the sexual transgressions of Phaedra and Oedipus are there, but detecting them is not easy. The ungoverned and unacceptable sexuality (the jealousy, suggestion of adultery and incest, the wrong choice of lovers) is influenced by similar attitudes and treatments in, especially, *Oedipus*, *Medea*, and *Hippolytus*, although Shakespeare offers an alternative to disaster in his comedy.

685v Laroque, François. "Ovidian Transformations and Folk Festivities in *A Midsummer Night's Dream, The Merry Wives of Windsor,* and *As You Like It.*" *Cahiers Elisabéthains,* 25 (1984), 23-36.

In each of these three comedies Shakespeare explored in three successive variations the common theme of comic or grotesque metamorphosis. In each case he used Ovid's text as one of his principal courses. Five paragraphs, repeating, for the most part, what has been said elsewhere, are devoted to the *Dream.* Items on the Ovidian influence are listed in item 599.

685w May, Steven W. "*A Midsummer Night's Dream* and the Carey-Berkeley Wedding." *Renaissance Papers 1983.* Ed. A. Leigh Deneef and M. Thomas Hester. Durham, N. C.: The Southeastern Renaissance Conference, 1984, pp. 43-52.

On 19 February 1596, Elizabeth Carey, daughter of Sir George Carey, married Thomas Berkeley in the bride's home at the Blackfriars, London. The timing of this wedding and the Carey family's connections with Shakespeare's company of players suggest this wedding as a likely occasion for the first performance of the *Dream.* A number of allusions (discussed) in the play fit the time and circumstances associated with this match. Moreover, the precipitous fashion in which this match was arranged helps to explain the laughably irreverent way that Shakespeare treats love and courtship in the play, for less than four months before the ceremony it had seemed almost certain that Mistress Carey would wed Lord Herbert, son and heir to the Earl and Countess of Pembroke. For items which treat this same suggestion see Index under Carey, Elizabeth.

686 Entry Deleted.

On sources, background, and date, see also items 2, 4, 16, 19, 54, 63, 155, 162, 182-3, 212, 280a, 284, 303, 355,

406, 410, 414, 457-58, 538, 544, 566, 715, 735, 738,
741a-42, 744, 746-47, 750, 754-55, 757, 759-60, 776, 802,
804, 807, 825, 854-55, 880, 897, 906, 913, 925, 931, 934,
960 and 1065c.

III. TEXTUAL STUDIES

687 Pollard, Alfred W. *Shakespeare Folios and Quartos: A Study in the Bibliography of Shakespeare's Plays 1594-1685.* London: Methuen, 1909. vii, 175 pp.

In Chapter 4, Pollard details his part and that of W. W. Greg in developing the hypothesis that the true printer and date of the so-called "Roberts quarto" (Q2) of "1600" were Jaggard and 1619. Pollard takes F1 to be based on a Q2 "in a copy which must have been used by the prompter" (p. 121), and Q1, from which Q2 was printed, to have been either itself used in the theatre or else brought afresh into accordance with a theatrical manuscript (p. 126).

688 _____. *Shakespeare's Fight with the Pirates and the Problems of the Transmission of His Text.* 2nd ed., rev. with an Introduction. Cambridge: University Press, 1920. xxviii, 110 pp. Reprint. New York: Haskell House, 1974.

Repeats (pp. viii-xii, 100-102) in brief the story already given in item 687 adding to it the corroborative studies of William Neidig.

689 Alexander, Peter. "Two Notes on the Text of Shakespeare." *Edinburgh Bibliographical Society Transactions,* 2, pt. 4 (1946), 409-13.

F1's "thou not" at II.i.77 should not be preferred to the "not thou" of the quartos.

690 Kirschbaum, Leo. "Shakespeare's Hypothetical Marginal Additions." *MLN,* 61 (1946), 44-49.

Rejects Wilson's theory (item 748) that the mis-lined
passages in V.1.1-84 represent marginal additions. They
could just as easily be examples of the compositor's
carelessness.

691 Munro, John. "Some Matters Shakespearian--II." *The Times
     Literary Supplement,* 27 September 1947, p. 500.

In the Griggs and Praetorius facsimile of Q2 (Roberts)
sigs. Bv and B2r of Q1 (Fisher) have been substituted for
the corresponding pages in Q2. Also belittles the
significance of Fleay's notice of the *Puck-Robin* variation,
the former being a common name, like *clown.* In *Huon*
Oberon has the power to raise storms, one of which is
described (quoted). See item 714.

692 Greg, W. W. *The Editorial Problem in Shakespeare: A
     Survey of the Foundations of the Text.* 2nd ed., with a
     New Preface. Oxford: Clarendon, 1951. lv, 210 pp.
     (First published in 1942)

His views (pp. 124-28) as summarized (pp. 184-85):
"Good Quarto: 1600: from a careful author's copy, possibly
with duplicate endings, with signs of alteration, and
annotations by the prompter. Reprint: '1600' = 1619. Folio:
from Q1619 with reference to the prompt-book in the stage
directions: divided into acts."

693 Parsons, Howard. *Shakespearian Emendations and
     Discoveries.* London: Ettrick, 1953. 136 pp.

Takes *quick* to be an adjective (I.i.[149]), argues for a
full-stop after *qualities* (I.i.231), and wonders why the
fairy sentinel does not give a cry of alarm (II.ii.[25]).
(Pp. 64-67) Parsons first made these points in *Forum:
Stories and Poems,* 1, no. 2 (1950), 44-47.

694 Williams, Philip. "Two Problems in the Folio Text of *King
     Lear.*" *Shakespeare Quarterly,* 4 (1953), 451-60.

Considers briefly details in the relationship between F1
and Q2 of *Dream* to support the suggestion that the *Lear* of
F1 is not based directly on the quarto.

695   Greg, W. W. *The Shakespeare First Folio: Its
         Bibliographical and Textual History.* Oxford: Clarendon,
         1955. xvi, 496 pp.

         Does not think (pp. 240-47) the alternation of
      Puck-Robin in Q1 indicates different periods of composition,
      rather the "habitual inconsistency of the author." Q1 does
      not represent a finished prompt-book, as Wilson thought
      (item 748), rather, more likely, foul papers. The addition
      at the beginning of Act 5 or the possibility of alternate
      endings need not suggest elaborate revision. The copy of
      Q2 used for F1 may have been compared with the
      prompt-book or else annotated to serve as one. Summarizes
      (pp. 9-17) the research by Alfred W. Pollard, William
      Neidig, and himself which established the facts about the
      "Roberts quarto" (Q2) of "1600."

696   Sisson, Charles Jasper. *New Readings in Shakespeare.*
         Shakespeare Problems, VIII. 2 vols. Cambridge:
         Cambridge University Press, 1956. Reprint. London:
         Dawson's of Pall Mall, 1961. Reprint. Birmingham,
         Alabama: Banner Press, 1965.

         Contains (Vol. 1, pp. 125-34) an "explanation and
      defence" of nineteen specific readings, including most of
      the difficult places in the text, which occur in his edition
      (item 825).

697   Martineau, Sir Wilfrid. "*A Midsummer Night's Dream*: The
         Original Text?" Copy of a typescript of 1958. The
         Shakespeare Centre Library at Stratford and elsewhere.

         Provides in thirty-eight pages a text based on the rimed
      portions of the play which are held to be remains of an
      early play. Argues that this substratum was the play the
      "King of Fairies," which Shakespeare also wrote, alluded to
      by Nashe and Greene.

698   Craig, Hardin. *A New Look at Shakespeare's Quartos.*
         Stanford Studies in Language and Literature, 22.
         Stanford: Stanford University Press, 1961. viii, 134 pp.

         Q1 was set from a revised copy of the manuscript; Q2
      set from Q1. F1 was set from the official playbook of the

company which reflected theatrical practice, not, as is usually thought, from a theatrical copy of Q2. (Pp. 90-120)

699   Turner, Robert K., Jr. "Printing Methods and Textual Problems in *A Midsummer Night's Dream* Q1." *Studies in Bibliography*, 15 (1962), 33-55.

Describes Q1 in detail and analyzes the probable method of composition and type distribution. He concludes: "The quarto was set largely by formes under adverse conditions probably caused by sections of difficult copy. The bibliographical evidence seems to me to point toward the kind of heavily revised manuscript described by Professor Wilson [item 748] as copy for the quarto, although it does not, of course, lend any support to his distinction of different levels of style in the revisions. . . . The presence of revision may lead one to think of late-stage foul papers as copy."

700   Hinman, Charlton. *The Printing and Proof-reading of the First Folio of Shakespeare*. 2 vols. Oxford: Clarendon, 1963.

The analysis of the typesetting and distribution for *Dream* (quires N and O) occurs in Volume 2, pages 415-26.

701   Lambrechts, Guy. "Proposed New Readings in Shakespeare: The Comedies (1)." *Bulletin de la faculté des Lettres de Strasbourg*, 43, no. 8 (1965), 952.

At V.i.91-2 for "noble respect / Takes it in might not merit" would read "a fault / Noble respect takes it in might, not merit."

702   Kable, William S. "Compositor B, The Pavier Quartos, and Copy Spellings." *Studies in Bibliography*, 21 (1968), 131-62.

Considers the evidence of Q2 as part of the discussion of how Compositor B's spelling habits were influenced by his copy. Assumes B to have composed all of the Paviers.

703 Spevack, Marvin. "A Concordance to *A Midsummer Night's Dream.*" *A Complete and Systematic Concordance to the Works of Shakespeare.* Vol. 1. Hildesheim: Georg Olms Verlagsbuchhandlung, 1968, pp. 632-65.

A complete concordance to the text of *Dream* is provided with tables indicating the word, its frequencies, its relative frequencies, whether in verse or prose, and the act-scene-line references. Line references are based upon the Riverside Shakespeare edited by G. Blakemore Evans (item 941). Cf. Spevack's *Harvard Concordance to Shakespeare* (1973) which incorporates the same material.

704 Bentley, Gerald Eades. "Eleven Shakespeare Quartos." *The Princeton University Library Chronicle,* 30 (1969), 69-76.

Describes the Chalmers-Rodd-Bain-Law copy of Q2 given to Princeton by Daniel and Donald L. Maggin.

705 Brooks, Harold F. "A Notorious Shakespearian Crux: *Midsummer Night's Dream,* V.i.208." *Notes and Queries,* n.s. 17 (1970), 125-27.

Q1's "Moon vsed" is a misreading of the autograph "mure rased." The annotator of Q2 must have written "wall downe"--"rall downe" to the compositor of F who then wrote "morall downe," drawing "mo" from the original "Moon." The usual emendations "murall downe" or "more all downe" cannot be justified. (Reprinted in Appendix II of the author's New Arden *Dream,* item 960)

706 [Howard-Hill, T. H., ed.] *"A Midsummer Night's Dream": A Concordance to the Text of the First Quarto of 1600.* Oxford Shakespeare Concordances. Oxford: Clarendon Press, 1970. iv, 227 pp.

A computerized concordance which deals with every word in the text, and "represents their occurrence by frequency counts, line numbers, and reference lines." The text used was the University Microfilms facsimile of the British Library copy (B.M.C.34.k.29) checked with the Bodleian Library copy (Malone 38).

707 Widmann, R. L. "Morgann's Copy of Theobald." *Notes and*
     Queries, n.s. 17 (1970), 125.

     Notices that a Folger Shakespeare Library copy of
     Theobald's 1733 edition of Shakespeare contains manuscript
     notes by Maurice Morgann which suggests that he projected
     an edition of his own. (*Dream* is interleaved and has a few
     notes.)

708 Miller, Paul W. "The 1619 Pavier Quartos of Shakespeare: A
     Recapitulation." *Michigan Academician*, 3, no. 1
     (1970-71), 95-99.

     Summarizes the story of the discovery of the facts of the
     volume's publication.

709 Widmann, R. L. "The Computer in Historical Collation: Use
     of the IBM 360/75 in Collating Multiple Editions of *A*
     Midsummer Night's Dream." *The Computer in Literary*
     and Linguistic Research. Ed. R. A. Wisbey. Cambridge:
     University Press, 1971, pp. 57-63.

     Describes the use of the computer and student card
     punchers to obtain a print-out of the full collation of about
     sixty important editions of *Dream*.

710 Andrews, John Frank. "The Pavier Quartos of
     1619--Evidence for Two Compositors." Ph.D.
     dissertation, Vanderbilt University, 1971. *DAI*, 32
     (1972), 6364A. Summarized in *Shakespeare Newsletter*, 22
     (Feb., 1972), 6.

     Assigns *Dream* not to B but to another compositor whom
     he calls F.

711 Blayney, Peter W. M. "'Compositor B' and the Pavier
     Quartos: Problems of Identification and Their
     Implications." *The Library*, 5th ser., 27 (1972), 179-206.

     Dream would seem to have been the seventh printed, not
     the tenth. Two compositors seemed to have worked on it,
     though it would be unwise to make a clear distinction on
     the basis of present evidence.

712 Widmann, R. L. "The Computer and Editing Shakespeare."
     Shakespearean Research and Opportunities, 5-6 (1972,
     for 1970/71), 53-59.

     An account of the computer method chosen, among
     several available, to assist with the historical collation of
     multiple editions of *Dream* for the New Variorum series.
     Followed by "List of Useful Works."

713 Widmann, R. L. "Compositors and Editors of Shakespeare
     Editions." *Papers of the Bibliographical Society of
     America*, 67 (1973), 389-400.

     Surveys types of variants turned up as a result of a
     computer collation of twenty-five editions against Q1. The
     first part looks in particular at variants found in Q2, the
     second at the great range of variants in other editions
     before the nineteenth century.

714 McCaughey, G. S. "A Midsommer night's Mare or What Was
     Griggs Up To?" *Humanities Association Review* [*La Revue
     de l'Association des Humanites*, formerly *Humanities
     Association Bulletin*], 26 (1975), 225-35.

     Makes the point Munro had already made in item 691
     concerning the Griggs and Praetorius facsimiles of Q2.

     See also items: 2, 11, 19, 49, 284, 410, 567, 576,
     727-35, 738, 742, 748, 752, 754, 756, 757, 759-60, 776, 804,
     825, 843, 855, 874, 880, 897, 906, 913, 934, 936, 941, 952,
     960.

IV. BIBLIOGRAPHIES

Bibliographies

715 Guttman, Selma. *The Foreign Sources of Shakespeare's Works: An Annotated Bibliography*. Morningside Heights, N. Y.: King's Crown Press of Columbia University, 1947. xxii, 168 pp.

Contains 22 references to studies of *Dream* between 1904 and 1940.

716 Smith, Gordon Ross. *A Classified Shakespeare Bibliography 1936-1958*. University Park: Pennsylvania State University Press, 1963. lviii, 784 pp.

References to 102 works on *Dream* are included (B5995-B6097, pp. 628-31), classified under Texts, Literary Genesis and Analogues, Use of Language, General Criticism of the Play, etc.

717 Berman, Ronald. "*A Midsummer Night's Dream*." *A Reader's Guide to Shakespeare's Plays: A Discursive Bibliography*. Glenview, Ill.: Scott, Foresman, 1965. Pp. 43-47. Rev. ed. 1973, pp. 48-51.

With sections on text, editions, sources, criticism, and staging. Gives a selection of references with brief annotations for some.

717a Coleman, Arthur, and Gary R. Tyler. *Drama Criticism. Volume One: A Checklist of Interpretation Since 1940 of English and American Plays*. Denver: Alan Swallow, 1966. 457 pp.

An alphabetical list without comment of fifty-four items (pp. 242-45).

718 Marder, Louis, ed. *"A Midsummer Night's Dream*: A
Supplementary Bibliography [1892-1965]*." A New
Variorum Edition of Shakespeare: "A Midsommer Night's
Dreame."* Ed. Henry Howard Furness. New York:
American Scholar, 1966, pp. 1-xviii.

An unannotated list of 200 or so items, mostly critical
studies.

718a Bate, John. *How to Find Out About Shakespeare.* Oxford:
Pergamon, 1968. xv, 161 pp.

The single paragraph (on p. 121) on *Dream* includes six
items (all articles) with brief comments.

719 Velz, John W. *Shakespeare and the Classical Tradition: A
Critical Guide to Commentary, 1660-1960.* Minneapolis:
University of Minnesota Press; London: Oxford
University Press, 1968. xiv, 459 pp.

Lists publications, usually with full annotations, which
make suggestions as to Shakespeare's use of classical
literature. Studies of *Dream* occur alphabetically by author
in the section on "The Comedies." The index is arranged
by topics: sources, theme, genre, and the like.

720 Habicht, Werner, ed. *English and American Studies in
German.* Summaries of Theses and Monographs. A
Supplement to *Anglia.* Tübingen: Max Niemeyer, 1969-

A yearly publication with the authors' own English
summaries.

720a Wells, Stanley W. *Shakespeare: A Reading Guide.* The
English Association. London: Oxford University Press,
1969. 44 pp.

Lists (pp. 26-27) without comment three editions and six
critical studies of *Dream.*

720b Gabler, Hans Walter. *English Renaissance Studies in
German 1945-1967: A Checklist of German, Austrian, and*

*Swiss Academic Theses, Monographs, and Book
Publications on English Language and Literature, c.
1500-1650.* Heidelberg: Quelle und Meyer, 1971. 77 pp.

There are 167 items on Shakespeare. Each is translated
but otherwise without annotation or description.

721 Howard-Hill, T. H. *Shakespearian Bibliography and Textual
     Criticism: A Bibliography.* Oxford: Clarendon Press,
     1971.

     Seven annotated entires are given (pp. 134-35).

722 *A Shakespeare Bibliography: The Catalogue of The
     Birmingham Shakespeare Library.* Parts 1 and 2. 7
     volumes. London: Mansell, 1971.

     Material on *Dream* appears in several places under
     several heads. Both parts (Accessions Pre-1932, Accessions
     Post-1931) have sections on English and Foreign Editions
     and Shakespeareana. Useful not only for the extensive
     holdings in printed studies of *Dream* included (and in many
     languages) but also for the numerous typescripts of radio
     and television programs which are either adaptations of or
     else about *Dream* and which are not listed elsewhere.

723 *Folger Shakespeare Library: Catalogue of the Shakespeare
     Collection.* 2 vols. Boston: G. K. Hall, 1972.

     The list of holdings on *Dream* (editions, translations,
     studies) is in Volume 1, pages 509-524.

724 Palmer, D. J. "The Early Comedies." *Shakespeare: Select
     Bibliographical Guides.* Ed. Stanley Wells. London:
     Oxford University Press, 1973, pp. 54-73.

     Presents various critical attitudes in several studies
     toward the early comedies of which *Dream* is taken to be
     the last and "his first major triumph." Calls special
     attention to discussions of Shakespeare's "synthesizing and
     transforming power," his preoccupation with his art, and
     his intentions in the Theseus-Hippolyta exchange

(V.i)--which is a focal point for two divergent approaches to the play. Gives a selected list of texts and criticism.

725 Bergeron, David M. "A Guide to Resources: Comedies." *Shakespeare: A Study and Research Guide*. New York: St. Martin's, 1975, pp. 40-55.

Discusses fifteen book-length studies with sections on *Dream*.

726 McManaway, James G., and Jeanne Addison Roberts. "*A Midsummer Night's Dream*." *A Selective Bibliography of Shakespeare: Editions, Textual Studies, Commentary*. Charlottesville: University Press of Virginia (for the Folger Shakespeare Library), 1975, pp. 134-36.

Lists without annotation 44 items on *Dream*.

726a McLean, Andrew M. "Teaching Shakespeare on Film: A Checklist" and "Audio-visual Resources for the Teaching of Shakespeare." *Shakespeare in the Classroom: Resources and Media Aids*. Ed. Andrew M. McLean. Kenosha: University of Wisconsin-Parkside, 1977, pp. 31-35, 36-46.

Superseded by item 726c.

726b Bevington, David. *Shakespeare*. Goldentree Bibliographies in Language and Literature. Arlington Heights, Ill.: AHM Publishing, 1978. xxii, 259 pp.

The section devoted to *Dream* lists without annotation 56 items (numbers 3571-3626) and directs us to 30 additional items most of which are essays in books which deal with a number of the comedies.

726c McLean, Andrew M. *Shakespeare: Annotated Bibliographies and Media Guide for Teachers*. Urbana, Ill.: National Council of Teachers of English, 1980. x, 277 pp.

Items ("as complete as possible through 1978"), usually with brief annotations, are divided into three

parts--Teaching Shakespeare in the Schools, Shakespeare in
Feature Films and on Television, and Guide to Media for
Teaching Shakespeare. A list of distributors of the
non-print material is included. The section on teaching
Shakespeare in the schools gives under *Dream* (pp. 58-59)
eleven items and references to thirteen others.

726d Wilbern, David. "William Shakespeare: A Bibliography of
      Psychoanalytic and Psychological Criticism, 1964-1975."
      International Review of Psycho-Analysis, 5 (1978):
      361-72. Revised and reprinted, "A Bibliography of
      Psychoanalytic and Psychological Writings on
      Shakespeare: 1964-1978." *Representing Shakespeare: New
      Psychoanalytic Essays.* Ed. Murray M. Schwartz and
      Coppélia Kahn. Baltimore and London: Johns Hopkins
      University Press, 1980, pp. 264-88.

V. EDITIONS AND TRANSLATIONS

Editions and Translations

727 Rowe, Nicholas, ed. *The Works of William Shakespeare*. 7 volumes. London: J. Tonson, 1709. Reprint. New York: AMS, 1967.

Based on the fourth folio of 1685. Provides scene divisions, certain locations, a *dramatis personae*, a number of emendations, and modernized punctuation and spellings. *Dream* appears in Volume 2, pages 465-522.

728 Pope, Alexander, ed. *The Works of William Shakespeare*. 6 volumes. London: J. Tonson, 1723-1725. Reprint. New York: AMS, 1969.

Uses Rowe's text (item 727) "corrected" in places to suit Pope's sensibility. There are a few explanatory notes.

729 Theobald, Lewis, ed. *The Works of William Shakespeare*. 7 volumes. London: A. Bettesworth and C. Hitch et al., 1733. Reprint. New York: AMS, 1968.

Volume 7 lists as "Editions of Authority" the first two folios and both quartos. Rowe (item 727) and Pope (item 728) are of "no Authority." Emendations occur at the foot of the page.

730 Hanmer, Thomas, ed. *William Shakespeare: The Works of Shakespeare*. 6 volumes. Oxford: Printed at the Theatre, 1743-1744. Reprint. AMS, 1969.

Uses Pope's text (item 728) altered according to Theobald's (item 729) and Hanmer's own judgments. Includes a large illustration of III.ii by F. Gravelot. *Dream* is in Volume 1, pages 76-141. There are a few notes and a *dramatis personae*.

731 Warburton, William, ed. *The Works of William Shakespeare*. 8 volumes. London: F. and P. Knapton, 1747. Reprint. New York: AMS, 1968.

Claims to reject Rowe (item 727), Theobald (item 729), and Hanmer (item 730), although he uses the latter two a good deal, while accepting much of Pope (item 728) whose notes he gives along with his own. His "Comment and Notes, Critical and Explanatory" are at the foot of each page. *Dream* is in Volume 1, pages 91-171.

732 Johnson, Samuel, ed. *The Works of William Shakespeare*. 8 volumes. London: J. and R. Tonson et al., 1765. Reprint. New York: AMS, 1968.

Uses the Roberts quarto, "very carefully collated, as it seems, with that of Fisher" (Vol. 1, p. 176). Based primarily on Warburton (item 731). Makes few emendations but does change punctuation freely. Notable for its explanations and for selected opinions of which the following (from the 1773 edition, Vol. 1, p. 107) is best known: "Wild and fantastical as this play is, all the parts in their various modes are well written, and give the kind of pleasure which the author designed. Fairies in his time were much in fashion; common tradition had made them familiar, and Spenser's poem had made them great." The notes include the comments of other editors and Johnson's reactions to these comments.

733 Steevens, George, ed. *Twenty of the Plays of Shakespeare*. 4 volumes. London: J. and R. Tonson, 1766. Reprint. New York: AMS, 1968.

Based on the Roberts quarto of 1619 collated with the Fisher of 1600. Alternate readings occur at the foot of each page. *Dream* appears in Volume 1, signatures A2-E2v.

734 Capell, Edward, ed. *Mr. William Shakespeare: His Comedies, Histories, and Tragedies: Set out by Himself in Quarto, or by the Players his Fellows in folio, and now faithfully republished from those Editions*. 10 volumes. London: J. and R. Tonson, 1767-1768. Reprint. New York: AMS, 1968; Burt Franklin, 1970.

The text for *Dream* is based on a comparison of both
quartos and the first folio. It is in Volume 3. Notes occur
in *Notes and Various Readings to Shakespeare*, Part 3
(1780), 99-118.

735 Malone, Edmund, ed. *The Plays and Poems of William
     Shakespeare.* 10 volumes. London: H. Baldwin, 1790.
     Reprint. New York: AMS, 1968.

     Dates *Dream* 1592 (Vol. 1, pp. 283-85). The text (Vol.
     2, pp. 449-539) is based on the first folio with the collation
     of both quartos. There are notes from previous editors at
     the bottom of the page, with additional notes in Volume 10,
     pages 577-81.

736 Boswell, James, the Younger, ed. *The Plays and Poems of
     William Shakespeare.* 21 volumes. London: F. C. and J.
     Rivington et al., 1821. Reprint. New York: AMS, 1966.

     Based on Malone's 1790 edition (item 735). *Dream* is in
     Volume 5. Extensive notes from earlier editions are printed
     with the text.

737 Campbell, Thomas, ed. *The Dramatic Works of William
     Shakespeare.* London: Edward Moxon, 1838. Reprint.
     New York: AMS, 1972. lxxx, 960 pp.

     Introduction (pp. xxxvi-viii) includes a brief
     appreciation of the play's delights. "Of all his works the
     Dream leaves the strongest impression on my mind, that
     this miserable world must have, for once at least, contained
     a happy man." Shakespeare knew we would dote on this
     play. Fairies have as good a right to be in old Greece as
     anywhere else. Nothing in the play approaches any pretense
     of history. The text is presented with no accompanying
     apparatus.

738 Halliwell[-Phillipps], James O., ed. *The Works of William
     Shakespeare.* 16 volumes. London: C. and J. Adlard,
     1853-65. Reprint. New York: AMS, 1970.

     Dream is in Volume 5 (1856). The introduction (pp.
     3-16) considers topical allusions--the foul weather

(II.i.81-117) and "death of learning" (V.i.52-53, which is a
reference either to Robert Greene's death or to Spenser's
Teares of the Muses)--sources, and text--the 1619 Roberts
quarto (imprinted "1600") is taken to be the first and the
uncorrected basis for the 1600 Fisher quarto. Halliwell finds
the fairies the heart of the piece and thinks it "better
fitted for the closet than the stage." *Dream* contains "the
sweetest poetry ever composed in any language." Alongside
his own, Halliwell gives the notes of earlier scholars.
Woodcuts are by F. W. Fairholt.

739   Clark, William George, John Glover, and William Aldis
      Wright, eds. *The Works of William Shakespeare*. The
      Cambridge Shakespeare. 9 volumes. Cambridge and
      London: Macmillan, 1863-65. Reprint. 1969. Rev. ed.
      1891-95. Reprint. New York: AMS, 1968. Re-edited by
      William George Clark and William Aldis Wright and
      reprinted in one volume, The Globe Edition. London:
      Macmillan, 1864. viii, 1079 pp. Reprint. New York: Blue
      Ribbon Books, 1940. 1233 pp.; New York: Garden City
      Publishing, 1940. xviii, 1527 pp.; Philadelphia:
      Blakiston, 1944. viii, 1527 pp.; New York: Grosset and
      Dunlap, 1951. 1420 pp.; 2 volumes. Franklin Center,
      Pa.: Franklin Library, 1952 and 1978; 2 volumes.
      Chicago: Encyclopedia Britannica, 1952 and 1955;
      London: Macmillan and New York: St. Martin's, 1956 and
      1961. viii, 1211 pp.; 2 volumes. Garden City, N. Y.:
      International Collector's Library, 1967; New York: AMS
      Press, 1970. viii, 1079 pp.

Dream, in Volume 2 (pp. 197-274) of the first edition, is
based on the Fisher quarto of 1600. This edition provides
collation for quartos and folios with the conjectural
emendations of others, critical notes, and lineation. Clark
and Wright revised the edition in 1891-93. *Dream* is in
Volume 2 (pp. 237-331), with textual notes at the foot of
the page and some few in back. A one-volume edition of the
text only, known as The Globe Shakespeare, was published
in 1864. Among the special features which occur in one or
another of the reprints of this volume are the Temple notes
of Israel Gollancz, illustrations by Rockwell Kent and
Robert Anning Bell, a preface by Edward Dowden, and a
glossary by J. M. Jephson.

740 Furness, Henry Howard, ed. *A New Variorum Edition of
     Shakespeare: "A Midsommer Nights Dreame."*
     Philadelphia: J. B. Lippincott, 1896. xxxiv, 357 pp.
     Reprint. New York: Dover, 1973; American Scholar,
     1966. With Supplementary Bibliography to 1965 to Louis
     Marder.

     The Preface briefly assesses received views on title,
     date, sources, text, and duration of the action. The text is
     that of the first folio. An Appendix excerpts and organizes
     attitudes of early (usually nineteenth-century) scholars
     toward text, date, sources, and duration of the action.
     Selections of comments are from English criticism on the
     play in general and on Bottom in particular, from German
     criticism, and on notable performances, costume, *Peter
     Squentz*, the comment by John Spencer alluding to a 1631
     performance before John Williams, Bishop of Lincoln, and on
     Purcell's *The Fairy Queen* (1693). Discussion of the date is
     arranged according to the allusions which furnish internal
     evidence; nine topics are covered, including the assumption
     that the play was intended to celebrate a noble wedding. A
     list of dates suggested by scholars is given. There are full
     textual and explanatory notes.

741 Gollancz, Israel, ed. *A Midsummer Night's Dream*.
     Illustrated by Robert Anning Bell. London: J. M. Dent,
     1895. li, 128 pp. Reprint. A Legacy Library Facsimile.
     Ann Arbor: University Microfilms, 1966.

     Gollancz (in a "Letter") gives a fanciful account of how
     Shakespeare came to write *Dream* through the inspiration,
     while he was young, of the Kenilworth festival (see item
     568). He demonstrates the structure of the play through
     the diagram of a wheel. Sketches are in red and black.

741a Craig, W. J., ed. *The Complete Works of William
     Shakespeare*. The Oxford Shakespeare. London: Oxford
     University Press; New York: Henry Frowde, 1904. viii,
     1264 pp. Reprint. London and New York: Oxford
     University Press, 1942, 1943, 1945, 1954, 1966, 1969,
     1971, 1973, 1978. viii, 1164.

     For Algernon Charles Swinburne, who has supplied a
     general introduction to the plays (reprinted in item 8),
     Dream is "outside as well as above all possible or imaginable

criticism. It is probably or rather surely the most beautiful work of man." Edward Dowden's brief introduction to the play dates it not earlier than 1593 or later than 1595. "Let us . . . give ourselves up to enjoy a quaint and charming piece of various-coloured tapestry." Of Bottom: "there is a gloriousness in his self-contented stupidity."

742 Cuningham, Henry, ed. *A Midsummer Night's Dream*. The Arden Shakespeare. London: Methuen, 1905. lxiii, 181 pp.

The introduction describes the quarto and folio versions, argues for a date of Autumn 1594 to 1595, and attempts to show, quoting at great length from an earlier unnamed critic, that the fairies are the primary conception of the play. The topical allusions are taken up one by one--Shakespeare (at V.i.52-53) refers to Robert Greene's death--and the various suggestions for allegorical readings of Oberon's speech (II.i.148-68) are detailed. Sources are discussed and appreciations quoted from several critics: William Hazlitt, Henry Hallam, Charles Knight, Thomas De Quincey, F. J. Furnivall, and Edward Dowden.

743 Rhys, Ernest, ed. *Shakespeare: The Comedies*. Everyman's Library, 153. London and Toronto: J. M. Dent; New York: E. P. Dutton, 1906. 847 pp. Numerous reprints.

Follows the text of Clark and Wright's Cambridge Shakespeare (item 739). Only the text and a glossary is provided. Later impressions include a prefatory note by D. C. Browning.

744 Hudson, Henry Norman, Israel Gollancz, and C. H. Herford, eds. *A Midsummer Night's Dream*. The Aldus Shakespeare. New York: Bigelow Smith, 1909. Reprint. New York: Funk & Wagnalls, 1967. xlv, 114 pp.

There is a preface by Israel Gollancz, an introduction by Henry Norman Hudson, comments on aspects of the play by various scholars and critics, a synopsis by J. Ellis Burdick, notes by Gollancz, Hudson, and Herford, a glossary by Gollancz, and study questions by Anne Throup Craig. Gollancz takes the allusion to the death of learning (V.i.52-53) to refer to Robert Greene and to be suggested

by Spenser's *Teares of the Muses,* and dates the play
1593-1595, that is, before *Romeo.* In his treatment of the
sources, which is extensive (pp. ix-xiii), he assumes "The
Knight's Tale" to be the chief, changes having been made
to create a "court drama" similar to those of Lyly. He gives
the certain and probable debts for the fairy material,
though he holds popular traditions (Teutonic and Celtic) to
be the main sources. His list resembles that offered by
others, including, for example, from before, Sidgwick (item
571) and after, Bullough (item 630). He takes the time
duration to be three (not four) days, the season to be May
Day, and the idea of a "dream drama" to be perhaps
suggested by Lyly's *Woman in the Moon.*

Hudson covers much the same ground, disagreeing with
the suggestion, originally made half-heartedly by Charles
Knight (see item 2), that Robert Greene is alluded to, and
dating the play 1594-1598. While he finds the style mixed,
there being passages "which relish strongly of an earlier
period," he does not think revision a likely theory. Hudson
believes the play could not have been successfully acted
and praises Shakespeare's originality in putting in the
fairies. He finds "a sort of lawlessness . . . indeed the
very law of the piece," and dwells on the appropriateness
of the absence of deep passion and of a certain moral
sensibility. The whole is like a dream. "The play, from
beginning to end, is a perfect festival of whatsoever
dainties and delicacies poetry may command--continued
revelry and jollification of soul, where the understanding is
put asleep that fancy may run riot, and wanton in
unrestrained carousel." In this vein, at some length,
Hudson describes the play. The section on comments by
scholars includes twenty-two excerpts on a variety of
topics.

745 Craig, W. J., ed. *The Comedies of Shakespeare.* The
     Oxford Shakespeare. London and New York: Oxford
     University Press, 1911. xxxviii, 1128 pp. Numerous
     reprints.

     This edition (with *Dream* on pp. 519-583) reprints the
     section on comedies from Craig's 1904 edition (item 741a).
     Several of the reprints include Swinburne's general
     introduction and Dowden's introduction to each play.

746   Brooke, C. F. Tucker, John William Cunliffe, and Henry
       Noble MacCracken, eds. *Shakespeare's Principal Plays.*
       New York: Century, 1914. Reprint. New York:
       Appleton-Century, 1941. 933 pp.

       The text is that of the first folio with modernized
spelling, corrections from the two quartos, and the Globe
lineation. Cunliffe's introduction has a section on sources,
which emphasizes the influence of Lyly's plays, on date,
suggesting 1594-1595, stage history, with a rather full
account of English and American productions, critical
comment (that is, of others), and the text. "On the whole,"
Cunliffe says, "German criticism has contributed less to the
elucidation of *Dream* than to that of almost any other
Shakespearean play." Notes are in back. An appendix
summarizes Halpin's theory (see item 568) that Oberon's
Vision (II.i.148-68) refers to the Kenilworth festivities.
Dream occupies pp. 5-36.

746a   *Shakespeare's Comedy of "A Midsummer Night's Dream."*
        With Illustrations by W. Heath Robinson. London:
        Minerva Press, 1916. 148 pp. Reprint. 1976.

        This book is distinguished by the many full-page,
black-and-white illustrations of Robinson. There is
otherwise no apparatus. The print is large.

747   Durham, Willard Higley, ed. *A Midsummer Night's Dream.*
       The Yale Shakespeare. New Haven: Yale University
       Press; London: Oxford University Press, 1918. 96 pp.
       Numerous reprints.

       The text is based on the Oxford Shakespeare, edited by
W. J. Craig (item 741a). Glosses are at the foot of the
page, notes in back. The brief appendix on sources
reminds us that "nothing has been found which may
properly be called the 'source.'" It lists Chaucer's
"Knight's Tale" and *Legend of Good Women*, Plutarch's "Life
of Theseus," Ovid's *Metamorphoses*, and Montemayor's *Diana
Enamorada.* A second appendix dates the play not earlier
than 1593 or later than 1595 and gives a short stage
history. A third notes the departures from Craig's edition.
A fourth suggests collateral reading. There is an index of
words glossed.

748 Quiller-Couch, Arthur, and John Dover Wilson, eds. *A
     Midsummer-Night's Dream*. New Shakespeare. Cambridge:
     Cambridge University Press, 1924. 176 pp. Reprint.
     1940; (with some revision) 1968.

     Introduction (by Quiller-Couch). Briefly discusses text,
     occasion, date, and sources, and provides (from *Notes on
     Shakespeare's Workmanship*, 1917, which is reprinted in
     Cambridge Lectures [London: J. M. Dent, 1943]) an
     impressionistic effort "to get at the workings of
     Shakespeare's mind and reason" during the process of
     composition. "Can anyone read the opening scene, or the
     closing speech of Theseus, and doubt that the occasion was
     a wedding?" Of the sources of the fairies: "When will
     criticism learn to allow for the enormous drafts made by
     creative artists . . . upon their childhood?" Concludes with
     the fantasy of an ideal performance, which begins, "The set
     scene should represent a large Elizabethan hall, panelled,
     having a lofty oak-timbered roof and an enormous
     staircase."

     Apparatus (after text, by Wilson). Takes Q1 to be
     printed from a theatrical prompt-book, presumably an
     autograph manuscript. Q1 was then reprinted in Q2, which
     then served as a prompt-book or else was "corrected"
     before it was itself reprinted in F. Reprints a page from Q1
     showing the disarranged verse of V.i.1-84. Argues that
     Shakespeare added the twenty-nine lines, including those
     having to do with "the poet," in his maturity, some time
     after he had written the other lines. *Dream* is a revised
     text. The double-ending and the *Robin-Puck* speech-prefix
     variation (both noticed by F. G. Fleay), along with other
     evidence, lead to the conclusion that the play was written
     in 1592 or before, much revised (the Bottom and the Robin
     fairy scenes added) in 1594, and then probably revised
     again in 1598 (as comparisons with *Merry Wives* suggest).
     The Stanley-Vere wedding (1595) seems not to have been
     the occasion, since the Queen was present for it; but the
     last revision (1598) may have been for the Southampton-
     Vernon wedding of 1598. The notes are followed by a note
     on the folio text (on the additions to Q1), a stage history
     by Harold Child, and a glossary. For other comments on
     the possibility of revision see items 16, 49, 284, 303, 574,
     576, 586, 598, 630, 634, 744, 752, 757, 760, 776, 843, 855,
     897, 913 and 960.

749 Losey, Frederick D., ed. *The Complete Poetic and Dramatic Works of William Shakespeare.* Philadelphia: John C. Winston, 1926. Reprint. The Kingsway Shakespeare. London: G. G. Harrap, 1949. 1331 pp.; The Red Letter Edition. Philadelphia: John C. Winston, 1952. xvi, 1344 pp.

A two-page introduction (pp. 196-97) considers how Shakespeare manipulates the groups of characters into a unified plot, demonstrating that nothing within the scope of the imagination is foreign to his art.

750 Craig, Hardin, ed. *Shakespeare: A Historical and Critical Study with Annotated Texts of Twenty-one Plays.* Chicago: Scott, Foresman, 1931. Rev. ed. 1958. vi, 1194 pp.

Uses the Globe text (see item 739) with slight changes. Introduction (pp. 96-100) treats date (1594-95), occasion, plots and sources, and, briefly, stage history. Both Kenilworth and Elvetham festivities seem to have influenced Shakespeare in Oberon's speech (II.i.148-68) and in the play in general, Edith Rickert's views (see item 594) on the Hertford influence and Elvetham being "sufficiently plausible to be worth repeating." The "changeling boy" may be the son of Lady Catherine Grey and the Earl of Hertford. Craig summarizes the plot (outlining the lovers' love chain) while suggesting how the various elements mix and what sources we know.

751 Calenza, Guilia, trans. *Sogno di una notte d'estate.* Biblioteca Sansoniana Straniera, 73. Florence: G. C. Sansoni, 1934. xxxiii, 233 pp. Reprint. 1949, 1965. (Italian and English--not seen)

752 Ridley, M. R., ed. *A Midsummer Night's Dream.* The New Temple Shakespeare. London: J. M. Dent, 1934; New York: E. P. Dutton, 1935. xiv, 104 pp. Reprint. 1957.

A revision of The Temple Shakespeare edited by Israel Gollancz. (*Dream* is, it seems, Volume 23 of the series.) The introduction has very brief sections on the text, sources and date, time of action (inconsistencies are the result of carelessness), and on criticism (with short

comments from several critics). The Fisher quarto (Q1) is
the basis for the text, and scene divisions occur "only
when there is an obvious change of scene." Ridley accepts
Dover Wilson's view (see item 748) that *Dream* was composed
in 1592, worked over again in 1594, and put into final
shape (perhaps for the wedding of the Earl of Southampton
to Elizabeth Vernon) in 1598. Notes and glossary follow the
text.

753   [Bullen, Arthur Henry, ed.] *The Works of William
       Shakespeare*. The Shakespeare Head Press Edition. New
       York: Oxford University Press, 1934. Reprint. 1940.
       1263 pp. London: Odhams Press, 1944. New York:
       Grolier, 1958.

The text is that prepared by Arthur Henry Bullen for
the Stratford Town Edition, first printed in 1904 by the
Shakespeare Head Press. No introduction or notes. A
synopsis of the play by Sir Paul Harvey follows the
glossary.

754   Kittredge, George Lyman, ed. *The Works of William
       Shakespeare*. Boston: Ginn, 1936. xx, 1561 pp.

A preface to the volume explains Kittredge's editorial
practices. He has based his edition on a fresh collation of
the original editions. In the two-page introduction (pp.
229-3), Kittredge dates the play between 1594 and 1596,
but thinks that the foul weather passage (II.i.81-117)
refers to the summer of 1594, and therefore prefers a date
for the play of 1595. He does not find (at V.i.52-52) an
allusion to the death of either Robert Greene or Tasso.
Kittredge takes the copy for the Fisher quarto of 1600 to
have been "probably" a manuscript prompt book, possibly
even in Shakespeare's own handwriting. Shakespeare may
have drawn from Chaucer and Plutarch, as he certainly did
from Ovid, but the fairy lore goes back to tales that he
had learned in childhood. Bottom's transformation need not
have derived from either Lukios of Patrae or Apuleius; the
story was generally known. Oberon's Vision (II.i.155-64) is
"the most famous of all tributes to Queen Elizabeth." See
items 760 and 787. *Dream* occurs on pages 231-55.

755 Harrison, G. B., ed. *A Midsummer Night's Dream*. The
Penguin Shakespeare. Harmondsworth, Middlesex:
Penguin Books, 1937. 100 pp. Reprint. 1953. Rev. ed.
1957. 106 pp. (not seen)

756 Holzknecht, Karl J., and Norman E. McClure, eds. *Selected
Plays of Shakespeare*. Volume 2. New York: American
Book Company, 1937. 739 pp.

The introduction (pp. 191-97) compares the play with
Love's Labour's Lost and *The Tempest* (all being without
source and designed for special audiences) and with *Romeo*
(both being lyrical). There are sections, offering commonly
held views, on sources, the unification of the material
(around the central theme of the amusing perplexities of
love), the fairies, date, and text. Q1 is the basis for the
text. The Globe lineation is used. Notes and glossary
appear at the foot of each page. *Dream* occupies pages
198-274. See items 59, 131 and 149 for similar comparisons.

757 Parrott, Thomas Marc, ed., with assistance from Edward
Hubler and Robert Stockdale Telfer. *Shakespeare:
Twenty-Three Plays and the Sonnets*. New York: Charles
Scribner's Sons, 1938. Reprint. Madison: Charles
Scribner's Sons (for the United States Armed Forces
Institute), 1944. Rev. ed. New York: Charles Scribner's
Sons, 1953. 1116 pp.

The text (pp. 135-61) is based on Q1 (the Fisher quarto
of 1600) with some modernizations, for purposes of clarity,
the volume being designed for students, a few corrections,
and the lineation of the Globe edition. Q1 was based on
Shakespeare's original manuscript prepared for acting by
the stage-manager. The introduction (pp. 131-34) dates the
play late 1594 or 1595, accepts the possibility of revision,
probably for performance in a public theatre, discusses the
sources, giving the customary list, and offers brief
discussions of construction, characterization, and the
poetry of the play. There is also a stage history. For
Parrott the unity of the play, which is organic, not
mechanical, grows out of the point of view of its "one
controlling idea": the irrational nature of love ("fancy").
Only very careless readers fail "to distinguish between the
warm-hearted quick-tempered little Hermia and her
sentimental spaniel-like rival in love." Bottom is

Shakespeare's "first fully realized, highly individual, and
unmistakably human character." (Much of this material
reappears in modified form in Parrott's *Shakespearean
Comedy,* 1949, item 63.)

757a   *The Complete Works of William Shakespeare.* The New
       Nonesuch Shakespeare. 4 volumes. London: Nonesuch;
       New York: Random House, 1939. Reprint. New York:
       Nonesuch, 1953.

       This edition is based on the text established by Herbert
       Farjeon (see item 758) for the Limited Editions Club. It
       provides a general introduction by Ivor Brown. The text
       for *Dream,* which is in Volume 1, pages 543-603, is based
       on the first folio with a limited number of readings from the
       quartos in the margins.

758   Farjeon, Herbert, ed. *The Comedies, Histories, and
       Tragedies of William Shakespeare.* 37 volumes. New York:
       Limited Editions Club, 1935-1941.

       The text of *Dream* (Volume 23, [1939]) is derived from
       the first folio "edited and amended where obscure." It is
       printed with large type and is without any notes. There are
       five water-colors by Arthur Rackham. There is a plot
       synopsis by Sir Paul Harvey, a preface by Benedetto
       Croce, from his *Ariosto, Shakespeare and Corneille* (item
       10), a note on the illustrator, and one on the
       reproductions.

759   Horwood, F. C., ed. *A Midsummer Night's Dream.* New
       Clarendon Shakespeare. London and New York: Oxford
       University Press, 1939. 192 pp. Numerous reprints.
       Overseas Edition. With supplement and questions by Alan
       Warner. 1968. xxiv, 192 pp.

       Horwood's introduction (pp. 7-32), which is divided into
       sections, deals with the several major issues which have
       occupied scholars and critics. He is concerned to present
       what is presumed by most to be true about the play's
       origins and its nature. He dates *Dream* as probably
       1595-1596--on the basis of topical allusions and its affiliation
       with other plays of the lyrical group (*Romeo* and *Richard
       II*). He does not think V.i.52-53 alludes to Robert Greene's

death. He describes the texts, gives the (customary) list of sources written and unwritten, provides a plot summary and a comment as to how the play would have gone on a Shakespearean stage. His critical appreciation assesses the extent to which the lovers are not fully realized as characters and defends this lack of substance. They illustrate a theme: the capriciousness and transforming power of love. The lovers seem absurd, yet love is not treated finally as a laughing matter. The poet has some fun at the expense of Theseus. Horwood concludes with praise of Bottom and Puck as creations and with a comment on the delight lovers of poetry take in the play. There are brief notes at the foot of the page, longer notes in back. Also in back are excerpts from critics on several aspects of the play, and appendices on Shakespeare's life (from E. K. Chambers) on his language (from C. T. Onions), and on his meter. Alan Warren's material (added to the 1968 edition, on pp. 1-xxiv) includes comments on how to study a play, on imagery and irony, and questions on *Dream*.

760 Kittredge, George Lyman, ed. *A Midsummer Night's Dream*. Boston: Ginn, 1939. xiv, 160 pp.

Reproduces the text of *The Complete Works* (item 745) with a slightly expanded introduction and full notes. The Roberts quarto (of 1619), based on the Fisher quarto (of 1600), with misprints and corrections, may have served as a prompt-book before becoming the basis for the first folio text. Is unconvinced by John Dover Wilson's theory of revision (see item 748). Takes May Day to be the season. An appendix on the fairies quotes from seven sources and lists others. See items 14 and 787.

761 *The Complete Works of William Shakespeare*. Art-Type Edition. New York: Books, 1940. 1300 pp.

Includes the Temple notes by Israel Gollancz and a glossary.

762 Doi, Kōchi, trans. [*A Midsummer Night's Dream*. Iwanami Pocket Library.] Tokyo: Iwanami Shoten, 1940. 198 pp. Reprint. 1950. (Japanese)

More literal and modern than the standard Shyōyō Tsubouchi translations (1915, revised 1934) which are widely used. Meant mainly for students to help them understand the original text.

763   Gerard, Brother, ed. *A Midsummer Night's Dream.* Shakespeare Head Publications. Sydney: W. E. Smith, 1940. 150 pp. Numerous reprints.

With a brief introduction (to p. 12) on the material of the play, poetry, etc., and with notes, glossary, and questions in back (pp. 78-150). Some reprints give only the play.

764   Macpherson, Guillermo, trans. *El sueño de una noche de verano.* Buenos Aires: Editorial Spena argentina, 1940. 150 pp. (Spanish--not seen)

765   Entry Deleted.

766   Robinson, F. W., ed. *A Midsummer Night's Dream.* The Australian Student's Shakespeare. Melbourne: Milford, 1940. (not seen)

767   *Shakespeare's First Folio of 1623.* Boston: Graphic Service, 1940.

A positive microfilm copy of the first folio with explanatory notes by William Dana Orcutt.

768   *Shakespeare's Masterpieces.* The World's Popular Classics. Art-Type Edition. New York and Boston: Books, 1940.

The play with no apparatus.

769   *Five Great Comedies by William Shakespeare.* With introductions by John Masefield. New York: Pocket Books, 1941. xi, 447 pp.

Masefield's introduction (pp. 93-95, from his 1911 *William Shakespeare*, published by Henry Holt) stresses the inspiration Shakespeare took from the English country and the spirit of the English. In *Dream* Shakespeare obviously turned his heart to the country, not so much to the squires and farm-folk, but to the land itself and the fairies. Athens is conceived as an English town. J. Walker McSpadden's synopsis is given. *Dream*, in Wright's Cambridge text (item 739), without notes, is on pages 98-163. A glossary is in back. See item 905.

770 Gozenpud, A., trans. *Son litnoyi nochi*. Kharkov: [n.p.], 1941. (Ukranian--not seen)

771 Schlegel, A. W., trans. *Ein Sommernachtstraum*. Reclams Univ.-Bibl., 73. Leipzig: Reclam, 1941. 64 pp. Reprints. 1948, 1961, 1962. Stuttgart: Reclam, 1950, 1959, 1960, 1963; edited by Dietrich Klose, 1972, 1975, 1977. 72 pp. (German--not seen)

772 *The Complete Works of William Shakespeare*. Forum Book Edition. Cleveland: World Syndicate Publishing Co., 1942. Reprint. 1960. lxxxvi, 1173 pp.

A reprint of the 1935 edition, itself apparently a revision of a 1930 edition. Includes the Temple notes, designs by T. M. Matterson, and engravings by Alexander Anderson.

773 Doorn, Willem van, ed. *A Midsummer Night's Dream: A Comedy in 5 Acts*. [With explanatory notes (in Danish).] Groningen: J. B. Wolters, 1942. Reprints. 1948, 1950, 1958. x, 101 pp. (not seen)

774 Farzād, Masūd, trans. [*A Midsummer Night's Dream*.] Tehran: [n.p.], 1942. viii, 162 pp. (Persian)

775 Marin, Luis Astrana, trans. *Sueño de una noche de San Juan*. Madrid: Espasa-Calpe, 1942. 143 pp. (Spanish--not seen)

776   Neilson, William Allan, and Charles Jarvis Hill, eds. *The
      Complete Plays and Poems of William Shakespeare*. The
      New Cambridge Edition. Boston: Houghton Mifflin, 1942.
      Reprint. 1970. xxviii, 1420 pp.

      Hill's revision of Neilson's Cambridge edition first
      published in 1906. Two-page introduction considers that the
      William Stanley, Earl of Derby, and Elizabeth Vere marriage
      of 26 January 1595 was the occasion, and Queen Elizabeth
      was present, that the foul weather of 1594 is referred to
      (II.i.81-117), and that the Lion material probably does not
      refer to events in the Scottish Court on 30 August 1594
      when a blackamoor was substituted for a lion to draw the
      triumphal car because James was frightened (as Edith
      Rickert had argued in item 574). Takes the possible
      alternate endings (of which three are found), but not the
      presence of inconsistent speech-headings, as proof of
      adaptation. Lists the sources and makes a brief critical
      observation of the accomplishment of the play, which
      includes the following: "There is perhaps no one
      achievement of his genius which has had so pervasive an
      effect as his treatment of fairies in the present play." The
      text is based on Q1. It is on pages 90-114.

777   Entry Deleted.

778   Castelain, Maurice, trans. *Le songe d'une nuit d'été*.
      Collection bilingue. Paris: Aubier, Éditions Montaigne,
      1943. 228 pp. (French and English--not seen)

779   *Prose and Poetry Individualized Program: The Drama*. With
      Introductions on the Drama and Notes. Syracuse, N. Y.:
      L. W. Singer, 1942. (not seen)

      Apparently includes *Dream*.

780   Davidowitz, Shalom Z. [Harry Solomon], trans. *Halom Leyl
      Ka'yitz*. [With introduction and notes.] Jerusalem:
      Tarshish, 1943. 100 pp. (Hebrew--not seen)

781   Puigmiguel, Ángel, trans. *El Sueno de una noche de
      Verano*. [Illustrated by Emilio Freixas.] Barcelona: Edit.
      Enrique Mesequer, 1943. (Spanish--not seen)

782 Piachaud, René-Louis, trans. *Le songe d'une nuit d'été.*
Collection des flambeaux, 3. Lausanne: Editions André
Gonin, 1944. (French--not seen)

> With eleven original woodcuts by Henry Bischoff. Loose
> leaves boxed.

783 Sevin, Nureddin, trans. *Bir yaz* dönümü gecesi rüyasi.
Ingiliz Klasikeri 9. Ankara: Maarif matbaasi, 1944. 96
pp. Reprint. Ankara: Milli Eğitim Basimevi, 1962.
(Turkish--not seen)

784 *Shakespeare: Seven Plays, The Songs, The Sonnets,
Selections from the Other Plays* The Viking Portable
Library. New York: Viking Press, 1944. 800 pp.
Reprint. 1956.

> *Dream,* on pages 397-465, without notes and individual
> introduction, is one of the seven plays. The text is that of
> George Lyman Kittredge (item 754). There is a "Key-Word
> Index" in back.

785 Neveux, Georges, trans. *Le songe d'une nuit d'été.* Paris:
Gallimard, 1945. 128 pp. Reprint. 1959/60. (French--not
seen)

> See item 176.

786 Bergstrand, Allan, trans. *En midsommarnatts dröm.*
Stockholm: Bröderna Lagerströms, 1946. 144 pp.
(Swedish--not seen)

787 Kittredge, George Lyman, ed. *Sixteen Plays of
Shakespeare.* With a preface by Arthur Colby Sprague.
Boston: Ginn, 1946. ix, 1541 pp.

> Contains the material of Kittredge's 1939 single-volume
> *Dream* (item 760). Text and introduction followed by notes
> are on pages 145-202. Textual notes are on pages 1409-12.
> See item 754.

788   Malakul, Dusdi, trans. [*A Midsummer Night's Dream*. With
      an introduction by Prem Purachatra. Bangkok: Teachers'
      Institute Press, 1946.] (Siamese--not seen)

789   Schlegel, A. W., trans. *Ein Sommernachtstraum*.
      Einzelausgaben der Berliner Klassiker, 1946, 1. Berlin:
      Dressler, 1947. 56 pp. (German--not seen)

790   Bogdanović, Milan, trans. *San ivanjske noci*. [Revised, with
      introduction and notes by Josip Torbarina.] Zagreb:
      Matica Hrvatska, 1947. 150 pp. Reprint. 1970.
      (Serbo-Croat--not seen)

791   Hazon, Mario, ed. *A Midsummer Night's Dream*. Milan:
      Garzanti, 1947. 58 pp. (not seen)

792   Patterson, R. F., and Ian J. Simpson, eds. *A Midsummer
      Night's Dream*. The Satchel Shakespeare. London and
      Glasgow: Blackie, 1947. 95 pp.

      With brief notes at the bottom of the page and
      appendices (pp. 72-95) on Shakespeare in general and
      Dream, its date, "Books which inspired," and questions.

793   Piachaud, René-Louis, trans. *Le songe d'une nuit d'été*.
      Beaux textes, textes rares, textes inedits, 9.
      Vésenaz-près-Genève: P. Gailler, 1947. 97 pp.
      (French--not seen)

794   Schlegel, A. W., trans. *Ein Sommernachtstraum*. [With
      silhouettes by Paul Konewka.] Wuppertal: Marées-Verl.,
      1947. 132 pp. (English and German--not seen)

795   _____, trans. *Ein Sommernachtstraum*. Klassiker der
      Weltliteratur. Offenburg and Mainz: Lehrmittelverl.,
      1947. xvi, 88 pp. (German--not seen)

796   _____, trans. *Ein Sommernachtstraum*. [With
      Annotations and afterword by Christian Jenssen.] Die

Garbe, 8. Hamburg: Laatzen, 1947. 76 pp. (German--not seen)

797 _____, trans. *Ein Sommernachtstraum*. Condor-Bibl., 5. Vienna and Innsbruck and Lindau: Apollo-Verlag, 1947. 64 pp. (German--not seen)

798 *Le songe d'une nuit d'été*. [Illustrated by Brunelleschi.] Paris: Guillot, 1947. (French--not seen)

799 Ayyar, Sri P. A. Subrahamanya, ed. *A Midsummer Night's Dream*. Madras: Kaviraja, 1948. (not seen)

800 Errante, Vincenzo, trans. *Il sogno di una notte d'estate*. Florence: G. C. Sansoni, 1948. 124 pp. (Italian--not seen)

801 *Four Great Comedies*. New York: Washington Square Press, 1948. x, 342 pp. Several reprints, including New York: Pocket Books, 1952.

The text and glossary (in back) are from Wright's Cambridge edition (item 739). The introduction (pp. 3-9) is by Mark Van Doren (from his *Shakespeare* [New York: Henry Holt, 1939]). For him the universe of *Dream* is large, roomy, and real, not "the tiny toy-shop" most such spectacles present. The poetry of the play is dominated by the words *moon* and *water* and by images of wet flowers (these three images are discussed). *Dream*, moreover, "as large as all imaginable life," echoes with "an ample music" (also discussed). Of Theseus' description of the hounds (IV.i.101-126): "Had Shakespeare written nothing else than this he still might be the best of English poets." The story by J. Walker McSpadden is given, and there are black line drawings by F. E. Banbery.

802 Harrison, G. B., ed. *Shakespeare: Major Plays and the Sonnets*. (Also issued as *Twenty-Three Plays and the Sonnets*.) New York: Harcourt, Brace, 1948. vi, 1090 pp.

Introduction dates the play late 1594 or early 1595, finds the William Stanley, Earl of Derby-Elizabeth Vere marriage of 26 January 1595 the most likely occasion, discusses sources and gives excerpts from some, including the passage on Pyramus and Thisbe from Golding. The foul weather speech (II.i.81-117) refers to the summer of 1594; Bottom's warning about the fear of lions alludes to James of Scotland's fear--on 30 August 1594, when his son was baptized; and Greene's death is the possible reference at V.i.52-53. The marriage of Hippolyta and Theseus, Harrison says, was "not a love match." She is "a haughty, muscular lady." At the playlet she is "bored and contemptuous, but Theseus remains gracious and encouraging." Harrison's text is based on the Globe (see item 739) with adjustments for "current American usage in spelling, punctuation, and capitalizations."

803 _____, ed. *Shakespeare: The Complete Works*. New York: Harcourt, Brace, World. 1948. Reprint. 1952, 1968. vi, 1668 pp.

An expansion of the editor's *Major Plays* (item 802) with the introductory material duplicated (pp. 511-15).

804 Jain, S. A., ed. *A Midsummer Night's Dream*. Madras: Madras Publishing, 1948.

A substantial introduction (to p. xlvii) on date, text, sources, characters, etc., with glossary at the foot of the page, notes and "typical questions" in back.

805 Suchtelen, Nico van, trans. *Een Midzomernacht Droom*. Amsterdam and Antwerp: Wereldbibliotheek, 1948. 82 pp. (Dutch--not seen)

806 *Best Loved Plays by William Shakespeare*. With Sixteen Original Illustrations by Marion Kunzelman. Chicago: Peoples Book Club, 1949. [xiv], 480 pp.

Dream (pp. 91-117) appears with no apparatus other than a *dramatis personae*.

807   Campbell, Oscar James, ed. *The Living Shakespeare:*
      Twenty-Two Plays and the Sonnets. New York:
      Macmillan, 1949. 1239 pp.

         The text (pp. 232-62) is that of the Globe, with
      glossary and notes at the foot of each page. The
      introduction to *Dream* (pp. 225-31) covers the circumstance
      of composition, topical allusions, date (1594-1595) and
      publication, sources, and stage history. Campbell thinks
      the Queen was present for the first performance and that
      the wedding was probably that of William Stanley, Earl of
      Derby, and Elizabeth de Vere, daughter of the Earl of
      Oxford, on 26 January 1595. For him, the "best critics are
      now agreed" that Oberon's Vision (II.i.148-68) and other
      elements in the play allude to the fête at Elvetham in 1591
      and the events surrounding it, the circumstances of which,
      as Edith Rickert had given them (in item 574), he recounts.
      He also takes Bottom's comment about how the ladies will be
      frightened by the lion to be an "indisputable piece of
      ridicule directed at King James," as Rickert had taken it
      (in item 574), although, he says, Bottom and James are not
      to be taken as identical. As for the theme of the play, it
      declares that "Love is a completely irrational passion, the
      slave of whim and fantastic caprice." Bottom is a lout first
      of all, but as a comic character he has progressed beyond
      malapropism and rustic stupidity into a kind of folly that
      makes him an eternal comic embodiment of the distinguishing
      characteristics of John Bull, the chief of which is English
      stability. (Much of this material reappears in slightly
      altered form in items 284 and 900.)

808   Hugo, François-Victor, trans. *Le songe d'une nuit d'été.*
      [Illustrated by Eduard Chimot.] Paris: Guillot, 1949. 114
      pp. (French--not seen)

809   Kalma, D., trans. *In Midsummernachtdream.* Drachten:
      Laverman, 1949. 96 pp. (Frisian--not seen)

810   Krog, Fritz, ed. *A Midsummer Night's Dream.* [With
      silhouettes by Paul Konewka.] Neusprachliche
      Textausgaben 2. Engl. Reihe. Frankfurt-am-Main:
      Hirschgraben-Verlag, 1949. 135 pp. Reprints. 1954,
      1958. (not seen)

811 Saudek, E. A., trans. *Sen noci svatojánské.* Prague: Umění
    lidu, 1949. 122 pp. (Czech--not seen)

812 Schlegel, A. W., trans. *Ein Sommernachtstraum.* Europ.
    Komödien. Berlin and Bielefeld: Cornelsen, 1949. 101 pp.
    Reprint. Schwalbenbuch, 44. 1949. (German--not seen)

813 Hochkofler, Mary de, trans. *Sogno di una notte di mezza
    estate.* L'Ulivo, 14. Florence: Salani, 1950. 106 pp.
    (Italian--not seen)

814 Kozmian, M., trans. *Sen nocy letniej.* Biblioteka accydziel
    Poezji i Prozy, 101. Krakow: Wydawnictwo M. Kot, 1950.
    100 pp. (Polish--not seen)

815 Kurijagawa, Fumio, ed. *A Midsummer Night's Dream.*
    Kenkyūsha Pocket English Series, 72. Tokyo:
    Kenkyūsha, 1950.

    Widely used as a classroom text. The annotator (the
    notes are especially full) is a specialist in Middle English
    and Medieval English literature; hence he provides some
    interesting historical explanations of peculiarly Elizabethan
    expressions.

816 Ojetti, Paola, trans. *Sogo di una notte d'estate.* Biblioteca
    Universale Rizzoli, 195. Milan: Rizzoli, 1950. 86 pp.
    (Italian--not seen)

817 Alexander, Peter, ed. *William Shakespeare: The Complete
    Works.* The Tudor Edition. London and Glasgow: Collins,
    1951, 1952. With numerous reprints, including New York:
    Random House, 1952, 1956; W. W. Norton, 1954. xxxii,
    1376 pp. Published as a box set (4 vols.) by Collins.
    Dream is in Volume One (*Comedies: William Shakespeare,
    pp. 372-416*). Reprint. Collins and Norton, 1958.

    The general introduction places *Dream* early in the
    "second period"--1595 to 1599--in the group with *Richard II*
    and *Romeo* called the "poetical plays." The lineation is that
    of the Cambridge edition of Clark and Wright (item 739).

Dream, with no notes, is on pages 198-222. There is a general glossary in back. Alexander's introduction to *Dream* in the box set is from his *Introductions to Shakespeare* (item 218).

818 Craig, Hardin, ed. *The Complete Works of Shakespeare*. Chicago: Scott, Foresman, 1951. xii, 1337 pp. Rev. ed. 1961.

As regards *Dream*, repeats with slight modification the 1931 edition (see item 750).

819 Brabander, Gerard den, trans. *Een midzomernachtdroom*. Amsterdam: van Kampen, 1952. Reprint. 1959. 96 pp. (Dutch--not seen)

820 Burgersdijk, L. A. J., trans., revised by F. de Backer and G. A. Dudok. *Een midzomernachtdrom*. Klassieke galerij, 71. Leiden: Sijthoff; Antwerp: Nederl. Boekhandlers, 1952. 84 pp. (Dutch--not seen)

821 Oikonomide, S. Kent and Gianne, trans. [*A Midsummer Night's Dream*.] Athens: Peter Dematrakos, 1952. 31 pp. (An abridgement in modern Greek)

822 Schlegel, A. W., trans. *Ein Sommernachtstraum*. Editiones Helveticae. Abt. Deutsche Texte, 20. Basel: Birkhäuser, 1952. 75 pp. (German--not seen)

823 Entry Deleted.

824 Mikami, Isao, trans. [*A Midsummer Night's Dream*.] Tokyo: Kawade Shobō, 1953. 150 pp.

Regarded by some as the most balanced Japanese version. Included in [*Selected Plays by Shakespeare*] (1977) along with other translations by the same author.

825   Sisson, Charles Jasper, ed. *William Shakespeare: The*
      Complete Works. New York: Harper, 1953, 1954; London:
      Odhams Press, 1954. lii, 1376 pp.

      One-page introduction (p. 207) treats the fairies,
      conventional qualities of the play, sources and date. "We
      are apt to take Shakespeare's fairy-world for granted. . .
      . But [the fairies] present many a problem." They are, for
      example, "certainly not Warwickshire fairies." *Dream*
      combines Masque and Anti-Masque. As for sources, "a great
      tossing of books, indeed, preceded the rolling of the poet's
      eye here." The text, a new one, is printed without
      explanatory notes. There is a list of "doubtful readings."

826   Zeynek, Theodor von, trans. *Ein Sommernachtstraum.*
      Stifterbibliothek, 24. Munich and Salzburg:
      Stifterbibliothek, 1953. 96 pp. (German--not seen)

827   Arnold, Paul, trans. *Songe d'une nuit d'été.* Revue
      Théâtrale, 25 (1954), 31-84. (French)

828   Guthrie, Tyrone, and G. B. Harrison, eds. *A Midsummer*
      Night's Dream. New Stratford Shakespeare. London:
      George G. Harrap, 1954. 121 pp.

      The text is that of Harrison's New Readers'
      Shakespeare. Guthrie has supplied an introduction on
      Shakespeare's theatre, a commentary, sections on scenery,
      lighting, costume, and on character. His commentary
      stresses the artificial qualities of the play: "it aims to
      increase our enjoyment by drawing attention to its own
      artificial and symmetrical design." Scenes are not to be
      played as naturalistic except in the case of the rustics,
      whose simplicity and earnestness should be at least as
      touching as it is funny. *Dream* resembles *Love's Labour's*
      Lost in that pattern (males and females, young and old,
      gentle and simple) is more important than story (see item
      59); it differs in the maturity of the verse and in the
      presence of the supernatural. We ought not to
      sentimentalize the play: there is in the fairies and nature of
      the play a magic which is not merely pretty but dark and
      dangerous. "The play is not well served if the ferocity, the
      greed, the sensuality and mischievous silliness of the

Fairies is played down in favour of daintiness and
respectability."

829   Kökeritz, Helge, and Charles T. Prouty, eds. *Mr. William
      Shakespeares Comedies, Histories, & Tragedies.* New
      Haven: Yale University Press; London: G. Cumberlege,
      Oxford University Press, 1954. xxix, 889 pp.

      A facsimile reproduction, with page size reduced by
      one-fifth, of the Henry Huth first folio in the possession of
      The Elizabethan Club of Yale University.

830   Lozinskii, M., trans. [*"A Midsummer Night's Dream":
      Comedy in Five Acts.*] Moscow: Iskusstuo, 1954. 91 pp.
      (Russian--not seen)

831   Lu Wing, trans. [*A Midsummer Night's Dream.* Peking:
      People's Literature Publishing House, 1954.] (Mandarin
      Chinese--not seen)

832   Sumardjo, Trisno, trans. *Impian ditengah musim.* Djakarta:
      Balai Pustaka, 1954. 116 pp. (Indonesian--not seen)

833   Kittredge, George Lyman, ed. *The Works of Shakespeare.*
      Players Illustrated Edition. 3 volumes. Chicago: Spencer
      Press, 1955. Reprint. (In one volume) New York:
      Grolier, 1958. xx, 1561 pp.

      In Volume 1. To the apparatus of the 1936 Complete
      Works (item 754) adds eight pages with photos of the Old
      Vic production with Robert Helpmann as Oberon, Moira
      Shearer as Titania, Philip Guard as Puck.

834   *A Midsummer Night's Dream.* Illustrated by Mary Grabhorn.
      San Francisco: The Grabhorn Press, 1955. 108 pp.

      Limited to 180 copies. In large print with eight colored
      plates.

835   Weifeng, Tsao, trans. [*A Midsummer Night's Dream.*
      Shanghai: New Literature Publishing Co., 1955.]
      (Mandarin Chinese--not seen)

835a *Complete Works of William Shakespeare.* Classics Club
      College Edition. Princeton, N. J.: D. Van Nostrand Co.,
      1956. 1312 pp. (not seen)

      A thin-paper volume, apparently, with an index of
      characters and a glossary. The text is taken from the
      Johnson-Steevens-Reed edition of 1803.

836   Dora, Asena, trans. *Bir yaz gecesi rüyasi.* Istanbul:
      Necmettin Salman Kitap Yayma Odasi, 1956.
      (Turkish--not seen)

837   Oldendorf, H. J., and H. Arguile, eds. *A Midsummer
      Night's Dream.* Cape Town: Maskew Miller, 1956. 161 pp.

      School text. With introductory sections on the play,
      characters, fairies, masque, etc., and with questions in the
      back.

838   Schlegel, A. W., trans. *Ein Sommernachtstraum.* [With five
      colored lithographs by Jack V. Reppert-Bismarck.] Duo-
      Bücher. Bern: Scherz, 1956. 134 pp. (German--not
      seen)

839   Stuart, Ian, ed. *A Midsummer Night's Dream.* New
      Simplified Shakespeare Series. Birmingham, Ala.:
      Vulcan, 1956. xv, 159 pp.

      With the story of the play from Charles and Mary Lamb
      as an introduction and notes facing the text.

840   Barnes, V., ed. *A Midsummer Night's Dream.* The
      Intermediate Shakespeare. Sydney: Shakespeare Head
      Press, 1957. (not seen)

841 Buning, J. W. F. Werumeus, trans. *Een
    midzomernachtsdroom*. Toneelfonds Maestro, 196.
    Amsterdam: Strengholt, 1957. 64 pp. (Dutch--not seen)

842 *A Midsummer Night's Dream*. Introduction by Sir Ralph
    Richardson. Designs by Oliver Messel. Text of The New
    Temple Shakespeare, ed. M. R. Ridley. [London:] The
    Folio Society, 1957. viii, 80 pp.

    Eight full-page, colored illustrations--the designs for
    Tyrone Guthrie's production at the Old Vic in 1937.
    Richardson writes briefly of stage history. "Even though I
    have never seen a bad production of the play, I have
    equally never seen a perfect one." With a glossary in back.
    Richardson's comments are reprinted in *Introductions to
    Shakespeare* (London: Michael Joseph, 1977). See item
    T1162.

843 Munro, John, ed. *The London Shakespeare*. 6 volumes.
    London: Eyre and Spottiswoode, 1957, 1958; New York:
    Simon and Schuster, 1957, 1958.

    The introduction (Vol. 1, pp. 337-41) sets out the
    relationship among the three texts (Q1, Q2, F1) which is
    generally accepted. Though reluctant to agree with it,
    Munro presents Dover Wilson's view of revision (see item
    748). Does not perceive a double ending. Offers as a
    tentative suggestion the date 1595. The text is in Volume 1.
    Notes are at the foot of each page.

844 Raghav, Rangeya, trans. [*A Midsummer Night's Dream*.]
    Delhi: [?p.], 1957. (Hindi--not seen)

845 Alexander, Peter, ed. *The Heritage Shakespeare*. Preface
    by Tyrone Guthrie and illustrations by Edward
    Ardizzone. 3 volumes. New York: Heritage Press,
    1958-1959.

    Reprints the text and general introduction of Alexander's
    1951 edition (item 817) in three volumes. *Dream*, with no
    notes, is in Volume 1 (*The Comedies*, 1958), pages 536-96.
    Alexander's introduction to *Dream* (pp. 531-35) is from his
    Introductions to Shakespeare (item 218).

846   _____, ed. *William Shakespeare: The Complete Works.*
       Players' Edition. London: Collins, 1958, 1964. xxxii,
       1376 pp.

       Alexander's Tudor Edition (item 817) with 24 illustrations
       of Shakespearean actors and actresses of the past and
       present.

847   Baldini, Gabriele, trans. *Sogno di una notte di mezza
       estate. Fiabe teatrali presentate da Diego* Valeri, 9.
       Turin: E. R. I., 1958. Reprint. Rome: A. Signorelli,
       1961. 155 pp. (Italian--not seen)

848   Bjerke, André, trans. *En Sommernattsdrom.* Oslo: H.
       Aschenhoug, 1958. 129 pp. (Norwegian--not seen)

849   *The Complete Works of William Shakespeare Comprising His
       Plays and Poems.* Preface by Donald Wolfit. Introduction
       and glossary by Bretislav Hodek. Feltham, Mass.:
       Spring Books, 1958. [xxii], 1081 pp. (not seen)

850   Deelen, Martin, trans. *Een midzomernachtdroom.* Beroemde
       Boeken in Woord en Beeld, 64. Bussum: Classics
       Nederland, 1958. 48 pp. (Dutch--not seen)

851   Kher, Bhālcandra Dattātray, trans. *Midsamar nāits drĩm.*
       Bombay: Vora, 1958. 51, 36 pp.
       (Paraphrase-Marathi--not seen)

852   Quiller-Couch, Arthur, and John Dover Wilson, eds. *A
       Midsummer Night's Dream.* Cambridge Pocket
       Shakespeare. Cambridge: Cambridge University Press,
       1958. 83 pp.

       The Cambridge Shakespeare text and glossary (item 748)
       in paperback.

853   Schlegel, A. W., trans. *Ein Sommernachtstraum.*
       [Illustrations with the text.] Illustrierte klassiker, 64.

Hamburg: Bildschriftenverlag, 1958. 48 pp.
(German--not seen)

854 Wright, Louis B., and Virginia A. LaMar, eds. *A
     Midsummer Night's Dream*. The Folger Library General
     Reader's Shakespeare. New York: Pocket Books,
     Washington Square Press, 1958. xxxv, 81, 81 pp.
     Reprint. Reader's Enrichment Series. Washington Square
     Press, 1966 (with "Reader's Supplement").

     Designed for inexperienced readers of Shakespeare. The
     brief introduction treats the masque-like properties, theme
     ("the whimsical and irresponsible aspects of love"),
     sources, and stage history. Notes face the page. The
     supplement to the 1966 edition (pp. 1-87), from which the
     original introduction is missing, by contributing editor
     Walter James Miller, is divided into two parts. The first has
     sections on Shakespeare's life, the publication of his plays,
     the stage history of the play, and the basis for his lasting
     appeal. In this last section, under "Dramatic
     Craftsmanship," is a summary of the structure of the play
     and ways in which it resembles a masque. The second part
     has sections on vocabulary, ideas for discussion,
     suggestions for further reading, and so on. There are a
     number of black-and-white cuts including those by Paul
     Konewka.

855 Doran, Madelaine, ed. *A Midsummer Night's Dream*. The
     Pelican Shakespeare. Baltimore: Penguin Books, 1959.
     119 pp. Rev. ed. Baltimore: Penguin Books, 1971. 115
     pp.

     Doran's introduction covers the occasion (probably the
     wedding of William Stanley and Elizabeth Vere), the date
     (1594 or 1595), each of the four components and how they
     blend, and the variety of source material which produces a
     play "classical in the Renaissance manner" with the theme of
     "love-blindness." In associating "literary" with folk fairies
     Shakespeare was not doing anything novel or incongruous,
     for fairy lore in his day was already an inextricable mixture
     of literary tradition (both medieval and classical), folk
     belief, religious teaching (which associated the fairies with
     evil spirits), and poetic invention. He enriched the blend
     and reduced their size. It is the poetry which creates the
     enchantment of the wood. Compared with similar but more

complicated later plays, *Dream* may seem a "pretty toy. But the lesser thing it does it does to perfection." There is a brief summary of its "lively but not very satisfactory acting history." Notes are at the foot of the page. In back a supplementary note on the text (pp. 116-19) suggests that Q1 was set up from Shakespeare's own working manuscript. There is some evidence for revision, it is noted, but the extent of that revision is impossible to decide. Q2 was based on Q1 with some corrections and sophistications and some new errors. And this Q2, with still more changes, was the copy for F1. A number of readings for stage directions in F1 must have come from the theatrical manuscript. The act divisions in F1 obstruct the management of the scenes since there are only seven (here described) in the quarto. Readings which depart from Q1 are listed. See item 921.

856 Schlegel, A. W., and Ludwig Tieck, trans. *Ein Sommernachtstraum*. [Ed. L. L. Schücking. With essay "Zum Verständnis des Werkes" and a bibliography by Wolfgang Clemen.] Rowohlts klassiker der Literatur und der Wissenschaft, 48. Engl. Literatur, 8. Hamburg: Rowohlt, 1959. Reprint. Reinbek: Rowohlt, 1966, 1968. 152 pp. (German and English--not seen)

857 Söderwall, Margreta, trans. *En midsommarnatts-dröm*. Stockholm: Bonniers, 1959. 190 pp. Reprint. Stockholm: Laromedelsforlag, 1970. (not seen)

A shortened edition with parallel English and Swedish texts for school performances. Preface and commentary by Söderwall. See item 200.

858 Superveille, Jean-Louis and Jules, trans. *Le songe d'une nuit d'été*. Paris: Le Club Français du livre, 1959. 76 pp. (French--not seen)

See item 176.

859 Cán-Huy-Tang, trans. *Giác mo' dêm trung-ha*. Saigon: Khai-Tri, 1960. 32 pp. (Vietnamese--not seen)

860 Courteaux, Willy, trans. *Midzomernachtdroom.* Klassieke
Galerij, 71. Antwerp: Nederl. Boekhandlers, 1960. xii,
82 pp. (Dutch--not seen)

861 Fergusson, Francis, and C. J. Sisson, eds. *A Midsummer
Night's Dream.* Laurel Shakespeare, LB 137. New York:
Dell, 1960. 159 pp.

Fergusson introduces the play (pp. 6-14) and has an
essay in back (pp. 130-150) on Shakespeare and his
theatre. For Fergusson, who trips lightly through the play
from start to finish, it is the idea of wedding which gives
the common motive to all elements in the play, and the
whole is like a Court Masque. See item 354 where this essay
is collected. The text is Sisson's (item 825, "further
revised"). Lincoln Kirstein has a comment (pp. 16-26) "on
Producing *A Midsummer Night's Dream*" based on his 1958
Stratford, Connecticut production. The essential aim was to
follow Shakespeare's original intention as closely as
possible, that is, to emphasize "the wizardry in the spoken
verse." The Great Hall in a country home (at Charlecote,
say) determined the style. H. H. Smith prepared the
glossary. See item T1193.

862 Fukuda, Tsuneari, trans. *Natsu no Yo no Yume.* Tokyo:
Shinchōsha, 1960. 196 pp. (Japanese)

Fukuda is, like Tsubouchi (see item 762), a leading
literary critic as well as a distinguished playwright. His
production of *Hamlet* (1956) in his own translation marked a
new epoch in the history of Shakespeare production in
Japan, and his translations have been much acclaimed as
worthy literary achievements. Now somewhat superseded by
that of Yushi Odajima (item 948).

863 Hodek, Břetislav, ed. *A Midsummer Night's Dream.* [With
photos from the Czech puppet-film (Jiří Trnka's) by Jiří
Vogta. With essays on the film by J. Brdečka, Břetislav
Hodek, and V. Bor.] Prague: Artia, 1960. 158 pp. With
essays translated into English by Sylva Součková.

London: Spring Books, 1960. 158 pp. A. W. Schlegel,
trans. [With essays translated into German by Kurt

Lauscher.] Prague: Artia, 1960. 164 pp. Pierre
Letourneur, trans. [With essays translated into French
by Yvette Joye.] Prague: Artia, 1960. 163 pp.
See items 883, 1028, T1185a and T1198.

863a János, Arany, trans. Szentivánéji *alom.* Budapest: Europa,
      1960. 107 pp. (Hungarian--not seen)

864   Josten, Walter, trans. *Ein Sommernachtstraum.* [Illustrations
      by Günter Schöllkopf.] Neujahrsgabe, 4. Sonderdruck
      des Verlag der Druckspiegel. Stuttgart: Der
      Druckspiegel, 1960. 90 pp. [Not for sale.] (German--not
      seen)

865   Entry Deleted.

866   Mahmoud, Hassan, trans. *Holm Lailat Saif.* Cairo: Dar
      al-Ma'aref, 1960. 366 pp. Reprint. 1968. (Arabic--not
      seen)

867   Arnold, Paul, trans. and ed. *Le songe d'une nuit d'été. La
      Tempête.* Paris: Club des Amis du Livre, [1961?]. 288
      pp. (French--not seen)

868   Bax, Peter, ed. *A Midsummer Night's Dream.* French's
      Acting Edition. London: Samuel French, 1961. xiii, 43
      pp.

      A reprint of the 1933 edition. Commentaries and
      glossaries by George Skillan are added to this edition. Bax
      based his version (the directions in the margins) on the
      production by Basil Dean at Drury Lane in 1924 (see items
      under Dean, Basil, in Index).

869   Jesenská, Z., and J. Rozner, trans. *Sen* májovej *noci.*
      Bratislava: SDILIZA, 1961. Reprint. 1963. 143 pp.
      (Slovak--not seen)

      Mimeographed edition for actors.

870   Lever, J. W., ed. *A Midsummer Night's Dream.* New Swan
      Shakespeare. London: Longmans, 1961. xxiv, 205 pp.

      A school text, with sections in the introduction (to p.
      xxiv) on story, characters, construction and ideas,
      language, imagery, and *Dream* in the theatre. Notes face
      the text. There is a synopsis before each scene, a glossary
      in back, and "Hints to Examination Candidates" by H. M.
      Hulme in back. The explanatory material is presented
      simply--"within the range of a specially chosen list of 3,000
      most commonly used English root-words." The introduction,
      which treats the basic components in the traditional way,
      notes incidentally that Theseus does not entirely support
      the demand of Egeus and that the characters of the play
      are just such people as might be present for a wedding at a
      big house. Reason and nature must unite, it is said, if love
      is to succeed.

871   Lodovici, Cesare Vico, trans. and ed. *Sogno d'una notte
      d'estate.* Turin: Guilio Einaudi, 1961. 114 pp.
      (Italian--not seen)

871a Barker, Sir Ernest, intro. *The Works of William
      Shakespeare.* London: Georges Newnes, [?1962]. [lxiv],
      1079 pp. (not seen)

872   Barrows, Marjorie Wescott, ed. *Currents in Drama.* Literary
      Heritage Series. New York: Macmillan; London:
      Collier-Macmillan, 1962. Rev. editions. 1968, 1974. xiv,
      327 pp.

      For secondary students. Includes a brief introduction, a
      glossary in back, and in Teacher's Guide versions a
      summary of the action of each scene.

873   Guthrie, Sir Tyrone, introduction and commentaries. *Ten
      Great Plays.* New York: Golden Press, 1962; London:
      Paul Hamlyn, 1963. 502 pp.

      The fourteen colored illustrations are by Alice and
      Martin Provensen. For the introduction to *Dream* Guthrie
      repeats some of the material in item 828.

874 Langford, W. F., ed. *A Midsummer Night's Dream.*
     Canadian Swan Shakespeare. Toronto: Longmans Canada,
     1962. lx, 119 pp.

     Prepared especially for use in secondary schools. The
     introductory pages (to p. lx) offer a variety of material.
     Comments on characters and the appeal of the play are
     quoted at length from a number of critics. There is a
     section with advice for actors and a scene (I.ii) in actor's
     handbook form, and sections on Shakespeare's life, times,
     and stage. Of more definite application to the play are the
     brief sections on the date (the style suggests 1594-1595,
     though other elements suggest 1592-1595), the early
     editions, the sources of the plot, the fairies, the time of
     action (three days, not the four Theseus mentions),
     Shakespearean verse and prose (lines are scanned), and a
     resume of the story of the play. There are photographs
     from performances of *Dream.* Glosses are at the foot of the
     page, commentary and long notes in the back along with
     review questions.

875 *A Midsummer Night's Dream.* With Glossary and Selection of
     Sonnets. Midget Classics. London: Burgess & Bowes,
     1962.

     No apparatus. The book will fit in a closed hand.

876 Mullik, B. R., ed. *Shakespeare's "A Midsummer Night's
     Dream."* Delhi: S. Chand, 1962. (not seen)

877 Verspoor, Dolf, trans. *Droom van een Midzomernacht.*
     Amsterdam: van Ditmar, 1962. 90 pp. (Dutch--not seen)

878 Entry Deleted.

879 Bonazza, Blaze Odell, and Emil Roy, eds. *Studies in Drama.*
     New York and Evanston: Harper & Row, 1963. 352 pp.

     Contains *Dream,* with study questions after each act.
     For college students.

880   Clemen, Wolfgang, ed. *A Midsummer Night's Dream*. The
      Signet Classic Shakespeare. New York and Toronto: New
      American Library, 1963. xxxvii, 186 pp. Included, with
      some revisions, in item 934a.

      Clemen's introduction emphasizes the way disparate
      elements are unified by the atmosphere (dream, illusion),
      by links of comparison and contrast, and by the main
      theme--"the transitoriness and inconstancy of love." The
      title would have suggested to Elizabethan audiences how the
      play should be understood--as an unrealistic creation of the
      imagination, a series of dream images, contradictory and
      inconsistent but having symbolic content. There are Masque
      and Anti-Masque elements of song, dance, and the
      supernatural, befitting the play's origin on the private
      stage. The lovers are intended to be puppets, not fully
      realized characters. (Clemen proceeds to discuss the
      various elements of the play, stressing the special effect of
      style.) A brief analysis of the opening scene is given in
      order to show how delicately and accurately the play's
      particular atmosphere, together with its theme and
      leitmotifs, is rendered from the beginning. There is a note
      on the sources and one on the text (Q1 is the basic text).
      There are excerpts from William Hazlitt, Edward Dowden,
      Enid Welsford, Henry Alonzo Myers, and John Russell
      Brown.

881   Evans, Bertrand, and James J. Lynch, eds., *"The
      Merchant of Venice" and "A Midsummer Night's Dream."*
      Literary Heritage. New York: Macmillan; London:
      Collier-Macmillan, 1963. xi, 249 pp.

      Designed for students. Introduction (pp. 131-35)
      imagines Shakespeare's thoughts when commissioned to
      compose the play. There are marginal glosses and footnotes
      and, in the back (pp. 227-38), comments, questions, and
      suggestions for composition.

882   Fergusson, Francis, and C. J. Sisson, eds. *Shakespeare's
      Comedies of Romance.* Delta Book. New York: Dell, 1963.
      415 pp.

      Includes *Dream*. Fergusson's introduction is the
      previously published Laurel preface (item 860), and Sisson's
      is the text (items 825, 860).

883   Greene, Jay E., ed. *"A Midsummer Night's Dream"* and
       "Berkeley Square." Noble's Comparative Classics. New
       York: Noble and Noble, 1963. 308 pp.

       Designed for schools with an emphasis on comparing the
       two plays. Introduction gives a general background and
       takes up such elements as versification, plot structure, and
       sources. There are numerous illustrations from productions,
       including some from the Jiří Trnka puppet motion picture
       (see items 863 and 1028). Provides various "aids"
       (questions, etc.) for understanding and appreciation.

884   Ichikawa, Sanki, and Takuji Mine, eds. *A Midsummer
       Night's Dream.* The Kenkyūsha Shakespeare Series.
       Tokyo: Kenkyūsha, 1963.

       Introduction covers the play, a synopsis, and
       characters; text follows the Globe; and there is an index to
       the notes. Mainly used as a text for reading in
       universities. Introduction and notes are eclectic or
       conventional, showing little originality.

885   Kim, Jaenam, trans. [*A Midsummer Night's Dream.*] Seoul:
       Yang Moon Pub. Co., 1963. (Korean--not seen)

886   Wright, Louis B., and Virginia A. LaMar, eds. *The Play's
       the Thing: Seventeen of Shakespeare's Greatest Dramas.*
       New York: Harper & Row, 1963. viii, 781 pp.

       Text and introduction to *Dream* (pp. 137-68) previously
       published in The Folger Library General Reader's
       Shakespeare (item 854).

887   Broido, Ephraim, trans. *Halom Leyl Ka'yitz.* [With
       introduction and notes.] Jerusalem: Bialik Institute,
       1964. II.i (an excerpt) was printed in *Ma'ariv* (Tel
       Aviv), 8 May 1964, and III.i-ii in *la-Merhav*, 22 May
       1964.

       See items 219, 248 and 254.

888 Carmi, Tcherni, trans. *Halom Leyl Ka'yitz.* Merchavia, Israel: Sifriyat Po'alim, 1964. Also printed in *Te'atron* (Haifa), ed. Mose Shamir, 9 (June 1964), 17-50, a special Shakespeare issue in connection with the Hebrew production of *Dream* at the Haifa Theatre. An excerpt (II.i) was printed in *I ha-Mishmar* (Tel Aviv), 24 April 1964. Reprint. Tel Aviv: Sifriyat Po'alim, 1979. (not seen)

889 *The Complete Works of William Shakespeare.* Abbey Library. London: Murray Sales and Service, 1964. Reprint. London: Rex Library, 1973. 1100 pp.

The foreword is by Dame Sybil Thorndike. The text is derived from Delius's German edition of 1854. There are no notes and apparatus.

890 Fried, Erich, trans. *Ein Sommernachtstraum.* Frankfurt: S. Fischer, 1964. 80 pp. (German--not seen)

890a Harrison, G. B., ed. *A Midsummer Night's Dream.* New York: Shakespeare Recording Society, 1964. 73 pp.

The complete text of the performance issued without apparatus with the recording. There are a few analytical notes by Harrison on the container.

891 Inani, M. M., trans. *Hulm Laylat Al-Sayf.* Cairo: Al-Masrah, 1964. (Arabic--not seen)

892 Ley, Charles David, and Joao Gaspar Simoes, trans. *Sonho de uma Noite de Verao.* Colecçao Classicos. Lisbon: Editorial Presença, 1964. (Portuguese--not seen)

893 Lhôte, Jean-Marie, ed. *Le songe d'une nuit d'été.* [With an introduction,] "*Le songe* dans le miroir des cartes a jouer." Marseille: Théâtre Universitaire de Marseille, 1964. 183 pp. (French--not seen)

Apparently based on the translations of Victor Hugo, Maurice Castelain, Pierre Messiaen and others. See item 310.

894   *A Midsummer Night's Dream.* London: University Microfilms, 1964. (unpaged)

Microfilm-Xerox copy of the Fisher Quarto in the British Library.

895   Munnik, Pauline de, ed. *A Midsummer Night's Dream.* The Students' Shakespeare. Johannesburg: Voortrekkerpers, 1964.

Intended primarily for use in South Africa by pupils whose home language is not English. A companion paraphrase is published separately (1964, item 1044). Contains an introduction to the plot, characters, Shakespeare's English, extensive marginal- and footnotes, and with questions in the back.

896   Rotas, Vassilis, trans. *Oneiro Therines Nuktos.* Athens: Ikaros, 1964. Reprint. 1973. 100 pp. (Greek--not seen)

897   Walter, J. H., ed. *A Midsummer Night's Dream.* The Players' Shakespeare. London: Heinemann Educational Books, 1964. Reprint. New York: Theatre Arts; Boston: Plays, 1966 (which is pasted over imprint). 183 pp.

School text in which glosses and comments (designed to suggest performance) face the text. A substantial introduction (pp. 1-28) assumes the play to be "a careful, serious work of art" whose aim is "virtue-breeding delightfulness." It has five plots: the wedding of Theseus and Hippolyta, the lovers' entanglements, the dispute between Oberon and Titania, Titania's infatuation with Bottom, and the interlude of Pyramus and Thisbe--all concerned with love, and in which the mature love of Theseus and Hippolyta stands as ideal. Throughout Shakespeare ridicules the "heady force of frantic love." The movement of each plot is shaped by the balance of opposing ideas either based on or else parallel with appearance and reality or reason and imagination. Each of the five plots is

discussed, with a good deal made of allegoric or symbolic
levels. Titania, for example, is sensual love; Oberon,
higher love; the changeling, a rational soul. The lovers are
dramatic pieces playing out a foolish pageant. They flee
from the judgment and order of parent and king. The
interlude reflects the disaster which may befall rash
elopements. Bottom may be a caricature of Will Kempe (but
probably not Robert Greene). Was Shakespeare mindful of
the ass who saw the angel in the way when his master
could not (Numbers 22:23)? There are also sections on
Elizabethan stage practice and the play, verse and prose,
imagery and vocabulary, and puns--all designed for
students. An appendix (pp. 175-83) gives the customary
list for the sources (although Walter does not accept "The
Merchant's Tale" as influential), describes Shakespeare's
theatre, and summarizes with comment Dover Wilson's theory
of revision (see item 748). Walter wonders whether simpler
explanations other than wholesale revision may account for
what Wilson sees as evidence. The disturbed lines, for
example, at the beginning of Act 5, may be the compositor's
device for covering bad casting off and rectifying an error
in setting up the pages in the G gathering.

898 Ward, A. C., ed. *A Midsummer Night's Dream*. Heritage of
   Literature, 65. London: Longmans, 1964. lxxix, 159 pp.

   With a general introduction to Shakespeare and one to
   Dream with sections on sources, date, craftsmanship, etc.
   Based on Q1. Gives Golding's "Tale of Pyramus and
   Thisbe." Notes face the text.

899 Yoh, S. K., ed. *A Midsummer Night's Dream*. Seoul:
   English Library Society of Korea, 1964. (not seen)

   Introduction and notes in Korean.

900 Campbell, Oscar James, Alfred Rothschild, and Stuart
   Vaughan, eds. *A Midsummer Night's Dream*. The Bantam
   Shakespeare Commemoration Editions. New York: Bantam
   Books, 1965. xiii, 160 pp. Large Type Edition. New
   York: Watts, 1965. xv, 229 pp.

   A foreword on the series is by Rothschild, an
   introduction by Campbell, and a note on Shakespeare's

theatre by Vaughan. Campbell's comments (pp. 1-10) are in substance (and often in phrasing) a repeat of material he used in his 1949 edition of Shakespeare (see item 807) and his 1966 *Reader's Encyclopedia* (see item 284). That is, they are largely a presentation of and defense of Edith Rickert's theory of the topical satire of the play (item 574). There are in back, along with notes and a bibliography, selected commentaries from William Hazlitt (1817, item 1), F. J. Furnivall (1877, his introduction to the Leopold Shakespeare), Thomas Marc Parrott (1949, item 63), Enid Welsford (1927, item 575), Muriel C. Bradbrook (1951, item 607), and C. L. Barber (1959), item 158).

901   Hirai, Masao, trans. [*A Midsummer Night's Dream.*] Tokyo: Chikuma Shobō, 1965. (Japanese)

       Similar in nature to that by Kochi Doi (item 762). Volume 1 of *The Collected Works of Shakespeare*, by various hands, mostly academic, the second complete translation. The first was by Tsubouchi (see item 762).

902   Pitt, David G., intro., with notes by Lucy M. Fitzpatrick. *A Midsummer Night's Dream*. Airmont Shakespeare Classics. New York: Airmont Publishing Company; Toronto: Ryerson Press, 1965. xxi, 105 pp.

       With a general introduction on Shakespeare, an introduction to *Dream*, study questions, and notes at the foot of the page. The introduction (divided into "An Early Play," "Four Stories in One," "The Love Theme," "The Title," and "The Characters") suggests that Shakespeare recommends a stable, married love, like that of Theseus and Hippolyta, not one based on fancy alone (the eyes) or parental choice. True marriage stabilizes both society and nature (Titania is the moon, Oberon the sun, the changeling boy the day). There is a prose summary before each act.

903   Schlegel, A. W., trans. *Ein Midsommernachtstraum*. [With illustrations by Gerhard Ulrich.] Hamburg: von Schröder, 1965. 101 pp. (German--not seen)

904 _____, trans. *Ein Sommernachtstraum.* [For members
of the Bertelsmann Book Club.] Gütersloh: Bertelsmann,
1965. 101 pp. (German--not seen)

905 *Three Comedies: "A Midsummer Night's Dream," "As You
Like It," "The Merchant of Venice."* With introductions
by John Masefield. Great Illustrated Classics. New York:
Dodd, Mead, 1965. xx, 266 pp.

Masefield's introduction (pp. 3-5) is from his 1954 *William
Shakespeare* (item 115), which resembles but is not identical
with the comment in his 1911 *William Shakespeare* (item
769). *Dream* occupies pages 6-75. There are five full-page
photographs: one of the titlepage of Q1, three of
performances, and one of Ashdown Forest. A general
glossary is in back. The text is that of the New Clarendon
Shakespeare.

906 Ribner, Irving, and George Lyman Kittredge, eds. *A
Midsummer Night's Dream.* The New Kittredge
Shakespeare. Waltham, Mass.: Blaisdell, 1966. xvii, 85
pp.

Ribner's revision of the 1939 Kittredge *Dream* (item 760)
taking into account recent attitudes toward the material.
Ribner's introduction presents, for the most part, received
views of text, occasion, date (1594-1595), and sources. He
thinks for the occasion the wedding of Sir Thomas Heneage
and Mary, Countess of Southampton, on 2 May 1594 to be
the most likely suggestion. He also says that "we may now
be fairly certain that Shakespeare was indebted to Anthony
Monday's *John a Kent and John a Cumber*," based on the
assumption that it was the earlier of the two plays (see item
623) and on Nevill Coghill's discussion of the two (see item
648). Theseus he finds "the ideal Elizabethan
gentleman--staid, rational, firm yet merciful in his rule."
Dream, he says in the section called "the shapes of love,"
explores "the meaning of love between men and women as
the most basic of all human relationships." Kittredge's text
and many of his notes remain.

907 Vnai, M. Madhava, trans. [*A Midsummer Night's Dream.*]
Kerala: Kottayam, 1966. (Malayalam--not seen)

908 Evans, A. A., ed. *A Midsummer Night's Dream*. London
     English Literature Series. London: University of London
     Press, 1967. 140 pp.

     With a lengthy introductory critical commentary (pp.
     9-43) stressing "its all-pervading gaiety and lightness of
     heart," finding the dramatic success in plot, unity, and
     dramatic irony, and commenting on the events of the play
     in the order of their occurrence.

909 Helsztyński, Stanisław, trans. *Sen nocy letniej Williama
     Szekspira*. Biblioteka Analiz Literackich, 24. Warsaw:
     Państwowe Zakłady Wydawnictw, 1967. 116 pp.
     (Polish--not seen)

910 Jolles, Frank. *A. W. Schlegels "Sommernachtstraum" in der
     ersten Fassung vom Jahre 1789*. Palaestra Series, 244.
     Göttingen: Vanderhoeck & Ruprecht, 1967. 248 pp.

     An annotated edition and study of the first version of
     Schlegel's translation and a comparison of the manuscripts.
     See item 25.

911 Kalocsay, Kálmán, trans. *Somermeznokta songô*. Stafeto:
     Beletraj Kajeroj, 30. La Laguna: J. Regulo, 1967.
     (Esperanto--not seen)

912 *"A Midsummer Night's Dream": A Comedy*. Magnatype
     Edition. Pittsburgh: Stanwix, 1967. xxxii, 187 pp.

     With a brief general introduction to Shakespeare, the
     story of the play, and synopses of the acts.

913 Wells, Stanley, ed. *A Midsummer Night's Dream*. New
     Penguin Shakespeare. Harmondsworth, Middlesex:
     Penguin, 1967, with reprints. 171 pp.

     The introduction (pp. 1-40) gives a brief stage history;
     considers as a likely date some time immediately before,
     during, or fairly soon after the theatres were closed for
     the plague (1593 and 1594); dismisses the view that
     Titania's weather speech must carry an allusion ("an

insultingly low view of Shakespeare's artistry"); groups
Dream because of common concerns with the other plays
(*Love's Labour's Lost* and *The Tempest*) without a clear
source; and finds it "credible that *Dream* was always
intended for the public theatres." ("The richness and
complexity of *Romeo and Juliet* cause it to be more usually
regarded as the later work.") A general comment discusses
the characters and the sources for them and then, quickly,
covers the several issues of the play as they emerge in the
action. Theseus is rather like an Elizabethan nobleman, a
benevolent landlord. His relationship with Hippolyta
suggests a basis of "maturity and common sense." The
tininess of the fairies derives from traditional beliefs. The
theme is "the irrationality of love." The wood is "a place of
liberation, of reassessment, leading through a stage of
disorganization to a fully increased stability." We get the
impression that the lovers have had a learning, significant
experience, though "it is difficult to rationalize this
impression." Following the text are a commentary, an
account of the text (there is no certain evidence for
revision), and the collation. For other discussions of the
issues covered here see items 14, 20, 59 and 149.

914 Castelain, Maurice, trans. *A Midsummer Night's Dream.* With
   Preliminary Study and Notes. Collection "Bilingue
   Aubier-Flammarion." Paris: Aubier, 1968. 192 pp.
   (French and English--not seen)

915 Fuller, Edmund, ed. *A Midsummer Night's Dream.* Invitation
   to Shakespeare. New York: Dell, 1968. 223 pp.

   Designed for high school students. With an introduction
   and, facing the text, detailed explanatory notes, quotations
   from various critics, and vocabulary definitions. The
   introduction (pp. 7-15) guides the teacher in selecting the
   themes which should be discussed with students at this
   particular level. *Dream* is "the most comical and beautiful
   fairy tale ever written. . . . It is not by *believing*, but by
   entering into the game of *pretending* . . . that we enjoy
   it." There are plot summaries at the beginnings of the acts.

916 Hagberg, Carl August, trans. *En Midsommarnatts-dröm.*
   [Introduction and commentary by Erik Frykman.]

Stockholm and Lund: Wahlström & Widstrand, 1968. 98
pp. (Swedish--not seen)

917 Hinman, Charlton, ed. *The First Folio of Shakespeare*. New
York: Norton; London: Paul Hamlyn, 1968. xvii, 928 pp.

This facsimile text reproduces the most fully corrected
state of the first folio publication as determined by a
collation of the copies of the folio in the Folger Shakespeare
Library.

918 Kokona, Vedat, trans. *Ëndra e një nata vere*. Prishtinë:
Rilindja, 1968. 103 pp. (Albanian--not seen)

919 Wright, Martin, ed. *A Midsummer Night's Dream*. Edited
from the Quarto of 1600. Shakespeare Workshop. London:
Ginn, 1968. 59 pp. Published with a second booklet by
Wright, *Notes on "A Midsummer Night's Dream."* 60 pp.

Old-spelling edition. The play is printed as an actor's
script. *Notes* contains brief sections on sources, copy,
characters, etc., a glossary, and "A Note on the Theme of
Sight," by Frank Kermode, a reprint from item 182.

920 Christie, Laurie, and Michael Davis, eds. *A Midsummer
Night's Dream*. Illustrated by Colin Winslow. The Kennet
Shakespeare. London: Edward Arnold, 1969. 175 pp.

A school text, with a one-page introduction, a dozen
black-and-white illustrations, and notes, which include
scores for the music by John H. Long, facing page.

921 Greenwood, J. L., ed. *"A Midsummer Night's Dream": A
Comedy by William Shakespeare*. The Montague
Shakespeare. London: Evans Bros., 1969. 169 pp.

A school text, based on F1, with modernized punctuation
and spelling and a two-page introduction. The notes (which
face the text) provide "a running commentary on the action
and motives so that the reader does not miss the dramatic
significance of what he is reading."

921a Harbage, Alfred, gen. ed. *William Shakespeare: The
      Complete Works.* The Complete Pelican Shakespeare.
      Baltimore: Penguin Books; London: Allen Lane and the
      Penguin Press, 1969. Reprint. New York: Viking, 1977.
      xxxii, 1481 pp.

      Dream is edited by Madelaine Doran and reprinted from
      her Pelican edition (see item 855).

922   Kim, Kap-Soon, ed. *A Midsummer Night's Dream.* Panmun
      Shakespeare. Seoul: Panmun Book Co., for The
      Shakespeare Society of Korea, 1969. xi, 167 pp. (not
      seen)

923   *A Midsummer Night's Dream.* Illustrated by Jack Wolfgang
      Beck. New York: Graphic Arts Typographers, 1969.
      (unpaged)

      The play illustrated but otherwise with no apparatus.

924   Østergaard, V., trans. *En Skoersommernatsdrøm.*
      Copenhagen: J. H. Schultz, 1969. 106 pp. (Danish--not
      seen)

925   Phillips, Ann, ed. *A Midsummer Night's Dream.* The South
      Bank Shakespeare. London: University Tutorial, 1969.
      vii, 160 pp.

      Based on the Alexander text (item 817). Designed for
      students, with notes facing the text and with an
      introduction (pp. 8-16) to plot, themes, language, and
      versification. Takes a traditional approach to the matter of
      the play. Its many disparate elements are harmonized by
      the dream atmosphere and by our laughter. It is a play
      bound up with crops and seasons and fertility. There is a
      comment on the text and a general discussion of the sources
      for each component which includes this remark:
      "Shakespeare, if he did take an idea from Chaucer, has so
      completely refashioned it as to make it unrecognizable--
      especially in that Chaucer's atmosphere of high romance and
      passionate chivalry is replaced by that of comedy."

926 Renč, Václav, trans. *Sen noci svatojánské.* Prague:
     DILIA, [1969?]. Reprint. 1977. (Czech--not seen)

     Mimeographed for actors.

927 Rodway, Allan, ed. *A Midsummer Night's Dream.* The New
     Warwick Shakespeare. London and Glasgow: Blackie,
     1969. ix, 63 pp.

     A school text, based on the quartos and folio, with
     modernized spelling and punctuation, with notes and
     commentary facing the text, and with a three-page
     introduction which calls the play a perfect example of "a
     celebratory comedy." The play is described as being about
     how "an imbalance of body, mind and emotions is
     undesirable." Though we are not to look for a fixed
     symbolic significance, something serious is there. "Its
     unrealism, like that of most dreams, is often meaningful
     (though sometimes simply pleasure-giving)."

928 Rothe, Hans, trans. *Ein Sommernachtstraum.* Theatertexte,
     9. Munich and Vienna: Langen-Müller, 1969. 75 pp.
     (German--not seen)

929 Scanlon, David, intro. *A Midsummer Night's Dream.*
     Riverside Literature Series. Boston: Houghton Mifflin,
     1969. xvii, 93 pp.

     A school text. Scanlon's introduction (pp. vi-xv), titled
     "The Special World of *Dream*," asks that inexperienced
     readers realize that the play was intended for acting and
     that its world is "unlike anything created before or since."
     Dream is mostly about love, but it takes on added dimension
     through the theme of the imagination. It "becomes finally a
     kind of hall of mirrors in which reality becomes confused
     and intermingled with its many reflections." Its meaning has
     to do with "how illusion can betray our common sense of
     what is truly desirable." In the back (pp. 7-91) George
     Prigmore gives suggestions (comments and questions) for
     reading and discussing the play as a whole and each scene.
     Paul Konewka's illustrations (black and white) are used.
     Notes are at the foot of the page.

930 Homan, Sidney, ed. *A Midsummer Night's Dream.* The
 Blackfriars Shakespeare. Dubuque, Iowa: William C.
 Brown, 1970. xvi, 54 pp.

 With a general introduction to Shakespeare's life and
 times and Homan's introduction to the play which is "a
 revised and somewhat abridged version" of his 1968
 Bucknell Review article (item 336). Uses the act-scene-line
 numbering of The Riverside Shakespeare (item 941) and the
 Through Line Numbering of Marvin Spevack's Shakespeare
 Concordances (item 703). Textual and explanatory notes are
 at the foot of the page.

931 Reese, M. M., ed. *A Midsummer Night's Dream.* Nelson New
 Shakespeare. London: Nelson, 1970. 155 pp.

 School text, with a brief introduction (pp. 7-10), a
 section on Elizabethan theatres (pp. 11-13), "Revision
 Questions" (pp. 152-53), and "General Questions" (pp.
 154-55). Reese dates the play 1595-1596 largely on the basis
 of its association with other plays of a lyrical group which
 includes *Romeo* and *Richard II.* Its style, that is, the
 nature of the verse, rhyme and obvious rhythm, and the
 emphasis on mood rather than character, suggests an early
 date. The theme is "that love is a highly irrational
 business." Shakespeare took "an enormous risk" introducing
 the fairies; they are not easy to present on stage. Realists
 do not get the final word: lovers are "better people" for
 their dream of love. Theseus is not permitted to deny the
 sovereignty of the imagination.

932 Tarnawski, Władysław, trans. *A Midsummer Night's Dream.*
 [With introduction and notes by Przemyslaw
 Mroczkowski.] Wrocław: Ossolineum, 1970. ciii, 139 pp.
 (Polish--not seen)

932a Bejblik, Alois, trans. *Sen svato jánské noci.* Prague:
 DILIA, 1971. 81 pp. (Czech--not seen)

 Mimeo edition for theatres.

932b Meszaros, Patricia Kerns. "Prolegomena for a Student's
 Dramatic Edition of Shakespeare, with an Edition of *A*

Midsummer Night's Dream. " Ph.D. dissertation, University of Maryland, 1971. *DAI,* 32 (1971), 3261A.

Adapted for high school and lower-level college students, the edition offers left-hand pages with expanded stage directions and stage diagrams "consistent with Elizabethan stage practice," and the commentary provides "alternative possibilities for stage movement" and space for the student's own diagrams.

933   Ribner, Irving, and George Lyman Kittredge, eds. *The Complete Works of Shakespeare.* Rev. ed. Waltham, Mass.: Ginn, Xerox College Publishing, 1971. 1743 pp.

Includes Ribner's 1966 revision of the 1939 *Dream* (item 906).

934   Sanders, Norman, ed. *A Midsummer Night's Dream.* The Macmillan Shakespeare. Basingstoke and London: Macmillan, 1971. 179 pp.

The introduction (pp. 1-24) gives what evidence there is external and internal, of allusion and style, for a date, suggesting 1594 (late)-1595, and for the circumstance of performance, reminding us that there is no strong external evidence for the theory of a private performance in honor of some nobleman's marriage. The critical comment discusses first those aspects of the play on which there is general agreement (The Young Lovers, Theseus and Hippolyta, The Mechanicals, especially how they provide an implicit comment on the situation of the lovers, The Fairies, and The Action and the Character Groups). A section on Critical Views presents briefly the approaches which find a thematic seriousness in the play (in the two themes "love and marriage" and "art"). No particular criticism is seen to be completely convincing in itself. There is a full note on the text. An appendix (pp. 176-179) describes the customs of the two folk holidays; Puck's associations; the fairies of the literary tradition, usually human or superhuman in size, and of the countryside, apt to be short, some even minuscule; and suggests that the general attitude then as reflected in literature has the fairies capable of being vicious but most commonly only mischievous. It concludes with the view that, whatever went before, Shakespeare's "has become the *only* fairy world of the English-speaking nations." See item 14.

934a Barnet, Sylvan, gen. ed. *The Complete Signet Classic Shakespeare.* New York: Harcourt Brace Jovanovich, 1972. 1776 pp.

       Reprints (pp. 524-54) with minor alterations Wolfgang Clemen's Signet Classic edition of 1963 (item 880).

935 Farrow, S. M., ed. *A Midsummer Night's Dream.* The Alexander Shakespeare. London and Glasgow: Collins, 1972. 213 pp.

       A school text, with introduction covering Shakespeare's theatre, life, and times, money, and, briefly, the play, and with notes facing the text. A "Summing Up" and "Theme Index" appear at the end. Based on Alexander's text (item 817). The introduction sees the play as "in praise of marriage (and in dispraise of obstinate virginity)" and among other things "a kind of spell against evil." Theseus and Hippolyta are "ideal lovers," a standard to judge other lovers by. Romantic love blots out the individuality of the young lovers. Acting is the play's second subject. Oberon and Titania are "an old married couple" who quarrel. There is a debate in the play between marriage and virginity, which marriage wins. The "Summing Up" (pp. 191-209) discusses the nature of love, how selfish and sexual it is, how unique the experience, how unreasonable--how all this is reflected in the play. "'Love' in fact is a violent impersonal force, that irons the humanity out of people, reducing them to animals, monsters, even things." Actors (the rustics) are as senseless and in many of the same ways as lovers.

936 Fraser, Russell, ed. *An Essential Shakespeare: Nine Plays and the Sonnets.* New York: Macmillan, 1972. 534 pp.

       With a note on the text before and an afterword (pp. 105-109) on how skepticism and approval of romantic love coexist in the play, with some comparisons between it and *Romeo.* See item 131.

937 Entry Deleted.

938 Craig, Hardin, and David Bevington, eds. *The Complete
     Works of Shakespeare.* Rev. ed. Glenview, Ill.: Scott,
     Foresman, 1973. [viii], 1447 pp.

     The notes are basically Craig's (see item 818), and the
     text is still based on the Globe edition (see item 739)
     "though carefully reviewed throughout and brought up to
     date on certain particulars." Bevington has revised the
     general introduction and supplied the introduction to
     Dream. He stresses the transitional nature of the play,
     noting that it resembles Shakespeare's early attempts in its
     lighthearted presentation of love's tribulations and that it
     suggests his later treatment by viewing love as an
     imaginative journey away from reality and back, one which
     contrasts the worlds of social order and escape. Each of the
     four main plots (taken up in turn) contains one or more
     pairs of lovers whose happiness is at issue. The lovers'
     story is a modified version of New Comedy; here the
     heroine chooses not the young over the old but rather the
     young over the young. Egeus' demand is arbitrary and
     unjust (he's the *alazon*). The forest experience suggests
     the universal power of love, its irrational nature and
     affinity to enchantment. Puck is like Cupid. The magic of
     the play is related to deep irrational powers and can do
     great harm, although the spirit of comedy keeps any threat
     at bay. Behind any explicit criticism of the fantasy, such
     as that of Theseus, we can hear Shakespeare's
     characteristically self-effacing defense of "dreaming."
     "Shakespeare leaves the status of his fantasy world
     deliberately complex; Theseus' lofty denial of dreaming is
     too abrupt." We emerge with our perceptions enlarged, led
     to wonder about it all.

939 Evans, Bertrand, ed. *The College Shakespeare: 15 Plays
     and the Sonnets.* New York: Macmillan, 1973. 744 pp.

     An afterword (pp. 50-53) quotes the fantasy of
     Shakespeare's conception of the play which occurs in Evans
     and Lynch, eds. (item 881), and treats the various
     components of the plot.

940   Lembcke, Edv., trans. *En skaersommernatsdrøm.* [With
      illustrations by Ludmilla Balfour.] Copenhagen: Selskabet
      Boguennerne, 1973. (Danish--not seen)

941   Evans, G. Blakemore, textual ed. *The Riverside
      Shakespeare.* Boston: Houghton Mifflin, 1974. xvi, 1902
      pp.

      According to Anne Barton's introduction (pp. 217-21),
      the play in the second half of our century (after much
      condescension) has finally received the acknowledgement it
      deserves as "a complex and exacting work of art." A good
      deal of general reading seems to underlie it, unified by its
      themes of transformation, love, and art. It suggests
      strongly two seasons (May Day and Midsummer's Eve), but
      mixes them so that they are not cleanly to be identified
      from moment to moment. The scenes and imagery of the play
      are richly complex, partly classical, partly English. The
      Young Lovers represent a deliberately generalized picture
      of unreason in love. Characters betray a penchant for
      list-making (as in Ben Jonson). Theseus is "a wise ruler
      and a good man but . . . there are other, important areas
      of human experience with which he is incompetent to deal."
      The fairies reappear to give the lie to his skepticism. We
      are protected from the images of death and sickness in
      Puck's penultimate speech by the immortality of procreation
      promised in the blessings of the fairies which follow it. We
      are also by these endings brought back to reality as the
      play closes.

      Evans gives a brief note on the text and textual notes
      (pp. 247-249). Q1 may have been printed from some sort of
      "fair copy" of the "foul papers," and the theatrical
      provenience of certain aspects of the copy text for F1 is
      unquestionable. The text of F1 is based on a copy of Q2
      which thus either itself had served as a prompt-book or,
      more probably, had been corrected against an official
      prompt-book.

942   *Midsomernag-Droom.* Kaapstad and Pretoria: Human &
      Rousseau, 1974. (Afrikaans--not seen--translator not
      given)

943 Nisar Ahamed, K. S., trans. [A Midsummer Night's Dream.
     Foreword by Masti.] Mysore: Prithui, 1974.
     (Kanarese--not seen)

944 Bevington, David, and Hardin Craig, eds. An Introduction
     to Shakespeare: Eight Plays and Selected Sonnets. Rev.
     ed. Glenview, Ill.: Scott, Foresman, 1975. 378 pp.

     Bevington has added Dream and his introduction (from
     The Complete Works, 1973, item 938).

945 Franke, Wolfgang, trans. A Midsummer Night's Dream. Ein
     Sommernachtstraum. Stuttgart: Reclam, 1975. 175 pp.
     Reprint. 1978. (English and German--not seen)

946 Lesberg, Sandy, ed. The Works of William Shakespeare.
     The Peebles Classic Library. New York and London:
     Peebles Press, 1975.

     The text of Dream is included in Volume 6.

947 A Midsummer Night's Dream. Little Blue Book, 251. Girard,
     Kansas: Haldeman-Julius, 1975. 251 pp. (not seen)

948 Odajima, Yūshi [Odajima Shuji], trans. [A Midsummer
     Night's Dream.] Tokyo: Hakusuisha, 1975. Reprint.
     1977. (Japanese)

     The most popular version at present. For stage
     productions it is almost exclusively used. Very lively,
     up-to-date in diction, and shows considerable ingenuity in
     rendering Shakespeare's wordplay. Odajima's translation of
     all the plays--the third complete translation of Shakespeare
     in Japanese--was completed in the summer of 1980.

949 Griffin, Alice, ed. Rebels and Lovers: Shakespeare's Young
     Heroes and Heroines: A New Approach to Acting and
     Teaching. New York: New York University Press, 1976.
     Pp. 1-78.

Classroom edition of *Dream* (and other plays). Relies on Q1 for punctuation--it being best for speaking. The introduction (pp. 1-10), which presents each of the elements of the play in the general, commonly accepted way, stresses the centrality of the young lovers, how *Shakespeare* understands and sympathizes with them, how the secondary characters provide additional viewpoints on love. Love gives the lovers a "special understanding (apprehension) that may go beyond what reason can grasp." Their woodland journey symbolizes their progress from youth to adulthood. There is a glossary at the foot of the page and textual notes in back.

950 Gunther, Frank, trans. *Ein Sommernachtstraum.* Köln: Theaterverlag Kiepenheuer & Witsch, [1976]. 85 pp. (German--not seen)

951 Auburn, Mark S., and Katherine H. Burkman, eds. *Drama through Performance.* Boston: Houghton Mifflin, 1977. 775 pp.

Designed for college students. With a brief introduction to the Renaissance and an "Action analysis and performance suggestions."

952 Halstead, William P. *Shakespeare as Spoken: A Collation of 5000 Acting Editions and Promptbooks* of Shakespeare. 12 volumes. Ann Arbor: For the American Theatre Association by University Microfilms International, 1977-79.

"A line-by-line collation of about 2500 printed acting editions and an equal number of promptbooks" drawn from William Jaggard's bibliography (1911), Charles Shattuck's *Shakespeare Promptbooks* (1965), and special library catalogues. The Globe text (item 739) is printed on the left pages, the variants on the right. *Dream* is in Volume 3.

952a Jusuf, Tjetje, trans. [*A Midsummer Night's Dream.*] Jakarta: Dunia Pustaka Jaya, 1977. 42 pp. (Indonesian--not seen)

953 Lemmer, André N., ed. *A Midsummer Night's Dream*. The
     Stratford Shakespeare Series. Cape Town: Maskew
     Miller, 1977.

     With an illustrated introduction to Shakespeare's life and
     times, theatre, texts, comedy, and the *Dream*. Glosses,
     which face the text, are accompanied by numerous photos
     from performances and cuts from the period. There are
     appendices with a bibliography and questions.

954 *A Midsummer Night's Dream*. With Illustrations by Arthur
     Rackham. London: Heinemann; New York: Viking, 1977.
     vii, 134 pp.

     Facsimile reprint of the 1908 edition, with forty pages of
     plates.

955 *A Midsummer Night's Dream*. Written out by Graily Hewitt.
     Illustrated by Arthur Rackham. London: Weidenfeld &
     Nicolson; New York: Abaris Books, 1977. 144 pp.

     A photoprint edition of the manuscript commissioned on
     11 April 1928 and now in the William Augustus Spencer
     Collection in the New York Public Library. Thirty color
     plates. "Its illustrations are very different from the edition
     published in 1908" (item 954).

956 *Ein Midsommernachtstraum*. [No translator given]
     Programmbuch. Württembergisches Staatstheater
     Stuttgart, Schauspiel 27. Stuttgart: Württemberg.
     Staatstheater, 1977. 156 pp. (German--not seen)

     Apparently a text.

956a Nunes, Carlos Alberto, trans. *Sonho de uma noite de
     verão* [A Midsummer Night's Dream]. O mercador de
     Veneza [The Merchant of Venice]. Rio de Janeiro:
     Tecnoprint, 1977. 196 pp. (Portuguese--not seen)

957 Pagnol, Marcel, trans. *Le songe d'une nuit d'été*. Monte
     Carlo: Pastorelly, 1977. (French--not seen)

958   Entry Deleted.

959   Rowse, A. L., ed. *The Annotated Shakespeare: The
       Comedies.* New York: Clarkson N. Potter; London:
       Orbis, 1978.

       Dream is on pages 230-277. With fifty black-and-white
       illustrations of various dimensions from Fuseli, W.
       Heath Robinson, Arthur Rackham, and others and from various
       productions. The introduction takes the Sir Thomas Heneage
       and Mary, Countess of Southampton marriage of 2 May 1594
       to be the occasion and assumes Queen Elizabeth did not
       attend; finds an allusion (at V.i.52-53) to the death of
       Robert Greene and (at II.i.81-117) to the foul weather of
       the summer of 1594 (the play having been revised
       thereafter for the public); and stresses the Warwickshire
       coloring.

960   Brooks, Harold F., ed. *A Midsummer Night's Dream.* The
       Arden Shakespeare. London: Methuen, 1979. cxliv, 165
       pp.

       Introduction. I. 1. The text. Brooks gives extensive
       evidence for the position (largely the same as Greg's) that
       Q1 is of the very highest quality, probably based on "foul
       papers," not on the prompt-book; that Q2 is a
       page-for-page reprint of Q1; and that F is based on Q2
       with some readings taken from a theatre document, probably
       a prompt-book derived, with changes, ultimately from
       Shakespeare's autograph and not, as Wilson thought (item
       748), a Q2 having been annotated as a prompt-book or
       compared with a Q1 which had been annotated as a
       prompt-book. The annotator who took these readings
       displays "demonstrable negligence and clumsiness." Thus F
       is "a substantive (that is, an evidential) text."

       2. Date and occasion. With consideration of the poetic
       style. Brooks dates the play "with confidence" between
       autumn 1594 and spring 1596 and offers as a hypothesis the
       specific period of winter 1595-96. He considers the various
       types of evidence, for examples, topical allusion (the
       "Scottish lion-incident" of autumn 1594 being the *terminus a
       quo*), possible sources (Spenser's *Amoretti*, 1595, among
       others), and style (the lyrical group of the mid-1590s,
       comprising *Richard II, Romeo,* and *Love's Labour's Lost*).

He discusses at length the *Dream*'s special combination of
rhetoric (with "schemes" given) and lyricism, and
speculates that the occasion was the Elizabeth Carey and
Thomas, son of Henry, Lord Berkeley wedding of 19
February 1596, while admitting the possibility that it was
that of Elizabeth Vere and William Stanley, Earl of Derby on
26 January 1596.

3. Sources and antecedents. Taking it to be "unlikely
that there was any comprehensive source," Brooks singles
out a few of the small but decisive borrowings from the
"dozen identifiable works" no one doubts Shakespeare drew
on; these include Chaucer, plays by Lyly, Ovid (especially
Golding), Apuleius (Adlington), Scot, Montemayor, Thomas
Mouffet, Anthony Munday (*John a Kent and John a
Cumber*--if it came before *Dream*), *Huon of Burdeux*, and
two sources heretofore neglected, Spenser (*Shepheardes
Calendar*) and Seneca (various plays). He assumes Oberon's
retrospective account of a courtly diversion (which might
suggest Kenilworth or Elvetham) represents a general
rather than a specific occasion, and looks at other courtly
pastimes and folk traditions as influential antecedents
(holidays, etc.). He believes that there were literary and
folk traditions for three sizes of fairies--full-, child-, and
(particularly in Welsh sources) diminutive--and for
benevolent fairies. And he notices selected features as they
were influenced by sources, including Theseus, the four
lovers, metamorphosis, Oberon, the moonlit wood, and
(accepting Muir's finding, item 615) "Pyramus and Thisbe."

II. The play. 1. The exposition. "Love in relation to
marriage" is the theme. "The profoundest source of the
play's unity is thematic: the dominance of that theme,
firmly established in the exposition." (The exposition ends
when Oberon declares what he means to do with the magic
flower.)

2. Design and plot. The design is masterly, with its
movement into the wood, reversed with a change--the
fairies' appearance at the end. Within the play the story of
each group is progressive, independent, yet interlocked
with each of the others, all involving threats posed and
averted. All draws to a climax in passion and comic folly
(*summa epitasis*) and then is resolved before the start of
Act V. The stories and groups are linked also by many
parallels (resemblances and contrasts).

3. Characters and comedy. Theseus' leading traits are reason, statemanship, and sympathy; he's "unhappy at the verdict he has to deliver." Titania is an offending wife Oberon must control. The play offers more justification for the operation of fairy benevolence (though not the wisps of gossamer) than it does for the sinister, even malevolent elements recently stressed (by Kott, Merchant, Wilson Knight, Young, and Fender; for the opposing view see Leggatt, Schanzer, Bertrand Evans, and Dent). Puck delights in the comic confusion, not in the pain. The two women, if not the men, are strongly contrasted, consistently conceived, and unfold before us. We commiserate somewhat with their distress. Our laughter at Bottom is mingled with admiration and affection. "Bottom's weft of absurdity is woven on a warp of practical ability and common sense." Much--here discussed--combines to make Bottom's a great comic role (he's compared with Falstaff), and to render the playlet burlesque.

4. Lyricism, music and dance. The music of the poetry and its variety (always appropriate) joins with the comic, and with the song and dance, to produce the charm of the play. (A long note considers that the two songs of the finale are not preserved.)

5. Setting: woodland and fairyland; moon. Through allusion and imagery the woodland scene is produced in the mind's eye and extended beyond the wood to all nature and the world, joining with the pastoral other literary (Ovidian) qualities.

6. The principal themes. Love and marriage is central: the renewal, adult love, and the conflicts and resolution of youthful love. The whole work affirms its value through these phases and a network of related themes, through alternatives (noble virginity) which are acknowledged, and through foes, obstacles, and aberrations which are exorcized. The play does not censure love as unreasonable (as some argue) but rather finds in love a mysterious power beyond the rational.

The imagination and related questions about illusion, appearance, and reality combine to form the other major theme. The play investigates planes of reality, the nature of perception and identity, and dramatic illusion. It neither equates the two realms of imagined and real nor discounts them. Theseus' too sweeping attack is answered *in* the play

and *by* the play which, by its success, can be "accepted as
a vision of truth, far more authentic than fancy's images."
"Theseus intends them as censure; but his eloquence,
summoned like Balaam to curse, blesses altogether."

Appendix I contains source materials from: 1) Chaucer,
2) North, 3) Golding, 4) Seneca, 5) *Huon of Burdeux*,
trans. by Lord Berners, 6) Reginald Scot, and 7) Golding.

Appendix II discusses four textual cruces: 1) thinks F's
merit as well as Q1's *friends* of I.i.139 may be
Shakespeare's, 2) reads *Odorous, odorous* for Q1's *Odours,
odorous* at III.i.79, and *Odorous* for Q1's *Odours* at 1.80,
3) notes the corruption not easily removed at III.ii.257-59,
4) suggests *mure rased* at V.i.204 for Qq's *moon vsed* and
F's *morall downe* (see item 705).

Appendix III discusses the mislined verse in Q1, V.i.

Appendix IV contains Quince's Prologue (V.i.108-16)
properly punctuated.

960a   Vessas, Halldis Moren, trans. *Ein midtsommarnattsdraum.*
       Oslo: Det Norske Samlaget, 1980. 92 pp. (Norse--not
       seen)

960b   Clemen, Wolfgang, ed. *A Midsummer Night's Dream.* In
       Types of Drama: Plays and Essays, ed. Sylvan Barnet,
       Morton Berman, and William Burto. Third and Fourth
       Editions. Boston: Little, Brown and Co., 1981 and 1984.

       Includes the text, with notes at the foot, questions, and
       a three-page comment--on two traditions, "critical" comedy
       and "romantic" comedy.

960c   Słomczyński, Maciej, trans. *Sen nocy letniej [A Midsummer
       Night's Dream].* Afterword by Juliusz Kydryński.
       Kraków: Wydawnictwo Literackie, 1982. 128 pp.
       (Polish--not seen)

960d   Rotas, Vasilis, trans. "*A Midsummer Night's Dream,* Act
       II, Sc. ii." *Nea Estia,* 113 (1983), 883-84. (Greek--not
       seen)

VI. ADAPTATIONS, ACTING EDITIONS, SYNOPSES, INFLUENCE

961 [Cox, Robert?], adapt. *The Merry Conceited Humors of Bottom the Weaver.* London: F. Kirkman and H. Marsh, 1661. Facsimile reprint. Ed. Stanley Wells. London: Cornmarket Press, 1970. [34 pp.]

The earliest extant stage adaptation. Reprinted in 1673 in Part 2 of Kirkman's two-part collection of drolls, *The Wits, or, Sport Upon Sport,* where Kirkman credits the actor Cox for some of the drolls.

962 [Settle, Elkanah?], adapt. *The Fairy-queen: An Opera.* Represented at the Queen's Theatre by their Majesties servants. London: J. Tonson, 1692. Facsimile reprint. London: Cornmarket Press, 1969. 52 pp.

The first in a long history of quasi-operatic adaptations. Henry Purcell's score is mostly for the four spectacular, intermezzi-like pieces appended to the ends of Acts II through V. Up to these points, the adapter follows Shakespeare closely, chiefly simplifying the verse with pedestrian and insensitive paraphrase. Settle is one candidate among many advanced (including Betterton and Congreve); the identity of the inventor(s) of the intermezzi is not settled either. See item T1101a.

963 [Leveridge, Richard], adapt. *The Comick Masque of Pyramus and Thisbe.* As it is Perform'd at the theatre in Lincoln's Inn Fields. London: W. Mears, 1716. Facsimile reprint. London: Cornmarket Press, 1969. [10], 16 pp.

A spoof on the newly fashionable Italian opera, using the "Pyramus and Thisbe" scenes. With nine songs by Leveridge. See item T1336.

964 Lampe, John Frederick. *Pyramus and Thisbe: A*
     Mock-Opera. Written by Shakespeare. Set to Musick by
     Mr. Lampe. Perform'd at the Theatre Royal in Covent
     Garden. London: H. Woodfall, Junior, 1745. vii, 23 pp.

     An expansion of Leveridge's spoof of 1716 (item 963),
     with fourteen songs. See item T1336.

965 [Garrick, David?, and John Christopher Smith?], adapts.
     The Fairies, An Opera. Taken from *A Midsummer Night's*
     Dream, Written by Shakespear. As it is Perform'd at the
     Theatre-Royal in Drury Lane. The Songs from
     Shakespear, Milton, Waller, Dryden, Lansdown,
     Hammond, & C. The music composed by Mr. Smith. 2nd
     ed. London: J. and R. Tonson and S. Draper, 1755.
     Facsimile reprint. London: Cornmarket Press, 1969. 48
     pp.

     Operatic adaptation using a few essentials of
     Shakespeare's lovers' and fairies' plots and omitting entirely
     Bottom and his friends and "Pyramus and Thisbe." In all,
     560 lines and twenty-eight songs, written by Smith,
     Handel's amanuensis, using a variety of lyrics, seven taken
     from Shakespeare's original text. See item T1336.

966 [Colman, George], adapt. *A Fairy Tale.* In Two Acts.
     Taken from Shakespeare. As it is Perform'd at the
     Theatre-Royal in Drury Lane. London: J. and R.
     Tonson, 1763. Facsimile reprint. Cornmarket Press,
     1969. 24 pp.

     Colman's reduction into an afterpiece of the 1763 version
     (item 967) with 400 lines and thirteen songs. See item
     T1336.

967 [Garrick, David, and George Colman], adapts. *A Midsummer*
     Night's Dream. Written by Shakespeare. With alterations
     and additions and several new songs. As it is Perform'd
     at the Theatre-Royal, Drury Lane. London: J. and R.
     Tonson, 1763. Facsimile reprint. London: Cornmarket
     Press, [1969]. 47 pp.

     Closer to the original than any stage version since the
     Restoration, though still half the length, with thirty-three

songs, interspersed, representing six composers, twelve of
which came from Smith's score of 1755 (item 965) and ten
from Charles Burney. The Folger Shakespeare Library copy
contains a table of songs and composers.

968 Lamb, Charles [and Mary]. "A Midsummer Night's Dream."
     Tales from Shakespeare. Designed for the Use of Young
     Persons. 2 volumes. London: T. Hodgkins, 1807.

     A children's story of the play which eliminates the
     business of the mechanicals. It is Oberon who claps the
     ass's head on Bottom, who is simply "a clown" who has lost
     his way in the wood. There are copper plates by W.
     Mulready. *Tales* has been published many times and in many
     languages.

969 Reynolds, Frederic, adapt. *A Midsummer Night's Dream.*
     Written by Shakespeare; with Alterations, Additions, and
     New Songs: As it is perform'd at the Theatre-Royal,
     Covent Garden. London: John Miller, 1816. Facsimile
     reprint. Ed. Stanley Wells. London: Cornmarket Press,
     1970. [59 pp.]

     Three-act operatic version, with interlinear cutting and
     re-arranging and an altered ending, all in the service of
     the twenty-four vocal pieces and scenic spectacle. Sir
     Henry Rowley Bishop arranged the score and was one of
     several composers of the songs used, many of which were
     brought over from the 1763 adaptation. Hazlitt's famous
     complaint (items 1, 1a) that the play and the stage were
     incompatible arose from this adaptation. The production was
     a grandparent to the century's scenic traditions for the
     play.

970 Vestris, Elizabeth. *A Midsummer Night's Dream.* As Revived
     at The Theatre Royal, Covent Garden, November 16th,
     1840. Correctly printed from the prompt copy, with
     exits, entrances, etc. . . . London: J. Pattie, [n.d.].
     46 pp.

     This edition is apparently based directly upon the
     promptbook of this successful and historically significant
     production of 1840-41, in which the full text of the play
     was performed for the first time since before the

Restoration and realized in the scenic terms of the developing romantic, pictorial realism. James Robinson Planché was credited by J. O. Halliwell-Phillipps with preparing the text; Planché also designed the Greek costumes. Vestris's staging, the scenery, music, and her portrayal of Oberon set the Victorian production style for this play, vestiges of which prevailed through the 1950s. Charles Kean's 1856 production (see item 973), documented in the well-known watercolors of his scene designers, is directly indebted to Vestris's staging. The Folger Shakespeare Library owns a copy of this rare volume. See also items T1312, T1352, T1418 and T1451.

971   [Vestris, Elizabeth, and Charles Kean.] *A Midsummer Night's Dream*. As performed at the Theatre Royal, Covent Garden, London, November 16th, 1840. *Lacy's Acting Plays*. Volume 28. London: Thomas Hailes Lacy, [n.d.]. 62 pp.

A catchpenny edition in Lacy's annual series, issued after Charles Kean's 1856 production (item 973) but *not* based on Kean's promptbook nor Vestris's exactly (see item 970). Lacy's edition offers a conflation of Vestris's stage directions, as represented in the Pattie edition (item 970), and Kean's; the Lacy text represents neither precisely, though it is closer to Vestris'. Kean issued his own acting edition (item 973). Clearly, the widely available Lacy editions must be used with some caution by Shakespeare stage historians. See items T1312, T1418 and T1451.

972   [Barry, Thomas.] *A Midsummer Night's Dream*. In Three Acts, by William Shakespeare. To which are added a Description of the Costume, Cast of the Characters, Entrances and Exist . . . as performed with great success for upwards of sixty consecutive nights at The Broadway Theatre. . . . New York: Samuel French, [n.d.]. 48 pp.

Thomas Barry's glittery, fairy-pantomime production opened in February, 1854, rivaling William Burton's more tastefully splendid version, which had opened at Burton's Chambers Street Theatre three days earlier. Both were probably inspired by Samuel Phelps's subtler, simpler successful London production of the previous fall. Both represent American attempts to come up to the mark of the

Macready and Kean spectacle. This edition is probably made
up from the thorough promptbook for the 1854 production of
Barry's stage manager, John B. Wright.

973   [Kean, Charles.] *Shakespeare's play of "A Midsummer
      Night's Dream."* Arranged for Representation at The
      Princess's Theatre, with Historical and Explanatory notes
      by Charles Kean. First Performed, Wednesday, October
      15, 1856. 3rd edition. London: John K. Chapman,
      [n.d.]. 60 pp. Facsimile reprint. Introduction by
      Stanley Wells. London: Cornmarket Press, 1970.

      Kean's 1856 production was one of the scenic highpoints
      of nineteenth century illustrated Shakespeare. The stage
      directions and texts of Kean's published acting editions are
      based on his promptbooks for the Shakespearean
      productions he did at the Princess's Theatre between 1850
      and 1859. Kean cut almost one-third of the text; only Laura
      Keene (see item 974) exceeded him in cuts in the century.
      Memorable watercolors of each scene, done by Kean's scenic
      staff, may be seen in the Harvard Theatre Collection's
      presentation promptbook, and separately, in larger format,
      in the Victoria and Albert Museum. The three editions are
      identical except for title page and cast list differences. See
      items T1270 and T1418.

974   [Keene, Laura.] *A Midsummer Night's Dream.* Arranged for
      representation at Laura Keene's Theatre. With historical
      and explanatory notes, collected from various authorities
      by Laura Keene. New York: Samuel French, 1863. 59
      pp.

      Keene produced the play in April, 1859, at her own
      theatre in New York; it was a derivative, scenically lavish,
      well-promoted affair, with some high-culture affectations
      and some popular pantomime effects. Her text was
      apparently based on Charles Kean's (item 973), with
      additional cuts, some based on Thomas Barry's edition (item
      972). Keene attempted to blend the historical scenery of the
      former with the fairy transformations of the latter. An
      earlier edition of her acting text was published in 1859 by
      O. A. Roorbach, New York. See also items T1315 and
      T1418.

975   [Calvert, Charles.] *A Midsummer Night's Dream.* Arranged
      for representation at the Prince's Theatre. Manchester,
      by Charles Calvert. As First performed on Saturday,
      2nd September, 1865. Manchester: A. Ireland, [n.d.].
      40 pp.

      Calvert's staging, scenery, and text were all derived
      from Charles Kean's 1856 production (item 973).

976   *Shakspeare's "Midsummer-Night's Dream."* As produced,
      With Mendelssohn's Music, At the Concerts of the New
      York Philharmonic Society. New York: Torrey Brothers,
      1869.

      An oversize volume (35 x 27 cm.) with the full text in
      large, bold type, intended for use of oral readers in a
      concert presentation of the play with Mendelssohn's music.

977   [Saker, Edward.] *Midsummer Night's Dream.* Produced at
      the Alexandra Theatre, Liverpool, Monday, March 29th,
      1880. Arranged for Representation by Edward Saker.
      Liverpool: [n.p.], 1880. 48 pp.

      Saker's production was in the Vestris-Kean tradition (see
      items 971 and 973), and he staged it, with a different cast,
      in London in this year also.

978   [Daly, Augustin.] *The Comedy of "A Midsummer Night's
      Dream."* Written by William Shakespeare and Arranged
      for Representation at Daly's Theatre by Augustin Daly.
      Produced there for the First Time, January 31, 1888.
      Privately Printed, 1888. 75 pp.

      Daly's text and stage directions with a preface by William
      Winter and seven tinted photographs of the production.
      Daly brought to bear on the play all the scenic resources
      America's Gilded Age could provide, both in the 1888
      premiere and later in London, in 1895. The production's
      chief virtues were Ada Rehan, John Drew, Otis Skinner,
      and Virginia Dreher as the quartet of lovers. Daly prepared
      the text himself, which involved some bold rearranging
      around the voyage of the ship with which he furnished the
      Argonaut, Theseus, in the fourth act. (The voyage was

new; the ship had sailed several times since 1816.) See also
items T1315 and T1418.

979 [Greet, Sir Ben.] *A Midsummer Night's Dream*. Arranged
     by Mr. Ben Greet. [n.p., n.d.]. 54 pp.

     For almost half a century, from 1886 to the early 1930s,
     Greet's touring companies, in which many of England's
     future stars got their early experience, carried this play
     from college gardens to Chautaqua circuits, from the Old
     Vic to Carnegie Hall. Greet played Bottom. This text (the
     Folger Shakespeare Library has a copy) is not helpful as to
     staging but does show some customary nineteenth century
     cutting. (Greet's *Dream* has been published frequently. A
     version, for example, in the series "for Young Readers and
     Amateur Players," was published by Musson of Toronto in
     1975.)

980 Smith, J. Moyr, ed. *A Midsommer Night's Dreame.* London:
     [n.p.], 1892.

     This is a standard text of the play with an introductory
     essay by Smith of special stage history importance. He
     provides an account of Samuel Phelps's production at
     Sadler's Wells in 1853, probably the most poetically effective
     of the nineteenth century. See item T1286.

980a Barrie, James M. *Dear Brutus* (A Comedy in Three Acts).
     Produced by Gerald du Maurier at the Wyndham's
     Theatre, London, in October, 1917. *The Plays of J. M.
     Barrie.* New York: Charles Scribner's Sons, 1922. There
     are several printings.

     Barrie's play is heavily influenced by the *Dream*. It
     begins with a group of visitors being entertained in the
     country house of a mysterious, diminutive host. The action
     soon shifts to an enchanted forest on Midsummer Eve where
     modern equivalents of Hermia, Demetrius, and Helena play
     out a love comedy under the magical influence of the host
     (Lob), who begins to look very like a latter-day Puck.

981   Barnouw, Erik, adapt. "'Pyramus and Thisbe': A Radio
      Version of the Comic Interlude in *A Midsummer Night's
      Dream.*" *Senior Scholastic*, 15 April 1940. (not seen)

982   Phillips, Leroy, and Mary Major Crawford, eds.
      Shakespeare for Today. London: George G. Harrap;
      Yonkers-on-Hudson, N. Y.: World, 1940. x, 454 pp.

      School text, with a three-page introduction to *Dream*,
      one of several plays included, with glosses, and with
      black-and-white illustrations by Ruth Creighton. *Dream* is
      somewhat modernized and selectively cut for "today's
      student."

983   Bennett, Rodney. *The Story of "A Midsummer Night's
      Dream."* Retold by Rodney Bennett. London: University
      of London Press, 1941.

      "Memorable passages" are quoted.

984   Robinson, Thomas P., adapt. *A Midsummer Night's Dream*.
      The Players' Shakespeare. New York: Viking, 1941. viii,
      135 pp.

      Text based on that of W. J. Rolfe with full stage
      directions within the text and with sections (pp. 97-135) on
      Traits of Characters, Scenery, Painting, Lighting,
      Costumes, Properties, Music, Organization (of Little Theater
      group), Direction, Language, and so on. Glossary and
      Notes on Music are by Donald Fay Robinson. The play is
      adapted and condensed. According to the preface, "anyone
      who doesn't believe in fairies shouldn't be allowed in the
      cast."

985   Thorp, Josephine. "The Enchanted Book-shelf." *The Magic
      of Books.* Ed. A. P. Sanford and Robert Haven
      Schauffler. New York: Dodd, Mead, 1941, pp. 245-340.

      Children's play containing an excerpt (pp. 323-38) from
      the material of the mechanicals. First published in 1929 and
      reprinted in 1938.

986 Davies, [William] Robertson. *Shakespeare for Young Players: A Junior Course.* Illustrated by Grant MacDonald. Toronto: Clarke, Irwin, 1942. Reprint. 1964. xv, 255 pp.

Presents two scenes (I.ii and III.i) with brief introductions and explanatory comments interpolated. Designed for young students to act.

987 Boas, Guy. *An English Book of Light Verse.* London: Macmillan, 1944. xx, 300 pp. Includes (pp. 20-24) much of the Pyramus and Thisbe playlet.

988 Bridie, James. "The Open-Air Drama" ("Midsummer Afternoon's Dream"). *Tedious and Brief.* London: Constable, 1944, pp. 65-72.

A play about a production of *Dream.*

989 Hollander, Lee M. "'Erlkönig' und *Sommernachtstraum.*" *Monatshefte für Deutschen Unterricht,* 36 (1944), 145-46.

Cites *Dream* II.i.86-105 and III.i.145-52 to demonstrate that the play was a source for Goethe's famous ballad.

990 Thomas [Schnittkind], Henry, ed. *"A Midsummer Night's Dream," Dramatized for Young People.* Boston and Los Angeles: Baker's Plays, 1944. 25 pp. (not seen)

991 Cady, Frank W., and Van H. Cartmell, eds. *Shakespeare Arranged for Modern Reading.* Illustrated by Rockwell Kent. New York: Doubleday, 1946. ix, 1165 pp. Reprint. Greenwich, Conn.: Fawcett Publications, 1963.

The famous passages are given (from Wright's Cambridge text, item 739) in their places within a narrated plot.

992 Deutsch, Babette. *The Reader's Shakespeare.* New York: Julian Messner, 1946. xiii, 510 pp. Numerous reprints.

A prose version, with decorations by Warren Chappell.

993 Field, Josephine, adapt. *"A Midsummer Night's Dream,"* by
     William Shakespeare. Retold for Young People.
     Crowther's Introduction to Good Reading. Bognor Regis:
     Crowther, 1946. 61 pp.

     Act 5 of the play is given.

994 Kingston, Waldo, ed. *The Shakespeare Companion: A
     Selective Anthology.* London: Saturn Press, 1947. vii,
     326 pp.

     Eleven excerpts (pp. 28-33).

995 Peat, R. C. *Presenting Shakespeare.* London: George G.
     Harrap, 1947. 247 pp. Reprint. 1949, 1977.

     Dream is one of three plays presented in reduced form
     with narrative bridges taken largely from the Lambs.
     Intended for schools.

996 Beckerlegge, Oliver A., ed. *The Youth Club Shakespeare.*
     Book 1. "Pyramus and Thisby." London: Epworth, 1948.
     31 pp.

     The mechanicals' plot adapted.

997 Gilbert, Mark. *A Midsummer Night's Dream.* The Short
     Story Shakespeare, 4. Bournemouth and London: William
     Earl, 1948. 53 pp.

     Prose rendering.

998 Glover, W. J., adapt. *Wedding Revels from "A Midsummer
     Night's Dream."* In *Glover's Short Plays from
     Shakespeare.* With Notes on Production and Costume.
     Stage Directions and Costumes Illustrated by Ethelwyn
     Shiel. London: George Philip & Son, 1948. 57 pp.

     The mechanicals' plot is worked into a simple playlet of
     six scenes.

999   Stanley, Arthur [pseud.], ed. *The Bedside Shakespeare: An Anthology.* London: Victor Gollancz, 1948. 287 pp.

Excerpts (pp. 181-93) are from several fairy scenes.

1000   Lussier, Claude, trans. and adapt. *Le songe d'une nuit d'été.* Montreal: Fides, 1949.

For French children.

1001   Smith, Logan Pearsall. *The Golden Shakespeare: An Anthology.* London: Constable, 1949; New York: Macmillan, 1950. xli, 700 pp.

Extracts from "the great luminous flood of poetry in *Dream*" occupy pages 70-101.

1001a   Delannoy, Marcel. *Puck, opera-féerique en trois actes inspiré du "Songe d'une nuit d'été" de Shakespeare.* Par André Boll. Musique de Marcel Delannoy. Traduction allemand de Pierre Hambourger et Alfred Berger. [*Puck, a fairy opera in three acts inspired by Shakespeare's "A Midsummer Night's Dream."* Adapted by André Boll. Music by Marcel Delannoy. German translation by Pierre Hambourger and Alfred Berger.] N.p.: n.p., [1950]. 253 pp.

Piano-vocal score of the opera, with lyrics in French and German. (See item T1107a.) This light romantic opera follows the play closely with the major exception of its treatment of the mechanicals' play and the ending. Shakespeare's text is followed closely in the lyrics, though considerably reduced. Hippolyta is a mute role here and the role of Puck is danced; he speaks only a few lines in the baiting of Lysander and Demetrius in the duel scene. There are twenty songs and four pieces for dances as well as introductory music for each act. The text is almost entirely sung, with a few spoken passages alternating. The "Prologue" and "Epilogue" are set in Theseus' palace; the "act unique" is set in the forest and is the longest of the three. The Oberon-Titania quarrel is over each other's infidelities, not the Indian boy. Where exposition is necessary because the role of Puck is played by a non-speaking dancer, a fairy provides it in addresses to the audience. At various points there is a mysterious offstage chorus of the Voices of the Forest. Puck is introduced with a special dance of sylphides for Titania's lullaby and a "Dance of the little asses" with Puck occurs after the four young lovers have been put to sleep. There is no discovery of the sleeping lovers by the Duke and his party. And so on. (See item T1113a.)

1002   Vazakas, Byron. "Midsummer Night's Dream." *Kenyon Review*, 12 (1950), 300-301.

        Poem.

1003   Windross, Ronald, adapt. *"A Midsummer Night's Dream." William Shakespeare, Three Comedies.* The Stories of These Abridged and Simplified. Tales from England, 2nd degree, 3. Illustrated by Greville Irwin. Paris and Brussells: Didier, 1950, pp. 1-33. Reprint. 1952.

1004   Bransom, Laura. *The Living Shakespeare.* Illustrated by Molly Bransom. London: Newnes Educational Publishing Co., 1951.

        Includes the play turned into a story. A Teachers' Companion is in a separate booklet.

1005   Rashbrook, R. F. "Keats, Oberon, and Freud." *Notes and Queries*, 196 (1951), 34-37.

        Detects reminiscences of lines by Shakespeare in certain of Keats's poems. See items 575a and 1083.

1006   Coxhead, Elizabeth. *A Play Toward.* London: Faber and Faber, 1952. 239 pp. (not seen)

        A novel apparently in part about a school production of *Dream.*

1007   Dodd, E. F. *Three Shakespeare Comedies.* Dodd's Supplementary Readers. London: Macmillan, 1953. Numerous reprints. 56 pp.

Dream told in story using a vocabulary of 2000 words, with a few black-and-white illustrations. Later included in the series Macmillan's Stories to Remember in Simple English.

1008 Klingmüller, Götz. *"Pyramus und Thisbe oder Die Premiere um acht." Ein Stück Shakespeare und ein Stück Schmierentheater züsammengefügt.* ["Pyramus and Thisbe or The Premiere at Eight." A Bit of Shakespeare and a Bit of Strolling-Player-Theater Combined]. Kassel: Bärenreiter, 1953. 54 pp. (German--not seen)

1008a *Midsummer Night's Dream* /filmstrip]. *Stories from Shakespeare.* Chicago: Encyclopedia Britannica Educational Corp., 1954. No. 8060, 49 fr., col., 35 mm. (not seen)

Through watercolor paintings of the scenes, condenses the play into a story. For secondary students.

1009 Price, N. M. [*"A Midsummer Night's Dream" and Other Stories from Shakespeare.* Translated into Hebrew by M. Ben-Eliezer.] Tel Aviv: Chachick, 1954. (not seen)

1010 Specking, Inez. *A Shakespeare for Children.* New York: Vantage, 1954. 95 pp.

The story of *Dream.*

1010a *A Midsummer Night's Dream* [filmstrip]. The Stories of Music Classics, No. 3. Detroit: Jam Handy Organization, 1955, 32 fr., col., 35 mm. (not seen)

Presents the story of *Dream,* using illustrations, to suggest how it inspired the music of Mendelssohn. See also item 1065a.

1011 Bjerke, André, trans. *"A Midsummer Night's Dream. En Sommernattsdrøm." Ordet* (Oslo), 6, no. 4 (1955), 181-88.

Extracts from the play as produced at Der nationale
scene, Bergen, in March 1955.

1012   Avinoam (Grossman), Reuben, ed. and trans. *Miv'har
       Shirat Anglia* [An Anthology of English Poetry]. 2nd ed.
       Tel Aviv: Massahad, 1956. (Hebrew--not seen)

       Includes excerpts from *Dream.*

1013   Chute, Marchette. *Stories from Shakespeare.* Cleveland:
       World Publishing Co.; New York: New American Library,
       1956. Reprint. New American Library, 1976. New York:
       Collins, 1979. 351 pp.

       The story of the play.

1014   Paris, Jean. *Connaissance de Shakespeare.* Présentation
       et traductions de Jean Paris. Cahiers de la Compagnie
       Madeleine Renard-Jean-Louis Barrault. Paris: René
       Julliard, 1956. 126 pp.

       Includes a translation from III.i. which is introduced by
       a speaking La Lune.

1014a *Scenes from Shakespeare* [phonodisc]. Read by Paul
       Rogers. Great Artists Series. New Rochelle, N. Y.:
       Spoken Arts, [1956]. SA 723. (not heard)

       Dream is one of six plays from which an excerpt is read.

1015   Taylor, Henry S., arr. *A Shorter Shakespeare: "A
       Midsummer Night's Dream."* London: Ginn, 1956. lx, 86
       pp.

       Arranged for classroom use with young students.

1016   Armour, Richard. *Twisted Tales from Shakespeare.*
       Illustrated by Campbell Grant. New York: McGraw-Hill,
       1957, etc. 5th printing 1963. 152 pp. Reprint. New
       York: New American Library, 1966. 128 pp.

Humorous redaction, with an introduction and questions in the same vein.

1017 Powell, Hugh, ed., with introduction and commentary. *Herr Peter Squentz.* Leicester: Leicester University College, 1957. 2nd ed. 1969. lix, 52 pp.

German text with notes in English. Introduction discusses the relationship between *Squentz* and the Quince episode in *Dream* (pp. 1-lx). The text reproduced is from the British Museum copy of the 1663 edition of Andreas Gryphius' work, for which the original titlepage reads *Absurda comica; oder, Herr Peter Squentz, Schimpff-Spiel.* See items 528, 1018 and 1040.

1018 Schenck zu Schweinsberg, Clotilde. *"Peter Squenz und die Pannen." Frei nach Shakespeare and Gryphius.* Munich: Höfling, 1957. Reprint. 1959. 56 pp. (not seen)

Apparently a blend of the two sources. See items 528, 1017 and 1040.

1019 Bennett, C. M., and C. V. Jackson, adapts. *Masters and Masterpieces: A Book of Classroom Plays Based on the Lives and Works of Five Great Writers.* Illustrated by Shirley Hughes. London: John Murray, 1958.

Contains the mechanicals' scenes (pp. 61-73) "slightly adapted."

1020 Burton, H. M. *Shakespeare and His Plays.* Illustrated by Richard G. Robinson. Methuen's Outlines. London: Methuen; New York: Roy Publishers, 1958. 68 pp.

The story (pp. 22-23), with two black-and-white illustrations.

1021 Cooper, Charles W., ed. *Shakespeare's "Julius Caesar," "A Midsummer-Night's Dream," "Romeo and Juliet." Modern Version.* Classics for Enjoyment. River Forest, Illinois: Laidlaw Brothers, 1958. vii, 335 pp.

Simplified, abridged teaching version.

1022   DeBerry, Frances C. *All the World's a Stage for
       Shakespeare's Comedies: A Modern Interpretation of the
       Bard's Humor.* New York: Exposition Press, 1958. 130
       pp.

       A synopsis. (Pp. 59-65)

1023   Forker, Charles R. *"A Midsummer Night's Dream* and
       Chapman's *Homer*: An Unnoted Shakespeare Allusion."
       Notes and Queries, 203 (1958), 524.

       In the phrase "rude Mechanicals" Chapman may recall
       Puck.

1024   Olfson, Lewy, adapt. *Radio Plays from Shakespeare.*
       Boston: Plays Inc., 1958. 193 pp. Also in *Plays: The
       Drama Magazine for Young People* (Boston), February,
       1959.

       The cast reduced to eight plus a narrator. Neither the
       plot of the fairies nor that of the mechanicals is retained.

1025   Young, Eleanor Patmore, ed. *Shakespeare for Young
       Actors: Forty-minute Versions of "A Midsummer Night's
       Dream"* [etc.] *for Secondary School Study and
       Production.* New York: Exposition Press, 1958. (An
       Exposition-University Book) 284 pp.

       Adapted into five scenes for junior high students. With
       introduction and comments.

1026   Adamson, Elgiva, with Kathleen V. Moore. *Notes on William
       Shakespeare's "A Midsummer Night's Dream."* Stratford,
       Ont.: Mirror Press, 1960. 45 pp.

       A running summary with occasional critical comments.

1026a Britten, Benjamin. *A Midsummer Night's Dream.* An Opera
       in three acts, opus 64. Libretto adapted from William

Shakespeare by Benjamin Britten and Peter Pears. Vocal Score by Imogen Holst and Martin Penny. London: Hawkes and Son, Ltd., 1960. 314 pp.

Score of the opera for voice, with piano accompaniment. See item T1188.

1027 Murray, Geoffrey. *Let's Discover More Shakespeare.* London: Hamish Hamilton, 1960. xii, 211 pp.

Dream told in simple prose.

1028 Petiška, Eduard. *A Midsummer Night's Dream.* With Photographs of Puppets by Jiří Trnka. Retold for Children by Eduard Petiška. Translated by Jean Layton. Prague: Artia, 1960; London: Books for Pleasure, 1961. 35 pp.

The photographs are of Trnka's puppet-film version of the play. See items 863, 883, and T1198.

1029 Selden, Samuel. *A Player's Handbook of Short Scenes.* New York: Holiday House, 1960. 201 pp.

Gives, with added acting directions, I.ii and III.i.

1030 M., A. J. [?Martinez, Antonio Jiménez-Landi]. *Teatro.* [Illustrated by Julio Castro.] Madrid: Aguilar, 1961. 104 pp. (Spanish--not seen)

Includes an adaptation of *Dream.*

1031 Anderson, Joy. "Poor Mr. Shakespeare!" *New Plays Quarterly,* no. 60 (1962). (not seen)

Apparently a comedy based on *Dream.*

1032 Langford, W. F., ed. *Shakespearean Festival.* Canadian Swan Shakespeare. Toronto: Longmans Canada, 1962. 219 pp.

Five excerpts (pp. 104-132) selected as notable for "sheer fun," introduced with a plot summary.

1033   Leonhardi, Arnold, ed. *A Midsummer Night's Dream*. Prepared and Abridged for Schools by Reinhold Arndt. Drama and Play. Gekürzte Ausg. Dortmund: Lensing, 1962. xiii, 57, 47, 20 pp. (not seen)

1034   Jolles, Frank. "Shakespeares *Sommernachtstraum* in Deutschland: Einige Betrachtungen über den Vorgang der Assimilation" [Shakespeare's *Dream* in Germany: Some Observations on the Process of Assimilation]. *German Life and Letters*, 16 (1962-63), 229-37. (German--not seen)

Compares Shakespeare's play's reception in German in the 18th and 19th centuries.

1035   Buckman, Irene. *Twenty Tales from Shakespeare*. With a Foreword by Dame Peggy Ashcroft. London: Methuen; New York: Random House, 1963. Reprint. Random House, 1965. 228 pp.

With illustrations from productions.

1036   Harbage, Alfred. "*A Midsummer Night's Dream*." *William Shakespeare: A Reader's Guide*. New York: Farrar, Straus and Giroux; Noonday Press, 1963. Reprint. Noonday Press, 1970. New York: Octagon, 1971, 1974, pp. 105-21.

Scene-by-scene summary of the play mixed with comment.

1037   Amir, Aharon, trans. "Nehash Nikundim" ["You spotted snakes with double tongue"]. *Keshet* (Tel Aviv), 6 (Summer, 1964), 89. (Hebrew--not seen)

1038   Evans, G. Blakemore, ed. *Shakespearean Prompt-books of the Seventeenth Century*. Volume 3. Charlottesville:

Bibliographical Society of the University of Virginia, 1964.

Part 1 provides a facsimile of a page of a folio text with cutting marks for a "nursery" version; part 2 gives an introduction and a collation of all cuts and notations of other such prompt-books. See item T1495.

1039 Goulden, Shirley. *Tales from Shakespeare.* Illustrated by Nardini. Splendour Book Series, 20. London and Milan: W. H. Allen, 1964. 55 pp. (not seen)

1040 Gryphius, Andreas, adapt. *Absurda Comica or Master Peter Squentz.* Translated from the German and introduced by Ernest Brennecke in his *Shakespeare in Germany 1590-1700, With Translations of Five Early Plays.* Chicago: University of Chicago Press, 1964, pp. 52-104.

Based on the Folger Shakespeare Library copy of the 1663 edition, and dated not later than 1657. Brennecke's introduction discusses seventeenth century German adaptations of the burlesque derived from Shakespeare based on what can be known of the version by Daniel Schwenter and on versions described by Johann Balthasar Schupp and Johannes von Rist. On Gryphius see items 528 and 1017-18.

1041 Kerman, Gertrude, ed. *Shakespeare for Young Players, from Tens to Teens.* Illustrated by Anne Lewis. Irvington-on-Hudson, N. Y.: Harvey House, 1964. vii, 242 pp.

A modified text (with lineation retained from the full text) suitable for a twenty-minute production.

1042 Miller, Katharine E., ed. *Five Plays from Shakespeare.* Illustrated by Lynd Ward. Musical Arrangements by Norman Cazden. Boston: Houghton Mifflin, 1964. 236 pp.

"Versions to be read and produced by young people. Each play is about half its original length."

1043   Moss, Arnold, ed. *Come, woo me! A Shakespearean
       Entertainment.* New York: H. S. Stuttman, 1964. 40 pp.
       (not seen)

       Dream apparently one of the ten plays from which
       excerpts are taken for this booklet.

1044   Munnik, Pauline de. *A Midsummer Night's Dream.* Retold
       by Pauline de Munnik. Everybody's Shakespeare.
       Johannesburg: Voortrekkerpers, 1964.

       Companion volume to The Students' Shakespeare (1964,
       item 895). An extended paraphrase with full-page
       photographs from the production of the Alexander Theatre,
       Johannesburg, March 1964.

1045   Serraillier, Ian. *The Enchanted Island: Stories from
       Shakespeare.* Illustrated by Peter Farmer. New York: H.
       Z. Walck, 1964. 201 pp.

       Paraphrase which includes numerous quotations.

1046   Sideris, I., ed. [Small Shakespeare Anthology.] *New
       Estia,* no. 887 (1964), 875-84. (Greek--not seen)

       Excerpts from *Dream* and other plays translated.

1047   Turner, W., ed. *A Midsummer Night's Dream.* Notes and
       paraphrase by T. Jagat and S. Bandyopādhyāy.
       Bombay: Educational-Publishers, 1964. lxvi, 258 pp. (not
       seen)

1048   Vandiver, Edward P. *Highlights of Shakespeare's Plays.*
       Great Neck, N. Y.: Barron's Educational Series, 1964.
       454 pp. Rev. ed. Woodbury, N. Y.: Barron's
       Educational Series, 1976. 564 pp.

       Quoted selections with prose bridges. There are two
       photographs of the 1960 Stratford, Ontario, production.

1049 Green, Roger Lancelyn. *Tales from Shakespeare.*
Illustrated by Richard Beer. Foreword by Christopher
Fry. London: V. Gollancz, 1964-65; New York:
Atheneum, 1965. 346 pp.

The play's story, with black-and-white drawings.

1049a Kates, N. *The Stories of Shakespeare's Plays.* Retold by
N. Kates. Oxford English Readers. Grade Two. London:
Oxford University Press, 1965. (not seen)

1050 McCutchan, J. Wilson. *Plot Outlines of Shakespeare's
Comedies: Scene By Scene.* Barnes & Noble Focus Books.
New York: Barnes & Noble, 1965. xviii, 174.

Dream is on pp. 38-46.

1050a *"Midsummer Night's Dream," by William Shakespeare*
[filmstrip]. Pleasantville, N. Y.: Educational
Audio-Visual, 1965. No. A3F0976, 41 fr., col., 35 mm.
(not seen)

A synopsis. With teacher's guide and description of
frames. Uses photographs of a production.

1051 Lothian, John M., arr. *Shakespeare's Charactery: A Book
of "Characters" from Shakespeare.* Oxford: Basil
Blackwell; New York: Barnes & Noble, 1966. xvi, 271
pp.

Gives ten excerpts from *Dream* totalling over one
hundred and fifty lines.

1052 Mayoux, Jean-Jacques. *William Shakespeare.* Paris: Éditions
Seghers, 1966. 192 pp.

A summary of the play. (Pp. 73-75)

1053 Thaler, Alwin. *Shakespeare and Our World.* Knoxville:
University of Tennessee Press, 1966. viii, 235 pp.

Lists (on pp. 196-203) over twenty "recollections" from
Dream in Milton's works. The passages are printed in
parallel columns. The play, according to A. W. Verity in
1923 (quoted by Thaler), was "constantly imitated by
Milton."

1053a   *"Midsummer Night's Dream"* *(With Magoo)* [film]. Mount
Vernon, N. Y.: Macmillan, 1967, 26 min., col., 16 mm.
(not seen)

This abbreviated cartoon features Mr. Magoo as Puck,
who recites an introduction, pulls a drape to show
scene-endings, and performs as a fleeting, mischievous
Puck. He repeats the phrase "What fools these mortals be"
throughout. Presumably the same as item T1262a and thus
produced in 1965.

1054   Schaller, Rudolf, trans. *Ein Sommernachtstraum.*
[Prompt-book, not for sale.] Berlin: Henschel, 1967.
(Typescript, German--not seen)

1055   Cullum, Albert. *Shake Hands with Shakespeare.* New York:
Citation Press, 1968. 320 pp.

An eight-scene adaptation of *Dream* for elementary
students, with an introduction.

1056   Hodges, Margaret, ed. *Constellation: A Shakespeare
Anthology.* New York: Farrar, Straus and Giroux, 1968.
(An Ariel Book) x, 225 pp.

Five substantial quotations with brief introductions.

1057   Usherwood, Stephen. *Shakespeare, Play by Play.*
Illustrated by Raymond Piper. London: Phoenix House,
1967; New York: Hill & Wang, 1968. viii, 99 pp.

Prose version with comment.

1058   Updike, John. *Bottom's Dream. Adapted from William
Shakespeare's "A Midsummer Night's Dream."* With Music

by Felix Mendelssohn and Illustrations by Warren
Chappell. New York: Alfred A. Knopf, 1969. 34 pp.
Reprint. Tokyo: Izumi Press, [1977].

Updike's prose version along with sections (adapted) of
Mendelssohn's score and with numerous colored and
black-and-white illustrations.

1059 Wright, Louis B., and Virginia A. LaMar. *The Folger
Guide to Shakespeare.* The Folger Library General
Reader's Shakespeare. New York: Washington Square
Press, Pocket Books, 1969. xii, 462 pp.

Plot summary with illustrations.

1060 Graczyk, Edward. *The Rude Mechanicals: A Play for
Young People, Freely Adapted from Shakespeare's "A
Midsummer Night's Dream."* Anchorage, Ky.: Anchorage
Press, 1970. 46 pp.

Titania's place is taken by Hippolyta. Sample of the
dialogue: *"Robin.* To the tangled wood I've been, and there
your bride I spied, lying on a hillside of clover, looking
very sad inside."

1061 Kochav, Yehoshua, trans. "Nishvi, Nishvi" ["Blow, blow"]
and "Al p'ney har" ["Over hill, over dale"]. *Parahim
mi-Mednot ha-Yam.* Tel Aviv: Ophir, 1971, pp. 26-27.
(Hebrew--not seen)

1062 Bentley, Nicolas. *Nicolas Bentley's Tales of Shakespeare.*
London: Mitchell Beasley, 1972; New York: Simon and
Schuster, 1973. 111 pp.

The story of the play in modern idiom.

1063 Fühmann, Franz. *Ein Sommernachtstraum.* [Narrated by
Franz Fühmann. With Colored Illustrations by Gertrud
Zucker.] Berlin: Kinderbuchverlag, 1972. 79 pp.
(German--not seen)

For a discussion of the influence of the *Dream* on this writer see item 1091e.

1064   Herendeen, Warren. "The Midsummer Eves of Shakespeare and Christina Rossetti." *Victorian Newsletter*, 41 (1972), 24-26.

Considers what the poet of *Goblin Market* took from *Dream* for the two girls who have experiences similar in nature to those of the supernatural beings in the play.

1065   Kartak, Thomas Clifford. "The Adapting of Shakespearean Comedies for Child Audiences with Acting Versions of Four Plays as Examples." Ph.D. dissertation, Northwestern University, 1971. *DAI*, 32 (1972), 4759A.

Discusses the suitability of adaptations for children, surveys twentieth century adaptations, and gives a version of *Dream* with notes on production (scene, costuming, etc.).

1065a   *"A Midsummer Night's Dream"--Mendelssohn* [filmstrip]. Pleasantville, N. Y.: Educational Audio-Visual, 1971. 70 fr., col. 35 mm. (not seen)

Presents scenes from a Royal Shakespeare Company performance to illustrate the inspiration for Mendelssohn's music (part of a music appreciation series). With teacher's guide. See also item 1010a.

1065b   *Understanding Shakespeare: His Stagecraft* [film]. Bristol, England: Gateway Educational Films, Ltd., 1971. Distributed by Coronet Films (Chicago, Ill.). Code no. 1997, 24.5 min., 16 mm. (not seen)

Episodes from *Dream* and other plays are given authentic staging, according to the catalogue description--that is, without scenery, on a simple, uncurtained stage.

1065c   *Understanding Shakespeare: His Sources* [film]. Bristol, England: Gateway Educational Films, Ltd., 1971.

Distributed by Coronet Films (Chicago, Ill.). Code no. 1999, 20 min., 16 mm. (not seen)

Episodes from *Dream* and other plays are given to show how the plays grew out of the sources.

1065d Styan, J. L. "*A Midsummer Night's Dream.*" *The Challenge of the Theatre: An Introduction to Drama.* Encino and Belmont, Calif.: Dickenson Publishing Co., 1972, pp. 201-206.

The playlet of Pyramus and Thisbe given as an illustration for students of the burlesque. The text is modernized with stage directions added.

1066 West, Michael. *Five Great Plays of Shakespeare.* Adapted and Brought Within the Vocabulary of New Method Reader 4 by Michael West. Illustrated by Hugh Marshall. London: Longman, 1972. 139 pp.

The vocabulary level is 1400 words.

1067 Bryan, Margaret B. "Shakespeare in the Puppet Theatre." *CEA Critic*, 35, no. 3 (1973), 31-32.

On a student production of III.i as puppet theatre.

1068 D'Avanzo, Mario L. "The Literary Sources of 'My Kinsman, Major Molineux': Shakespeare, Coleridge, Milton." *Studies in Short Fiction*, 10 (1973), 121-36.

Finds echoes of *Dream* in Hawthorne's story: the two Robins, Midsummer Eve, and madness. Cf. item 1091g.

1068a Anderson, Poul. *A Midsummer Tempest.* Garden City, N.Y: Doubleday, 1974. 207 pp. Reprint. New York: Ballantine Books, 1975; London: Severn House, 1976; New York: Tom Doherty Associates, 1984. There is also a phonodisc by the same name read by Alan Haines. New York: American Foundation for the Blind, 1974.

Apparently a fantasy based on the two plays combined. According to the catalogue description, the phonodisc "recreates a world where Shakespeare's plays become reality. Shows a world in which the Bard is known as the Historian. The dialogue is in iambic pentameter and Oberon, Titania, Puck, Ariel, and Caliban all materialize to help Prince Rupert."

1069   [Brook, Peter.] *Peter Brook's Production of William Shakespeare's "A Midsummer Night's Dream" for the Royal Shakespeare Company.* The Complete and Authorized Acting Edition. Ed. Glenn Loney. Stratford-upon-Avon: Royal Shakespeare Company; Chicago: Dramatic Publishing Co., 1974. 128, 85a, 85b pp.

Includes the text of the play annotated with detailed notes and diagrams on blocking and stage business, cues for music, sound, lights, and flying. The 128 pages of materials, in addition to the annotated text, include cast lists for the Stratford-upon-Avon opening in 1970, and the New York and world tour productions (see item T1314); lists of properties, costumes, musical instruments, and all scenic and lighting equipment for the world tour; production photographs, and set and costume designs. There are essays by or interviews with Peter Brook, designer Sally Jacobs, actors John Kane, Alan Howard, and others in which the concept, development, and rehearsal techniques of the production are discussed. In the history of Shakespeare production, there has never been a comparable record of a significant production published; one looks to the Berliner Ensemble's *Modelbücher* for comparisons. The edition itself is evidence of the impact of and interest in the Brook production, which signified a break with illusionistic staging traditions for this play, emphasized the young love world of the play and interaction between audiences and actors, caught the emotions of the 1960s on the fly, and set in motion new forces in Shakespearean staging and directorial interpretation.

1070   Gates, Barbara T. *The Explicator*, 32 (1974), item 68.

The "raging moon" of Dylan Thomas' "In My Craft or Sullen Art" suggests a reading of the poem, not merely a

possible source, that strongly recalls Theseus' speech
(V.i.2-17).

1071   Ahačič, Draga, adapt. *Sen kresne noci [A Midsummer
       Night's Dream].* [Translated into Slovene by Oton
       Zupančič. Adapted for Youth by Draga Ahačič.
       Introduction by Draga Ahačič. Illustrated.] Ljubljana:
       Oddelek za gledališko vzgojo in ritmiko pri pionirskem
       domu, 1975. (not seen)

1072   Clayton, J. Douglas. "Emblematic and Iconographic
       Patterns in Pushkin's *Eugene Onegin*: A Shakespearean
       Ghost?" *Germano-Slavica*, 6 (1975), 53-66.

       Traces many similarities in emblematic qualities between
       Tatiana and Titania, especially the Diana/moon/chastity
       complex.

1073   Fleissner, Robert F. "Shakespeare Again in Xanadu."
       Research Studies (Washington State University), 43
       (1975), 193-96.

       Cites parallels (an influence, not a source) between
       Theseus' speech on the imagination and Coleridge's poem.

1074   Keersmaekers, A. "Frederik van Eeden's *Kleine Johannes
       I*, Shakespeare en Andersen." *De Nieuwe Taalgids*
       (Groningen), 68 (1975), 275-81.

       On van Eeden's reading of and admiration of
       Shakespeare, especially *Dream*.

1075   Rathan, S. N. "The East and the West in Radhanath Ray's
       'Kedara-Gauri.'" *Indian P.E.N.*, 41, nos. 9-10 (1975),
       1-5. (not seen)

       On the influence on this Oriya poet of *Dream*.

1076   Rose, Margaret A. "Carnival and 'Tendenz': Satiric Modes
       in Heine's 'Atta Troll. Ein Sommer-Nachtstraum.'"

Journal of the Australasian Universities Language and Literature Association, 43 (1975), 33-49.

Heine's bear hero, who is both satiric object and satirist in comment on certain political movements of the 1840s, is a combination of Bottom (object) and Puck (satirist). The subtitle is "A Midsummer Night's Dream."

1077   Hoge, James O., Jr. "Tennyson on Shakespeare: His Talk about the Plays." *Texas Studies in Literature*, 18 (1976), 160-61.

Gives Tennyson's praise of two passages in II.i: Titania's "His mother was a votaress" and Oberon's "That very time I saw."

1078   Jacobs, Henry E., and Claudia D. Johnson. *An Annotated Bibliography of Shakespearean Burlesques, Parodies, and Travesties*. New York: Garland Publishing, 1976. 202 pp.

Annotates twenty adaptations which either ridicule or else use as the basis for ridicule 1) the play as a whole (three), 2) scenes from the play (ten), or 3) specific passages in it (seven).

1079   Miles, Bernard. *Favourite Tales from Shakespeare*. Illustrated by Victor G. Ambrus. London: Hamlyn; Chicago: Rand McNally, 1976. 125 pp.

A full retelling with a colored illustration on every page.

1080   Rennert, Hellmut Hal. "An Exploration of Eduard Mörike's Reading with Emphasis on Shakespeare." Ph.D. dissertation, University of Washington, 1975. *DAI*, 37 (1976), 958A.

Dream was one of Mörike's favorite plays.

1081   Harris, Aurand, and William Shakespeare. *Robin Goodfellow*. New Orleans: Anchorage Press, 1977. 36 pp. (not seen)

"A children's play based on the folk tales of Robin
Goodfellow and scenes from *A Midsummer Night's Dream*."

1082 Weil, Lisl. *Donkey Head*. New York: Atheneum, 1977. 40
      pp.

      Text and illustrations retell the adventures of Bottom,
      Titania, Oberon, Puck, and other characters from *Dream*.

1083 Candido, Joseph. *"A Midsummer Night's Dream* and 'Ode to
      a Nightingale': A Further Instance of Keats's
      Indebtedness." *American Notes and Queries*, 16 (1978),
      154-55.

      Finds Stanza 5 strongly reminiscent in tone and language
      of Oberon's speech at II.ii.248-54. See also items 575a,
      1005, and 1091j.

1084 Evans, Gareth Lloyd and Barbara Lloyd. *Everyman's
      Companion to Shakespeare*. London: J. M. Dent, 1978.
      xiv, 368 pp. Published as *The Shakespeare Companion*
      by New York: Scribner, 1978.

      Gives an extract ("I know a bank . . . .") and plot
      summary (pp. 239-40).

1085 Love, Harold. "Dryden's 'Unideal Vacancy.'"
      Eighteenth-Century Studies, 12 (1978), 74-89.

      Mentions a passage in Dryden's and Nathaniel Lee's
      Oedipus, 1679, and another from Lee (not identified),
      developed on the model of Titania's season speech
      (II.i.81-117).

1086 Ofrat, Gideon. [*Miss Julie* and *A Midsummer Night's
      Dream*.] *Bikoret u-Parshanut* [Criticism and
      Interpretation] (Ramat-Gan, Israel), 11-12 (1978),
      269-84. (Hebrew)

      The plays are similar in that both involve the swapping
      of social positions for one night and on the same festive
      occasion and in a diabolic atmosphere. Both plays deal with

engaged couples who swap around during that night and both are based on the symbolic struggle between the forces of light (society, morality) and the forces of the night (sex, violation of society's norms). In Julie's forest-kitchen, "sex and madness jubilate, just as in Shakespeare's forest." And the scene near the end when Jean wrings the pet bird's neck functions in the same way as the artisans' playlet in the conclusion. Strindberg was obviously influenced by Shakespeare. *Dream*, however, ends in order; *Miss Julie* does not. (There is a summary in English on pp. xviii-xx.)

1087   Davidson, Diane, adapt. *A Midsummer Night's Dream*. Shakespeare Simplified for the Leisure Reader, 5. Fair Oaks, Calif.: Swan Books, 1979. xvi, 99 pp. (not seen)

1088   Goodwin, John. *A Short Guide to Shakespeare's Plays*. London: Heinemann, 1979. 80 pp.

A two-page guide, "simply to indicate the story and general flavour."

1089   Hignett, D. J. *Shakespeare's "A Midsummer Night's Dream."* G.C.E. Set Book. Notes for O Level Students. Formby, Merseyside: [n.p.], 1979. 20 pp.

Plot summary with interpretive comment.

1089a   Johnson, Diana L. *Fantastic Illustration and Design in Britain, 1850-1930*. Providence, R. I.: Rhode Island School of Design, 1979. 240 pp. Also published as *Bulletin of Rhode Island School of Design: Museum Notes*, 65, no. 5 (1979).

Several of the plates included (mostly given in black and white and reduced) are of matter inspired by the *Dream*: nos. 6 (Thomas Allen), 17 (Robert Anning Bell), 66 (Francis Danby), 129 (Maxwell Gordon Lightfoot), 154 (Sir Joseph Noël Paton), 164 and 175 (Arthur Rackham), and 214 (John Simmons).

1090   Peyton, K. M. *A Midsummer Night's Death.* London:
        Oxford University Press; Cleveland: Collins, 1979. 138
        pp.

        A novel of detection set in an English public school. In
        a class session students are cast for roles in *Dream.*

1090a   *A Midsummer Night's Dream* [audio-cassette]. [197?].
        Distributed by National Center for Audio Tapes
        (Boulder, Colo.). Cassette 7950-06, 30 min. (not heard)

        A synopsis of the play narrated by Richard Baker.

1091   Amblard, Marie-Claude. "Nodier et Shakespeare." *Europe,*
        58, Nos. 614-615 (1980), 110-16.

        Cites the influence of the *Dream* on two major tales,
        "Smarra" and "Trilby" (of 1821-1822), of Charles Nodier.

1091a   Pedicord, Harry William and Frederick Louis Bergmann,
        eds. *The Plays of David Garrick.* A Complete Collection
        of the Social Satires, French Adaptations, Pantomimes,
        Christmas and Musical Plays, Preludes, Interludes, and
        Burlesques, to which are added the Alterations and
        Adaptations of the Plays of Shakespeare and Other
        Dramatists from the Sixteenth to the Eighteenth
        Centuries. 4 volumes. Carbondale: Southern Illinois
        University Press, 1980.

        Volumes three and four include the texts of the
        adaptations of the *Dream* done at Garrick's Drury Lane:
        The Fairies (1755) and *Midsummer Night's Dream* (1763),
        both of which were quasi-operatic adaptations. There are
        editorial notes on the omissions of Shakespeare's lines and
        reproductions of the title pages. (For the original editions
        see items 965 and 967.)

1091b   Wangenheim, Gustav von. "*Ein Sommernachtstraum.*"
        Shakespeare Jahrbuch (Weimar), 116 (1980), 120-31.

        This first publication of a chapter from a novel by von
        Wangenheim, "*Sommernachtstraum bei Reinhardt,*" focuses
        almost exclusively on Max Reinhardt's charismatic

personality and ignores almost completely his famous production of the *Dream* at the Deutsches Theatre in Berlin.

1091c   Rogers, June Walker, David Rogers, and Alan Menken. *The Dream on Royal Street*. A Full-length Musical. Chicago: The Dramatic Publishing Company, 1981.

An adaptation of the *Dream* set in the present in the Royal Street Hotel in New Orleans on Mardi Gras night. Rex (Theseus) is King of the Carnival and Hippolyta is his press secretary in disguise. Egeus manages the hotel and wants Hermia to marry his assistant manager, Demetrius, but she is in love with the desk clerk, Lysander. Oberon and Titania are Las Vegas rock stars with a back-up group called the Fly-by-Nights, and under their manager, Puck, are playing the hotel's night club. Bottom is the Head Doorman, Snout and Flute are bell captains, and Quince, Starveling and Snug are bellmen. They all seek to put together an act and audition for the nightclub. There are love ballads ("The Course of True Love"), a New Orleans jazz version of "What Fools These Mortals Be," rock songs ("Thief of Love"), and Pyramus and Thisbe is performed as a country and western song. There are three settings and a cast of twenty. Playscript can be purchased; music on request. Royalties for performance.

1091d   Nicholson, David. "Hauptmann's *Hannele*: Naturalistic Fairy Tale and Dream Play." *Modern Drama*, 24 (1981), 282-91.

Hauptmann's dream play is similar to Shakespeare's in that the spirit world is used to comment on the real world; but with Hauptmann we return in the end firmly to a naturalistic world, which is not the case with Shakespeare. Several comparisons are drawn between the two plays.

1091e   Seehäse, Georg. "Franz Fühmanns Märchen vom *Sommernachtstraum*." *Weimer Beiträge: Zeitschrift für literaturwissenschaft*, 1 (1982), 120-31.

Discusses Fühmann's adaptations and his understanding of Shakespeare, one tale in particular, *Sommernachtstraum* (see item 1063), being based on the play. In the fairy-tale element Fühmann includes a personal and historical element that goes beyond Shakespeare. Comparisons are made with other adaptations of Shakespeare.

1091f Stewart, Diana, adapt. *A Midsummer Night's Dream*. Illustrated by Charles Shaw. Milwaukee, Wis.: Raintree Pubs., 1982. 48 pp. (not seen)

Apparently an adaptation in which fairy creatures meddle with varying results in the lives of human beings wandering in the woods.

1091g Van Deusen, Marshall. "Sex and Religion in Hawthorne's 'My Kinsman, Major Molineux.'" *American Notes & Queries*, 21 (1982), 11-12.

In his Freudian reading of "My Kinsman" in *The Sins of the Fathers*, Frederick Crews might have made more of the phallic associations of the name Robin which are there in the *Dream* and elsewhere. Cf. item 1068.

1091gg Besoyan, Rick. *Babes in the Wood*. New York: Broadway Play Publishing, Inc., 1983. 54 pp.

Script of an adaptation of *A Midsummer Night's Dream* produced off-Broadway in 1964 (see T1229b and T1248b). There are two acts, nineteen musical numbers, and a cast of eight. Theseus and Hippolyta are omitted. Bottom is the only remaining member of the original six mechanicals and "Pyramus and Thisbe" is not done. Also omitted are Egeus, Philostrate, and Peaseblossom and company. The spirit of the adaptation is that of a modern spoof, though there are some earnest, romantic songs for the young lovers. It opens in the forest with Titania angry at Oberon's infidelities; the Indian boy is not mentioned. After she departs, Oberon asserts himself singing "This State of Affairs," assisted by Puck. Titania later sings of how women can rule men. And so on. The score and a cassette tape (and the performance rights) are available separately from the publisher.

1091h Boyle, Robert, S. J. "Joyce and Faith." *Work in Progress: Joyce Centenary Essays*. Ed. Richard F.

Peterson, Alan M. Cohn, and Edmund L. Epstein.
Carbondale and Edwardsville, Ill.: Southern Illinois
University Press, 1983, pp. 132-44.

In several places in *Finnegans Wake* where faith is at
issue, Joyce seems to be building specifically on Bottom's
attempt to express his "most rare vision."

1091i   Fontane, Marilyn Stall. "Under the Net of *A Mid-summer
         Night's Dream.*" *Publications of the Arkansas Philological
         Association*, 9, no. 1 (Spring, 1983), 43-54. (not seen)

         Apparently argues for the *Dream* as "the most influential
         literary work" on Iris Murdoch's novel *Under the Net*,
         especially in the matter of plot.

1091j   Spiegelman, Willard. "Keats's 'Coming Muskrose' and
         Shakespeare's 'Profound Verdure.'" *ELH*, 50 (1983),
         347-62.

         The *Dream*, which Keats called "a piece of profound
         verdure"--may have inspired the "midnight vision at the
         heart of his [Nightingale] ode." "The very confusions, as
         well as incidental details, loud echoes, and thematic
         parallels, point us toward a source for much in the ode."
         For another account of an indebtedness see item 1083.

1091k   Straus, Botho. *Der Park.* Drama. Munich and Vienna:
         Carl Hanser, 1983. 127 pp. (not seen)

         Apparently a drama inspired by the *Dream*.

1091l   Garlick, Kenneth. "Illustrations to 'A Midsummer Night's
         Dream' before 1920." *Shakespeare Survey*, 37 (1984),
         41-53.

         Notices the range in tastes reflected and the shift in
         content treated, from the frontispiece to Rowe's 1709 edition
         to the illustrations of Heath Robinson and Arthur Rackham,
         in a series of brief comments made about each of seventeen
         particular illustrations (reproduced in black and white and
         in reduced form). "The illustrations range from the ethos of
         the baroque masque through the academic restriction of the

late eighteenth century to the kind of historical and un-Shakespearian approach of the mid and late nineteenth century which is implied in the word 'revival.'" The illustrations reflect a popular image of the play--a coalescence of English romanticism and German fairy sentiment--which has become almost a part of our folklore. When recent productions have underplayed or ignored this enchantment, they have lost significance.

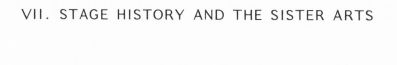

VII. STAGE HISTORY AND THE SISTER ARTS

The format of this section of the bibliography includes annotated production entries, with review listings, for thirty-four selected productions of *A Midsummer Night's Dream* on the English-speaking stage within the frame of our coverage, 1940-1983. Films, operas, and ballets derived from the play are also given production entries (without reviews). These entries, like those for publications, are listed alphabetically in any given year under the play title (or the title of the adaptation, if different).

For quick reference, an abbreviated listing of the stage, film, and television productions of the play itself (not the opera and ballet adaptations) is provided below, giving for each its item number, the year date, the name of the theatre or company, and the name of the director. (For further information on the coverage and format here, see the Introduction.)

T1093 1942 Shakespeare Memorial Theatre, Stratford-upon-Avon. B. Iden Payne.

T1096 1943 Shakespeare Memorial Theatre, Stratford-upon-Avon. Baliol Holloway.

T1097 1944 Shakespeare Memorial Theatre, Stratford-upon-Avon. Robert Atkins.

T1099 1945 Haymarket Theatre, London. Nevill Coghill.

T1110 1949 Shakespeare Memorial Theatre, Stratford-upon-Avon. Michael Benthall.

T1120 1951 Old Vic Theatre, London. Tyrone Guthrie.

T1138 1954 Old Vic Company and Sadler's Wells Ballet, Edinburgh
Opera House and New York Metropolitan Opera House.
Michael Benthall.

T1140 1954 Shakespeare Memorial Theatre, Stratford-upon-Avon.
George Devine.

T1160 1957 Old Vic Theatre, London. Michael Benthall.

T1172 1958 American Shakespeare Festival Theatre, Stratford,
Connecticut. Jack Landau.

T1183 1959 Shakespeare Memorial Theatre, Stratford-upon-Avon.
Peter Hall. Revived through 1963.

T1194 1960 Festival Theatre, Stratford, Ontario. Douglas
Campbell.

T1196 1960 Old Vic Theatre, London. Michael Langham.

T1204 1961 New York Shakespeare Festival, Wollman Memorial
Skating Rink, New York City. Joel Friedman.

T1215 1962 English Stage Company, Royal Court Theatre,
London. Tony Richardson.

T1216 1962 New Shakespeare Company, Open Air Theatre,
Regent's Park, London. David William.

T1253 1964 New York Shakespeare Festival, on tour in New York
City. Jack von Sydow.

T1269 1966 Actor's Workshop Company, Marines' Theatre, San Francisco, California. John Hancock. Revived in Pittsburgh and New York, 1967.

T1277 1967 American Shakespeare Festival Theatre, Stratford, Connecticut. Cyril Ritchard.

T1278 1967 Popular Theatre Company, Edinburgh Festival and Saville Theatre, London. Frank Dunlop.

T1288 1968 Festival Theatre, Stratford, Ontario. John Hirsch.

T1301 1969 Royal Shakespeare Company, 35 mm. film. Peter Hall.

T1314 1970 Royal Shakespeare Company, StratforduponAvon. Peter Brook. New York and world tour through 1973.

T1332 1972 Guthrie Theatre, Minneapolis, Minnesota. John Hirsch.

T1373 1975 New York Shakespeare Festival, Mitzi E. Newhouse Theatre, Lincoln Center, New York. Edward Berkeley.

T1374 1975 Yale Repertory Theatre, New Haven, Connecticut. Alvin Epstein. Revived in Boston, 1980.

T1396 1976 Festival Theatre, Stratford, Ontario. Robin Phillips. Revived and revised in 1977.

T1411 1977 Royal Shakespeare Company, StratforduponAvon. John Barton.

T1479 1980 Bristol Old Vic Company, Old Vic Theatre, London. Richard Cottrell.

T1498 1981 Royal Shakespeare Company, Stratford-upon-Avon.
Ron Daniels. Revived in London, 1982.

T1499 1981 Arena Stage Company, Arena Stage, Washington, D.
C. David Chambers.

T1499a 1981 BBC Television series, "The Shakespeare Plays."
Elijah Moshinsky.

T1516 1982 New York Shakespeare Festival, Delacorte Theatre,
Central Park, New York City. James Lapine.

T1516a 198? Television version of the 1982 New York Shakespeare
Festival production. Emile Ardolino.

T1517 1982 National Theatre of Great Britain Acting Company,
Cottesloe Theatre. Bill Bryden.

T1092   Spencer, Hazelton. "Mr. Pepys is Not Amused," *ELH*, 7
        (1940), 163-76.

        Assesses the character of Samuel Pepys and surveys his
        visits to productions of Shakespeare in London theatres.
        Pepys famous comment about an otherwise unknown
        production of *A Midsummer Night's Dream* at the King's
        theatre in 1662 ("the most insipid ridiculous play that ever
        I saw in my life") is discussed. Spencer, who generally
        defends Pepys's critical taste, suggests that some of the
        comic portions of the play might have been cut to make
        room for the dancing to which Pepys refers. Spencer says
        Pepys was likely "too much the Restoration man to savor
        the delicacy of the fairy scenes," but suggests that his
        response may be attributable to a performance failure as
        much as to the play itself.

T1092a   Bentley, Gerald Eades. *The Jacobean and Caroline
         Stage.* 7 volumes. Oxford: Clarendon Press, 1941-1968.
         Illustrated.

Continuation of E. K. Chambers *The Elizabethan Stage*
(1923), covering companies, players, playwrights, and
theatre buildings, 1616 to 1642. As to the particulars of
performance coverage of *A Midsummer Night's Dream*,
Volume I (pp. 27-28) cites a rare document that shows a
King's Men performance of it at Hampton Court, October 17,
1630. Volume II (p. 590) provides biographical information
on William Tawyer, immortalized in the First Folio stage
direction of the play, "Tawyer with a trumpet before them,"
in V.i. It also includes (pp. 621-22) biographical
information on John Wilson and Henry Wilson, one of which
may have been the "cunning musician" who planned the
entertainment for Bishop Lincoln referred to below. Volume
V (pp. 1153-54) discusses James Shirley's *The Triumph of
Beauty* (1646), the first part of which is derived from the
first scenes of the Athenian mechanicals in the play. Volume
VII notes (pp. 33-34) the publication of the so-called
Collection of 1619, containing *A Midsummer Night's Dream*,
and in a performance calendar (p. 71) records the
performance of a play, perhaps *A Midsummer Night's
Dream*, on a Sunday in September of 1629 or 1631 before
John Williams, Bishop of Lincoln, and his guests, probably
at Buckden Palace, near Huntingdon. (The documents may
be seen in E. K. Chambers, *Shakespeare, A Study of Facts
and Problems* [1930], II, 348-50.)

T1093   *A Midsummer Night's Dream* presented at the Shakespeare
         Memorial Theatre, Stratford-upon-Avon, beginning 4
         April 1942. Director, B. Iden Payne. Designer, Peggy
         Neale. *Oberon*, George Hays. *Bottom*, Jay Laurier.
         Puck, Roy Siddons. *Titania*, Sarah Jackson.

         A conventionally romantic production during the war
         years, with local dancers in the fairy retinues and with
         Mendelssohn's music. The set was in the simple, suggestive
         pictorial style, with Theseus' palace represented by a
         symmetrical, classically pillared veranda. Laurier's Bottom
         was criticized for resorting at times to the easy comic tricks
         of the Christmas pantomime but praised for his awakening
         from the dream.

         Reviews: *The Times*, 6 April 1942; *New York Times*, 12
         April 1942. (See also items T1096, T1097, T1104, T1110,
         T1249, T1481 and T1508.)

T1094   Webster, Margaret. *Shakespeare Without Tears.*
        Introduction by John Mason Brown. New York:
        Whittlesey House, McGraw Hill, 1942; rev. ed.,
        Cleveland: World Publishing Company, 1955; reprint,
        Capricorn Books, G. P. Putnam's Sons, 1975; re-issued
        as *Shakespeare Today*, London: J. M. Dent and Sons,
        Ltd., 1957. ix, 319 pp.

        The experienced actress and director and descendent of
        an old English theatrical family offers commentary on the
        plays and some pioneering considerations of a practical,
        performance-oriented nature. Some of her commentary is
        based on her experiences with the plays in production. The
        commentary on staging *A Midsummer Night's Dream* (pp.
        155-58) runs from wishful thinking about the scenery and
        the atmosphere necessary for the play to some practical
        advice on the characters. She notes that actors find the
        lovers better differentiated than literary critics do, and she
        stresses that the play will lose effectiveness if the lovers'
        humanity is not established. She mentions some traditional
        business for the mechanicals such as Starveling being deaf
        and Thisbe falling on Pyramus's scabbard instead of his
        sword. She urges directors to be judicious and not let the
        mechanicals' business go on interminably.

T1095   Agate, James. *Brief Chronicles: A Survey of the Plays of
        Shakespeare and the Elizabethans in Actual Performance,
        1923-1942.* London: Cape, 1943; New York: Benjamin
        Blom, 1971. 311 pp.

        Includes the *Sunday Times*'s critic's pieces on three
        productions of *A Midsummer Night's Dream*. He disapproved
        of the version directed by Donald Calthrop at the Kingsway
        Theatre in 1923, a production influenced by Harley
        Granville-Barker (in whose production of 1914 Calthrop
        played Puck), with somewhat simplified settings and
        costumes designed by Norman Wilkinson. He also objected to
        the quartet of lovers for speaking and acting poorly and to
        Baliol Holloway's Bottom for being too much the egotistic
        bully. Neither did he approve of Basil Dean's staging at
        Drury Lane in 1924, a traditionally lavish affair with acres
        of scenery only a step removed from Tree's and hydraulic
        platforms that left a massive *corps de ballet* somewhat more
        than a step from where they should have been. He found
        "extraordinarily effective" the production at the Old Vic in
        1929, directed by Harcourt Williams. This production,

influenced by Granville-Barker, had its virtues in Paul Smyth's simple scenery, fairy costumes inspired by Inigo Jones, John Gielgud's Oberon, Margaret Webster's Hermia, Gyles Isham's Bottom, and Leslie French's Puck.

T1096   *A Midsummer Night's Dream* presented at the Shakespeare Memorial Theatre, Stratford-upon-Avon, 21 April 1943. Director, Baliol Holloway. Designer, Charles Reading. *Bottom*, Baliol Holloway. *Oberon*, Charles Reading. *Titania*, Christine Adrian. *Helena*, Patricia Jessel.

A conventional moonlight-and-Mendelssohn production with some less-than-adequate performances that critics tolerated in the war years when many young actors were in military service.

Reviews: *The Observer*, 25 April 1943. (See also items T1104, T1110, T1249, T1481 and T1508.)

T1097   *A Midsummer Night's Dream* presented at the Shakespeare Memorial Theatre, Stratford-upon-Avon, 8 May 1944. Director, Robert Atkins. Scene design, Guy Sheppard. Costume design, Norman Wilkinson (from the Stratford production of 1932). *Bottom*, Cliff Weir. *Puck*, Mary Honer.

Atkins had directed the play frequently at Regent's Park in the 1930s. He headed the Festival at Stratford in the 1944 and 1945 summer seasons. Sheppard's settings featured a Quince's workshop out of a Durer engraving and a sharply silhouetted forest. Otherwise, it was a conventional production in which fairies danced to Mendelssohn. (See items T1104, T1110, T1249, T1481, T1508 and T1125.)

T1098   Sprague, Arthur Colby. *Shakespeare and the Actors: The Stage Business in His Plays (1660-1905).* Cambridge: Harvard University Press, 1944; reprint, New York; Russell and Russell, Inc., 1963. xxv, 442 pp.

Regarded as one of the classics in the field of Shakespearean performance history because of its sensitive and meticulous scouring of promptbooks and reviews to identify significant, telling moments of stage business and vocal inflections in major productions of most of the plays.

"Through business, actors became commentators, critics," said Sprague in 1944, and "through business, Shakespeare's plays could be brought nearer us and our own experience--could be made more like 'modern' plays." Of the six chapters, the first is devoted to the comedies and six of its seventy-five pages are concerned with *A Midsummer Night's Dream* productions up through the end of the nineteenth century, including those of Elizabeth Vestris, Charles Kean, Samuel Phelps, William Burton, Augustin Daly, and Sir Herbert Beerbohm Tree. Theseus has entered in a galley; Puck has entered by rising on a mushroom or coming out of a flower. The waking Bottom has discovered hay in his pouch, Moonshine has pulled along a wooden dog on wheels, and the fairies have danced in the finale with illuminated lamps.

T1099   *A Midsummer Night's Dream* presented at the Haymarket Theatre, London, opening 25 January 1945. Director, Nevill Coghill. *Oberon*, John Gielgud. *Titania*, Peggy Ashcroft. *Puck*, Max Adrian. *Bottom*, Leslie Banks. *Quince*, Miles Malleson. *Theseus*, Leon Quartermaine. Music by Leslie Bridgewater.

A moderately successful production with critics, featuring Gielgud as an overly sonorous Oberon, somewhat sinister in appearance, and Max Adrian as a large but nimble Puck. The design and music evoked a Jacobean world for reviewers. "Back to Mendelssohn," cried critic James Agate.

Reviews: Agate, *Sunday Times*, 21 January and 4 February, 1945; Ivor Brown, *The Observer*, 28 January 1945; *The Times*, 26 January 1945; *New York Times*, 25 March 1945; *The Sketch*, 21 March 1945. (See also item T1100.)

T1100   Agate, James. *The Contemporary Theatre, 1944 and 1945*. London: George G. Harrap, 1946. 259 pp.

Contains two of his pieces on the production at the Haymarket Theatre, London, in January of 1945. (See item 1099.) He found some pleasures in this version, directed by Nevill Coghill, whose cast included John Gielgud as Oberon (whose sinister appearance Agate found frightening), Peggy Ashcroft as Titania (whose delivery he criticized) and Max

Adrian as Puck (whom he disliked). But his chief topic was his displeasure at the absence of Mendelssohn's score behind the play (Leslie Bridgewater had provided the production's music).

T1101   Loewenberg, Alfred. *"Midsummer Night's Dream* Music in 1763." *Theatre Notebook,* 1 (1946), 23-26.

Discusses the identity of the composers of the thirty-three vocal numbers in the 1763 production of *A Midsummer Night's Dream,* the second of three operatic adaptations done at Garrick's Drury Lane. Garrick and George Colman, the elder brought this out with thirty-three songs from six composers; some of these were carried over from John Christopher Smith's score for the 1755 adaptation, *The Fairies.* Loewenberg, citing a rare Table of Songs in a British Museum copy of the published libretto, shows that Charles Burney composed fourteen of the songs and probably arranged the 1763 score. (See also items 965-967, T1351 and T1446. For an analysis of Garrick's part in the preparation of the texts of these productions, see George Winchester Stone's *"A Midsummer Night's Dream* in the Hands of Garrick and Colman," *PMLA,* 54 (1939), 467-82.)

T1101a   Purcell, Henry. *The Fairy Queen,* presented by the Sadler's Wells Ballet and the Covent Garden Opera House, London, opening 12 December 1946. Produced by Frederick Ashton and Malcolm Baker Smith. Adapted by Constant Lambert. Designer, Michael Ayrton. Choreography, Frederick Ashton. *Titania,* Margaret Rawlings. *Oberon,* Robert Helpmann. *Puck,* James Kenny. *Fairy,* Joan Sheldon. *Speaking Fairy,* Olive Dyer. *Fairies,* Anne Negus, Pauline Clayden, Joan Sheldon, Avril Navarre. *Sleep,* David Franklin. *Secrecy,* Gladys Palmer. *Mystery,* Constance Shacklock. *Night,* Audrey Bowman. *Bottom,* Michael Hordern. *Quince,* Harcourt Williams. *Snug,* Cyril Wheeler. *Flute,* Douglas Seale. *Snout,* Gordon Crier. *Starveling,* Ronald Richie. *Spirits of the Air,* Muriel Burnet, Margot Fonteyn, Michael Somes. *Spring,* Moira Shearer. *Summer,* Beryl Grey. *Autumn,* Michael Somes. *Winter,* David Paltenghi. *Four Chinese Dancers,* Alexis Rassine, John Hart, Pauline Clayden, Margaret Dale. *Chinese Man and Woman,* Olive Dyer, Hubert Norville. *A Chinese*

Priestess, Audrey Bowman. *Two Chinese Children*,
Veronica Vail, Peter Clegg. *Hymen*, Richard Ellis.
Phoebus, David Davenport. Soloists and chorus of the
Covent Garden Opera House. The Covent Garden
Orchestra conducted by Constant Lambert.

This revival was the first major London staging of the
work since the discovery of the lost Purcell score in this
century (see T1229a). In Lambert's adaptation, the young
lovers were excluded, and the focus was upon Titania and
Oberon and the scenic spectacles and dances of the four
masque-like entertainments that are brought out by the
fairy royalty. (See T1106 and 962.) Lambert's adaptation
was arranged in three acts. I.i was set in a Grove Near
Athens, and included the "Ballet of the Birds." Act I.ii was
set in The Wood and included "The Masque of Night," with
the dance of the characters Sleep, Secrecy, Mystery, and
Night. In II.i, the mechanicals met in The Wood, and there
was a transformation to The Enchanted Lake for II.ii, the
setting for "The Masque of Love," with the Spirits of the
Air and the Savages. III.i was set in The Wood, and after
the scene with Oberon, Puck, Titania and Bottom, a
transformation took the scene to A Chinese Garden, where
"The Masque of the Seasons" was danced. There were then
dances by several Chinese characters. The production then
ended with the apotheosis, featuring Hymen and Phoebus.
Among the notable dancers in the cast were Margaret
Rawlings, Robert Helpman, Margot Fonteyn, and Moira
Shearer. Notable among the speaking cast were Michael
Horden, as Bottom, and Harcourt Williams, as Quince. For a
photographic record of the production, see T1106.

T1102   Stahl, Ernst Leopold. *Shakespeare und das Deutsche
        Theater: Wanderung und Wandelung seines Werkes in
        dreiundeinhalb Jahrhunderten* [Shakespeare and the
        German Theatre: The Migration and Transformation of
        His Work over Three and a Half Centuries]. Stuttgart:
        W. Kohlhammer Verlag, 1947. 768 pp. Illustrated.

        Surveys Shakespeare's plays on the German stage from
the early seventeenth century to about 1947, providing a
bibliography of selected works at the end of each chapter.
Discusses Andreas Gryphius's three act *Absurda Comica
oder Herr Peter Squenz* and the early English troupes in
Germany. There is a chapter on Ludwig Tieck's productions
that includes a general characterization of his *Ein*

Sommernachtstraum in Potsdam in 1843, with set designer J. C. Gerst and composer Felix Mendelssohn-Bartholdy. Tieck here drew upon ideas he had worked out in his earlier novel, *The Young Carpenter,* and he may also have been influenced by Goethe's ideas for a Shakespearean-type stage. The setting featured an architectural structure of steps and levels, which was used in combination with pictorial elements for certain scenes, such as that in Quince's workshop. The costumes were an anachronistic mix of Greek, old German, Spanish and the fantastic. There are brief characterizations of Karl von Holtei's 1826 production; Heinrich Laube's in 1854; Franz Dingelstadt's in 1850; Eduard Devrient's in 1855; Reinhardt's in Berlin in 1905, and in Munich in 1909, in Berlin in 1921, and in Salzburg in 1925. There are brief references to the play in the chapter on Shakespeare in opera and incidental music. The chapter on Shakespeare on film very briefly characterizes the German film versions of 1913 and 1925 and the 1935 Reinhardt film. Among the illustrations are two of Gerst's designs for Tieck's production (Theseus' palace and Quince's workshop), a design for Theseus' palace for an 1893 Berlin production, photographs of Carl Ebert's 1930 production in Darmstadt and of an outdoor, night-time performance at the Heidelberg Festival of 1926.

T1103   Watkins, Ronald. *Moonlight at the Globe.* An Essay in Shakespearean Production Based on the Performance of *A Midsummer Night's Dream* at Harrow school by Ronald Watkins. Drawings by Maurice Percival. Foreword by R. W. Moore. London: Michael Joseph, 1947. [vi], 136 pp.

In 1945, the Harrow School boys under Watkins' direction performed *A Midsummer Night's Dream* on the quasi-Elizabethan platform stage he set up at the school. Watkins, influenced by Granville-Barker, William Poel, and John Cranford Adams' *The Globe Playhouse,* offers here a discussion of the staging of the play that "outlines a modern production on the pattern of a supposed performance at the Globe." He employs "the study" for the bower and the hawthorne brake, does away with Mendelssohn and employs Elizabethan music (using Byrd's lullaby for the fairies). The music called for in the play is reproduced here, including a hunting horn call. The chapters consider the staging, setting, music and costumes. The drawings include costume sketches and blocking suggestions. There are detailed suggestions on line

readings, gestures, blocking, and stage business both in
the text and in the appendix. (See items T1115, T1363 and
T1515.)

T1103a   Byrne, Muriel St. Clare. *A Pictorial History of
         Shakespearean Productions in England, 1576-1946.*
         Freeport, New York: Books for Libraries, 1970. A
         revision of *A History of Shakespearean Productions in
         England. Part I: 1700-1800.* Scenes and Characters in
         the Eighteenth Century. London: Common Ground, 1948;
         rpt., Freeport, New York: Books for Libraries Press,
         1970. 35 pp.

         Catalogue of an exhibition presented by the Arts Council
         of Great Britain and the Society for Cultural Relations with
         the U. S. S. R. at the National Book League in January
         and February, 1948. (The exhibit materials were then
         deposited with the University of Bristol Drama Department.)
         There are brief annotations on each of the exhibit items.
         Among them were the frontispiece to the Rowe edition of *A
         Midsummer Night's Dream*; three watercolors of Charles
         Kean's production of the play--Theseus' palace by W.
         Gordon and F. Lloyds, the Dance of Fairies by Lloyds; and
         the meeting of Oberon and Titania by Lloyds; a photograph
         of Norman Wilkinson's setting for W. Bridges Adam's
         production of the play at Stratford-upon-Avon in 1932;
         photographs of productions there in 1934, 1937, and 1938,
         in which Wilkinson's settings were again used; and a
         photograph of the 1945 *A Midsummer Night's Dream* directed
         by Nevill Coghill at the Haymarket Theatre, London, with
         décor by Hal Burton.

T1104   Ellis, Ruth. *The Stratford Memorial Theatre.* London:
         Winchester Publications, 1948. xiii, 162. Illustrated.

         The survey of the theatre's history includes photographs
         of the interior and exterior of the old and new (1932)
         theatres, and there is an appendix giving the titles of the
         plays produced over the seasons and the casts of the
         birthday productions from 1879-1948. The latter includes
         twenty-four productions of *A Midsummer Night's Dream* here
         in 1880, 1888, 1903, 1906, 1910, 1911, 1912, 1914, 1916,
         1919, 1921, 1923, 1924, 1926, 1928, 1930, 1932, 1933, 1934,
         1937, 1938, 1942, 1943 and 1944.

T1105   "International News." *Shakespeare Survey*, 1 (1948),
        112-17.

        News from Shakespearean correspondents on scholarly
        and theatrical activities includes brief notices of recent
        various productions of *A Midsummer Night's Dream* in
        various nations, including Poland, Belgium, The
        Netherlands, Switzerland, Austria, Finland, and Spain.

T1106   [Mandinian, Edward.] *Purcell's "The Fairy Queen" as
        Presented by the Sadler's Well's Ballet and the Covent
        Garden Opera.* London: John Lehmann, Ltd., 1948. 96
        pp. Illustrated.

        Provides a photographic record of the production of *The
        Fairy Queen*, as adapted by Constant Lambert, done in 1946
        at Covent Garden (see T1101a). There are about sixty
        black and white production photographs by Mandinian and
        also photos of Michael Ayrton's design sketches for the
        scenery and costumes. The book contains three short
        essays. Edward Dent provides a history of the Purcell
        score, rediscovered in this century; Lambert discusses the
        Purcell music and the problems of adaptation of the original
        work, which combined *A Midsummer Night's Dream* with four
        elaborate masque-like spectacles at the ends of the acts.
        (See also 962.) Designer Michael Ayrton comments on the
        scenery and costumes.

T1107   Byrne, Muriel St. Clare. "Fifty Years of Shakespearean
        Production: 1898-1948." *Shakespeare Survey*, 2 (1949),
        1-20.

        Surveys acting and production in English productions
        from late Victorianism to the advent of the director's
        theatre. Victorian antiquarianism in costumes and settings
        may be seen in the productions of Charles Kemble, Charles
        Kean, and Herbert Beerbohm Tree. Samuel Phelps and
        Frank Benson offered simpler scenery and fuller texts of
        the plays. Spectacular realism can be seen in Max
        Reinhardt's 1905 *A Midsummer Night's Dream*. The setting
        of Harley Granville-Barker's production of the play in 1914
        is briefly described with review excerpts. His general stage
        arrangement is said to be similar to those already used in
        Germany. Byrne praises his unabridged texts and the speed
        and continuity of playing that his setting allowed.

Granville-Barker is said to have offered a happy compromise
between the severe platform staging of scholarly enthusiasts
and the elaborate pictorial scenery to which the public was
accustomed. The article also mentions briefly the
productions of the play by Harcourt Williams (1929) and
Tyrone Guthrie (1937).

T1107a   Delannoy, Marcel. *Puck, opera-feérique en trois actes
         inspiré du "Songe d'une nuit d'été" de Shakespeare*
         [Puck, a fairy opera in three acts inspired by
         Shakespeare's "A Midsummer Night's Dream"]. Premiered
         at the Municipal Theatre of Strasbourg, France, 29
         January 1949. Composer, Marcel Delannoy. Adaptation,
         André Boll. Director, Roger Lalande. Costume and Scene
         Design, André Boll. Choreographer, Jean Combes.
         Musical Director, Ernest Bour. *Puck*, Roland April
         (dancer). *Titania*, Mme. Monda-Million
         (coloratura-soprano). *Oberon*, Georges Jongejans (bass).
         Theseus, Roger Barnier (tenor). *Hippolyta* (mute role),
         Eveline Miscke. *Demetrius*, Paul Derenne (light tenor).
         Helene, Marika-Stephanides (mezzo soprano). *Lysander*,
         Georges Verguet (*barytone-Martin*). *Hermia*, Jacqueline
         Drozen (light lyric soprano). *Quince*, N. Kedroff (comic
         tenor). *Snug*, B. Akiaroff (comic baritone). *Flute*, B.
         Borissoff (comic bass). *Egeus*, Paul Parmentier (actor).
         The Voices of the Forest.

         The premiere of the Delannoy opera. For the piano-vocal
         score and plot summary, see item 1001a..

T1108   Farjeon, Herbert. *The Shakespearean Scene, Dramatic
         Criticisms*. London, New York: Hutchinson, 1949. 195
         pp.

         This collection of Farjeon's reviews of Shakespearean
         productions in London, 1918-44, includes four of his pieces
         on productions of *A Midsummer Night's Dream*. In two of
         these he severely criticizes the 1924 London production
         directed by Basil Dean for its heavily cut text, cut to make
         room for more Mendelssohn music, and for its scenic
         contraptions. He writes approvingly of the Victorian-style
         staging of Tyrone Guthrie's production at the Old Vic in
         1937-38. He does not like Robert Atkins's Elizabethan style
         of producing the play; this is mentioned in some random

notes on staging problems in *A Midsummer Night's Dream* (p. 28).

T1109 "International News." *Shakespeare Survey*, 2 (1949), 126-29.

News of Shakespearean activities, scholarly and theatrical, from correspondents includes brief mentions of productions of *A Midsummer Night's Dream* in Austria and Italy in the past year.

T1110 *A Midsummer Night's Dream* presented at the Shakespeare Memorial Theatre, Stratford-upon-Avon, opening 23 April 1949. Director, Michael Benthall. Scene design, James Bailey. *Bottom*, John Slater. *Theseus*, Harry Andrews. *Helena*, Diana Wynyard. *Snug*, George Rose.

A lavishly staged production that critics found to be somewhat oddly disparate, with its heroic, Renaissance Athens, its dark menacing forest world, and its tulle-skirted fairies dancing to Mendelssohn.

Reviews: Harold Hobson, *Sunday Times* 24 April 1949; Bryan Harvey, *Birmingham Evening Dispatch*, 25 April 1949; *Birmingham Sunday Mercury*, 24 April 1949; *Yorkshire Post*, 25 April 1949; *Wolverhampton Express and Star*, 25 April 1949; *The Times*, 25 April 1949; *Guardian*, 25 April 1949; *Liverpool Post*, 25 April 1949; *Daily Telegraph*, 25 April 1949; *Birmingham Gazette*, 28 April 1949; *Stage*, 28 April 1949; *Royal Leamington Spa Courier*, 29 April 1949; *Punch*, 4 May 1949. (See also items T1119 and T1481.)

T1111 Williams, Harcourt. *Old Vic Saga.* London: Winchester Publications, 1949. 240 pp. Illustrated.

A history of the Old Vic Theatre, Williams' account includes coverage of his 1929 production of *A Midsummer Night's Dream*, memorable for his fresh direction and the several major talents in the cast. Among the cast were John Gielgud as Oberon, Leslie French as Puck, Margaret Webster as Hermia, and Gyles Isham as Bottom. Williams, whose direction bore the influences of William Poel and Harley Granville-Barker, sought in his productions to break from the traditional, slow rate of delivery of Shakespeare's

language and from the heavy accretions of pictorial scenery
and actor business. His belief that this play had been
written for a court wedding was reflected in Paul Smyth's
settings and costumes, which were suggestive of a Jacobean
court masque, and in the replacement of Mendelssohn's
music by English folk tunes. The production was revived in
1931 with Ralph Richardson as Bottom, wearing an
innovative ass's head that did not cover his face. Williams
comments here upon his general principles for
Shakespearean direction; more details on this production
will be found in Williams' *Four Years at the Old Vic* (1935).
Old Vic Saga includes photographs of Ralph Richardson as
Bottom and of Robert Helpmann as Oberon in the later Old
Vic production of 1937-38, directed by Tyrone Guthrie.
Williams briefly characterizes that production. (See item
T1306.)

T1112   Henriques, Alf. "Shakespeare and Denmark: 1900-1949."
        Shakespeare Survey, 3 (1950), 107-115.

        Provides an overview of Danish translations, criticism,
        and productions of the plays. In the discussion of the
        latter, there are brief mentions of stagings of *A Midsummer
        Night's Dream*; the play has been the most popular of the
        sixteen Shakespearean plays performed by the Royal
        Theatre since 1813.

T1113   "International News." *Shakespeare Survey*, 3 (1950),
        116-19.

        News from correspondents includes brief notices of at
        least four productions of *A Midsummer Night's Dream*,
        amateur and professional, in 1948-1949, including versions
        in Austria, Canada, Germany, Norway, and Poland. The
        production at the Norwegian Theatre in Oslo, directed by
        Sandro Malmquist, is admiringly described by Lorentz
        Eckhoff. The lovers fought and loved at a breath-taking
        pace. Trees and shrubs metamorphosed into human shapes.
        There were great-rooted trees and elves' dresses sewn with
        flowers.

T1113a Raeck, Kurt. "Shakespeare in the German Open-Air
        Theatre." *Shakespeare Survey*, 3 (1950), 95-97.

Reports that German open air theatre repertory has come to rely mainly upon Shakespeare's plays, including *A Midsummer Night's Dream*. The reason is the poet's reliance on the spoken word. The Elizabethan stage has been rediscovered in our time after being subordinated to the illusionary traditions of the continent. *A Midsummer Night's Dream* has proved to be by far the most popular play for open air production; however, such stages do pose a problem. Shakespeare's wood should be one of the imagination and "only the enclosed theatre can create the stage symbols necessary for its proper interpretation." The reality of a natural setting can distract.

T1114   Sandoe, James. "The Oregon Shakespeare Festival." *Shakespeare Quarterly*, 1 (1950), 5-11.

Describes briefly the nine summer seasons of Shakespeare at the Ashland Festival to date. Sandoe, who was a director there, comments on the quasi-Elizabethan Festival stage and on various productions, including a 1949 *A Midsummer Night's Dream* done in Elizabethan style costumes, without Mendelssohn's music, and with simple suggestive scenic pieces, such as a semi-circular green platform with a green baize covered bench for Titania's "bank." The text was "sharply cut." The production was indebted to the Harrow school production of Ronald Watkins. (It was reviewed in the *Ashland Daily Tidings*, 27 August 1949. See also items T1103 and T1115.)

T1115   Watkins, Ronald. *On Producing Shakespeare*. With drawings by Maurice Percival. London: Michael Joseph, [1950]. vi, 335 pp. Illustrated.

Pleads for rebuilding Shakespeare's Globe and staging the plays under the conditions for which they were created. Watkins, a disciple of Granville-Barker and William Poel and working from J. C. Adams' *The Globe Playhouse*, staged the plays at Harrow School for boys on a quasi-Elizabethan platform stage. *A Midsummer Night's Dream*, which he produced several times there, figures in the discussions of setting, costume ("The courtiers will be Elizabethan courtiers, the craftsman good Londoners"), gesture, characterization, and the "architecture" of the plays in their continuity. Percival's numerous drawings show possible blocking arrangements. (See also item T1103.)

T1116   "Current Theater Notes." *Shakespeare Quarterly*, 2
        (1951), 343-51.

        The editors began in this issue a listing of productions
        of the plays in professional, university, and community
        theatres in the U. S. and abroad; the listings seem to have
        been informally gathered and dependent upon
        correspondents. Twelve productions of *A Midsummer Night's
        Dream*, mostly amateur, are briefly noticed here. The two
        professional productions listed are those of the Old Vic in
        London and the Bankside Players in Regent's Park under
        the direction of Robert Atkins, with Atkins as Bottom. Such
        notices of productions are given in various formats in
        various issues hereafter.

T1117   Eisner, Doris. "Sieben Jahre Shakespeare in Öesterreich,
        1945-1951." *Shakespeare-Jahrbuch*, 87-88 (1951-52),
        180-97.

        Lists productions of Shakespeare's plays in Austria
        between 1945 and 1951, noticing some eight productions,
        school or professional, of *A Midsummer Night's Dream*.
        Among these were a 1947 production of Richard Flatter's
        translation of the play with Mendelssohn's music and, in the
        cast, Hugo Thimig as Bottom, Judith Holzmeister as Titania,
        and Curt Jürgens as Theseus; and a production for a Max
        Reinhardt seminar in Vienna in 1951.

T1118   "International Notes." *Shakespeare Survey*, 4 (1951),
        123-28.

        News from correspondents on Shakespearean activity,
        scholarly and theatrical, includes brief notices of frequent
        (unspecified) productions of *A Midsummer Night's Dream* in
        Germany in 1949 and of the Young Vic of London production
        in Oslo in 1949.

T1119   McBean, Angus. *The Shakespeare Memorial Theatre,
        1948-1950. A Photographic Record*, with forewords by
        Ivor Brown and Anthony Quayle. London: Reinhardt and
        Evans, 1951. 59 pp. Illustrated.

        Includes the cast list and ten black and white production
        photographs in large format of scenes from the 1949

Stratford-upon-Avon production, directed by Michael
Benthall (see item T1110).

T1120   *A Midsummer Night's Dream* presented at the Old Vic
        Theatre, London, 26 December 1951, Director, Tyrone
        Guthrie. Designer, Tanya Moiseiwitsch. *Bottom*, Paul
        Rogers. *Helena*, Irene Worth. *Theseus*, Douglas
        Campbell. *Quince*, Alan Badel.

        The setting was coolly romantic and Oberon and Titania
        somewhat sinister. Bottom and the setting pleased critics,
        but the production seemed to lack unity.

        Reviews: Ivor Brown, *The Observer*, 30 December 1951;
        The Times, 27 December 1951; *The Sketch*, 15 January
        1952. (See also items T1124, T1249 and T1166.)

T1120a Trewin, John Courtenay. *The Theatre Since 1900.*
        Illustrated from the Ray Mander and Joe Mitchenson
        Theatre Collection. London: Andrew Dakers, 1951. xvi,
        339 pp. Illustrated.

        Survey includes a favorable assessment of the Harley
        Granville-Barker Shakespearean productions at the Savoy
        Theatre (pp. 100-102): "He mounted the plays with beauty
        but also with simplicity . . . . He taught playgoers to hear
        the plays as they had never heard them before." Trewin
        describes the forest setting of Granville-Barker's *A
        Midsummer Night's Dream* and praises its simplicity. The
        1924 production of the play, directed by Basil Dean at
        Drury Lane, is unfavorably mentioned in passing, and the
        1945 Haymarket production, with John Gielgud as Oberon
        ("less enchanted than he used to be") is briefly
        characterized. There is also a favorable commentary on J.
        M. Barrie's *Dear Brutus* (1917), derived from *A Midsummer
        Night's Dream*.

T1121   Hogan, Charles Beecher. *Shakespeare in the Theatre,
        1701-1800.* 2 vols. Oxford: Clarendon Press, 1952-57.

        A chronological list of Shakespearean performances in
        London (Volume I: 1701-1750; Volume II: 1751-1800). Cast
        lists are given for each performance; there are charts
        showing the relative popularity of each play; and box office

receipts are given. Included are the performances of *A Midsummer Night's Dream* and its adaptations in 1716, 1755, and 1763. (See also item T1187.)

T1122   "International Notes." *Shakespeare Survey,* 5 (1952), 111-18.

News from correspondents on Shakespearean activities, scholarly and theatrical, includes brief notices of at least five productions of *A Midsummer Night's Dream* in four different countries in 1950-1951, including Germany, Czechoslovakia, and the U. S., where it was among the most often produced of the plays.

T1123   "Shakespeare Productions in the United Kingdom: 1950." *Shakespeare Survey,* 5 (1952), 119-20.

Included in the annual listing, compiled by the Shakespeare Memorial Library in Birmingham, are three productions of *A Midsummer Night's Dream* in 1950: by the Renegade Company at Ilford Town Hall; by the Oxford University Drama Society in New College Gardens, Oxford; and in Pittville Gardens, Cheltenham, directed by Leslie French.

T1124   Trewin, John Courtenay. *A Play To-night.* London: Elek Books, 1952. 220 pp.

Contains his generally favorable review (pp. 153-56) of the Old Vic production of *A Midsummer Night's Dream* directed by Tyrone Guthrie. (See item T1120.) He praises especially the Bottom of Paul Rogers and the "elegantly austere" setting of Tanya Moiseiwitsch. Rogers' Bottom, speaking in a full mid-Dartmoor accent, is monstrously sincere" and never attempts desperately to be funny. Guthrie was less successful with the fairies.

T1125   Crosse, Gordon. *Shakespeare Playgoing, 1890-1952.* London: A. R. Mowbray, 1940; reissued, 1941; rev. ed., Illustrated from the Raymond Mander and Joe Mitchenson Theatre Collection, 1953. 159 pp. Illustrated.

Included in this often-cited diary of a long-time Shakespearean playgoer are many details and judgments on several significant productions of *A Midsummer Night's Dream*. There are also discussions of the staging and acting style in general in the late Victorian theatre of Henry Irving and Herbert Beerbohm Tree and of the staging and acting in the post-World War I era. He recalls the landmark production of *A Midsummer Night's Dream* by Tree and Tree's too-elaborate Bottom. He recalls fondly the Bottom of Robert Atkins, whom he saw in the role nine times over the years, and comments on Regent's Park Open Air Theatre productions. From the 1929-31 Old Vic production, directed by Harcourt Williams, he recalls Ralph Richardson's Bottom; he was too sweet and refined for "bully Bottom," but there was an appealing wistful manner that gave "a new edge" to his scenes with Titania.

T1126 "Current Theatre Notes." *Shakespeare Quarterly*, 4 (1953), 61-75.

Annual listing of productions of Shakespeare's plays includes brief notices of nineteen productions of *A Midsummer Night's Dream*, some with a few notes on the productions or casts and production credits. Among those listed are productions by several U.S. universities, by the Old Vic, in the round in Dallas (directed by Margo Jones), by an Australian touring company, by the National Theatre of Greece in Athens, in Budapest, Zurich, and Liverpool (with costumes after Botticelli), and in Avon, Connecticut (with costumes after Arthur Rackham's illustrations of the play and court processions inspired by Max Reinhardt).

T1127 Guthrie, Tyrone and Robertson Davies. *Renown at Stratford: A Record of the Shakespeare Festival in Canada.* Toronto: Clarke Irwin and Company, 1953. viii, 127 pp. Illustrated.

Provides historical background on the development of the festival and the then unique open stage upon which *A Midsummer Night's Dream* would be produced in 1960, 1968, 1976, and 1977.

T1128 "International Notes." *Shakespeare Survey*, 6 (1953), 117-25.

News from correspondents includes brief notices of at least thirteen productions of *A Midsummer Night's Dream* in eight different nations in 1951-1952, including Australia, Austria, Czechoslovakia (4), Germany, Italy (at the Teatro Valle directed by Guido Salvini and designed by Giulio Coltellacchi), The Netherlands, and New Zealand. Marcel Delannoy's new opera, *Puck* (based on *A Midsummer Night's Dream*) was staged in Berlin. The production of the play at the Flensburg, Germany, theatre was "hyper-modern in concept," with a setting in the style of Oscar Kokoschka and the actors costumed "in bikini shirts, samba socks and sun glasses."

T1129   Kemp, T. C., and John Courtenay Trewin. *The Stratford Festival: A History of the Shakespeare Memorial Theatre.* Birmingham: Cornish, 1953. xxiii, 269 pp. Illustrated.

Provides a chronological history of the Shakespeare Memorial Theatre with brief characterizations of major productions and major performers. There are some cast lists, and the appendices include lists of plays performed at the festivals from 1879-1953 and lists of players in the festival companies. Photos of the interiors of the old and new Memorial Theatres are included. There are brief descriptions of the productions of *A Midsummer Night's Dream* in the following years: 1888, directed by Frank Benson; 1932, directed by W. Bridges-Adams, with scenery by Norman Wilkinson; 1937, directed by E. Martin Browne; 1942, directed by B. Iden Payne; 1944, directed by Robert Atkins; and 1949, directed by Michael Benthall. (See also items T1093, T1097, T1110 and T1481.)

T1130   Miller, Edwin Haviland. "Shakespeare at the Brattle Theatre." *Shakespeare Quarterly*, 4 (1953), 59-60.

For a production of *A Midsummer Night's Dream*, the director (unnamed) of the professional repertory theatre company at the Brattle Theatre in Cambridge, Massachusetts, utilized "a highly ornate, neo-classical eighteenth century setting," with Oberon and Titania entering in elaborate chariots, Puck as a neoclassical Mercury on winged feet, the royal party with parasols and high heels, and a forest with neoclassical doorways and an elaborate chandelier above stage center. Bottom (actor unnamed) was done in the Groucho Marx vein. Miller says too much emphasis upon décor overwhelmed the action and poetry, and he found the rustics striving desperately to be hilarious. Directors should trust to Shakespeare, and simplicity is preferable to ostentation and precious artificiality.

T1131   "Shakespeare Productions in the United Kingdom: 1951." *Shakespeare Survey*, 6 (1953), 126-28.

Included in the annual listing, compiled by the Shakespeare Memorial Library, Birmingham, are four productions of *A Midsummer Night's Dream* in 1951, the three of which elsewhere unnoticed in this bibliography are those at the Open Air Theatre, Regent's Park, directed by Robert Atkins; at Walpole Park, Ealing, by the First Folio Theatre Company, directed by Kenneth McClellan; and at the Playhouse, Nottingham, directed by Guy Verney.

T1132   Sprague, Arthur Colby. *Shakespearian Players and Performances*. Cambridge: Harvard University Press, 1953. vii, 222 pp.

Discusses the changing trends in Shakespearean staging from William Poel through Harley Granville-Barker. There are brief references to the outdoor productions of *A Midsummer Night's Dream* of Sir Philip Ben Greet and to the productions of *A Midsummer Night's Dream* at the Harrow school by Ronald Watkins. (See also items T1103 and T1515.)

T1132a   Cohen, Selma Jeanne. "*A Midsummer Night's Dream*, Many Composers Have Attempted Musical Settings." *Musical America*, 74, 11 (September 1954), 5, 18.

Surveys musical treatments of the play from Shakespeare's day to the 1940s. The article was written on the occasion of the upcoming Old Vic and Sadler's Wells Ballet production at the Metropolitan Opera House. Cohen notes that it was probably the Children of the Chapel who did the singing fairies for the original performance, and points out that in the 1661 *Merrie Conceited Humours of Bottom the Weaver*, Titania's lullaby is marked "Fayries first dance and then sing"; that Bottom's tongs and bones request is followed by the designation "Musik Tongs Rurall

Musik"; and that the Bergomask dance is indicated. Briefly
Cohen characterizes musical adaptations of the play from
Purcell through the eighteenth century down to the 1816
Reynolds opera. Mendelssohn's incidental music and
overture are characterized at more length. Among the
contemporary productions whose musical scores are briefly
discussed here are the Reinhardt film of 1935, Ronald
Watkins' Elizabethan production, with madrigals, at Harrow
School in 1945, and Jacques Ibert's setting for a 1942
production at Chateau Montredon in Marseilles. The author
says the play is susceptible to many different conceptions
in musical settings and so has inspired many composers.

T1133   "Current Theatre Notes." *Shakespeare Quarterly*, 5
        (1954), 51-69.

        Includes (p. 63) brief notices of fifteen productions of *A
Midsummer Night's Dream, amateur and professional, in the
U. S. and Europe. With some there are brief notes on the
staging features or partial casts and production credits.
Notable on this list is a production with a company of
nearly 100 on the grounds of the Bishop's Palace in
Norwich, England, directed by Nugent Monck, who
announced it as his final production.

T1134   *Enciclopedia dello Spettacolo*, s. v. "William Shakespeare,
        7a-g, 'Fortuna.'"

        Provides seven, separate signed entries (in Italian) on
the stage history of the plays in England, France, Italy,
Spain, Germany, Russia, and the United States. A selected
bibliography follows each. Each makes brief mention of one
or two major productions of *A Midsummer Night's Dream*.
Among the photographs in the copiously illustrated volume
will be found one of the Birmingham Repertory Theatre's
1936 production of the play showing the forest, with Bottom
and Titania, with setting and costumes by Paul Shelving.

T1135   Fallois, Bernard de. "Shakespeare á Paris." *La Revue de
        Paris*, March 1954, pp. 91-96.

        Includes a review of *A Midsummer Night's Dream* in
Paris. Not seen.

T1136 *Grove's Dictionary of Music and Musicians*, 5th edition.
s. v. "William Shakespeare."

Lists composers of songs and incidental music composed
for each of Shakespeare's plays including operas and
adaptations. Twenty-eight composers are listed under *A
Midsummer Night's Dream* including Arne, Aylward, Bishop,
Castelnuovo-Tedesco, Cooke, Delannoy, Purcell, Hüe,
Křenek, Mendelssohn, Nixon, Orff, Satie, Smith, Suppé,
and Vaughn Williams. For additional composers, see items
T1230 and T1324.

T1137 Helpmann, Robert. "Formula for Midsummer Magic."
Theatre Arts, 38, 9 (September 1954), 76-77, 95.

Discusses dance style problems faced in the 1954
production of *A Midsummer Night's Dream* by the Old Vic
and Sadler's Wells ballet, directed by Michael Benthall. (See
item T1138.) Helpmann, who danced the role of Oberon (and
who had played it in the 1937-1938 Old Vic production
directed by Tyrone Guthrie), writes that Benthall wanted
the production to be based on classical Greece as seen
through Elizabethan eyes and that completely classical Greek
fairies were in conflict with the romantic ballet traditions of
Les Sylphides, in which the fairies wear the customary
short skirts and point shoes. In this production, point
shoes were reserved for Titania (danced by Moira Shearer).
Helpmann believed casting classically trained dancers in the
roles of Oberon and Titania (for the first time in this
production) would make the characters more "otherworldly."

T1137a "International Notes." *Shakespeare Survey*, 7 (1954),
107-117.

Included in the news from correspondents are notices of
(at least) twelve productions of *A Midsummer Night's Dream*
in 1952-53 in Belgium, Czechoslovakia, Germany, Greece,
Italy, Malaya, South Africa, Sweden, Switzerland, and
Turkey. Notable among these were the production directed
by Gustav Rudolf Sellner at Darmstadt, with Carl Orff's
music; the Greek National Theatre's production in Athens,
directed by Charles Koun with sets and costumes by S.
Vassiliou and music by M. Hatzidakis; the outdoor
production in Kuala Lumpur, directed by David Lyttle; and
a production at the National Theatre of Ankara, directed by

Carl Ebert, which used a Turkish verse translation by
Nureddi Sevin, and was the first production of the play in
Turkish.

T1138   *A Midsummer Night's Dream.* Presented at the Edinburgh
Opera House, 31 August 1954, and subsequently at the
New York Metropolitan Opera House, 21 September 1954,
and on a tour of major U. S. and Canadian cities, 1954.
Produced by the Old Vic Company. Director, Michael
Benthall. Choreographers, Robert Helpmann and
Frederick Ashton. Design, Robin and Christopher
Ironside. *Oberon,* Robert Helpmann. *Titania,* Moira
Shearer. *Bottom,* Stanley Holloway.

A scenically lavish, romantic production with the
combined forces of the Old Vic Company, the Sadler's Wells
Ballet, an orchestra of sixty for Mendelssohn, and thirteen
tons of pictorial scenery. It enjoyed considerably popular
success and media coverage, although some New York
critics found it a monumental betrayal of Shakespeare's play
and anachronistic. RCA Victor recorded the full production
on a three-record album. (See item T1139.)

Reviews: W. A. Darlington, *New York Times,* 1
September 1954; *The Times,* 1 September 1954; Brooks
Atkinson, *New York Times,* 22 and 23 September; Walter
Kerr, New York *Herald Tribune,* 23 September 1954; John
McClain, *Journal American,* 22 September 1954; Richard
Watts, Jr., New York *Post,* 22 September 1954; *New York
Times Magazine,* 19 September 1954; John Chapman, New
York *Daily News,* 22 September 1954; Robert Coleman, New
York *Daily Mirror,* 22 September 1954; William Hawkins, *New
York World-Telegram and The Sun,* 22 September 1954;
Arthur Colby Sprague, *Shakespeare Quarterly,* 6 (1955),
423-27.

T1139   *A Midsummer Night's Dream.* [Recording of the 1954
production of the Old Vic and the Sadler's Wells Ballet.]
Director, Michael Benthall. *Oberon,* Robert Helpmann.
Titania, Moira Shearer. *Bottom,* Stanley Holloway.
Mendelssohn's music performed by the BBC Symphony
Orchestra, conducted by Sir Malcolm Sergeant. Three
33-1/3 rpm phonodiscs. RCA Victor LM-6115. Recorded
in England *circa* 1954.

Accompanying album brochure includes photos of three designs for the settings and costumes of the production. A note on the text indicates that several small cuts have been made and that IV.ii has been omitted entirely. (See item T1138.)

T1140   *A Midsummer Night's Dream* presented at the Shakespeare Memorial Theatre, Stratford-upon-Avon, 23 March 1954. Director, George Devine. Designer, Motley. Music, Roberto Gerhard. *Oberon,* Powys Thomas. *Titania,* Muriel Pavlow. *Bottom,* Anthony Quayle. *Theseus,* Keith Michell. *Quince,* Leo McKern. *Flute,* Ian Bannen. *Helena,* Barbara Jefford. *Puck,* David O'Brien.

In Motley's setting of stylized, metallic trees, Oberon and Titania were costumed as if from the world of exotic birds, and Puck appeared to be from the insect world. Some critics were impressed by the new approach and the visual beauty; some were alienated by the birds, insects, and the chilling November landscape.

Reviews: *The Times,* 24 March and 1 April 1954; *Daily Worker,* 24 and 26 March 1954; *Daily Telegraph,* 26 March 1954; *Bolton Evening News,* 26 March 1954; T. C. Worsley, *New Statesman,* 27 March 1954; *The Observer,* 28 March 1954; Richard David, *Shakespeare Quarterly,* 5 (1954), 385-94 (photo); Richard David, *Shakespeare Survey,* 8 (1955), photographs. (See also T1481.)

T1141   "Shakespeare Productions in the United Kingdom: 1952." *Shakespeare Survey,* 7 (1954), 118-20.

Included in the annual listing, compiled by the Shakespeare Memorial Library, Birmingham, are notices of three productions of *A Midsummer Night's Dream* in 1952: at the Harrow School, directed by Ronald Watkins; at The Playhouse by the Liverpool Repertory Theatre, directed by Willard Stoker (with settings and costumes after Botticelli); and at the Theatre Royal, Windsor, by the Windsor Repertory Company, directed by Leslie French and John Counsell.

T1142   Speaight, Robert. *William Poel and the Elizabethan Revival.* London: William Heinemann, 1954. (Annual

Publication for the Society for Theatre Research for
1951-52.) 302 pp. Illustrated.

Describes Poel's experiments with an unlocalized,
Elizabethan platform stage and his emphasis upon the poetic
values of the plays of Shakespeare when played on such a
stage. Both of Poel's thrusts influenced many actors and
directors in the late Edwardian and post-World War I
theatre in England, despite some of his personal
eccentricities. Among the Poel-influenced directors who
broke with nineteenth century pictorial illustration of the
plays was Harley Granville-Barker. Poel himself never
produced *A Midsummer Night's Dream*. There are appendices
listing his productions and articles about his work. (See
also items T1232 and T1345.)

T1143   Sprague, Arthur Colby. *The Stage Business in
        Shakespeare's Plays: A Postscript.* London: The Society
        for Theatre Research, 1954. 35 pp.

The pamphlet, which continues the work Sprague began
in *Shakespeare and the Actors: The Stage Business in His
Plays (1660-1905)* (T1098), includes mention of one piece of
business in Ronald Watkins's Harrow School production of *A
Midsummer Night's Dream*. Hippolyta was shown savoring
the possibility of the hunt with Theseus by practicing a few
spear thrusts. She was then disappointed when the hunt
was interrupted by the discovery of the lovers.

T1144   Stroedel, Wolfgang. "90th Anniversary Celebration of the
        Deutsche Shakespeare-Gesellschaft." *Shakespeare
        Quarterly*, 5 (1954), 317-22.

Describes a production of *A Midsummer Night's Dream*
directed by Gustav Rudolf Sellner, with new music by Carl
Orff, which was performed at the ninetieth anniversary
meeting of the German Shakespeare Society in Bochum.
Sellner's staging of Schlegel's translation was derivative of
a notable, well-received production that he had done in
Darmstadt in 1952, but on this occasion there was new
scenery by the same designer, Franz Merz. The conception
was that *A Midsummer Night's Dream* is not a playful love
story, but "deals with man confronted by elemental forces,
as represented in a world of fairies and elves." Oberon,
Titania, and Puck were horned (photograph). The stage

was a circular, tilted disc, changed for the forest scenes only by the addition of large leaves on wire frames and atmospheric lighting. The lovers were in modern dress; Bottom was accompanied always by a double bass player. The quality of the acting is praised in general terms.

T1144a Boas, Guy. *Shakespeare and the Young Actor: A Guide to Production.* London: Rockliff Publishing Corporation, 1955. xii, 126 pp. Reprint. London: Baurie and Rockliff, 1961. xi, 140 pp.

Describes productions of Shakespeare's plays with the boys at Sloane School in Chelsea. The former headmaster argues that we should not view Shakespeare's use of boys in women's roles as a second-best arrangement and suggests that the classical drama is in some ways better suited to school stages than to commercial theatres. In production method, Boas offers an alternative to Ronald Watkins's style, which used an Elizabethan bare platform at Harrow School for boys. Boas offers a permanent two arch scenic structure on a proscenium stage, a structure that can be variously painted and is used with various painted drops behind (diagram). His suggestions on costumes range from historical costumes to modern dress. Chapter four describes his staging of twelve of the plays including *A Midsummer Night's Dream*. Walter de la Mare wrote its program notes, which stressed the intensity of the love interest of the quartet of young lovers. The production reflected this and sought to raise the rustics to a higher comic level. Bottom woke to strains from *Der Rosenkavalier* and Boas also drew on music by Purcell, Byrd, Mendelssohn, and Stravinsky. Of major interest for Boas's case for the effectiveness of boy performances is a long letter to Boas from Sean O'Casey who saw a Sloane School performance of *A Midsummer Night's Dream*: "I've never seen a fresher or more charming performance of a Shakespeare play. . . . In all performances by professional actors we see him through a glass darkly; here, for once in a while, we met him face to face." There are also five photographs of scenes from the Sloane production of the play.

T1145 "Current Theatre Notes." *Shakespeare Quarterly,* 6 (1955), 67-88.

Included in this annual listing of productions of the
plays, are twenty-six productions of *A Midsummer Night's
Dream* in the 1954-1955 season, including American and
European productions. Among them is a production at the
University of Texas at Austin, directed by B. Iden Payne;
the issue contains a photograph of this production. Some
entries in the listing include brief notes on the staging
and/or partial cast lists and production credits.

T1146   Guthrie, Sir Tyrone. "Shakespeare at Stratford,
         Ontario." *Shakespeare Survey*, 8 (1955), 127-31.

Characterizing the planning and the goals of the
Canadian festival, Guthrie describes the architectural thrust
stage of the Festival Theatre that he and Tanya
Moiseiwitsch designed. *A Midsummer Night's Dream* was done
on this stage, which featured functional Elizabethan
features with no scenery, in 1960 and 1968, and on the
modified version of it in 1976 and 1977. Guthrie also speaks
of its advantages: it stresses the "ritual" rather than the
"illusionary" quality of performance; it is easier to arrange
groupings and flow of movement on it; both soliloquies and
conversational scenes work effectively on it; and the
auditorium that nearly surrounds it accommodates more
spectators.

T1147   "International Notes." *Shakespeare Survey*, 8 (1955),
         118-22.

Included in the news from correspondents are brief
notices of four productions of *A Midsummer Night's Dream*
in four countries in 1953-54. Notable among these were an
elaborately staged production by the Royal Flemish Theatre
on April 27, 1954, to celebrate the company's centenary; a
swift-moving two setting production by the Finnish National
Theatre that celebrated its eightieth year with this play,
which had been in this theatre's repertory since 1891; and
a production in Belgium by the Theatre Royal du Park of
Brussels that used a translation by Jacques Copeau and
which was directed by Oscar Lejeune.

T1148   Long, John H. *Shakespeare's Use of Music. A Study of
         the Music and Its Performance in the Original Production*

of Seven Comedies. Gainesville: University of Florida
Press, 1955. xv, 213 pp.

Examines the music called for in the text of *A Midsummer
Night's Dream*, in which more music is required than in the
previous plays), and envisions a performance of the play
for a noble wedding at Sir George Carey's home, with music
by John Dowland. Long suggests some contemporary song
settings and instrumentation. For "You spotted snakes with
double tongue" (the fairy lullaby), which Long suggests
Shakespeare himself might have provided the original melody
for, Long recommends a 1599 lullaby by Anthony Holborne.
The music for it is provided. He also provides a melody for
the Bergamask. In his discussion of the problem of "The
Song," debated by editors and scholars since Samuel
Johnson, he disagrees with Richmond Noble (*Shakespeare's
Use of Song*, 1923), who suggested that the song is to
begin with "Now until the break of day." Long believes it
begins with "Through this house give glimmering light,"
and adds that Oberon and Titania might have intoned rather
than sung their lines. He believes it would not have been
in character for royalty to sing in public, fairy or
otherwise. He would have the musicians hidden during
performance, so as not to break the illusion of fairies and
"supernatural melodies."

T1149   Purdom, C. B. *Harley Granville-Barker: Man of the
        Theatre, Dramatist and Scholar.* London: Rockliff, 1955.
        xiv, 322 pp.

Traces Granville-Barker's career in a documented,
chronological biography. Included are descriptions of his
three Shakespearean productions at the Savoy Theatre in
London between 1912 and 1914. Among these was his
controversial *A Midsummer Night's Dream* with the golden
fairies, designed by Norman Wilkinson. With his suggestive,
non-illusionistic scenic decor, Granville-Barker sought the
fluidity that would put the emphasis upon Shakespeare's
word music; his text for the production was virtually
uncut. The actors spoke rapidly, and much customary
business was cut. Purdom describes the staging and sets
briefly, samples the critical responses, both in London and
New York, and includes four photographs of the production
showing the different settings. (See also items T1366, T1392
and T1401.)

T1150   Robinson, Horace W. "Shakespeare, Ashland, Oregon."
        Shakespeare Quarterly, 6 (1955), 447-51.

        Reviews favorably the 1955 production of *A Midsummer
        Night's Dream* at the Ashland, Oregon, festival, directed by
        James Sandoe. There was a "nice balance of all elements.
        Gay, elegant, bawdy, and wistful by turn . . . ." But it
        is also said that the lovers "became a dominant comic
        element" and that the Bottom of Richard T. Jones was
        broadly given and "grossly effeminate." Puck was zestful
        but did not handle the verse well. Douglas Russell's
        costumes provided opulence for the court and "gossamer
        lightness" for the fairies.

T1151   "Shakespeare Productions in the United Kingdom: 1953."
        Shakespeare Survey, 8 (1955), 123-26.

        Included in the annual listing by the Shakespeare
        Memorial Library, Birmingham, are two productions of *A
        Midsummer Night's Dream* in 1953, one directed by Nugent
        Monck in the Palace Gardens at Norwich, and one at the
        Library Theatre, Manchester, directed by Stuart Latham.

T1152   Sprague, Arthur Colby. "Shakespeare on the New York
        Stage, 1954-1955." *Shakespeare Quarterly*, 6 (1955),
        423-27.

        Characterizes, with well-selected details, the Old Vic
        production of *A Midsummer Night's Dream* in 1954 (see
        T1138), among other offerings of the season. Sprague found
        it ponderous and anachronistic in its pictorial scenery and
        its use of Mendelssohn and a *corps de ballet*. Puck led
        Demetrius and Lysander up and down behind a gauze
        curtain on which a spider's web was painted, and Titania
        brought Bottom on in a sort of gondola. Bottom
        sentimentally awoke to find a rose in his hair rather than
        hay in his pouch. Act IV.ii was cut, and the text generally
        was poorly spoken.

T1153   Felheim, Marvin. *The Theatre of Augustin Daly: An
        Account of the Late Nineteenth Century American Stage.*
        Cambridge: Harvard University Press, 1956. ix, 329 pp.
        Illustrated.

Coverage of Daly's career includes (Chapter 6) descriptions of his productions of Shakespeare. Felheim describes and is critical of Daly's 1888 production of *A Midsummer Night's Dream* that featured exceptionally lavish Grecian palaces and forests, a galley ship that Theseus employed to bring the lovers home to Athens (with a diorama), and blinking electric lights in the hair of the fairies. "In Daly's hands," he says, the play "became a spectacle, not a play at all." Daly cut many of the best poetic passages, and there were also some prudish cuts, such as the omission of the phrase "virgin patent." Daly's comedians were unable to handle the verse well, according to the critics cited. William Winter is said to have been responsible for the cutting of some of the Shakespeare plays Daly produced. (See also items T1437 and T1351.)

T1154   Hewes, Henry. "Broadway Postscript: No Great Shakes." *Saturday Review*, 18 January 1956, p. 18.

Coverage includes an unfavorable review of a production of *A Midsummer Night's Dream* off-Broadway by a group called the Shakespearewrights.

T1155   [McBean, Angus, and Ivor Brown.] *Shakespeare Memorial Theatre, 1954-56.* A photographic record, with a critical analysis by Ivor Brown. Photographs by Angus McBean. London: Max Reinhardt, 1956. 66 pp. Illustrated.

Includes in the review of the two seasons a brief characterization of the 1954 *A Midsummer Night's Dream* at Stratford-upon-Avon, directed by George Devine, the cast list, and six production photos. (See item T1140.) Brown notes that it did not suit romantics. There was no Mendelssohn in the production, which featured Oberon and Titania costumed as birds and Puck costumed as an insect-like creature. Alan Dent is quoted as saying that Roberto Gerhard's score was "a not unpleasing mixture of frogs croaking and the horns of elfland faintly blowing."

T1156   Pearson, Hesketh. *Beerbohm Tree: His Life and Laughter.* London: Methuen, 1956. xiv, 250 pp. Illustrated.

This biography provides background for, and some brief characterization of, Tree's production of *A Midsummer Night's Dream* in 1900. Pearson says Tree's portrayal of Bottom "was a comment on the actor-manager system, the 'star' actor, as it were, pulling his own leg." He cites Henry Arthur Jones as saying "Tree as Bottom had a blank wall of vanity . . . ."

T1157   Sellman, Priscilla M. "The Old Globe's Sixth Season in San Diego." *Shakespeare Quarterly*, 7 (1956), 419-22.

Reviews the amateur production of *A Midsummer Night's Dream* at the San Diego National Shakespeare Festival, directed by Peter Bucknell. The fairies wore Kabuki-inspired costumes and were accompanied by oriental music. Theseus and Hippolyta wore regal attire of a contemporary Western cut, the lovers were in petticoats and Napoleonic uniforms, and Bottom and the mechanicals were in Elizabethan dress. "A ripe sense of display, in Mr. Bucknell's case, tended to obscure the meaning of the play." Photograph of the fairies opposite p. 429.

T1157a   Taubman, Howard. "Music: Midsummer Night." *New York Times*, 20 July 1956, p. 9.

Reviews favorably a production of *A Midsummer Night's Dream* in the tent of the Empire State Music Festival in Ellenville, New York, in the Catskills. The chief feature of it was Carl Orff's music for the play; this was its American premiere. Leopold Stokowski conducted the Symphony of the Air and a choral group. Orff's score is characterized as offering some quasi-Elizabethan melodies at times, as sparingly instrumented, and as generally designed to keep Shakespeare in the foreground. Mendelssohn's score, says Taubman, is "more rewarding when heard by itself on a symphonic program." Basil Langton directed, Basil Rathbone played Oberon and Nancy Wickwire, Titania. Red Buttons played Bottom "like a vaudevillian about to plunge into a buck and wing."

T1158   "International Notes." *Shakespeare Survey*, 10 (1957), 115-22.

News from correspondents on scholarly and theatrical Shakespearean activities includes mention of four productions of *A Midsummer Night's Dream* in three different nations in 1955: one by the National Theatre of Sweden, directed by Karl Rognar Gierow; one in Bern, Switzerland; and one at the Shakespeare Festival in Ashland, Oregon (see T1150).

T1159   Mander, Raymond, and Joe Mitchenson. *A Picture History of the British Theatre.* London: Hulton Press, 1957. 160 pp. Illustrated.

Includes a black and white reproduction of the watercolor of the quarrel scene between Oberon and Titania as staged in the Charles Kean production of 1856. Also reproduced is a photo of the same scene from the 1914 production directed by Harley Granville-Barker. There is also a photograph of Bottom and Titania in the Old Vic production of 1937, directed by Tyrone Guthrie.

T1160   *A Midsummer Night's Dream* presented by the Old Vic, London, in repertory opening 23 December 1957 and closing 15 February 1958. Director, Michael Benthall. Designer, James Bailey. Music by Mendelssohn. *Oberon*, Derek Godfrey. *Titania*, Joyce Redman. *Puck*, Keith Taylor. *Bottom*, Frankie Howerd. *Helena*, Coral Browne.

A very pretty, neo-romantic production, given for the Christmas season, that was generally critically praised as "delightful" and that proved popular (sixty-three performances). James Bailey's setting employed simplified Corinthian pillars with rich swag draperies for Theseus' palace and a very delicate, elegant wood, with what Muriel St. Clare Byrne called "a Charles Kean moon." Coral Browne, who was simple-minded Helena, and Frankie Howerd, a well known music hall comedian who played Bottom, were the main features of the cast.

Reviews: *The Times*, 25 December 1957; *Sunday Times*, 29 December 1957; Peter Roberts, *Plays and Players*, February 1958, with photographs by Angus McBean; "F. S.," *Theatre World*, 54 (February 1958), with five photographs by Tony Armstrong Jones; Muriel St. Clare Byrne, *Shakespeare Quarterly*, 9 (1958), 507-30. See also items T1168, T1169 and T1249.

T1161   "Shakespeare Productions in the United Kingdom: 1955."
        Shakespeare Survey, 10 (1957), 123-25.

        Included in the annual listing compiled by the
        Shakespeare Memorial Library, Birmingham, are two
        productions of *A Midsummer Night's Dream*, that at the
        Open Air Theatre, Regent's Park, directed by Robert
        Atkins, and that by the Windsor Theatre Guild, directed by
        Charles Hunt.

T1162   Shakespeare, William. *A Midsummer Night's Dream*. With a
        New Introduction by Sir Ralph Richardson. Designs in
        Colour by Oliver Messel. London: Folio Society, 1957. 88
        pp. Illustrated.

        Included in this edition of the play are eight color plates
        reproducing Messel's designs for the 1937-1938 Old Vic
        production of the play, directed by Tyrone Guthrie, which
        returned to all the Victorian iconography for the play, with
        the fairies as a gauzy *corp de Sylphides* and the
        Mendelssohn score. Robert Helpmann was Oberon. Vivian
        Leigh played Titania, and Ralph Richardson was Bottom.

T1163   Shedd, Robert G. "Shakespeare at Antioch, 1957: Past
        Record and Present Achievement." *Shakespeare
        Quarterly*, 8 (1957), 521-25.

        Includes a generally favorable review of the *A
        Midsummer Night's Dream* at the Antioch Shakespeare
        Festival, Yellow Springs, Ohio, in 1957, directed by Ellis
        Rabb. Notable among the cast were Patrick Hines, who
        offered Bottom as a sweetly solicitous bumpkin, Grace
        Chapman as Helena, Clayton Corzatte as Oberon, and Chase
        Cooley as Titania.

T1164   Sorell, Walter. "Shakespeare and the Dance."
        Shakespeare Quarterly, 8 (1957), 367-84.

        Includes a discussion of the historical background of the
        Bergomask dance, called for at the end of *A Midsummer
        Night's Dream*, and there is some discussion of romantic
        ballet traditions attached to the play, with concern
        expressed that Mendelssohn and the ballet may overshadow
        the play. There is also a description of a baroque-style

staging of Purcell's *The Fairy Queen* in an adaptation by
John Reich and Nicholas Goldschmidt, presented by the
Columbia University Theatre Associates in cooperation with
the Columbia Department of Music, on November 28th, 1956.

T1165   Speaight, Robert. "The Dream in South Bend:
        Shakespeare in the Middle West." *Tablet*, 27 April 1957,
        pp. 393-94.

        Relates his experiences as a guest director of *A
        Midsummer Night's Dream* in the new Arts Center at St.
        Mary's College in South Bend, Indiana.

T1166   Williamson, Audrey. *Old Vic Drama 2, 1947-1957.* London:
        Rockliff, 1957. xii, 224 pp. Illustrated.

        Includes a brief description of Tyrone Guthrie's Old Vic
        production of *A Midsummer Night's Dream* of 1951. (See item
        T1120.)

T1167   Brett-Evans, D. "Der 'Sommernachtstraum' in
        Deutschland, 1600-1650." *Zeitschrift für deutsche
        Philologie*, 77 (1958), 371-83. Not seen.

T1168   Byrne, Muriel St. Clare. "The Shakespeare Season at the
        Old Vic, 1957-58, and Stratford-upon-Avon, 1958."
        Shakespeare Quarterly, 9 (1958), 507-30.

        Includes her description of the popular Old Vic
        production of *A Midsummer Night's Dream* in 1957, directed
        by Michael Benthall, which she found delightful. (See item
        T1160.) Especially praised are James Bailey's settings (with
        "a Charles Kean moon"), the Bottom of music-hall and
        pantomime star, Frankie Howerd, and Coral Browne's
        "romantic, beautiful, statuesque Helena."

T1169   Clarke, Mary. *Shakespeare at the Old Vic.* London:
        Hamish Hamilton Limited, 1958. 58 pp. Illustrated.

        Included in this photo-illustrated account of the Old
        Vic's 1957-58 season is a detailed description of the popular
        1957 production of *A Midsummer Night's Dream* at the Old

Vic, directed by Michael Benthall (see entry T1160). "There were snatches of Mendelssohn, dancers from the Royal Ballet School tripping about as fairies, wonderful fooling from all the mechanicals, and several outstandingly good performances," among which, she says, was that of music hall comedian Frankie Howerd in the role of Bottom. The cast list is provided. There are five photographs of the production, including one of James Bailey's "exquisitely pretty setting" for the forest. There is also a note on a private performance of the last act for Queen Elizabeth II on March 18, 1958.

T1170   Griffin, Alice. "Current Theatre Notes, 1956-1957." *Shakespeare Quarterly,* 9 (1958), 39-58.

Included in the annual listing of productions of Shakespeare's plays are twelve productions of *A Midsummer Night's Dream,* including American university and regional theatre productions and several European productions. There are occasionally a few notes on a production and/or a partial cast list.

T1171   "International Notes." *Shakespeare Survey,* 11 (1958), 117-23.

Included in the news of theatrical and scholarly activity in 1956 from Shakespearean correspondents are brief notices of thirteen productions of *A Midsummer Night's Dream* in six different nations, including Czechoslovakia (6), Germany, Japan, South Africa, Sweden, and the U. S.

T1172   *A Midsummer Night's Dream* presented at the American Shakespeare Festival Theatre, Stratford, Connecticut, by the Festival Company, opening 20 June 1958 and in repertory. The production was revived here in 1959 and toured the U. S. in 1960-1961. Director, Jack Landau. Scenery by David Hays and Peter Wexler. Costumes by Thea Neu. Lighting by Will Steven Armstrong. Music and Songs by Marc Blitzstein. Dances originated by George Balanchine. *Oberon,* Richard Waring, *Titania,* June Havoc (Nancy Wickwire in 1959). *Bottom,* Hiram Sherman (Bert Lahr on tour). *Quince,* Morris Carnovsky (Patrick Hines on tour). *Snout,* Will Geer. *Starveling,* Ellis Rabb (Al Corbin on tour). *Lysander,* John Colicos (Douglas

Watson on tour). *Puck*, Richard Easton (Clayton Corzatte on tour). *A Master of Revels*, Russell Oberlin.

The first significant American production of the play in over half a century. Visually, the motif was that of an Elizabethan-Jacobean wedding masque in the costumes and the Hays-Wexler setting of an arched gallery, with stairways, from which wagon stages moved on the modified thrust stage. The most memorable feature of the production was the comedy of the mechanicals, played by an exceptionally strong cast. Counter-tenor Oberlin sang songs in Blitzstein's Jacobean-style score.

Reviews: Brooks Atkinson, *New York Times*, 23 June 1958; Herbert Whittaker, *Herald Tribune*, 23 June 1958; Henry Hewes, *Saturday Review*, 5 July 1958; Harold Clurman, *Nation*, 5 July 1958; *Theatre Arts*, July 1958; Claire McGlinchee, *Shakespeare Quarterly*, 9 (1958), 539-42; *New York Times*, 3 June 1959; McGlinchee, *Shakespeare Quarterly*, 10 (1959), 573-76; Boston *Morning Globe*, 27 September 1960. (See also entry T1180.)

T1173   "Shakespeare Productions in the United Kingdom: 1956." *Shakespeare Survey*, 11 (1958), 125-27.

Included in the annual listing, compiled by the Shakespeare Memorial Library, Birmingham, are two productions of *A Midsummer Night's Dream* in 1956, those of the Northampton Repertory Theatre and of the Perth Repertory Theatre at Perth and Kirkcaldy.

T1174   White, Eric Walter. "Early Theatrical Performances of Purcell's Operas, with a Calendar of Recorded Performances, 1690-1710." *Theatre Notebook*, 13 (1958/59), 43-65.

Provides a calendar of London performances of Purcell's operas and the plays for which Purcell composed incidental music, 1690-1710. Among these are adaptations of *Timon of Athens*, *The Tempest*, *Henry IV*, and his opera, *The Fairy Queen*, which was produced in 1692. He shows that Queen Mary and her Maids of Honor attended *The Fairy Queen* on February 16, 1693. White draws upon primary sources for the cost of the expensive production and its cast. He discusses its possible designer and librettist. He also

provides eighteenth century references to two performances
of portions of the opera--the first act in 1703 and a dance
from it done in 1704. The loss of the complete Purcell score
is also discussed.

T1175   Whiting, Frank. "Shakespeare to GI's in Europe." *Players
        Magazine*, 34 (1958), 106.

        Describes a U. S. State Department sponsored tour of a
        University of Minnesota student production of *A Midsummer
        Night's Dream*, playing at Army and Air Force bases in
        Germany and France. The author directed.

T1176   Brown, Ivor. *Shakespeare Memorial Theatre, 1957-1959.* A
        Photographic Record, with an Introduction by Ivor
        Brown and Photographs by Angus McBean. London: Max
        Reinhardt, 1959. 112 pp. Illustrated.

        Includes nine photographs and the cast list of *A
        Midsummer Night's Dream* as produced at Stratford-upon-
        Avon in 1959, directed by Peter Hall. (See item T1183.)

T1177   Byrne, Muriel St. Clare. "The Shakespeare Season at the
        Old Vic, 1958-59, and Stratford-upon-Avon, 1959."
        Shakespeare Quarterly, 10 (1959), 545-67.

        Includes her review of the *A Midsummer Night's Dream*
        at Stratford-upon-Avon, directed by Peter Hall. (See
        T1183.) Byrne took strong exception to Hall's handling of
        the lovers, who "galumph" through the forest and the
        verse, and to the "lapse of taste" in the barefooted fairies,
        who otherwise were dressed well in Jacobethan costumes,
        and to the suggestion of the sexual by Bottom when he
        woke from his dream.

T1178   Evans, G. Blakemore. "Garrick's '*The Fairies*' (1755):
        Two Editions." *Notes and Queries*, n. s. 6 (1959),
        410-11.

        Points out that there were two editions of the 1755 *The
        Fairies*, the Garrick adaptation of *A Midsummer Night's
        Dream*, both printed by J. and R. Tonson and S. Draper,
        and not one as previously supposed. The "first" does not

contain Garrick's prologue, lacks Lansdowne's name among
the poets whose lyrics are used, shows some slight
differences in lyrics, and a somewhat different cast list.
Listed in the first edition's cast is a Miss Poitier who, by
the time the second edition was printed, had married and
changed her name. Poitier and Vernon were the Helena and
Demetrius of Garrick's production. (See also item 965.)

T1179 "Free Will--Adult Western Version." *Time,* 8 June 1959,
p. 48.

Reviews a London performance of a Western-style
adaptation of *A Midsummer Night's Dream,* produced by
students of Howard Payne College, a Baptist school near
Waco, Texas. The director was Alex Reeve, a former
director at the Royal Theatre and Opera House,
Northampton, England. The play was set on an 1880s ranch
and the costumes included stetsons, bandannas, and
bustles, with Hippolyta as an Indian princess in white
buckskin. The production represented the U. S. at
Bristol's International Festival of University Theatre and
was played on tour in other cities in England and Scotland.

T1180 Houseman, John, and Jack Landau. *The American
Shakespeare Festival. The Birth of a Theatre.* New
York: Simon and Schuster, 1959. 96 pp. Illustrated.

This history of the first years of the festival includes
(pp. 57-8) a brief description of the setting by David Hays
for the festival's 1958 production of *A Midsummer Night's
Dream,* directed by Landau. (See item T1172.) There are
photographs of two set designs for it and two photos of
corresponding scenes from the production (p. 68). There
are numerous other photos of the production throughout
(especially, pp. 24-26). There is a detailed description of
Rouben Ter-Aruturian's modified thrust stage and a ground
plan of it (p. 48). The cast and production staff of the
Landau production are listed on pp. 92-93.

T1181 Kennedy, Joseph F. "Filmstrips." *Shakespeare Quarterly,*
10 (1959), 241.

Notices of 35 mm. filmstrips, in color, of productions of
Shakespeare's plays by the Old Vic. Includes one filmstrip

of an unidentified production of *A Midsummer Night's Dream* (1953?). The filmstrips were produced in London by Educational Productions, Ltd., 1958.

T1182   Merchant, W. Moelwyn. *Shakespeare and the Artist.* Oxford: Oxford University Press, 1959. Illustrated. xxx, 254 pp.

Discusses major individual artists' works dealing with Shakespearean subjects and the scenic art in Shakespearean productions (and the "interplay" among these), from Shakespeare's time to the mid-twentieth century. There are references to *A Midsummer Night's Dream* throughout. For example, he compares Torelli's settings to those that seem to be required for Purcell's *The Fairy Queen* (1692), discusses William Blake's watercolors and drawings based on the play, and he traces the development of English scene painting from the beginning of the nineteenth century to Harley Granville-Barker's productions (1912-1914), discussing the watercolors of the sets for Charles Kean's *A Midsummer Night's Dream* at the Princess's Theatre in 1856. Among the illustrations are the frontispiece to Rowe's 1709 edition of the play, Blake's watercolors, and a watercolor of a Kean setting. There is a chapter on "The Boydell Venture," and an appendix listing paintings from the Boydell gallery including works by Fuseli, Reynolds, and Blake.

T1183   *A Midsummer Night's Dream* presented at the Shakespeare Memorial Theatre, Stratford-upon-Avon, 2 June 1959. Revived (with cast changes) at Stratford, 17 March 1962, and at the Aldwych Theatre, London, 13 June 1963. It toured England in 1963. It was televised by NBC and shown in the U.S.A. in 1959; Hall's film of 1969 was derivative of this production (see item T1301). Director, Peter Hall. Designer, Lilla de Nobils. Music, Raymond Leppard. *Lysander*, Albert Finney. *Helena*, Vanessa Redgrave (Diana Rigg in 1962 and 1963). *Bottom*, Charles Laughton (Paul Hardwick in 1962 and 1963). *Puck*, Ian Holm. *A Fairy*, Zoe Caldwell. *Oberon*, Robert Hardy. *Titania*, Mary Ure.

A popular, significant production in its time and historically interesting, for it was an evolving production, marking the formative years for the Royal Shakespeare

Company. It showed signs of the move away from romantic illusion and of the developing emphasis upon Shakespeare informed with the spirit of contemporary culture. A simplified Tudor Hall setting converted to a simple forest; the fairies were in Jacobethan dress except that they went barefoot; and the lovers were confused, ungraceful, and anxious in a discordant world. But it also had a traditional star in Laughton in the 1959 premiere.

Reviews: *The Times*, 3 June 1959; W. A. Darlington, *Daily Telegraph* and *New York Times*, 3 June 1959; Cecil Wilson, *Daily Mail*, 3 June 1959; *Financial Times*, 3 June 1959; Milton Shulman, *Evening Standard*, 3 June 1959; Felix Barker, *Evening News* (London); 3 June 1959; J. C. Trewin, *Birmingham Post*, 3 June 1959; Philip Hope-Wallace, *Guardian*, 4 June 1959; J. W. Lambert, *Sunday Times*, 7 June 1959; *The Observer*, 7 June 1959; Peter Forster, *Spectator*, 12 June 1959; J. C. Trewin, *Illustrated London News*, 13 June 1959; *Time and Tide*, 13 June 1959; Caryl Brahms, *Plays and Players*, July 1959, and production photos, September 1959; Muriel St. Claire Byrne, *Shakespeare Quarterly*, 10 (1959), 545-67, with photographs; Gareth Lloyd Evans, *Guardian*, 18 April 1962; Kenneth Tynan, *The Observer*, 22 April 1962; *The Times*, 18 April 1962; *New York Times*, 18 April 1962; J. C. Trewin, *Birmingham Post*, 19 April 1962; Roger Gilbert, *New Statesman*, 21 April 1962; Anthony Mervyn, *Stage and Television Today*, 26 April 1962; Bamber Gascoigne, *Spectator*, 17 April 1962; *Theatre World*, July and August, 1962 (photos); Charles Marowitz, *Theatre Arts*, September 1962; Bertram Joseph, *Drama Survey*, 2 (1962); J. C. Trewin, *Shakespeare Quarterly*, 13 (1962), 505-19. *The Times*, 14 June 1963; *Guardian*, 14 June 1963; *Evening News*, 14 June 1963; *Daily Mail*, 14 June 1963; *Daily Express*, 14 June 1963; *Sunday Times*, 16 June 1963; *The Observer*, 16 June 1963; *Punch*, 26 June 1963; *Plays and Players*, August 1963; *Theatre Arts*, August 1963; John Russell Brown, *Shakespeare Survey*, 16 (1963), 143-51. (See also items T1189, T1232a, T1235, T1413, T1421, T1481, T1508; on the Hall film, see items T1301, T1406, T1376.)

T1184   Monck, Nugent. "The Maddermarket Theatre and the Playing of Shakespeare." *Shakespeare Survey*, 12 (1959), 71-75.

Describes his directing career and his ideas on the
staging of Shakespeare's plays on the platform stage in the
Fortune-like theatre space he fashioned. Monck (who died
shortly after this article) produced all of Shakespeare's
plays, including *A Midsummer Night's Dream*, at the
Maddermarket between 1921 and 1933. He suggests here that
A Midsummer Night's Dream "should be treated as a
masque--the forestage for the rude mechanicals, the centre
stage for the court and also the forest, the [upper] gallery
for the sleeping Titania and Bottom; for the wedding scene,
the Duke and Hippolyta are on the balcony."

T1185   Nagler, Alois Maria. *A Source Book in Theatrical History.*
         New York: Dover Publications, Inc., 1959.

Included in this anthology of primary source materials
from antiquity to the twentieth century are excerpts from
critic Henry Morley's review of Samuel Phelps's *A
Midsummer Night's Dream* at Sadler's Wells in 1853, probably
the most poetically successful production of the nineteenth
century and sensitively described by Morley, and excerpts
from descriptions of Charles Kean's *A Midsummer Night's
Dream* of 1856 at the Princess's Theatre, a highwater mark
of pictorial illustration of Shakespeare in the century.
These descriptions are those of Kean's biographer, J. W.
Cole, who praised it for its lavish antiquarian pictures, and
Morley, who found all this "damaging to the poem."

T1185a   *Sen Noci Svatojánské [A Midsummer Night's Dream].* 35
         mm color film in Cinemascope. A Ceskoslovensky Film
         made in Czechoslovakia, 1959. 80 minutes. Released by
         Showcorporation. Producer, director, and screenwriter,
         Jiří Trnka. Animators, Jan Karpoš, Stansilav Latal.
         Photographer, Jiří Vojta. Art Director, Jiří Trnka.
         Editor, Hana Walachová. Music, Václav Trajan.
         Re-release in 1961 with an English sound track (74
         minutes). Director of the English adaptation, Howard
         Sackler. *Narrator*, Richard Burton. *Lysander*, Tom
         Criddle. *Hermia*, Ann Bell. *Demetrius*, Michael Meacham.
         Egeus, John Warner. *Helena*, Barbara Leigh-Hunt.
         Theseus, Hugh Manning. *Quince*, Joss Ackland. *Bottom*,
         Alec McCowen. *Flute*, Stephen Moore. *Titania*, Barbara
         Jefford. *Oberon*, Jack Gwylim. *Puck*, Roger Shepherd.
         Hippolyta, Laura Graham.

The 1959 film used marionettes that mimed Shakespeare's plot and characters; there was no dialogue. Director Jiri Trnka's intent was to create not a textual adaptation but a version conceived for the silent puppets. The film was re-released in 1961 with an English soundtrack. Richard Burton narrated the film, and English actors provided the lines for the scenes. Several of the English cast came from the 1960 Old Vic production of the play (see T1196). (See also 862.)

T1186   Strvska, J. "Sen noci svatojánské." *Tvorba* (Prague), 24 (1959), 1100-1101.

    Not seen. (In Czechoslovakian.) Reviews the filmed, puppet version of *A Midsummer Night's Dream* by Jiří Trnka. (See above entry and item 862.)

T1186a   Whitesell, J. Edwin. "The Wits Drolls: Were they Meant to be Acted?" *Tennessee Studies in Literature*, 4 (1959), 73-90.

    Argues that the drolls, including *Bottom the Weaver*, were acted during the Commonwealth and that Marsh and Kirkman published them to be used as acting scripts as well as for reading. Whitesell draws upon internal evidence, such as the prefaces to the editions of 1673, and upon external evidence, including various accounts of the actor Robert Cox mentioned in the preface. His conclusion is the opposite of that of John James Elson, in his 1932 edition of *The Wits*, that the drolls were primarily for a reading public. Whitesell points out that the preface to *Bottom the Weaver* claims that it had been produced and notes three stage directions in it that are not found in *A Midsummer Night's Dream*.

T1187   Avery, Emmet L., William Van Lennep, Arthur H. Scouten, George Winchester Stone, Jr., and Charles Beecher Hogan, eds. *The London Stage 1660-1800: A Calendar of Plays, Entertainments and Afterpieces, Together with Casts, Box-Receipts, and Contemporary Comment.* 11 volumes. Carbondale: Southern Illinois University Press, 1960-1968. Illustrated.

Provides performance calendars for the era's theatres
and primary source material essential for the performance
history of the musical adaptations of *A Midsummer Night's
Dream* in the Restoration and eighteenth century, from
Purcell's opera through the Garrick era adaptations.
Introductory essays to each part provide background on all
aspects of theatre production, such as performers,
theatres, scenery, audiences, finances, and social history.
Each volume is indexed, there is a computer-generated
index volume, edited by Ben Ross Schneider, Jr. (Southern
Illinois University Press, 1979), and an associated computer
search service is available.

T1188   Britten, Benjamin. *A Midsummer Night's Dream*, an Opera
        in three Acts, opus 64, with libretto adapted by Britten
        and Peter Pears, presented at Jubilee Hall at the
        Aldeburg Festival, 11 June 1960. Also performed at the
        Holland Festival in July 1960, with some cast changes.
        Director, John Cranko. Design, John Piper, assisted by
        Carl Toms. *Oberon* (counter-tenor or alto), Alfred
        Deller. *Titania* (soprano), Jennifer Vyvyan. *Puck*
        (speaking role), Leonide Massine II (later, Nicholas
        Chagrin). *Theseus* (bass), Forbes Robinson (later,
        Roger Stalman). *Hippolyta* (alto), Johanna Peters.
        Bottom (bass), Owen Brannigan (Forbes Robinson).
        Flute (tenor), Peter Pears. .The English Opera Group
        Orchestra, conducted by Britten and George Malcolm.

        The premier of the Britten opera, written for the
        opening of the rebuilt Jubilee Hall at the Aldeburgh
        Festival. For piano-vocal score and plot summary, see item
        1026a. (See also T1447 and T1526.)

T1189   Brown, John Russell. "Three Adaptations." *Shakespeare
        Survey*, 13 (1960), 137-45.

        Characterizes texts and performances of several
        adaptations of Shakespeare's plays, from the Dryden and
        Davenant version of *The Tempest*, played by the Old Vic in
        1959, through Tyrone Guthrie's rewritten *All's Well That
        Ends Well*, played at Stratford-upon-Avon in 1959, to Peter
        Hall's production of *A Midsummer Night's Dream* at
        Stratford-upon-Avon in 1959. (Adaptation here is
        understood in a broad sense as applying to both textual
        changes and new directorial concepts.) Of Hall's production

he says: "As well as ignoring the humanity and poetry of Shakespeare's comedy, Peter Hall also missed its width of appeal," having pursued "liveliness" too thoroughly. (Two photographs of the Hall production will be found in Plate VII.)

T1190   Griffin, Alice. "Current Theatre Notes, 1959-1960." *Shakespeare Quarterly*, 12 (1960), 73-85.

Includes a listing of twelve productions of *A Midsummer Night's Dream* in 1960, academic and professional, and notes the premiere of Benjamin Britten's opera at the Aldeburgh Festival.

T1191   Hitchman, Percy J. "*The Fairy Queen* at Nottingham." *Theatre Notebook*, 14 (1960), 92-99.

Describes in detail the staging mechanics of a 1959 production of Purcell's opera for the Purcell tercentenary by the University of Nottingham in collaboration with the Nottingham Playhouse and various city groups. The 1692 text was used, and the scenery was created in the late eighteenth century style. Hugh Willat directed and the musical director was Ivor Keys. The author describes the hand operated shutters and flats-in-grooves, the painted cloths and gauzes, and provides a ground plan of the placement of scenic elements, elevation sketches of the cloths, and three photographs of the production.

T1192   Joseph, Bertram. *Acting Shakespeare.* London: Routledge & Kegan Paul, 1960. 199 pp.

Suggests ways of preparing to act in Shakespeare's plays, with special attention to reading and speaking the score. *E.g.*, the structure of this line of Theseus suggests its proper reading: "Our sport shall be to *take* what they *mistake*" (V.i.90).

T1193   Kirstein, Lincoln. "On Producing *A Midsummer Night's Dream*," in *A Midsummer Night's Dream*, Francis Fergusson and Charles Jasper Sisson, eds. New York: Dell Publishing Company (The Laurel Shakespeare), 1960. Pp. 16-27 (item 861).

Discusses how a production of the play should evoke the
atmosphere of a noble wedding in a Tudor Great Hall (an
idea that John Masefield had advanced in 1923 and which
influenced English productions). There are a few allusions
to the elements of the successful production at the American
Shakespeare Festival in 1958 (which occasioned this
contribution from Kirstein, then on the Festival's production
committee. See item T1172.) Kirstein says this production
attempted "to follow Shakespeare's intention as closely as
possible." His essay provides some suggestive source
materials on dances, music, and fairies.

T1194   *A Midsummer Night's Dream* presented by the Stratford
         Shakespeare Festival at the Festival Theatre, Stratford,
         Ontario, Canada, in repertory beginning 28 June 1960.
         Director, Douglas Campbell. Designer, Brian Jackson.
         Music, Harry Sommers. *Oberon*, Bruno Gerussi. *Bottom*,
         Tony van Bridge. *Theseus*, Max Helpmann. *Helena*, Kate
         Reid. *Lysander*, Leo Ciceri. *Demetrius*, Peter Donat.

         The Canadian Festival's first production of the play on
         its innovative thrust stage designed by Tanya Moiseiwitsch
         and Tyrone Guthrie. It was costumed by Jackson in
         Elizabethan style. It was otherwise not a noteworthy
         production; the reviews were mixed.

         Reviews: Brooks Atkinson, *New York Times*, 30 June
         1960; Judith Crist, *Herald Tribune*, 30 June 1930; Herbert
         Whittaker, *Toronto Globe and Mail*, 19 June 1960; Burke
         Martin, *London Evening Free Press*, 29 June 1960; Arnold
         Edinborough, *Shakespeare Quarterly*, 11 (1960), 455-59;
         Detroit News, 29 June 1960; *Toronto Telegram*, 29 June
         1960. (See also items T1127, T1146, T1291.)

T1195   *A Midsummer Night's Dream*. [Recorded performance of
         the play.] By the Marlowe Society and Professional
         Players, directed by George Rylands. Three 33 1/3 rps
         phonodiscs, stereo. Argo RG 250-252. *circa* 1960.

         For a moderately favorable review, see Margaret Willy,
         "Shakespeare on Record," *English*, 13 (1961), 188-89.

T1196   *A Midsummer Night's Dream* presented by the Old Vic
         Company at the Old Vic Theatre, London, opening 20

December 1960. Director, Michael Langham. Scene design, Carl Toms. *Bottom,* Douglas Campbell. *Hermia,* Judi Dench. *Helena,* Barbara Leigh-Hunt. *Oberon,* Alec McCowen. *Puck,* Tom Courtenay.

Langham wanted to emphasize the discordant elements in the play's world. Hippolyta was manacled, and the lovers quarreled violently. Robert Speaight found it a satisfying production, but Kenneth Tynan did not. The palace settings offered an Athens seen through Renaissance eyes.

Reviews: *The Times,* 21 December 1960; Kenneth Tynan, *The Observer,* 25 December 1960; *Plays and Players,* February 1961; Robert Speaight, *Shakespeare Quarterly,* 12 (1961), 425-41. (See also item T1249.)

T1197   "Shakespeare Productions in the United Kingdom: 1958." *Shakespeare Survey,* 13 (1960), 134-36.

Included in the annual listing, compiled by the Shakespeare Memorial Library, Birmingham, are five productions of *A Midsummer Night's Dream* in 1958, including productions by the Library Theatre, Manchester; the People's Theatre in Newcastle-upon-Tyne; the Bristol University Dramatic Society; and the Oxford Play House Company (which toured Europe after a performance in Cambridge).

T1198   Entry Deleted.

T1198a   Trewin, John Courtenay. *Benson and the Bensonians.* With a foreword by Dorothy Green. London: Barrie and Rockliff, 1960. 302 pp. Illustrated.

Describes the career of English actor-manager Sir Frank Benson. From the mid-1880s to the early 1930s, the robust Benson sustained Shakespeare's plays and developed new young talent on provincial tours, in London, and at Stratford-upon-Avon, where he headed the festival during most of its first two decades. Trewin characterizes Benson's staging and his acting in general and follows the company's tours down to 1933. *A Midsummer Night's Dream* was always in the repertoire, from the first showing of 1887 (pp. 56-57), and featured Lady Benson as Titania (photo) and costumes by Benson's brother, William. It was staged in the "moss-rose and velvet manner," with a lush forest, "coveys of elves and fairies," and a fight between a spider and a wasp. Otho Stuart, as Oberon, suffered acid burns from the battery powered electric light he wore on his head. The London success of the production in 1889 is described and reviews sampled (pp. 61-63).

T1199   Baldwin, T. W. *The Organization and Personnel of the Shakespearean Company.* Princeton, New Jersey: Princeton University Press, 1927; New York: Russell and Russell, 1961. 463 pp.

Suggests that *A Midsummer Night's Dream*'s trains of fairies for Oberon and Titania would have made unusual casting demands on the Lord Chamberlain's Men and entailed the recruiting of auxiliary players. He allots the roles to members of the company, assigning Demetrius to Burbage, Theseus to Phillips, Bottom to Kemp, Quince to Thomas Pope, Oberon to Goffe, Titania to Gilburne, Puck to Tooley, Hippolyta to Ned Shakespeare, Flute to Sly, and Hermia and Helena to Eccleston and Cooke, boy actors. He suggests that Quince, in pursuit of his duties managing "Pyramus and Thisbe," is an example of the Elizabethan company's "bookkeeper-prompter."

T1200   Burnim, Kalman A. *David Garrick, Director.* Pittsburgh: University of Pittsburgh, 1961. 234 pp. Illustrated.

Illustrates Garrick's theory and practice in the mounting of plays at Drury Lane during his management there from 1747 to 1776, drawing extensively upon reviews, prints, paintings, correspondence, promptbooks, and printed texts of the plays. Five chapters deal with personnel, rehearsal procedures, costuming, scenic arrangements, and lighting. There are chapters reconstructing the staging and acting of Garrick's *Macbeth, Romeo and Juliet, King Lear,* and *Hamlet,* and *The Provoked Wife.* Essential to the study of Garrick's management, during which time three versions of *A Midsummer Night's Dream* were produced at Drury Lane, though these are not discussed here.

T1201   Horn, Robert. "Shakespeare and Ben Jonson--Ashland, 1961." *Shakespeare Quarterly,* 12 (1961), 415-18.

Includes review coverage of the Ashland Festival's 1961 production of *A Midsummer Night's Dream*, directed by B. Iden Payne, with Angus Bowmer, Festival founder and producer, as Quince and Rod Alexander as Bottom (photo), both of whom are praised. But Helena was equipped with a lisp, and the production lacked romantic charm and love-ardor.

T1202   "International Notes." *Shakespeare Survey*, 14 (1961), 116-25.

News of recent Shakespearean activities from correspondents includes brief notes on some twelve different productions of *A Midsummer Night's Dream* in nine countries, including Australia (two), Canada, Czechoslovakia, France, Hungary, Italy, Kenya, The Netherlands, Poland (two), and the U.S. Notable among these were Jean Vilar's production with the Théâtre National Populaire at Avignon, a production in the Roman theatre at Osia, Italy, and a production Texas-style in the U.S. in which Puck wore a coon-skin cap and lassoed fairies.

T1203   Merchant, W. Moelwyn. "*A Midsummer Night's Dream: A Visual Re-creation.*" *Early Shakespeare.* Stratford-upon-Avon Studies 3. Ed. John Russell Brown and Bernard Harris. London: Edward Arnold, 1961; reprint, New York: Schocken, 1966, pp. 165-85.

Surveys the visual interpretations of *A Midsummer Night's Dream* in the illustrations, paintings, and the stage scenery of selected productions. Merchant argues that the scenery for the original *Fairy Queen* (1692) was borrowed from the Teatro Olimpico stage setting and from Torelli's designs for Corneille's *Andromède,* one engraving of which is reproduced. He suggests that the Rowe frontispieces of 1709 and 1714 are probably based on the production of Purcell opera, given their dramatic and masque-like nature. He also finds an illustration of it in the Vauxhall painting, *Fairies Dancing* (reproduced here). He describes Hayman's drawings (engraved by Gravelot) for the Hanmer edition of the plays in 1744 (reproduced), analyzes Fuseli's large painting, *Titania and Bottom in the Wood* (in the Tate Gallery), and four other Fuseli illustrations of the play, including his *Oberon Awaking Titania.* Also briefly discussed are engravings of Puck by James Parker and of

Titania by Rhodes for the 1805 Rivington Shakespeare;
drawings by William Blake; engravings by Smirke in 1825;
Sir J. Noël Paton's painting, *Reconciliation of Oberon and
Titania*; and Paul Nash's drawings for the play in the 1923
Players' Shakespeare. Among the other productions whose
scenery is briefly characterized are those of Elizabeth
Vestris (1840), Samuel Phelps (1853), Charles Kean (1856),
Harley Granville-Barker (1914), the Old Vic (1937), and
Nevill Coghill's production at the Haymarket in 1945. Also
briefly discussed are the 1944 revival at Covent Garden of
The Fairy Queen and John Piper's scenic effects for
Benjamin Britten's opera at the 1960 Aldeburgh Festival.
Britten's opera is assessed as "the richest and most faithful
interpretation of Shakespeare's intentions . . . that the
stage has seen in our generation." [Some inaccuracies in
the article are noted by G. Blakemore Evans in a review of
this collection of essays in the *Shakespeare Quarterly*, 14
(1963), 70-73.] This item is also annotated at 183.

T1204   *A Midsummer Night's Dream* presented by the New York
         Shakespeare Festival at the Wollman Memorial Skating
         Rink, New York City, 2 August 1961. Producer, Joseph
         Papp. Director, Joel Friedman. Stage and scenery
         design, Eldon Elder. *Oberon*, James Earl Jones. *Titania*,
         Kathleen Widdoes. *Puck*, John Call. *Bottom*, Albert
         Quinton. *Helena*, Margaret Hall. *Hermia*, Ann Fielding.
         Costumes, Theoni V. Aldredge. Music, David Amram.

         The production was characterized as youthful,
         fast-paced, and broadly funny. It featured very amusing
         lovers, a Puck who was a clumsy bumpkin, the
         "silver-tongued," satanic Oberon of James Earl Jones (*New
         York Tribune*), and the fluttery, swooping Titania of
         Kathleen Widdoes.

         Reviews: Joseph Morgenstern, New York *Herald Tribune*,
         3 August 1961; Lewis Funke, *New York Times*, 3 August
         1961; Jim O'Connor, *New York Journal American*, 3 August
         1961; New York *Daily News*, 3 August 1961; New York
         World Telegram and Sun, 3 August 1961; Henry Hewes,
         Saturday Review, 19 August 1961.

T1205   Moore, Robert Etheridge. *Henry Purcell and the
         Restoration Theatre.* London: Heinemann, [1961];

reprint, Westport, Connecticut, Greenwood Press, 1974.
xv, 223 pp. Illustrated.

Chapter four is devoted to a detailed study of *The Fairy
Queen*. The author argues that Elkanah Settle was probably
the playwright who did the adaptation of Shakespeare's text
(the librettist is unnamed in the published text). Etheridge
also presents the case that the unidentified scene painter
was Robert Robinson, "painter of Chinoiserie." There is a
detailed explanation of how the scenic demands of the four
elaborate masques could have been accommodated with
Restoration stage machinery, and there is a discussion of
selected, significant musical features of the score.

T1206 *Shakespeare in Art. A Visual Approach to the Plays.
Paintings, drawings and other Works devoted to
Shakespearian subjects from the seventeenth century to
the present day and including Designs for Stage-Sets
and Illustrated Editions of the plays.* Introduction by W.
Moelwyn Merchant. Nottingham University Art Gallery,
1961. 58 pp.

Catalogue of an exhibition at the Nottingham University
Art Gallery. Included in the exhibition were the frontispiece
to *A Midsummer Night's Dream* in the Rowe edition;
Hogarth's two paintings [supposedly derived] from Purcell's
The Fairy Queen; Sir Joshua Reynold's *Puck*; George
Romney's *Titania's Attendants Chasing Bats*; W. Gordon's
watercolor for the backdrop for "A Wood Near Athens,"
used in II.i of Charles Kean's 1856 production; a sketch by
Paul Nash for the illustrated Players Shakespeare edition of
the play (1923); and some preliminary drawings by John
Piper for the settings for the premiere production of
Benjamin Britten's opera, *A Midsummer Night's Dream*
(1960). Each of these is briefly annotated but none is
reproduced in the catalogue.

T1207 "Shakespeare Productions in the United Kingdom: 1959."
Shakespeare Survey, 14 (1961), 126-28.

Included in the annual listing, compiled by the
Shakespeare Memorial Library, Birmingham, are four
productions of *A Midsummer Night's Dream* in 1959: at
Stratford-upon-Avon, directed by Peter Hall; in the Open
Air Theatre in Regent's Park, directed by Robert Atkins;

at the Nottingham Repertory Theatre, directed by Val May;
and that of the Oldham Repertory Theatre Club, Oldham,
England.

T1208   Tynan, Kenneth. *Curtains: Selections from the Drama
        Criticism and Related Writings.* London: Longmans,
        Green and Company, Ltd.; New York: Atheneum 1961.
        [xii], 495 pp.

        Included in this collection of the British critic's theatre
        reviews and related essays is his evaluation of the 1959
        production of *A Midsummer Night's Dream* at Stratford-
        upon-Avon, directed by Peter Hall (pp. 238-39). Hall's
        fairies are compared to the lost boys of *Peter Pan* and
        Oberon to Peter. He disapproves of Charles Laughton's
        Bottom; he "behaves throughout . . . like a rapscallion
        Uncle dressed up to entertain children at a Christmas
        party." He also disliked the broad, unfunny, physical
        business in the young lovers' scenes. (See also item
        T1183.)

T1209   Chatenet, Jean. *Shakespeare sur la scène française
        depuis 1940.* Paris: Lettres Modernes, 1962. 124 pp.

        Brief discussions of translations, staging trends, and
        the productions of both the traditional and the younger,
        innovative French companies. There are a few very brief
        allusions to productions of *A Midsummer Night's Dream*. The
        Appendix includes a chart of major productions of
        Shakespeare's plays in Paris between 1940 and 1954, which
        includes four stagings of *Le songe d'une nuit d'été*. (See
        also item T1238.)

T1210   Hapgood, Robert. "West Coast Shakespeare, 1961." *Drama
        Survey,* 1 (1962), 344-50.

        Included in the coverage is a review of the production of
        A Midsummer Night's Dream at the 1961 Ashland, Oregon,
        Shakespeare Festival. The reviewer describes it as
        "educational theatre par excellence," since its casts and
        staff came from college drama departments. *A Midsummer
        Night's Dream* was directed by B. Iden Payne; the
        performances praised by the reviewer were those of Rod
        Alexander as Bottom (with movable ears on the ass's head),

William Kinsolving as "a beautifully spoken Oberon," and Angus Bowmer as "a sweet-tempered, longsuffering Quince." The production was, however, badly marred by a babytalking Helena, some bad musicians on oboe and recorder, and some hackneyed stage business. (See also item T1201.)

T1211   "International Notes." *Shakespeare Survey,* 15 (1962), 131-43.

Included in the news from correspondents on Shakespearean activities, scholarly and theatrical, are brief notices of some nine or more productions of *A Midsummer Night's Dream* in eight different countries in 1961: Austria (two), Germany (several), Hungary, Kenya, Sweden, the U.S., and Yugoslavia (two).

T1212   Marowitz, Charles. "The Three Theatres of Peter Hall." *Theatre Arts,* September 1962, pp. 62-64.

Includes a brief characterization of Peter Hall's *A Midsummer Night's Dream* at Stratford-upon-Avon, 1959-62 (see T1183). Bottom and company were given a new twist in Hall's production. Paul Hardwicke's Bottom was good-hearted and slow-witted, a believable tradesman on amateur night, not a raging egocentric. There was in general in the clowns a gain in pathos and whimsy rather than in comedy. Fairyland was etherealized with uncanny music, elfin children, and silvery cobwebs.

T1213   *A Midsummer Night's Dream.* [Recorded Performance of the Play.] A condensed version of the play, featuring Sarah Churchill as *Helena* and Stanley Holloway as *Bottom.* Text of the play included in the album. Two 33 1/3 rpm phonodiscs. Living Shakespeare SND 19A-20A. *circa* 1962.

T1214   *A Midsummer Night's Dream.* [Recorded Performance of the Play.] An Eamonn Andrews Studio Production, performed by the Dublin Gate Theatre. Includes incidental music sung and played on the harp and recorded by Christopher Casson. Recorded in Dublin.

Three 33 1/3 phonodiscs. Spoken Word SW
A5(SW131-133). *circa* 1962?

T1214a *A Midsummer Night's Dream*. Ballet adaptation by George
Balanchine for the New York City Ballet, premiered at
the New York City Center, 17 January 1962. In
repertory thereafter. Choreographer, George Balanchine.
Scene design, David Hays. Costume design, Karinska.
Music, Felix Mendelssohn. *Oberon*, Edward Villella.
Titania, Melissa Hayden. *Puck*, Arthur Mitchell.

Balanchine's ballet, in two acts and six scenes, is based
on the play but was actually inspired by Mendelssohn's
score for the play. Other music by Mendelssohn was added
by Balanchine to provide for the danced action of the whole
play (see T1402a). Act I opens in the wood with the
quarrels of Oberon and Titania and ends with Theseus'
discovery of the sleeping lovers. Act II begins with a
processional of the court to Mendelssohn's "Wedding March"
into a pavilion set up in the forest for the nuptial
festivities. Then a series of divertissements are danced for
the entertainment of the wedding guests. At the end, the
court retires, and the forest becomes the fairies' domain
again, with Oberon and Titania entering while a fairy choir
sings. At the end Puck sweeps the stage with his broom.
The ballet was filmed by Columbia Pictures in 1967; see
T1276b. (See also T1409.)

T1215   *A Midsummer Night's Dream* presented by the English
Stage Company at the Royal Court Theatre, London,
opening 24 January 1962. Director, Tony Richardson.
Helena, Lynn Redgrave. *Hermia*, Rita Tushingham.
Bottom, Colin Blakely. *Flute*, Nicol Williamson. *Titania*,
Samantha Eggar. *Snout*, David Warner.

This production by the company that made the Royal
Court a center of new and disturbing drama was not
well-received by critics, but it is of interest because in
this young cast there was evidence of the trend of a new
generation of actors to eschew the traditional classical
approach to Shakespeare. Critics said the verse was spoken
without music, "flatfootedly" (*The Times*), or "rushed and
chopped," with "no rubato" (*The Observer*).

Reviews: *The Times*, 25 January 1962; *The Observer*, 28 January 1962; Bamber Gascoigne, *The Spectator*, 2 February 1962; J. C. Trewin, *Illustrated London News*, 10 February 1962; F. S., *Theatre World*, March 1962 (photos); Roger Gellert, *New Statesman*, 2 February 1962. (See also T1218.)

T1216   *A Midsummer Night's Dream* presented by the New Shakespeare Company at the Open Air Theatre, Regent's Park, London, opening 4 June 1962. Director, David William. Set design, Henry Bardon. Costumes, Dwan Pavitt. Choreography by Geraldine Stephenson. Lighting, Richard Pilbrow. *Oberon*, David William. *Bottom*, Patrick Wymark. Revived 17 July 1963.

The high-spirited young lovers who romped across the wide stage were reported to be more successful in this fresh, better-than-routine production than the grotesquely masked fairies or the sometimes unrestrained mechanicals.

Reviews: *The Times*, 5 June 1962; Irving Wardle, *The Observer*, 10 June 1962; Bamber Gascoigne, *The Spectator* 15 June 1962; Howard Taubman, *New York Times*, 2 July 1962; Mark Taylor, *Plays and Players*, August 1962; A. C., *Theatre World*, July 1962; Malcolm Rutherford, *Plays and Players*, September 1963; *The Times*, 18 July 1963; *The Observer*, 21 July 1963; L. V. M., *Theatre World*, September 1963; *Tablet*, 27 July 1963.

T1217   *A Midsummer Night's Dream* presented by the Royal Shakespeare Company at the Royal Shakespeare Theatre, Stratford-upon-Avon, 17 March 1962. Director Peter Hall. Design, Lila de Nobili.

A revival, with some cast changes and modifications, of the 1959 production directed by Hall. Reviews of the 1962 and 1963 versions will be found under the 1959 listing of this production; see item T1183. (For the Hall film of 1969, see item T1301.)

T1218   Richardson, Tony. "Spare, Simple and Naive." *Plays and Players*, 9, 5 (February 1962), 5.

Discusses in a transcribed interview the 1962 production
of *A Midsummer Night's Dream* that he directed with the
English Stage Company at the Royal Court Theatre,
London. (See T1215.) He chose the play because it was his
favorite Shakespeare comedy. There were virtually no cuts,
apart from a few lines in V.i, where Theseus reads the list
of alternative entertainments. The basic problem of a
director doing this play is to "present it so its very
disparate elements weave together and yet preserve a sort
of light magical romantic atmosphere." Also, "it is a play
about the theatre, which is why it is so much fun to do.
All that one has felt about the theatre is in this play." He
wanted the staging to be fluid, and there was only very
suggestive scenery used. The costuming placed the play
definitely in Greece. The cast was very young, and
Richardson emphasized the youth of the lovers and even of
Bottom. For some of the cast, the text was worked through
line by line in rehearsals, even marked for breathing. He
preferred to cast actors with freshness and youth to more
experienced actors.

T1219   "Shakespeare Productions in the United Kingdom: 1960."
        Shakespeare Survey, 15 (1962), 144-46.

        Included in the annual listing, compiled by the
Shakespeare Memorial Library, Birmingham, are four
productions of *A Midsummer Night's Dream* by the Norwich
Players at the Maddermarket Theatre, Norwich; by the
Harrow School; by the Old Vic; and by the Royal Academy
of Dramatic Art at Hurley Manor, Surrey.

T1220   Shattuck, Charles H., ed. *William Charles Macready's
        "King John," a Facsimile Prompt-book.* Urbana:
        University of Illinois Press, 1962. 75 pp. plus facsimile
        text. Illustrated.

        Reconstructs the pictorially illustrated production of
King John by Macready in 1842 at Drury Lane Theatre and
shows the relationship to it of the Charles Kean productions
of 1846, 1852, and 1858, which were much indebted to
Macready's. Shattuck analyzes six different promptbooks
from related mid-century productions, reproduces the Kean
promptbook in facsimile, and includes thirty-four
black-and-white reproductions of the watercolor scene
designs for both the Macready and the Kean productions

and reproductions of the costume designs. Many notable
scene painters were involved in the productions, including
William Telbin and Thomas H. Grieve. The Macready
production costumes were designed by Colonel Charles
Hamilton Smith and derived from James Robinson Plánche,
who had designed the Charles Kemble production of *King
John* in 1823, a landmark in the historically accurate
costuming of Shakespeare in the theatre. There are
discussions here of scene-shifting and other technical
practices and notes on the mysteries of promptbook
markings. Shattuck also provides information on several of
the key stage managers who were the keepers of these
promptbooks and the purveyors of staging traditions in
Shakespeare as they or their promptbooks traveled from
producer to producer. Many of the painters and stage
managers involved here are involved in productions of *A
Midsummer Night's Dream* from 1840 to 1888.

T1221   Felton, Felix. "Max Reinhardt in England." *Theatre
        Research/Recherches Theatrales*, 5 (1963), 134-42.

        Remembers several Reinhardt productions and provides
several vivid pictures of Reinhardt's outdoor staging with
the Oxford University Dramatic Society in the summer of
1933, in which the author played Bottom. The
internationally known Herr Doktor Professor sent advance
requests for "eighty extras and a lake." Felton's waking
from Bottom's dream included the business of seeing the
reflection of himself in the lake *sans* ass's ears and running
off into the surrounding woods, joyous and relieved.

T1222   Hadamowsky, Franz. "Max Reinhardt and Austria."
        Trans. Stanley Radcliffe. *Theatre Research/Recherches
        Theatrales*, 5 (1963), 120-27.

        Provides an overview of Reinhardt's career, noting his
various productions of *A Midsummer Night's Dream* between
1905 and 1927 and commenting briefly on their significance
in his career.

T1222a "International Notes." *Shakespeare Survey*, 16 (1963),
        132-39.

News of recent Shakespearean activities, scholarly and
theatrical, includes brief mentions of nine productions of *A
Midsummer Night's Dream* in Austria, Czechoslovakia (four),
Germany, Greece, and the U.S. Notable among them were
Karl-Heinz Stroux's production at the Düsseldorf
Schauspielhaus that stressed the effects of the love
enchantment. Puck raised the sleeping lovers as if they
were puppets on strings and led them in a ballet to their
right partners. Britten's opera had its first performance in
Germany at Hamburg. B. Iden Payne's production of the
play at Ashland, Oregon, was the best of the season at
that Shakespeare festival.

T1223   Knudsen, Hans. "Max Reinhardt in Berlin." *Theatre
        Research/Recherches Theatrales*, 5 (1963), 128-33.

        Includes a brief description of Reinhardt's use of the
        revolving stage (invented by Karl Lautenschläger in 1905)
        for his Berlin production of *A Midsummer Night's Dream* in
        1905, the feature that made the production memorable for
        audiences. "It seems that at 9 p.m. people looked at their
        watches and said: 'Reinhardt's wood is revolving now.'"
        (See item T1225.)

T1224   [Odell, George C. D.] *Index to the Portraits in Odell's
        "Annals of the New York Stage."* New York: American
        Society for Theatre Research, 1963. 179 pp.

        Indexes all the engravings and photographs of
        performers and productions in the fifteen volume *Annals*
        that covers the New York theatre from 1700 to 1894,
        including theatre, opera, vaudeville, ballet, and concert
        events. *E.g.*, for Augustin Daly's *A Midsummer Night's
        Dream* of 1888 one will be guided to Odell's volume thirteen
        for photos of individual cast members and photos of scenes
        from the production. The index was derived from a file in
        the Princeton University Theatre Collection and provides
        access to the illustrations by an interfiled, alphabetical list
        of personal names, role names, and play titles.

T1225   Pinthus, Kurt. "Max Reinhardt and the U.S.A." *Theatre
        Research/Recherches Theatrales*, 5 (1963), 151-63.

Discusses, in this issue devoted to essays on the German director, his productions in the U.S., including (briefly) his production of *A Midsummer Night's Dream* with his German company in New York in 1927, using a baroque setting derived from an earlier staging in Salzburg. The performance in German, the overpowering scenery, and the restless motion that characterized the acting provoked negative reviews, says the author. He also briefly discusses the staging of the play by Reinhardt in the Hollywood Bowl in 1934 and the subsequent tour of that production to several U.S. cities. The critical response to Reinhardt's 1935 film of the play, co-directed by William Dieterle, one time Reinhardt pupil, is briefly sampled. Critics found it "as spectacular a show in a big way as anything you will see," but audiences found it "too long and too slow," says the author. Reinhardt staged the play "more than a dozen times in his career, always in new idioms." Pinthus says Reinhardt's aim of uniting "the expressional powers of the realistic theatre with his own romantic-fantastic" stagecraft culminated in his 1905 production, which used a three-dimensional forest on a revolving stage.

T1226   Prosser, Eleanor. "Shakespeare at Ashland and San Diego." *Shakespeare Quarterly*, 14 (1963), 445-54.

Included in the coverage is a favorable review of the production of the 1963 San Diego National Shakespeare Festival, directed by Ellis Rabb, with Stephen Joyce as Puck, Jacqueline Brooks as Helena, and Ed Flanders as Bottom. After beginning unpromisingly, the play came alive in the forest. The lovers were wonderfully idiotic, with the two lads nibbling ecstatically at Helena's fingertips or facing off, chin to chin, in their quarrel. The fairies were a family, with unaffected children as fairies around the adult Oberon and Titania. Oberon sang Titania to sleep. Bottom had superhuman energy. Cautious Quince threw up his hands at the catastrophe of the performance of "Pyramus and Thisbe," in which Thisbe's mantle caught on Moon's thornbush. At the finale, the child fairies threw gold dust in the fading light.

T1227   "Shakespeare Productions in the United Kingdom: 1961." *Shakespeare Survey*, 16 (1963), 140-42.

Included in the annual listing, compiled by the Shakespeare Memorial Library, Birmingham, are two productions of *A Midsummer Night's Dream*: at the Everyman Theatre, Cheltenham, directed by David Giles, and at the Opera House, Harrowgate, by the White Rose Company, directed by Robert Chetwyn.

T1228   Shirley, Frances Ann. *Shakespeare's Use of Off-Stage Sounds*. Lincoln: University of Nebraska Press, 1963. xv, 258 pp.

Surveys the use of off-stage sound effects and music as indicated in the texts and stage directions of Shakespeare's plays. Discusses the Renaissance methods of producing those effects (e.g., "thunder runs"--troughs for cannonballs). Effects in *A Midsummer Night's Dream* are sampled at various points in the discussion, such as the rude, percussive metal tongs and bones that Bottom mentions and the possibility of a birdcall before Puck's "I do hear the morning lark." The appendix listing, by play, of lines or stage directions seeming to require some music or sound effects includes thirteen for *A Midsummer Night's Dream*.

T1228a   Spencer, Hazelton. *Shakespeare Improved: The Restoration Versions in Quarto and On the Stage*. Cambridge, Massachusetts: Harvard University Press, 1927; reprint, 1963. xii, 406 pp. Illustrated.

Examines the texts of the plays in the adaptations in which they were performed on the Restoration stage, 1660-1710. Samuel Pepys's response to a 1662 performance of *A Midsummer Night's Dream* is recorded. Spencer suggests that the play Pepys saw was probably unaltered, and then says, "I find no other mention of this play before 1692, when it was tortured into an opera, under the title of *The Fairy Queen*" (p 42). He describes the textual changes in the opera and cites in full the stage directions for its major spectacles (pp. 318-24). Its scenic lavishness is said to be more celebrated than Purcell's music. He notes that Hyppolyta is cut and that the performance of "Pyramus and Thisbe" is moved to what was originally the forest rehearsal scene. This makes way for the spectacle of the Chinese garden and dance in the last scene. The play ends with Oberon and Titania complimenting wits, critics, beaux, and

cits "as pertly as in any epilogue" to a Restoration play.
The scenic and musical embellishments "do not call for
serious criticism," says Spencer, who concludes citing as an
amusing parallel the extraneous spectacle in a Hollywood
bowl production of the play in 1922.

T1229   Trewin, John Courtenay. *The Birmingham Repertory
Theatre, 1913-1963.* London: Barrie and Rockliff, 1963.
xvi, 272 pp. Illustrated.

Mentions briefly the theatre's 1936 production of *A
Midsummer Night's Dream*, staged by Paul Shelving "in the
intricacy of a glistening, glimmering wood, to whose magic
Charles Victor, as the Weaver, responded with the best wit
of any handicraft man in Athens." The appendices include
lists of plays produced in each season from 1913 to 1962
and of performances by the company in other cities.

T1229a Zimmerman, Franklin B. *Henry Purcell 1659-1695: An
Analytical Catalogue of His Music.* London: Macmillan and
Company, Ltd.; New York: St. Martin's Press, 1963. 575
pp.

Provides in entry number 629, on *The Fairy Queen*, the
first bars of the opera's major songs, overtures, and dance
pieces; a census of manuscripts of the score; a list of
editions of songs from it; a section of commentary; and a
bibliography. The commentary provides contemporary
sources on the first performance of 1692, traces the history
of the publication of the text and selected songs, noting
the rediscovery of the lost autograph score in the twentieth
century, and lists the music still missing (if ever composed)
for certain situations, *e.g.* the Clowns' Dance in Act II.

T1229b Besoyan, Rick. *Babes in the Woods*, presented at the
Orpheum Theatre, New York City, opening 28 December
1964. Producers, Sandy Farber, Aaron Schroeder.
Director, Rick Besoyan. Costumes, Howard Baker.
Scenery and lighting, Paul Morrison. Adaptation, music,
and lyrics, Rick Besoyan. Arrangements, Arnold Goland.
Musical director, Natalie Charlson. *Oberon*, Richard
Charles Hoh. *Titania*, Carol Glade. *Robin Goodfellow*,
Elmarle Wendel. *Lysander*, Don Stewart. *Hermia*, Joleen
Fodor. *Bottom*, Kenneth McMillan. *Helena*, Ruth Buzzi.

An off-Broadway spoof of *A Midsummer Night's Dream* by
the author and composer of the successful musical spoof on
melodrama *Little Mary Sunshine.* The two-act adaptation
requiring one setting cuts the original cast to eight
characters and features nineteen musical numbers. These
include romantic songs for the young lovers, quarrel songs
for Oberon and Titania, and a song Bottom sings about
preferring his mother to the girls of today which is done in
the Al Jolson, "Mammy" style. For a complete synopsis, see
1091gg. *New York Times* critic Howard Taubman disliked it,
with the exception of some of Besoyan's melodies (see
T1248b); the reviews of the other New York daily papers
included praise of it as a fresh and funny spoof, with good
tunes.

T1230   Boustead, Alan. *Music to Shakespeare. A Practical
         Catalogue of Current Incidental Music, Song Settings,
         and Other Related Music.* London: Novello; New York:
         Oxford University press, 1964. 40 pp.

         Catalogues, by play, the song settings, incidental music
         and other music somehow related to the plays. (There is
         also a section on music related to the sonnets and other
         poems.) Done on the occasion of the quadricentennial of
         Shakespeare's birth, the catalogue includes music scores
         that are reasonably accessible from publishers. Under *A
         Midsummer Night's Dream* will be found a listing of
         composers of incidental music, individual song settings, and
         a category of "other music" that includes derivative operas
         and vocal or instrumental music inspired by the play. For
         each of the song settings, Boustead lists the publisher(s)
         from whom it is available. Some fifty-five composers are
         represented. No fewer than twenty have set "Ye spotted
         snakes with double tongues" and eighteen have set Oberon's
         "I know a bank . . . ." Under "other music" will be found
         some twenty-three composers other than those numbered
         above. Here is listed Benjamin Britten's opera and
         overtures by Felix Mendelssohn and Maria
         Castelnuova-Tedesco. For additional listings, including
         composers not included here, see items T1136 and T1324.

T1231   Carter, Huntly. *The Theatre of Max Reinhardt.* New
         York: Mitchell Kennerley, 1914; reprint, New York:
         Benjamin Blom, 1964. 332 pp. Illustrated.

This early work on the innovations of the German director includes brief references to two of Reinhardt's productions of *A Midsummer Night's Dream* prior to 1914. There is a reproduction of Karl Walser's sketch of his design for the last act of the *A Midsummer Night's Dream* that Reinhardt staged in the Kunstler Theater in Munich in 1909 (mislabelled in the caption).

T1231a *The Dream.* Ballet adaptation by Sir Frederick Ashton for the Royal Ballet Company. Premiered at Covent Garden Opera House, 2 April 1964. Choreographer, Sir Frederick Ashton. Scene design, Henry Bardon. Music, Felix Mendelssohn. *Oberon*, Anthony Dowell. *Titania*, Antoinette Sibley. *Puck*, Keith Martin. *Bottom*, Alexander Grant.

Created on the occasion of the quartercentenary of Shakespeare's birth, Ashton's *The Dream* shared the evening's bill with Robert Helpmann's ballet, *Hamlet*, and *Images of Love*, a suite of love vignettes inspired by passages from Shakespeare. *The Dream* condenses the play and Mendelssohn's score, focussing impressionistically on Oberon and Titania's quarrel, Bottom's transformation, and Puck's mischief among the four young lovers. Theseus and Hippolyta were omitted. In Oberon and Puck, Ashton created strong male dancer roles. Titania and Oberon danced a *pas de deux* to the music of the Nocturne, with allusions to winged flight. The fairy lullaby was sung from the orchestra pit by the London Boy Singers. (See T1246a.)

T1232 Glick, Claris. "William Poel: His Theories and Influence." *Shakespeare Quarterly*, 15 (1964), 15-25.

Discusses the influence of Poel's experiments with the unlocalized Elizabethan platform stage for Shakespeare's plays and his emphasis upon the word music. Poel influenced many subsequent directors, Harley Granville-Barker and B. Iden Payne among them. There is some consideration of Poel's ideas in relation to the work of Gordon Craig and Max Reinhardt. The author sees some modern stages and quasi-Elizabethan settings as descendents of the Poel experiments, including Peter Hall's set for *A Midsummer Night's Dream* in 1959 (see T1183). (See also items T1142 and T1345.)

T1232a Goodwin, John, ed. *Royal Shakespeare Company*
        1960-1963. London: Max Reinhardt, 1964. 334 pp.
        Illustrated.

        Includes photographic record of the RSC productions in
        the 1960-63 seasons and cast lists. There are four
        photographs of and the cast list for the 1962 revival at
        Stratford-upon-Avon of the 1959 production of *A Midsummer*
        Night's Dream (pp. 128-31), directed by Peter Hall (see
        item T1183). There are also brief excerpts from two reviews
        of it. There is an essay by Hall on directing Shakespeare
        in which he speaks of the RSC goal of informing
        Shakespeare with the spirit of contemporary culture, the
        spirit of "our world of contradictions." Hall is convinced
        that many Shakespearean productions in his experience were
        far more Victorian than Elizabethan and that new directorial
        interpretations are a necessity. (See T1235.)

T1233   H., R. "National Youth Theatre in '*The Dream*'.
        Queen's." *Theatre World*, October 1964, pp. 33-34.

        Favorable review of a London production "ablaze with
        romance and imagination, played with a style and assurance
        that was positively awesome." Helena was played by Helen
        Mirren, Hermia by Diana Quick, Oberon by Jeremy
        Anthony, Puck by Tim Haunton, and Bottom by Ken
        Cranham. Paul Hill directed.

T1234   Hainaux, René, and Yves-Bonnat. *Stage Design*
        Throughout the World since 1950. New York: Theatre
        Arts, 1964. 276 pp. Illustrated.

        Includes in its illustrated survey of design two
        photographs of settings for the 1959 production of *A*
        Midsummer Night's Dream designed by József Cseltnyi for
        the József Szinhay Theatre in Kecskemet, Hungary; one
        photograph of the setting designed by Stellan Mörner for
        the 1956 production at the Kungliga Theatre, Stockholm;
        and one photograph of the forest setting designed by John
        Piper for Benjamin Britten's opera as produced at the Royal
        Opera House, Covent Garden, London, in 1961. (See also
        item T1338.)

T1235   Hall, Peter. "Shakespeare and the Modern Director."
        Royal Shakespeare Company, 1960-1963, ed. John
        Goodwin. London: Max Reinhardt, 1964, pp. 41-48.

   Stresses the importance of making Shakespeare's plays
responsive to the contemporary world, arguing that
Shakespearean staging to the mid-twentieth century had
been largely Victorian in temper. This emphasis has been a
keystone of RSC philosophy from Hall, one of its founders,
through the RSC directors of the 1980s. Hall directed the
RSC's *A Midsummer Night's Dream* in 1959 (see item T1183).

T1235a Hartnoll, Phyllis, ed. *Shakespeare in Music. Essays by*
        John Stevens, Charles Cudworth, Winton Dean, and
        Roger Fiske. With a Catalogue of Musical Works. London:
        Macmillan and Company, Ltd.; New York: St. Martin's
        Press, 1964. ix, 333 pp.

   Stevens, in his essay on "Shakespeare and the Music of
the Elizabethan Stage: An Introductory Essay," describes
the dramatic function of the music required in *A Midsummer*
Night's Dream as providing the distinction between the
play's natural and supernatural worlds. He suggests that
originally a consort of mixed instruments was used: lute,
pandora and cittern, and trebel and bass viols. Dean, in
"Shakespeare and the Opera," discusses briefly the opera
adaptations of the play from Purcell through the eighteenth
and nineteenth century versions of Leveridge, Lampe,
Smith, and Mancinelli. He concludes with descriptions of the
works of Benjamin Britten and Carl Orff. Dean's fullest
discussions and assessments are of Mancinell's opera of 1917
("nothing remains of Shakespeare's spirit"), Orff's two
scores of 1939 and 1952 (consisting of incidental music and
a few songs, some of which are to be played by onstage
musicians), and the Britten opera ("the most successful
Shakespearean opera since Verdi"). Charles Cudworth, in
his article on the song settings of Shakespeare's lyrics,
1660-1960, discusses briefly songs for the eighteenth
century's adaptations and songs for the nineteenth
century's productions of the play itself. Roger Fiske, in
"Shakespeare in the Concert Hall," characterizes
Mendelssohn's overture to the play, explaining the
descriptive function of major passages (*e.g.*, themes for
each group of characters and musical passages for each of
the four lovers to enter the forest, lie down, and go to
sleep). Fiske argues that descriptive music need not be

inferior by nature, as is commonly assumed. Mendelssohn's
overture proves "that a literary programme need not
preclude the writing of great music." There is a catalogue
of compositions relating to the play (most of which have
been published), including the operas and other musical
adaptations, songs for the play, incidental music, concert
hall music, and single lyric song settings. (See also items
T1230 and T1136.)

T1236   Hayter, Alethea. "La mise en scène Shakespearienne en
        Grand-Bretagne, aujourd'hui." *Revue D'Histoire Du
        Théâtre* (1964), pp. 471-81.

        Surveys contemporary staging styles for Shakespeare in
        Britain. Included is a description and a photograph of Lila
        de Nobili's setting for Peter Hall's production of *A
        Midsummer Night's Dream* at Stratford-upon-Avon in 1959.
        The 1937-38 production of the play in Victorian style at the
        Old Vic, directed by Tyrone Guthrie, is praised for
        bringing that charm to the fairies that only the ballet can
        provide. The lovers and the artisans, however, suffered
        from the treatment. Guthrie's direction is said to be
        sometimes rewarding and sometimes exasperating as he seeks
        new treatments for the well-known plays.

T1237   Isaac, Winifred F. E. C. *Ben Greet and the Old Vic: A
        Biography of Sir Philip Ben Greet.* With forewords by
        Dame Sybil Thorndike, Malcolm Morley, and Leslie
        French. London: Published for the author by The
        Greenbank Press, 1964. xxii, 238 pp. Illustrated.

        Provides a worshipful account of the life and career of
        the fondly regarded actor and manager in whose touring
        companies many famous English actors began their careers.
        Greet produced *A Midsummer Night's Dream* at the Old Vic
        and his touring companies carried it in their repertoire from
        1816 onward for half a century, during much of which time
        Greet performed in the role of Bottom. His production was
        widely seen in England and the U.S. The play was often
        performed during his stewardship at the Old Vic from 1914
        to 1918. The biography includes many brief references
        throughout to touring performances of *A Midsummer Night's
        Dream* and an occasional cast list (pp. 14, 221). Isaacs also
        describes productions at the Open Air Theatre, Regents
        Park, which Greet founded with Robert Atkins and Sidney

Carroll in 1933. An Atkins production of *A Midsummer Night's Dream* is described in the cast of which was Jessica Tandy (Titania), Leslie French (Puck) and Phyllis Neilson Terry (Oberon), and there are two photos of it.

T1238   Jacquot, Jean. *Shakespeare en France, mises en scène d'hier et d'aujourd'hui.* Paris: Le Temps, 1964. 142 pp. Illustrated.

Illustrated survey of styles in French Shakespearean staging from the nineteenth century to 1964, with concentration on major directors such as André Antoine, Aurélien-Marie Lugné-Poë, Michel Saint-Denis, and Roger Planchon. There are photographs of the production of *A Midsummer Night's Dream* directed by Camille de Sainte Croix (1910-1911), and a few brief references to other productions of the play. (See also item T1209.)

T1239   Kindermann, Heinz. "Shakespeare und das Burgtheater." *Sitzungberichte, österreichische Akademie der Wissenschaften, philosophisch-historische Klasse* (Vienna), 240 [1964], 1, 1-40. Illustrated.

Survey of productions of Shakespeare's plays in the Vienna Burgtheater from 1770 to 1964. Not seen.

T1239a   [Kopáčová, Ludmila, ed.] *Theatre in Czechoslovakia, William Shakespeare.* Trans. Jiří Harrer. Theatre Institute, Prague, Publication No. 60. [Prague: Divadelní Ústav, *ca.* 1964.] 61 pp. Illustrated.

Surveys Shakespeare in translations, productions, music, and art in Czechoslovakia. In the essay "William Shakespeare in Three Generations of Czech art," by Jaromir Pečírka, there is a brief description of the lyrical, free illustration of *A Midsummer Night's Dream* by Karel Svolinký in 1938. In the essay "Musical Inspiration," Vladimír Lébel mentions an unproduced opera based on *A Midsummer Night's Dream* by composer Jaroslav Doubrava. A listing of first Czech productions of Shakespeare's plays shows *A Midsummer Night's Dream* was first done in Prague in 1855. There are photos (pp. 42-45) of five productions of the play between 1943 and 1963, reflecting five different styles, from post-war romanticism through austere modernism in the setting of Josef Svoboda.

T1240   Lippmann, Max, ed. *Shakespeare im Film.* Aus Anlass des vom Deutschen Institut für Filmkunde, vom 2, bis 8. Wiesbaden: Saaten-Verlag, 1964. 132 pp. Illustrated.

Provides (in German) a filmography of Shakespeare on film (films in all languages) and essays on filming the plays, on film music techniques in Shakespearean films, and on the general history of Shakespeare on film from 1899 to 1964. Among the early films of *A Midsummer Night's Dream* were an adaptation of the play in 1909 by the Vitagraph Company, directed by J. Stuart Blackton; a French film of 1909 by Le Lion studios; a German film of 1913 by Deutsche Bioscop Limited, directed by Stellan Rye; fairy scenes from the play, filmed by Harmonie-Film in 1917, which consisted of dances to Mendelssohn's music by the ballet company of the Berlin Opera; and a German film of the play of 1925 by Neumann Productions Limited, directed by Hans Neumann. Also listed are the Warner Brothers version of 1935, directed by Max Reinhardt and William Dieterle, and a Czechoslovakian puppet performance for film, directed by Jiří Trnka in 1959 (see T1183a). There are two photographs of scenes from the 1935 Reinhardt film and one photo from the Czech film.

T1241   M., H. G. "Shakespeare for Schools, *A Midsummer Night's Dream* at the Comedy Theatre." *Theatre World,* 60 (May 1964), 36.

Reviews favorably the Ipswich Arts Theatre production of *A Midsummer Night's Dream* presented by Shakespeare for Schools Ltd., commencing 22 April 1964 . Robert Chetwin was the director and Geoffrey Scott designed the settings; the costumes were from the Royal Shakespeare Company.

T1242   *A Midsummer Night's Dream.* [Recorded Performance of the Play.] Presented by the Folio Theatre Players, starring Eithne Dunn and Eve Watkinson. An abridgment of the play. Recorded at Stapleton Studios, Dublin. Two 33 1/3 rpm phonodiscs. Spoken Arts 882. *circa* 1964.

T1243   *A Midsummer Night's Dream* presented by the New York
        Shakespeare Festival, Joseph Papp, producer, on tour in
        New York City's five boroughs, beginning 26 June 1964.
        Director, Jack von Sydow. Caravan stage designed by
        Ming Cho Lee. Music, David Amram. *Titania*, Ellen Holly.
        Oberon, Ted van Griethuysen. *Puck*, Clyde M. Burton.
        Bottom, Clifford James. *Helena*, Susan Carr.

        Papp's mission with this truck-stage tour was to bring
        Shakespeare to the streets and parks of the City, making
        him accessible to audiences who otherwise would not see the
        plays in performance. The production played for
        neighborhood audiences fifty-eight times in thirty-nine
        locations on the portable stage, the lights for which were
        powered by portable generators. A black actress played
        Titania, and there was special interest in the response of
        Harlem audiences to the production. Critics praised the
        mission while finding some of the performances overly
        broad. A derivation of this production was taken indoors
        for City school audiences in the fall of 1964.

        Reviews: Howard Taubman, *New York Times*, 30 June
        and 12 July 1964; Marlies K. Danziger, *Shakespeare
        Quarterly*, 15 (1964), 419-22; John Molleson, *New York
        Herald Tribune*, 16 October 1964. (See also items T1255 and
        T1256.)

T1244   *A Midsummer Night's Dream.* [Recorded Performance of
        the Play.] Presented by the Shakespeare for Students
        Company, directed by Milt Commons. Arranged for this
        performance by James Dursell. Music composed and
        played by Gary Filsinger. Text of play included in
        slipcase. Two 33 1/3 rpm phonodiscs. Folkways Records
        FL 9872. *circa* 1964.

T1245   *A Midsummer Night's Dream.* [Recorded Performance of
        the Play.] Presented by the Shakespeare Recording
        Society, featuring Paul Scofield as *Oberon* and Joy
        Parker as *Titania.* Directed by Howard Sackler. Album
        notes by G. B. Harrison. Text of play included in
        album. Three 33 1/3 rpm phonodiscs, stereo.
        Shakespeare Recording Society SRS 208. 1964.

T1246   Orff, Carl. "Musik zum *Sommernachtstraum*: Ein Bericht."
        Shakespeare Jahrbuch (Heidelberg), 100 (1964), 117-34.

        Provides an account of his experiences composing music
        for six different productions of the play from 1917 to 1964.
        The fifth of these was a production at the Empire State
        Music Festival in Ellenville, New York, in 1956, directed by
        Basil Langton, with Basil Rathbone as Oberon, Nancy
        Wickwire as Titania, and Red Buttons as Bottom. Leopold
        Stowkowski conducted. (See item T1157a.)

T1246a "The Royal Ballet Celebrates Shakespeare's
        Quartercentenary: *The Dream, Hamlet,* and *Images of
        Love* Presented at Covent Garden." *Illustrated London
        News,* 11 April 1964, pp. 578-79.

        Included in this photo feature is one photo of a piece
        created by Sir Frederick Ashton entitled *The Dream,* using
        Mendelssohn's score. (See T1231a.)

T1247   Salomaa, Pekka. "Max Reinhardt's Productions of *A
        Midsummer Night's Dream.*" *Players Magazine,* 9 (1964),
        256-59.

        Describes briefly five of Reinhardt's productions of the
        play, from his 1905 staging in Berlin Neues Theater to his
        1927 production at the Salzburg Festival. The theatres in
        which he staged the play ranged from the huge Grosses
        Schauspielhaus in Berlin (1921) to the theatre in der
        Josefstadt in Vienna.

T1248   *Shakespeare und das Deutsche Theater.* Köln:
        Theaterwissenschaftliches Institut der Universität Köln,
        1964. 73 pp. 43 plates. Illustrated.

        Includes a list of Shakespearean productions in Germany.
        Not seen.

T1248a Simpson, Donald Herbert. *Shakespeare and the
        Commonwealth.* London: The Royal Commonwealth
        Society, 1964. 18 pp. Illustrated.

Included in this essay written on the occasion of the 400th anniversary of Shakespeare's birth is a survey of plays in performance, professional and amateur, by actors past and present in the Commonwealth. Productions of *A Midsummer Night's Dream* are among those noted briefly. The New Zealand Players, a group in existence from 1953-60, produced it, and in Mauritius there was a production of a musical version by Ambroise Thomas entitled *Le songe d'une nuit d'été*. The play was performed in Sierra Leone in 1917 and in Uganda in 1950.

T1248b   Taubman, Howard. "The Theatre: A Lampoon." *New York Times*, 29 December 1964, 21:2.

Very unfavorable review of Rick Besoyan's *Babes in the Wood*, a musical adaptation of *A Midsummer Night's Dream*, which opened at the Orpheum Theatre, New York City, 28 December (see 1091gg amd T1229b). Taubman says the author, who wrote the successful musical *Little Mary Sunshine*, turned *A Midsummer Night's Dream* "to graceless and profitless account." His spoof of the lovers' confusions and of Oberon and Titania is described as vulgar. (The fairies were cut except for Oberon, Titania, and Puck.) Puck was "just another musical comedy dim-wit," and Bottom was "converted into an effeminate sort who is looking for a girl like the kind his mother was." (Bottom appeared without any of the other mechanicals.) Puck mistakenly turned him into a lion and then into a gorilla. Helena, says Taubman, behaved like a slap-stick musical comedy comedienne; Titania did a "joyless" suggestive dance with Bottom; and in general Besoyan is said to have robbed the play of enchantment. Taubman has praise for Besoyan's flair for flowing, singable melodies.

T1248c   Trewin, John Courtenay. "Out of the Pigeonhole." *Illustrated London News*, 7 March 1964, p. 364.

Includes a generally favorable review of the Birmingham Repertory Theatre's production of *A Midsummer Night's Dream*, directed by John Harrison. There are objections to the representation of the fairies by mobiles and to the forest of painted, moveable screens, but high praise for the cast's attention to the delivery of the language, especially Angela Pleasence as Titania and Robert Robinson as

Oberon. The mechanicals, with Derek Smith as Bottom, were "not tediously overfooled."

T1249   Trewin, John Courtenay. *Shakespeare on the English Stage, 1900-1964.* London: Barrie and Rockliff, 1964. x, 328 pp. Illustrated.

Characterizes briefly the major British Shakespearean productions within the years indicated, including the major productions of *A Midsummer Night's Dream* in the West End Theatres, at the Old Vic, and at Stratford-upon-Avon. Characterized are productions of the play directed by Herbert Beerbohm Tree (1900), Frank Benson (tours), Harley Granville-Barker (1914), Robert Courtneidge (1901), Donald Calthrop (1923), Basil Dean (1924), Harcourt Williams (1929), Tyrone Guthrie (1937-38 and 1951), Michael Benthall (1957), Peter Hall (1959), Tony Richardson (1962), and David William (1963). There is a photograph by Angus McBean of the 1959 Stratford production, directed by Peter Hall. There are check lists of productions that include partial or full casts; there is a lengthy bibliography and a thorough index. The West End checklist includes the revivals of *A Midsummer Night's Dream* by Donald Wolfit and Robert Atkins. The survey takes Trewin from the Victorian pictorial traditions to the beginnings of the Shakespeare revolution in the early 1960s. He did not like the Hall production of 1959 and calls it "tone-deaf." The book's last paragraph uses the production history of the play as a paradigm.

T1250   Trilling, Ossia. "Shakespeare at the Paris Festival." *Theatre World*, June 1964, p. 28.

Reviews unfavorably a production of *A Midsummer Night's Dream* presented by the British Council and H. M. Tennent Ltd. at the Theatre of the Nations for the annual Paris festival. Mendelssohn's score was used, and director Wendy Toye "swamped the stage with prancing fairies." There was little music in the speaking of the poetry. The production toured in repertory in six European capitals and in Central and South America.

T1251   *World Theatre*, 13, 1-2 (Summer 1964), 111.

Contains a photograph of a 1956 production of *A Midsummer Night's Dream* in Stockholm and one of a 1964 production in Beograd, Yugoslavia, the latter showing Oberon on stilts.

T1252 Brustein, Robert. "Defects and Virtues," *Seasons of Discontent, Dramatic Opinions 1959-1965.* New York: Simon and Schuster, 1965, pp. 228-31.

Brustein found Joe Friedman's *A Midsummer Night's Dream* at the 1961 New York Shakespeare Festival badly mauled, grossly sensual, and badly cast.

T1253 Creux, Antoinette. "Shakespeare at Maynardville." *Lantern* (Pretoria), 15 (1965), 55-59.

Reviews favorably two Shakespearean productions, including one of *A Midsummer Night's Dream*, at the Open Air Theatre, Wynberge, Capetown, South Africa, directed by René Ahrenson and Cecilia Sonnenberg.

T1254 Dean, Winton. "Shakespeare in the Opera House." *Shakespeare Survey*, 18 (1965), 75-93.

Surveys the operas based on Shakespeare's plays and provides a listing of them. He lists fourteen based on *A Midsummer Night's Dream*. Dean suggests that for the quasi-operas of the English Restoration such as *The Fairie Queen*, two separate casts were used, one for the acting and one for the singing. He notes that in *The Fairies* (1755), Lysander has a large part, which was sung by the famous castrato, Guadagni, the creator of Orfeo in Gluck's opera. But Demetrius does not sing at all, probably because only a non-singing actor was available. Britten's *A Midsummer Night's Dream* is perhaps the only successful full-length opera derived from the play that manages to preserve the text and create its own musical design. The intensely concentrated style of Britten's opera helps, and it "has a sinewy quality, a refusal to luxuriate in emotion, which I think is essential for a Shakespearian [*sic*] subject." (See also T1136, T1230, and T1324.)

T1255   Faust, Richard, and Charles Kadushin. *Shakespeare in
        the Neighborhood*. Audience Reaction to *A Midsummer
        Night's Dream* as produced by Joseph Papp for the
        Delacorte Mobile Theatre. New York: Twentieth Century
        Fund for the Bureau of Applied Social Research of
        Columbia University, 1965. 73 pp.

        Describes the audiences' responses to the New York
        Shakespeare Festival's 1964 production of *A Midsummer
        Night's Dream*, which toured the five boroughs of New York
        City in a self-contained caravan stage, playing in parks
        and streets. This report by the two authors who observed
        performances includes audience head counts, classifications
        according to race, age and sex, and interviews with forty
        audience members. Of the adults, more women attended than
        men. Some neighborhood audiences were predominantly
        black; some were Caucasian. About half of the audiences
        were children and about twenty percent were teenagers.
        Four of the fifty-seven performances had to be stopped
        because of the throwing of rocks, eggs, fruit, or the
        setting off of firecrackers. (See also items 292a and T1243.)

T1256   Griffin, Alice. "The New York Shakespeare Festival
        1965." *Shakespeare Quarterly*, 16 (1965), 335-39.

        Included in the review's coverage is a report on the
        Festival's mobile theatre unit that offered *A Midsummer
        Night's Dream* admission-free in 1964 to 70,000 spectators in
        the city's parks and playgrounds. She summarizes the
        Faust-Kadushin survey of those audiences (see item above
        and T1243).

T1257   Hoffman, D. S. "Some Shakespearean Music, 1660-1900."
        Shakespeare Survey, 18 (1965), 94-101.

        Surveys the songs and incidental music used with the
        plays since the Restoration. Among the numerous references
        to *A Midsummer Night's Dream*, he briefly discusses *The
        Fairies* (1755) and Lampe's *Pyramus and Thisbe* (1745). The
        only Lampe song that is funny is "The Lion's Song," which
        uses "a kind of musical roar--a vocal vibrato." From the
        nineteenth century productions of the play, C. E. Horn's
        setting of "I know a bank" deserves a hearing as does H.
        R. Bishop's setting of "By the simplicity of Venus's doves."

T1258   "International Notes." *Shakespeare Quarterly*, 18 (1965), 119-35.

Included in the extensive news from correspondents of Shakespearean activities, scholarly and theatrical, in 1964, the quartercentenary year, are brief notices of twelve productions, professional and amateur, of *A Midsummer Night's Dream* in nine different nations: Austria, Finland, Germany, Israel, South Africa, Sweden, Turkey, the U.S., and Yugoslavia. The production of the play in Hamburg was double celebration, for it was first performed there in 1864. In Antwerp, the play was staged in the courtyard of Ruben's house. The Haifa Theatre in Israel offered a novel Bottom who was youthful and mischievous, a human counterpart of Puck. In the U.S., Hofstra College did an adaptation for children called *Puck and the Tinkers*.

T1259   Kelly, Helen M. T. "The Granville-Barker Shakespeare Productions. A Study Based on the Promptbooks." Ph.D. Dissertation, University of Michigan, 1965, *DAI*, 27 (1966), 547A.

Analyzes the three Harley Granville-Barker productions at the Savoy Theatre in London, 1912-1914, providing information on some production details of his *A Midsummer Night's Dream* (1914) drawn from his promptbooks at the University of Michigan. (See also items T1366, T1392, and T1401.)

T1260   Kitchin, Laurence. "Shakespeare on the Screen." *Shakespeare Survey*, 18 (1965), 70-74.

Included in this brief and general survey of filmed Shakespeare are some of the author's responses to Max Reinhardt's 1935 film of *A Midsummer Night's Dream*. "The best sequences have more to do with Mendelssohn than Shakespeare." It is "true cinema," but only Ian Hunter (Theseus) can speak the verse. Cagney's Bottom is highly praised.

T1261   Entry Deleted.

T1262   Mendelssohn-Bartholdy, Felix. *Ein Sommernachstraum*
         musik zu Shakespeares Schauspiel, opus 21 und opus 61.
         Rafael Kubelik conducting the Orchester des Bayerischen
         Rundfunks, with Edith Mathis, soprano, Ursula Boese,
         alto, and choir. Program notes by Willy Haas in German,
         French, and English. Two 33 1/3 rpm phonodiscs,
         stereo. Deutsche Grammophone Gesellschaft SLPM
         138,959. *circa* 1965.

T1262a   *A Midsummer Night's Dream.* A 26 minute animated
         cartoon adaptation, featuring Mister Magoo as Puck. A 16
         mm. color film produced by Fleetwood Films, released in
         1965. (not seen)

         Mister Magoo recites an introduction, pulls a drape to
         show scene-endings and performs as a fleeting and
         mischievous Puck, repeating throughout, "What fools these
         mortals be." Rentals are available from various professional
         and university film distributors including: Audio Brandon
         Films at 34 MacQuesten Parkway, Mt. Vernon, New York, or
         at 3868 Piedmont Avenue, Oakland, California; Oklahoma
         State University, Audio-visual Center, Stillwater, Oklahoma,
         74074; and the A. Krasker Memorial Film Library, Boston
         University, Boston, Ma. This is the film at 1053a,
         presumably.

T1263   "Shakespeare Productions in the United Kingdom:
         1962-4." *Shakespeare Survey*, 18 (1965), 136-46.

         Included in the annual listing, compiled by the
         Shakespeare Memorial Library, Birmingham, are twenty-five
         productions of *A Midsummer Night's Dream* in 1962-64,
         including the following which are not otherwise noted in
         this bibliography: by the Citizens Theatre, Glasgow; by the
         Birmingham University Guild Theatre Group; by the Windsor
         Theatre Guild; by the London Academy of Music and
         Dramatic Art; by the Birmingham Repertory Theatre; by
         the Playhouse, Liverpool; by the Library Theatre,
         Manchester; by the Oxford University Dramatic Society at
         the Alveston Manor Hotel, Stratford-upon-Avon; by the
         Marlowe Society at the Arts Theatre, Cambridge; by the
         Bristol Old Vic Company at the Theatre Royal, Bristol; at
         the Marlowe Theatre, Canterbury; at Richmond Theatre; at
         the Gateway Theatre, Edinburgh; and at the Open Air
         Theatre, Regent's Park, directed by David William.

T1264   Shattuck, Charles. *The Shakespeare Promptbooks: A
        Descriptive Catalogue.* Urbana: University of Illinois
        Press, 1965. [x], 553 pp.

        Lists by play, with annotations, some 2000 individual
promptbooks associated with Shakespearean productions from
the 1620s to the early 1960s and that are accessible in
public collections. "Promptbook" is used here in the
broadest sense to include any hand-annotated copy of a
play associated with a professional production; these include
stage managers' workbooks; rehearsal promptbooks; the
fully annotated promptbooks from which stage managers run
productions nightly; annotated, illuminated souvenir copies;
and studybooks or preparation copies of actors, with
occasional marginal notes. The author combed the major
theatre collections and theatre archives in England, the
United States, and Canada. He identifies each promptbook
(some are correctly identified for the first time here) as to
the production(s) it reflects and the date, city, and
theatre. The library and call number are noted and the
basic, identifying bibliographic features are given. The
contents and usefulness of each are described; often the
author notes the various productions that a cumulative
promptbook seems to reflect after passing from hand to
hand, production to production. The introductory material
provides useful notes on the symbols and abbreviations from
the cryptic, efficient, and sometimes mysterious language
used in the backstage world. The section on *A Midsummer
Night's Dream* (pp. 322-32) lists over fifty promptbooks,
dating from the 1670s to the 1960s. (See also item T1303.)

T1265   Shedd, Robert G. "The Great Lakes Shakespeare
        Festival." *Shakespeare Quarterly,* 16 (1965), 341-42.

        The review coverage includes a brief, favorable mention
of the summer Festival production of *A Midsummer Night's
Dream,* directed by David Hooks, which was later
transferred to the McCarter Theatre, Princeton, New
Jersey, for the 1965-66 season. Hooks is praised for his
emphasis on the lovers and some of the original stage
business; he "satisfied all the traditional expectations and
yet made the play seem freshly new."

T1266   Stephens, Frances, ed. *Theatre World Annual: 1965.*
        London: Iliffe Books for Theatre World, 1965.

Includes in the pictorial review of the 1963-64 season, photographs of the Royal Shakespeare Company production of *A Midsummer Night's Dream* directed by Peter Hall (revival).

T1267   Brown, John Russell. *Shakespeare's Plays in Performance.* London: Edward Arnold Limited, [1966]. 244 pp. Illustrated.

Analyzes the texts of selected plays and productions to show inherent production values, alternating between close reading and stage history. He argues that in Oberon's "We are spirits of another sort," meter, rhythm, diction, syntax, and inherent phrasing in the passage will provide "the long controlled sound" that gives the fairy king authority. In an analysis of Bottom's character, his inner nature is said to be revealed to us in a sequence that is progressively intimate, leading ultimately to our full, amused understanding of his performance as Pyramus. There are a few brief references to stage business in the 1959 production of *A Midsummer Night's Dream* at Stratford-upon-Avon in 1959, directed by Peter Hall.

T1267a   Grice, Maureen. "Midsummer Night's Dream, A: Stage History," s.v. *A Midsummer Night's Dream*, in *The Reader's Encyclopedia of Shakespeare*, edited by Oscar J. Campbell and Edward G. Quin. New York: Thomas V. Crowell Company, 1966, pp. 545-48.

Provides brief descriptions and assessments of major productions of the play on the English and American stage from 1595 to 1964. For some productions of importance, staging features and principal cast members are provided. There are relatively longer descriptions of the 1958 production of the American Shakespeare Festival (see item T1172) and those of the 1961 and 1964 New York Shakespeare Festival (see items T1204 and T1243).

T1268   Gouhier, Henri. "De l'Adaption Théâtrale, Théâtre et cas de conscience." *La Table Ronde*, 216-17 (1966), 115-18.

Includes an unfavorable review of a production of *A Midsummer Night's Dream* at the Comedie-Française that used an adaptation by Charles Charras.

T1269   *A Midsummer Night's Dream* presented by the Actor's
        Workshop Company at the Marines' Theatre, San
        Francisco, 11 March 1966, and subsequently at the
        Pittsburgh Playhouse, 25 November 1966, and at the
        Theatre de Lys, New York City, 29 June 1967, as a
        production of the Circle in the Square, Theodore Mann
        and Paul Lubin, producers. Director, John Hancock.
        Settings and costumes designed by Robert La Vigne after
        drawings by Jim Dine. *Theseus/Oberon*, Alvin Epstein.
        Hippolyta/Titania, Gloria Foster. *Hermia*, Susan
        Anspach. *Helena*, Robert Benson. *Bottom*, Alan Manson.

        An anti-romantic, anti-establishment production of the
        play in the spirit of the American avant-garde of the
        sixties, with powerful, satiric imagery of an erotic and
        decadent world. Well known artist Jim Dine provided set
        designs that included a proscenium painted in a
        house-enamel rainbow and costume designs that borrowed
        upon "hippie" culture clothes for the mechanicals. Helena
        was played by a female impersonator, Titania was dressed
        as the comic strip Wonder Woman, and Puck was a weary,
        worn Cupid.

        Reviews: George Oppenheimer, *Newsday*, 30 June 1966;
        The Valley Independent (Pittsburgh), 23 November 1966;
        Pittsburg Post-Gazette, 18 November 1966; Dan Sullivan,
        New York Times, 30 June 1967; *Newark Evening News*, 30
        June 1967; Alan Bunce, *Christian Science Monitor*, 3 July
        1967; *Variety*, 5 July 1967; Jerry Tallmer, *New York Post*,
        5 July 1967; Richard Cooke, *Wall Street Journal*, 1 July
        1967; Michael Smith, *Village Voice*, 6 July 1967; Whitney
        Bolton, New York *Morning Telegraph*, 1 July 1967; Mildred
        C. Kuner, *Shakespeare Quarterly*, 18 (1967), 411-15. (See
        also items T1285 and T1312.)

T1270   Odell, George Clinton Densmore. *Shakespeare from
        Betterton to Irving.* 2 Volumes. New York: Charles
        Scribner and Sons, 1920; reprint, With a new
        Introduction by Robert Hamilton Ball, New York: Dover
        Publications, Inc., 1966.

        Surveys chronologically the major figures, major theatre
        companies, and major trends in the production of
        Shakespeare's plays in England from the Restoration to
        1914. The coverage includes descriptions, ranging from
        brief to lengthy, of many important productions of *A*

Midsummer Night's Dream. He discusses the operatic
versions from Purcell (1692) through Garrick (1755 and
1763) to Reynolds (1816) and (at greater length) the
Victorian productions of Vestris (1840), Phelps (1853),
Kean (1856), Daly (1888), and Tree (1900). Playbills,
reviews, and stage directions from published acting editions
are often cited at length; the considerations of these
productions are divided into discussions of texts, acting,
and scenic and costuming practices. A Victorian taste for
the star actor-manager and for elaborate pictorial
illustration of the plays prevails here; praise is lavished on
the scenically lavish Victorian productions of *A Midsummer
Night's Dream.* The summit of all for Odell was Tree's
production; he loathed the Granville-Barker production of
1914, with its modern décor, and closed his history with a
scathing denunciation of it as an ominous indication of the
future. Odell's methodology, documentation, and
enthusiastic narrative have made the work a classic in the
bibliography of staged Shakespeare.

T1271   Scorer, Mischa. "*A Midsummer Night's Dream,* 1962." *To
         Nevill Coghill from Friends.* Ed. John Lawlor and W. H.
         Auden. London: Faber and Faber, 1966, pp. 103-18.

         Recounts the author's experience with Coghill in the
Worcester College production of. *A Midsummer Night's
Dream.* "This was to be the central theme of the
production--harmony and disharmony, stability and
instability in nature and in man, and the coming together of
the two worlds in the solemn and mysterious sacrament of
marriage." The atmosphere was one of "awful beauty and
magic."

T1272   "Shakespeare Productions in the United Kingdom: 1965."
         Shakespeare Survey, 19 (1966), 108-110.

         Included in the annual listing, compiled by the
Shakespeare Memorial Library, Birmingham, are five
productions of *A Midsummer Night's Dream,* including those
at the Playhouse, Salisbury, directed by Derek Martinus; at
the Flora Robson Playhouse, Newcastle-upon-Tyne, directed
by Julian Herington; at the Alveston Manor Hotel,
Stratford-upon-Avon, by the Amateur Dramatic Club of
Cambridge; and at the Tower Theatre, London, by the
Tavistock Repertory Company, directed by Jessica Taylor.

T1273   Smith, Peter D. "The 1966 Festivals at Ashland, Oregon, and San Diego, California." *Shakespeare Quarterly*, 17 (1966), 407-17.

Reviews seven productions and offers a fairly favorable assessment of the *A Midsummer Night's Dream* at the previous summer's Ashland Festival, "a workmanlike and enjoyable production," if not a memorable one. Hugh C. Evans directed and Angus L. Bowmer, the Festival's founder, was Peter Quince; he is praised as especially effective, not only as a "home-town impresario" but as an anxious director who won sympathy throughout. There is an unusually forthright discussion of critical standards for festivals seemingly insulated from contemporary trends in Shakespearean production elsewhere and commentary on the matter of the limitations of amateur performers.

T1274   Sprague, Arthur Colby. *Shakespeare and the Audience.* A Study in the Technique of Exposition. Harvard University Press, 1935; reprint, Russell and Russell, 1966. xi, 327 pp.

Shows how Shakespeare keeps character and plot clear for an audience watching and listening to a performance. In chapter two, "Time and Place," he explains how Shakespeare sets the stage and communicates the sense of the hour. He points to the night and dawn scenes in *A Midsummer Night's Dream* that are prepared for in many lines, and shows how each of the groups of characters in the play are carefully introduced when we first meet them.

T1275   Britten, Benjamin. *A Midsummer Night's Dream.* [Recording of the Britten opera.] Libretto adapted from William Shakespeare by Benjamin Britten and Peter Pears. Benjamin Britten conducting the London Symphony Orchestra, with Alfred Deller as *Oberon*, Elizabeth Harwood as *Titania*, Peter Pears as *Lysander*, Thomas Hemsley as *Demetrius*, and Owen Brannigan as *Bottom.* Three 33 1/3 rpm phonodiscs, stereo. London OSA 1385. 1967.

See item T1188.

T1275a   Fontane, Theodor. *"Causerian über Theatre,"* in
         Samtliche Werke, Band 22, Dritter Teil. München:
         Nymphenburger Verlagschandlung, 1967, pp. 61-65.

         This collection of essays on theatre performances by the
         prolific nineteenth century German author includes his
         accounts of many London theatre productions that he saw in
         the 1850s, including several of Charles Kean's at the
         Princess's Theatre. Among these was Kean's *A Midsummer
         Night's Dream,* which Fontane describes in some detail. He
         was impressed by Kean's settings and wholly charmed by
         the fairy spectacle of the closing scene of the production.
         The collection also includes his essays on German
         productions of the play in 1877, 1880, and 1882.

T1276   Fuerst, Walter René, and Samuel J. Hume. *Twentieth
         Century Stage Decoration.* With an Introduction by
         Adolphe Appia. 2 volumes. London: Alfred Knopf, Ltd.,
         1929; reprint, New York: Benjamin Blom, Inc. and Dover
         Publications, Inc. (paperback), 1967. Illustrated.

         Discusses the major achievements in theory and practice
         of early twentieth century scenic and lighting design.
         Among the major theorists and directors considered are
         Adolphe Appia, Gordon Craig, Konstantin Stanislavski, Max
         Reinhardt, and Harley Granville-Barker. Among the dozens
         of designers whose works are discussed and reproduced is
         Norman Wilkinson, who designed the settings for
         Granville-Barker's 1914 production of *A Midsummer Night's
         Dream.* Two photographs of the production are reproduced,
         showing Wilkinson's set for Titania's bower (a green mound,
         backed with painted draperies) and for a scene in the
         lovers' chase in the forest (stepped forestage, with a large
         impressionistically painted curtain backing it).

T1276a   Heliodora, Barbara, C. de M. F. de Almeida.
         "Shakespeare in Brazil," *Shakespeare Survey,* 20 (1967),
         121-24.

         Mentions a 1949 production of *A Midsummer Night's
         Dream* by students and "fairly good" productions of the
         play by amateurs in 1964, using a new translation by Maria
         de Sauda de Cortesão.

T1276ab *A Midsummer Night's Dream.* Color film of the ballet
adaptation by George Balanchine, featuring the New
York City Ballet Company, 1967. 93 minutes. Producer,
Richard Davis. Director, Dan Eriksen. Choreographer
and Production Conception, George Balanchine.
Photographer, Arthur J. Ornitz. Art Director, Albert
Brenner. Editor, Armond Lebowitz. Music, Felix
Mendelssohn. Orchestra of the New York City Ballet
conducted by Robert Irving. *Titania,* Suzanne Farrell.
Oberon, Eduard Villella. *Puck,* Arthur Mitchell. *Helena,*
Mimi Paul. *Theseus,* Francisco Moncion. *Hippolyta,* Gloria
Govrin. *Bottom,* Richard Rapp. (See items T1214a and
T1409.)

T1277 *A Midsummer Night's Dream* presented by the American
Shakespeare Festival Theatre and Academy, Stratford,
Connecticut, 17 June 1967. Director, Cyril Ritchard.
Setting, William and Jean Eckart. Lighting, Tharon
Musser. Costumes, Robert Fletcher. *Theseus,* Myles
Eason. *Oberon/Bottom,* Cyril Ritchard.

A conventionally romantic production, somewhat
anachronistic for 1967, with a few novelties. Notable chiefly
for the three roles Cyril Ritchard took upon himself as
Oberon, Bottom and director, none of which made the
production exceptional according to critics, though his
doubling as Oberon and Bottom was unique in the play's
stage history.

Reviews: Walter Kerr, *New York Times,* 18 June 1967;
Julius Novick, *Nation,* 25 September 1967; Bernard
Beckerman, *Shakespeare Quarterly,* 18 (1967), 405-408.

T1278 *A Midsummer Night's Dream* presented by the Popular
Theatre Company at the Edinburgh Festival, 21 August
1967, and subsequently at the Saville Theatre, London,
26 September 1967. Director, Frank Dunlop. *Bottom,* Jim
Dale. *Theseus/Oberon,* Robin Bailey. *Hippolyta/Titania,*
Cleo Laine. *Quince,* Bernard Bresslaw.

An untraditional production in "modern dress." Theseus
wore the white uniform of a modern Greek general, and
Bottom wore a leather jacket and motorcycle helmet. Jazz
vocalist Cleo Laine was most effective when singing the jazz
idiom songs composed for her to sing as Titania. One

reviewer characterized it as a vigorous and good natured production in which "a kind of cocky fun" prevailed.

Reviews: *The Times*, 22 and 27 August 1967; *The Observer*, 27 August 1967; *Illustrated London News*, 2 September 1967; J. W. Lambert, *Drama*, 87 (Winter 1967), 18-31.

T1279   Rosenfeld, Sybil. "The Grieves' Shakespearean Scene Designs." *Shakespeare Survey*, 20 (1967), 107-111.

Discusses on the occasion of an exhibit at Stratford of designs by the Grieves, the contributions to Shakespearean production in the nineteenth century by members of this notable family of scene painters. (They painted scenery for notable productions of *A Midsummer Night's Dream*, including the Reynolds opera of 1816, Vestris' 1840 production, and Kean's of 1856.) This article includes a reproduction and discussion of the exhibited Grieves' design for a masque entitled "Oberon and Robin," which was inserted into Act I of Charles Kemble's 1832 production of *All's Well That Ends Well* at Covent Garden.

T1280   Rowell, George. *The Victorian Theatre, A Survey.* Oxford: Clarendon Press, 1967. 209 pp. Illustrated.

Surveys the major theatres, production trends, plays, playwrights, and producers from 1792 to 1914. There is mention of Elizabeth Vestris' production of *A Midsummer Night's Dream* (1840) and a brief characterization and one photograph of the Granville-Barker staging (1914). There is an exceptionally full bibliography for students of Victorian theatre.

T1281   Seng, Peter J. *The Vocal Songs in the Plays of Shakespeare. A Critical History.* Cambridge: Harvard University Press, 1967. xix, 314 pp.

Collects the textual and analytical commentary of many scholars on the lyrics, early extant song settings, and musical terminology used in the plays, together with the author's own considerations of the dramatic functions of the songs. In the section on *A Midsummer Night's Dream*, the fairy lullaby for Titania and Bottom's "woosel cock" song are discussed. Titania's request for "a rondell" elicits a round or dancing song, far removed from the more sophisticated rondel. Terms and names in the lullaby are glossed. The source of Bottom's song is reported to be "A poem of a Mayde forsaken," by (probably) Richard Edwards.

T1282   Styan, J. L. *Shakespeare's Stagecraft.* Cambridge: Cambridge University Press, 1967. 244 pp.

Analyzes Shakespeare's plays as performance scripts, stressing the importance of exploring their theatrical dimensions. Several scenes from *A Midsummer Night's Dream* come into the analyses that are arranged thematically and that consider such matters as acting conventions, vocal inflections, pauses, pace changes, and blocking. In his chapter, "The Full Stage," for example, Styan discusses what Shakespeare achieves in scenes of "multiple-centered interest," such as occur when diverse types of characters all converge on stage in resolution scenes (as at the end of *A Midsummer Night's Dream*). The analysis envisions the plays on the Elizabethan open stage. There are a few references to present-day stage practices.

T1283   Willis, Ronald A. "Shakespeare in the Rockies." *Shakespeare Quarterly*, 18 (1967), 417-20.

Coverage of the Colorado Shakespeare Festival includes an unfavorable review of the production of *A Midsummer Night's Dream*, directed by Martin Cobin, who reportedly approached it as a simple play likely to be obscured by hair-splitting analysis. It was "an amiable diversion," but there was little interplay among characters, which encouraged audiences to respond to the roles as individual creations, and it lacked a clear overall design in movement on the stage of the outdoor theatre.

T1283a   Ball, Robert Hamilton. *Shakespeare on Silent Film: A Strange Eventful History.* London: George Allen and Unwin, Ltd., 1968. 403 pp. Illustrated.

This chronological history of Shakespeare on silent film comments on seven early silent film versions of *A Midsummer Night's Dream* (which are identified by the

names of the following companies, directors, or actors): Le
Lion (1909), Vitagraph (1906 and 1909), Lubin (1912),
Deutsche Bioscop (1913), Tommasi-Hubner (1913?), and
Neumann (1925). One of the earliest, that of Le Lion, which
has not survived, reportedly was an interpretation by a
French clown, his sons, and a Russian woman dancer. The
successful eight minute 1909 Vitagraph version, which
survives, is praised by Ball as being "fairly intelligible,"
with sharp photography. It was "more of a movie than a
photograph of a play," and it achieved, with its outdoor
backgrounds, "a kind of pastoral poetry." He also praises
the Italian film of 1913, whose only known credits are the
names Socrate Tommasi and Bianca Maria Hubner. The
Deutsche Bioscop film of 1913, *Ein Sommersnachtstraum*, was
a successful re-working of parts of the play written by
Hanns Heinz Ewers and directed by Stellan Rye. The Hans
Neumann version of 1925, with titles by Klabund [Alfred
Henschke], was forbidden for juveniles and is described by
reviewers excerpted here in conflicting terms ranging from
"charming" to "Rabelasian." Ball says it was the second
German film of the play "to seize on Shakespeare and then
treat him brutally." Four frames from the 1909 Vitagraph
film are reproduced and a photo from the Neumann film
shows Pyramus, Lion, and Wall. In a section entitled
"Explanations and Acknowledgements," Ball provides data on
the location of prints of films, biographical information on
cast members (including some from interviews), and
documentation of published notices of films that he was
unable to view.

T1284   Brook, Peter. *The Empty Space*. London: MacGibbon and
        Kee; New York: Atheneum, 1968; New York: Avon
        [1969]. 128 pp.

        Characterizes "the deadly theatre" and suggests ways of
revitalizing the art. The innovative, influential English
director, who was a key figure in the creation of the Royal
Shakespeare Company and the International Center for
Theatre Research, says that Shakespeare's plays should be
staged in a non-illusionistic manner and should be informed
by the spirit of contemporary society. This philosophy was
manifest in his world-renowned productions of *King Lear*
and *A Midsummer Night's Dream*, landmarks in the history
of staged Shakespeare in this century. The personal,
impressionistic essays explore Artaud and Brecht, who
influenced Brook, and other major twentieth century

experimenters in theatre and drama, including Vsevelod
Meyerhold, Merce Cunningham, Jerzy Grotowski and Samuel
Beckett. These comments are characteristic: "In the
theatre, every form once born is mortal; every form must
be reconceived, and its new conception will bear the marks
of all the influences that surround it. . . . Yet a great
theatre is not a fashion house; perpetual elements do recur
. . ." (p. 15). "Today the theatre of doubting, of unease,
of trouble, of alarm, seems truer than the theatre with a
noble aim" (p. 40). "In the theatre the audience completes
the steps of creation" (p. 113). "I do not for one moment
question the principle of rewriting Shakespeare--after all,
the texts do not get burned--each person can do what he
thinks necessary with a text and still no one suffers" (p.
74). (See also item T1314.)

T1285   [Dine, Jim.] *Jim Dine Designs for "A Midsummer Night's
         Dream."* Introduction by Virginia Allen. New York:
         Museum of Modern Art, 1968. Illustrated. 32 pp.

         Reproduces thirty-two of Dine's designs for the costumes
         and sets for the controversial, anti-romantic production of
         A Midsummer Night's Dream of 1966 directed by John
         Hancock. Some of these designs are in the Museum of
         Modern Art's theatre arts collection; several are reproduced
         here in color. The booklet also includes six production
         photographs. (See also item T1269.)

T1285a   Downes, John. *Roscius Anglicanus, or an Historical
         Review of the Stage . . . from 1660 to 1706.* London: H.
         Playford, 1708; With additions by Thomas Davis, London:
         Printed for the Editor, 1789; facsimile reprint of the
         1708 edition with a preface by Joseph Knight, London:
         J. W. Jarvis and son, 1886; Montague Summers, ed.,
         London: The Fortune Press [1928]; reprint, New York:
         Benjamin Blom, 1968. xiii, 286 pp.

         Downes was the prompter for the Duke's Men from 1661
         to 1706, and included in his brief notes on their
         productions (his account is only fifty-two pages long, to
         which Summers provided 223 pages of notes) is his
         characterization of Purcell's *The Fairy Queen* of 1692 (pp.
         42-43), which he says was very expensively produced in
         scenery and costumes and very well performed in the

portions composed by Purcell. "But the expenses in setting out being so great, the Company got very little by it."

T1286   Foulkes, Richard. "Samuel Phelps's *A Midsummer Night's Dream*, Sadler's Wells--October 8th, 1853." *Theatre Notebook*, 23 (1968/69), 55-60.

Reconstructs Phelps's successful production in detail, drawing on reviews, biographies, and a newly discovered source--an account by Frederick Fenton, Phelps's scene designer. Foukes shows with this evidence how Phelps achieved the dream-effect of his forest scenes with a stage-wide gauze and new gas lighting. *A Midsummer Night's Dream* had not, Foulkes contends, had "such a fine and appropriate staging as that by Samuel Phelps" before and "probably not since." Phelps is seen as a precursor of modern directors, having harmonized the theatre's arts into a whole in this production.

T1287   Gascoigne, Bamber. *World Theatre, an Illustrated History*. London: Eberry Press, 1968. 335 pp. Illustrated.

Included in this well-illustrated survey is a photograph (black and white) of the watercolor of the Charles Kean production's setting for Quince's workshop (1856). Also it reproduces Goethe's sketch of a stage for a production of *A Midsummer Night's Dream* that features a fixed structure of three levels, with staircases and arches, and which foreshadows that used by Ludwig Tieck in his production of 1843.

T1288   *A Midsummer Night's Dream* presented by the Stratford Shakespeare Festival at the Festival Theatre, Stratford, Ontario, Canada, beginning in repertory 12 June 1968. Director, John Hirsch. Designer, Leslie Hurry. Music, Stanley Silverman. *Theseus*, Kenneth Pogue. *Hermia*, Tedde Moore. *Lysander*, Christopher Walken. *Helena*, Jane Casson. *Quince*, Bernard Behrens. *Bottom*, Douglas Rain. *Puck*, Barbara Byrne. *Titania*, Martha Henry.

A production influenced by Jan Kott's *Shakespeare, Our Contemporary* that suggested some erotic decadence at

Theseus' court and emphasized the sexual and sensual side of the forest and fairy world.

Reviews: Dan Sullivan, *New York Times*, 13 June 1968; Richard Coe, *Washington Post*, 13 June 1968; Herbert Whittaker, *Toronto Globe and Mail*, 13 June 1968; Kevin Kelley, *Boston Globe*, 14 June 1968; *Toronto Star*, 13 June 1968; *Toronto Telegram*, 13 June 1968; Walter Kerr, *New York Times*, 23 June 1968; Arnold Edinborough, *Saturday Night*, August 1968; Edinborough, *Shakespeare Quarterly*, 19 (1968), 381-84, with two photos opposite p. 378; John Pettigrew, *Journal of Canadian Studies*, III (1968). (See also items 239 and T1291.)

T1289   Nicoll, Allardyce. *English Drama, A Modern Viewpoint.* London: George G. Harrap and Company, Ltd., 1968. vi, 184 pp. Illustrated.

Includes some discussion of modern trends in Shakespearean production. While acknowledging that there is a darker side of Shakespeare's fairy world in *A Midsummer Night's Dream*, he suggests that the modern emphasis on it is a reaction to Victorian sentimentalism, and Nicoll believes that replacing Mendelssohn with "modern discords" leads us no closer to "Shakespeare's complete vision."

T1290   Purcell, Henry. *The Works of Henry Purcell.* Volume 12: *The Fairy Queen*, rev. ed. Anthony Lewis. London: Novello and Company, Ltd., for the Purcell Society [1968]. xxvi, 224 pp.

A revised edition of the complete score based on newly discovered manuscripts. All that was published of the score in Purcell's lifetime was a volume of twelve pages. The discovery in 1903 of a major portion of manuscript score led to its publication then, edited by J. S. Shedlock. Other sections of the score, both vocal and instrumental came to light prior to the publication of this revised edition. The introductory material includes the 1903 preface that gives an account of the development and the sources of the score. There is a new preface and a list of the sources used for this revised edition. The score is preceded by a condensation of the text with the song lyrics and the stage

directions, cited in full, for the intermezzi-like spectacles
which the music accompanied.

T1291   Raby, Peter, ed. *The Stratford Scene, 1958-1968.* With
         an introduction by Michael Langham. Toronto: Clarke,
         Irwin and Company, Ltd., 1968. 256 pp. Illustrated.

    Includes a section on the Canadian Festival's production
of *A Midsummer Night's Dream* in 1968, directed by John
Hirsch, with pre-rehearsal notes of the director, an essay
by Robertson Davies that is part stage history and part
description and assessment of the 1968 production, and nine
large photographs of the production. (See also item T1288.)
Hirsch's notes call for the fairies to be flower children,
"children of the loins of night"; the court was to be "a
society of fossils sprinkled with the dust of law books,
tomes of death," and the actors were to play "not the
humour of the mechanicals but their reality." Davies, in his
assessment, is critical of the director's rendering of the
court and says the fairies, led by a beautiful, noble
Titania, "made the night splendid."

T1291a   Beerbohm, Sir Max. *More Theatres, 1898-1903.* With an
         Introduction by Rupert Hart-Davis. London: Hart-Davis;
         Foreword by Louis Kronenburger, New York: Taplinger
         Publishing Company, 1969. 624 pp.

    Included in this collection of Beerbohm's *Saturday
Review* theatre reviews is an often-cited review (pp.
113-16) of an Oxford University Drama Society production
of *A Midsummer Night's Dream* that is devoted in large part
to praise of the play itself. "Throughout the *Midsummer
Night's Dream* we see [Shakespeare] in his slippers . . .
which, in sheer gaiety and lightness of heart, he kicks up
into the empyrean and catches again on the tip of his toe
upturned." He has praise for the production, noting that
the play, with its even distribution of parts, means it is a
happy one for amateurs. In this collection there is also his
review of Herbert Beerbohm Tree's 1900 production of the
play, which he found "charming." The fairies "*were* fairies
for me." He defends the scenically pictorial style of staging
over the scenery-less methods advocated by Sidney Lee.

T1292   *Contemporary Foreign Theatre: Controversial Ideas and Trends. A Collection of Essays.* Moscow: Nauka, 1969.

Essays in Russian include discussion of the music for *A Midsummer Night's Dream* composed by Carl Orff and Benjamin Britten. Not seen.

T1293   Entry Deleted.

T1294   Hall, Peter. "Why the Fairies Have Dirty Faces." *The Sunday Times*, 26 January 1969, p. 55.

Discusses his handling of the 1969 filming of *A Midsummer Night's Dream*, a film derivative of his production with the Royal Shakespeare Company, 1959-63. (See T1301.) Shakespeare is essentially non-cinematic because he is "a verbal dramatist, relying on the associative and metaphysical power of words." A good film, by comparison, depends upon "contrasting visual images"; what is spoken is of secondary importance. Film directors seek "to capture the general image of the play, its story and mood, with a deliberate simplification of text." Hall's film used actors from his stage production of the play, but the film was not intended as a reproduction of the stage presentation. People and places had to be concrete. The play is more Elizabethan than Greek, with Theseus an English country Duke, and the fairies are not classical "but sprites of Hallowe'en." In Hall's film, shot at Compton Verney in Warwickshire in rainy cold September weather, the dialogue was studio-recorded and synchronized with the film. The film was thus edited to the text, with shots changing at line or phrase ends. The film text was actually fuller than the text used on the stage, and the film was shorter than the stage version, because actors spoke more quickly and there was no time taken by entrances and exits. Hall wanted to "bend the medium of the film to reveal the full quality of the text. . . . It therefore may not be a film at all." Four photos of the fairies accompany the article.

T1295   Hunt, Hugh. "Granville-Barker's Shakespearean Productions." *Theatre Research/Recherches Theatrales*, 10 (1969), 44-49.

Describes Granville-Barker's three Shakespearean productions at the Savoy Theatre, London, 1912 to 1914, which included his *A Midsummer Night's Dream* with the famous golden fairies. (See also item T1149.) He contrasts the staging with that of Victorian tradition. "Above all it was the fairies that caught popular attention." In their bronze and gold costumes, moving like marionettes, "they were sinister and menacing creatures from another world." Puck, dressed in scarlet with a yellow wig, "became a link between the exotic mythology of Shakespeare's conception of the Eastern world and the Elizabethan conception of the spirit of mischief."

T1296   Hurtgen, Charles. "The Operatic Character of Background Music in Film Adaptations of Shakespeare." *Shakespeare Quarterly*, 20 (1969), 53-64.

Included in this consideration of the nature and techniques of film music scoring is a discussion of Eric Korngold's arrangement of Mendelssohn's music for Max Reinhardt's film of *A Midsummer Night's Dream* (1935) and the methods of coordinating the action and the music. The most popular Mendelssohn passages were used, including the "Wedding March," which was used for a mimed mock wedding of Oberon and Titania in a procession from forest to palace. This contradicted the general wisdom of not using familiar music for films that will either distract or sound hackneyed.

T1297   Jorgens, Jack C. "Staging Shakespeare in 1969." *Shakespeare Newsletter*, 19 (1969), 4-5.

Surveys briefly the productions of some eight different theatre groups, including the productions of *A Midsummer Night's Dream* in 1968 and 1969, respectively at the Stratford, Ontario, Shakespeare Festival, directed by John Hirsch (see item T1288), and at the Cape May, New Jersey, Shakespeare Festival, directed by Paul Barry. Both seemed to have been influenced by Jan Kott's essay on the play. At Cape May, Oberon was hippie god of love and Titania a faded movie queen of the 1930s. Some of the fairies were go-go girls and the music was adapted from the Supremes. The mechanicals were "Kiwanis club types."

T1298   Lewis, Allan. "*A Midsummer Night's Dream*--Fairy Fantasy
        or Erotic Nightmare?" *Educational Theatre Journal*, 21
        (1969), 251-58.

        Describes and compares two recent productions of *A
        Midsummer Night's Dream*--the anti-romantic production
        directed by John Hancock at the Theatre de Lys, New York
        City, 1967, and the traditional, romantic production
        directed by Cyril Ritchard at the Stratford, Connecticut,
        Shakespeare Festival, 1967. (For characterizations of these,
        see items T1269 and T1277.) The Ritchard version,
        "stemming from Calvinistic rejection of emotional exuberance
        and contradictorily adding the romantic idealism of
        Coleridge, with the grace and outward elegance of
        Pre-Raphaelite lyricism, aptly belongs to the Age of
        Victoria." The erotic nightmare of Hancock provoked a
        re-examination of accepted myths and a questioning of the
        love relationships: "its forerunners are Freud, McLuhan,
        and the hydrogen bomb." "Contradictory interpretations are
        inevitable," Lewis says and argues against such extremes as
        the joyless cynicism of Jan Kott or the banality of a fairy
        tale production. He asks for "respect for the script and
        avoidance of gimmickry." This essentially conservative essay
        is an early American entry in the developing debate about
        directorial freedoms with Shakespeare. For another
        annotation of this item see 340.

T1298a McManaway, James G. "The Renaissance Heritage of
        English Staging (1642-1700)," in *Studies in Shakespeare:
        Bibliography, and Theatre*. Ed. Richard Hosley, Arthur
        C. Kirsch, and John W. Velz. New York: The
        Shakespeare Association of America, 1969, pp. 223-39.

        Reprint of a 1964 article reviewing English staging
        practices from 1642 to 1700--stages, scenery, machines, and
        lighting, citing evidence illustrative of normal and special
        practices from stage directions. Among the matters
        discussed are the importation of French machinery, the use
        of curtains, proscenium doors, wings and shutters, gauze
        transparencies, and "relieves." Analyzes the stage direction
        in *Fairy Queen* describing a garden fountain and suggests
        that one large fountain was practical, comparing it to
        hydraulic spectacles at London fairs. Suggests, in a
        discussion of Settle's *The World in the Moon* (1697), that
        the English were attempting to catch up with continental
        practices.

T1299 Mendelssohn-Bartholdy, Felix. *A Midsummer Night's Dream, Complete Incidental Music.* Rafael Frübeck De Burgos conducting the New Philharmonia Orchestra, Hanneke Van Bork, Alfreda Hodgson, and the Ambrosian Singers. One 33 1/3 phonodisc, stereo. Decca OS 26017. 1969. Reissued in 1979 as Decca Jubilee JB72.

Contains the overture and the complete incidental music, recorded in fourteen separate cuts.

T1300 Mendelssohn-Bartholdy, Felix. *A Midsummer Night's Dream": Incidental Music.* Peter Maag conducting the London Symphony Orchestra, with Jennifer Vyvyan and Marion Lowe, sopranos, and the female chorus of the Royal Opera House, Covent Garden. Program notes by Robert Boas and the texts of the vocal portions printed on the slipcase. Two 33 1/3 rpm phonodiscs, stereo. London STS 15084. *circa* 1969.

Contains the overture, opus 21, and excerpts from the incidental music, opus 61: numbers 1, 3, 5, 7, 9, 11, and 12.

T1301 *A Midsummer Night's Dream.* 35 mm. color film produced by the Royal Shakespeare Company, Michael Birkett, producer. Opened 30 January 1969. Director, Peter Hall. Photography, Peter Suschitzky. Design, John Bury and Ann Curtis. Music, Guy Woolfenden. *Theseus*, Derek Godfrey; *Lysander*, David Warner; *Helena*, Diana Rigg; *Hermia*, Helen Mirren; *Oberon*, Ian Richardson; *Titania*, Judi Dench; *Puck*, Ian Holm; *Bottom*, Paul Rogers.

This first full-length film of the play in English since the Max Reinhardt-William Dieterle film for Warner Brothers in 1935 was a radical departure from the moonlight and Mendelssohn traditions. The film was derivative of Hall's evolving production with the RSC, 1959-63 (see T1183), but employed innovative, unconventional techniques in the film medium. For example, Hall shot the forest scenes in a cold September rain to capture a vision of nature in disharmony such as Titania describes. Also, a handheld camera was used in the chase scenes. Said Hall of his approach to the play in this film: "It is not a pretty balletic affair, but erotic, physical, down to earth." (See T1294.) The film was shown on CBS television, 9 February 1969. (See also items T1183, T1294, T1323, T1376 and T1406.)

T1302   Rischbieter, Henning, compiler. *Art and the Stage in the Twentieth Century, Painters and Sculptors Work for the Theatre.* New York: New York Graphic Society, 1969. 306 pp. Illustrated.

Discusses and documents the theory and practice of major painters and sculptors of the twentieth century who have designed for the theatre. Their work represents a wide variety of scenic styles and experiments. The 256 illustrations plates include a color reproduction of a forest setting by Karl Walser for Max Reinhardt's 1909 *A Midsummer Night's Dream* at the Munich Kunstlertheater and an unrealized design by Oscar Kokoschka for a forest scene for a production by the Shakespeare Memorial Theatre, Stratford-upon-Avon. Also reproduced (in black and white) are six of Jim Dine's designs for the 1966 Actors' Workshop production, San Francisco, directed by John Hancock. See also the Catalogue of Productions in Rischbieter's appendix for notes on these productions and guides to sources for further study. (See also item T1269.)

T1303   Shattuck, Charles H. "The Shakespeare Promptbooks: First Supplement." *Theatre Notebook,* 24 (1969), 5-17.

Provides a promised supplement to his 1965 catalogue, *The Shakespeare Promptbooks* (T1264), in which he lists and annotates three more important promptbooks of *A Midsummer Night's Dream* productions--that of Alfred Bunn (which opened in 1833), that of Charles Kean (which opened in 1856), and that of Harley Granville-Barker (which opened in 1914).

T1304   Stephan, Erika. "Zweierlei Haltung zu Shakespeare." *Theater der Zeit,* 24, 3 (1969), 31-35.

Reviews a production of *A Midsummer Night's Dream* in Weimar, directed by Fritz Bennewitz. Not seen.

T1305   Vassiliou, Spyros. *Lights and Shadows.* Athens, 1969. Illustrated.

Included among the illustrations of the work of this Greek scene designer are several of his designs for several of Shakespeare's plays, *A Midsummer Night's Dream* among them. Not seen.

T1306   Webster, Margaret. *The Same Only Different: Five Generations of a Great Theatre Family.* London: Gollancz; New York: Alfred A. Knopf, 1969. xviii, 409 pp. Illustrated.

Webster's stories about the theatre careers of the actors and actresses in the Webster family included her reminiscences about her own experiences in the Old Vic production of *A Midsummer Night's Dream* in 1929. Webster then did Hermia under the direction of Harcourt Williams. She tells of his use of the uncut text and his emphasis upon good verse speaking and rapid delivery--goals of the highest priority for Williams who was very influenced by Harley Granville-Barker. Of verse delivery, she says Williams "wanted a truth with music in it." She reports that Williams read to his cast the proofs of Harley Granville-Barker's *Prefaces to Shakespeare* and says Granville-Barker once wrote Williams saying that his actors should "let the verse seem to be carrying them along and not . . . be so damned explanatory." There is a photo of Webster at age fourteen as Puck in a school production.

T1307   Ansorge, Peter. "Director in Interview: Peter Brook." *Plays and Players,* 18 (October 1970), 18-9.

Brook discusses his approach to his famous 1970 production of *A Midsummer Night's Dream* with the RSC. (See also item T1314.) Having worked on a series of violent, dark plays, he longed to do a work of pure celebration, and this play is "amongst other things, a celebration of the arts of the theatre." While today we do not believe in magic, spirits, and fairies, we can discover the real play, "the hidden play," behind the artificial, unreal elements. The stage imagery serving it today must be different than that of the past. The magic of the play must come from the hidden life of the performer; the necessary beginning is for the production to drop stage tricks. Actors must present themselves as men like all other men. On his doubling of several roles in the production, Brook says it was done because "each scene is like a dream

of a dream; the interrelation between theme and character
is more mysterious than at first sight." Theseus and
Hippolyta try to discover what constitutes a true union,
and in Oberon and Titania we have a man and a woman
coming together through a concord found out of a discord.
Oberon and Titania "could easily be sitting inside the minds
of Theseus and Hippolyta." Asked if he shared Jan Kott's
conception of the play, Brook replies that Kott "fell into
the trap of turning one aspect of the play into the whole."
The play is a very powerful sexual play, with "something
more amazing than in the whole of Strindberg" at the
center. "It's the idea, which has been so easily passed over
for centuries, of a man taking the wife whom he loves
totally and having her fucked by the crudest sex machine
he can find."

T1307a   Beerbohm, Sir Max. *Last Theatres, 1904-1910.* With an
         introduction by Rupert Hart-Davis. London: Hart-Davis;
         New York: Taplinger Publishing Company, 1970. 553 pp.

Included in this collection of *Saturday Review* theatre
reviews by Beerbohm is an unfavorable review of a 1908
production of *A Midsummer Night's Dream* (pp. 344-47). He
discusses the problems and responsibilities of reviewing
amateur productions and then says that he never saw one
worse than this, directed at Oxford by W. R. Foss. He
criticizes the "aloof" Oxford students for being "tame and
dull" and apparently afraid of demeaning themselves. There
is severe criticism of the delivery of the poetry which "is
the first and foremost thing in Shakespeare."

T1307b   Brown, Ivor. *Shakespeare and the Actors.* London: The
         Bodley Head, 1970. 208 pp. Illustrated.

Considers the contingencies of professional theatre
production that affected Shakespeare's company and the
plays, arguing that the words were "the flexible material of
a theatrical effect, written by an actor for actors." He
infers from Theseus' speech "The best in the kind are but
shadows" that Shakespeare was keenly aware of the
ephemeral nature of his craft. Of Puck's "If we shadows
have offended," Brown says it points to the necessity for
actors in Shakespeare's time "to be extremely careful in the
presence of the great," and points to what he believes to

be the likelihood that the play was originally performed for a nobleman's marriage.

T1308   *Catalogue of Pictures and Sculpture.* Royal Shakespeare
        Theatre Picture Gallery. 6th edition. Stratford-upon-
        Avon, 1970. 73 pp.

        Contains an annotated listing of works in the RST
        collection, among which are George Romney's oil painting
        "Titania reposing with her Indian Votaries (*Midsummer
        Night's Dream*)" and a pen-and-ink caricature by Ronald
        Searle of a scene from the RSC's production of *A
        Midsummer Night's Dream* in 1959, directed by Peter Hall.
        (Neither work is among those reproduced in the catalogue.)

T1309   Cushman, Robert. "*A Midsummer Night's Dream.*" *Plays
        and Players*, 17 (August 1970), 45-6.

        Reviews the New Shakespeare Company's "workmanlike"
        production of *A Midsummer Night's Dream* at the Open Air
        Theatre, Regent's Park, London, directed by Richard Digby
        Day. He characterizes it as being, in some part, the first
        "post-Kott" production of the play, with Titania nearly
        raping Bottom. The Bottom was deeply disappointing, the
        First Fairy extremely funny. The lovers get mixed reviews.
        Cushman objects to staging the play outdoors at all, despite
        the popularity of this play at the Park each year, and also
        says, "I have seen, I think, too many *Dreams*. . . .
        Tradition lies heavy on each scene, every line."

T1310   Dean, Basil. *Seven Ages. An Autobiography 1888-1927.*
        London: Hutchinson, 1970. 340 pp. Illustrated.

        Devotes a full chapter to "My Christmas Dream," his
        production of the play at Drury Lane Theatre at Christmas,
        1924. It was an elaborately staged affair in the tradition of
        Tree's, with an elaborate palace, forest, sunrise effect,
        hunting party, and dozens of fairy children aboard
        hydraulic lifts. But among its strong cast were Edith Evans
        as Helena, Hay Petrie as Puck, Leon Quartermain as
        Lysander, Miles Malleson as Snout, and Wilfrid Walter as
        Bottom. (See item T1095.)

T1311 Elson, Louis C. *Shakespeare in Music: A Collation of the Chief Musical Allusions in the Plays of Shakespeare, with an Attempt at their Explanations and Derivations. Together with Much of the Original Music.* London: David Nutt, 1901; reprint, Freeport, New York: Books for Libraries, 1970. 354 pp. Illustrated.

Commenting on the songs and dances in *A Midsummer Night's Dream* (pp. 126-33), Elson says Titania's mention of a "roundel" refers not to a round but to dancers dancing in a circle while they sing. Bottom's invitation to the Duke to "hear" a Bergomask dance is not inaccurate, for many of the old dances were accompanied by songs or chanted verses. For it, Elsom reproduces a piano score of a French "air de danse," entitled "La Romanesca."

T1312 Jorgens, Jack J. "Studies in the Criticism and Stage History of *A Midsummer Night's Dream.*" Ph.D. dissertation, New York University, 1970. 552 pp. *DAI*, 31 (1971), 4719A-4720A.

Inquires into the popularity of *A Midsummer Night's Dream* in each age from Shakespeare's time to the late 1960s. He surveys the criticism and the theatrical representation of the play with varying emphases, depending upon critical themes, staging styles, the treatment of the play by painters, or the relationships among these. It is suggested that the Elizabethans enjoyed the play's artifice and language. Purcell's *Fairy Queen* is said to further translate the play into idioms of traditional love-lyrics, classical mythology, and the pastoral and is a monument to Baroque taste. The eighteenth century, seeing no unifying principle in the play, played only separate parts of the play, as in Garrick's *The Fairies* or in the Lampe and Leveridge mock operas that used the mechanicals. Special attention is given to Elizabeth Vestris' production of 1840, which restored the text, and her printed promptbook is drawn on (for the first time) for the discussion of the staging. Other major nineteenth century productions are surveyed. Close attention is given to the Reinhardt-Dieterle film of 1935 and to the radical rebellion against the romantic staging traditions for this play in John Hancock's production, with designs from Jim Dine, in 1967-1968. There is a checklist of productions.

T1313   Leach, Joseph. *Bright Particular Star, The Life and
        Times of Charlotte Cushman.* New Haven: Yale University
        Press, 1970. 453 pp. Illustrated.

        Describes briefly the American actress's successful
        appearance as Oberon in the Park Theatre production of *A
        Midsummer Night's Dream* of 1841 in New York, under
        Edmund Simpson, a musical adaptation derived from the
        Reynolds opera of 1816. (It was mounted by Simpson in the
        season following the success in London of Elizabeth Vestris'
        production in which Vestris played Oberon.)

T1314   *A Midsummer Night's Dream* presented by the Royal
        Shakespeare Company at the Royal Shakespeare Theatre,
        Stratford-upon-Avon, 27 August 1970; in New York (20
        January 1971), Boston, and London (10 June 1971), and
        World Tour, 1972-1973. Director, Peter Brook. Design,
        Sally Jacobs. Music, Richard Peaslee with the actors and
        Felix Mendelssohn. The original Stratford cast included:
        Theseus/Oberon, Alan Howard; *Hippolyta/Titania*, Sara
        Kestelman; *Philostrate/Puck*, John Kane; *Bottom*, David
        Waller; *Hermia*, Mary Rutherford; *Helena*, Frances de la
        Tour.

        A major theatrical event of the explosive 1960s,
        internationally influential, and a reference point in every
        discussion of trends in staged Shakespeare in the two
        decades since. In setting and costume, it departed radically
        from romantic, illusionistic traditions with its all white,
        gym-like setting, fairies on trapezes, accompanying
        musicians visible on catwalks above the stage, and actors in
        colorful, blousy jumpsuits or tie-die shirts. It emphasized
        the young love world of the play, making the quartet of
        lovers contemporaries of the youth of the 'sixties, anxious
        for the survival of innocence, honesty, and sincerity.
        Received rapturously by audiences world-wide, it also
        caused wide critical controversy. (See item 1069.)

        Reviews: Irving Wardle, *The Times*, 28 August and 9
        September, 1970; J. C. Trewin, *Birmingham Post*, 28
        August 1970; Rosemary Say, *Financial Times*, 28 August
        1970; John Barber, *Daily Telegraph*, 28 August 1970; Clive
        Barnes, *New York Times*, 28 August 1970; Peter Lewis,
        Daily Mail, 28 August 1970; *The Guardian*, 28 August 1970;
        The Times, 29 August 1970, interview with Peter Brook;
        Harold Hobson, *Sunday Times*, 30 August 1970; *The*

Observer, 30 August and 13 December, 1970; Benedict Nightingale, *New Statesman*, 4 September 1970; Charles Marowitz, *New York Times*, 13 September 1970; J. C. Trewin, *Illustrated London News*, 12 September 1970; Jeremy Kempton, *Punch*, 4 September 1970; John Barber, *Daily Telegraph*, 14 September 1970; Peter Roberts, *Plays and Players*, October 1970, with eight photographs; Christopher Porterfield, *Time*, 19 October 1970; Ronald Bryden, *The Observer*, 13 December 1970; Douglas Watt, New York *Daily News*, 21 January 1971; Richard Watts, *New York Post*, 21 January 1971; Clive Barnes, *New York Times*, 22 January 1971; Martin Gottfried, *Women's Wear Daily*, 22 January 1971; John J. O'Connor, *The Wall Street Journal*, 22 January 1971; Walter Kerr, *New York Times*, 31 January 1971; Jack Kroll, *Newsweek*, 1 February 1971; T. A. Kalem, *Time*, 1 February 1971; Henry Hewes, *Saturday Review*, 6 February 1971; Jack Kroll, *New York Times*, 7 February 1971; Stanley Kauffmann, *New Republic*, 20 February 1971; John Simon, *New York*, 21 February 1971; *Life* (photos), 9 March 1971; *Variety*, 27 March 1971; *Herald Traveler* (Boston), 7 April 1971; *The Globe* (Boston), 7 April 1971; Elliot Norton, *The Record American* (Boston), 9 April 1971; *Christian Science Monitor*, 8 April 1971; Irving Wardle, *The Times*, 11 June 1971; *Daily Mail*, 11 June 1971; *Daily Express*, 11 June 1971; *Daily Telegraph*, 11 June 1971; Milton Shulman, *Evening Standard*, 11 June 1971; Ronald Bryden, *The Observer*, 13 June 1971; Harold Hobson, *Sunday Times*, 13 June 1971; *Plays and Players*, August 1971; Bernard Levin, *The Times*, 30 September 1971; J. Richardson, *Commentary*, 51 (1971), 76-78; J. W. Lambert, *Drama*, 102 (1971), 15-30; Donald Richie, *The Drama Review*, 15 (1971), 330-34; Bernard Dukore, *Educational Theatre Review*, 23 (1971), 93-94; *Massachusetts Review*, 12 (1971), 821-33; John Russell Brown, *Shakespeare Survey*, 24 (1971), 127-35; Peter Thomson, *Shakespeare Survey*, 24 (1971), 117-26, with three photos; Yu Fridstein, *Teatr* (Russia), 10 (1971), 181-83; Matthieu Galey, *Les Nouvelles, littéraires*, 2347 (1972), 18; *Literaturen Front* (Sofia), 45 (1972); Gábor Mihályi, *Nagyvilág* (Budapest), 1973, no. 1, 128-33; *Otečestven Front* (Sofia), 8730 (1972); George Banu, *Secolul* (Bucharest), 20, 8 (1972); *Theater heute*, 13, 1 (1972); *Theater der Zeit*, 27, 12 (1972); J. C. Trewin, *Contemporary Review*, 221 (November 1972). (See also items T1307, T1329a, T1358a, T1284, T1356, T1481, T1508, T1521 and T1524ab.)

T1315   Odell, George Clinton Densmore. *Annals of the New York
        Stage*. 15 volumes. New York: Columbia University
        Press, 1927-49; reprint, New York, AMS Reprint, 1970.
        Illustrated.

        This detailed narrative history of the New York Stage,
        from about 1699 to 1894, season by season and at times
        company by company, includes brief characterizations of
        major Shakespearean productions, including those of *A
        Midsummer Night's Dream*. Covered here in varying detail
        are the early productions at the Park Theatre of 1826 and
        1841; those of William Burton and Thomas Barry in 1853 at
        the Chambers Street Theatre and the Broadway Theatre,
        respectively; Laura Keene's production of 1859; James
        Hayes's at the Olympic in 1867; Mrs. Conroy's in Brooklyn
        in 1865; Augustin Daly's two productions in 1873 and 1888
        (photographs), and John Albaugh's in 1888. (For more
        details on these, especially the Burton and Barry
        productions, see Odell's "*A Midsummer Night's Dream* on the
        New York Stage," in *Shaksperian Studies*, edited by
        Brander Matthews and A. H. Thorndike (New York, 1916),
        pp. 119-62.) For more on the Daly production, see item
        T1270.

T1316   Sprague, Arthur Colby, and J. C. Trewin. *Shakespeare's
        Plays Today: Some Customs and Conventions of the
        Stage*. Columbia, South Carolina: University of South
        Carolina Press, 1970. 147 pp. Illustrated.

        Discusses stage business and line readings in produc-
        tions of *A Midsummer Night's Dream* in the nineteenth and
        twentieth centuries, noting some traditional and innovative
        practices in the role of Bottom and in the performing of
        "Pyramus and Thisbe" (Chapter 4). The authors also trace
        the use of an actor to represent the much-talked of Indian
        boy (Chapter 3). American actor-manager William Burton
        may have been the first to put him on stage in his New
        York production of 1853. Reproduced is an engraving from
        the *Illustrated London News* of 1856 that shows the Indian
        boy in Charles Kean's production of that year. There is
        also a photograph of the quartet of lovers in Basil Dean's
        1924 production and a discussion of memorable actors in
        these roles in Chapter 6.

T1317   Entry Deleted.

T1318   Allen, Shirley S. *Samuel Phelps and Sadler's Wells Theatre*. Middletown, Connecticut: Wesleyan University Press [1971]. xvi, 354 pp. Illustrated.

Describes Phelps's career during his management of Sadler's Wells from 1844 to 1862, concentrating chiefly on his acting performances. There is a section on Phelps's staging of Shakespeare's plays that draws upon reviews and promptbooks; Allen argues that Phelps's methods were sensitive to Shakespeare's poetry and ran counter to the trends of lavish, literal spectacle. She sees him as a forerunner of modern directors. *A Midsummer Night's Dream* was one of the most successful of the thirty-one of Shakespeare's plays which he mounted; Allen shows that Phelps's staging was praised by critic Henry Morley for serving the poetry of the play rather than overwhelming it with scenery. One feature of it was a dream-like rendering of the forest scenes by the use of a green gauze across the proscenium. Another feature was Phelps's portrayal of Bottom, which Allen describes, drawing on contemporary reviews. She also argues that one of Phelps's most important textual restorations was *A Midsummer Night's Dream*, pointing out that he omitted the customary extraneous songs (pp. 223-24).

T1319   Carey, Robin. "Oregon Shakespearean Festival, Spring Season." *Educational Theatre Journal*, 23 (1971), 348-49.

Describes the festival, its new indoor theatre, and briefly reviews the season's productions, which included *A Midsummer Night's Dream*. It was performed in the new Angus Bowmer Theatre, a 600 seat indoor theatre with a semi-thrust stage convertible to proscenium. The production achieved several things; among them, it attracted the festival's established audience for Shakespeare and was well suited to the festival's educational goals for regional school audiences. (Cast and credits are not given.)

T1319a   Coursen, Herbert R., Jr. "Shakespeare in Maine: Summer, 1971." *Shakespeare Quarterly*, 22 (1971), 389-92.

Coverage includes a review of *A Midsummer Night's Dream*, directed by Robert Joyce, at the Theatre at Monmouth. William Meisle and Lee McClelland as Oberon and

Titania are praised as conveying very effectively "the
play's central comic transition from discord to harmony."
Oberon's relaxation of revenge with his awakening
understanding of Titania's true nature as he saw her asleep
with Bottom was the moment at which all other complications
were set right. The Bottom is criticized for hilarious
clowning that so dominated the Pyramus and Thisbe play as
to make the lovers irrelevant and undermine the fairy
finale. The problem--a lack of dramatic integration--was a
directorial one and characteristic of the second summer
Shakespeare season at Monmouth.

T1319b   Coveney, Michael. *"A Midsummer Night's Dream,*
         Regent's Park." *Plays and Players*, 18 (September 1971),
         48.

Assess the production at the Open Air Theatre, Regent's
Park, London, directed by Richard Digby Day. It was
traditional and glassy-eyed, with a few half-hearted sexual
novelties added. "Oberon and his cronies look like the last
of the Mohicans," and Titania's fairies looked like "a bunch
of unpleasant hags." The sexually active Titania nearly
mounted Bottom's ass's head. But there was a glimmering
torch light effect in the palace, and Marily Taylerson's
Helena was "delicious." Coveney protests against the
continued use of traditional costumes for the play.

T1319c   Dehn, Paul. "The Filming of Shakespeare." *Talking of*
         Shakespeare, ed. John Garrett. London: Hodder and
         Stoughton, with Max Reinhardt, 1954; reprint, Freeport,
         New York: Books for Libraries, 1971, pp. 49-72.

Promising to offer ways that teachers of Shakespeare
may assess whether a particular Shakespearean film will
help introduce young people to Shakespeare, the author
provides personal assessments of particular films. The 1935
Reinhardt-Dieterle film of *A Midsummer Night's Dream* was a
faithful recording of a Reinhardt open air production of the
play at Oxford in 1933 in which the author played
Philostrate. The Puck in the film (played by Mickey
Rooney) is "an eradicably German Puck," nearer
Rumpelstiltzskin than Shakespeare's Robin Goodfellow.
Bottom (James Cagney) is a German peasant suffering
"quite unBritish hysteria" in his metamorphosis from ass
back to man. One haunting image from the film is Oberon

carrying off the First Fairy over his shoulder, with a spotlight focussed on her fluttering hands as he moves into darkness.

T1320 Eidenier, Elizabeth. "Bottom's Song: Shakespeare in Junior High." *English Journal,* 60 (1971), 208-211.

Describes a production of *A Midsummer Night's Dream* with a cast of American eighth grade students.

T1321 Hayman, Ronald. *John Gielgud.* New York: Random House, [1971]. 276 pp. Illustrated.

Traces Gielgud's acting career. He reports Gielgud's memories of the 1945 production of *A Midsummer Night's Dream* at the Haymarket Theatre, directed by Nevill Coghill, in which Gielgud played Oberon (for a second time) and Peggy Ashcroft played Titania. The actor recalls painfully some over-indulgence in the sonorous sound of the poetry as he delivered it. (See item T1099.)

T1322 Horobetz, Lynn K. "Shakespeare at the Old Globe, 1971." *Shakespeare Quarterly,* 22 (1971), 385-87.

Included in the coverage is a favorable review of a production of *A Midsummer Night's Dream* directed by Eric Christmas at the San Diego National Shakespeare Festival's Old Globe Theatre. (Photograph.) It combined "the dreamy nostalgia of a past era with a mysterious, captivating group of fairies." The palace scenes and the costumes were Victorian. The forest was eerie, with phosphorescent hangings and fairies who were not insipid sprites. "This was a dream which could turn into nightmare at any moment."

T1323 Manvell, Roger. *Shakespeare and the Film.* London: J. M. Dent; New York: Praeger Publishers, 1971; rev. ed., South Brunswick and New York: A. S. Barnes, 1979. xvi, 182 pp. Illustrated.

Discusses the film version of *A Midsummer Night's Dream* directed by Max Reinhardt and William Dieterle for Warner Brothers in 1935 in Chapter 3 (pp. 25-27). The one-and-a-half million dollar film was the most spectacular attempt of the decade to present Shakespeare on the screen. Its cast included Victor Jory as Oberon, Mickey Rooney as Puck, and Olivia de Haviland as Hermia. Manvell says the elaborate choreography and special effects give the film its principal value as film; he cites as an example Oberon's absorption of the fairy train into his long cloak at dawn. The film was basically nineteenth century in its romantic concept; even a miniature orchestra of dwarfs was shown in the forest. The text was cut by half in the 140 minute film and the scene order changed in the interest of continuity. Manvell is critical of some of the acting and the lack of harmony. Manvell also discusses Peter Hall's 1969 film of the play (pp. 119-27), derived from his Royal Shakespeare Company production of 1959-63 (see item T1183). Hall, in an interview with Manvell, told him he wanted to use close-ups to scrutinize coolly the marked ambiguity of the text and to experiment with a less rhetorical delivery style. He shot much of the forest chase in a cold rain to emphasize the dissonance in nature that Titania describes. Thus he rejected fully the romantic approach. The film was poorly received by critics because, says Manvell, they wanted Reinhardt. There are four photographs from the Reinhardt film and six from Hall's. (See also T1301 and T1406.)

T1324   "Music scores, *A Midsummer Night's Dream,* Collections."
         A Shakespeare Bibliography. The Catalogue of the Birmingham Shakespeare Library. Vol. 5, pp. 1370-77.
         London: Mansell Information and Publishing Ltd., 1971.

Lists the library's holdings of published scores of songs and incidental music composed for or inspired by the play, with information on the publishers. Includes scores by Britten, Mendelssohn, J. C. Smith, Aylwood, Stevens, Horn, Bishop, Vaughn Williams, Blitzstein, and Purcell. (See also entries T1136 and T1230.)

T1325   Pfeiffer, Rolf. "Bildliche Darstellung der Elfen in Shakespeares 'Sommernachtstraum.'" Ph.D. dissertation, Marburgh, 1971. 111 illustrations.

Surveys the representation of the fairies in *A Midsummer Night's Dream* in illustrated editions of the play and in paintings. Not seen.

T1326 Purcell, Henry. *The Fairy Queen.* [Recording of the
       Opera.] Anthony Lewis conducting the Boyd Neel
       Orchestra, with Jennifer Vyvyan and Elsie Morison,
       sopranos; John Whitworth, countertenor; Peter Pears,
       tenor; and Thomas Hemsley, bass. Three 33 1/3 rpm
       phonodiscs, stereo. Éditions de l'Oiseau-Lyre OL 5
       121-23. *circa* 1971.

T1327 Salaman, Malcolm. *Shakespeare in Pictorial Art.* Edited by
       Charles Holme. London: Studio, 1916; reprint, New
       York: Benjamin Blom, 1971. 183 pp. Illustrated.

       Includes in the plates section (pp. 49-183) reproductions
       of two drawings from W. Heath Robinson's illustrations of *A
       Midsummer Night's Dream*; Sir Noel Paton's oil painting *The
       Reconciliation of Oberon and Titania*; William Blake's
       Oberon, Titania, with Puck and Fairies Dancing; H. Fuseli's
       painting of Titania and Bottom; and the engraving by L. P.
       Simon of Fuseli's painting, showing Titania and Bottom with
       fairies, Act IV.i.

T1328 Shpet, L. G. *Soviet Theater for Youth and Children:
       Pages from its History, 1918-1945.* Moscow: Iskusstvo,
       1971.

       Includes descriptions of some productions of *A
       Midsummer Night's Dream* in these years. In Russian. Not
       seen.

T1329 Toth, John W. "The Actor-Manager Career of Sir Frank
       Benson in Perspective: An Evaluation." *DAI*, 32 (1971),
       223A (Ohio State).

       Traces Benson's career from 1879 to 1916, with special
       focus upon his work as a director at the Shakespeare
       Memorial Theatre in Stratford-upon-Avon, during which time
       he staged *A Midsummer Night's Dream* in eight different
       seasons.

T1329a Trewin, J. C., *Peter Brook: A Biography.* London:
        Macdonald and Company, 1971. 216 pp. Illustrated.

Provides in Chapter 13 (pp. 173-90) a description and
favorable assessment of Brook's production of *A Midsummer
Night's Dream* with the RSC in 1970 (see item T1314).
Trewin provides a brief stage history of the play as a
preface to explaining Brook's shedding of the stage
traditions associated with it. He briefly traces the
influences behind the production, touching on Vsevold
Meyerhold, a Chinese circus that Brook saw in Paris, and
Jan Kott's interpretation. He briefly describes some of the
rehearsal process and Brook's quest for "the hidden play
behind the text." The staging and acting are characterized
admiringly; Trewin says the production opened the eyes of
audiences to the play as if it were new and unfamiliar. The
circus techniques are defended: "The more closely we
watched the actors' unexpected virtuosity, the more we
heard of the play . . . ." Brook "demolished thoughtless
conventions." Reviewers' reactions to the production are
sampled, and there are four production photographs.

T1330   Brown, John Russell. "Originality in Shakespeare
         Production." (Delivered as one of The Society for
         Theatre Research Annual Lectures, May 1971.) *Theatre
         Notebook*, 26 (1972), 107-115.

         Assesses the recent trend toward directorial invention
         and reconception in the production of Shakespeare's plays.
         He draws upon the work of several directors, including
         Peter Brook. In reference to Brook's production of *A
         Midsummer Night's Dream* Brown asks "how profitable is it
         to . . . have actors jump offstage to greet individual
         members of the audience with smiles and handshakes."
         Brown will mount his full argument against this trend and
         for an actor-centered theatre in his *Free Shakespeare*
         (1974). (See item T1355.)

T1330a   Eckert, Charles, ed. *Focus on Shakespearean Films*.
         Englewood Cliffs, New Jersey: Prentice Hall, 1972. viii,
         184 pp. Illustrated.

         An anthology of essays by various authors who consider
         the problems of putting Shakespeare's plays on film or who
         offer critical evaluations of particular films. There are two
         essays from the mid-1930s that discuss the Max
         Reinhardt-William Dieterle film of *A Midsummer Night's
         Dream* (1935). Allardyce Nicoll, in "Film Reality: Cinema

and the Theatre" (1936), argues that the cinema, if used in ways more imaginative than it had been up to that time, could provide a means of expression akin to the spirit of modern novelists and poets (pp. 43-47). The Reinhardt-Dieterle film is alluded to as illustrating some possibilities. In it, passages of verse that had become rhetoric in vast modern theatres were invested with intimacy and directness. Film has the power to present visual symbols to accompany language, and this is especially a boon to the modern audience which is less attuned to the word as spoken than were Elizabethans. Richard Watts, Jr., in "Films of a Moonstruck World" (1935) offers several points about Shakespeare film-making relating to the Reinhardt film. Actors will need to be better trained in verse speaking than were Anita Louise (Titania) and Mickey Rooney (Puck). Reinhardt's film was directorially heavy-handed and too long. He suspects it may not prove popular.

T1331   Johnson, Albert and Bertha. *Shakespeare at My Shoulder.* South Brunswick and New York: A. S. Barnes; London: Thomas Yoseloff, 1972. 143 pp. Illustrated.

Chapter 3 describes the Redlands (California) Bowl productions, done year after year, and the directing concept behind them. They were "replete with large cast, symphony orchestra, chorus, and corps de ballet," in a natural amphitheatre setting; "the language of the play furnished all necessary scenery." With photos.

T1332   *A Midsummer Night's Dream* presented by the Guthrie Theatre, Minneapolis, Minnesota, beginning in repertory on 4 July 1972. Director, John Hirsch. Costumes, Carl Toms. Setting, John Jensen. Songs and incidental music, John Duffy. Lighting, Gil Wechsler. *Theseus/Oberon,* Frank Langella (replaced in late August by Len Cariou); *Hippolyta/Titania,* Roberta Maxwell; *Puck/Philostrate,* Edward Zang (replaced in late August by Barbara Byrne); *Hermia,* Dianne Wiest; *Bottom,* James Blendick.

This was the first production of *A Midsummer Night's Dream* on the Guthrie Theatre stage, occurring in the theatre's tenth season, and the director, John Hirsch, sought to be assertively contemporary with near-nude,

sensual costumes for Titania and Oberon and some stress
upon the erotic in the fairy kingdom. There were other
modish touches in the elaborate staging, such as a lucite
and chrome set and a score influenced by rock music. It
was better received by local critics than by Barnes (New
York), Norton (Boston), or Christiansen (Chicago).

Reviews: Clive Barnes, *New York Times*, 2 August 1972;
Elliot Norton, *Boston Record American*, 9 July 1972;
Richard Christiansen (Chicago *Daily News* Service) in the
Evening Star (Washington, D. C.), 30 July 1972; William
Glover, Associated Press, in the *News American*
(Baltimore), 3 September 1972; Martin Gottfried, *Women's
Wear Daily*, 17 July 1972; John H. Harvey, *St. Paul
Dispatch*, 8 July 1972 and 7 September 1972; Mike Steele,
Minneapolis Tribune, 9 July 1972 and 28 August 1972; Peter
Altman, *Minneapolis Star*, 8 July 1972; Nick Baldwin, *Des
Moines Register*, 9 July 1972; Roy M. Close, *Minneapolis
Star*, 26 August 1972; *Mankato Free Press*, 10 July 1972;
Gregory Gordon, United Press International, in the *Santa
Ana Register* (Evening Edition), 11 July 1972; George E.
Bogusch, *Educational Theatre Journal*, 24 (1974), 449-50.

T1332a   Pollack, Daniel B. "Peter Brook: A Study of a Modern
         Elizabethan and His Search for New Theatrical Forms."
         Ph.D. Dissertation, New York University, 1972. 405 pp.
         DAI, 34 (1973), 447a.

Traces Brook's career through 1971, describing his major
productions, including *A Midsummer Night's Dream*. (See
T1314.) In Chapter 10 (pp. 342-71), he describes Brook's
intentions, the influences on the staging, and the
rehearsals. The production is then described in some detail.
Brook stripped away traditional trappings and sought to
celebrate the arts of the theatre. The bright white box
setting of Sally Jacobs was a way of bringing every action
into the open. The set proved to evoke comparisons with
the Elizabethan stage. The costumes were not to refer to
any period but to be very simple tunic dresses and working
trousers; they were ultimately in the informal boutique style
of the 1970s. In the last act, the court appeared in silk
robes of rich colors, with ostrich feather collars. The
doubling of characters arose from Brook's interest in the
dream-like relationship of theme and character. The
Titania-Bottom scene, played for raw sensuality, was
inspired by Jan Kott. Some of the physical feats of the

performers amazed audiences, from the trapeze work of Oberon and Puck to Hermia's attempt to block Lysander's exit by throwing herself across a doorway horizontally. The actors came into the audience at the end of the play after delivering the final lines to them. Pollack notes some differences between the Stratford-upon-Avon and New York staging. He surveys the New York critical responses, praising *Newsweek*'s Jack Kroll for seeing Brook as a director who was renewing Shakespeare. (See also T1307 and T1357.)

T1333   Purcell, Henry. *The Fairy Queen,* [Recording of a Performance of] a new version for concert performance. Devised by Peter Pears. Music edited by Benjamin Britten and Imogen Holst. Britten conducting the English Chamber Orchestra and Ambrosian Opera Chorus, with Jennifer Vyvyan, soprano; Peter Pears, tenor; and Owen Brannigan and John Shirley-Quick, basses. Two 33 1/3 rpm phonodiscs, stereo. London OSA 1290 (S26221-26222). *circa* 1972.

T1334   Sullivan, John. "O desbatere shakespeareană: Brook şi Visul unei nopti de vară." *Secolul,* 20, 8 (1972).

Contains six short articles on the Peter Brook production of *A Midsummer Night's Dream* (which toured the world in 1972-1973) by Brook, Alan Howard (Oberon), Andrei Brezeanu, Florian Potra, Virgil Nemoianu, and George Barm. Not seen. (See item T1314.)

T1335   Volbach, Walther R. "Memoirs of Max Reinhardt's Theatres 1920-1922." *Theatre Survey,* 13, 1a [monograph] (Fall 1972). 86 pp. Illustrated.

Volbach spent two seasons on Reinhardt's staff from 1920 through 1922 and recalls some of the German director's notable productions, including Reinhardt's *A Midsummer Night's Dream* in 1921 at the Grosses Schauspielhaus. There is a photograph of Hermann Thimig as Bottom in the role of Pyramus in that production. The clowns reportedly made up for many flaws in staging, set, and the cast otherwise. Appendix I outlines Reinhardt's career.

T1335a Webster, Margaret. *Don't Put your Daughter On the Stage.* New York: Knopf, 1972. xix, 379 pp. Illustrated.

Recalls, in this autobiography, the amusing, frustrating experience of directing short versions (her adaptations) of four of Shakespeare's comedies, including *A Midsummer Night's Dream,* at the New York World's Fair of 1939. The forty minute versions were performed at the "Merrie England concession" on a "pint-size" replica of the Globe stage, an experience Webster found not wholly satisfying. In her epilogue, "Letter to a Young Actress," she notes (p. 375) in her argument for getting good classical training, that in Peter Brook's production of *A Midsummer Night's Dream* with the RSC, the company spoke the text "with veracity, penetration, and beauty." It was for that reason that it became "a great and memorable production."

T1336 Fiske, Roger. *English Theatre Music in the Eighteenth Century.* London: Oxford University Press, 1973. xiv, 684 pp. Illustrated.

Discusses the quasi-operatic adaptations of *A Midsummer Night's Dream* in this survey of theatre music from 1695 to 1800. Purcell's *The Fairy Queen* (1692) is briefly described, as in Richard Leveridge's *The Comique Masque of Pyramus and Thisby* (1716). More attention is paid to John Frederick Lampe's *Pyramus and Thisbe* (which expanded upon Leveridge's satire of Italian opera) in which Wall gets an aria; the aria is here reproduced from the published score (pp. 157-59). In Chapter 6, the Garrick-produced adaptation, *The Fairies* (1755), with music by Handel's amanuensis, John Christopher Smith, is discussed at some length (pp. 243-45). Fiske briefly treats the lyrics (*e.g.,* Oberon's "When that gay season did us lead" is freely adapted from Milton's *L'Allegro*), characterizes some portions of the score (*e.g.,* all the arias are in *Da Capo* form except those for the boy singers), and assesses the music: "One can say little more . . . than that it is in a rather tepid good taste." The versions of the play produced at Drury Lane in 1763 are briefly treated (p. 317). (See items 963-66.)

T1337 Georges, Jr., Corwin Augustin. "Augustin Daly's Shakespearean Productions." Ph.D. dissertation, Ohio State University, 1973. *DAI,* 33 (1973), 4578A. 185 pp.

Provides an overview of Daly's Shakespearean
productions in his two management periods between 1869
and 1899. There are statistics on their performances within
his total repertory, a discussion of the collaboration
between Daly and critic William Winter on textual cutting,
and a description of Daly's staging methods. His *Taming of
the Shrew* is closely examined; his 1888 production of *A
Midsummer Night's Dream* is dealt with at some points.

T1338 Hainaux, Rene, compiler with Yves-Bonnat. *Stage Design
       Throughout the World Since 1960.* Text and Illustrations
       collected by the National Centres of the International
       Theatre Institute. New York: Theatre Arts Books, 1973.
       239 pp. Illustrated.

A collection of photographs of settings and scenes from
productions of plays and operas in the 1960s and 1970s,
with some discussion of design trends in the text. Included
are seven black-and-white photographs of the Royal
Shakespeare Company production of *A Midsummer Night's
Dream* in 1970, directed by Peter Brook, including a
photograph of Sally Jacobs's model of the setting. There
are photographs of a production of the play at Bucknell
University in 1969, designed by James D. Lyons, Jr., and
directed by Phillip S. Johnson, and of a production at the
Stadsschouwberg, Amsterdam, in 1961, designed by Nicolaas
Wijnberg. (See also item T1234.)

T1339 Highfill, Jr., Philip H., Kalman A. Burnim, and Edward
       A. Langhans. *A Biographical Dictionary of Actors,
       Actresses, Musicians, Dancers, Managers, and Other
       Stage Personnel in London, 1660-1800.* 8 Volumes, 12
       projected. Carbondale: Southern Illinois University
       Press, 1973--. Illustrated.

Biographical articles, alphabetically listed, on about
8,500 persons connected with the Restoration and
Eighteenth century stage, including some musicians not in
Grove's Dictionary. Portraits may accompany the articles
and, in the case of notable figures such as David Garrick,
an annotated iconography. Each volume contains an
appendix in which are reproductions of maps, engravings of
theatre interiors and exteriors, and various kinds of
documents such as accounts and playbills. Eight volumes
were completed through 1982, the eighth covering Hough to

Keyse. The work is an essential companion to *The London Stage, 1660-1800* (see T1187) for information on the personnel associated with the operated adaptations of *A Midsummer Night's Dream*, from Purcell through Garrick.

T1339a Jamieson, Michael. "Shakespeare in the Theatre." *Shakespeare: Select Bibliographical Guides*, edited by Stanley Wells. London: Oxford University Press, 1973, pp. 25-43.

Provides a general, basic survey (and occasional assessments) of the scholarship on the staging practices and the construction of the public and private playhouses of the Elizabethan and Jacobean periods and also surveys the scholarship on Shakespeare in the theatre from 1660 to 1970. Includes bibliographies of basic works in these categories.

T1340 Jorgens, Jack J. "Champlain Shakespeare Festival 1973." *Shakespeare Quarterly*, 24 (1973), 428-34.

Coverage includes a favorable, detailed review of a Festival production of *A Midsummer Night's Dream*, directed by Festival producer Edward J. Feidner: "a resolutely simple one, playful, charming, rapidly paced, very funny, and having few of the darker overtones and little of the mystery or complexity of other modern versions." The lovers were the funniest the reviewer had ever seen, especially the Hermia of Marjorie Lyne Feiner, who whined, pouted, and vainly primped her black curls. Randy Kim's Puck was a goblin with a pipe in his mouth, and Thomas Wagner's Bottom is praised for his energy and likeable egotism.

T1340a Lombardo, Agostino. "Nuovi registi Shakespeariani." *Biblioteca Teatrale*, 6/7 (1973), 120-27.

Coverage of three new Shakespearean productions includes a review of a production of *A Midsummer Night's Dream*. Not seen.

T1341 Price, Joseph G. "The Interpretation of Shakespeare in the Theatre," in *Directions in Literary Criticism:*

Contemporary Approaches to Literature. Festschrift for
Henry W. Sams. Eds., Stanley Weintraub and Philip
Young. University Park and London: Pennsylvania State
University Press, 1973, pp. 70-84.

Suggests that there is a new mutual respect between
scholars and theatre artists and illustrates the point with
examples in publications (*e.g.,* Stanley Wells's introduction
to his recent edition of *A Midsummer Night's Dream*) and in
scholarly conferences, particularly the World Shakespeare
Conference in Vancouver in 1971. Shakespearean critics are
increasingly turning to the theatre for answers to critical
dilemmas in the plays. Productions are to be seen as
explications. The 1970 Royal Shakespeare Company
production of *A Midsummer Night's Dream* is a case in
point. Director Peter Brook "framed his text, regenerating
through an outer form a play long suffocating in
excessively romantic encrustments." The production was
"the rejection of a strangling stage tradition." Price
characterizes the set and staging. Brook's goal is said to
be to render important Shakespearean themes in terms of
contemporary beliefs and attitudes: "Cupid's blindness
became Freudian suppression. Subliminal passions first were
freed in the sexual rough-and-tumble midsummer madness,
then matured in the sexual reality of the marriages which
end the play." For answers to questions about the
existential and psychological depths beneath the surface of
Shakespeare's plays, future criticism will turn "more
frequently and seriously" to the theatre than it has in the
past.

T1342   Purcell, Henry. *The Fairy Queen.* [Recording of the
        opera.] Alfred Deller conducting the Deller Consort and
        the Stour Music Chorus and Orchestra. Performance
        based on the 1692 version of the opera with some
        additions from the 1693 version. Two 33 1/3 rpm
        phonodiscs, stereo. Vanguard SRV 311-31250. *circa* 1973.

T1343   Rosenfeld, Sybil. *A Short History of Scene Design in
        Great Britain.* Oxford: Basil Blackwell, 1973. xviii, 214
        pp. Illustrated.

        Accompanying this brief history are black-and-white
reproductions of watercolors of scenes from Charles Kean's
production of *A Midsummer Night's Dream* (1856) and

photographs of the Harley Granville-Barker production
(1914).

T1343a   Savage, Roger. "The Shakespeare-Purcell *Fairy Queen*."
         Early Music, I (1973), 201-21.

         Argues that Purcell's *Fairy Queen* can be very effective
         in the theatre, based on his recent experience of staging it
         at Edinburgh University, where it was critically
         well-received. Recounting the customary objections to it by
         scholars and musicians past and present, among which are
         that it is a semi-opera, that it tampers with sacred
         Shakespeare but ultimately has little to do with the play,
         and that it is scenically unstageable and over long, Savage
         refutes each objection. He contends that the work marries
         the pre-Commonwealth popular stage and the courtly
         allegorical tradition of elaborate song and dance, which was
         present in the Jonson-James masques and which prevailed in
         France. He speculates that a committee created it and that
         Congreve had some part in it. The chief argument is that
         the work has an integrity of its own, with each end-of-act
         masque developing upon a theme in the act and each song
         thematically linked to the play. In his argument that it was
         designed to bring the play alive for its age, he compares it
         to the 1970 Peter Brook staging, drawing parallels between
         trapezes and flying machines, for example. He demonstrates
         that the playing time of the *Fairy Queen* would be less than
         four hours; analyzes the text to argue that not all the
         changes are perversions and that there are compensations
         in the masques; and suggests that the spectacle called for
         in the stage directions can be simplified. (See also item
         T1348.)

T1344   Shandler, Donald David. "American Shakespeare Festival
         Theatres: A Sense of Occasion." Ph.D. dissertation,
         Ohio State University, 1972. *DAI*, 33 (1973), 4581A. 258
         pp.

         Discusses the festival phenomenon, providing some
         history and characterization of each of the several festivals
         studied. (This could be useful background for the study of
         particular productions of *A Midsummer Night's Dream* in
         these festivals.) Those examined are the National
         Shakespeare Festival at San Diego; the Oregon Shakespeare
         Festival at Ashland; The American Shakespeare Festival at

Stratford, Connecticut; the Colorado Shakespeare Festival at Boulder; the Champlain Shakespeare Festival at Burlington, Vermont; and the Great Lakes Shakespeare Festival at Cleveland, Ohio.

T1345   Speaight, Robert. *Shakespeare on the Stage, An Illustrated History of Shakespearian Performance.* London: Collins; Boston: Little, Brown, and Company, 1973. 304 pp. Illustrated.

Surveys Shakespearean production from the Restoration through the Royal Shakespeare Company's production of *A Midsummer Night's Dream* in 1970, discussing selected major figures and major trends in England, the United States, France, Italy, Germany, and Russia. There are brief characterizations of the productions of *A Midsummer Night's Dream* of Charles Kean (1856), Augustin Daly (1888), Sir Herbert Beerbohm Tree (1900), Sir Frank Benson (1900), Harley Granville-Barker (1914), Harcourt Williams at the Old Vic (1929), Tyrone Guthrie at the Old Vic (1937), Michael Benthall at the Old Vic (1953), Robert Atkins at Regent's Park (1933), Nugent Monck at the Maddermarket Theatre, and Peter Hall and Peter Brook at Stratford-upon-Avon (1959 and 1970, respectively). Theatre critics' responses are briefly sampled in the accounts of productions, and the author ventures his own on latter-day productions. Discussing the RSC's 1970 production, he finds good in the work of Peter Brook, closing his book by saying "the magic had been found, far beyond the spinning saucers and Titania's bright-red feather-bed, where Shakespeare had put it and where it must always be rediscovered--in the alchemy of the spoken word."

T1346   Sprague, Arthur Colby. "Plays at Kilruddery." *Theatre Notebook*, 27 (1973), 113-14.

A brief note on Sir Walter Scott's account of outdoor, amateur performances of scenes from *A Midsummer Night's Dream* in his *St. Ronan's Well*, which may have been based on Scott's 1825 visit to Kilruddery, the Wicklow estate of Lord Merth, where there is a theatre.

T1347   Sprague, Arthur Colby. "Robert Atkins as a
        Shakespearian Director." *Shakespeare Jahrbuch*
        (Heidelberg), 109 (1973), 19-33.

        Surveys Atkins' career as a director of Shakespearean
        plays. Atkins died in 1972 at the age of eighty-five. He
        had frequently directed *A Midsummer Night's Dream* at the
        Old Vic, Regent's Park, Stratford-upon-Avon, and in
        London. Atkins began his career under Sir Herbert
        Beerbohm Tree and was a link with Sir Henry Irving and
        Sir Frank Benson. But his ideas of staging were also
        influenced by William Poel. (See also items T1249 and
        T1508.)

T1348   Stitt, Ken. "Newcastle." *Plays and Players*, 20, 6 (March
        1973), 54.

        Reviews, briefly and favorably, a production of Purcell's
        The Fairy Queen, combined with *A Midsummer Night's
        Dream* in a version by Gareth Morgan and Keith Statham,
        "with additional and linking text" by John Barton. Morgan
        directed the production by the Tyneside Theatre Company
        at the University Theatre, New Castle-upon-Tyne, with the
        Newcastle Festival Chorus and Northern Sinfonia Orchestra
        conducted by Meredith Davies. Puck was played by Ben
        Kingsley and Bottom by Bill Wallis. The production played
        12-20 January 1973.

T1349   Weaver, Janet H. "Utah Shakespearean Festival, 1973."
        Shakespeare Quarterly, 24 (1973), 444-45.

        Includes review coverage and a photograph of a
        production of *A Midsummer Night's Dream* directed by
        Festival producer Fred C. Adams for the twelfth annual
        season at Southern Utah State College. It was "filled with
        much action--falling, tackling, double takes, and wild
        gestures . . . ." The production won much laughter and
        applause and a standing ovation at the end. There were
        strengths in the pathos of the Helena of Janet Ellen
        Brennan; in the Bottom of English actor Derek Weeks; and
        in the loveable Puck of Robert St. John.

T1350 Williams, Clifford John. *Madame Vestris--a Theatrical Biography.* London: Sidgwick and Jackson, 1973. xii, 240 pp. Illustrated.

Discusses Vestris' professional life as an actress and manager, crediting her especially for her work as a manager at the Olympic and Covent Garden Theatres. Some attention is given to her notable 1840 production of *A Midsummer Night's Dream* (pp. 171-74). The abundant, well-reproduced illustrations include the engraving of Vestris as Oberon and the playbill for the opening performance of *A Midsummer Night's Dream.* Also given is the full text of a *Theatrical Journal* review of 1841 (by "E. R. W."), which is a long, impressionistic account of her production, praising the staging and the acting. (See also item T1354, T1418 and T1451.)

T1351 Williams, Gary Jay. "'The Concord of this Discord,' Music in the Stage History of *A Midsummer Night's Dream.*" *Yale/Theatre*, 4, 3 (Summer 1973), 40-68.

Surveys the music used in productions of *A Midsummer Night's Dream* or the adaptations of it from the Restoration to 1970. Describes the general nature of the adapted texts of the play from Purcell's opera through those of 1755 and 1763 at Garrick's Drury Lane, characterizing lyrics and identifying eighteenth century composers. Included among these composers and adapters were Richard Leveridge, John Frederick Lampe, John Christopher Smith, and Charles Burney. The major productions of the nineteenth century are treated in more detail, from the Reynolds-Bishop opera of 1816 through the productions of the play proper from Elizabeth Vestris (1840) to Harley Granville-Barker (1914). The Tieck-Mendelssohn production of 1843 is briefly considered, and the use of Mendelssohn's score is followed down to the early 1950s, after which time it was dropped from major productions. Other composers considered in this section range from Charles Edward Horn to Cecil Sharp. In the general survey of twentieth century productions, there are brief references to Marc Blitzstein, David Amram, and Carl Orff.

T1352   Addenbrook, David. *The Royal Shakespeare Company:*
        The Peter Hall Years. With a foreword by Peter Hall and
        afterword by Trevor Nunn. London: William Kimber and
        Company, Limited, 1974. xviii, 334 pp.

        Provides a production history of the RSC, showing its
        development from 1959 to 1973. In Part I, there are
        chapters on major productions and major innovations in
        design and directorial concepts. Part II consists of
        interviews with directors (including Peter Hall) and others.
        Among the productions discussed in Part I is the RSC's *A*
        Midsummer Night's Dream of 1959, directed by Peter Hall,
        which was in the RSC repertoire over a period of ten years
        (see T1183). It was made into a full length color film,
        directed by Hall, in 1969 (see T1301). Lila de Nobili's
        romantic Elizabethan setting is described as are many of
        Hall's unconventional touches, such as his treatment of the
        lovers as modern teenagers, his emphasis on the comic
        aspects of the play, and the sexy, wicked fairies. There
        are sampling of reviews and director and actor interviews
        incorporated into Addenbrook's discussion and three photos
        of the 1959 production. For the RSC's production of 1970,
        directed by Peter Brook, the setting, staging, and acting
        are characterized and reviews are sampled. There are three
        photos of it. Addenbrook argues that Brook did not endorse
        entirely Jan Kott's interpretation of the play. There are ten
        appendices, including organizational charts, box office
        receipts, seasonal production lists, a statement of RSC
        policy, a list of RSC awards since 1960, and a
        bibliography.

T1353   Akin, Lew Sparks. "Ben Greet and His Theatre
        Companies in America: 1902-1932." Ph.D. dissertation,
        University of Georgia, 1974. 392 pp. *DAI*, 35 (1975),
        6846A-47A.

        Covers Sir Philip Ben Greet's tours of the U.S. in the
        period designated, during which time *A Midsummer Night's*
        Dream was a staple in the company's repertoire, showing
        his cultivation of a new audience for Shakespeare, his
        contribution to actor training, his opposition to the star
        system, his frequent open-air theatre productions (*A*
        Midsummer Night's Dream being among them often), and his
        interest in simplified staging after William Poel's Elizabethan
        manner. Akin suggests that Greet's work influenced
        Shakespearean production in the U.S. thereafter.

T1354   Appleton, William. *Madame Vestris and the London Stage.*
        New York: Columbia University Press, 1974. x, 230 pp.
        Illustrated.

        Included in this documented biography of Elizabeth
        Vestris is coverage of her management of Covent Garden
        Theatre, with her husband, Charles Mathews, in the years
        1839-41. There is some discussion of her important
        production of *A Midsummer Night's Dream* in 1840, and the
        author places the staging in the context of her other
        relevant productions, such as *Sleeping Beauty.* He very
        briefly characterizes the restoration of the text, the music
        used, and the scenery, which struck "an uneasy balance
        between historical accuracy and Victorian convention." The
        responses of critics are sampled, and the author notes that
        the public crowded the theatre nightly for months to see
        this production. (See also items T1350, T1418 and T1451.)

T1355   Brown, John Russell. *Free Shakespeare.* London:
        Heinemann Educational Books, Limited, 1974. vi, 113 pp.

        Criticizes the current trends in Shakespearean
        production toward "one-sided" directorial interpretations
        (behind which he sees academic Shakespearean criticism).
        In the interest of ensuring that audiences experience the
        plays fully and imaginatively, Brown urges an alternative
        approach, a theatre in which the plays would not be
        expertly packaged and pinned down to a single view. He
        envisions an actor-centered, communal theatre in which
        talented, well-prepared professionals, free of directors and
        designers, "would provide an encounter with Shakespeare's
        plays at which everything was at risk, and from their
        prepared positions the actors, with the audience, could
        probe, penetrate, and ride high upon the plays in their
        moment to moment life" (p. 112). In the course of the
        argument against a director's theatre, many examples are
        drawn from productions of the 1960s and 1970s, including
        the RSC productions of *A Midsummer Night's Dream* in 1959
        and 1970.

T1356   Crouch, J. H. "Colorado Shakespeare Festival."
        Shakespeare Quarterly, 25 (1974), 422-24.

        Review coverage includes favorable comments on a
        production of *A Midsummer Night's Dream*, directed by
        Robert Baruch. It was "fast, funny, and discerning." It
        realized all the guises of love in the play--jealous married

love, foolish romantic love, mock-heroic love, and self-love.
There is general praise for most of the cast. Titania was
delightfully sensual; Oberon was eloquent and capricious;
Puck was unfortunately played for low comedy.

T1357   Croyden, Margaret. *Lunatics, Lovers, and Poets: The
         Contemporary Experimental Theatre*. New York: McGraw
         Hill Company, 1974. xxvi, 321 pp. Illustrated.

         Surveys in Chapter Ten ("The Achievement of Peter
         Brook: From Commercialism to the Avant-Garde") Brook's
         work from 1960 to 1973. This includes an eight page,
         enthusiastic description of the interpretation and staging of
         Brook's 1970 *A Midsummer Night's Dream*. There are four
         black-and-white production photographs. (See also item
         T1314.)

T1357a   Fuller, Peter. "Richard Dadd: A Psychological
         Interpretation." *Connoisseur*, 186 (July 1974), 170-77.

         Provides an existential, psychological analysis of
         paintings by Richard Dadd (1817-1886), including three
         works based on *A Midsummer Night's Dream*. (A decade of
         revived interest in Dadd had recently culminated in an
         exhibition at the Tate Gallery in London in 1964.) Fuller
         sees in Dadd's works the psychotic expressions of the man
         who murdered his father, including expressions of
         reparation for patricide. Discussed and reproduced here (in
         black and white) are Dadd's 1841 *Puck and the Fairies*, a
         circular composition in which a nude baby-like Puck sits on
         a toadstool while small nude male and female figures dance
         around beneath him; Dadd's *Titania Sleeping* of 1841 in
         which a classical nude figure of Titania sleeps, attended by
         two standing women, beneath an arch made up of grotesque
         elfin figures and bluebells, with dancing figures at left;
         and Dadd's *Contradictions--Oberon and Titania*, painted
         between 1848 and 1858, an oval composition thickly peopled
         with fairy attendants and framed by enormous foliage. Also
         reproduced is his *The Fairy Feller's Master Stroke*,
         1855-1864. The author suggests the fairy paintings provided
         an internal, fantasy reality for the artist and that in
         Oberon's kingdom there is reconciliation and no need for
         vengeance.

T1358 Kovnatskaya, L. G. *Benjamin Britten.* Moscow: Sovetskii kompozitor, 1974.

Devotes Chapter Six to a discussion of Britten's opera, *A Midsummer Night's Dream.* Not seen.

T1358a Loney, Glenn, ed. *Peter Brook's Production of William Shakespeare's "A Midsummer Night's Dream" for the Royal Shakespeare Company.* Stratford-upon-Avon: Royal Shakespeare Company; Chicago: Dramatic Publishing Co., 1974. 126 pp. a play text of 85 pp. Illustrated.

Contains the promptbook for the 1970 production (see item T1314), together with interviews with or essays by the director, designer, composer, and several actors. There are productions photos and sketches throughout. (See also the annotation of item 1069.)

T1359 Morley, Henry. *The Journal of a London Playgoer from 1851 to 1866.* London: George Routledge & Sons, Ltd., 1866; reprint, 1891; reprint, with an introduction by Michael R. Booth, Leicester: Leicester University Press, 1974. xxv, 316 pp.

This collection of criticism by the critic of the *Examiner,* containing reviews written between 1851 and 1866, includes valuable reviews of two of the most famous Victorian productions of *A Midsummer Night's Dream*--those of Samuel Phelps at Sadler's Wells in 1853 and Charles Kean at the Princess's in 1856. Morley praised Phelps for achieving the vision of a dream and thus for never losing sight of "the main idea which governs the whole play." He doubted that there was any value for the play in Kean's elaborate pictures of Periclean Athens. Michael Booth's twenty-page introduction provides a brief biography of Morley and background on the actors and companies which he reviewed. The photographic reprint includes the index of the 1891 edition.

T1360 Reinhardt, Max. *Schriften: Briefe, Reden, Ausätze, Interviews, Gesprache, Auszüge aus Regiebüchern*[Writings: Letters, Talks, Essays, Interviews, Dialogues, Excerpts from Promptbooks.] Ed. Hugo Fetting. Berlin: Henschel-verlag, 1974. 527 pp.

Not seen.

T1361   Shattuck, Charles, ed. *John Philip Kemble Promptbooks.*
        Charlottesville: Published for the Folger Shakespeare
        Library by the University Press of Virginia, 1974. 11
        vols.

        Provides photo-facsimiles of the actor-manager's
        promptbooks for twenty-six Shakespearean plays and six
        non-Shakespearean plays that he staged at Drury Lane and
        Covent Garden. Kemble's Shakespearean texts were used by
        many actors and managers thereafter. *A Midsummer Night's
        Dream* is not included here; Sir Frederick Reynolds'
        operatic adaptation was done at Covent Garden in 1816, in
        the last years of Kemble's reign there, but he does not
        seem to have had a direct hand in the text or the
        production. Relevant, however, are the textual and staging
        practices represented in the other Kemble promptbooks.
        Shattuck provides an introduction to each promptbook;
        these include comments on Kemble's performance, on the
        distinctive features of the acting version, on the staging,
        and on the significance of the particular promptbook
        selected for reproduction and its relation to others.

T1362   Shattuck, Charles H. "Shakespeare's Plays in
        Performance from 1660 to the Present." In *The Riverside
        Shakespeare*, ed. G. Blakemore Evans. Boston: Houghton
        Mifflin Company, 1974, pp. 1799-1825.

        Surveys production trends from the Restoration to about
        1970, touching on many major productions of the plays with
        details on adaptations, scenery, and individual
        performances. In addition to the chronological coverage,
        there are topical divisions, including sections on "The
        Modernist Revolt," "The Festival Theatres," and
        "'Interpreting' Shakespeare: Six Modes and Masters." In the
        latter section the author characterizes the various
        interpretive devices of various major directors, including
        Sir Barry Jackson, Michael Benthall, Tyrone Guthrie,
        Franco Zeffirelli, Theodore Komisarjevsky, Jonathan Miller,
        and Peter Brook. He suggests that anachronistic settings
        and costumes and other interpretive devices "are not crimes
        unless they are badly used," and finds an ideal balance in
        Glen Byam Shaw's productions at Stratford-upon-Avon,
        1953-59. Most of the major productions of *A Midsummer*

Night's Dream in the eighteenth and nineteenth century are briefly alluded to; there are brief characterizations of the twentieth century productions of Granville-Barker and Tyrone Guthrie (1937), and some discussion of the 1970 *A Midsummer Night's Dream* directed by Peter Brook as representing latter day trends. There is also a section on Shakespeare on film, which briefly characterizes a satiric, modern dress, German film of the play in 1925, directed by Hans Neumann; the Reinhardt-Dieterle film of 1935; and the Peter Hall version of 1969. The volume's bibliography includes a section on Shakespearean stage history (p. 1897).

T1362a   Söderwall, Margreta. *Barn och ungdom i skapande Verksamhet.* Umeå: Shakespearesällskap; Solna: Seelig, 1974. 121 pp. Illustrated.

Provides a history of the studies and productions of plays, mostly Shakespeare, of the Umea Shakespeare Society, the dramatic society of a secondary school in Umea in northern Sweden. For twenty years (1952-72) under the author's direction, boys and girls presented nine of Shakespeare's plays in Swedish, including *A Midsummer Night's Dream.* Performed in an open air theatre, this play became a traditional feature of the Umea midsummer celebration, and in 1965 was staged using Lapland scenery and Lappish attire. In 1966, music by the popular singing group "The Who" was used in a pop version of the play. The school also performed a popular Christmas play derived in some part from *A Midsummer Night's Dream.* Söderwall describes her methods of work, which included four to five month rehearsal periods, movement exercises, and the use of properties early in rehearsals. As evidence of the success of productions, she cites letters from pupils and headmasters of schools where the group performed, an academic study based on an audience questionnaire, and excerpts from reviews. There is a section in Swedish on the society's productions of *A Midsummer Night's Dream* (pp. 9-12) and nineteen photographs of these productions which date between 1954 and 1968. There is a brief concluding summary of the book in English.

T1363   Watkins, Ronald, and Jeremy Lemmon. *In Shakespeare's Playhouse. A Midsummer Night's Dream.* Newton Abbot:

David and Charles; Totowa: Rowman and Littlefield,
1974. 150 pp.

Reconstructs the play in performance as imagined in
Shakespeare's day on the Elizabethan stage by daylight.
(The book is one of a series of such reconstructions by the
authors.) The introduction sets forth the conditions,
drawing upon standard scholarship on the Elizabethan
public stage, and offers some speculations. *E.g.*, the
fairies are to be dressed as miniature copies of the
Athenian mortals and, for the music of Titania's lullaby,
Pilkington's "Rest, sweet Nymphs" is suggested. An
analysis of the play then proceeds scene by scene,
sometimes line by line, with suggestions of line readings,
characterizations, blocking and business. Special attention
is given to the essential information or emotional content of
the lines; *e.g.*, at the end of Act IV, "The testy Egeus,
barking his iterations with the explosive style with which
John Heminges was clearly the master (and Shakespeare's
inspiration), invokes again the cruel justice of the earlier
scene: 'Enough, enough, my Lord: you have enough . . .
.'" When Puck overcasts the night, the authors write, "His
ritual, accompanied by magicianly gestures of fog-raising,
has the repetitions proper to incantation . . . ." (See also
item T1103.)

T1364   Williams, Gary Jay. "Our Moonlight Revels: *A Midsummer
        Night's Dream* on the English-Speaking Stage,
        1662-1970." Ph.D. dissertation, Yale University, 1974.
        DAI, 35 (1974): 3934A-3935. 384 pp.

        Reconstructs major productions of the play or
        adaptations of it, analyzing playing texts, staging,
        performances, scenery, costumes, and music, and sampling
        the critical responses. The fullest reconstructions are of
        the major nineteenth century productions, including those
        of Elizabeth Vestris (1840), who restored the text and set
        many production precedents for the rest of the century,
        Samuel Phelps (1853), William Burton (1853), Charles Kean
        (1856), Augustin Daly (1888), Sir Herbert Beerbohm Tree
        (1900), and Harley Granville-Barker (1914), who broke from
        the nineteenth century scenic traditions for the play. Major
        twentieth century productions are more briefly
        characterized, including those at the three Stratfords, the
        Old Vic, Regent's Park, in New York (on and
        off-Broadway), and the West End. Among the twentieth

century versions given relatively more detailed attention are
the productions of Max Reinhardt (1927), W. Bridges Adams
(1921-1931), Harcourt Williams (1929), Tyrone Guthrie
(1937), Michael Benthall and the Old Vic-Sadler's Wells
(1954), Jack Landau (1958), Peter Hall (1959-1963), John
Hancock (1966), and Peter Brook (1970). There are thirty
illustrations representing productions from 1840 to 1914 and
a production checklist.

T1365   Aaron, Jules. [Review.] *Educational Theatre Journal* 27
         (1975), 267-68.

    Reviews the production of *A Midsummer Night's Dream* at
the Berkeley Repertory Theatre, Berkeley California, which
opened on 6 December 1974. Douglas Johnson, the director,
viewed the play "as a dream of summer in the cold of
winter." The setting was surrealistic and Dali-like. The
lovers were each costumed from different periods. The
acting is praised, there were "marvelous" directorial
touches throughout, but the reviewer found that a clear,
consistent, darker directorial vision was lacking. The cast
and other credits are not given.

T1366   Barbour, Charles M. "Up Against A Symbolic Painted
         Cloth: *A Midsummer Night's Dream* at the Savoy, 1914."
         Educational Theatre Journal, 27 (1975), 521-28.

    Discusses the Harley Granville-Barker production. After
providing some background on and some description of the
Norman Wilkinson setting, which departed from pictorial
practices and sought, as Granville-Barker put it, "a new
hieroglyphic language of scenery," the author provides
details on the blocking, business, and line readings from
the Granville-Barker promptbook at the University of
Michigan. Stresses the importance of "the motif of
kneeling": "Kneeling is one of the dramatic expressions of
loves' uncertain vision which links the play's various
actions." In the scenery, in the costumes of the golden
fairies and the red-suited Puck, and in the blocking and
business, Granville-Barker's productions stressed,
correctly, theatrical artifice. Barbour enthusiastically
concludes that in Granville-Barker's staging "theatre is the
root metaphor for the heightened states of love and
imagination," and that "the theatre best represents the
peculiar character and energy of romantic love, for its

artificiality corresponds to the workings of the erotic imagination which is itself an outrageous combination of the sublime and the ridiculous, whose inevitable mode of expression is simultaneously gross and graceful." (See items T1149, T1392 and T1401.)

T1367   Bowmer, Angus. *As I Remember, Adam: An Autobiography of a Festival.* Ashland, Oregon: The Oregon Shakespeare Festival Association, 1975. 272 pp. Illustrated.

Included in these personal memoirs by the founder of the Ashland Festival are photographs of the Ashland theatres and of some productions, including two photos of scenes from early Festival productions (undated) of *A Midsummer Night's Dream.*

T1368   Grebanier, Bernard. *Then Came Each Actor: Shakespearean Actors, Great and Otherwise, Including Players and Princes, Rogues, Vagabonds, and Actors Motley, From Will Kempe to Olivier and Gielgud and After.* New York: David McKay Company, 1975. xii, 626 pp.

Surveys Shakespearean production history in a personal, sometimes eccentric style. There is some sampling of reviews, and the author provides, from memory, some selected staging details of productions he has seen and gives his judgments, which might be characterized as those of a traditionalist. The style and judgments may be illustrated by his comments on the Royal Shakespeare Company production of *A Midsummer Night's Dream* in 1970, directed by Peter Brook. He found it "shocking . . . for the outrageous vulgarity visited upon a work which has the refinement of the music Mendelssohn later wrote for it." No production of recent years was, for the author, "more revolting," more full of obscenities and gimmickry vulgarity (pp. 524-25).

T1369   Griffiths, Trevor R. "*A Midsummer Night's Dream* and *The Tempest* on the London Stage, 1789-1914." Ph.D. dissertation, University of Warwick, 1975.

Not seen. (See also items T1392 and T1451.)

T1370 Loney, Glenn, and Patricia MacKay. *The Shakespeare Complex: A Guide to Summer Festivals and Year-round Repertory in North America.* New York: Drama Book Specialists, 1975. 182 pp. Illustrated.

Briefly characterizes each of the major North American Shakespeare festivals and other Shakespeare producing groups. The photographs of productions include several of stagings of *A Midsummer Night's Dream,* in which can be seen a variety of approaches to costume and set design for the play. The quality clearly varies, too.

T1371 Marshall, Norman. *The Producer and the Play.* [3rd ed.] London: Davis-Poynter, 1975. 355 pp.

Discusses the development of the director, characterizing the staging practice of major eras and the work of major modern figures. There are three short chapters on the production of Shakespeare in the theatre from the seventeenth century to modern times. Productions of *A Midsummer Night's Dream* are occasionally drawn upon for examples of directorial approaches, with some attention being given to the versions of the play of Max Reinhardt (1905), Granville-Barker (1914), and Peter Brook (1970).

T1372 [Marder, Louis.] "A Musical Dream." *Shakespeare Newsletter,* 25 (1975), 24.

Brief review of a recent production of *A Midsummer Night's Dream* at Chicago's Ivanhoe Theatre, a "delightful blend of zany modern and zany Shakespeare," staged by Rudolf Tallman and Steven MacKenroth. There were modern songs, good acting, a mix of classical and modern costumes, an Oberon who was a magician, and an Egeus dressed like Kentucky Fried Chicken's amiable colonel.

T1373 *A Midsummer Night's Dream* presented by the New York Shakespeare Festival, Joseph Papp, producer, at the Mitzi E. Newhouse Theatre, Lincoln Center, 19 January to 16 March 1975. Director, Edward Berkeley. Musical staging by Donald Sadler. Design by Santo Loquasto. Lighting design, Jennifer Tipton. Music, William Penn. *Oberon,* George Hearn. *Titania,* Kathleen Widdoes. *Puck,* Larry Marshall. *Bottom,* Richard Ramos. *Theseus,* Dan

Hamilton. *Hippolyta*, Marlene Warfield. *Hermia*, Toni
Wein. *Demetrius*, Richard Gere. *Flute*, Edward
Herrmann. *Snout*, Roberts Blossom. *Quince*, Tom Toner.

A relatively simple, off-Broadway production,
contemporary in spirit and set design and broad in its
humor, it received reviews that varied from Gussow's praise
for "a youthful frolicsome approach to a classic" to Mallet's
criticism of the director, who "interred the play in 20th
century sentimentality. The actors do their own thing and
the play becomes farce." There was a suggestion of "mod"
decadence in the chrome thrones of Theseus and Hippolyta.
Large frosted globes set atop a few slender aluminum poles
and slid down part way and emitted a greenish glow for the
forest scenes. Puck was played in the manner of a hip
street Arab disdainful of Oberon; the lovers were
contemporary and sassy; and there was broad clowning in
Pyramus and Thisbe. There were complaints about the
handling of the language.

Reviews: Mel Gussow, *New York Times*, 20 January 1975;
Martin Gottfried, *New York Post*, 20 January 1975; Douglas
Watt, *Daily News*, 20 January 1975; John Beaufort,
Christian Science Monitor, 30 January 1975; Christopher
Sharp, *Women's Wear Daily*, 20 January 1975; Gina Mallet,
Time, 3 February 1975.

T1374   *A Midsummer Night's Dream* presented by the Yale
        Repertory Theatre, Robert Brustein, Artistic Director,
        in association with the Yale School of Music at the Yale
        Repertory Theatre, New Haven, opening 14(?) May 1975
        and running through 31 May. Revived October 1975 and
        revived again in 1980 at Cambridge, Massachusetts (see
        item T1478). Director, Alvin Epstein. Setting, Tony
        Straiges. Costumes, Zack Brown. Lighting, William
        Warfel. Music from Henry Purcell's *The Fairy Queen*,
        adapted and conducted by Otto-Werner Meuller. *Oberon*,
        Christopher Lloyd. *Titania*, Carmen de Lavallade. *Puck*,
        Linda Atkinson. *Bottom*, Charles Levin. *Helena*, Meryl
        Streep. *Theseus*, Jeremy Geidt. *Hippolyta*, Franchelle
        Stewart Dorn.

        The production was informed by a dark and ironic
        directorial conception (probably somewhat Kott-influenced)
        and featured Purcell's music counterpointing, even
        contradicting the universe of sexual combat of the

production, "a nebula of intertwining seductions" (Kroll). A lizard-like Oberon had a sexual appetite touched with sadism, and the sensuous Titania was both "bait and bird of Prey" (Clurman). The mechanicals were rendered as vaudeville types, with a Harpo Marx-like Bottom. The set was a lunar landscape with a silver popcorn moon. A controversial production, it was much noticed in 1975, and revived in 1980 on the occasion of Brustein's removal from Yale and his new start at Harvard. (See item T1478.)

Reviews: Mel Gussow, *New York Times,* 15 May 1975; Walter Kerr, *New York Times,* 25 May 1975; Michael Feingold, *New York Times,* 8 June 1975 (rejoinder to Kerr's review); Harold Clurman, *The Nation,* 31 May 1975; Jack Kroll, *Newsweek* 20 October 1975.

T1375   Entry Deleted.

T1376   Mullin, Michael. "Peter Hall's *Midsummer Night's Dream* on Film." *Educational Theatre Journal,* 27 (1975), 529-34.

Briefly characterizes first the 1959 stage production of the play by Hall, which the author says reduced the play, and then Hall's 1962 reworking of it, which the author says kept the strengths of the original production and corrected its faults. He then analyzes the techniques of the film, an extension of the RSC production, explaining the effects of the "documentary" technique of the hand-held camera used in some scenes, and praises the surreal special effects achieved by cutting and coloring, which "induces something like the lovers' unbalanced state of mind." From these and other techniques which are exampled, the author concludes that Hall's film, "like the play itself, . . . challenges its audience to set their notions of conventional film aside." He finds Hall's film a "true rendering" of Shakespeare's play and is puzzled by the poor reception it had from film critics (whose reviews are sampled). (See also items T1183, T1301, T1323 and T1406.)

T1377   *Nederlands Theater-en Televisie Jaarboek: Toneel, Televisie-drama, Opera, Ballet.* No. 23, Seizon 1973/1974. Amsterdam: Doneto, 1975.

Survey of theatrical productions of 1973-1974 season that includes references to two Dutch productions of *A Midsummer Night's Dream*. Not seen.

T1378   Nightingale, Benedict. "The Royal, Risk-taking Shakespeare Company." *New York Times*, February 2, 1975, D, 5, 26.

Discusses the approaches and the successes of the RSC, providing some characterization of its major productions, including the 1970 *A Midsummer Night's Dream* directed by Peter Brook (photograph). (See item T1314.)

T1379   Price, Joseph G., ed. *The Triple Bond, Plays, Mainly Shakespearean, in Performance*. University Park: Pennsylvania State University Press, 1975. xiv, 312 pp.

Within the sixteen essays by American and English scholars that comprise the volume, there are a few references to productions of *A Midsummer Night's Dream*, including a reference by Kenneth Muir to the Titania of an undated Stratford-upon-Avon production and Stanley Wells's reference to the RSC's of 1970, directed by Peter Brook. The volume is dedicated to a Shakespearean stage history pioneer, Arthur Colby Sprague, and a bibliography of his works is provided.

T1380   Entry Deleted.

T1381   *The Riverside Treasury of Music: Music of England and the Continent in Shakespeare's Time and Music Inspired by Shakespeare*. Two-record album. Boston: Houghton Mifflin, 1975.

Includes arias from Benjamin Britten's opera, *A Midsummer Night's Dream*, and Felix Mendelssohn's overture (opus 21) for the play.

T1382   Rowell, George. "Tree's Shakespeare Festivals (1905-1913)." *Theatre Notebook*, 29 (1975), 74-81.

Discusses the development of the annual festivals, the productions given, and the companies who visited His Majesty's Theatre for them. Tree's production of *A Midsummer Night's Dream*, staged in 1900, was revived for the festival in 1911.

T1383   Salgãdo, Gãmini. *Eyewitnesses of Shakespeare: First Hand Accounts of Performances 1590-1890.* London: Chatto and Windus for Sussex University Press, 1975. 360 pp. Illustrated.

Reproduces in the section on *A Midsummer Night's Dream* very abridged versions of William Hazlitt's damning review of the 1816 operatic version of the play by Sir Frederick Reynolds, Henry Morley's enthusiastic review of Samuel Phelps's production in 1853, and G. B. Shaw's disapproving review of Augustin Daly's production of 1895 in London. There are also excerpts from the autobiographies of James Robinson Planché, who designed for Elizabeth Vestris' 1840 production, and Ellen Terry, and illustrations showing Terry's Puck and the last scene of the Charles Kean production of 1856, in which Terry played.

T1384   Simon, John. "Spring 1971." *Uneasy Stages, A Chronicle of the New York Theatre, 1963-1973.* New York: Random House, Incorporated, 1975, pp. 315-22.

Deplores the 1970 production of *A Midsummer Night's Dream* of the Royal Shakespeare Company, directed by Peter Brook and any such Artaud-influenced "no more masterpieces" approach to Shakespeare. "The enchantment stamped out, the performances divested of magic, love turned into lust, the *Dream* changed into nightmare--what remains when everything is overthrown, dismantled, shattered: There remains the supreme magician Peter Brook, who fancies himself the Prospero of the occasion but is really its Sycorax." Simon warns, "We must not allow our justified indignation with boring productions or complacent spectators to goad us into senseless retaliatory measures that cannot reclaim a blasé or boorish audience, but may obscure and destroy the meaning and beauty of a play." (See also item 1314.)

T1385   Stein, Elliott. "The Art of Art Direction." *Film Comment*,
        11, 3 (1975), 32-35.

        Accompanying the brief text are illustrations of settings
        by Metzner and Grot, respectively, for the German films of
        the play directed by Hans Neumann in 1925 and by Max
        Reinhardt and William Dieterle in 1935.

T1386   Styan, J. L. *Drama, Stage and Audience*. London:
        Cambridge University Press, 1975. viii, 256 pp.

        Stresses the different factors affecting the production of
        the drama, from the actor to the *Zeitgeist*, emphasizing the
        actor and audience relationship that textual study has
        ignored. The author believes "the 'futurist' productions of
        A Midsummer Night's Dream by Granville-Barker with his
        stylized gold fairies (1914) and by Brook with his magic
        circus (1970)--both shockingly untraditional--were
        outstandingly true to the original because directed
        accurately at their contemporary audiences" (p. 10). In the
        general discussions of production values in the drama, often
        examples are drawn from Shakespeare's plays; the "Pyramus
        and Thisbe" play is drawn upon in a discussion of the
        complicity between actors and audience in the putting on of
        a play.

T1387   Williams, David Terry. "An Analysis of Representative
        Productions of Sir Frank Benson." *DAI*, 35 (1975),
        6852A (Indiana).

        Reconstructs Benson's *A Midsummer Night's Dream* in
        detail and four other of his Shakespearean productions,
        using promptbooks, photographs, and reviews--most of
        which are in the Shakespeare Centre Library at
        Stratford-upon-Avon. Benson's *A Midsummer Night's Dream*
        illustrates his attempt to imitate the lavish productions of
        his mentor, Sir Henry Irving, and to compete with Sir
        Herbert Beerbohm Tree. Benson's staging is viewed here in
        the context of the turn-of-the-century changes in
        Shakespearean production style.

T1388   Willson, Robert F., Jr. *"Their Form Confounded":
        Studies in the Burlesque Play from Udall to Sheridan*.
        The Hague: Mouton, 1975. xiv, 170 pp.

Includes a discussion of "Pyramus and Thisbe" in *A Midsummer Night's Dream* showing that it incorporates conventions of the burlesque play form. Shakespeare wittily comments on misconceptions about drama's representation of reality, about audience-actor relationships, and even parodies romance conventions in this farce. There is a detailed analysis of "Pyramus."

T1388a Anderegg, Michael A. "Shakespeare on Film in the Classroom." *Literature/Film Quarterly*, 4, 2, (Spring 1976), 176-86.

Discusses his experiment in teaching Shakespeare and films of the plays. Peter Hall's 1969 film of *A Midsummer Night's Dream* (see T1301) is used as an example of a film adhering closely to the text. Reinhardt's 1935 film of the play is discussed as to the Victorian and Hollywood influence on it. Anderegg's students preferred the Hall film.

T1389 Forsyth, James. *Tyrone Guthrie, a Biography*. London: Hamish Hamilton, 1976. xi, 372 pp. Illustrated.

Authorized biography of the director's life and professional career includes a brief description of his 1937-38 Old Vic production of *A Midsummer Night's Dream* in Victorian style. There is a lengthier discussion of his development of the open stage for the Stratford, Ontario, theatre with Tanya Moiseiwitsch.

T1390 Fuhrich-Leisler, Edda, and Gisela Prossnitz. *Max Reinhardt in America*. Publikation der Max Reinhardt-Forschungsstätte 5. Salzburg: Otto Verlag, 1976. 456 pp. Illustrated.

Devotes one chapter (pp. 205-22) to a discussion of and documents relating to the 1935 Reinhardt-Dieterle film of *A Midsummer Night's Dream* for Warner Brothers. The chapter excerpts selected reviews, a teacher's manual that Warner Brothers published for the film, and letter to Reinhardt from his son, Gottfried. There are also comments from some of Reinhardt's associates in the making of the film. Another chapter (pp. 180-204) provides documents pertaining to his productions of the play at the Hollywood Bowl in 1932 and

in Berkeley's Greek theatre and San Francisco's War
Memorial Opera House in 1934. These include
correspondence about the arrangements, with some letters
from Reinhardt.

T1390a   Fuhrich-Leisler, Edda, and Gisela Prossnitz. *Max
          Reinhardt in Europa und Amerika.* Austellung der
          Max-Reinhardt-Forschungs- und Gedenkstätte, Salzburg
          unter Mitwirkung der Botschaft der Vereinigten Staaten
          von Amerika in Wien und dem Kulturamt der Stadt Wien.
          26. Juli bis 30 August 1976, Salzburg, Schloss
          Arenberg. 9. November bis 7. Dezember 1976, Wien,
          Haus des Buches. Salzburg: Reischl-Druck, 1976. 74 pp.
          Illustrated.

          Exhibition catalogue for exhibits in 1976 in Vienna and
          Salzburg of photographs and documents of Reinhardt
          productions includes illustrations representing eight
          different productions of *A Midsummer Night's Dream*
          directed by Reinhardt. There is a sketch and two photos of
          Oskar Strnad's setting for the production in New York in
          1927. The playbill is also reproduced; among the cast were
          Lili Darvas as Titania, Vladimir Sokoloff as Puck, and
          Alexander Moissi as Oberon. There is a photo of a model of
          Ernst Stern's forest setting for the Berlin production of
          1905; the forest moved on a revolving stage. There are
          three sketches for the productions of 1909 (Munich) and
          1921 (Berlin), a photo of the lovers discovered in the wood
          in the outdoor production at Oxford in 1933, and a photo of
          the finale in the Berkeley production of 1934 in Berkeley's
          outdoor Greek theatre. There are also two photos from the
          1935 Reinhardt-Dieterle film.

T1391   Gielgud, Sir John. *Early Stages.* London: Falcon Press
          [1948]; new and rev. ed., with a preface by Ivor Brown
          [1953]; rev. ed., London: Heinemann, 1974; New York:
          Taplinger Publishing Company, 1976. xiv, 210 pp.
          Illustrated.

          Included in this autobiography is some discussion of his
          performance as Oberon in the 1929 Old Vic production of *A
          Midsummer Night's Dream*, directed by Harcourt Williams (p.
          100). "I was learning to speak verse well at last . . .
          beginning to control the lovely language which at rehearsals
          moved me so much that tears would spring to my eyes." He

says Lilian Baylis was not in sympathy with Williams' break from Mendelssohn nor the Elizabethan costumes in Athens. He recalls, dimly, the Harley Granville-Barker production.

T1392   Griffiths, Trevor. "Tradition and Innovation in Harley Granville-Barker's *A Midsummer Night's Dream.*" *Theatre Notebook,* 30 (1976), 78-87.

Contends that Granville-Barker's production was a mixture of traditional and innovative elements and seeks to correct the customary characterizations of it as wholly innovative. Such characterizations usually disparage earlier revivals. There were innovations: Granville-Barker offered "a virtually unaltered text . . . which was the most significant textual advance since Madame Vestris' [revival] in 1840"; uncomplicated scenery that allowed for the flow of scenes; and the dropping of Mendelssohn's music for Cecil Sharp's folk songs. But there were traditional elements: an opening procession of the court; some of the comic business of the fairies and of the mechanicals (such as the conception of "poor, old, timid Starveling"); and the chalice of rose petals for the final fairy blessing. The latter is seen as but a step away from Benson's use of an altar and priests for the last act opening. (See also items T1149, T1392 and T1401.)

T1392a   Homan, Sidney. "A Cinema for Shakespeare." *Literature/Film Quarterly*, 4, 2 (Spring 1976), 176-86.

Discusses responses of students in his course on Shakespeare on film to the question "can the plays be translated into the medium of film?" Their responses ranged from the purist's rejection to the film enthusiast's belief that the verbal life of the plays can and must be replaced by visual cinemagraphic equivalents. Homan suggests the profitable questions in the debate have to do with whether the theatre and the film medium are antithetical. He thinks not, because "the camera's eye is never realistic," and he believes that some common ground can be found between Shakespeare and the cinema. Peter Hall's 1969 film of *A Midsummer Night's Dream* (see item T1301), which critics regarded less as genuine film than a compelling filmed play, says Homan, is cited as an example of the issues in the debate.

T1393   Jensen, Ejner J. [Review.] *Educational Theatre Journal*,
         28 (1976), 558-59.

         Review coverage includes a favorable assessment of a
         youthful production of *A Midsummer Night's Dream* by the
         Royal Academic of Dramatic Art at the Vanbrugh Theatre,
         London, 16 June 1976. The costumes ranged from 1940s
         formal wear for Theseus and Hippolyta to 1970s street wear
         for the lovers. So costuming was "a matter of genre rather
         than period." The staging and acting style were also used
         to suggest a genre--the elegance and wit of 1940s films.

T1394   Kauffmann, Stanley. *Persons of the Drama: Theater
         Criticism and Comment.* New York: Harper and Row,
         1976. 397 pp.

         Included in this anthology of Kauffmann's essays on
         theatre in the *New Republic*, the *New York Times*, and
         elsewhere between 1964 and 1975, is his 1971 review of the
         Royal Shakespeare production of *A Midsummer Night's
         Dream*, directed by Peter Brook, an essay on Harley
         Granville-Barker's career, with some discussion of his 1914
         production, and an essay on Joseph Papp's career with the
         New York Shakespeare Festival. Papp is characterized as an
         "insistent cultural phenomenon," a figure of major stature
         in art "without one single achievement of major stature in
         that art." Peter Brook's production is described as having
         been spoken traditionally but anti-traditional in its staging
         and spectacle; it is doubted if there is a synthesis. Of
         Granville-Barker, he concludes: "The theatre proved too
         prosaic for Barker to discover his god in it, but before and
         after he left it, he did work that still helps those stubborn
         enough to hope."

T1395   Lewis, Peter Elfed. "Richard Leveridge's *The Comick
         Masque of Pyramus and Thisbe.*" *Restoration and
         Eighteenth Century Theatre Research*, 15, 1 (May 1976),
         33-41.

         Describes Leveridge's 1716 afterpiece, which used the
         play-within-the-play to mock the Italian opera, then
         enjoying popularity in London. Discusses both the textual
         and musical humor of the burlesque and relates it to other
         burlesques of the Restoration and eighteenth century. Lewis
         says it may be the best of the period's burlesques on the

Italian opera, and he sees it in the tradition of the dramatic
burlesque descending from *The Rehearsal.*

T1396   *A Midsummer Night's Dream* presented by the Stratford
         Shakespeare Festival at the Festival Theatre, Stratford,
         Ontario, in repertory 18 August to 16 October 1976.
         Director, Robin Phillips. Designer, Susan Benson,
         Bottom, Hume Cronyn. *Titania/Hippolyta,* Jessica Tandy.
         Theseus/Oberon, Jeremy Brett. *Hermia,* Mia Anderson.
         Puck, Tom Kneebone. Revived for the 1977 festival
         (opening 6 June 1977) with revisions and cast changes:
         Bottom, Alan Scarfe. *Titania/Hippolyta,* Maggie Smith.
         Theseus/Oberon, Barry MacGregor. *Helena,* Martha
         Henry.

         The 1976 production was Elizabethan in its elaborate
costumes and visual motifs. The doubling of the roles of
Theseus/Oberon and Hippolyta/Titania was emphasized, with
Jessica Tandy costumed to suggest Queen Elizabeth I. The
play seemed to be Elizabeth's dream. This was enlarged
upon visually in the 1977 staging, with Queen Elizabeth
present at the play's "presenter." The suggestion was that
Shakespeare wrote the play for a wedding entertainment and
as an homage to his sovereign, the "fair vestal throned by
the west," a wellspring of romantic devotion.

         Reviews: *London Evening Free Press,* 19 August 1976;
Toronto Globe and Mail, 20 August 1976; *Vancouver Sun,* 21
August 1976; Arnold Edinborough, *Performing Arts in
Canada,* Summer 1976; Brian Arnott, *MacLean's,* 28 June
1976; John Pettigrew, *Journal of Canadian Studies,* II, 4
(1976), 33-48; *London Evening Free Press,* 7 June 1977;
Toronto Star, 7 June 1977; Richard Eder, *New York Times,*
8 June 1977; Kevin Kelly, *Boston Globe,* 8 June 1977;
Robert Cushman, *The Observer,* 19 June 1977; T. A.
Kalem, *Time,* 20 June 1977; Samantha Dean, *New York
Times,* 3 July 1977; *Saturday Night,* July-August 1977; B.
A. Young, *Plays and Players,* 24, 2 (August 1977);
Berners A. W. Jackson, *Shakespeare Quarterly,* 28 (1977),
197-206; Ronald Bryden, *MacLean's,* 11 July 1977; Eric
Salmon, *Queen's Quarterly,* 84 (1977), 31-46; Michael
Crabb, *Performing Arts in Canada,* 14, 4 (1978), 8; Ralph
Berry, *Shakespeare Quarterly,* 29 (1978), 222-26, cover
photo; Roger Warren, *Shakespeare Survey,* 31 (1978),
141-53, with two photographs of Maggie Smith.

T1397   Shakespeareana. [A Catalogue of Works to be Auctioned.]
        *Paintings, Watercolors, Drawings, Ceramics, and
        Tapestries.* The Property of the American Shakespeare
        Theatre, Stratford, Connecticut. New York: Sotheby
        Parke Bernet Inc., 1976. 62 pp. Illustrated.

        Includes nine art works depicting scenes from *A
        Midsummer Night's Dream,* among which is a sketch of Sir
        Herbert Beerbohm Tree as Bottom by J. B. Booth (1900),
        the only performance-derived art work here. Also included
        in the catalogue are paintings and drawings by Arthur
        Rackham (two drawings are reproduced), Philipp William
        May, and Frances Wheatley, whose large oil, *Theseus and
        Hippolyta Discover the Lovers,* is reproduced.

T1398   Shattuck, Charles H. *Shakespeare on the American
        Stage, From the Hallams to Edwin Booth.* Washington, D.
        C.: The Folger Shakespeare Library, 1976. xiv, 170 pp.

        Included in the chronological history is a characterization
        of one of the major nineteenth century American productions
        of *A Midsummer Night's Dream,* that of William Burton in
        1854. Promptbooks and reviews are drawn upon and the
        Chambers Street Theatre playbill for the production is
        reproduced, as is a contemporary engraving of Burton as
        Bottom. The production is briefly compared to that of
        Thomas Barry that opened three days later at the Broadway
        Theatre. There is a brief allusion to Charlotte Cushman's
        appearance as Oberon in the Park Theatre's production of
        1841.

T1399   Trewin, John Courtenay. *The Edwardian Theatre.*
        Oxford: Basil Blackwell, 1976. xiv, 193 pp. Illustrated.

        Survey of major figures of the era includes sketches of
        these British producers of *A Midsummer Night's Dream:* Sir
        Herbert Beerbohm Tree, Sir Frank Benson, Oscar Asche,
        and Harley Granville-Barker. Includes a photograph of the
        Harley Granville-Barker production of 1914, showing Titania
        and Bottom asleep on the forest knoll with Oberon and Puck
        looking on (following p. 98).

T1400   Wearing, J. P. *The London Stage 1890-1899. A Calendar
        of Plays and Players.* 2 volumes. Metuchen, New Jersey,
        and London: The Scarecrow Press, Inc., 1976.

        Provides annual calendars of professional play
        performances in the major London theatres in the decade
        1890-99. Entries include dates of runs, partial casts,
        production credits, and, for some productions, a listing of
        some newspaper reviews. There is an entry for the
        Augustin Daly production in London of *A Midsummer Night's
        Dream* in 1895. This calendar is the first in a series of
        three by the author covering London theatre to 1919. (See
        items T1505 and T1524b.)

T1401   Williams, Gary Jay. "*A Midsummer Night's Dream*: The
        English and American Popular Traditions and Harley
        Granville-Barker's 'World Arbitrarily Made.'" *Theatre
        Studies*, 23 (1976/77), 40-52.

        Reconstructs the Granville-Barker production and
        describes the critical response to its London premiere of
        1914 and its New York showing of 1915. With Norman
        Wilkinson's non-illusionistic scenic decor, the folk music
        score by Cecil Sharp that replaced Mendelssohn, and the
        rapid delivery of the verse, it was a considerable departure
        from the theatrical traditions for the play, seen in ripeness
        recently in the Tree and Daly productions. But the famous
        golden fairies, which were among the Granville-Barker-
        Wilkinson solutions to the problem of creating a new visual
        vocabulary for the play, called much attention to
        themselves. One American critic found the new world for
        the play "a world arbitrarily made." Traditionalists such as
        Odell and Winter denounced the production as a desecration
        of Shakespeare. From those critics who gave it a warmer
        reception there were complaints about its lack of unity and
        Granville-Barker's intellectuality and "perfect sanity." (See
        also items T1149, T1366 and T1392.)

T1401a Willson, Robert F., Jr. "Ill Met by Moonlight:
        Reinhardt's *A Midsummer Night's Dream* and Musical
        Screwball Comedy." *Journal of Popular Film and
        Television*, 5 (1976), 185-97.

        Shows that in the Reinhardt-Dieterle film, Warner
        Brothers attempted to capture an audience for the film by

using some of the techniques of the successful film comedies of the period, such as *Footlight Parade* and *It Happened One Night*. Critics need to study Shakespeare on film in the context of contemporary films and social history, as well as studying the subject relative to literary and stage traditions.

T1402   Allen, Shirley S. "Notes and Queries." *Theatre Notebook*, 31, 3 (1977), 38.

Against Trevor-Griffith's assertion (see item T1392) that Harley Granville-Barker's 1914 production of *A Midsummer Night's Dream* was the most significant advance since Elizabeth Vestris' in 1840, Allen enters Samuel Phelps' staging of 1853. (See also items T1286 and T1318.)

T1402a   Balanchine, George, and Francis Mason. *Balanchine's Complete Stories of the Great Ballets*. Revised and enlarged edition. Garden City, New York: Doubleday and Company, 1977. 838 pp. Illustrated.

Provides synopses of two ballets based on *A Midsummer Night's Dream*, Frederick Ashton's and Balanchine's. Balanchine writes (pp. 359-61) of his creation of his ballet, which premiered in 1962 (see item T1214a). The play had been a childhood favorite of his in Russia, but the ballet was actually inspired by Mendelssohn's score for the play. To fill out the music for the danced action of the whole play, Balanchine incorporated other Mendelssohn music: in Act I, the overtures to *Athalie*, *The Fair Melusine*, and *The First Walpurgis Night*, and in Act II, the *Symphony No. 9* and the overture to *Son and Stranger*. He provides a scene by scene synopsis of the two-act, six-scene ballet. The principals of the ballet's premiere are given, and there are two photographs. (See also item T1409.) Also provided is a synopsis and production history (pp. 183-84) of Ashton's one-act ballet that premiered at the Royal Opera House, Covent Garden, on April 2, 1964, as part of the Royal Ballet's observance of the 400th anniversary of Shakespeare's birth. (See also item T1246a.) It, too, uses the Mendelssohn score. It begins with the Oberon-Titania quarrel in the forest and does not include Theseus and Hippolyta. The premiere's principals are given and also those of a 1973 revival by the Joffrey ballet.

T1403   Berry, Ralph. *On Directing Shakespeare: Interviews With
        Contemporary Directors.* London: Croom Helm; New
        York: Barnes and Noble, 1977. 135 pp. Illustrated.

        Berry interviews Jonathan Miller, Robin Phillips, Konrad
Swinarski, Trevor Nunn, Michael Kahn, Giorgio Strehler,
and Peter Brook. The book had its origins in a letter
(reproduced here) by Jonathan Miller to *The Times* in 1971
on the occasion of criticisms of Peter Brook's production of
A Midsummer Night's Dream with the RSC, discussing the
modern directorial approaches to Shakespeare. Brook's
production is referred to throughout the other interviews,
and he himself comments on the creating of it and on
audience responses to it. The English resented the sexual
suggestions (such as the miming of Bottom's phallus) but
Americans did not object. On the other hand, Americans
found the company unattractive and "scruffy" while the
English found it made up of vigorous young people. Brook
says, "we want the very bright but uninformed audience,
with no prejudices . . . who's interested if its interesting,
and not otherwise." "What I'm interested to see," says
Brook, "is not the historical sense but the actual, what
makes a meaning for me." He says he did not cut the text
of the play in his production. Swinarski comments at some
length on a production of *A Midsummer Night's Dream* that
he directed in Krakow, which was colored by his experience
in Poland. He believes Shakespeare, in the fifth act
play-within-the-play, meant to hold a mirror up to the
court through the workers and that Quince is attempting to
bring to the court a truth about the corruption of human
feeling by state power. The fairies in his production were
in costumes representing various body parts (photo).

T1404   Booth, Stephen. "Shakespeare in California and Utah."
        Shakespeare Quarterly, 28 (1977), 229-44.

        Review coverage includes a brief characterization of a
production of *A Midsummer Night's Dream* by the South
Coast Repertory, directed by Dan Sullivan. It and two
other productions are characterized as "hyped-up,
condescending production[s]," the kind that derive from
contempt both for the play produced and for audiences. It
included a magic show, a puppet show, an essay on Greek
Americans in the nineteenth century, and an electric Walt
Disney forest backdrop.

T1405   Coursen, H. R. "The Theater at Monmouth." *Shakespeare Quarterly*, 28 (1977), 206-207.

Coverage includes a brief, very favorable review of a production of *A Midsummer Night's Dream* at the Shakespearean Theatre of Maine in the summer of 1976, directed by Earl McCarroll. Cheryl Moore's Titania is reported to have charged her speech to Oberon on their quarrel with lyric power, Dana Mills's Oberon was a rich baritone, and both characterizations were enhanced by stylized movement. The reviewer says "the artisans were the best I've seen since Morris Carnovsky played Quince many seasons ago at Stratford, Connecticut." Principals in the cast and production credits are listed.

T1406   Jorgens, Jack J. *Shakespeare on Film.* Bloomington: Indiana University Press, 1977. xii, 337 pp.

Analyzes, in Chapters Two and Three, the two major films of the play, Max Reinhardt and William Dieterle's of 1935 and Peter Hall's of 1969. The descriptions and critical assessments of the main text are organized around themes and are accompanied by an appendix in which detailed scene-by-scene synopses of the action will be found. Full credits will be found there, also. Hall's textual cuts are given in notes to Chapter Three. Eleven black and white photographs from the two films are included. Discussing the Reinhardt film, whose cast included Victor Jory·as Oberon, Anita Louise as Titania, James Cagney as Bottom, Mickey Rooney as Puck, and Olivia de Havilland as Hermia, Jorgens points out its interpretive freedom, which included some stress on the erotic aspects of the play. He notes the relation of its lavish spectacle to the nineteenth century stage traditions for the play, and notes the surprising freedom of its American actors from declamatory traditions. In the discussion of the Hall film, he points out its unconventional cinematic vocabulary, which stressed a disjunctive, dream world vision, and Hall's stress on the erotic and down-to-earth elements. (See also items T1323 and T1376.)

T1407   Kemme, H. -M. "Ludwig Tiecks Bühnenreformplace und--versuche und ihre Wirkung auf die Entwicklung des deutschen theaters im 19. und 20. Jahrhunderts." Ph.d.

dissertation, Freie University, Berlin. 1977, Freie University, Berlin.

Discusses Tieck's theories on and experiments with a Shakespeare stage, that is to say an Elizabethan type of stage, and Tieck's influence on German production thereafter. Tieck produced *A Midsummer Night's Dream* in 1843 at the Neues Theater in Potsdam, using a setting that had some non-pictorial, architectural features.

T1408   Laroque, François. *Cahiers Élisabéthains,* 12 (1977), 87-88.

Favorable review of an "enjoyable" production of *A Midsummer Night's Dream* by the Folger Theatre Group in Washington, D.C. in June, 1977. The director and the company highlighted the comic and farcical aspects of the play at the expense of the sophistication, poetry and magic, however. "But this genial production reminded us that this is also one of Shakespeare's jolliest comedies." Oberon was played as a sort of Mephistophelean mock-villain who sneezed with hay fever when smelling the magic flower. The physiques of the actresses playing Hermia and Helena were of such extremes of tall and short as to create caricatures. Demetrius was black, which for the reviewer resulted in unexpected touches, such as on Hermia's line to him, "O, wilt thou darkling leave me?" There was doubling in the roles of Theseus/Oberon, Hippolyta/Titania and Philostrate/Puck. The production opened and closed with the company dancing a merry jig and a morris dance, respectively.

T1409   Lassalle, Nancy, ed. *"A Midsummer Night's Dream": The Story of the New York City Ballet's Production.* Told in Photographs by Martha Swope. Introduction by Lincoln Kirstein. New York: Dodd, Mead, 1977. 64 pp. Illustrated.

Provides seventy performance photographs of the ballet created by George Balanchine. It premiered in New York City, 17 January 1962, at New York City Center, with Titania and Oberon danced by Melissa Hayden and Edward Villella and Puck danced by Arthur Mitchell (see item T1214a). David Hays designed the scenery and Karinska the

costumes. These photographs are of a 1976-1977 company
and include Kay Mazzeo or Suzanne Farrell as Titania and
Helgi Tomasson or Peter Schaufuss as Oberon. Balanchine's
ballet, in two acts and six scenes, is based on the play but
inspired chiefly by Mendelssohn's score; he used the full
incidental score and added other music by Mendelssohn to
it. (Balanchine had staged dances for the 1958 production
of the play by the American Shakespeare Festival; see item
T1172). Balanchine's first act follows Shakespeare's plot up
through the discovery of the lovers in the wood by
Theseus. The second act begins with a processional to
Mendelssohn's Wedding March into a pavilion set up in the
forest for the nuptial festivities. Then a series of
divertissements are danced for the entertainment of the
wedding guests. At the end, the forest elves mingle with
the departing guests, Oberon and Titania enter while the
choir of fairies sings, the stage becomes a nest of
flickering fireflies, and Puck sweeps the stage with a
broom. (The ballet was filmed in 1967 by Columbia Pictures;
see item T1276b.)

T1410   Mendelssohn-Bartholdy, Felix. *A Midsummer Night's
        Dream. Incidental Music.* Andre Previn conducting the
        London Philharmonic Orchestra, with soloists and a
        children's choir. One 33 1/3 phonodisc, stereo. London
        HMV (sq) ASD 3377 and Angel S 37268. *circa* 1977.

T1411   *A Midsummer Night's Dream* presented by the Royal
        Shakespeare Company at the Royal Shakespeare Theatre,
        Stratford-upon-Avon, beginning in repertory 3 May
        1977. Moved to the Aldwych Theatre, London, 25 June
        1977, and back to Stratford-upon-Avon, 22 March 1978.
        Director, John Barton, with choreographer Gillian
        Lynne. Designer, John Napier. Music, Guy Woolfenden.
        Oberon, Patrick Stewart. *Titania*, Marjorie Bland.
        Bottom, Richard Griffiths. *Puck*, Leonard Preston.
        Hermia, Pippa Guard. *Helena*, Marilyn Galsworthy.

        The first RSC production of the play in the seven years
since the pre-emptive impact of the Brook production of
1970, it managed to make a mark with another kind of
impressive staging, in which there was an emphasis upon
romantic, exotic enchantment. Most notable were its
strange, ancient, wizened-face fairies; the nearly nude,
masculine figure of Stewart's *Oberon*, resembling a bronzed

Aztec Indian; the contrasting formal court, all in black and white; the quiet leadership of Griffiths' *Bottom*; and Woolfenden's beguiling score, which included a moving song for *Bottom* to sing in "Pyramus and Thisbe."

Reviews: John Barber, *Daily Telegraph*, 9 May and 22 June, 1977; Michael Billington, *Guardian*, 9 May 1977; Garry O'Connor, *Financial Times*, 9 May 1977; Irving Wardle, *The Times*, 9 May 1977; Gareth Lloyd Evans, *Stratford-upon-Avon Herald*, 13 May 1977; Robert Cushman, *Observer*, 15 May 1977; Bernard Levin, *Sunday Times*, 15 May 1977; John Elsom, *Listener*, 19 May 1977; Sally Aire, *Plays and Players*, July 1977, with two photographs; Jean Fuzier, *Cahiers Élisabéthains*, 12 (1977), 73-74; G. M. Pearce, *Cahiers Élisabéthains*, 13 (1978), 114; Roger Warren, *Shakespeare Survey*, 31 (1978), 141-53, with photograph. (See also items T1481 and T1508.)

T1411a   *A Midsummer Night's Dream* presented by the Stratford Shakespeare Festival at the Festival Theatre, Stratford, Ontario, opening 6 June 1977. Director, Robin Phillips. *Titania*, Maggie Smith.

This was a revival, with revisions in concept and new cast members, of the festival's 1976 production. For a characterization and reviews for both seasons, see item T1396.

T1412   Payne, Ben Iden. *A Life in a Wooden O.* New Haven: Yale University Press, 1977. xvii, 204 pp. Illustrated.

His reminiscences about his long career as an actor in and director of Shakespeare's plays includes his memory of playing Egeus in Sir Frank Benson's production of *A Midsummer Night's Dream*. He recounts Benson's last scene, with the lovers entering to Mendelssohn's wedding march and doing obeisance to an altar on which there burned a low flame.

T1412a   Radice, Mark. "Some Observations on Purcell's *The Fairy Queen*." *Bach*, 8, 1 (1977), 12-15.

Argues that the operatic treatment of Shakespeare's play was not unusual for the era and that this work, more than

any other Purcell opera, shows the English masque tradition
and not the Continental opera tradition, though Purcell was
well aware of the latter. He contends that Elkanah Settle,
whom he accepts as the librettist, dictated the final musical
form and chauvinistically elected to strive for a native
English opera. Purcell than made "the aesthetic viewpoint of
the librettist his own," and provided widely varying music
adapted to the play's requirements.

T1413 Styan, J. L. *The Shakespeare Revolution: Criticism and
       Performance in the Twentieth Century.* Cambridge:
       Cambridge University Press, 1977. ix, 292 pp.
       Illustrated.

       Discusses the development of twentieth century
       explorations of Shakespeare, noting the increasing variety
       of interpretation in literary criticism and theatrical
       production. The chief argument is that since Shakespeare's
       plays are essentially non-illusory in nature, twentieth
       century production since Granville-Barker is closer to
       Shakespeare than was Victorian production (and criticism),
       which was misguided in its pictorial realism. Twentieth
       century directors are successful or not depending how well
       they understand "non-illusion." Styan finds the
       Granville-Barker and Brook productions of the play *A
       Midsummer Night's Dream* (1914 and 1970) more metaphorical
       and closer to Shakespeare than the Hall production of 1959
       and so praises Granville-Barker and Brook for giving
       twentieth century audiences insight into what Shakespeare
       had achieved. In his chapter on Victorian staging, he
       briefly samples stagings of *A Midsummer Night's Dream* from
       the Reynolds opera (1816) to the Tree production (1900).
       In Chapter Five, devoted to Granville-Barker's productions,
       he describes his *A Midsummer Night's Dream* and samples
       critical responses. There are chapters on Sir Barry Jackson
       and his modern dress experiments, on Tyrone Guthrie and
       the open stage, and on "non-illusion." Contains
       photographs of the dance of fairies in Kean's 1856 *A
       Midsummer Night's Dream* and of scenes from the Barker
       and Brook productions.

T1414 Teague, Francis. "Odessa Shakespeare Festival."
       Shakespeare Quarterly, 28 (1977), 226-28.

Coverage includes a generally favorable review, with descriptive detail, of a summer 1976 production of *A Midsummer Night's Dream* at the Odessa Globe Shakespeare Festival, directed by Charles D. McCally, with James Bottom as a fine Bottom. McCally conceived of the play as "Bottom's Dream," and placed his speech, "I have had a most rare vision," at the end of the play. Theseus and Hippolyta bathed in a bath in the center trap at the play's opening; this became a pool for the forest scenes. There is high praise for the quality of acting, for the reading of the verse, and for the director's use of the open thrust stage.

T1415   Troeber, Hans-Joachim. "Shakespeares 'Sommernachtstraum' auf der Bühne des 20. Jahrhunderts. Dargestellt an ausgewählten deutschen und englischen Inszenierungen" [Shakespeare's 'A Midsummer Night's Dream' on the Twentieth Century Stage. Illustrated by reference to German and English Productions]. Ph.D. dissertation, University of Trier, 1977. 275 pp. Illustrated.

Discusses in the first part the problems in the stage realization of the play in scenery, music, acting, and translation. A survey of German language productions from 1905 to 1976 shows Schlegel's translation to be the most popular. In the second part, he reconstructs ten important twentieth century productions, drawing on reviews, promptbooks, pictures, and interviews: Max Reinhardt (Berlin, 1905), Harley Granville-Barker (London, 1914), Reinhardt (Salzburg, 1927), Otto Falckenberg (München, 1940), Gustav Rudolf Sellner (Darmstadt, 1952), Karl Heinz Stroux (Düsseldorf, 1961), Peter Hall Stratford-upon-Avon, 1962), Leopold Lindtberg (Salzburg, 1966), Gustav Rudolf Sellner (Recklinghausen, 1972), and Peter Brook (Stratford-upon-Avon, 1970). He discusses the influence of Reinhardt upon English producers, and argues that Falckenberg "laid the foundations for de-romanticizing" the play by "stripping the stage of any superfluous scenery." Sellner, in collaboration with composer Carl Orff, created "a comedy of panic enchantment." The author sees Peter Brook as finally understanding Shakespeare's *A Midsummer Night's Dream* as "a celebration of the art of acting," saying that "body, gesture, mime, and language constituted a central unity," and that Brook aimed at social harmony by blending the three levels of court, fairies, and mechanicals.

T1416 Tynan, Kenneth. "Profiles: At Three Minutes Past Eight
You Must Dream." *New Yorker*, 53, 1 (1977), 45-75.

The British critic characterizes the acting of Ralph
Richardson, using examples from many of his roles among
which is Bottom, which he played under Harcourt Williams
at the Old Vic in 1931 and again at the Old Vic in 1938, in
the revival of the 1937 production directed by Tyrone
Guthrie.

T1417 Entry Deleted.

T1418 Williams, Gary Jay. "Madame Vestris' *A Midsummer
Night's Dream* and the Web of Victorian Tradition."
Theatre Survey, 18, 2 (November 1977), 1-22.

Reconstructs in detail, using promptbooks, reviews, and
other sources, the 1840 Covent Garden production of
actress-manager Elizabeth Vestris. In it, the full text of
the play was used in the theatre for the first time since
before the Restoration; James Robinson Planché was Vestris'
editor. It was embellished with fourteen songs, most of
which Vestris--as *Oberon*--sang. Her staging, in which she
has the collaboration of Planché, set many precedents for
the play's life on the Victorian stage in scenery, costuming,
music, and casting (*Oberon* was played by a woman
thereafter well into the twentieth century). The particular
indebtedness of Charles Kean's better known production of
1856 is shown, and there are also comparisons with other
major nineteenth productions, including comparative figures
for the textual cuttings in these productions. There are
four illustrations, showing Vestris' *Oberon* and three scenes
from Kean's production. (See also items T1312, T1418,
T1451 and T1354.)

T1418a Blackstone, Mary Anna. "The Eighth Fairy: Stage Music
and *A Midsummer Night's Dream* to 1800." Ph.D.
dissertation, University of New Brunswick. *DAI*, 39
(1978), 1188A-89A.

Study of the use of music in the original play and in
adaptations of the play to 1800, including Purcell's opera;
the short comic operas by Leveridge and Lampe; the three
versions at Garrick's Drury Lane--*The Fairies*, *Midsummer*

Night's Dream, and *A Fairy Tale;* and other more distant relatives, such as *The Fairy Prince.* The dissertation evaluates the works under consideration both musically and dramatically and shows music designed first as subordinate to dramatic structure and then becoming dominant in opera and spectacular production.

T1419   Booth, Stephen. "Shakespeare in the San Francisco Bay Area." *Shakespeare Quarterly,* 29 (1978), 267-78.

Review coverage of thirteen Shakespearean productions includes an unfavorable assessment of the *A Midsummer Night's Dream* production of the touring Oxford and Cambridge Shakespeare Company, Ltd. ("cheap in its conception and ineptly executed," a "rip-off" on both names), and a generally favorable assessment of a performance of the play by school children directed by Paul Barnes at the Lincoln Summer Theatre in Stockton, California, June 1977. The Oxford/Cambridge production was marked by "smug mindlessness, unctuous sleasiness, and counterfeit sophistication," while the performance of the children provided four lovers who could be funny and touching, a stunningly confident Puck, and well-spoken poetry. (See also item T1434.) A listing of the principals in the cast and on the production staff is included.

T1420   Cutts, John P. "A Shakespearean Tribute to Ben Jonson in Garrick's Operatic Version of *A Midsummer Night's Dream.*" *Comparative Drama,* 12 (1978), 233-48.

Identifies the sources of the lyrics used in each of the twenty-eight songs in the operatic version of *A Midsummer Night's Dream* that Garrick produced at Drury Lane Theatre in 1755, called *The Fairies,* with music by J. C. Smith. Notably, the author shows that Garrick employed an air from Ben Jonson's masque, *Oberon, The Faery Prince,* although Jonson's name does not occur in the list of authors given on the title page of the original edition. The article includes the musical setting of Jonson's lyrics by Ferrabosco. The author also notes that there are no lyrics in *The Fairies* taken from Dryden, though his name is in the list of authors.

T1421   David, Richard. *Shakespeare in the Theatre*. Cambridge:
        Cambridge University Press, 1978. xv, 263 pp.

        In part an expansion of the author's annual critical
        essays on Shakespeare in the British theatre for
        Shakespeare Survey, the book includes detailed discussions
        of the Royal Shakespeare Company's productions from 1971
        to 1976. There is a brief introduction on the theatrical
        values in Shakespeare and on production trends in general,
        especially the matter of the contemporary practice of
        classical plays being "translated" for modern audiences. The
        author may be described as disinclined to admire those
        productions heavily informed with contemporary meanings.
        The essays, which are marked by careful attention to
        performance values and are especially detailed on line
        readings, include references throughout to the productions
        of *A Midsummer Night's Dream* by Harley Granville-Barker,
        Peter Hall, and Peter Brook.

T1422   Gates, Joanne E. [Review.] *Educational Theatre Journal*,
        30 (1978), 559-60.

        Unfavorable review of a Smith College Theatre
        Department production of *A Midsummer Night's Dream* in
        1978, directed by Kenny McBain, guest director, which
        borrowed much, but not well, from the Peter Brook
        production of 1970. That this tame and flawed copy pleased
        audiences with its "moment to moment gimmickry," puzzles
        the reviewer who draws comparisons between the
        productions.

T1423   Habicht, Werner. "Shakespeare in West Germany."
        Shakespeare Quarterly, 29 (1978), 296-99.

        Review coverage includes a brief mention of Wilfried
        Minks's "emphatically disharmonious" production of *A
        Midsummer Night's Dream* in Frankfort in 1977.

T1424   Hapgood, Robert. "Shakespeare in New York and
        Boston." *Shakespeare Quarterly*, 29 (1978), 230-31.

        Coverage includes a brief characterization of the "over
        animated and under-felt" production of *A Midsummer Night's
        Dream* in the 1976-1977 season by the young Boston

Shakespeare Company (production credits and partial cast provided), whose work the author finds as yet undistinctive though generally deserving some attention.

T1425   Jackson, Berners A. W. "The Shakespeare Festival: Stratford, Ontario, 1953-1977." *Shakespeare Quarterly,* 29 (1978), 164-91.

Brief history of the development of the festival, with characterizations of the administrations of different periods, of the stage directors, and of the facilities. With photographs of the theatre and of major figures.

T1425a   Jackson, Russell. "Shakespeare in Liverpool: Edward Saker's Revivals, 1876-81." *Theatre Notebook,* 32 (1978), 100-109.

Reviews Saker's career in which he earned acclaim for several sumptuous Shakespearean revivals in the tradition of Charles Kean and Saker's friend, Charles Calvert. Among them was his 1880 *A Midsummer Night's Dream,* seen in Liverpool and in London, at Sadler's Well Theatre. The production is characterized as to Saker's text, the scenery in general, and the performances of some of the principals.

T1426   Littlefield, Tom. "Second Company Lives up to a Great Script." *Kite* (Schenectady, New York), 19 July 1978, pp. 9-10.

Review of a production of *A Midsummer Night's Dream* at Union College by the Williamstown Second Company. Not seen.

T1427   _____. "The World's the Stage for Shakespeare: New Lenox Group Plays *A Midsummer Night's Dream* on the Hills and Woods." *Kite* (Schenectady, New York), 19 August 1978, pp. 8-9, 12.

Review of a production by Shakespeare and Company which opened 21 July 1978. Not seen.

T1428   Marowitz, Charles. "A Royal Season for the Royal
        Shakespeare." New York Times, 19 March 1978, section
        D, pp. 5, 38.

        Survey of the Royal Shakespeare Company's 1977-1978
        season, including characterizing comments on the production
        of A Midsummer Night's Dream directed by John Barton.
        (See item T1411.)

T1428a McClellan, Kenneth. Whatever Happened to Shakespeare?
        New York: Barnes and Noble, 1978. 230 pp.

        Surveys the sins of directors and actors against
        Shakespeare, from the Commonwealth to the 1970s. McClellan
        argues for textual purity and "straight" representations,
        saying that audiences should not encounter masterpieces for
        the first time in a mangled form and that interpretative
        selection "must be confined to what can reasonably be
        deduced from the text." In regard to A Midsummer Night's
        Dream in particular, he forgives the fugitive companies of
        the Commonwealth their drolls. Purcell's music fortunately
        can be separated from the adaptation of The Fairy Queen.
        There is a brief review of its production from Garrick's The
        Fairies (1755) through Tree's 1900 production, most of
        which versions are disapproved of. Among the twentieth
        century productions dealt with very briefly are those of
        Granville-Barker (1914), Harcourt Williams (1929), the Max
        Reinhardt film (1935), Tyrone Guthrie (1937-38), Nevill
        Coghill (1945), Peter Hall (1959) and Peter Brook (1970).
        He dismisses most of these as impertinences. He was
        distressed by the lovers in Hall's production, whom he
        describes as "modern hippy teenagers" with no manners.
        Coming to Brook's RSC production of 1970 he writes: "1970
        was possibly the worst year the Bard has ever suffered in
        his native town" and his assessment is: "Ability to perform
        tricks [on ropes and trapezes] took precedence over ability
        to act or speak verse."

T1429   Mendelssohn-Bartholdy, Felix. A Midsummer Night's
        Dream: Incidental Music, opus 21 and opus 61. Bernard
        Haitink conducting the Concertgebouw Orchestra of
        Amsterdam. Philips Festivo 6570021. 1978 reissue of the
        1965 recording.

T1430   _____. *A Midsummer Night's Dream: Incidental
         Music*, opus 21 and opus 61. Eugene Ormandy conducting
         the Philadelphia Orchestra. One 33 1/3 phonodisc,
         stereo. RCA Red Seal (A) RL1208A. *circa* 1978.

T1431   Planché, James Robinson. *The Recollections and
         Reflections of J. R. Planché: A Professional
         Autobiography.* London: Tinsley Brothers, 1872; rev.
         ed., London: Solow, Marston, and Company, Ltd., 1901;
         reprint, New York: De Capo Press, 1978. xxiii, 464 pp.
         Illustrated.

         The noted costume historian and author of the libretto of
         Oberon and many fairy plays was the supervisor of
         costumes for Elizabeth Vestris during her management of
         Covent Garden when she revived *A Midsummer Night's
         Dream* in 1840. He recalls his association with Vestris and
         his staging of the last fairy scene of *A Midsummer Night's
         Dream*, which was highly praised by critics. (See also items
         T1350, T1354, T1418, and T1451.)

T1432   Roberts, Jeanne Addison. "Shakespeare in Washington,
         D. C." *Shakespeare Quarterly*, 29 (1978), 234-38.

         Review coverage includes a generally positive assessment
         of the Folger Theatre Group's 1977 production of *A
         Midsummer Night's Dream*, directed by Harold Scott. There
         was "youthful humor and earthiness" and some Peter Brook
         influence in the doubling of roles (Theseus/Oberon,
         Hippolyta/Titania, and Philostrate/Puck) and in the kinetic,
         physical nature of the staging. "Unquestionably the levels
         were flattened out; but it was a very funny play . . . ."
         Helena was so tall and Hermia so short that they were face
         to face only when Helena dropped to her knees. Demetrius
         was played by a black actor, which offered "a solution to
         the perennial problem of the indistinguishable male lovers
         and one that added an allowable edge to Demetrius's
         castigation of Hermia as "thou Ethiope." A modern note was
         struck in "the female solidarity" throughout the production.
         The fairies were not ethereal, and the mechanicals usurped
         the focus; Terry Hinz's Bottom and David Cromwell's Peter
         Quince are praised.

T1433   Rowell, George. *Queen Victoria Goes to the Theatre*.
        London: Paul Elek, 1978. 144 pp. Illustrated.

        Draws upon the Queen's diaries at Windsor Castle for
        her criticism of various Shakespearean productions including
        her astute responses to the production of *A Midsummer
        Night's Dream* of Elizabeth Vestris at Covent Garden in the
        1840-1841 season and the production of Charles Kean at the
        Princess's Theatre in the 1856-1857 season.

T1434   Ryan, Thomas. [Review.] *Educational Theatre Journal*, 30
        (March 1978), 112.

        Review of *A Midsummer Night's Dream* presented by the
        Oxford and Cambridge Shakespeare Company, on tour in
        the U.S., at the University of California at Santa Barbara,
        in October, 1977. The author found that the production,
        directed by Peter Farago, reduced the play "to triviality
        and dullness," and says the directorial intent seems to have
        been "the projection of a violent and sadistic nightmare, to
        which was added a touch of punk-rock, a pinch of
        fashionable perversity, and a passing glance at the text."
        (See also item T1419.)

T1435   Treglown, Jeremy. "*A Midsummer Night's Dream*, Open
        Air Theatre." *The Times*, 6 June 1978, p. 13.

        Reviews the New Shakespeare Company's production of
        the play at the Open Air Theatre, Regent's Park, London,
        directed by David Conville. It employed traditional Greek
        costumes, music, and dances, and was set around the time
        of George Byron. There were writhing, hissing fairies, and
        the robust lovers had "a kind of groping sexuality directed
        at, though rather remote from the eroticism noted in the
        play by Jan Kott, who is quoted in the program." But
        otherwise this was a traditional and traditionally enjoyable
        production." The fairies' costumes and the mechanicals'
        business "could have come from any one of a dozen '50s
        production." The metaphors of the play survived the literal
        natural surroundings, the unpredictable rain, and the jet
        planes overhead.

T1436   Trewin, John Courtenay. *Going to Shakespeare*. London:
        George Allen and Unwin, 1978; reissued 1979. 288 pp.

This collection of essays on each of Shakespeare's plays in performance includes one on *A Midsummer Night's Dream* (pp. 98-106). There are comments in appreciation of the play together with notes on selected pieces of stage business and selected line readings from productions on the late Victorian stage to the RSC production directed by Peter Brook in 1970. These details are from the author's own recollections from the late 1920s onward and he makes some observations on staging trends in his lifetime. For example, he remembers the quartet of young lovers being played as straight romantics as late as the 1920s, when Edith Evans in 1924 became one of the first of a new order of comic Helenas. He comments on the change in Bottom's ass's head from a large, full head piece to a skeletal construction. He touches briefly on the productions of Charles Kean (1856), Frank Benson (1890s), Augustin Daly (1888), Herbert Beerbohm Tree (1900), Harley Granville-Barker (1914), Basil Dean (1924), Harcourt Williams (1929), W. Bridges-Adams (1920s), Nevill Coghill (1945), Michael Benthall (1954) and Peter Hall (1959).

T1437   Ventimiglia, Peter. "The William Winter Correspondence and the Augustin Daly Shakespearean Productions of 1885-1898." *Educational Theatre Journal* , 30 (1978), 220-28.

New York *Tribune* theatre critic William Winter played a major role in editing and cutting the texts of most of the ten Shakespearean plays Daly produced. Using correspondence between the two, the author makes clear that in the case of Daly's lavishly staged *A Midsummer Night's Dream* of 1888, Daly himself did the cutting. Among other things, the cuts accommodated a fourth act panorama for a boat trip by Theseus, the Argonaut, back to Athens with the young Lovers. Daly sent his cutting to Winter, who made emendations and gave approval.

T1438   Warren, Roger. "Comedies and Histories at Two Stratfords, 1977." *Shakespeare Survey*, 31 (1978), 141-53.

Provides detailed characterizations of both the Royal Shakespeare Company production of *A Midsummer Night's Dream* of 1977, directed by John Barton, and the Stratford, Ontario, version of 1976-1977, directed by Robin Phillips.

The author finds much to admire in both, though more to
disapprove of in the Ontario production. "The achievement
of both . . . was to leave you marvelling at the sheer
richness of the play itself . . . ." (See items T1396 and
T1411.) In the Barton production, there was a clear
contrast, but a balanced one, between the court and forest
worlds. There was a mixture of wood sprites and pagan
deities such as David Young has described in *Something of
Great Constancy* (item 303, which the RSC program cited).
The Oberon of Patrick Stewart and the Bottom of Richard
Griffiths are praised as the chief strengths of the cast. In
the Ontario production the play was seen as a dream of
Elizabeth I. This entailed making Hippolyta Elizabeth's
look-alike. Theseus' speech on imagination went to her,
which puzzles Warren. There were many cross-references in
the stage business between the dream world and the real
world. The mechanicals lacked spontaneity but the lovers
were wholly funny. Martha Henry's Helena symbolized the
production, though. While it was an elaborate tour de
force, it lacked the simpler humanity of the RSC Helena,
who was obviously inexperienced.

T1439   Bablet, Marie-Louise, and Denis Bablet. *Le Théâtre du
         Soleil ou la Quête du Boneur*. Paris: SERDDAV/Centre
         National de la Recherche Scientifique, 1979. Text, 99
         pp., plus a guide to the 84 accompanying slides and disc
         recording.

         Describes (in French) the origins and the productions of
the internationally well known French experimental theatre
group headed by Ariane Mnouchkine. The documentation of
the group's history from 1964 to 1975 includes seventy-five
color slides and a disc recording. There is a chapter
describing the successful 1968 production of *Le songe d'une
nuit d'été* (pp. 26-30), staged by Mnouchkine. The stage
floor was covered with fur pelts and the intent was to
suggest a forest of unconscious desires, to emphasize the
erotic and the diabolic. The play, said Mnouchkine in an
interview quoted here, is "la pièce la plus sauvage, la plus
violente dont on puisse rêver. Un fabuleux bestiaire des
profondeurs dont le sujet n'est rien moins que ce 'Dieu
furieux' qui sommeille dans le coeur des hommes." [The
play is more savage, more violent than one could fantasize.
A fabulous bestiary of profundities, the subject of which is
nothing less than the furious God that sleeps in the heart
of man.] There are two slides of the production included.

Characteristically, the emphasis was more upon theatrical imagery than upon the written word.

T1440   Barlow, Graham, and Priscilla Seltzer. "Shakespeare in Scotland." *Shakespeare Quarterly*, 30 (1979), 160-63.

Includes a brief, unfavorable review of a production of *A Midsummer Night's Dream* by Edinburgh Festival Productions at that city's international festival in the summer of 1978: "a heavy-footed production" that "suffered in general from clichéd Shakespearean acting and false vocal affectations." Production credits, a partial cast list, and a photograph are included.

T1441   Beechey, Gwilym. "Shakespeare and Music: A Bibliographical Guide." *Musical Opinion*, 102 (1979), 207-208.

An annotated list of studies in English of music in Shakespearean plays, studies done in about the last fifty years. Not seen. (See items T1230, T1230 and T1324.)

T1442   Berkowitz, Gerald M. "The Shakespearean Fringe: London and Edinburgh." *Shakespeare Quarterly*, 30 (1979), 163-67.

Includes a mention of the Edinburgh Festival production of *A Midsummer Night's Dream* in 1978 (competently done but without excitement or spirit) and a favorable review of the 1978 production of the play by the Company Worktheatre in Edinburgh, which was less polished and professional but far more charming and spirited. It had a female Puck, with some sexual tension between her and Oberon; a Mistress Flute, who was a concession to limited resources; and convincing young lovers. Cast principals and production personnel are listed.

T1442a   Bingham, Madeleine. *The Great Lover: The Life and Art of Herbert Beerbohm Tree.* New York: Atheneum, 1979. 293 pp. Illustrated.

Included in this undocumented biography is a short anecdotal description of the rehearsals of Tree's production

of *A Midsummer Night's Dream* (1900) and a characterization
of his portrayal of Bottom: "He portrayed the weaver with a
blank wall of vanity that was impassable" (p. 108).

T1443   Booth, Stephen. "Speculations on Doubling in
         Shakespeare's Plays," in *Shakespeare: The Theatrical
         Dimension*. Ed. Philip C. McGuire and David A.
         Samuelson. New York: AMS Press Incorporated, 1979,
         pp. 103-31.

         Argues for the doubling of the roles of Theseus/Oberon
         and Hippolyta/Titania in *A Midsummer Night's Dream*, citing
         the Royal Shakespeare Company production of 1970,
         directed by Peter Brook, as an example of its success.

T1444   *The Boydell Shakespeare Prints*. With an Introduction by
         A. E. Santaniello. New York: Benjamin Blom, 1968;
         reprint, New York: Arno Press, 1979. 9, 120
         unnumbered pages of plates. Illustrated.

         Reproduces two large engravings after paintings by H.
         Fuseli of Oberon and Titania and of Titania and Bottom,
         taken from the Boydell Gallery engravings (Volume I, plates
         20 and 21), originally published by John and Josiah Boydell
         in 1803. Also reproduced here are two small engravings
         depicting scenes from *A Midsummer Night's Dream*, after
         Fuseli and Joshua Reynolds, done for George Steevens's
         "National" edition of Shakespeare's plays, published in nine
         volumes by the Boydells in 1802.

T1445   Brissenden, Alan. "Shakespeare in Adelaide."
         Shakespeare Quarterly, 30 (1979), 267-70.

         Review coverage includes a brief description of the
         production of *A Midsummer Night's Dream* by the Adelaide
         University Theatre Guild in July of 1978. Seeking a modern
         counterpart to the patriarchal society of Act I, director Jim
         Vilé set the play among the oilwell dominions of modern
         Arabia. Theseus was an oil mogul in sun glasses, and
         Hippolyta was his camera-toting American wife. The fairies
         were derelicts among the derricks. "The text managed to
         survive through the assurance of the direction," says the
         author.

T1445a   Cotes, Alison. [Review.] *National Times* (Brisbane),
         Weekend of 29 September 1979, p. 58.

   Reviews a production of *A Midsummer Night's Dream* by
   the Queensland Theatre Company in the open air in Albert
   Park, Brisbane, Queensland, Australia, in September, 1979.
   It was directed by Alan Edwards and the Queensland
   Theatre orchestra was conducted by Brian Stacey; some of
   the fairies were played by members of the Queensland
   Opera Company, the Queensland Ballet Company, and the
   Australian Youth Ballet. Not seen.

T1446   Cutts, John P. "Garrick's Use of Milton in His Versions
        of *A Midsummer Night's Dream.*" *Neuphilologische
        Mitteilungen*, 80 (1979), 78-80.

   Discusses the use of lines from Milton's "L'Allegro," set
   to music by J. C. Smith, in the operatic adaptation of *A
   Midsummer Night's Dream* called *The Fairies* at Garrick's
   Drury Lane in 1755. They also were in the fuller version of
   the play, with a derivative but expanded score, done there
   in 1763.

T1447   Evans, Peter Angus. *The Music of Benjamin Britten.*
        London: Dent; Minneapolis: University of Minnesota
        Press, 1979. 564 pp. Illustrated.

   Analyzes Britten's work musicologically and dramatically.
   Chapter Twelve is devoted to his opera *A Midsummer
   Night's Dream* (1960). Britten's *Dream* is not Shakespeare's.
   Where Shakespeare sets up contrasts between the levels of
   characters, "with no unifying cosmography," Britten "has
   chosen to employ means of intra-musical unity that
   inevitably have the effect of subsuming the specific
   incidents, as though offering a view that embraces all."
   Evans characterizes it as a chamber opera on every count,
   except the economic one. The original Aldeburgh production
   used a small string group along with the rest of the
   delicate, exotic instrumentation (celeste, two harps,
   harpsichord, oboe, piccolos, and bassoon among others) and
   subsequent productions in large opera houses, such as
   Covent Garden, have used a large complement of strings "to
   the detriment of the work's characteristically fragile but
   very bright timbres." The countertenor role (Oberon) is
   impossibly demanding in a large house. (See item T1188.)

T1448   Fielding, Eric. "The Prague Quadrennial, '79: Theatre
         Architecture and Design on Display." *Theatre Crafts*,
         13, 3 (1979), 24-25.

         Discusses exhibits by various nations and these included
         designs of various artists for Shakespearean productions.
         Awarded the Grand Prix was Great Britain's display of
         designs of current shows, which included the John Napier
         design for the RSC's *A Midsummer Night's Dream*. (See
         T1411.) The current British designs are said to be
         characterized by clarity of vision, creative economy, and a
         cutting back to necessities.

T1448a   Gammond, Peter. *The Illustrated Encyclopedia of
         Recorded Opera.* London: Salamander Books; New York:
         Harmony Books (Crown, Inc.), 1979. 256 pp.

         Provides synopses of major operas, including Purcell's
         The Fairy Queen and Benjamin Britten's *A Midsummer
         Night's Dream*, and information on recordings of them,
         including company album numbers and casts.

T1449   Goodfellow, William S. "Utah Shakespearean Festival."
         Shakespeare Quarterly, 30 (1979), 229-31.

         Included in the coverage of three of the festival's
         productions in the summer of 1978 is a favorable assessment
         of the staging of *A Midsummer Night's Dream* by Brian
         Hansen, which pleased audiences as much as any. Hansen
         emphasized "the orderly philosophical universe of the
         playwright's day" by presenting "a world of tiers," in
         which each sphere influenced that immediately below it.
         Hansen employed a multi-leveled Elizabethan stage to
         advantage and was imaginative in stage business. Hippolyta
         was an angry, captive bride, Egeus kept forgetting his
         prospective son-in-law's name, and Puck dragged the
         unknowing lovers on stage using an invisible rope.
         "Pyramus and Thisbe" may have been over-burlesqued, but
         it pleased audiences. Partial lists of the cast and production
         staff are included.

T1450   Gow, Gordon. "A Feeling in the Throat: John Hancock in
         an Interview with Gordon Gow." *Films and Filming*, 25, 1
         (1979), 12-15.

In this interview on the occasion of Hancock's film, *California Dreaming*, Hancock briefly touches on some of the ideas behind his off-Broadway production of *A Midsummer Night's Dream* in 1966-67 (see T1269). "My fairies were puppets, and great hairy bats, dolls with wings, worked by zombies. We used a lot of ultra-violet light." Hancock says he sought to follow Shakespeare's play and "so long as it is stuck in fairyland, in tutus and gauze, I felt it wasn't what Shakespeare wanted."

T1451   Griffiths, Trevor. "A Neglected Pioneer Production: Madame Vestris' *A Midsummer Night's Dream* at Covent Garden, 1840." *Shakespeare Quarterly*, 30 (1979), 386-96.

Seeks better recognition of Elizabeth Vestris' production of the play that restored the text to the stage after nearly two centuries of operatic adaptations of it in the theatre. Griffiths provides explanations for the cuts she made and praises the production for its comparative textual fidelity. The loss of four hundred lines is regrettable, but we should regard the production primarily for its reclamation of seventeen hundred lines. Vestris' use of music was sparing relative to previous operatic adaptations, and the score she used was thematically unified.

T1452   Habicht, Werner. "Shakespeare in West Germany." *Shakespeare Quarterly*, 30 (1979), 295-300.

Describes and compares two 1978 productions of *A Midsummer Night's Dream*. Both broke from the Peter Brook model without denying indebtedness to it. The Hamburg Schauspielhaus version, directed by Franz Marijnen, using Schlegel's translation, featured a clinically cold court setting for Theseus' court, whose white tiles suggested a head, and an Athenian wood that was a labyrinth of blue balloons and subdued light, which suggested a landscape of the soul. There seemed to be two kinds of oppressiveness--that of the conventional world and that of nightmarish affliction. There were specter-like fairies, touches of homosexuality in Oberon, an ugly ass's head that made Titania's infatuation seem horrible, and a maliciously writhing Puck. The Munich Kammerspiele production, directed by Dieter Dorn, used a new translation by Michael Wachsmann and Dorn. The production "firmly and

successfully established Dorn as a new name among
Shakespearean directors." It combined ritual and
psychology. Hippolyta/Titania was unbandaged like a
monumental mummy at the opening of the play, revealing a
fantastically tattooed naked body--"mythical raw material for
both the Queen of Amazons and the Queen of Fairies." Love
and hatred were shown as coexisting in all the main
characters, with an emphasis upon plausible psychological
foundations. A simple, open stage was used, with simple
devices such as a network of strings for Titania's bower.
The fairies were wizened dwarfs and muscular wrestlers as
well as attractive girls; the Puck was bulky and
complacent. Included are lists of principals and production
staffs of both productions and a photo of a scene from
each.

T1453   Jacobs, Laurence H. "Shakespeare in the San Francisco
        Bay Area." *Shakespeare Quarterly*, 30 (1979), 246-53.

        Coverage of thirteen productions includes a brief,
        unfavorable assessment of the 1978 production of *A
        Midsummer Night's Dream* by the Diablo Valley College
        Department of Performing Arts. Director Raymon Stansbury

T1453a Manvell, Roger. *Theater and Film. A Comparative Study
        of the Two Forms of Dramatic Art, and of the Problems
        of Adaptations of Stage Plays into Films*. Rutherford,
        New Jersey: Fairleigh Dickinson University Press;
        London: Associated University Presses [1979]. 303 pp.
        Illustrated.

        Discusses, in the first of two chapters on Shakespeare
        in film (pp. 164-71), the Peter Hall film of *A Midsummer
        Night's Dream* released in 1969 (see item T1301). Hall
        wanted to take advantage of the medium to prove that
        Shakespeare's speeches are "antirhetorical" and meant to be
        spoken "very tight to his audience." Hall wanted to rid
        himself of the traditional romantic concept of the play and
        saw it as "a Halloween entertainment" (Puck as a
        mischievous goblin), as erotic (Titania and the fairies were
        almost nude), and he stressed the disharmony among the
        lovers. Manvell assesses the film as "among the freshest,
        simplest, and most contemporary of film productions based
        on Shakespeare," with a strong cast. There are four
        photographs from the film.

did not trust the play. The mechanicals' play was overlaid
with unnecessary and distracting business and was not
funny. Kenneth Hein's set was versatile and evocative--a
two-leveled scaffold structure of unfinished wood and slat
walkways. A partial listing of the cast and production staff
is included.

T1454   Oz, Avraham. "Shakespeare in Israel." *Shakespeare
         Quarterly*, 30 (1979), 279-81.

Included in the coverage is a generally unfavorable
review of a production of *A Midsummer Night's Dream* by
the Habimah Company at the Habimah National Theatre in
1978, directed by Omri Nitzan. There were some seeds of
Peter Brook's staging and Jan Kott's erotic interpretation of
the play. Oberon and Titania were "the black id versions of
Theseus and Hippolyta." Their quarrel animated an
otherwise silent, spooky world of the fairies "with passion,
youth and sexuality." Ezra Dagan's "impish, masterly Puck"
is said to be the best ever seen on the Israeli stage: "he
hovered about the scene like some elemental power, a
fleeting spirit, scarcely touching the ground." Stress upon
the pathos of the young lovers "inadvertently turned I.i
into a mock-melodrama . . . ." The court was all in white
velvet in a white tent; the tent fell away to reveal a black
velvet wood.

T1455   Parker, Barry M. *The Folger Shakespeare Filmography*.
         Washington, D. C.: Folger Books, 1979. 64 pp.

Provides a directory of 1) feature-length films (with
sound) of the plays; 2) film adaptations or derivations; 3)
musical, operatic, or dance versions of the plays on film;
and 4) some educational and/or abridged versions of the
plays on film. There are also appendices listing
miscellaneous Shakespeare-related films. The entries for the
feature-length films provide cast lists, studio and
production staff credits, release dates, timings and some
comments. For the instructional films, distributors'
addresses are provided. (Video tapes are not included.)
Among the listed films of *A Midsummer Night's Dream* (or
derived from it) are The Max Reinhardt-William Dieterle film
of 1935, the Czech puppet Film by Jiri Trnka of 1959 (see
T1183a), the Peter Hall film of 1969 (see T1301), and the
film of the Balanchine ballet by Columbia Pictures, 1967

(see T1276a). There is a photograph of James Cagney as Bottom from the 1935 Reinhardt film. (See a review of this filmography in *Shakespeare Quarterly*, 31 [1980], 296-99.)

T1456   Reinhardt, Gottfried. *The Genius, A Memoir of Max Reinhardt By His Son.* New York: Alfred A. Knopf, 1979. 420 pp. Illustrated.

Includes impressionistic accounts of Reinhardt's 1905 production of *A Midsummer Night's Dream* at the Neues Theatre in Berlin (pp. 279-81), of the 1927 production of the play in New York with his German company, of the staging of the play in the Hollywood Bowl in 1934, and of the making of the 1935 Warner Brothers film of the play. There are two photos of his version of the play done in 1905, a photograph of pages from one of his *A Midsummer Night's Dream* promptbooks, and two photos of scenes from the 1935 film.

T1457   Riehle, Wolfgang. "Shakespeare in Austria." *Shakespeare Quarterly*, 30 (1979), 304-306.

Describes the 1978 production of *A Midsummer Night's Dream* in Graz and the 1978 productions of *A Midsummer Night's Dream* and *The Fairy Queen* at the festival in Helbrunn in 1978. The deromanticizing version at the Graz Schauspielhaus, directed by Kurt Joseph Schildkneckt, was influenced by Jan Kott's criticism, Freud, and Peter Brook's RSC staging. The stress was on the sexual instincts. Puck and Titania were seen as materializations of the sexual drive. There were "pop-star fairies who acted as if they were part of a variety show." Hippolyta looked like Elizabeth I from the waist up, but her farthingale frame was without material covering. In the forest setting, tree trunks supported a large circular trampoline that was encompassed in part by an esplanade. The festival at Helbrunn, a complementary event to the Salzburg Festival, featured a seven-and-a-half hour "collage" of scenes from *A Midsummer Night's Dream*, from Andreas Gryphius' *Absurda Comica oder Herr Peter Squentz*, and from Henry Purcell's *The Fairy Queen*. These were performed in various open-air settings, the audience moving from one site to another, goaded on by green-leaved elves and fairies. A partial list of the cast and production staff is included.

T1458   Salisbury, Judy. "Shakespeare at 'The Mount.'"
        Shakespeare Quarterly, 30 (1979), 177-78.

Gives high praise to the 1978 production of *A Midsummer
Night's Dream* by Shakespeare & Company, directed by Tina
Packer, outdoors on the grounds of Edith Wharton's summer
home, "The Mount," in Lenox, Massachusetts. The terrace
became the palace; wood scenes were played in pine woods
below the audience in a natural amphitheatre; fairies lit
candles in each window of the house at the end. There is
praise for fidelity to the text, for clarity of delivery
(under Kristin Linklater's coaching), for lovers who were
lusty and youthful, fairies who were spritely but healthy,
mechanicals who were "endearing stumblebums," and an
ensemble performance in general. "Packer directed her
company to present Shakespeare classically, for the people,
. . . with emphasis on the word."

T1459   Schoenbaum, Samuel. *Shakespeare, the Globe and the
        World.* New York, Oxford: Published by Oxford
        University Press in association with the Folger
        Shakespeare Library, 1979. 208 pp. Illustrated.

Published to accompany the touring exhibition of the
same title, this lavishly illustrated book, which draws upon
the Folger archives, includes a twenty-four page section on
the plays in performance, featuring playbills, programs,
photographs, prints, paintings and posters, many in color.
Here and in the epilogue section will be found many
reproductions relevant to *A Midsummer Night's Dream* in the
theatre, including sketches from Charles Kean's scrapbooks,
Henry Fuseli's paintings, Kean's playbill, a photograph from
the Max Reinhardt film, and a photograph of a scene from
the Peter Brook production of 1970.

T1459a Stodder, Joseph H., and Lillian Wilds. "Shakespeare in
        Southern California." *Shakespeare Quarterly*, 30 (1979),
        232-45.

Included in the review coverage of twenty-two
productions is a favorable account of a musical adaptation of
A Midsummer Night's Dream at the Los Angeles Shakespeare
Festival in 1978, and a favorable assessment of the
production of the play at the San Diego National
Shakespeare Festival in 1978. Kim Friedman directed the

musical version, "a dazzler," with "first rate" music by
Charles Fox and lyrics by Norman Gimbel. It was set in a
seaside hotel in turn-of-the-century Britain and featured a
much rewritten text, with the emphasis upon farce: the
lovers quarreling on the beach, the mechanicals as hotel
employees trying to make a movie, and Bottom as a bellboy.
The reviewers question Friedman's apparent assumption that
Shakespeare's play is inaccessible and boring. The San
Diego festival production was staged by Jack O'Brien on the
new outdoor stage, the previous Old Globe having been
recently destroyed by fire. Robert Morgan's setting and
costumes are described in detail; the setting consisted of a
bare stage with two tall posts up center right and left,
with winding iron staircases around them, which only the
fairies moved on. The Athenians were in eighteenth century
costumes, and the fairies' costumes were skewed,
cobwebbed mirror images of them. A partial listing of the
casts and production staffs of both productions are
included, and there is a photo of the Globe production.

T1460   Stříbrný, Zdeněk. "Shakespeare in Czechoslovakia."
         Shakespeare Quarterly, 30 (1979), 285-89.

     Survey of productions includes reviews of two
anti-romantic, aggressively modern versions of *A Midsummer
Night's Dream* (two of six productions of the play in
Czechoslovakia in 1977-1978). Jan Kačer directed the
production at the Ostrava State Theatre (opening in
December 1976), the most important of these productions
(translation by Alois Bejblík). It emphasized the
dream-like--and modern--juxtaposition of the comic and
serious, passion and pain, chance and abrupt change, and
featured an aging, over-burdened Puck, modern lovers,
some Fellini-like flashes of decadence, and the presence of
a changeling boy. Kačer "does not force Shakespeare to
turn into our contemporary at all costs," however, says the
reviewer. He "endeavors to give Shakespeare's astounding
universality and complexity full voice, creating an
invigorating tension between our modern sensibility and the
mighty Renaissance upsurge of thought and imagination."
Jiří Fréhar directed a production at the E. F. Burian
Theatre in Prague (opening in May 1977) which was
"vehemently anti-romantic" and which was reportedly more
dazzling than thought-provoking (photo). Partial cast lists
and production credits for both productions are included.

T1461 "Summer Shakespeare Festivals--1979." *The Shakespeare Newsletter*, 29 (1979), 1.

Lists forthcoming summer seasons at twelve Shakespearean festival theatres. *A Midsummer Night's Dream* was being produced by five of them in Colorado, Texas, North Carolina, Oregon, and Virginia.

T1462 Thaiss, Christopher J. "Summer Shakespeare in Philadelphia." *Shakespeare Quarterly*, 30 (1979), 191-92.

Reviews favorable a production of *A Midsummer Night's Dream* by the Philadelphia Company, directed by Robert Hedley, in the City Hall courtyard in the spring and summer of 1978. The emphasis was on sensuality over dreamy illusion, and there were generous amounts of exuberant "running, colliding, hugging, and falling," but the business was well timed and fitted to the lines. The mechanicals were the dominant element of the company. "The puns, the knockabout, and the bright spirits sent the [mixed] audience home happy." The poetry was lost in the poor acoustics of the square, open to Saturday night strollers, but the reviewer recommends the "innyard" atmosphere.

T1463 Trewin, J. C. "Shakespeare in Britain." *Shakespeare Quarterly*, 30 (1979), 151-58.

Surveys sixteen current productions and includes a brief, favorable mention of the "straight" production of *A Midsummer Night's Dream* by the New Shakespeare Company at the Open Air Theatre, Regent's Park, London, in repertory from 29 May through August, 1978, directed by David Conville. A partial list of the cast and production staff is included. (See also T1435.)

T1464 Entry Deleted.

T1465 Zarkin, Robert. "*A Midsummer Night's Dream*." *Plays and Players*, 26, 10 (July 1979), 34-35.

Favorable review of the production of the New Shakespeare Company, at the Open Air Theatre, Regent's

Park, directed by David Weston and designed by Tim
Goodchild. It achieved a "blend of mysticism, happiness,
frustration and eroticism." Oberon was a bare-chested
centaur. The lovers were in eighteenth century costumes
that became increasingly dusty in the chase in the wood.
The park's natural outdoor stage is the perfect setting for
this play: "The stone building behind the trees can easily
be Theseus' palace. . . . The sun sets, the stage comes
closer to us; we begin to be involved in the dream. We
could even start to believe in fairies." Miranda Fellows
choreographed "a magical reconciliation scene," and the
mechanicals did a Greek dance for their Bergomasque at the
end of the play. Included is a listing of the full cast and
production staff.

T1466   Barber, Lester E. "Great Lakes Shakespeare Festival."
        Shakespeare Quarterly, 31 (1980), 232-35.

        Coverage includes a favorable review of the 1980
production of *A Midsummer Night's Dream* at the Cleveland
Playhouse, directed by Paul Lee: "a faithful interpretation
without idiosyncratic biases." Designer Gary C. Eckhart
provided a revolving setting with tree stumps, stone steps,
and a cave, and Estelle Painter provided elaborately
worked, romantic fairy costumes, with Oberon's train as
animal-like creatures and the other fairies blending with the
landscape in their costumes and elaborate poses (photo). A
partial list of the cast and production staff is provided.

T1467   Christopher, Georgia B. "Shakespeare in Virginia."
        Shakespeare Quarterly, 31 (1980), 211-12.

        Review coverage includes favorable reviews of two
productions of *A Midsummer Night's Dream* (production
credits and partial casts given). An outdoor production in
Richmond in 1979 by the Shakespeare Players, Inc., a
semi-amateur group, featured Edwardian costumes,
well-choreographed children as the fairies, and a Teddy
Roosevelt-like Bottom. The Virginia Shakespeare Festival
production, seen at William and Mary College in 1979, was
endearing for its young lovers and its fairies, played and
costumed as gypsies. This put Oberon and Titania's quarrel
over the stolen child in a new light.

T1467a   Correll, Laraine. "Federal Theatre Project Records at George Mason University." *Performing Arts Resources*, 6 (1980), 1-177.

Lists research materials for FTP productions of several Shakespearean plays, including a puppet version of *A Midsummer Night's Dream*.

T1468   Dessen, Alan C. "Oregon Shakespearean Festival." *Shakespeare Quarterly*, 31 (1980), 278-85.

Reviews several productions, including a production of *A Midsummer Night's Dream* at the festival's Elizabethan Stagehouse, in repertory from 8 June to 28 September 1979, directed by Dennis Bigelow. The author marvels at the variations and contrasts in emotional tones and such features as the feminist approach to Hippolyta, the permutations of sexual fantasies, and the menacing fairies with knives, who later sang Titania asleep with a lovely song. A moving rendition of Bottom's return to his comrades capped the fine ensemble work of the mechanicals. Textual adjustments included a rearranged placement of Bottom's dream at the point just before the lovers are awakened and the notable omission of some lines, including the V.i exchange that contains "the best in this kind are but shadows." A partial listing of the cast and production staff is included.

T1469   Dryden, Daniel. "San Diego National Shakespeare Festival." *Theatre Crafts*, 14, 4 (September 1980), 38, 121-22.

Sketches the operation of this festival in an issue devoted to brief descriptions and photos of California theatres, including the state's several Shakespeare festival theatres. This article includes a photograph of a setting for a recent production of *A Midsummer Night's Dream* at this festival.

T1470   Foulkes, Richard. "J. B. Fagan: Shakespearean Producer." *Theatre Notebook*, 34 (1980), 116-23.

Discusses Fagan's Shakespearean productions between 1918 and 1924, including his *A Midsummer Night's Dream* at the Court Theatre, London, in 1920. Fagan's principles of fidelity to the text, continuous action, more rapid delivery of the lines, the stripping away of traditional business, and more simplified settings influenced later directors such as Guthrie, according to the author. He describes in some detail Fagan's setting for *A Midsummer Night's Dream,* which was sparse relative to the usual lavish treatments of the play. He used a single forest setting, consisting of four large, gnarled oaks with impressionistic leaves, a simplified palace for Theseus, with two fluted pillars against a colored sky, and a quaint shanty for Quince's house. Members of Fagan's company included Arthur Clark (Bottom), Miles Malleson (Quince and Egeus), and H. O. Nicholson (Starveling).

T1471   Frey, Charles. "Shakespeare in Seattle." *Shakespeare Quarterly,* 31 (1980), 285-86.

Review coverage includes detailed characterizations of two 1979 productions of *A Midsummer Night's Dream.* Jack Sydow's production with University of Washington Drama School students, who were "adequate if unremarkable," was "stylized . . . toward mannerist elegance and a kind of dreamy inconsequence, . . . a light opera or tone poem neatly contained in a single style of courtesy." There was also "an edge of self-reflexiveness and near-parody that suggested the theatre ritually reconsidering one of its ancient monuments." The Floating Theatre Company's production, directed by Arne Zaslove, was sprinkled with popular songs from 1957 and set in a high school of 1957, with bobby sox lovers, the royalty as school administrators, and the mechanicals as janitors. Partial cast lists and production credits are included.

T1472   Gielgud, Kate Terry. *A Victorian Playgoer.* With forewords by John, Val, and Eleanor Gielgud. Edited by Muriel St. Clare Byrne. London: Heinemann, 1980. 126 pp.

Sir John Gielgud's mother wrote descriptions of plays she attended for a housebound friend. Her "reviews" of London theatre, 1892-1903, include her enthusiastic response to Sir Herbert Beerbohm Tree's *A Midsummer Night's Dream* in January of 1900 at Her Majesty's Theatre, with Tree as Bottom and Julia Neilson (Terry) as Oberon.

T1473   Hildy, Franklin Joseph. "Reviving Shakespeare's
        Stagecraft: Nugent Monck and the Maddermarket
        Theatre, Norwich, England." Ph.D. Dissertation,
        Northwestern University, 1980. *DAI*, 41 (1981):
        3781-3782.

Documents Monck's fifty-seven year career as a director,
drawing upon Monck's papers and interviews with his
associates over the years. Monck, who was influenced by
William Poel and Harley Granville-Barker, produced all of
Shakespeare's plays between 1921 and 1933 at his
proscenium-less stage in the Maddermarket Theatre,
including *A Midsummer Night's Dream*. The appendices
include a list of his productions.

T1474   Holmin, Lorrie. "Shakespeare in Sweden." *Shakespeare
        Quarterly*, 31 (1980), 432-34.

Includes brief, favorable reviews of two reportedly
inventive productions of *A Midsummer Night's Dream* in 1979
by the Stockholm City Theatre and the Skånska Teatern in
Landskrona. The Stockholm production featured "a
masterpiece of translation" by the director, Göran O.
Eriksson. Its setting was controversial. Athens was a city
at war, blackened by artillery fire, and Hippolyta was
brought in imprisoned in a net. The forest was created with
a deep-pile fur floor, and Puck was a somewhat devil-like
creature of fifty-three, vested in fur (photo). The Skånska
Theatre's production featured a circus tent and sawdust
floor for the forest and an athletically skilled young
company. Partial listings of the casts and production staffs
are included.

T1475   Jacobs, Laurence H. "Shakespeare in the San Francisco
        Bay Area." *Shakespeare Quarterly*, 31 (1980), 274-78.

Coverage includes a brief, favorable review of *A
Midsummer Night's Dream* as produced in the John Hinkel
Park Amphitheatre by the Berkeley Shakespeare Festival in
August and September of 1979, directed by Mary Rae
Thewlis. It was "entirely traditional" and popular,
"emphasizing a pastoral simplicity in the play and
capitalizing on the sylvan setting in a city park on a
summer evening." Gail Chugg's Bottom stood out, especially
in the depth of mystery he suggested in "I have had a

dream." A partial list of the cast and production staff is
provided.

T1475a   Joseph, Bertram. *A Shakespeare Workbook: Volume 2:*
         Comedies and Histories. New York: Theatre Arts Books,
         1980. 287 pp.

         Aims at helping modern actors understand and
         communicate the meanings of Shakespeare's texts. An
         introduction offers some suggestions about Shakespeare's
         language, Elizabethan vocabulary, and considerations of
         imagery and meter. Joseph than takes the actor through
         selected scenes from ten of the comedies and five of the
         history plays. The section on *A Midsummer Night's Dream*
         (pp. 43-56) explains who Theseus is and paraphrases some
         passages and explains others in Theseus' opening speech
         and in other portions of I.i. *E.g.*, there are notes on
         "abjure," "avouch," "self-affairs," "Phoebe," "virgin
         patent," "livery," "belike," and "lode-star." There are also
         some explications of selected words and portions of the plot
         in II.i, II.ii, and III.ii.

T1476   Loney, Glenn M. "Europe in the Seventies." *Theatre*
         Crafts 14, 1 (January/February 1980), 23, 86-92, 97.

         Characterizes ten recent Royal Shakespeare Company
         productions including, briefly, the 1970 *A Midsummer*
         Night's Dream directed by Peter Brook, in this survey of
         trends in theatre architecture and scene design. The Brook
         production, "with its circus air of trapezes, clownlike
         costumes, and juggling props, took place in a white box, a
         Brookian Empty Space. . . . Narrow slits downstage at
         each side of the box . . . were actually to permit the
         asbestos curtain behind the masked proscenium arch to
         descend in full view of the audience, as required by British
         law."

T1477   McNeir, Waldo F. "Shakespeare in Texas." *Shakespeare*
         Quarterly, 31 (1980), 243-48.

         Survey of seven productions includes a favorable review
         of *A Midsummer Night's Dream* produced at the Dallas
         Shakespeare Festival, directed by Kenneth Frankel, festival
         Artistic Director. A rotating mirror ball cast reflections on

the Band Shell stage in the park; Bottom and crew and the four lovers were the strengths of the cast. A partial listing of the cast and production staff is included.

T1478   *A Midsummer Night's Dream* presented by the American Repertory Theatre at the Loeb Drama Center, Cambridge, Massachusetts. 21 March to 17 May 1980, and at the Wilbur Theatre, Boston, 26 October to 27 November 1980. Video-taped by WGBH, Boston. Artistic Director, Robert Brustein. Director, Alvin Epstein. Designer, Tony Straiges. Music by Henry Purcell, adapted by Otto-Werner Meuller. Orchestra and chorus of the Banchetto Musicale directed by Daniel Stepner. *Theseus*, Robert Brustein. *Titania*, Carmen de Lavallade. *Bottom*, John Bottoms. *Flute*, Max Wright. *Helena*, Lisa Sloan.

This was essentially a revival of the Yale Repertory Theatre production of 1975, offered as the first production by the newly-formed ART in residence at Harvard under Robert Brustein, former Dean of the Yale School of Drama. Three of the original cast appeared in the revival; there were some modifications in staging and costuming. For a characterization of the 1975 production and its reviews, see item T1375.

Reviews: Mel Gussow, *New York Times*, 24 March 1980; Jack Kroll, *Newsweek*, 28 April 1980; Elizabeth H. Hageman, *Shakespeare Quarterly*, 32 (1981), 190-93.

T1479   *A Midsummer Night's Dream* presented by the Bristol Old Vic Company at the Old Vic Theatre, London, beginning 2 July 1980. Director, Richard Cottrell. Settings, Bob Crowley. Costumes, Bob Ringwood. Lighting, John A. Williams. *Oberon*, Robert O'Mahoney. *Titania*, Meg Davies, *Puck*, Nickolas Grace. *Theseus*, Andrew Hilton. *Hermia*, Caroline Holdaway. *Helena*, Louise Jameson. *Bottom*, Clive Wood.

A well-received minor production, designed in high Renaissance style. The lovers and the romantic dream qualities were less emphasized than was the polarity between the dark, dangerous side of the wood and the very funny comedy of the mechanicals.

Reviews: Don Carleton, *Plays and Players*, 27, 8
(August 1980); John Elsom, *Listener*, 104 (3 July 1980);
G. M. Pears, *Cahiers Elisabéthains*, 18 (October 1980),
100-101; John Russell Taylor, *Drama*, 138 (October 1980),
17-26.

T1480 Moehlmann, John. "North Carolina Shakespeare Festival."
       Shakespeare Quarterly, 31 (1980), 214-16.

       Describes in some detail the 1979 production of *A
       Midsummer Night's Dream* in this new festival, directed by
       Malcolm Morrison. "The play was conceived as taking place
       in rural Elizabethan England, where both mortal and
       immortal worlds existed as ordered hierarchies." The fairies
       were gnomes, with a Puck with a pot belly and a pipe.
       Theseus was a cultured lord of the manor, and the
       mechanicals were very well-restrained bucolic artisans.
       Fidelity to an uncut text, economy of movement, and
       startling contrasts in Mark Pirolo's costumes combined to
       make it a memorable production. A partial listing of the cast
       and production staff is included, and there is a photograph
       of Puck and Oberon.

T1481 Mullin, Michael, and Karen Morris Muriello. *Theatre at
       Stratford-upon-Avon. A Catalogue-Index to Productions
       of the Shakespeare Memorial/Royal Shakespeare Theatre,
       1879-1978.* 2 Volumes. Westport, Connecticut: Greenwood
       Press, 1980.

       Lists alphabetically every play, Shakespearean or
       non-Shakespearean, produced at Stratford-upon-Avon and
       at the Aldwych, the RSC's London base, giving the date of
       each opening, the production credits, the cast, and a list
       of reviews in newspapers and popular periodicals. The
       review lists were compiled from the clippings books kept by
       the Shakespeare Centre Library. The number of reviews
       varies from a few in the early years to as many as forty
       reviews of the significant productions of the last decade. In
       the nearly 100 years covered, there were thirty-one
       productions of *A Midsummer Night's Dream* at Stratford-
       upon-Avon, representing the work of these directors: Sir
       Frank Benson, Patrick Kirwan, W. Bridges-Adams, B. Iden
       Payne, E. Martin Browne, Andrew Leigh, Baliol Holloway,
       Robert Atkins, Michael Benthall, George Devine, Peter Hall,
       Peter Brook, and John Barton.

T1481a   Proudfoot, Richard. "Peter Brook and Shakespeare," in
         Drama and Mimesis, ed. James Redmond. Cambridge:
         Cambridge University Press, 1980, pp. 157-89.

         Provides a brief history of the Shakespeare productions
         directed by Brook, characterizing the major ones, including
         his *Measure for Measure* (1950), *Titus Andronicus* (1955),
         King Lear (1962), *A Midsummer Night's Dream* (1970), and
         Antony and Cleopatra (1978). For Brook's *A Midsummer
         Night's Dream,* he describes the setting and representative
         moments in the staging, such as the use of the trapezes by
         Oberon and Puck, the magic flower being represented by a
         spinning platter, and the quarrel of the kinetic lovers. He
         argues that the solemn ending, in which the actors shook
         hands with the audience, was at odds with the festivity
         suggested in the text and contends that while verbally the
         production was faithful to the text, Brook had a "hidden
         play" beneath it. He believes the production's "rejection of
         a sentimentalizing stage tradition was dearly bought," that
         the performances were "robbed of human particularity," and
         that "Brook in his turn risked a sentimental reduction of
         the play, a confinement of its range and fantasy with a
         setting as modishly pretty and as thoroughly distracting as
         a whole forest of palpable-gross Beerbohm Trees."

T1482   Riehle, Wolfgang. "Shakespeare in Austria." *Shakespeare
         Quarterly,* 31 (1980), 424-27.

         Coverage of seven productions in 1978-1979 includes a
         fairly favorable review of a production of *A Midsummer
         Night's Dream* at the Burgtheater, Vienna, directed by
         Jonathan Miller. A. W. Schlegel's translation was used. The
         approach was reportedly generally conservative, though
         there were some modernizing touches as in Hippolyta's
         emphatic, feminist gesture of disapproval of the sentence
         Theseus passes on Hermia. This theme was not, however,
         taken further. The trees in Patrick Robertson's forest
         setting suggested sexual symbols and a world taken from
         Hieronymus Bosch. A partial list of the cast and production
         staff is provided.

T1483   Rosen, Carol. "Shakespeare in New Jersey." *Shakespeare
         Quarterly,* 31 (1980), 202-205.

Includes in the coverage a favorable review of the New
Jersey Shakespeare Festival *A Midsummer Night's Dream*,
directed by Paul Barry. It is characterized as "lively and
refreshingly un-Jan Kottish. Instead of suggesting a murky
psychic terrain, . . . the forest . . . suggested a
deep-sea discothèque, verdant, aglow, and pleasurably
weightless. . . . A disco version of this play, where you
can't tell the dancer from the dance, made concrete sense
in the summer of 1979." It was "highly imaginative and
illuminating, as well as trendy." Much attention is given to
the acting, with Oberon (Eric Tavaris) and Bottom
(Clarence Felder) being praised highly. Titania was fussy
and overstylized, and Puck was incomprehensible. A partial
list of the cast and production staff is included.

T1484   Rossi, Alfred. *Astonish Us in the Morning.* London:
        Hutchinson and Company, Ltd., 1977; reprint, Detroit:
        Wayne State University Press, 1980. 309 pp. Illustrated.

This collection of "conversations" Rossi had with those
who worked with director Tyrone Guthrie over the years
includes an interview with Paul Rogers, who talks of
Guthrie's direction of the 1951 Old Vic production, in which
Rogers played Bottom. (See T1120.) Rogers says Guthrie
was embarrassed by the success of his Victorian style *A
Midsummer Night's Dream* in 1937-38. Guthrie is said to
have been an effective teacher of verse speaking to the
quartet of lovers. In the 1951 production, it was Guthrie's
idea that the ass's head should be an open structure to
allow the audience to see Bottom's face. Rogers believes
this was a mistake, one perpetuated when Peter Hall
borrowed the idea for his 1959 production.

T1485   Smith, Susan Harris. "Shakespeare Makes a Comeback in
        Shanghai." *New York Times*, 14 September 1980, Section
        D. pp. 3, 9.

An American exchange professor recounts her experience
producing *A Midsummer Night's Dream* in Shanghai with a
Chinese cast.

T1486   Stodder, Joseph H., and Lillian Wilds. "Shakespeare in
        Southern California and Visalia." *Shakespeare Quarterly*,
        31 (1980), 254-74.

Coverage of thirty-three productions includes brief, glowing accounts of two productions of *A Midsummer Night's Dream* in 1980. At the Globe Playhouse, Los Angeles, the popular Shakespeare Society of America production, directed by Lane Davies, featured scantily clad, chirping, chipmunk like fairies. At the Will Geer Theatricum Botanicum, in Topanga Canyon, in the production directed by Mary Ann Dolcemascolo, Hippolyta entered the open-air theatre, which was surrounded by woods and trails, riding on a snorting, pawing palomino. A dozen school children played fairies, coached by actor Will Geer's widow who also played the First Fairy in long silver tresses. Oberon and Puck overlooked their domain from a large tree at center stage.

T1486a   "Summer Shakespeare Festivals--1980." *The Shakespeare Newsletter*, 30 (1980), 1.

Lists the forthcoming summer seasons of twenty-one Shakespeare festival theatres, three of which were staging *A Midsummer Night's Dream*: the American Players Company, Spring Green, Wisconsin; the California Shakespeare Festival, Visalia; and the Champlain Shakespeare Festival, Vermont.

T1487   Turner, Jerry. "Colorado Shakespeare Festival." *Shakespeare Quarterly*, 31 (1980), 249-51.

Includes a mixed review of the 1979 production of *A Midsummer Night's Dream* by the festival at the Mary Rippon Outdoor Theatre in Boulder, directed by Ronald E. Mitchell. While the festival's productions are reported to be becoming more contemporary in interpretation, stepping out of the "academic cocoon," the style for *A Midsummer Night's Dream* was simple and unforced. There was the now common doubling of Theseus and Oberon, Hippolyta and Titania, and Puck and Philostrate but the reviewer objects; the actors did not do both roles well. The scenery was "a cross between Walt Disney and busy Sixties psychodelia." Includes partial cast list, production credits, and a photograph.

T1487a   Veitch, Andrew. "Midsummer Night's Dream." *The Guardian*, 8 July 1980, p. 9.

Very favorable review of the New Shakespeare Company's production of *A Midsummer Night's Dream* at the Open Air Theatre, Regent's Park, London. Directed by Celia Bannerman and designed by Tim Goodchild, it was set in the early nineteenth century. It is described as "a merry dream" that "bustles along," climaxing in Bernard Bresslaw's "truly awful Pyramus." There is a production photograph on page one of the *Guardian* of 1 July 1980.

T1488   Ward, Michael. "Kenyon Copying a Winner." *The Plain Dealer* (Cleveland), 27 July 1980, pp. D-1, 3.

Review of *A Midsummer Night's Dream* at the Kenyon College Festival Theatre. Not seen.

T1488a   Ashton, Geoffrey, with members of the staff. *Shakespeare and British Art.* New Haven: Yale Center for British Art, 1981. viii, 126 pp. Illustrated.

Catalogue for the exhibition at the Yale Center for British Art, April 23-July 5, 1981. The first section consists of numbered annotations (1-165) of paintings, drawings, and single sheet engravings, arranged alphabetically by artist. The second section of entries (166-90) consists of annotations describing illustrated editions of Shakespeare's works. The annotations include information on the type, size, and provenance of the work, and, where relevant, on attribution problems. There are lists of works related to those exhibited, some commentary on the subjects in the works, and lines from the plays corresponding to the works in exhibition are sometimes given. In the plate section of the catalogue (pp. 76-126) are over 100 black-and-white reproductions of selected works from the exhibition. Among them are three works depicting scenes from *A Midsummer Night's Dream*, including Thomas Stothard's *Oberon and Titania* (1806) and Francis Danby's painting of the same title (1837).

T1489   Babula, William. *Shakespeare in Production, 1935-1978. A Selective Catalogue.* New York and London: Garland Publishing Company, 1981. x, 383 pp.

Provides a chronological listing of productions of each of the plays throughout the period indicated in the title (forty-one productions of *A Midsummer Night's Dream*), together with a listing of some reviews for them, some of which are excerpted with the intent of characterizing the productions and sampling the responses. Four books on Shakespearean stage history have been referenced in this selection also.

T1490   Barlow, Graham, and Priscilla Seltzer. "Shakespeare in Scotland." *Shakespeare Quarterly*, 32 (1981), 168-71.

Coverage includes reviews of two 1980 productions of *A Midsummer Night's Dream*: at the University of Stirling by the London-based New Shakespeare Company on tour, directed by David Conville, and in Perth by the Perth Theatre Company, directed by Joan Knight. In the simple, touring production of the New Shakespeare Company, there was an attempt to represent Titania's fairies as invisible, buzzing spirits (a kazoo sound), with their flight paths being suggested by those who "watched" them. But the device was not well carried out. The Perth production set the play in Edinburgh, "the Athens of the North," in the early nineteenth century, with Demetrius and Lysander in full dress kilts. But it was reportedly "an unimaginative and dour production," ending on a somewhat happier note with a "Scottische" dance done by the mechanicals.

T1490a   Berry, Ralph. "The Aesthetics of Beerbohm Tree's Shakespeare Festivals." *Nineteenth Century Theatre Research*, 9 (1981), 23-51.

Challenges the view that Tree was "a successful flâneur," who overelaborated in ostentatious productions of Shakespeare. Berry praises his nine consecutive years of Shakespeare festivals (1905-1913), which ran between two and five weeks in length and which saw fourteen of the plays performed. Tree is seen as a very successful marketer of Shakespeare "in a way his public would appreciate," and praised for the "sense of genre and decorum" that governed his pursuit of detailed illusion, *i.e.*, "realism." Several of Tree's Shakespearean productions are characterized, including his *A Midsummer Night's Dream* (1900 and revived for the 1911 festival). Berry stresses Tree's treatment of it as a children's fairy play and suggests that "the genre of Tree's *Dream* . . . can be thought of as Disney." Stage directions and some

critical responses to the production are included in the
discussion. Berry suggests in conclusion that economic
factors played a role in the changing production
styles--that extras and spectacle became too expensive, and
he argues that most modern theatre historians have failed to
see in the outward form of Tree's staging that "realization
of the spiritual" that G. Wilson Knight attributed to Tree.

T1491   Booth, Michael R. *Victorian Spectacular Theatre,
        1850-1910*. Boston, London: Routledge & Kegan Paul,
        1981. 190 pp. Illustrated.

   Discusses Shakespeare and the Victorian pictorial stage
in Chapter Two, noting some of the paintings, prints, and
book illustrations that have sprung from *A Midsummer
Night's Dream*, and Booth briefly describes (citing from key
primary sources) the productions of the play by Elizabeth
Vestris (1840), Samuel Phelps (1853), and Charles Kean
(1856). He places these in the context of the fairy
painting, fairy ballets, and fairy tales prevalent in the
Victorian era. In Chapter Five, devoted to a reconstruction
of Sir Herbert Beerbohm Tree's *Henry VIII*, he
characterizes other Tree productions briefly, including his
A Midsummer Night's Dream of 1900.

T1491a Burridge, Christina J. "'Music, Such as Charmeth
        Sleep': Benjamin Britten's *A Midsummer Night's Dream*."
        University of Toronto Quarterly, 51 (1981-82), 149-60.

   Analyzes portions of Britten's opera to demonstrate the
success that the author claims for its combined musical and
dramatic effects. Britten overcame the problems involved in
trying to provide musical unity for a work whose verbal
integrity could not be violated. In Britten's work, the
musical and dramatic structure coincide, enabling him to
create "a motivic structure," a musical shorthand that, in
its complexity, "obviated the need for any wholesale
translation of poetic images into musical equivalents."
Britten's emphasis is on the world of the wood--which is
virtually a character--and its power of sleep, which Oberon
uses to resolve the complications of the night. In the
opera, the Oberon-Tytania [*sic*] quarrel is the generating
force of the action, and Oberon's jealousy and desire for
revenge dominate Acts I and II. The lovers are more
developed in the opera than in Shakespeare's play, being

more obsessed with love; Oberon, in Britten's opera, has power over the human world, the humans being almost puppets. Burridge answers the frequent criticism of Britten's pairing of a countertenor Oberon with a Tytania who is a coloratura. She argues that this involves a delicate balance that makes the work essentially a chamber opera, most effective in a small house or a recording. She objects to Britten's treatment of "Pyramus and Thisbe" as a parody of opera; while it is funny, the parody jars because it is not the work of the rustics themselves. Nevertheless, she says Britten synthesizes all in his ending and reminds us of the layers of reality and illusion with an imaginative musical stroke that uses a motif from the play-within-the-play for Theseus' line, "the iron tongue of midnight has told twelve."

T1491b   Clark, Leroy. "*A Midsummer Night's Dream.*" *Theatre Journal*, 33 (1981), 541-43.

Favorable review of a production by the Alaska Repertory Theatre in Anchorage in April, 1981. Directed by Walton Jones, the play was reportedly well staged and strongly acted by the company that provides the state's only professional theatre. Some of the costume designs of William Ivey Long were inspired by Inigo Jones; the "abstract" setting employed a raked stage and ramps, and individual scenes were lighted in different colors.

T1492   Conville, David. "Turkish Dream." *Drama*, 2nd Quarter, 1981, pp. 7-9.

The British director describes his experience directing *A Midsummer Night's Dream* with Turkish actors at the State Theatre in Istanbul. Matters discussed include language problems, rehearsal procedures, and stage business.

T1493   Dunbar, Mary Judith. "*Dream* at Santa Cruz." *Shakespeare Quarterly*, 32 (1981), 262-63.

Describes a student production of *A Midsummer Night's Dream* directed by Audrey Stanley at the University of Santa Cruz in May 1980. It was done in an outdoor theatre amid a ring of redwood trees. There is high praise for the director's work in developing student actors who offered refreshing directness and thoughtful verse delivery, the result of two months of work on the language before rehearsals began. They were also inventive. The ensemble composed the music that was used, basing it on sounds of the grove around them and played on simple hand-held instruments. In a shortened version entitled *Bottom's Dream*, the production toured ten colleges and universities. It was performed using circular staging, with the audience seated on parachute silk, resewn into a circle. A photograph and partial listing of the cast and production staff is included.

T1493a   Farmer, Patrick A. "*A Midsummer Night's Dream.*" *Theatre Journal*, 33 (1981), 405-406.

Unfavorable review of a production of the play by the Guthrie Theatre touring company, seen at the Civic Center, Des Moines, Iowa, 5 November 1980. The play was adapted and directed by Stephen Willems who cut it considerably (only Bottom remained of the mechanicals and the fairies were simulated with taped sounds), and conceived of it as a 1930s movie fantasy. It was set on a 1930s tropical isle, and the characters became period screen idols; *e.g.*, Oberon and Titania were reflections of Fred Astaire and Ginger Rogers. Puck was a South Seas goblin, brandishing maracas. Bottom did "Pyramus and Thisbe" as a one-man show. The designers established the climate, but the adaptation and most of the cast were reportedly not up to the standards of excellence expected of the Guthrie.

T1493b   Linzer, Martin. "*A Midsummer Night's Dream* in East Germany." *The Drama Review*, 25, 2 (1981), 45-54.

Describes two 1980 East Berlin productions that he suggests provide material for discussion of how the classics "can confront the world of today." In the production at the Deutsches Theatre, directed by Alexander Lang, both the court and forest worlds were male-dominated, with Oberon feeling threatened by the possible liberation of his Titania, who was a Marilyn Monroe-like sex object. The young lovers experienced extremes of lust, anxiety, and pain and finally were reduced to paralysis by Puck. The love drugs were used manipulatively. In the production at the Maxim Gorky Theatre, directed by Thomas Langhoff, there was something of a circus and variety show atmosphere. Oberon and

Titania swung over the stage on ropes, and the stage floor
was part trampoline on which the shaky lovers tripped and
staggered, propelled by abruptly changing emotions. In
both productions, the young lovers were seen as
capitulating to the adult establishment in Act V.

T1493c   Elsom, John, ed. *Post-War British Theatre Criticism.*
          With drawings by Feliks Topolski. Boston: Routledge &
          Kegan Paul; London: Boston and Henley, 1981. 270 pp.

          Portions of four reviews of the 1970 RSC production of *A
          Midsummer Night's Dream*, directed by Peter Brook (see
          T1314), are included in this anthology of British theatre
          reviews since World II, which is arranged by production.
          Irving Wardle of *The Times* (28 August 1970) sees the
          production as the apex of the RSC's work. He describes
          enthusiastically the highlights of the staging, from Puck's
          magic flower being represented by a spinning juggler's
          plate, to the nuptials for Titania and Bottom. In the last
          act, the audience is not encouraged to join with the nobility
          in sneering at the mechanicals. He praises the actors'
          knowledge of the text. John Barber of the *Daily Telegraph*
          (28 August 1970) says Brook "found new ways of giving
          form to [the play's] latent poetry and power" and describes
          some stage business. Peter Lewis of the *Daily Mail* (28
          August 1970) describes the production as a circus, saying
          "once you get used to it, it seems natural." Benedict
          Nightingale of the *New Statesman* (4 September 1970),
          deplores the production as "Mickey Mouse" or perhaps "the
          Dream, 2001." He objects to Brook's presumption that the
          play would otherwise be dull. The effect of Brook's
          interpretation is not to escape tradition so much as "to
          sentimentalize [the play] once again and in a new, more
          insidious way. His manic decoration has deprived it of the
          suffering, fear, horror, and apart from one moment, when
          Bottom's phallus is crudely mimed by the fairies, even of
          lust." "Only a humorless man could have staged this."

T1494   Labriola, Albert C. "Shakespeare in Pittsburgh."
         Shakespeare Quarterly, 32 (1981), 202-206.

         Coverage includes a favorable review of a university
         production of *A Midsummer Night's Dream* presented in the
         Duquesne Union Ballroom by the Red Masquers, directed by
         James Berry, who played Oberon. The staging in the round

had the green-clad fairies providing formations of forest
growth, orchestrated by Puck. "Visually and auditorily they
created a maze within which the sudden infatuations of
Demetrius, Lysander, Hermia and Helena were seen as the
onset of primitive urges of sensuality, the dark underside
of human nature where reason does not shine." Peaseblossom
and company were portrayed by handpuppets operated by
the other fairies. A partial listing of the cast and
production staff is included.

T1495   Langhans, Edward A. *Restoration Promptbooks.*
         Carbondale: Southern Illinois University Press, 1981. 535
         pp.

         Examines promptbooks of professional London Theatre
productions dating between 1660 and 1700. While those
promptbooks represented in the discussions and in the
eleven facsimile promptbooks included are
non-Shakespearean, the analysis of this rare material is
instructive for study of any of this era's plays in
performance, including as it does considerations of stages,
auditoriums, scene shifting, prompter markings, and acting
conventions. (See also item 1038.)

T1496   Littlefield, T. H. "Shakespeare in Upstate New York."
         Shakespeare Quarterly, 32 (1981), 187-88.

         Includes in the coverage an unfavorable review of the
Lexington Conservatory Theatre's production of *A
Midsummer Night's Dream,* directed by Michael J. Hume,
which emphasized sexual battles and sensual sexual
encounters throughout. Mating calls and hoarse sighs filled
the forest. Demetrius was played as lust personified, and
the costumes revealed a lot of bare male breasts and female
thighs. The costumes were apparently inspired by
science-fiction comic strip superheroes. A partial listing of
the cast and production staff and a photo are included.

T1497   Mazer, Cary M. *Shakespeare Refashioned: Elizabethan
         Plays on Edwardian Stages.* Ann Arbor, Michigan: UMI
         Research Press, 1981. xiv, 267 pp. Illustrated.

         Discusses sceneography in the Edwardian era, beginning
with the late Victorian traditions and then analyzing the

intentions and aesthetics of 1) the Elizabethan revival, led
by William Poel; 2) the "new stagecraft"; and 3)
Granville-Barker's productions and theories. Within these
discussions will be found mentions of scenic effects for the
productions of *A Midsummer Night's Dream* of Tree (1900),
Benson (1888 and after), Patrick Kirwan (1914), and
Granville-Barker (1914). Among the arguments advanced
are: that Granville-Barker's Savoy production did not so
much radically depart from tradition as resourcefully
integrate disparate features of various Edwardian trends;
that the modern "Director's Theatre" owes some of its
assumptions to the Edwardian developments, including the
assumption that there is a single authorial intention
discernible in Shakespeare's plays; and that the principle of
unity in production, as seen in theory of Gordon Craig and
the practices of the new stagecraft designers and directors,
contributes to the development of the concept of the theatre
artist as Great Man and Genius Director.

T1498   *A Midsummer Night's Dream* presented by the Royal
        Shakespeare Company at the Royal Shakespeare Theatre,
        Stratford-upon-Avon, in repertory beginning 9 July
        1981. Entered in repertory at the Barbican Arts Centre,
        London, 16 June 1982. Director, Ron Daniels. Designer,
        Maria Bjornson. Puppet Master, Barry Smith. Music,
        Stephen Oliver. *Theseus/Oberon*, Mike Gwilym.
        Hippolyta/Titania, Juliet Stevenson. *Puck*, Joe Marcell.
        Hermia, Jane Carr. *Bottom*, Geoffrey Hutchings.

The production's most distinctive feature was the fairies,
represented by small, broken doll puppets, operated by
actors in black against black stage hangings. Scenically,
the production was theatrically self-reflexive, with
dream-like images of the play in a Victorian theatre. The
lovers were lost in a backstage forest world of nineteenth
century flats and properties. In an atmosphere of
anxiousness about love and faith, reconciliation was a major
concern, as in Oberon and Titania's dance of reconciliation.
The production seemed to suggest that beauty and meaning
can exist in a shadow-world by virtue of what imagination
and love may do. Some critics were hostile to what they felt
was a directorially perverse reading and to the grotesque
fairies; some took the Victorian imagery as an invitation to
nostalgia; a few found it very affecting and contemporary.

Reviews: *The Times*, 3 July 1981 (pre-opening feature); Michael Coveney, *Financial Times*, 17 July 1981; Michael Billington, *Guardian*, 17 July 1981; John Barber, *Daily Telegraph*, 17 July 1981; Robert Cushman, *Observer*, 19 July 1981; Robert Hewison, *Sunday Times*, 19 July 1981; Benedict Nightingale, *New Statesman*, 24 July 1981; John Elsom, *Listener*, 106 (30 July 1981); Sheridan Morley, *International Herald Tribune*, 30 July 1981; Nicholas Shrimpton, *Times Literary Supplement*, 31 July 1981; Gareth Lloyd Evans, *Drama*, 142 (Winter 1981), 10-12; Irving Wardle, *The Times*, 17 June 1982; Gareth Lloyd Evans, *Shakespeare Quarterly*, 33 (1982), 184-88; A. Masters, *Plays and Players*, August 1982 (photos); Gary Jay Williams, *Theater*, 13, 2 (Summer 1982), 60-64; Roger Warren, *Shakespeare Survey*, 35 (1982), 141-52, with two photographs. (See also items T1481, T1524a, T1524ab and T1525d).

T1499   *A Midsummer Night's Dream* produced by Arena Stage in the Arena Theatre, Washington, D. C., 4 December 1981 to 10 January 1982. Director, David Chambers. Setting, Heidi Landesman. Costumes, Marie Anne Chiment. *Theseus/Oberon*, Avery Brooks. *Hippolyta/Titania*, Kathleen Turner. *Philostrate/Puck*, Charles Janasz. *Bottom*, Mark Hammer. *Hermia*, Christina Moore.

Titania's realm was at the edge of a deep, practical pool in one corner of the arena stage, with Oberon and Puck occupying the metal pipe canopy over the whole stage. The ass's head became a seahorse's head, and Bottom followed Titania (played by a currently prominent movie starlet) in a plunge into the pool. The production achieved some notoriety for its ambitions and novelty but mixed reviews and responses.

Reviews: David Richards, *Washington Post*, 14 December 1981; Megan Rosenfeld (feature), *Washington Post*, 12 December 1981; Julius Novick, *Village Voice* (New York City), 6-12 January 1982; Jeanne Addison Roberts, *Shakespeare Quarterly*, 33 (1982), 229-32, with two photographs.

T1499a   *A Midsummer Night's Dream* presented by BBC Television for the Time-Life series, "The Shakespeare Plays," produced by Jonathan Miller and shown in the

U.S. on 13 December 1981 and 19 April 1982. Director, Elijah Moshinsky. Designer, David Myerscough-Jones. Music, Stephen Oliver. *Titania*, Helen Mirren. *Oberon*, Peter McEnery. *Puck*, Phil Daniels. *Bottom*, Brian Glover. *Helena*, Cherith Mellor. *Hermia*, Pippa Guard.

A romantic production that juxtaposed a fantasy forest world, with a horned moon and gypsy-like fairies, with a meticulous television realism for the scenes at court and for the mechanicals gatherings--in a pub. It offered special strengths in the performances of Oberon--a virile McEnery on a black horse and Titania--Mirren warmly attentive to her gypsy children fairies around a campfire. The psychological anxieties of the lovers were emphasized. The solemnity of the playing of "Pyramus and Thisbe" annoyed some reviewers. There were some objections also to the Liverpool punk Puck, who was seldom comprehensible.

Reviews: Nicholas Shrimpton, *Times Literary Supplement*, 25 December 1981; John J. O'Connor, *New York Times*, 19 April 1982; G. M. Pearce, *Cahiers Elisabéthains*, 21 (April 1982); Scott Colley, *Shakespeare on Film Newsletter*, 8, 1 (December 1982). (See also item T1524a.)

T1500   Murray, Christopher. "Shakespeare at the Abbey." *Shakespeare Quarterly*, 32 (1981), 173-76.

Coverage includes a brief review of the Abbey production of *A Midsummer Night's Dream* in the spring of 1979, directed by Tomás MacAnna, who is more traditional than not. It was "not an adventurous production," but there were pleasant features in the pretty girl fairies, a finale with lighted tapers, and the mechanicals as Irish peasants. "It may well be that the Abbey, rooted as it is in a tradition radically at odds with England's, is fated never to present on the main stage a production that is a disinterested and innovative interpretation of a Shakespeare play." A partial listing of the cast and production staff is provided.

T1501   Pollack, Rhoda-Gale. "Shakespeare in Wisconsin." *Shakespeare Quarterly*, 32 (1981), 236-38.

Includes a review of a production of *A Midsummer Night's Dream* presented by the American Players Theatre

in an outdoor theatre in a rural area outside Spring Green,
Wisconsin. There were some well-staged moments and some
cast strengths in the production in the natural
amphitheatre, but there was a lack of synthesis between the
three worlds of the play, perhaps because it was the
product of two directors, Anne Occhiogrosso and her
replacement, Edward Berkeley. One of the company's
founders, Randall Duk Kim, was an elfish, impish Puck,
who added the dimensions of weariness and frustration. The
production had some charm and wit and was well-reviewed
in local newspapers, but this reviewer found it to be
uneven in pace and spirit. A partial listing of the cast and
production staff is included.

T1501a   Reid, Christopher. "Television." *Listener*, 105 (5
          February 1981), 186-87.

          Unfavorable review of a production of *Dear Brutus* by
James M. Barrie, by BBC 1-TV, shown in England in
January of 1981. Barrie's play has its base in *A Midsummer
Night's Dream*. It features an ancient elfin character called
Lob, another name for Robin Goodfellow, who arranges for
the dream-like refreshing of the loves and marriages of
several pairs of lovers by leading them upon adventures in
a strange wood on midsummer's eve. Matey the Butler is,
perhaps, a semi-Bottom. There were reportedly able
performances from Alan Webb as Lob and Stratford Johns as
Matey, but these and the expensive costumes and sets
"were not enough to revitalize this old crock." See item
980a.

T1502   Roberts, Jeanne Addison. "Shakespeare in the Nation's
         Capital." *Shakespeare Quarterly*, 32 (1981), 206-210.

         Included in the coverage is a brief, mixed review of *A
Midsummer Night's Dream* presented at the outdoor Sylvan
Theatre by the Shakespeare Summer Festival, sponsored by
the National Park Service. The casual ambience of
picnicking families and holiday loungers who occupied the
ground in front of the stage and the buffering effects of
microphones distanced the audience from the performance.
The production was acceptably acted. There were
"spectacular" costumes by Marjorie Slaiman that put Oberon
in a white cloak, with a silver ruff and a feathered,
broad-brimmed hat, and Titania in a headdress with white

swans soaring on it. A partial list of the cast and
production staff is included.

T1503   Rothwell, Kenneth S. "Champlain Shakespeare Festival."
         Shakespeare Quarterly, 32 (1981), 185-87.

         Offers in the coverage a generally favorable review of a
         traditional, exuberant staging of *A Midsummer Night's
         Dream*, directed by Jennifer A. Cover. The company is
         credited with ensemble playing, and the doubling of
         Theseus/Oberon and Hippolyta/Titania is said to have been
         adroitly carried off by Bill Christ and Kate Goldsborough.
         Amusing as it was, the horseplay in "Pyramus and Thisbe"
         passed over the thin line between slapstick and hysteria."
         A partial listing of the cast and production staff is
         included, and there is a photo of a scene from "Pyramus
         and Thisbe."

T1504   Simon, John. "Perky Penzance, Soporific Dream." *New
         York Magazine*, 14 (26 January 1981), 44-46.

         Very unfavorable review of a Brooklyn Academy of Music
         production of *A Midsummer Night's Dream*, produced by
         Harvey Lichtenstein and directed by David Jones, with sets
         and costumes by Santo Loquasto and music by Bruce
         Coughlin. Among the many things Simon criticized was the
         casting of blacks in roles in which he found them
         inappropriate. The production is further discussed in his
         column in the issue of 23 February 1981. Letters to the
         editor protesting against Simon's review for inherent racism
         may be found in the issue of 16 March 1981. The letters are
         from Lichtenstein and Jones, Willard Swire, and Richard
         Harper, and there is a rejoinder from Simon. (See also item
         T1516.)

T1504a   Smith, Ronn. "The Acting Company, a tour de force."
         Theatre Crafts, 15, 5 (May 1981), 22-25, 50-56.

         Discusses sets and lighting for John Houseman's Juilliard
         Acting Company touring production of *A Midsummer Night's
         Dream*. There is a photograph showing Heidi Landesman's
         circular, pipe-structure setting and a light plot.

T1504b   Sylvander, Carolyn. "*Titus Andronicus* and *A Midsummer Night's Dream*." *Theatre Journal*, 33 (1981), 256-57.

Praises in general terms a production of *A Midsummer Night's Dream* as seen in the outdoor theatre and natural setting at Spring Green, Wisconsin. The play was produced in repertory by the American Players Company, Randall Duk Kim, Artistic Director. No listing of the cast or production staff is provided. (See T1501.)

T1505   Wearing, J. P. *The London Stage 1900-1909. A Calendar of Plays and Players*. 2 volumes. Metuchen, New Jersey, and London: The Scarecrow Press, Inc., 1981.

Provides annual calendars of professional play performances in the major London theatres of the decade 1900-09. Entries include dates of runs, partial casts, production credits, and, for some productions, a listing of some newspaper reviews. The entires include productions of *A Midsummer Night's Dream* directed by Herbert Beerbohm Tree (1900), Frank Benson (1900), and Oscar Asche (1905). This calendar is the second in a series of three by the author covering London theatre from 1890 to 1919. (See items T1400 and T1524b.)

T1506   Wheeler, Richard P. "Illinois Shakespeare Festival." *Shakespeare Quarterly*, 32 (1981), 233-36.

Included in the review coverage is a favorable assessment of a traditional production of *A Midsummer Night's Dream* by the festival, sponsored by Illinois State University, at Ewing Manor, Bloomington. The energetic young actors who played the young lovers put these four characters at the center of the play. The humor of the mechanicals was one dimensional, and the actor playing Bottom did not provide the sense of mystery upon his awakening from his dream.

T1507   Wilds, Lillian. "Shakespeare in Southern California." *Shakespeare Quarterly*, 32 (1981), 250-60.

Includes a glowing review of a production of *A Midsummer Night's Dream* at the College of the Sequoias

Theatre in Visalia by the California Shakespearean Festival, in repertory in the summer of 1980, directed by Mark Lamos. Its features included a furious fight among the four lovers in the forest (photo), a lizard-like Oberon, some insect-like fairies, some elaborate choreography in which the fairies carried Oberon and Titania as if in flight, and an enormous, silhouetted moon. A partial list of the cast and production staff is included.

T1508   Beauman, Sally. *The Royal Shakespeare Company, A History of Ten Decades.* Oxford, New York: Oxford University Press, 1982. xii, 388 pp. Illustrated.

Documented, chronological history of the world famous company that has its origins in the summer productions of the first Shakespeare Memorial Theatre at Stratford-upon-Avon in 1879. It charts the administrative struggles and artistic achievements of the major figures of all eras since then at Stratford-upon-Avon, from Sir Frank Benson through William Bridges-Adams, Sir Barry Jackson, and Glen Byam Shaw, to the founding of the RSC and the work of Peter Hall, Peter Brook, and Trevor Nunn. It characterizes the production philosophy of each of the major figures. Among the productions of *A Midsummer Night's Dream* that are briefly described are those of Benson, Bridges-Adams (there is a photograph of the Norman Wilkinson setting for Theseus' palace in Bridges-Adams's 1932 production), Hall, and Brook (with a photograph of Bottom hoisted on the shoulders of the fairies).

T1509   Berkowitz, Gerald M. "Edinburgh: Festival and Fringe." *Shakespeare Quarterly*, 33 (1982), 191-97.

Coverage includes a generally favorable review of a production of *A Midsummer Night's Dream* by the Leicestershire Youth Theatre in August of 1981. The teenage cast reportedly had the confidence and presence of professionals and were effective as young lovers and young mechanicals. Theseus and Hippolyta were played as Prince Charles and Lady Diana, which yielded some interpolated humor at the expense of royal dignity. Puck was divided into four roles, all energetically acted.

T1509a   Brockett, Oscar G. *History of Theatre.* 4th ed. Boston: Allyn and Bacon, Inc., 1982. 768 pp. Illustrated.

This widely respected textbook draws upon several productions of *A Midsummer Night's Dream* in the course of its chronological and national coverage to illustrate staging practices in several periods. The innovative, Elizabethan-influenced set of the 1843 production of Ludwig Tieck is briefly described and a contemporary lithograph of it is reproduced (p. 435). The successful forest setting for the 1853 production of Samuel Phelps is briefly described (pp. 503-04). Herbert Beerbohm Tree's 1900 production, with its heavily literal forests, is briefly characterized and a photo of the meeting of Tree's Oberon and Titania is reproduced (pp. 557-58). Harley Granville-Barker's Shakespeare productions at the Savoy Theatre are characterized, with examples taken from his *A Midsummer Night's Dream* of 1914; a photo of the bower scene in that production is reproduced (pp. 572-73), and a portion of a review of it is given (p. 590). Peter Brook's 1970 production with the Royal Shakespeare Company is described as to staging and interpretation, and a photo of Titania and Bottom in the bower is reproduced (pp. 691-92).

T1510   Charney, Maurice, and Arthur Ganz. "Shakespeare in New York City." *Shakespeare Quarterly,* 33 (1982), 218-22.

Included in the coverage is a favorable review of a production of *A Midsummer Night's Dream* at the Brooklyn Academy, directed by David Jones, in repertory from January through March of 1981. Jones drew somewhat on the dark reading of Jan Kott's essay. Puck was wanton, and the fairies were "amoral nature spirits." Titania was a sexy enchantress, and Gerry Bamman's Bottom was a loveable ass. Santo Loquasto designed a "lovely pastoral setting" that somewhat suggested "that we can get spiritually ensnared in the forest." A partial listing of the cast and production staff is included. (See also T1504.)

T1511   Christopher, Georgia B. "Shakespeare in Virginia." *Shakespeare Quarterly,* 33 (1982), 233-34.

Includes a favorable, brief review of the Virginia
Museum Theatre's *A Midsummer Night's Dream* in Richmond
in January and February of 1981, directed by Tom Markus.
Spectacle was king, with the fairies in pale-blue satin
tights and ostrich feathers, sliding down poles from a
circular, aerial platform to the raked stage. A partial list of
the cast and production staff is provided.

T1511a Elkin, Saul. "A 'Hollywood' *Midsummer Night's Dream.*"
        On Stage Studies, 6 (Summer 1982), 115-19.

Not seen. Reviews a production at the Shakespeare
Festival at Delaware Park in Buffalo, New York, 8-20 July
1980. Includes the reproduction of a review of this
production from the *Buffalo Evening News*, 10 July 1980.

T1511b Fulton, R. C. "Alabama Shakespeare Festival, 1981."
        Shakespeare Quarterly, 33 (1982), 345-52.

Included in the coverage is a favorable review of the
festival's *A Midsummer Night's Dream*, reportedly the best
of its four productions. There is detailed description of and
praise for every aspect of the production, directed by
Martin L. Pratt. Michael Stauffer's simple blue-carpeted
setting curved toward the audience and provided risers and
platforms upstage right and left. The four sets of
characters were very distinctly rendered, most especially in
movement, but ultimately they all blended in a weaving
together of styles. The fairies were in film and gauze;
Oberon and Titania were attractively, tastefully sexual. One
of the comic highlights was the mechanicals' rehearsal in the
woods. Charles Antalosky's Bottom "ought to stand as a
pattern for the role." There are photographs of the
mechanicals and of Bottom in the ass's head. A partial
listing of the cast and production staff is included.

T1512 Hodnett, Edward. *Image and Text. Studies in the
       Illustration of English Literature.* London: Scolar Press,
       1982. vii, 271 pp. Illustrated.

Analyzes the work of major English artists in selected
illustrated editions of major English authors. In Chapter
Three, "Images of Shakespeare," he discusses the
development and the quality of the art work in the Nicholas

Rowe and Thomas Hanmer editions of Shakespeare. He also examines Fuseli's illustrations of Shakespeare and William Gilbert's illustrations of Howard Staunton's edition of the plays. (None of the *A Midsummer Night's Dream* scenes by these artists are among those reproduced here.) Points out the need for a comprehensive study of the illustrated editions on Shakespeare.

T1513   Jackson, Russell. "Alfred Thompson, 1831-1895: A
        Forgotten Talent." *Theatre Notebook*, 36 (1982), 72-82.

Traces the career of Thompson, an author of burlesques and a costume designer. Thompson designed the costumes for the 1875 production of *A Midsummer Night's Dream* at the Gaiety Theatre, London, in which Samuel Phelps appeared as Bottom. Accompanying the article is a reproduction of an *Illustrated London News* engraving of a scene from the production, showing Bottom, Titania, and her fairies.

T1514   Jackson, Russell. "Before the Shakespeare Revolution:
        Developments in the Study of Nineteenth Century
        Shakespearian Production." *Shakespeare Survey*, 35
        (1982), 1-12.

Surveys the scholarship on nineteenth century Shakespearean production, with special attention given to the growth of the field since Odell (see entry T1270). Characterizes some of the notable contributions and their methodologies and makes suggestions about problems in the field and about further needs and opportunities. Among the assessments of the work to date, the author writes: "Nor can it be said that many theatrical subjects have given rise to works possessing the intellectual scope and vigour of Painter's Proust or of Ellman's Joyce."

T1515   Mallalieu, Huon, ed. *The Harrow Achievement, 1941-1981.*
        With Contributions from Herbert Harris, Jeremy Lemmon,
        Michael Levete, and Simon Welfare. Illustrations by
        Maurice Percival. Plymouth and London: The Bowering
        Press, 1982. 222 pp.

Describes the Shakespearean productions by the boys at Harrow School from 1941 to 1981. The book is dedicated to

Harrow theatre director Ronald Watkins by "the old
Harrovians." Watkins, influenced by Harley
Granville-Barker, William Poel, and J. C. Adams's *The
Globe Playhouse*, staged the plays in the school's Speech
Room on an Elizabethan platform stage, complete with
rushes strewn on the stage floor. He emphasized a
non-illusionistic stage and the well-spoken text. Over the
years, professional London critics praised the Harrow
productions for their simple staging and the standard of
acting. *A Midsummer Night's Dream* was performed by the
boys in 1945, 1952, 1960 (the latter with Stanley Holloway's
son as Bottom; Holloway, senior had performed the role
with the Old Vic in 1954), and 1974. The descriptions of
these often include excerpts from two or three reviews. The
book also includes a history of the plays produced at the
eighteenth century Haddo estate, near Aberdeen, where
Watkins and Lemmon staged plays (including *A Midsummer
Night's Dream*) after the Elizabethan manner. (See also
items T1103, T1115 and T1363.)

T1516   *A Midsummer Night's Dream* presented by the New York
Shakespeare Festival, Joseph Papp, producer, at the
Delacorte Theatre, Central Park, New York City, 3
August to 5 September 1982. Director, James Lapine.
Design, Heidi Landesman. Costumes, Randy Barcelo.
Lighting, Frances Aronson. Music, Allen Shawn.
Choreography, Graciela Daniele. *Oberon*, William Hurt.
Titania, Michelle Shay. *Puck*, Marcell Rosenblatt.
Bottom, Jeffrey DeMunn. *Helena*, Christine Baranski.
Lysander, Kevin Conroy.

Directed for Papp by a rising experimental director, this
production was generally neo-romantic with some
contemporary sassiness. It garnered reviews mixing praise
for an enchanting play and setting with strong disapproval
of some of the cast and direction. Its virtues and novelties
were a pastoral setting consisting of carefully landscaped
real trees and real grass, "a little Central Park" (Tallmer),
and the comic Helena of Christine Baranski, in white gloves
and picture hat (the young lovers' costumes were roughly
Edwardian). Lapine wanted fairies "from every culture and
all kinds of myth"; Oberon was costumed like an Indian
brave and the black Titania was in sequins and veils.
There were objections to this disparateness, to the absence
of magic, and to idiosyncratic directorial flourishes. (See
video tape recording, item T1516a.)

Reviews: Jennifer Dunning, *New York Times*, 8 August 1982 (pre-opening interview with Lapine); Mel Gussow, *New York Times*, 16 August 1982; Patricia O'Haire, *Daily News*, 16 August 1982; Jerry Tallmer, *New York Post*, 16 August 1982; Howard Kissel, *Women's Wear Daily*, 16 August 1982; John Beaufort, *Christian Science Monitor*, 18 August 1982; Leslie Bennetts, *New York Times*, 20 August 1982 (interview with Baranski); Edith Oliver, *New Yorker*, 23 August 1982; Michael Feingold, *Village Voice*, 24 August 1982; Richard Schickel, *Time*, 30 August 1982; John Simon, *New York*, 30 August 1982, and see also the letter objecting to Simon's review in *New York*, 4 October 1982; Robert Brustein, *New Republic*, 20-27 September 1982; Marjorie Oberlander, *Bulletin of the New York Shakespeare Society*, 1 4 (October 1982); Arthur Ganz, *Shakespeare Quarterly*, 34 (1983), 103-107.

T1516a   *A Midsummer Night's Dream*. Television version of the 1982 production of the play directed by James Lapine at the Delacorte Theatre, Central Park, New York City (see T1516). Released 1985? Directed for television by Emile Ardolino. Design, Heidi Landesman. *Oberon*, William Hurt. *Titania*, Michelle Shay. *Puck*, Marcell Rosenblatt. *Bottom*, Jeffrey DeMunn. 2 hours, 45 minutes. Available on video tape, 1/2 inch VHS or Beta, purchase or rental, from Films for the Humanities, Box 2053, Princeton, New Jersey, 08540.

T1517   *A Midsummer Night's Dream* presented by the National Theatre of Great Britain Acting Company at the National Theatre's Cottesloe Theatre, opening 25 November 1982. It also played in Bristol and Cardiff in December and in Glascow in January of 1983. Director, Bill Bryden. Set design, Bob Crowley. Costume design, Deidre Clancy. Lighting, William Bundy. Music, John Tams, Howard Evans. Choreography, David Busby. *Oberon*, Paul Scofield. *Titania*, Susan Fleetwood. *Puck*, Jack Shepherd. *Bottom*, Derek Newark. *Helena*, Jennifer Hall. *Hermia*, Bernadette Shortt. *Lysander*, Karl Johnson. *Theseus*, Edward DeSouza.

A production generally very well-received by critics as enchanting and reflective, this was the National Theatre's first *A Midsummer Night's Dream*. It was distinctive in its centuries-old fairies, led by the grizzled, ancient, paternal

Oberon of Scofield and an earthy Titania, all of whom
moved with watchful benevolence among the mortals and
amid the audience, which sat on the stage amid a carpet of
dead leaves or on backless benches in the house. The court
was in quasi-Edwardian dress and the setting suggestive of
a country manor house in midsummer. There were objections
to the absence of sexuality, fear or magic and to the
artificiality of the actor-audience mingling.

Reviews: Irving Wardle, *The Times*, 26 November 1982;
Michael Coveney, *Financial Times*, 26 November 1982;
Michael Billington, *Guardian*, 27 November 1982; Robert
Cushman, *Observer*, 28 November 1982; James Fenton,
Sunday Times, 5 and 19 December 1982; R. Findlater, *Plays
and Players*, February 1983; P. Roberts, *Plays and
Players*, June 1983; Roger Warren, *Shakespeare Quarterly*,
34 (1983), 334, with a photo of Titania.

T1517a   *A Midsummer Night's Sex Comedy.* 35 mm. color film
produced by Orion Pictures. 85 minutes. Released
through Warner Brothers and opened 16 July 1982.
Producer, Robert Greenhut. Written and directed by
Woody Allen. Director of photography, Gordon Willis.
Editor, Susan E. Morse. Music, Felix Mendelssohn.
Andrew, Woody Allen. *Ariel*, Mia Farrow. *Leopold*, Jose
Ferrer. *Duley*, Julie Hagerty. *Maxwell*, Tony Roberts.
Adrian, Mary Steenburgen.

Inspired in part by *A Midsummer Night's Dream* and in
part by Ingmar Bergman's film "Smiles of a Summer Night,"
this romantic film features a changing dance of partners
among three couples at an elegant country summer house in
upstate New York just after the turn of the century. The
occasion is a wedding party hosted by the earnest Andrew
(Allen), a Wall Street broker and inventor, and his wife,
Adrian, whose sexual interest in him is waning. An object
of desire of all the men is Ariel, Andrew's old flame. Among
the eccentric inventor's creations is a metal beach ball-like
device designed to contact the spirit world. There are
spirits in the Tinkerbell tradition that the six principal
characters come to believe in, though the critics did not.
The film was given a soft-focus, romantic look, a Renoir
palette, and Edwardian costumes; it opens with strains of
Mendelssohn. But the couples are clearly ancestors of
Woody Allen's comically anxious urban Americans of the

later twentieth century, though apparently to be taken in earnest.

T1517b   Mustanoja, Tauno. "Shakespeare in Finland."
         Shakespeare Quarterly, 33 (1982), 522-24.

Includes a brief review of the 1980 Finnish National Theatre production of *A Midsummer Night's Dream* on its studio theatre stage, a theatre in the round with a few tiers of seats along the walls. Scenery consisted of rope work above the actor's heads, and "much of the acting took place in the air." Young actors of the theatre's academy made up the cast. Though well-received by the press, spectators queried by this critic were less enthusiastic. Production credits and cast list are included.

T1518   *New Grove Dictionary of Music and Musicians*, 6th
        edition, s. v. "Music in Shakespeare's Plays," by F. W.
        Sternfeld.

Discusses Shakespeare's indicated music under the general categories of functional music, magic music, character music, and atmospheric music. Stresses Shakespeare's integration of music into his text and his careful use of the musical performers available to him. Closes by saying, "In Shakespeare, music is never a divertissement for which another piece might easily be substituted; its effect is carefully calculated in dramatic and poetic terms." Bibliography follows.

T1519   *New Grove Dictionary of Music and Musicians*, 6th
        edition, s. v. "Shakespeare and Music Since 1616," by
        Eric Walter White.

Surveys music composed for Shakespeare's plays and the major derivative operas, ballets, overtures, and symphonies to about 1960. Notes that, of the twentieth century Shakespearean operas, "the one that succeeded in establishing itself most firmly in the current repertory was Britten's *A Midsummer Night's Dream* (1960)." A bibliography follows. (See items T1136, T1230 and T1324.)

T1519a   Oba, Kenji, "Shakespeare in Tokyo." *Shakespeare Quarterly*, 33 (1982), 498-99.

Included in the review coverage is a very brief characterization of the 1982 production of *A Midsummer Night's Dream* by the Haiyuza Company in Tokyo, directed by Toshikiyo Masumi. It was like its 1978 predecessor, *As You Like It*, directed by Masumi, a rock-and-roll version, "but the mirth was not so abundant or lively," and the frequent topical jokes inappropriate. A new, effective translation by Yushi Odashima was used. A partial listing of the cast and production staff is included.

T1520   Paulson, Ronald. *Book and Painting: Shakespeare, Milton, and the Bible. Literary Texts and the Emergence of English Painting*. Knoxville: University of Tennessee Press, 1982. xi, 236 pp. Illustrated.

Devotes Chapter Two to a study of "Shakespearean painting," in which he argues a point made in the introduction: "There is a real sense in which English painting . . . was a branch of literature rather than art." He suggests that there is an "Englishness" of English art in the awareness of the discrepancy between the word and the painted image. There are discussions of Blake and Fuseli (though not of their work inspired by *A Midsummer Night's Dream*), and Fuseli's *Titania and Bottom* is reproduced.

T1520a   Roberts, Alan. [Review.] *The Advertiser* (Adelaide), 10 May 1982, p. 26.

Not seen. Reviews a production of *A Midsummer Night's Dream* by the Lighthouse, the State Theatre Company of South Australia, directed by Jim Sharman, 1-15 May 1982.

T1521   Selbourne, David. *The Making of Peter Brook's "A Midsummer Night's Dream."* An eye-witness account of Peter Brook's production from first rehearsal to first night. With an introductory essay by Simon Trussler. London: Methuen London Ltd., 1982. xxxvii, 327 pp. Illustrated.

Records in a daily diary the rehearsals of the landmark 1970 production by the Royal Shakespeare Company under the direction of Peter Brook. (See item T1314.) The author offers detailed descriptions of the director's methods and of the tides of the emotions of the director and company throughout the sometimes exhilarating and sometimes disheartening rehearsals. The play text is reprinted on pages opposite the description of the rehearsal of that portion of the play. The author, at the time an aspiring playwright, is sometimes unsympathetic with Brook's "director's theatre," with his coaching methods, and with his interpretation of Shakespeare. Brook is seen in the accounts as attempting to make actors rid themselves of clichés and be spontaneous; he is also seen as being unclear at times. There are descriptions of exercises stressing company interplay, of experiments with musical instruments, of gymnastic exercises, and the experiment of reading the last act of the play by candlelight in a darkened hall. The production evolved toward a vision of the play as a passage from barren Athens "to an underworld of freer emotion," peace and authenticity. "Yet to get there," the author writes, "performance and performance alone tells us we must all pass through refining fire . . . ." Trussler's introductory essay surveys Brook's career. There are twenty-four photographs of scenes from the final production.

T1522   "Shakespeare Festivals--1982." *The Shakespeare
         Newsletter*, 32 (1982), 1-2.

         Lists the seasonal repertoires of twenty-seven Shakespeare festival companies, six of which were planning to produce *A Midsummer Night's Dream*: the American Players Company, Spring Green, Wisconsin; the Shakespeare Theatre at Monmouth, Maine; the Royal Shakespeare Company at the Barbican Theatre, London; Shakespeare in the Park in Fort Worth, Texas; the Santa Cruz Shakespeare Festival, California; and the Stratford festival, Ontario, Canada.

T1522a   Skura, Meredith. "The Houston Shakespeare Festival."
         Shakespeare Quarterly, 33 (1982), 370-72.

         Includes an unfavorable review of the festival's production of *A Midsummer Night's Dream*, directed by Sidney Berger, "a straightforward yet nervously inventive production." Many of the inventions only added as much

violence, knock-about, and local comedy as would fit.
Oberon was angry and loud; the lovers were still raucous
at dawn in the forest after being discovered; the fairies
involved themselves in invented tangles of their own. The
bustle went on into the closing scene. There was no sense
of the night's strangeness, the forest's distinctness, or of
a return to Athenian order at the end of the play. A
partial listing of the cast and production staff is included.

T1523 Styan, J. L. *Max Reinhardt.* Cambridge and New York:
       Cambridge University Press, 1982. 171 pp. Illustrated.

       Includes a short account of Reinhardt's Shakespearean
productions (pp. 128-56 and see also pp. 51-58). Devotes
eight pages to accounts of Reinhardt's first production of *A
Midsummer Night's Dream* (the German director's favorite
play), a neo-romantic version employing a revolving stage,
produced in 1905 at the Neues Theater in Berlin
(photograph) and to his production with the Oxford
University Dramatic Society at Oxford in 1933. There is a
career chronology and a list of Reinhardt's productions,
with dates of openings.

T1524 Tanitch, Robert. *A Pictorial Companion to Shakespeare's
       Plays.* London: Frederick Muller Limited, 1982.
       128 pp. Illustrated.

       Represents each play by several pages of photographs of
major productions. In this large format book, the five page
section on *A Midsummer Night's Dream* contains several
black-and-white photographs of the 1970 Royal Shakespeare
Company production, directed by Peter Brook; two from the
1935 film directed by Max Reinhardt; two of the 1937 Old
Vic production, directed by Tyrone Guthrie (not John
Gielgud, as given); and one photograph each of the
Stratford-upon-Avon production of 1954 and the Royal
Shakespeare Company production of 1977, directed by
George Devine and John Barton, respectively.

T1524a Trussler, Simon. *Royal Shakespeare Company 1981/82.*
        London: RSC Publications, 1982. 136 pp. Illustrated.

        Provides a record of the 1981-82 season's productions in
essays and photographs, including coverage (pp. 28-31) of

the 1981 production of *A Midsummer Night's Dream* directed
by Ron Daniels. (See item T1498.) A brief essay surveys
the critics' responses to the production, providing brief
excerpts from reviews. A full list of the cast and
production staff and seven black and white photos of the
production are provided.

T1524ab   Warren, Roger. "Interpretations of Shakespearian
           Comedy, 1981." *Shakespeare Survey*, 35 (1982), 141-52.

Included in the survey is a very favorable assessment of
Peter Hall's direction of Benjamin Britten's *A Midsummer
Night's Dream* at Glyndebourne in 1981 and a very
unfavorable assessment of the 1981 RSC production of the
play, directed by Ron Daniels (see T1498). Hall's version of
the opera is seen as complex and absorbing, and a further
development upon Hall's 1959 production of the play itself
(see T1183), in which the court and the wood were closely
related. Here, Oberon was in Elizabethan court garb, but
with more non-human touches in costume and make-up. The
young lovers, physical and comic in the 1959 staging, were
toned down here, but without any loss of humor. "These
were the best performances of these parts I have seen
anywhere, greatly helped by the composer." The fairies'
return at the end was magical. They gathered outside the
windows, and the sense of the country house surrounded
by a wood was powerful. The Ron Daniels' production was
full of contradictions in directing, acting, and design.
Theseus' palace might have been a Victorian stage setting,
but the wood was the stage of a Victorian theatre. The
fairies were small, sinister, hideous dolls, out of a horror
film. Oberon and Titania, in Arabian nights glamour, were
scarcely sinister at all. Among the haphazard effects were
the artisans in raincoats in the forest, tree borders being
flown in, a prop trunk tree for Titania's bower, and a play
scene that "was a mixture of pantomime (Pyramus in
harlequin tights and Thisbe as the 'Dame'), music hall (a
piano commentary), and morris-dance (with Bottom, of
course, wearing the horse's head). The strengths and
weakness of the company seemed almost unrelated to the
directorial approach. Mike Gwilym and Juliet Stevenson are
praised for fine delivery of the text. Jane Carr's Hermia
was "a screeching housemaid." There are two photos of
each production.

T1524b   Wearing, J. P. *The London Stage 1910-1919: A Calendar of Plays and Players.* 2 volumes. Metuchen, New Jersey, and London: The Scarecrow Press, 1982.

Provides annual calendars of professional play performances in the major London theatres in the decade 1890-99. Entries include dates of runs, partial casts, production credits, and, for some productions, a listing of some newspaper reviews. Productions of *A Midsummer Night's Dream* listed, with reviews, include the 1911 revival of Herbert Beerbohm Tree's production, the 1914 Harley Granville-Barker production, a Frank Benson production at the Court Theatre in 1915, and there are several listings for Old Vic productions, including those of Ben Greet. This calendar is the third in a series of three by the author extending back to 1890. (See items T1400 and T1505.)

T1524c   Wells, Stanley. "Television Shakespeare." *Shakespeare Quarterly*, 33 (1982), 261-77.

Discusses the circumstances of the productions of the plays in the BBC Television series, "The Shakespeare Plays," and assesses the performances. Questioning the video "bank" concept behind it all he asks, "has there ever in the whole history of television [or film], been a production of Shakespeare which has borne repetition more than a few years after it was made?" He also discusses textual cutting, and scenic and staging considerations. At several points he refers to the *A Midsummer Night's Dream* of the series, which he found one of the weaker productions. Chiefly, it offered some beautifully composed pictures and a too-seriously played "Pyramus and Thisbe."

T1524d   Wilds, Lillian. "Shakespeare in Southern California." *Shakespeare Quarterly*, 33 (1982), 380-93.

Includes two favorable reviews of two professional productions of *A Midsummer Night's Dream* in July-August 1981 in the coverage of twenty Shakespearean productions in 1981, the "Shakespeare Year in Southern California," which corresponded to the visit to Los Angeles of the Folger Shakespeare Library exhibit "Shakespeare: The Globe and the World." The Garden Grove Shakespeare Festival production, staged in an amphitheatre, was reportedly characterized by an exuberant young cast and

directorial inventiveness. Oberon and Titania observed the
opening scene at court, Theseus and Hippolyta rode in on a
white horse, and Helena made comic attempts at suicide,
including taking pills. The Sherwood Shakespeare Festival
production, directed by David Hammond, with settings
designed by Ralph Funicello, is described as attractively
mounted and well acted, but, for the reviewer, derivative
of recent regional productions. The rustics are praised and
some bawdy business on Thisbe's kissing of Wall's "stones"
in "Pyramus and Thisbe" is described. Production credits
and cast list are included.

T1524e   Williams, Gary Jay. "A Dance for Our Disbeliefs: The
         Current *A Midsummer Night's Dream* of the RSC."
         Theater 13, 3 (Summer/Fall 1982), 60-64.

         Favorable review and analysis, with detailed description
and two photographs, of the 1981-82 RSC production
directed by Ron Daniels. It featured puppet fairies and
scenic evocations of the Victorian theatre. (See T1498.)
Daniels' world for the play seemed "one filled with
apprehension . . . and his intuitions very dark at the
edges." An ineffable sadness clung to the spectre-like,
broken doll puppets, who were "like souls no longer prayed
for," waiting in eternity "for the mending of a world long
broken." There were a number of images of reconciliation,
chiefly the dance between Oberon and Titania after he had
awakened her. "It is not so very beautifully danced . . .
and we and they know it is not. It is rather, made for us
to allow it and them to be pretty, and it ends in Titania
and Oberon's anxious, close embrace, as if this were indeed
the one dance left to dance upon the edge of a vanishing
enchantment." There was in the dance the suggestion of
"the existential sense behind the play" that Daniels had
spoken of. Williams concludes: "Poets and lovers, actors
and spectators can, probably, with imagination and faith,
create order and purpose in a shadow world: but it is a
precarious dance."

T1525   Williams, John T. *Costumes and Settings for
         Shakespeare's Plays*. Drawings by Jack Cassim-Scott.
         London: Batsford Academic and Educational Ltd.; Totswa
         [*sic*], New Jersey: Barnes and Noble, 1982. 120 pp.
         Illustrated.

Intended as a practical guide to production, this book provides, first, a brief survey of Shakespeare in the theatre from the Globe to about the mid-twentieth century, including brief explanations of Elizabethan era costuming and nineteenth century antiquarianism. In part two, the author explains a staging and costuming approach to each of ten plays; these are accompanied by full page drawings of major characters in costumes. For *A Midsummer Night's Dream* (pp. 23-32), he offers a late Victorian or Edwardian style of costume and staging. Theseus and Hippolyta are shown in drawings dressed in Victorian hunting habits; the mechanicals are pictured in Victorian jackets and trousers; Wall wears a checked waistcoat and heavy watchchain. Hermia's Victorian dress is to be in pale green and white to suggest youthful freshness. The sketch of the fairies shows Oberon in a cape, crown, tight-fitting shirt open to the waist, and ballet-type shoes. The author considers the setting briefly for either outdoor or indoor productions. For the latter, the palace is to be a box set.

T1525a   Adam, Donald G. "Shakespeare in Pittsburgh." *Shakespeare Quarterly*, 34 (1983), 111-12.

Characterizes a production of *A Midsummer Night's Dream* by the Pittsburgh Public Theatre in July-August, 1982, directed by Stephen Kanee. A "Jan Kottish" interpretation made Puck and the fairies medieval devils who encouraged venal pleasures, and this "fairy world of appetite" was contrasted with an "Athens of ordered intelligence." The setting was a dappled green quilt over an arena stage, on which the lovers played rambunctiously and the fairies "writhed in autotelic sexuality." Includes a partial listing of the cast and production staff.

T1525b   Coursen, H. R. "Shakespeare in Maine." *Shakespeare Quarterly*, 34 (1983), 96-98.

Reviews a "superb" production of *A Midsummer Night's Dream* by the Theatre of Monmouth in July-August, 1982, directed by Richard Sewell. Theseus' court was Victorian, with Lysander as a young Tennyson, jotting down verses, and Demetrius a light brigade lieutenant. Maryann Plunkett's Titania, in large wings and modeled on the Paul Konewka silhouette, is praised for her acting and singing (in II.ii). Ted Davis's Oberon "was a limping and grotesque

Richard III of the woods, à la *Huon of Bordeaux*," and he
underwent a transformation himself when he released
Titania. Helena watched "Pyramus and Thisbe" with a
recognition of the lovers' problems that linked it to the
young lovers' night in the forest. There is a photo of
Oberon and Titania and a partial listing of the cast and
production staff.

T1525ba   Kolin, Philip C., ed. *Shakespeare in the South: Essays
           on Performance*. Jackson: University Press of
           Mississippi, 1983. 279 pp. Illustrated.

Thirteen essays comprise a collection aimed at
documenting and evaluating Shakespearean performances in
the South, from colonial to contemporary times. Linwood E.
Orange's essay, "Shakespeare in Mississippi, 1814-1980,"
mentions college performances of *A Midsummer Night's
Dream* in 1956 and in the 1970s. Larry Champion's essay,
"'Bold to Play': Shakespeare in North Carolina," reports on
the Montford Players Company in Asheville, which has
performed *A Midsummer Night's Dream* and other plays to
racially mixed audiences. He describes a Jan Kott-influenced
production of the play at the University of North
Carolina--Asheville that was, like the Peter Brook and John
Hancock productions (see item T1314 and item T1269), a
reaction to the romantic tradition for staging the play. Earl
L. Dachslager reports on the popularity of the play at the
Globe of the Great Southwest. Stuart E. Omans and Patricia
H. Madden describe a Shakespeare program co-sponsored by
the National Endowment for the Humanities and the
University of Central Florida (see item 565). Student
participation was stressed in the studying of the plays as
plays; the program involved, among other things, the study
and production of *A Midsummer Night's Dream*. The novice
actors, many of whom were high school teachers,
constructed costumes, composed music, and acted. Among
the program's felicitous results, the authors believe, was
the creation of new teaching strategies that stress the
students' discovering the plays by doing the plays.

T1525c   Streitberger, W. R. "Shakespeare in the Northwest:
          Ashland and Seattle." *Shakespeare Quarterly*, 34 (1983),
          347-54.

Coverage of ten productions includes a very brief characterization of the 1981-1982 production of *A Midsummer Night's Dream* by the Bathhouse Theater, Seattle, "the longest-running non-commercial show in Seattle theatre history." Directed by John Aylward and Arne Zaslove, it was set in the gym of Athens High School on graduation night in 1957 and was complemented by rock music from the era. A partial list of the cast and production staff is included.

T1525d Trussler, Simon. *Royal Shakespeare Company 1982/83.* London: RSC Publications, 1983. 114 pp. Illustrated.

Provides a record of the 1982-83 RSC season's productions in essays and photographs. Included is coverage of the production of *A Midsummer Night's Dream* directed by Ron Daniels that premiered at Stratford-upon-Avon in 1981 and moved into the Barbican Theatre in London in 1982. A brief essay samples the critics' responses, there are eight black and white photographs of the production, and a listing of the cast and production staff.

T1525e Warren, Roger. *A Midsummer Night's Dream: Text and Performance*, Text and Performance Series, vol. 8. [London:] The MacMillan Press, Ltd., 1983. 77 pp. Illustrated.

Designed for sixth form and undergraduate students, the aim of the series is to show the vitality of major dramatic works in criticism and performance and so promote recognition of how both the scholar and the artist, the critic and director "can enhance our enjoyment of the play." Warren in Part I (pp. 9-43) discusses "how the play works as a play," eschewing discussion of abstract themes to focus on the dramatic techniques with which Shakespeare characterizes the four distinct worlds of the play and on the ways in which he brings them together. The language sets the stage and establishes plot and characters. Passages that establish the fairy world are placed at dramatically important points. Shakespeare does not treat the fairies as sinister; he draws them from Elizabethan folklore and literature. In Part Two, on performances of the play, directorial trends of the past thirty years are summarized, and then Warren characterizes the Peter Hall production of

1959 (see T1183) and Hall's production of the Benjamin
Britten opera (pp. 47-54). He also makes comparisons with
Hall's 1969 film of the play (see T1301). He describes the
RSC production of 1970 (pp. 55-61), directed by Peter
Brook (see T1314), the Stratford, Ontario, production of
1976-77 (pp. 62-66), directed by Robin Phillips (see
T1396), and the 1981 BBC Television version (pp. 67-73),
directed by Elijah Moshinsky (see T1499a). The different
directorial approaches are described, and Warren shows
which elements of the play the directors chose to emphasize
and which were de-emphasized or ignored. There is a brief
characterization (p. 46) of the 1981 RSC production
directed by Ron Daniels. There are several photos of the
Hall, Brook, Phillips and Moshinsky productions and
reading lists on the criticism and performance history of the
play.

T1526   White, Eric Walter. *Benjamin Britten, His Life and
        Operas.* London: Faber and Faber; Berkeley: University
        of California Press, 1970; 2nd edition, John Evans, ed.,
        Berkeley: University of California Press, 1983. 322 pp.
        Illustrated.

        Devotes Chapter Eleven to a critical appreciation of the
score of Britten's *A Midsummer Night's Dream*, noting that
the opera reduces Shakespeare's play by about half, that it
simplifies it by beginning in the forest sequence with the
quartet of lovers, and that the time sequence of the play
has been adjusted. The action of the opera seems to take
place within two consecutive nights. Discusses how
"Pyramus and Thisbe" is made into an opera buffa ("shades
of Leveridgea"), with fourteen songs in it that satirize the
nineteenth century romantic opera. White argues that the
poetry of the original play has not been harmed, and he
sees Britten's opera as comparable to Verdi's *Macbeth,
Othello,* and *Falstaff* in that it is among the works that are
fully satisfying Shakespearean operas. (See also item
T1447.)

T1526a White, Eric Walter. *A History of English Opera.* London:
        Faber and Faber, 1983. 472 pp. Illustrated.

        Surveys English opera, defined as a stage action with
vocal and instrumental music written by a British composer
to a libretto in English, offering some discussion of

Purcell's *The Fairy Queen* (pp. 121-24), passing references
to the eighteenth century opera adaptations of *A Midsummer
Night's Dream*, and a brief characterization of Benjamin
Britten's opera version (pp. 426-27). Purcell's work marks
regress rather than progress in the development of English
opera, for though the composer's genius shines steadily in
the score, the players and singers are divorced from each
other since the music is confined to the four separate
masques ending Acts II through V. Dancing played a more
important part in *The Fairy Queen* than in Purcell's *The
Prophetess* or *King Arthur.* Britten was attracted to
Shakespeare's play by many features, including the contrast
between natural and supernatural elements. The opera was
written for "medium sized orchestral forces" and the 1960
Covent Garden production of the opera, which followed its
premiere in the confined setting of Aldeburgh, showed the
opera to be "thoroughly viable as a medium scale opera."
(See also item T1526 and T1526a.)

T1526b   White, Eric Walter, compiler. *Register of First
         Performances of English Operas and Semi Operas from
         the 16th Century to 1980.* London: Society for Theatre
         Research, 1983. vi, 130 pp.

         Originally planned as an appendix to White's *History of
         English Opera* (see item T1525e), this is a selective list,
         giving titles, composers, librettist, premier dates, and
         theatres. Publication of scores or libretti are noted. There
         are brief notices of Purcell's *The Fairy Queen*, the *Pyramus
         and Thisbe* adaptations of Richard Leveridge and J. F.
         Lampe, the Henry Rowley Bishop and Frederic Reynolds
         version, and the Benjamin Britten opera.

T1527   Wood, Robert E. "Shakespeare in Atlanta." *Shakespeare
         Quarterly*, 34 (1983), 340-341.

         Describes the Alliance Theatre Company's production of
         A Midsummer Night's Dream in April and May of 1982,
         reportedly one of the company's most successful productions
         of recent years. Director Charles Abbott put the young
         lovers at the center of his exuberant staging, cutting the
         text heavily and subtitling it, "A Conspiracy for Lovers."
         There is special praise for the portrayals of Hermia and
         Helena. The mechanicals were reportedly a mixed success,
         and Theseus was parodied as a pompous monarch. The

fairies were acrobats and dancers, who freely used a setting that included a long slide, a gymnast's rope, and a trampoline. The reviewer points to an absence of any mature love in the production, and the staging and cutting left no strong image of Titania as the fairy queen in love with the man in the ass's head. But on the whole, the reviewer finds virtue in the directorial approach. A partial listing of the cast and production staff is provided.

T1528   Patenall, Andrew J. G. *Playing Shakespeare.* Canada:
        The Ontario Educational Communications Authority, 1984. '
        x, 164 pp. Illustrated.

A guide designed for use with *Playing Shakespeare*, a series of nine television programs written and presented by John Barton, Associate Director of the Royal Shakespeare Company and produced by London Weekend Television. The programs feature the RSC in rehearsal, showing the ways in which the plays are shaped into productions. The three-part guide by Professor Patenall includes notes on each program, passages from the plays used in each program, and photos from various productions or from the series itself. In the fourth program, on "Set Speeches and Soliloquies," Helena's speech in *A Midsummer Night's Dream,* Act II.ii ("How happy some o'er other some can be") is explored. There is one photo each of the productions of the play at Stratford, Ontario, in 1968 and 1976 (see T1288 and T1396), and at Stratford-upon-Avon in 1970 (see T1314). There are biographies on the actors in the series and a suggested reading list. The guide and information on the series is available from: TVOntario Marketing, Box 200, Station Q, Toronto, Ontario, M4T 2T1; telephone (416) 484-2613.

Index

References are to item numbers

Aaron, Jules, T1365
Abbey Theatre (Dublin), T1500
Absurda Comica; oder Peter Squentz, see Gryphius
Ackland, Joss, T1185a
Actability of the play, 1-5, 9, 16, 28, 63, 567, 738, 744, 842
Actaeon, 670, 685c
Acting Company (Juilliard), T1504a
Action, see Duration of Action
Actor's Workshop Company, T1269
Adams, Donald E., T1525a
Adams, John Crawford, T1103, T1115
Adams, W. Bridges, T1103a
Adamson, Elgiva, 1026
Addenbrook, David, T1352
Adland, David, 418
Adlington, William (translator), 591-92, 630, 672, 685i, 960; see also Apuleius
Adolf, Helen, 603
Adonis, 192
Adrian, Max, T1099, T1100
Afrikaans (translation), 942
Agate, James, T1095, T1099, T1100
Ahačič, Draga, 1071

Ainslie, Douglas, 10
Aire, Sally, T1411
Airmont Shakespeare Classics, 902
Akiaroff, B., T1107a
Akin, Lew Sparks, T1353
Alabama Shakespeare Festival, T1511b
Alaska Repertory Theatre, T1491b
Albanian (translation), 918
Albaugh, John, T1315, T1364
Alchemist, The, see Jonson, Ben
Aldeburg Festival, T1188
Aldred, C., 16
Aldredge, Theoni V., T1204
Aldus Shakespeare, The, 744
Aldwych Theatre (London), see Stratford-upon-Avon Shakespeare Memorial Theatre/Royal Shakespeare Theatre
Alençon, François Hercule, Duc D', 586, 649a, 673
Alexander, Craig Jon, 565
Alexander, Marguerite, 549
Alexander, Peter, 19, 73a, 218-18a, 689, 817, 845-46, 925, 935
Alexander, Rod, T1201
Alexander Shakespeare, The, 935

587

Snodgrass, W. D., 481
Socrates, 566q, 621
Söderwall, Margreta, 200, 857
Solomon, Harry (Davidowitz, Shalom Z.), 780
Somes, Michael, T1101a
Sommers, Harry, T1194
Songs, see Music
Sonnets, The (Shakespeare's), 563, 645
Sorell, Walter, 149, T1164
Sorum, Judith Ann, 435
Součková, Sylva, 862
Sources, 16, 34, 63, 182, 212, 280a, 284, 303, 355, 410, 414, 457, 567, 587-87a, 615, 630-31, 639-40, 650, 657a, 660a, 685a-w, 715, 738, 742, 744, 746-48, 750, 752, 754, 756, 757, 759-60, 776, 802, 804, 807, 825, 854-55, 880, 897, 906, 913, 925, 960, 1065c
South Africa, T1137a, T1171, T1253, T1258
South Bank Shakespeare, The, 925
South Coast Repertory (California), T1404
Southampton, Henry Wriothesley, third Earl of, 38, 574, 576, 645, 748, 752
Southampton, Mary, Countess of, 517, 576, 644-45, 906
Spain, T1105, T1134
Spalding, J. J., 106
Spanish (translation), 764, 775, 781, 1030
Spanish Tragedy, The, 357
Speaight, Robert, 517, T1142, T1165, T1196, T1345
Specking, Inez, 1010
Spence, Lewis, 597

Spencer, Hazelton, 23, T1092, T1228a
Spencer, John, 62, 740
Spencer, T. J. B., 617, 646
Spencer, Edmund, alluded to, 2, 670, 738, 744; *Amoretti,* 960; *Epithalamion,* 685d; *Faerie Queene,* 14, 89, 110, 153, 500, 570, 670, 673, 732; *Hymne in Honour of Beautie,* 187; influence on the diction of *Dream,* 620; satirized, 122; *Shepheardes Calendar,* 960; similar use of political allegory, 574, 673; *Teares of the Muses,* 2, 670, 738, 744
Spevack, Marvin, 703, 930
Spiegelman, Willard, 1091j
Spisak, James W., 685t
Sports, 44, 421a
Sprague, Arthur Colby, 787, T1098, T1132, T1138, T1143, T1152, T1274, T1316, T1346-47, T1379
Spurgeon, Caroline F. E., 17, 575a
Srinivasa Iyengar, K. R., 235
Stage History, 183, 284, 355, 567, 576, 746-47, 750, 757, 807, 854-55, 913 (see also various entries in Stage History section of Bibliography)
Staging (suggestions for, descriptions of specific productions), 9, 11, 25, 48, 84a, 108a, 119, 144, 149, 210, 310, 324, 350, 371, 418, 460, 480a, 820, 828, 842, 860, 868, 874, 937, 951, 984, 998, 1029, 1065, 1065b, 1069 (see also Stage History in index and various entries under